Instant Java™ Servlets

Phil Hanna

McGraw-Hill
New York   San Francisco   Washington, D.C.
Auckland   Bogotá   Caracas   Lisbon   London
Madrid   Mexico City   Milan   Montreal   New Delhi
San Juan   Singapore   Sydney   Tokyo   Toronto

McGraw-Hill

A Division of The McGraw·Hill Companies

Copyright © 2000 by The McGraw-Hill Companies, Inc. All rights reserved.
Printed in the United States of America. Except as permitted under the United
States Copyright Act of 1976, no part of this publication may be reproduced or
distributed in any form or by any means, or stored in a data base or retrieval
system, without the prior written permission of the publisher.

1 2 3 4 5 6 7 8 9 0   AGM/AGM   0 5 4 3 2 1 0

P/N 0-07-212423-7
ISBN 0-07-212425-3

*The sponsoring editor for this book was Francis J. Kelly, the editing supervisor
was Penny Linskey, and the production supervisor was Clare Stanley. It was set
in Century Schoolbook by Don Feldman of McGraw-Hill's Professional Book
Group composition unit in cooperation with Spring Point Publishing Services.*

Printed and bound by Quebecor/Martinsburg.

*Throughout this book, trademarked names are used. Rather than put a trade-
mark symbol after every occurrence of a trademarked name, we used the names
in an editorial fashion only, and to the benefit of the trademark owner, with no
intention of infringement of the trademark. Where such designations appear in
this book, they have been printed with initial caps.*

 This book is printed on recycled, acid-free paper containing a minimum
of 50% recycled de-inked fiber.

To Mom and Dad

CONTENTS

Contents

PREFACE

Purpose

As Java development has moved from the client side to the server side, it has gained stability, credibility, and a host of new adherents. More than ever before, Java is proving to be the platform of choice for new server side e-commerce projects.

There are a number of Java books that deal with the Java language, applet development, graphics, and GUI development, but relatively few that discuss server-side Java. The purpose of this book is to help you develop competence in writing Java servlets and JavaServer Pages. It does this by providing an easy-to-use reference to hundreds of techniques and solutions to commonly encountered problems.

Organization

This is not a book of plug-in software. What you will find are techniques for solving problems. The book consists of two sections: a three-chapter introduction to the web programming environment and Java servlets, and then the main substance—the servlet cookbook. Each chapter of the servlet cookbook consists of an overview section, followed by a number of problems with their solution techniques described and discussed. In the discussion sections, you will find program listings and screenshots that walk you step-by-step through the solution. Since every server installation is different, with different application products and database systems, you will need to study these techniques and adapt them to your own environment.

PHIL HANNA

ACKNOWLEDGMENTS

Writing this book has been an arduous but rewarding project. It would not have been possible without the collaboration and support of a number of people.

I would first like to thank my editor at McGraw-Hill, Franny Kelly. His skills and abilities were invaluable, as was his willingness to help with so many of the details. Thanks also to Penny Linskey for her editorial supervision, and to Maria Tahim for her work on the cover. My technical reviewers, Karl Moss and Chris Bailey, provided insight and helpful comments all along the way. Chris contributed his ability to look at problems from a completely fresh point of view, and prodded me to go the extra mile where necessary. I owe a great debt of gratitude to Karl for his advice and detailed comments, not only about the book but about the entire process.

I am most thankful to the people at Allaire Corporation for their help with JRun, in particular, Dan Smith, Barbara Duchesne, and Paul Colton. Thanks also go to Vince Bonfanti at New Atlanta Communications, Ltd. for his help with ServletExec. My thanks to Ellen B. Looney of E. Looney Graphics for drawing the cornucopia used in the *Internet Premium Food Market* logo. David J. Carlson, Director of the Atmospheric Technology Division of the National Center for Atmospheric Research, Boulder, Colorado, kindly gave permission to include data from the NCAR Foothills Laboratory Web site. The National Center for Atmospheric Research receives funding from the National Science Foundation.

I am very appreciative of the support and encouragement I received from my managers at SAS Institute, Alan Eaton, Deva Kumar, and Keith Collins, throughout this project. Thanks, too, to Perry Scherman, my friend and former business partner, for his highly original thinking about application development and undertaking new challenges.

Most of all, I'd like to thank my wife, Mary, and my children Eleanor and John for their devotion, their understanding, and for tolerating an out-of-phase husband and father through the long months it took to write this book.

Introduction
to Servlets

1

Introduction

The Java Revolution

Since its inception in 1995, use of the Java programming language and related technology has experienced explosive growth. According to Alan Baratz, president of Sun Microsystems' JavaSoft Division[1]:

- Java applications are running on more than 70 million computers.
- There are nearly 1 million Java developers.
- Almost half of all businesses worldwide are developing Java applications.

---

[1]Source: *http://java.sun.com/javaone/javaone98/keynotes/baratz/transcript_baratz.html.*

The reasons for Java's success are compelling. It is truly platform-independent, a universal programming language for any operating system. It is completely object-oriented, leveraging advances in the software engineering and component technology disciplines. Its security model is mature and robust, in stark contrast to its virus-prone alternatives.

Where Does Java Fit In?

The first wave of Java technology that caught attention was Java applets—small downloadable applications hosted by a Web browser. Applets have met with some disappointment, however. Browser incompatibilities lead to complexity, and download time can be significant. Security considerations can restrict the ability to perform necessary services. Applets' graphics capabilities land them in too many frivolous "eye candy" settings.

However, as with other immensely popular technologies, the second wave is where the real value becomes apparent. In this case, it is the server side of the enterprise that has emerged as the most significant arena for Java. There are several reasons for this:

- The server environment is where the database and business applications reside. Integration at this level is crucial, and Java's reliability, platform independence, and database connectivity are key considerations.
- The security environment is more manageable.
- There is no graphical user interface (GUI) to worry about.

The most remarkable factor driving server-side Java, however, is the phenomenal growth of electronic commerce.

The Role of E-Commerce

What was not envisioned as few as 5 years ago was the emergence of e-commerce as a significant business model. Estimates of market share as recently as a year ago consistently underestimated the growth. According to the U.S. Department of Commerce, the proportion of U.S. companies that sell products over the Internet is expected to grow from

24 percent in 1998 to 56 percent during 2000.[2] Online sales of computer products, stock trades, travel booking, mortgage loans, and retail products have all exceeded expectations. Compared with these business-to-consumer transactions, growth in business-to-business e-commerce is even more significant, with estimates of a staggering $1.3 trillion worldwide market by 2003.[3]

The convergence of three trends has been a key factor crucial to the rise of e-commerce:

1. Widespread access to the Internet at home and at work—as much as 37 percent of the U.S. population[4]
2. Online facilities for secure financial transactions
3. Availability of Web-connected application server software

It is the last of these factors that is creating the demand for server-side Java. The Gartner Group reports that Java servlets likely will be the most popular form of server-based Java because of the large volume of simple Internet application needs.[5] This is the subject that this book addresses.

What This Book Is About

This book deals with Java servlets and JavaServer Pages. Servlets are Java components that dynamically extend the capabilities of a Web server. JavaServer Pages (JSPs) are Web pages that contain both Hypertext Machine Language (HTML) and Java statements that handle application logic and database connectivity. Topics that are covered in detail include

- *HTML clients.* Using HTML to capture user input and convey it to a server.
- *Database access.* How Java Database Connectivity (JDBC) provides Java with industry-standard Structured Query Language (SQL) access to database management systems.

---

[2]Source: *The Emerging Digital Economy,* U.S. Department of Commerce, June 1999.

[3]Source: Forrester Research, press release, December 17, 1998 (*http://www.forrester.com*).

[4]Source: *The Emerging Digital Economy II,* U.S. Department of Commerce, June 1999.

[5]Source: Gartner Analytics SPA-04-0735.

- *Debugging*. Detailed information about tools and techniques for troubleshooting servlet problems.
- *Session management*. Leveraging Java's object management capabilities to maintain persistent user sessions.
- *Life-cycle issues*. Understanding the event-driven Web environment.
- *Threading issues*. Taking advantage of Java's built-in support for parallel processing to maximize performance.
- *Interservlet communication*. Techniques for servlet chaining, request dispatching, HTTP requests, and redirection to organize a group of servlets for more complex tasks.
- *Other clients*. How servlets cooperate with Java applets, XML systems, Perl scripts, and stand-alone Java applications.
- *Other servers*. Making use of servlets to access operating system functions, file systems, CGI programs, ASP scripts, FTP servers, and distributed-object systems such as CORBA.
- *Applications*. Using servlets for system administration, to send and receive mail, to handle images, to download spreadsheets, and to solve puzzles.

What You Need to Know

This book is not an introduction to Java itself. There are any number of good basic books and online resources that will help you if you are just starting out. One of the best is the online Java Tutorial at *http://java.sun.com/docs/books/tutorial*. Besides the Java language itself, no special knowledge is required. It would be helpful to have a basic understanding of network programming and database access, but studying the examples and consulting the application programming interface (API) reference should provide you with all the details you need to get your programs working.

Organization

This book is intended as a practical solutions-oriented resource for Java servlet programmers. Unlike a tutorial or an API reference, it focuses on workable solutions to programming problems, providing templates that bridge the gap between a basic understanding of the API and working applications.

Part I provides an overview of the Web programming environment, the HTTP protocol, and an introduction to the servlet API. Part II, which is the main substance of the book, consists of a set of approximately 100 real-world problems organized into 11 main topic areas for ease of reference. The model for each chapter is a brief overview of the topic followed by 8 to 12 solved problems. For each problem, a short description of the solution technique is presented, followed by a detailed discussion of the issues involved and one or more complete examples. The problems range in complexity, so beginning, intermediate, and advanced programmers will each encounter solutions to problems they have likely faced or will face in the future.

Summary

Just as e-commerce is driving the Internet, server-side applications are driving e-commerce. A successful server application is usually more than just a program—it may consist of a group of Internet-worked components that handles its business logic, its database access, and its content delivery. We will see throughout this book that Java servlets provide the glue that makes all these parts work together.

Programming in the Web Environment

The World Wide Web

Television often has been mentioned as the twentieth-century technology that has had the most significant sociologic and cultural impact. It is possible, however, that the effects of the Internet may be even more profound. Virtually all our commercial, government, cultural, and educational organizations are accessible at some level to anyone with a computer. The Internet expedites communication between individuals and groups of people having common interests. The World Wide Web acts as a universal, continuously updated library of all human knowledge. Given its pervasiveness, it is hard to believe that it is barely 10 years old.

Origins of the Web

The basic outlines of the Web and its Hypertext Transfer Protocol (HTTP) trace their origin to 1990. Working on a distributed hypermedia project at the European Laboratory for Particle Physics (CERN), Tim Berners-Lee developed both a networking protocol for distributing documents over the Internet (HTTP) and the first Web browser. The system was adopted at CERN and other high-energy physics laboratories and universities throughout 1991 and 1992. With the development in 1993 of the popular Mosaic browser at the National Center for Supercomputer Applications (NCSA) at the University of Illinois, Web access spread at an exponential rate. By 1994, there were 10,000 Web servers in use[1] and nearly 10 million users.

Evolution of the Web Application

As Web use has grown, so has its role as an application environment. Originally, it served mainly as a document repository with an improved means of navigation. With the advent of the Common Gateway Interface (CGI) in the NCSA HTTPd Web server, this changed significantly.

CGI introduced the idea of *dynamic content*. Instead of simply retrieving stored documents, a CGI script generates the equivalent of a Web

---

[1]As of this writing, the number of Web servers worldwide is estimated to be between 10 and 15 million.

page "on the fly." Scripts can be written in any language (although Perl and C are the most common choices) and in general have access to databases, system services, and most other application resources. This allows CGI scripts to generate and deliver highly selective information to the desktop on an up-to-the-minute basis. Searchable data sources about theater schedules, product specifications, and inventory levels can be made widely available at the click of a mouse button. Without question, the ability to deliver dynamic content has been a prime factor in the growth of the Web.

It is noteworthy that no change to the client/server protocol is required to implement CGI—a Web browser requests a CGI script using the same "language" as it uses for requesting a document. The browser is not even aware of whether the document that is returned came from a file or was created specifically in response to the request.

While the client side of the Web application continues to evolve, with Java applets, ActiveX controls, dynamic HTML, and JavaScript, these are essentially improvements to the user interface. To the extent they try to do serious work, they run into trouble with browser incompatibilities and security. The most useful improvements have come from server-side technologies like Active Server Pages, PHP, Cold Fusion, JavaServer Pages, and Java servlets. While each of these have their adherents, this book proposes that Java technologies have the most to offer in terms of platform independence, reliability, and functionality.

Hypertext Transfer Protocol (HTTP)

To understand Web application programming, we need a basic understanding of the protocol used to implement it. Web servers and Web browsers communicate over TCP/IP networks according to a set of rules for requesting content and responding to these requests. The rules provide the means for

- Specifying documents to be retrieved
- Negotiating the data formats to be used
- Authenticating user access to resources
- Indicating the date and time a document was last updated
- Returning status codes to indicate success or reasons for failure

The set of rules, known as the *Hypertext Transfer Protocol* (HTTP), is formally documented in the Internet standards referred to as RFC1945, RFC2068, and RFC2616.[2] Each of these is a complete specification of the standard; the latter two are updates of their predecessors.

Web Browser-to-Web Server Interaction

A Web browser or client requests a document from a Web server by opening a TCP/IP socket, writing a request message and possibly metadata about the request, and then reading the contents of the requested document from the socket's input stream. Both the request and the response are written in ordinary human-readable ASCII text.

Figure 2-1 shows a basic example of how this works. When the user of a Web browser such as Microsoft Internet Explorer or Netscape Navigator clicks on a hyperlink or opens the Uniform Resource Locator (URL) for *http://www.ipfoods.com/newsletter/Video.html,* the browser does the following:

1. Analyzes the URL for its individual components:
   - Protocol: `http`
   - Host name: `www.ipfoods.com`
   - File name: `/newsletter/Video.html`
2. Opens a socket connection to `www.ipfoods.com` using the default HTTP port number 80
3. Writes an HTTP GET request for the document requested:

   ```
   GET /newsletter/Video.html HTTP/1.0
   ```

4. Reads the HTTP response headers and the contents of the document:

   ```
   HTTP/1.1 200 OK
   Date: Sat, 19 Feb 2000 18:24:29 GMT
   Server: Apache/1.3.9 (Win32)
   ```

---

[2]An RFC (Request for Comments) is a document (usually the specification of a standard) that is published by the Internet Engineering Task Force (IETF) and widely accepted in the Internet research and development community. RFCs are numbered and never change once issued. Updates to a standard involve the publication of a new RFC. RFCs are available from a number of online sources; nicely formatted HTML versions can be found at *http://www.freesoft.org/CIE/index.htm.*

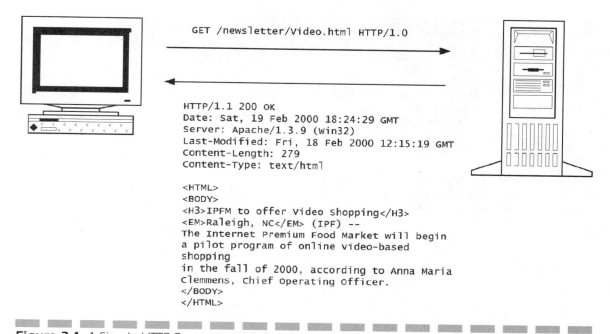

```
GET /newsletter/Video.html HTTP/1.0


HTTP/1.1 200 OK
Date: Sat, 19 Feb 2000 18:24:29 GMT
Server: Apache/1.3.9 (Win32)
Last-Modified: Fri, 18 Feb 2000 12:15:19 GMT
Content-Length: 279
Content-Type: text/html

<HTML>
<BODY>
<H3>IPFM to offer Video Shopping</H3>
<EM>Raleigh, NC</EM> (IPF) --
The Internet Premium Food Market will begin
a pilot program of online video-based
shopping
in the fall of 2000, according to Anna Maria
Clemmens, Chief Operating Officer.
</BODY>
</HTML>
```

Figure 2-1 A Simple HTTP Request and Response.

```
Last-Modified: Fri, 18 Feb 2000 12:15:19 GMT
Content-Length: 279
Content-Type: text/html

<HTML>
<BODY>
<H3>IPFM to offer Video Shopping</H3>
<EM>Raleigh, NC</EM> (IPF) —
The Internet Premium Food Market will begin
a pilot program of online video-based
shopping
in the fall of 2000, according to Anna Maria
Clemmens, Chief Operating Officer.
</BODY>
```

5. Formats and displays the resulting document in the browser window, as shown in Figure 2-2.

6. Closes the socket connection.

Let's examine the request and response in a little more detail.

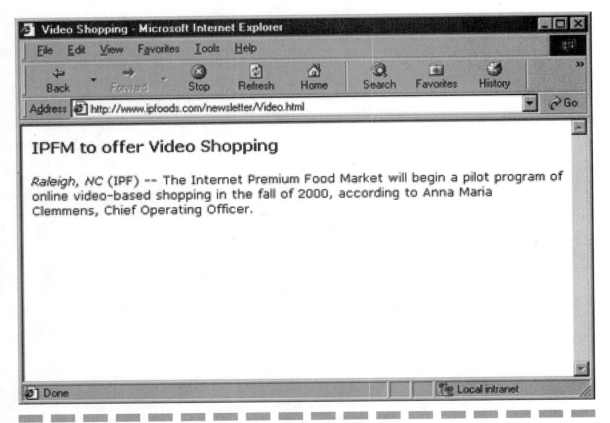

Figure 2-2 The Requested Document as Displayed by the Web Browser.

HTTP Requests

An HTTP request consists of up to three elements:

- *The request line.* This is a line containing exactly three fields:
    1. The request method
    2. The name of the resource (the Uniform Resource Identifier, or URI), and
    3. The lowest HTTP version supported for further communication.

    HTTP defines seven request methods: OPTIONS, GET, HEAD, POST, PUT, DELETE, and TRACE, but only two of these are commonly encountered—GET and POST—and these are the only methods dealt with in this book.[3] GET is used for simple retrieval requests, possibly with parameters tacked onto the resource name. POST indicates that the request contains a message body to be processed by the program named in the URI. Chapter 4 covers both these methods in detail. In our example, the request method was GET, the resource name was /newsletter/Video.html, and the HTTP version was HTTP/1.0.

▣ *Request headers,*[4] *if any.* These are a means for the client to pass on additional information about the request and about itself. These headers are simple key-value pairs, such as

```
User-Agent: Mozilla/4.0 (compatible; MSIE 5.0; Windows NT; DigExt)
```

The key field is terminated with a colon (:), and whatever follows on the same line is the value. Each request header appears on a line by itself, and the end of the request header section is indicated by an empty line (a line consisting of just a CRLF).

▣ *An optional message body.* If the request method is POST, the request data are written as a stream of bytes following the empty line that terminated the request header section. The length of this data stream should be passed in the Content-Length header.

HTTP Responses

An HTTP response also consists of up to three elements:

The status line. This is a line containing the highest HTTP version that the server supports, a three-digit return code,[5] and a human-readable text description of the return code. In our example, the HTTP version was HTTP/1.1, the return code was 200, and the text description was OK.

▣ *Response headers,*[6] *if any.* These are corresponding means for the server to pass on additional information about the response and about

---

[3]HTTP PUT is considered briefly in Chapter 12. The other methods are explained in RFC2616 and its predecessors.

[4]A complete list of request headers is given in Appendix B.

[5]These return codes are described in Appendix B.

[6]A complete list of response headers is given in Appendix B.

itself. Like request headers, response headers are simple key-value pairs. In our example, the headers were

```
Date: Sat, 19 Feb 2000 18:24:29 GMT
Server: Apache/1.39 (Win32)
Last-Modified: Fri, 18 Feb 2000 12:15:19 GMT
Content-Length: 279
Content-Type: text/html.
```

Each response header appears on a line by itself, and the end of the response header section is indicated by an empty line (a line consisting of just a `CRLF`).

■ *The message body.* The contents of the document itself.

Compound Requests

Frequently, HTML documents consist of more than just text and hyperlinks, the most common example being one that includes GIF or JPEG images. Figure 2-3 shows the two-way interaction between client and server for this kind of document.

Rather than cobbling text and binary image data together into a single request, the browser makes multiple requests, one for the text and one each for any images referred to. When the user clicks on a hyperlink or opens the URL for *http://www.ipfoods.com/gallery/IPFM_History.html,* the browser does the following:

1. Analyzes the URL for its individual components:
   ■ Protocol: `http`
   ■ Host name: `www.ipfoods.com`
   ■ File name: `/gallery/IPFM_History.html`
2. Opens a socket connection to `www.ipfoods.com` using the default HTTP port number 80.
3. Writes an HTTP `GET` request for the document requested:

```
GET /gallery/IPFM_History.html HTTP/1.0
```

4. Reads the HTTP response headers and the contents of the document:

```
HTTP/1.1 200 OK
Date: Sat, 19 Feb 2000 22:31:40 GMT
```

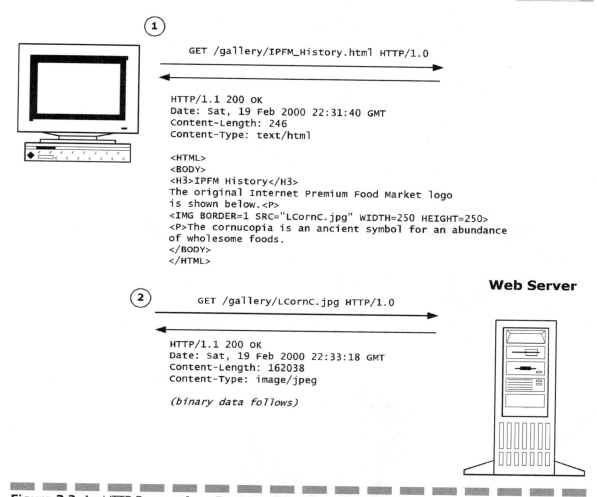

Figure 2-3 *An HTTP Request for a Document Including an Image.*

```
Content-Length: 246
Content-Type: text/html

<HTML>
<BODY>
<H3>IPFM History</H3>
The original Internet Premium Food Market logo
is shown below.<P>
<IMG BORDER=1 SRC="LCornC.jpg" WIDTH=250 HEIGHT=250>
<P>The cornucopia is an ancient symbol for an abundance
of wholesome food.
</BODY>
</HTML>
```

5. Closes the socket connection.[7]

6. Scans the text for any image URLs (such as `LCornC.jpg`). For each one that is found, repeats steps 1 to 5 using the image URL.

7. Formats and displays the resulting document in the browser window, as shown in Figure 2-4.

---

[7]HTTP/1.1 introduced the idea of persistent connections to cover this text-and-images scenario. If the client sends a `Connection: Keep-Alive` header, the server may keep the connection open for a short time for additional requests. (See RFC2068 for further details.)

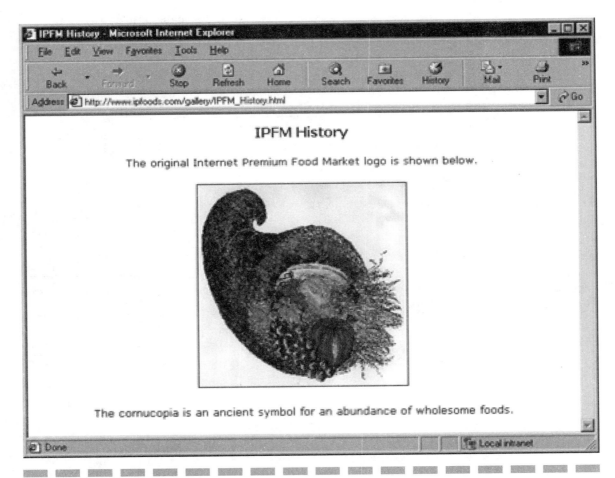

Figure 2-4 The Document with the Embedded Image.

Summary

We have traced the origin and evolution of Web applications from simple retrieval of static documents to highly interactive Web browsers accessing dynamic content. A key idea developed throughout this book is that there is nothing magical about either side of the HTTP client/server model, being a Web browser or Web server—you can emulate either one with a program or even manual input without the other side being able to tell the difference as long as you adhere to the HTTP protocol. The next chapter will introduce the Java servlet model, which uses HTTP to its fullest as a vehicle for complete Web applications.

3

Servlet Overview

The Basics

Java servlets were introduced in 1997, and their use has increased steadily ever since. Platform-independent, scalable, and offering better performance than Common Gateway Interface (CGI) scripts, servlets are a critical component of the Java 2 Enterprise Edition and have an enthusiastic following. This chapter examines servlets and their environment, considers their basic operations, and looks at a complete example.

What Is a Servlet?

A *servlet* is a Java class that dynamically extends the function of a Web server. Because it is written in Java, it has full access to Java's advanced features—database connectivity, network awareness, object orientation, and built-in support for multithreaded processes. These features can be used to deliver full-functioned applications to Web clients without requiring any special client-side configuration. Because they use ordinary Hypertext Transfer Protocol (HTTP) as their interface, they run the same in any browser environment.

A servlet runs in a Java virtual machine managed by a servlet engine. Like a CGI script, it is invoked to handle a request from a Web client, but unlike CGI, which requires a new process to be created for each request, a servlet remains loaded in the virtual machine, available to handle new requests. Each new request uses the same copy of the servlet in memory while running in its own thread of execution for optimal performance.

Figure 3-1 illustrates the main components of the servlet environment. A servlet engine, which is typically a third-party add-on, is connected by some vendor-specific means to a Web server. The servlet engine intercepts specific HTTP requests that it recognizes as servlet requests. Other requests are handled by the Web server in its usual manner. The servlet engine loads the appropriate servlet if it is not already

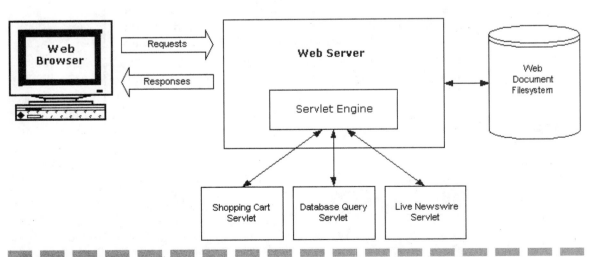

Figure 3-1 Servlets Managed by a Servlet Engine.

running and then assigns an available thread to handle the request, sending the servlet output back to the requesting Web client.

There are two Java packages that contain the application programming interface (API) for servlets: `javax.servlet.*` and `javax.servlet.http.*`. To be a servlet managed by a servlet engine, a Java class must implement the `javax.servlet.Servlet` interface, either directly or, as is more commonly done, by extending `javax.servlet.GenericServlet` or its subclass `javax.servlet.http.HttpServlet`. Usually, a servlet author will need to override only one or two superclass methods to implement the particular functionality that the servlet provides.

The Servlet Life Cycle

Like their client-side applet counterparts, servlets follow a strict life cycle. There are three types of events in the life of each servlet instance, and they correspond to three methods that are invoked by the servlet engine:

- `init()`. When a servlet is first loaded, the servlet engine calls its `init()` method exactly once. If a servlet has any special initialization needs, such as resetting a counter or establishing a database connection, the servlet author can override the `init()` method to perform the work. This is an optional method; if a servlet has no need for initialization, its superclass `init()` method will be called by default. A servlet is guaranteed not to be called to handle any requests until its `init()` method has completed successfully.

- `service()`. This is the heart of the servlet, the place where requests are actually handled. For each request, the servlet engine will call the servlet's `service()` method, passing it references to a servlet request object and a servlet response object. The request object, which implements the `ServletRequest` interface, encapsulates information about the client and the particulars of the request. Similarly, the response object, which implements `ServletResponse`, contains a reference to the output stream that will be used to write results back to the client.

- `destroy()`. This is the optional counterpart to `init()`, called by the servlet engine when the servlet is about to be unloaded. This is the place to clean up and release any resources allocated in the `init()` method.

Ordinarily, servlet classes remain loaded and active until the servlet engine is shut down. However, if the servlet engine detects that a servlet has been recompiled since the last time it serviced a request, the new servlet class will be loaded, replacing the old one.

Servlets and HTTP

In principle, servlets can operate in any networked request-response model, but by far the most common setting is HTTP. The API provides specialized subclasses for the servlet, servlet request, and servlet response objects in the HTTP environment:

- `HttpServlet`. This is an abstract class for handling HTTP requests. Its only public method is `service()`, which is a thin wrapper around specific methods for each HTTP method—`doGet()` for GET requests, `doPost()` for POST requests, and so on. It is common practice to override the `doGet()` or `doPost()` methods, not the `service()` method itself.

- `HttpServletRequest`. This is a subinterface of `ServletRequest`. It provides methods to access the request line, the request headers, any form parameters, and any message data passed with the request.

- `HttpServletResponse`. This is a subinterface of `ServletResponse`. It provides access to the output stream that the requesting client will read and allows the servlet to set response headers.

A Complete Example

To gain a clearer picture of how this all works, let's examine a servlet in detail. Figure 3-2 shows the source code for a servlet that extracts the HTTP request headers with which it is invoked and displays them in an HTML table.

To begin with, the program declares the packages that contain classes it will use. Two of them are the traditional input-output (I/O) and utilities packages, and the other two contain the Java servlet API.

```
import java.io.*;
import java.util.*;
import javax.servlet.*;
import javax.servlet.http.*;
```

██ ██ ██ ██
Figure 3-2
A Servlet That
Returns
Information About
Its Requests.

```java
import java.io.*;
import java.util.*;
import javax.servlet.*;
import javax.servlet.http.*;

/**
 * A basic servlet that echoes details about the
 * HTTP request that invokes it back to the client
 * that requested it.
 */
public class EchoRequestServlet extends HttpServlet
{
    /**
     * Handles an HTTP GET request
     */
    public void doGet(
            HttpServletRequest request,
            HttpServletResponse response)
        throws ServletException, IOException
    {
        response.setContentType("text/html");
        PrintWriter out = response.getWriter();

        out.println("<HTML>");
        out.println("<HEAD>");
        out.println("<TITLE>Request Headers</TITLE>");
        out.println("</HEAD>");
        out.println("<BODY>");
        out.println("<H3>Request Headers</H3>");
        out.println
            ("<TABLE BORDER=1 CELLPADDING=4 CELLSPACING=0>");
        Enumeration enames = request.getHeaderNames();
        while (enames.hasMoreElements()) {
            String name = (String) enames.nextElement();
            String value = request.getHeader(name);
            if ((value != null) && (!value.equals(""))) {
                out.println("<TR>");
                out.println("<TD>" + name + "</TD>");
                out.println("<TD>" + value + "</TD>");
                out.println("</TR>");
            }
        }
        out.println("</TABLE>");
        out.println("</BODY>");
        out.println("</HTML>");
    }
}
```

The class declaration defines the servlet class name to be
EchoRequestServlet and indicates that it is a subclass of
javax.servlet.http.HttpServlet:

```java
public class EchoRequestServlet extends HttpServlet
```

The class name is not necessarily the alias by which it will be invoked in a URL—this is not part of the servlet specification and is determined by the servlet engine vendor. This book follows the convention of appending `Servlet` to all servlet class names but using the unadorned name in the alias employed to invoke the servlet. Thus `ABCServlet.java` will contain a class named `ABCServlet` that will be invoked as *http://hostname/servlet/ABC*.

Most servlets extend `HttpServlet`, either directly or indirectly, because it provides basic support for the HTTP request and response environment. A somewhat less common choice is `GenericServlet`, which is `HttpServlet`'s immediate parent. `GenericServlet` may be an appropriate superclass for servlets that do not implement the `doGet()` or `doPost()` methods but only the `service()` method directly with no HTTP-specific behavior.

The only method that we need to implement in `EchoRequestServlet` is `doGet()`. It has the following signature:

```
public void doGet(
      HttpServletRequest request,
      HttpServletResponse response)
   throws ServletException, IOException
```

`doGet()` is a public method because it needs to be called by the servlet engine. It has two parameters, one for the request object and one for the response object. It must declare that it can potentially throw either a `javax.servlet.ServletException` or a `java.io.IOException`.

At the beginning of the `doGet()` method, we set the `Content-Type` response header to `text/html` so that the browser will know to interpret output as HTML rather than plain text or something else:

```
response.setContentType("text/html");
```

The servlet engine creates an output stream to which the Web output is written. Inside the `doGet()` method, this output stream is accessible in either of two forms—as a `ServletOutputStream`, used primarily for binary data, or as a `java.io.PrintWriter`, for ordinary character data. The response object provides two methods for this purpose, `getOutputStream()` and `getWriter()`, respectively. Either one can be called, but never both in the same request-handling method. In our case, we access a character stream using `getWriter()`:

```
PrintWriter out = response.getWriter();
```

Once we have a reference to the output stream, we can begin generating HTML using ordinary `println()` statements:

```
out.println("<HTML>");
out.println("<HEAD>");
out.println("<TITLE>Request Headers</TITLE>");
out.println("</HEAD>");
out.println("<BODY>");
out.println("<H3>Request Headers</H3>");
```

An HTML table is used to show the request headers. The servlet request object provides a pair of methods that will let us step through the list: `getHeaderNames()`, which returns a `java.util.Enumeration` of all known headers, and `getHeader(String name)`, which returns the value of the specified header (or `null` if it was not sent with the request):

```
out.println("<TABLE BORDER=1 CELLPADDING=4 CELLSPACING=0>");
Enumeration enames = request.getHeaderNames();
while (enames.hasMoreElements()) {
    String name = (String) enames.nextElement();
    String value = request.getHeader(name);
```

For each value that is nonnull and nonblank, we generate a table row containing the header name and header value:

```
if ((value != null) && (!value.equals(""))) {
    out.println("<TR>");
    out.println("<TD>" + name + "</TD>");
    out.println("<TD>" + value + "</TD>");
    out.println("<TR>");
    }
```

All that remains is to generate the closing tags for the table and the document body:

```
out.println("</TABLE>");
out.println("</BODY>");
out.println("</HTML>");
```

Invoking the Servlet   Servlets are registered with the servlet engine and can then be invoked by a URL from a Web browser. The means by which this registration is done is specific to each servlet engine vendor and is described in the vendor's documentation. Typically, the URL by which a servlet is invoked contains the string `/servlet` followed by the registered name of the servlet. In our case, the `EchoRequestServlet` is invoked with the *http://hostname/servlet/EchoRequest* URL and produces the results shown in Figure 3-3.

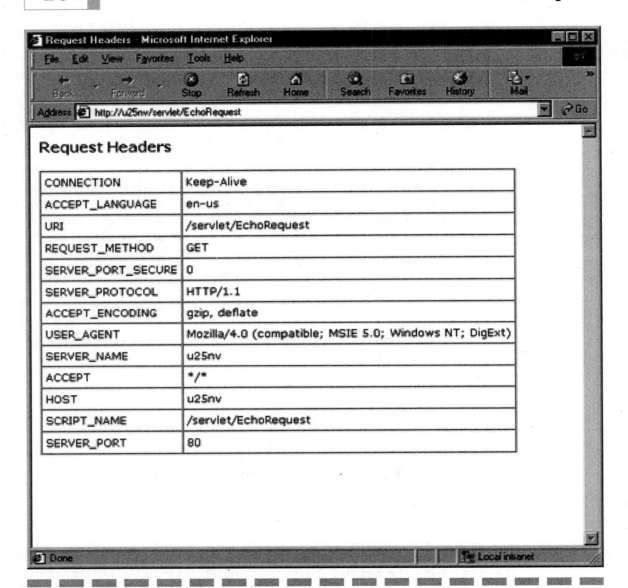

Figure 3-3 Output of the `EchoRequest` Servlet.

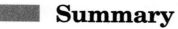 # Summary

We have described the servlet environment—the Java classes that servlets relate to and the servlet engine that manages them. We have examined the way in which servlets are loaded and executed and an example of the Java code they contain. Equipped with this basic understanding, we are now ready to embark on Part II of the book—the problems, techniques, and discussions that make up the "servlet cookbook."

2

The Servlet Cookbook

4

HTML Clients

Overview

If Hypertext Markup Language (HTML) is the universal language of the World Wide Web, then HTML forms are what make it a two-way conversation. If you have ever used an Internet search engine, ordered a book online, or registered a product on the Web, you probably did it with an HTML form like the one shown in Figure 4-1.

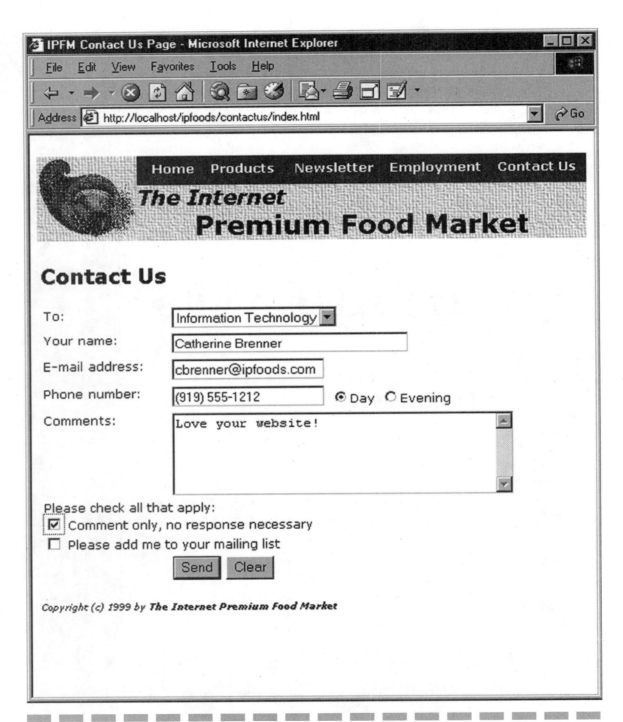

Figure 4-1 A typical HTML form.

Forms are likely to be the starting point for most Web applications you will write. This chapter will show you

- How to use HTML to capture user input and convey it to an application on the server
- How to interpret data sent by a form to your servlet
- How to create Web pages to be returned to the browser
- How to handle errors and control the online conversation

Forms and Input Elements

An HTML form is simply a section of a document that begins with a <FORM> tag, followed by any number of input elements or other valid HTML form and a closing </FORM> tag. The HTML used to create the "Contact Us" form in Figure 4-1 is shown in Figure 4-2.

Data that the user enters in a form are sent to the server program as a set of NAME=VALUE pairs that are encoded for transmission over the network. The resulting data stream can be interpreted by the server program to retrieve the individual fields, as shown in Figure 4-3.

This section describes how to use the <FORM> element and its associated input element tags. Note that the elements listed in this section are the ones used most commonly. There are others; a comprehensive treatment of the subject can be found in the official World Wide Web Consortium HTML 4.0 specification at *http://www.w3.org/TR/1998/ REC-html40-19980424/ interact/forms.html*. Be aware, however, that not all elements are supported equally well in all browsers. In particular, browsers differ in their use of default values. When in doubt, if you are relying on particular default values, you should specify all pertinent attributes instead of letting the browser choose them by default. And of course, test your form in all the environments in which it needs to operate.

The <FORM> Tag

The syntax of the <FORM> tag is fairly simple:

```
<FORM ACTION=url METHOD=GET|POST ENCTYPE=content type>
```

where

Figure 4-2
The HTML used in
the "Contact Us"
form.

```
<FORM METHOD=GET ACTION="/servlet/EchoParms">

<TABLE BORDER=0 CELLPADDING=2 CELLSPACING=0 WIDTH=550>

    <TR VALIGN=TOP>
       <TD>To:</TD>
       <TD>
          <SELECT NAME="to" SIZE=1>
             <OPTION VALUE="CS">Customer Service
             <OPTION VALUE="EX">Executive
             <OPTION VALUE="FI">Finance
             <OPTION VALUE="HR">Human Resources
             <OPTION VALUE="IT">Information Technology
             <OPTION VALUE="MK">Marketing
             <OPTION VALUE="FA">Facilities
             <OPTION VALUE="PC">Purchasing
             <OPTION VALUE="SP">Shipping
          </SELECT>
       </TD>
    </TR>

    <TR VALIGN=TOP>
       <TD>Your name:</TD>
       <TD><INPUT NAME="from" TYPE="text" SIZE=32></TD>
    </TR>

    <TR VALIGN=TOP>
       <TD>E-mail address:</TD>
       <TD><INPUT NAME="email" TYPE="text" SIZE=20></TD>
    </TR>

    <TR VALIGN=TOP>
       <TD>Phone number:</TD>
       <TD>
       <INPUT NAME="phone" TYPE="text" SIZE=20>
       <INPUT NAME="dayphone" TYPE="radio" VALUE="1" CHECKED>Day
       <INPUT NAME="dayphone" TYPE="radio" VALUE="0">Evening
       </TD>
    </TR>

    <TR VALIGN=TOP>
       <TD>Comments:</TD>
       <TD>
       <TEXTAREA NAME="comments" ROWS=5 COLS=40>
       </TEXTAREA>
       </TD>
    </TR>

    <TR VALIGN=TOP>
       <TD COLSPAN=2>
       <FONT SIZE=-1>
       Please check all that apply: <BR>
       <INPUT NAME="category" TYPE="checkbox" VALUE="1">
           Comment only, no response necessary <BR>
       <INPUT NAME="category" TYPE="checkbox" VALUE="2">
           Please add me to your mailing list
       </FONT>
          </TD>
       </TR>
          </TD>
       </TR>


    <TR VALIGN=TOP>
       <TD> </TD>
       <TD>
          <INPUT TYPE="submit" VALUE="Send">
          <INPUT TYPE="reset" VALUE="Clear">
       </TD>
    </TR>
    </TABLE>

    </FORM>
```

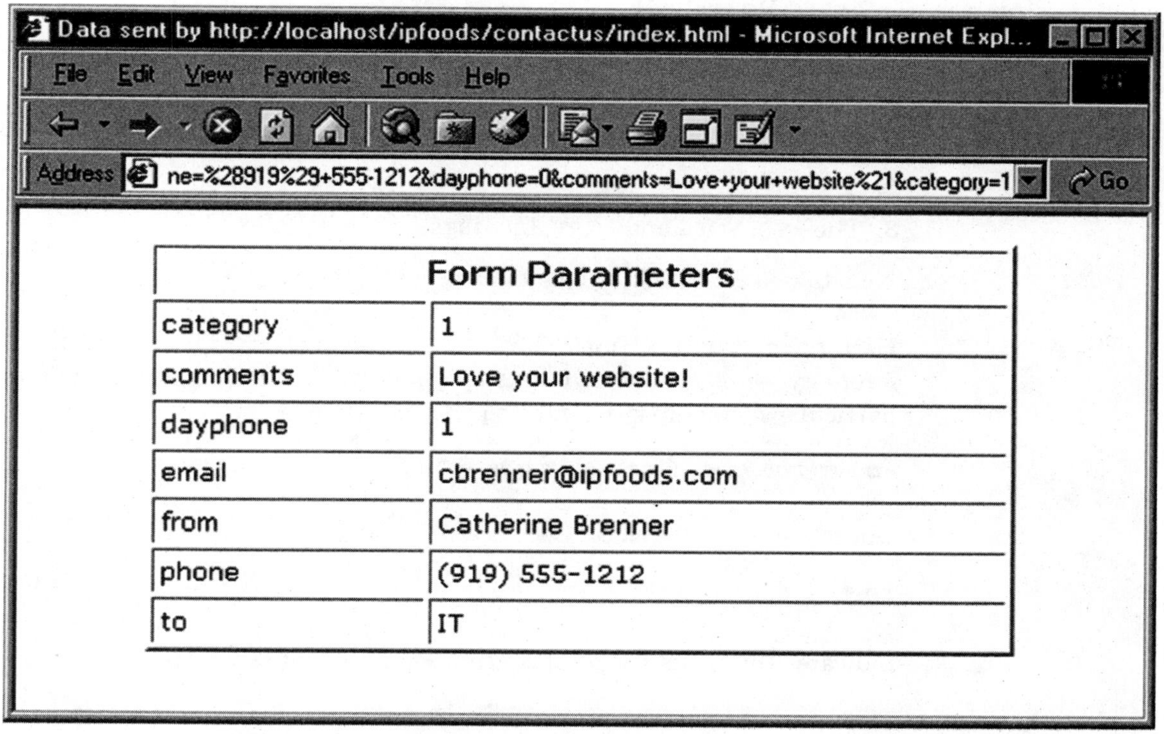

Figure 4-3 Data fields recovered from the "Contact Us" form.

ACTION=*url*

identifies the server-side program that processes the form.

METHOD=GET | POST

optionally specifies the means by which the server program receives the form data. GET causes the data to be appended to the URL as an encoded string, whereas POST makes it available in a data stream that follows the HTTP request. GET is the default value of this attribute.

ENCTYPE=*content type*

is the optional content type, which defaults to application/x-www-form-urlencoded.

Of the three, ACTION is the only required attribute.

Input Elements

The input elements within a form can be specified in any of three ways:

1. The `<INPUT>` tag
2. The `<TEXTAREA>` tag
3. The `<SELECT>` and `<OPTION>` tags

Let's take a brief look at how to use each of these.

Using the `<INPUT>` Tag   The `<INPUT>` tag is used for a number of different types of elements. It has optional attributes that are specific to particular element types, but its general format is

`<INPUT TYPE=`*type* `NAME=`*name* `VALUE=`*value*`>`

where

`TYPE=`*type*

indicates the specific type of control. Possible values for are

TEXT	A single-line text field. Use a `SIZE=` attribute to indicate the visible length of the field and/or a `MAXLENGTH=` attribute to specify the maximum number of characters that the field can contain.
PASSWORD	Same as `TEXT`, but characters typed will not be echoed to the screen. Instead, asterisks (*) will appear in place of what is typed.
CHECKBOX	An element representing a single Boolean value. Use the `CHECKED` attribute to indicate that this element should be preselected when the form is first displayed.
RADIO	Similar to a checkbox but used with a group of mutually exclusive attributes. When a user clicks any radio button in a group, all the others are deselected automatically. You can specify the set of buttons to be grouped together by giving them the same `NAME=` attribute.
SUBMIT	A pushbutton that the user clicks to cause the form to be submitted to the form's action handler. You can code a `VALUE=` attribute to give this button a label of something other than "submit."

RESET   A pushbutton that the user clicks to restore the default values of all the elements in the form. This button also can have a VALUE= attribute that gives it a different label.

FILE   A file selection box, typically with a BROWSE button shown next to it.

IMAGE   A submit button with a graphic image. When an IMAGE element is clicked, the x and y coordinates of the mouse click are sent to the server program.

HIDDEN   A read-only value invisible to the user that can be used to specify a hard-coded form value.

NAME=*name*

specifies the name by which the element will be known to the server program. This name is also visible to any client-side scripts in the Web page so that the elements of the form can be validated before being submitted to the server.

VALUE=*value*

is the initial value of the element.

The "Contact Us" form in Figure 4-2 illustrates several typical uses of the <INPUT> tag, including TEXT elements (the "from," "email," and "phone" fields), RADIO buttons (the choices for the "dayphone" field), CHECKBOX elements (the "category" fields), and the RESET and SUBMIT buttons.

Using the <TEXTAREA> Tag   A second type of input element is the <TEXTAREA> tag. This element allows you to create a multiline text field. Its basic format is

```
<TEXTAREA NAME=name ROWS=nrows COLS=ncols>
data line 1
data line 2
...
data line n
</TEXTAREA>
```

where

NAME=*name*

is the name by which the text field will be known to the server-side program named in the ACTION attribute of the <FORM> tag.

ROWS=*nrows*

indicates the number of visible rows. Note that this is only a visual suggestion to the user; the actual number of lines typed can be greater.

COLS=*ncols*

indicates the width of each row in the text field.

```
data line 1
data line 2
...
data line n
```

are the optional initial contents of the field.

Unlike the <INPUT> element, a <TEXTAREA> requires an ending </TEXTAREA> tag. This allows you to provide an initial set of lines to be displayed in the text area. Figure 4-2 shows a <TEXTAREA> being used for the comments a user wants to submit to the Web site.

Using the <SELECT> and <OPTION> Tags You can use the <SELECT> and <OPTION> tags to create scrollable list boxes. A list box created with these tags consists of three elements:

1. A <SELECT> tag specifying the name, size, and selection characteristics of the list

2. Any number of <OPTION> tags with their labels and values

3. An ending </SELECT> tag

The <SELECT> tag has the following syntax:

<SELECT NAME=name **SIZE**=size **[MULTIPLE]**>

where

NAME=*name*

indicates the field name that will contain the value of the selected option.

SIZE=*size*

specifies the number of rows that should be visible at one time.

MULTIPLE

if specified, allows the user to select more than one item from the list. All three attributes are optional (although it does not make much sense to omit the NAME).

Between the <SELECT> and </SELECT> tags comes the set of items that should be included in the list. These are coded with <OPTION> tags having the following syntax:

<OPTION VALUE=*value* **[SELECTED]>** *label*

where

VALUE=*value*

indicates the value that will be associated with the field named in the <SELECT> tag if this option is selected.

SELECTED

if specified, preselects this option when the list box is first displayed.

label

contains the text that should be displayed in the list for this option.

We have covered the syntax of the <FORM>, <INPUT>, <TEXTAREA>, <SELECT>, and <OPTION> tags. Familiarity with these elements is really all that is required for basic HTML form development. In actual practice, you most likely would want to perform client-side validation of your forms using JavaScript. I have not gone into all these details here because this is a book about servlets, not HTML. If you would like a more in-depth treatment of the subject, some good resources are *HTML: The Complete Reference*, by Thomas A. Powell, published by Osborne McGraw-Hill, December 1997 (ISBN 0078823978), and *JavaScript Annotated Archives*, by Jeff Frentzen, Henry Sobotka, and Dewayne McNair, published by Osborne McGraw-Hill, April 1998 (ISBN 0078823641). The remainder of this chapter consists of specific examples of how to process HTML forms with servlets.

4.1 Extracting Parameter Values

Problem

My servlet processes an HTML form. How do I know what fields the form contains and what their values are?

Technique

Use the request object's getParameterNames() method to get the field names and its getParameter(String name) method to retrieve the value of each field.

Discussion

The "Contact Us" form shown in Figure 4-1 has eight data fields:

1. The "To" department
2. The user's name
3. The user's email address
4. The phone number
5. Whether the phone number is a day or evening number
6. The user's comments
7. A checkbox to indicate that the question does not require a response
8. A checkbox for the user to ask to be put on the mailing list

When the user clicks the Send button, the Web browser transmits the field names and values to the program (i.e., your servlet) specified in the ACTION attribute of the <FORM> tag. In the HTML listing in Figure 4-2, we can see the names of each of these fields, but how exactly are these transmitted to the servlet?

The short answer is that the field names and values are concatenated into NAME=VALUE pairs that are separated by the ampersand character (&). This concatenated string is either appended to the URL as a query string if the form's METHOD attribute is GET or passed as an input stream if METHOD=POST. This is not quite the full answer, however. If the form's data values contain embedded blanks or other characters (such as the ampersand or equal sign) that have special meaning in the HTTP protocol, the data stream can be garbled or truncated. For this reason, field names and values are encoded according to the following rules:[1]

1. Nonalphanumeric characters are replaced by %xx, where xx represents the two-digit hexadecimal value of the character.

2. All spaces are replaced by a plus sign.

The resulting URL generated by the "Contact Us" form is

```
http://localhost/servlet/EchoParms
    ?to=IT
    &from=Catherine+Brenner
    &email=cbrenner@ipfoods.com
    &phone=%28919%29+555-1212
    &dayphone=1
    &comments=Love+your+website%21
    &category=1
```

NOTE *The URL is actually all one line with no spaces. It is shown here on multiple lines for ease of reference.*

The server program unwinds this process by applying it in reverse, splitting NAME=VALUE pairs along ampersand boundaries and then converting the plus signs to spaces and %xx to the corresponding ASCII characters.

The good news is that you do not have to be concerned with this in your servlet—the servlet engine takes care of it for you. Figure 4-4 shows how you can extract forms parameters from the HttpServletRequest object.

The ParmsExtractorServlet first gets an enumeration of the form's field names as follows:

```
Enumeration eParmNames = request.getParameterNames();
```

Then for each name in the list, it gets the corresponding field value by calling the request object's getParameter() method:

---

[1]A full description of how this is done can be found in RFC1738, *Uniform Resource Locators (URL)*, Section 2.2. The text of this RFC is available at *http://www.freesoft.org/ CIE/RFC/1738/index.htm*.

Figure 4-4

Extracting param-
eter names and
values.

```
package ijs.forms;

import java.io.*;
import java.util.*;
import javax.servlet.*;
import javax.servlet.http.*;

/**
 * ParmExtractorServlet
 */
public class ParmExtractorServlet extends HttpServlet
{
    /**
     * Handles a GET request
     * @param request the servlet request object
     * @param response the servlet response object
     * @exception ServletException if a servlet exception occurs
     * @exception IOException if an I/O exception occurs
     */
    public void doGet(
                    HttpServletRequest request,
                    HttpServletResponse response)
      throws ServletException, IOException

    {
        response.setContentType("text/plain");
        ServletOutputStream out = response.getOutputStream();

        // Get the names of all the form parameters

        Enumeration eParmNames = request.getParameterNames();

        // Iterate through the list retrieving the value
        // of each parameter

        while (eParmNames.hasMoreElements()) {
            String name = (String) eParmNames.nextElement();
            String value = request.getParameter(name);
            out.println(name + " = " + value);
        }
    }
}
```

```
while (eParmNames.hasMoreElements()) {
    String name = (String) eParmNames.nextElement();
    String value = request.getParameter(name);
    out.println(name + " = " + value);
}
```

The results are shown in Figure 4-5.

We have actually cheated a bit getting the values, but this is the subject of the next section.

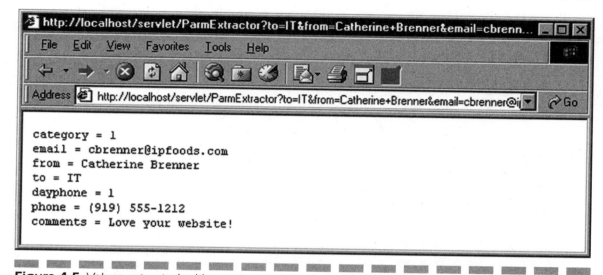

Figure 4-5 Values extracted with `getParameter`.

4.2 Handling Multivalued Parameters

Problem

The form my servlet is processing has checkboxes and multiple-selection list boxes. How can I retrieve multiple values of the same field?

Technique

Use the request object's `getParameterValues(String name)` method.

Discussion

The "Contact Us" form shown in Figure 4-2 has two checkboxes with the same name:

```
<INPUT NAME="category" TYPE="checkbox" VALUE="1">
   Comment only, no response necessary <BR>
<INPUT NAME="category" TYPE="checkbox" VALUE="2">
   Please add me to your mailing list
```

If the user checks both of them, the query string sent by the browser will contain (among other things) two NAME=VALUE pairs with a name of "category" as follows:

```
category=1&category=2
```

Similarly, if the "From:" list box is changed to a multiple-selection list box:

```
<SELECT NAME="to" SIZE=3 MULTIPLE>
    <OPTION VALUE="CS">Customer Service
    <OPTION VALUE="EX">Executive
    <OPTION VALUE="FI">Finance
    <OPTION VALUE="HR">Human Resources
    <OPTION VALUE="IT">Information Technology
    <OPTION VALUE="MK">Marketing
    <OPTION VALUE="FA">Facilities
    <OPTION VALUE="PC">Purchasing
    <OPTION VALUE="SP">Shipping
</SELECT>
```

and the user selects the Executive, Information Technology, and Marketing Departments, the browser will send three NAME=VALUE pairs each having a name of "to":

```
to=EX&to=IT&to=MK
```

This presents a problem if you naively use ServletRequest. getParameter(String name) to retrieve the value. The Servlet API documentation declares that in this case, the servlet engine will choose the value (no doubt one not to your liking). To avoid this problem, use the getParameterValues(String name) method, which returns an array of String objects rather than a single String value:

```
while (eParmNames.hasMoreElements()) {
    String name = (String) eParmNames.nextElement();
    String[] values = request.getParameterValues(name);
    if (values != null) {
        for (int i = 0; i < values.length; i++) {
            String value = values[i];
            out.println(name + " = " + value);
        }
    }
}
```

4.3   Handling Both GET and POST Requests

Problem

My servlet needs to process both GET and POST requests, and I would like to avoid duplicate code.

Technique

Call doGet(request, response) directly from doPost(request, response), or vice versa.

Discussion

To extract the raw query string from an HTML form, CGI programs typically employ logic something like this, either directly or indirectly:

```
my $query = "";
if ($ENV{'REQUEST_METHOD'} eq "POST") {
    read(STDIN, $query, $ENV{'CONTENT_LENGTH'} );
}
elsif ($ENV{'REQUEST_METHOD'} eq "GET") {
    $query = $ENV{'QUERY_STRING'} ;
}
```

The same logic is required in a servlet, but all the work is done by the servlet engine, which encapsulates the query data in an HttpRequest object and then calls the servlet's service() method. The service method either calls the doPost() method directly or conditionally executes the doGet() method, depending on whether the request contains an IF-MODIFIED-SINCE header. You can override the service() method if you wish, but it is simpler just to call doPost() from within doGet(), or vice versa:

```
/**
 * Handles a POST request
 * @param request the servlet request
 * @param response the servlet response
 * @exception ServletException if a servlet exception occurs
```

```
 * @exception IOException if an I/O exception occurs
 */
public void doPost(
      HttpServletRequest request,
      HttpServletResponse response)
   throws ServletException, IOException
{
   doGet(request, response);
}
```

The only caveat is that HTTP GET requests are considered to be idempotent operations, meaning that they can be executed multiple times with no adverse side effects (like 1 OR 1 OR 1 OR...), whereas POST requests do not have this property (like 1 PLUS 1 PLUS 1 PLUS...). This is why your browser occasionally nags you about deciding whether or not to repost form data. In most cases, however, the choice of GET versus POST is a matter of taste. GET requests can clutter up the address line with a long string of ampersands and hex digits and may run into length restrictions on some servers.

4.4   Creating Web Pages to Be Returned

Problem

After my servlet processes a request, how do I generate the HTML to be returned to the client?

Technique

Set the content type header

```
response.setContentType("text/html");
```

And write lines of text to the servlet output stream:

```
PrintWriter out = response.getWriter();
out.println("<HTML>");
out.println("<HEAD>");
out.println("<TITLE>Hello, world</TITLE>");
out.println("<BODY>");
out.println("<H1>Hello, world</H1>");
out.println("</BODY>");
out.println("</HTML>");
```

Discussion

The `javax.servlet.http.HttpServletResponse` object that is passed to every servlet encapsulates the HTTP response headers and output stream that the server uses to send a Web page back to the requesting browser. You set response headers using the response object's `setHeader()` method or one of its specialized `setContentLength()`, `setContentType()`, `setDateHeader()`, or `setIntHeader()` methods. At a minimum, you need to specify the content type (usually `text/html` for ordinary Web pages).

After you have set the desired headers, you simply start writing HTML statements with the `println()` method, either to a `ServletOutputStream` or to a `PrintWriter` (but never both):

```
ServletOutputStream out = response.getOutputStream();
out.println("<HTML>");
...
out.println("</HTML>");
```

or

```
PrintWriter out = response.getWriter();
out.println("<HTML>");
...
out.println("</HTML>");
```

The `PrintWriter` approach will use the character encoding you may have specified in the `charset=` property of the `setContentType()` method, whereas the `ServletOutputStream` will write unencoded binary data. In practice, there is little difference between these two choices.

There are a number of HTML generation tools available on the Internet. Whether you use these tools or not is a matter of personal preference. My own experience has been that they never generate exactly what you want, and you cannot fine tune them to the degree that you could if you simply wrote the HTML yourself—it is not that difficult.

4.5 Structured HTML Generation

Problem

Writing large amounts of HTML with `println()` statements is tedious and prone to error. How can I simplify the process but still keep control over the output?

Technique

Using an inner class, create a parameter structure that is local to your
doGet() method and that contains all your local variables. Then generate your HTML with a hierarchy of methods that corresponds to the document hierarchy. Pass the structure as each method's only parameter.

Discussion

Suppose you have a shopping cart application that produces the nice-
looking Web page illustrated in Figure 4-6. The HTML behind the Web
page is shown in Figure 4-7. The HTML is very busy-looking, full of the
<TR>'s and <TD>'s that you need to get the layout just right. Of course,
you do not mind all the detail because the HTML is generated by your
ShowCart servlet. This servlet (see Figure 4-8) generates the required
tables entirely within its doGet() method.

Suppose now, to your dismay, that while adding some enhancements
to the code, you inadvertently delete a couple of crucial lines:

```
out.println("</table>");    // This line
out.println(
  "<H4>There are "
  + ((nItems == 0) ? " no" : ("" + nItems))
  + " items in your cart:</H4>");
if (nItems > 0) {
  // ... and the line below
  out.println("<TABLE BORDER=1 CELLPADDING=5 WIDTH=546>");
  out.println("<TR>");
```

Look at the awful result, shown in Figure 4-9. You have lost an ending
table tag and thrown off your alignment and borders.

This is a fairly easy error to make, but in this case, it is also fairly easy
to correct. If you are dealing with two or three levels of nested tables,
however, being "one off" in your opening and closing tags can be quite
exasperating.

An obvious solution to this problem is to break down the monolithic
code that generates the HTML into a hierarchy of subroutines, each of
which has the opening and closing tags in close proximity. Figure 4-10
shows a logical decomposition of the ShowCart servlet.

A subtle difficulty with this approach, however, is that servlets are not
by default thread safe. There is usually a single instance of a running

Figure 4-6 The ShowCart servlet in operation.

Figure 4-7

The HTML that produces the ShowCart Web page.

```
<HTML>
<HEAD>
<TITLE>ShowCartServlet</TITLE>
<LINK REL="stylesheet" HREF="/ipfoods/style.css">
</HEAD>
<BODY>
<TABLE BORDER=0 CELLPADDING=0 CELLSPACING=0
       BACKGROUND="/ipfoods/images/texture.jpg">
<TR>
   <TD ROWSPAN=3>
      <MAP NAME="logo">
         <AREA SHAPE="rect" COORDS="0,0,96,96"
            HREF="/ipfoods/index.html">
      </MAP>
      <IMG
         USEMAP="#logo"
         SRC="/ipfoods/images/logo.jpg"
         ALT="The Internet Premium Food Market"
         ALIGN=LEFT BORDER=0 VSPACE=0 HSPACE=0>
   </TD>
   <TD ALIGN=LEFT VALIGN=TOP>
      <MAP NAME="toolbar">
         <AREA SHAPE="rect" COORDS="0,0,65,30"
            HREF="/ipfoods/index.html">
         <AREA SHAPE="rect" COORDS="66,0,145,30"
            HREF="/ipfoods/products/index.html">
         <AREA SHAPE="rect" COORDS="146,0,245,30"
            HREF="/ipfoods/newsletter/index.html">
         <AREA SHAPE="rect" COORDS="246,0,355,30"
            HREF="/ipfoods/employment/index.html">
         <AREA SHAPE="rect" COORDS="356,0,450,30"
            HREF="/ipfoods/contactus/index.html">
      </MAP>
      <IMG
         USEMAP="#toolbar"
         SRC="/ipfoods/images/toolbar.jpg"
         ALT="Toolbar"
         ALIGN=LEFT BORDER=0 VSPACE=0 HSPACE=0>
   </TD>
</TR>
<TR>
   <TD ALIGN=LEFT VALIGN=TOP>
      <FONT SIZE=+2><I><B>The Internet</B></I></FONT><BR>
   </TD>
</TR>
<TR>
   <TD ALIGN=CENTER VALIGN=TOP>
      <FONT SIZE=+3><B>Premium Food Market</B></FONT><BR>
   </TD>
</TR>
</TABLE>
<P>
<TABLE BORDER=0 CELLPADDING=0 CELLSPACING=0 WIDTH=546>
<TR>
<TD><H2>Shopping Cart</H2></TD>
<TD WIDTH=120 VALIGN=TOP>
<A HREF="/ipfoods/products/index.html">
```

Figure 4-7
(Continued)

```
<IMG BORDER=0 SRC="/ipfoods/images/search.gif">
</A>
</TD>
<TD WIDTH=120 VALIGN=TOP>
<A HREF="/servlet/IPFShowSearchResults">
<IMG BORDER=0 SRC="/ipfoods/images/viewsearch.gif">
</A>
</TD>
</TR>
</TABLE>
<H4>There are 3 items in your cart</H4>
<TABLE BORDER=1 CELLPADDING=5 WIDTH=546>
<TR>
<TH ALIGN=CENTER VALIGN=MIDDLE>Item<BR>Code</TH>
<TH ALIGN=CENTER VALIGN=MIDDLE>Description</TH>
<TH ALIGN=CENTER VALIGN=MIDDLE>Price</TH>
<TH ALIGN=CENTER VALIGN=MIDDLE>Quantity</TH>
<TH ALIGN=CENTER VALIGN=MIDDLE>Total</TH>
<TH ALIGN=CENTER VALIGN=MIDDLE>Change<BR>Quantity</TH>
</TR>
<TR>
<TD ALIGN=LEFT    VALIGN=TOP>K0250</TD>
<TD ALIGN=LEFT    VALIGN=TOP>FRUIT BASKET, LARGE</TD>
<TD ALIGN=RIGHT   VALIGN=TOP>$29.99</TD>
<TD ALIGN=RIGHT   VALIGN=TOP>1</TD>
<TD ALIGN=RIGHT   VALIGN=TOP>$29.99</TD>
   <TD ALIGN=CENTER VALIGN=TOP>
   <A HREF="/servlet/IPFAddToCart?itemCode=K0250">
   <IMG ALT="Cart" SRC="/ipfoods/images/cart.gif"></A>
   <A HREF="/servlet/IPFRemoveFromCart?itemCode=K0250">
   <IMG ALT="Cart" SRC="/ipfoods/images/nocart.gif"></A>
   </TD>
</TR>
<TR>
<TD ALIGN=LEFT    VALIGN=TOP>K0372</TD>
<TD ALIGN=LEFT    VALIGN=TOP>JOHN'S PIES - KEY LIME</TD>
<TD ALIGN=RIGHT   VALIGN=TOP>$10.49</TD>
<TD ALIGN=RIGHT   VALIGN=TOP>2</TD>
<TD ALIGN=RIGHT   VALIGN=TOP>$20.98</TD>
   <TD ALIGN=CENTER VALIGN=TOP>
   <A HREF="/servlet/IPFAddToCart?itemCode=K0372">
   <IMG ALT="Cart" SRC="/ipfoods/images/cart.gif"></A>
   <A HREF="/servlet/IPFRemoveFromCart?itemCode=K0372">
   <IMG ALT="Cart" SRC="/ipfoods/images/nocart.gif"></A>
   </TD>
</TR>
<TR>
<TD ALIGN=RIGHT VALIGN=MIDDLE> </TD>
<TD ALIGN=RIGHT VALIGN=MIDDLE><B>Order Total</B></TD>
<TD ALIGN=RIGHT VALIGN=MIDDLE> </TD>
<TD ALIGN=RIGHT VALIGN=MIDDLE> </TD>
<TD ALIGN=RIGHT VALIGN=MIDDLE>$50.97</TD>
<TD ALIGN=RIGHT VALIGN=MIDDLE>
   <A HREF="/servlet/IPFCheckout">
   <img border=0 src="/ipfoods/images/checkout.gif"></A>
</TD>
</TR>
</TABLE>
<P>
<font size=-2>
<em>Copyright (c) 1999 by
<b>The Internet Premium Food Market</b></em>
</font>
</BODY>
</HTML>'
```

■■■ ■■■ ■■■ ■■■
Figure 4-8

The monolithic
ShowCart servlet.

```java
package ipfoods;

import java.io.*;
import java.net.*;
import java.text.*;
import java.sql.*;
import java.util.*;

import javax.servlet.*;
import javax.servlet.http.*;

/**
 * ShowCartServlet
 */
public class ShowCartServlet extends HttpServlet
{
    /**
     * This servlet lists the items currently in the
     * shopping cart in tabular format.
     *
     * @param request the servlet request object
     * @param response the servlet response object
     * @exception ServletException if a servlet exception occurs
     * @exception IOException if an I/O exception occurs
     */
    public void doGet(
            HttpServletRequest request,
            HttpServletResponse response)
        throws ServletException, IOException
    {
        // Set content type to raw-html to invoke the servlet
        // chain that adds standard HTML header section.

        response.setContentType("text/raw-html");

        // Get or create the shopping cart

        HttpSession session = request.getSession(true);
        ShoppingCart cart =
            (ShoppingCart) session.getValue("cart");
        if (cart == null) {
            cart = new ShoppingCart();
            session.putValue("cart", cart);
        }

        // Start writing the HTML

        ServletOutputStream out = response.getOutputStream();
        out.println("<HTML>");
        out.println("<HEAD>");
        out.println("<TITLE>ShowCartServlet</TITLE>");
        out.println("<LINK REL=\"stylesheet\""
            + " HREF=\"/ipfoods/style.css\">");
        out.println("</HEAD>");
        out.println("<BODY>");

        // If there are no items, say just that
```

Figure 4-8

(Continued).

```java
int nItems = cart.getQuantity();

out.println("<P>");
out.println("<table border=0 cellpadding=0"
    + " cellspacing=0 width=546>");
out.println("<tr>");
out.println("<td><H2>Shopping Cart</H2></td>");
out.println("<td width=120 valign=top>");
out.println("<A HREF=\"/ipfoods/products/index.html\">");
out.println(
    "<img border=0 src=\"/ipfoods/images/search.gif\">");
out.println("</A>");
out.println("</td>");

Vector searchResults =
    (Vector) session.getValue("searchResults");
if (searchResults != null) {
    out.println("<td width=120 valign=top>");
    out.println(
        "<A HREF=\"/servlet/IPFShowSearchResults\">");
    out.println("<img border=0"
        + " src=\"/ipfoods/images/viewsearch.gif\">");
    out.println("</A>");
    out.println("</td>");
}

out.println("</tr>");
out.println("</table>");
out.println(
    "<H4>There are "
    + ((nItems == 0) ? " no" : ("" + nItems))
    + " items in your cart:</H4>");

if (nItems > 0) {

    out.println(
        "<TABLE BORDER=1 CELLPADDING=5 WIDTH=546>");
    out.println("<TR>");
    out.println("<TH ALIGN=CENTER VALIGN=MIDDLE>"
        + "Item<BR>Code</TH>");
    out.println("<TH ALIGN=CENTER VALIGN=MIDDLE>"
        + "Description</TH>");
    out.println("<TH ALIGN=CENTER VALIGN=MIDDLE>"
        + "Price</TH>");
    out.println("<TH ALIGN=CENTER VALIGN=MIDDLE>"
        + "Quantity</TH>");
    out.println("<TH ALIGN=CENTER VALIGN=MIDDLE>"
        + "Total</TH>");
    out.println("<TH ALIGN=CENTER VALIGN=MIDDLE>"
        + "Change<BR>Quantity</TH>");
    out.println("</TR>");

    // Get a list of the item codes of the items
    // in the cart

    Enumeration cartKeys = cart.keys();
```

Figure 4-8
(Continued).

```java
while (cartKeys.hasMoreElements()) {

    // Get the item associated with this code

    String itemCode = (String) cartKeys.nextElement();
    CartItem item = (CartItem) cart.get(itemCode);
    Product product = item.getProduct();

    // Print a row for the item

    out.println("<TR>");
    out.println("<TD ALIGN=LEFT    VALIGN=TOP>"
        + itemCode + "</TD>");
    out.println("<TD ALIGN=LEFT    VALIGN=TOP>"
        + product.getItemDesc() + "</TD>");
    out.println("<TD ALIGN=RIGHT   VALIGN=TOP>"
        + Util.toCurrencyString(product.getPrice())
        + "</TD>");
    out.println("<TD ALIGN=RIGHT   VALIGN=TOP>"
        + item.getQuantity() + "</TD>");
    out.println("<TD ALIGN=RIGHT   VALIGN=TOP>"
        + Util.toCurrencyString(item.getExtendedPrice())
        + "</TD>");
    out.println("    <TD ALIGN=CENTER VALIGN=TOP>"

        + "<A HREF=\""
        + "/servlet/IPFAddToCart?itemCode="
        + itemCode
        + "\">"
        + "<IMG ALT=\"Cart\""
        + " SRC=\"/ipfoods/images/cart.gif\">"
        + "</A>"

        + "<A HREF=\""
        + "/servlet/IPFRemoveFromCart?itemCode="
        + itemCode
        + "\">"
        + "<IMG ALT=\"Cart\""
        + " SRC=\"/ipfoods/images/nocart.gif\">"
        + "</A>"

        + "</TD>");
    out.println("</TR>");
}

out.println("<TR>");
out.println("<TD ALIGN=LEFT    VALIGN=TOP>"
    + " </TD>");
out.println("<TD ALIGN=LEFT    VALIGN=TOP>"
    + "<B>Order Total</B></TD>");
out.println("<TD ALIGN=RIGHT   VALIGN=TOP>"
    + " </TD>");
out.println("<TD ALIGN=RIGHT   VALIGN=TOP>"
    + " </TD>");
out.println("<TD ALIGN=RIGHT   VALIGN=TOP>"
    + Util.toCurrencyString(cart.getExtendedPrice())
    + "</TD>");
```

Figure 4-8
(Continued).

```
        out.println("<TD ALIGN=RIGHT  VALIGN=TOP>");
        out.println("<A HREF=\"/servlet/IPFCheckout\">");
        out.println("<img border=0"
            + " src=\"/ipfoods/images/checkout.gif\">");
        out.println("</A>");
        out.println("</TD>");
        out.println("</TR>");
        out.println("</TABLE>");
    }

    // Done

    out.println("</BODY>");
    out.println("</HTML>");

    out.flush();
    out.close();
}

/**
 * Handles a POST request
 * @param request the servlet request object
 * @param response the servlet response object
 * @exception ServletException if a servlet exception occurs
 * @exception IOException if an I/O exception occurs
 */
public void doPost(
        HttpServletRequest request,
        HttpServletResponse response)
    throws ServletException, IOException
{
    doGet(request, response);
}
```

servlet that handles all requests for its registered name.[2] As a consequence, multiple requests by different users for the same servlet may be handled at the same time, so any instance variables that a servlet may have are shared and possibly can be corrupted. This means that any data required by a subroutine must be passed as a method parameter somehow. But this creates its own problems: If you need access, say, to the request object several levels down in your call stack, you need to pass it through all the methods above it. You very quickly start creating method calls with six or seven parameters.

An efficient way around this is to use an inner class to create a parameter structure in the top-level method (e.g., doGet()) and store all working variables in it by name. This parameter structure then becomes the only parameter you need to pass. Figure 4-11 illustrates this technique in connection with the ShowCart servlet.

---

[2]See Chapter 9 for a more detailed discussion of threading issues.

Figure 4-9 The ShowCart servlet corrupted.

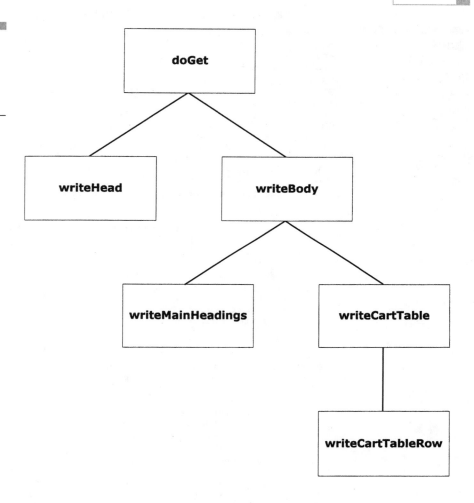

Figure 4-10
Generating
ShowCart with
hierarchy of
method calls.

4.6 Sending Error Messages Back to the Client

Problem

If my servlet is in the middle of writing to the response output stream and then detects an error, how can I cancel what I have written and send an error message back to the client?

Figure 4-11

Using a parameter structure in a hierarchy of method calls.

```java
package ipfoods;

import java.io.*;
import java.net.*;
import java.text.*;
import java.sql.*;
import java.util.*;

import javax.servlet.*;
import javax.servlet.http.*;

/**
 * ShowCartServlet2
 */
public class ShowCartServlet2 extends HttpServlet
{
    /**
     * Inner class for passing parameters between methods
     */
    class Parameters {
        HttpServletRequest request;
        HttpServletResponse response;
        ServletOutputStream out;
        HttpSession session;
        ShoppingCart cart;
        String itemCode;
    }

    /**
     * This servlet lists the items currently in the
     * shopping cart in tabular format.
     */
    public void doGet(
            HttpServletRequest request,
            HttpServletResponse response)
        throws ServletException, IOException
    {
        // Create the local parameter structure

        Parameters parms = new Parameters();
        parms.request = request;
        parms.response = response;

        // Get or create the shopping cart

        HttpSession session = request.getSession(true);
        parms.session = session;

        ShoppingCart cart =
            (ShoppingCart) session.getValue("cart");
        if (cart == null) {
            cart = new ShoppingCart();
            session.putValue("cart", cart);
        }
        parms.cart = cart;

        // Write the web page
```

Figure 4-11

(Continued)

```java
        response.setContentType("text/raw-html");
        ServletOutputStream out = response.getOutputStream();
        parms.out = out;

        out.println("<HTML>");
        writeHead(parms);
        writeBody(parms);
        out.println("</HTML>");

        out.flush();
        out.close();
    }

    /**
     * Writes the HEAD section
     */
    protected void writeHead(Parameters parms)
        throws ServletException, IOException
    {
        ServletOutputStream out = parms.out;

        out.println("<HEAD>");
        out.println("<TITLE>ShowCartServlet2</TITLE>");
        out.println("<LINK REL=\"stylesheet\""
            + " HREF=\"/ipfoods/style.css\">");
        out.println("</HEAD>");
    }

    /**
     * Writes the BODY section
     */
    protected void writeBody(Parameters parms)
        throws ServletException, IOException
    {
        ServletOutputStream out = parms.out;
        ShoppingCart cart = parms.cart;

        out.println("<BODY>");
        out.println("<P>");

        writeMainHeadings(parms);

        // If there are no items in the cart,
        // say just that.

        int nItems = cart.getQuantity();
        if (nItems == 0)
            out.println
                ("<H4>There are no items in your cart</H4>");

        // Otherwise, display the contents of the cart

        else {
            out.println
                ("<H4>There are " + nItems
                + " items in your cart</H4>");
```

Figure 4-11

(Continued)

```
        writeCartTable(parms);
    }

    out.println("</BODY>");
}

/**
 * Writes the main page headings
 */
protected void writeMainHeadings(Parameters parms)
    throws ServletException, IOException
{
    ServletOutputStream out = parms.out;
    HttpSession session = parms.session;

    out.println(""
        + "<TABLE"
        + " BORDER=0"
        + " CELLPADDING=0"
        + " CELLSPACING=0"
        + " WIDTH=546>"
        + "<TR>"
        + "<TD><H2>Shopping Cart</H2></TD>"
        + "<TD WIDTH=120 VALIGN=TOP>"
        + "<A HREF=\"/ipfoods/products/index.html\">"
        + "<IMG BORDER=0 SRC=\"/ipfoods/images/search.gif\">"
        + "</A>"
        + "</TD>"
    );

    Vector searchResults =
        (Vector) session.getValue("searchResults");
    if (searchResults != null) {
        out.println(""
            + "<TD WIDTH=120 VALIGN=TOP>"
            + "<A HREF=\"/servlet/IPFShowSearchResults\">"
            + "<IMG BORDER=0"
            + " SRC=\"/ipfoods/images/viewsearch.gif\">"
            + "</A>"
            + "</TD>"
        );
    }

    out.println("</TR>");
    out.println("</TABLE>");
}

/**
 * Writes the cart section
 */
protected void writeCartTable(Parameters parms)
    throws ServletException, IOException
{
    ServletOutputStream out = parms.out;
    ShoppingCart cart = parms.cart;

    // Start the table
```

Figure 4-11

(Continued)

```
out.println("<TABLE BORDER=1 CELLPADDING=5 WIDTH=546>");

// Write the column headings

String[] headings = {
   "Item<BR>Code",
   "Description",
   "Price",
   "Quantity",
   "Total",
   "Change<BR>Quantity",
};

out.println("<TR>");
for (int i = 0; i < headings.length; i++)
   out.println("<TH ALIGN=CENTER VALIGN=MIDDLE>"
       + headings[i] + "</TH>");
out.println("</TR>");

// Get a list of the item codes of the items in the cart
// and write a row for each

Enumeration cartKeys = cart.keys();
while (cartKeys.hasMoreElements()) {
   String itemCode = (String) cartKeys.nextElement();
   parms.itemCode = itemCode;
   writeCartTableRow(parms);
}

// Write the column footings

String[] footings = {
   " ",
   "<B>Order Total</B>",
   " ",
   " ",
   Util.toCurrencyString(cart.getExtendedPrice()),
   "<A HREF=\"/servlet/IPFCheckout\">"
   + "<img border=0"
   + " src=\"/ipfoods/images/checkout.gif\">"
   + "</A>",
};

out.println("<TR>");
for (int i = 0; i < footings.length; i++)
   out.println("<TD ALIGN=RIGHT VALIGN=MIDDLE>"
       + footings[i] + "</TD>");
out.println("</TR>");

// End the table

out.println("</TABLE>");
}

/**
* Writes a row in the cart section
```

Figure 4-11

(Continued)

```
*/
protected void writeCartTableRow(Parameters parms)
    throws ServletException, IOException
{
    ServletOutputStream out = parms.out;
    ShoppingCart cart = parms.cart;
    String itemCode = parms.itemCode;

    CartItem item = (CartItem) cart.get(itemCode);
    Product product = item.getProduct();

    // Write a row for the item

    out.println("<TR>");

    out.println(""
        + "<TD ALIGN=LEFT"
        + "    VALIGN=TOP>" + itemCode + "</TD>"
        + "<TD ALIGN=LEFT"
        + "    VALIGN=TOP>" + product.getItemDesc() + "</TD>"
        + "<TD ALIGN=RIGHT  VALIGN=TOP>"
        + Util.toCurrencyString(product.getPrice()) + "</TD>"
        + "<TD ALIGN=RIGHT  VALIGN=TOP>"
        + item.getQuantity() + "</TD>"
        + "<TD ALIGN=RIGHT  VALIGN=TOP>"
        + Util.toCurrencyString(item.getExtendedPrice())
        + "</TD>"
        );

    out.println("   <TD ALIGN=CENTER VALIGN=TOP>"

        + "<A HREF=\""
        + "/servlet/IPFAddToCart?itemCode=" + itemCode
        + "\">"
        + "<IMG ALT=\"Cart\""
        + " SRC=\"/ipfoods/images/cart.gif\">"
        + "</A>"

        + "<A HREF=\""
        + "/servlet/IPFRemoveFromCart?itemCode=" + itemCode
        + "\">"
        + "<IMG ALT=\"Cart\""
        + " SRC=\"/ipfoods/images/nocart.gif\">"
        + "</A>"

        + "</TD>");

    out.println("</TR>");
}


/**
 * Handles a POST request
 */
public void doPost(
        HttpServletRequest request,
        HttpServletResponse response)
    throws ServletException, IOException
    {
        doGet(request, response);
    }
}
```

Technique

Use a `java.io.StringWriter` or `java.io.ByteArrayOutputStream` as a holding buffer in place of the response output stream. If all goes well, write the contents of the buffer to the real servlet output stream. Alternatively, use `sendRedirect()` to cause an error page to be displayed.

Discussion

There are two `sendError()` methods provided in the Servlet API, but these are really for system-level messages (i.e., internal server errors) rather than application messages. For an application error message, you can simply generate an appropriate Web page.

The actual contents of the error Web page are, of course, up to you. But the mechanics of producing it instead of the original document require a little thought. Consider a servlet that accesses the employee database to generate an organization chart, as illustrated in Figure 4-12.

If an SQL exception occurs while the report is being generated, the servlet could generate partial results intermingled with an error message or stack trace. We would rather have "all-or-nothing" behavior—either a complete report or only an error message. This can be done by buffering the output that we generate until it is complete and then writing the buffer to the servlet response output stream all at once. If an error occurs instead, we simply throw away the buffer and send the desired message directly. Figure 4-13 shows how this technique is used.

Another approach to this same problem is detailed in the next section.

4.7 Redirecting the User to a Different Web Page

Problem

I have a set of related servlets, and I need to control the order in which they are accessed.

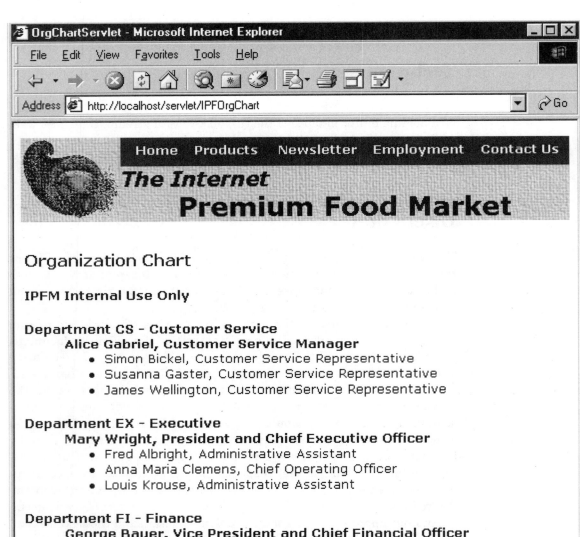

Figure 4-12 The IPFM organization chart.

▬▬▬ ▬▬ ▬▬ ▬▬
Figure 4-13
Buffered output for
the IPFM organiza-
tion chart.

```java
try {

    // Create a StringWriter to hold the output

    StringWriter sw = new StringWriter();

    // Filter it through a PrintWriter so that
    // the println() method can be used

    PrintWriter out = new PrintWriter(sw);

    // Start writing the document

    out.println("<HTML>");

    // ... do the real work here ...

    // Finish the document

    out.println("</HTML>");

    // Extract the contents of the buffer

    sw.flush();
    String webpage = sw.toString();
    out.close();

    // Finally, write the real web page

    response.setContentType("text/raw-html");
    out = response.getWriter();
    out.println(webpage);
    out.flush();
    out.close();
}
catch (SQLException e) {

    // But if an error happens, generate
    // a stack trace instead of the report

    response.setContentType("text/html");
    PrintWriter out = response.getWriter();
    e.printStackTrace(out);
    out.flush();
    out.close();
}
```

Technique

Use `HttpServletResponse.sendRedirect()` to instruct the HTTP client to go to a different Web page.

Discussion

Most applications involve a back-and-forth dialog with the user, with several different Web pages being used at different points in the dialog. A login prompt, for instance, may be required before any of the subsequent pages are accessible. However, each page has a URL, and there is nothing to prevent a user from bookmarking a URL and requesting it later out of sequence. To prevent this, a servlet can use session tracking to determine whether the user has started at the proper entry point. If not, the user has to be redirected to another page.

The HTTP protocol handles redirection by sending a return code of 302, followed by a `Location` header that specifies the correct URL:

```
HTTP/1.1 302 Moved Temporarily
Date: Mon, 11 Oct 1999 00:49:13 GMT
Server: Apache/1.3.9 (Win32)
Location: /ipfoods/infosys/Login.jsp
Connection: close
Content-Type: text/html
```

When the Web browser receives this response, it automatically generates another HTTP request for the URL specified in the `Location` header. For the servlet writer, all that is needed to trigger the redirection shown here is the following method call:

```
response.sendRedirect("/ipfoods/infosys/Login.jsp");
```

4.8 Servlet-Generated Frames

Problem

I would like to create a Web page with multiple frames, one to provide for navigation and one to display the data.

Technique

Use three servlets: one for the navigation frame, one for the main data frame, and one to generate the <FRAME> and <FRAMESET> tags that coordinate their activity.

Discussion

You can accomplish this in several ways, particularly if you want to use client-side features like JavaScript, but there is really no need to leave the servlet realm. Anything you can code manually in HTML you can have a servlet generate instead, including a cooperating set of URLs that perform a larger task.

Figure 4-14 demonstrates this with a frame-based application for viewing and clearing servlet log files. This application consists of three servlets:

LogViewerData	The main data display panel, shown in Figure 4-15.
LogViewerList	The navigation servlet, shown in Figure 4-16.
LogViewer	The frame handler, shown in Figure 4-17.

Let's examine how each servlet operates in conjunction with the others. The LogViewer servlet simply creates a frameset with two vertical columns:

```
out.println("<FRAMESET COLS=\"220,*\">");
out.println("<FRAME NAME=\"LIST\" SRC=\"/servlet/LogViewerList\">");
out.println("<FRAME NAME=\"DATA\" SRC=\"/servlet/LogViewerData\">");
out.println("</FRAMESET>");
```

The left- and right-hand frames are given the names LIST and DATA, respectively.

When the client browser receives this frameset, it recognizes two more URLs that it needs to request from the server. The first of these is /servlet/LogViewerList, which is the navigation panel. It is loaded into the frame named LIST. The other URL is /servlet/LogViewerData, the main data display servlet, which is loaded into the DATA frame.

When the LogViewerList servlet is invoked, it checks for an initialization parameter that gives it the list of file names it needs to make available:

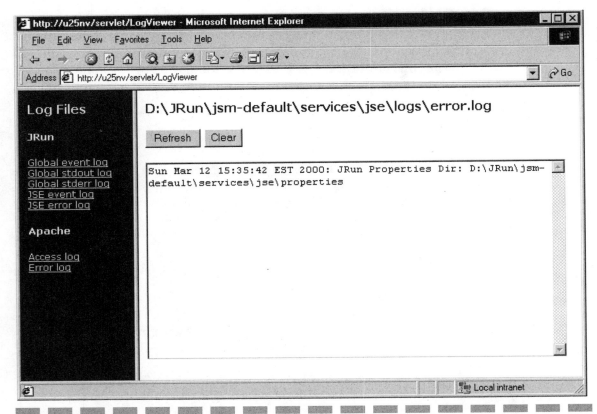

Figure 4-14 The LogViewer window.

```
String fileNames = getInitParameter("fileNames");
```

The parameter value is a semicolon-delimited list of file names relative to the current directory. The servlet uses a java.util.StringTokenizer to extract the individual file names. Then, for each name, it generates a hyperlink to the LogViewerData servlet giving it the file name and specifying that it should be displayed in the right-hand frame (the one named DATA):

▬▬ ▬▬ ▬▬ ▬▬
Figure 4-15

The LogViewer
main data display
servlet.

```java
package logviewer;

import java.io.*;
import java.net.*;
import java.util.*;
import javax.servlet.*;
import javax.servlet.http.*;

/**
 * DataServlet
 */
public class DataServlet extends HttpServlet
{
    /**
     * Handles a GET request
     */
    public void doGet(
            HttpServletRequest request,
            HttpServletResponse response)
        throws ServletException, IOException
    {
        Hashtable parms = new Hashtable();
        parms.put("request", request);
        parms.put("response", response);

        response.setContentType("text/html");

        ServletOutputStream out = response.getOutputStream();
        parms.put("out", out);

        // If no name parameter exists, prompt for it

        String name = request.getParameter("name");
        if (name == null) {
            out.println("<HTML>");
            out.println("<BODY>");
            out.println
            ("<H3>Select log file name at left</H3>");
            out.println("</BODY>");
            out.println("</HTML>");
            return;
        }
        parms.put("name", name);

        // Verify that the log file exists

        File logFile = new File(name);
        if (!logFile.exists()) {
            out.println("<HTML>");
            out.println("<BODY>");
            out.println("<H3>" + logFile.getPath()
                + " does not exist</H3>");
            out.println("</BODY>");
            out.println("</HTML>");
            return;
        }
        parms.put("logFile", logFile);
```

Figure 4-15
(Continued)

```java
// Clear the file if requested

String command = request.getParameter("command");
if (command != null)
   if (command.equals("Clear"))
      clearFile(parms);

// Create the HTML document to be returned

out.println("<HTML>");
out.println("<BODY>");
out.println("<H3>" + logFile.getPath() + "</H3>");

// Use an HTML form to handle the buttons

out.println("<FORM");
out.println(" METHOD=\"GET\"");
out.println(" ACTION=\""
   + request.getRequestURI() + "\"");
out.println(">");

// Hidden field with the log file name

out.println("<INPUT");
out.println(" TYPE=\"HIDDEN\"");
out.println(" NAME=\"name\"");
out.println(" VALUE=\"" + logFile.getPath() + "\"");
out.println(">");

// Refresh button

out.println("<INPUT TYPE=\"SUBMIT\""
   + " NAME=\"refresh\" VALUE=\"Refresh\">");

// Clear button

out.println("<INPUT TYPE=\"SUBMIT\""
   + " NAME=\"command\" VALUE=\"Clear\">");

// Contents of the file

out.println("<P>");
out.println("<TEXTAREA ROWS=24 COLS=80>");
BufferedReader in =
   new BufferedReader(
   new FileReader(name));
for (;;) {
   String buffer = in.readLine();
   if (buffer == null)
      break;
   out.println(buffer);
}
in.close();
out.println("</TEXTAREA>");

out.println("</FORM>");
```

Figure 4-15
(Continued)

```
    out.println("</BODY>");
    out.println("</HTML>");
}

/**
* Clears the log file
* @param parms the parameter hashtable
*/
public void clearFile(Hashtable parms)
{
    HttpServletRequest request =
        (HttpServletRequest) parms.get("request");
    File logFile = (File) parms.get("logFile");
    try {
        new FileOutputStream(logFile).close();
    }
    catch (Exception e) {
        log("Exception in clearFile for "
            + logFile.getPath(), e);
    }

}


String url = "/servlet/LogViewerData"
    + "?name="
    + URLEncoder.encode(logFile.getPath());

String tag = "<A"
    + " HREF=\"" + url + "\""
    + " TARGET=\"DATA\""
    + ">"
    + name
    + "</A>";

out.println(tag + "<BR>");
```

The hyperlink is encoded to prevent problems with embedded spaces, backslashes, and other special characters in the file name.

When the user clicks on a file name in the left frame, the browser invokes the LogViewerData servlet, passing it the name of selected file. LogViewerData opens the file and writes its contents in a <TEXTAREA> ... </TEXTAREA> block. It generates an HTML form with two submit buttons, one for refreshing the view and one for clearing the file.

This specific example makes use of a pair of frames for explorer-like applications, but the same general technique can be extended to handle framesets of arbitrary complexity.

Figure 4-16
The LogViewer
navigation servlet.

```java
package logviewer;

import java.io.*;
import java.net.*;
import java.util.*;

import javax.servlet.*;
import javax.servlet.http.*;

/**
 * ListServlet
 */
public class ListServlet extends HttpServlet
{
    /**
     * Handles a GET request
     */
    public void doGet(
            HttpServletRequest request,
            HttpServletResponse response)
        throws ServletException, IOException
    {
        Hashtable parms = new Hashtable();
        parms.put("request", request);
        parms.put("response", response);

        response.setContentType("text/html");

        PrintWriter out = response.getWriter();
        parms.put("out", out);

        // Get the properties file name

        String propFileName = getInitParameter("properties");
        if (propFileName == null) {
            response.sendRedirect("/servlet/LogViewerError?msg="
                + URLEncoder.encode(
                "No properties file name found"));
            return;
        }

        // Get the properties file itself

        Properties prop = new Properties();
        parms.put("prop", prop);
        try {
            prop.load(new FileInputStream(propFileName));
        }
        catch (Exception e) {
            response.sendRedirect("/servlet/LogViewerError?msg="
                + URLEncoder.encode(
                "Could not load properties file: "
                + e.getMessage()));
            return;
        }

        // Get the background color
```

```java
String bgcolor = prop.getProperty("bgcolor");
if (bgcolor == null)
    bgcolor = "#003194";

// Write the page

out.println("<HTML>");
out.println("<HEAD>");
out.println("<TITLE>ListServlet</TITLE>");
out.println("<STYLE>");
out.println("body, td {");
out.println(" color: #FFFFC0;");
out.println(" background-color: " + bgcolor + ";");
out.println(" font-family: Verdana,Arial,sans-serif;");
out.println(" font-size: 9pt;");
out.println("}");
out.println("a:link { color: #E0E0E0; }");
out.println("a:visited { color: #E0E0E0; }");
out.println("</STYLE>");
out.println("</HEAD>");
out.println("<BODY>");
out.println("<H3>Log Files</H3>");
writeList(parms);
out.println("</BODY>");
out.println("</HTML>");
}

/**
* Writes the list of log files
* @param parms the parameter hashtable
* @exception ServletException if a servlet exception occurs
* @exception IOException if an I/O exception occurs
*/
public void writeList(Hashtable parms)
    throws ServletException, IOException
{
    HttpServletRequest request =
        (HttpServletRequest) parms.get("request");
    PrintWriter out = (PrintWriter) parms.get("out");
    Properties prop = (Properties) parms.get("prop");

    // Get the max number of categories

    String catKey = "category";
    int maxCategories = Integer.parseInt(
        prop.getProperty(catKey + ".max", "0"));
    for (int i = 0; i < maxCategories; i++) {
        String catKeyIndex = catKey + "." + i;
        String category = prop.getProperty(catKeyIndex);
        if (category == null)
            continue;
        out.println("<H4>" + category + "</H4>");

        // Get the file names in this category

        int max = Integer.parseInt(
```

Figure 4-16
(Continued)

```
            prop.getProperty(category + ".max", "0"));
   for (int j = 0; j < max; j++) {

      String fileKeyIndex =
         category + "." + j + ".file";
      String name = prop.getProperty(fileKeyIndex);
      if (name == null)
         continue;
      name = name.trim();

      String labelKeyIndex =
         category + "." + j + ".label";
      String label = prop.getProperty(labelKeyIndex);
      if (label == null)
         continue;
      label = label.trim();

      File logFile;
      if (name.startsWith("/")
         || name.startsWith("\\")
         || (name.indexOf(":/") >= 0)
         || (name.indexOf(":\\") >= 0))
         logFile = new File(name);
      else
         logFile = new File(
            System.getProperty("user.dir"), name);
      String url = "/servlet/LogViewerData"
         + "?name="
         + URLEncoder.encode(logFile.getPath());
      String tag = "<A"
         + " HREF=\"" + url + "\""
         + " TARGET=\"DATA\""
         + ">"
         + label
         + "</A>";
      out.println(tag + "<BR>");
   }
  }
 }
}
```

Figure 4-17

The `LogViewer` frame-handling servlet.

```java
package logviewer;

import java.io.*;
import java.net.*;
import java.util.*;
import javax.servlet.*;
import javax.servlet.http.*;

/**
 * FrameServlet
 */
public class FrameServlet extends HttpServlet
{
    public void doGet(
        HttpServletRequest request,
        HttpServletResponse response)
        throws ServletException, IOException
    {
        response.setContentType("text/html");
        PrintWriter out = response.getWriter();
        out.println("<FRAMESET COLS=\"200,*\">");
        out.println("<FRAME NAME=\"LIST\""
            + " SRC=\"/servlet/LogViewerList\">");
        out.println("<FRAME NAME=\"DATA\""
            + " SRC=\"/servlet/LogViewerData\">");
        out.println("</FRAMESET>");
    }
}
```

Database Access

Overview

If your work involves more than writing Fahrenheit to Celsius conversion tables, at some point you will need to communicate with a database. Java provides a comprehensive framework for doing this—the Java Database Connectivity (JDBC) interface.

JDBC provides access to a wide variety of relational database management systems (RDBMS) using Structured Query Language (SQL) and a standard Java API. If you are Web-enabling a legacy application, it is likely that the database access portion is already written in SQL; this part of your conversion task will be straightforward. The syntax and semantics of the SQL statements used in a batch mainframe application will not change when you convert the application to a set of Java servlets.

Using JDBC is fairly simple. There are usually four steps involved, depending on the nature of the task at hand:

1. Loading a JDBC driver for your database management system
2. Using that driver to open a connection to a particular database
3. Issuing SQL statements through the connection
4. Processing the result sets returned by the SQL operations

These steps are illustrated in Figure 5-1.

Main JDBC Classes

The API consists of eight interfaces, six classes, and three exception types[1]—small enough to learn in a few days. Some of the classes are of interest primarily to JDBC driver developers; the ones you will use most often are these:

- `Connection`—An active link to a database. A `Connection` object allows you to determine the structure and capabilities of the database, to read from and write to its tables, and to control its transaction boundaries. You establish a connection by invoking the static `getConnection()` method of the `Drive rManager`.

- `Statement`—An object that sends SQL statements to a database over an active connection and returns the results. There are three types of `Statement` objects:

    `Statement`—Used to execute a string containing static SQL.

    `PreparedStatement`—A subclass of `Statement` that allows you to precompile an SQL statement and execute it multiple times with different input parameters.

    `CallableStatement`—A subclass of `PreparedStatement` that provides access to stored procedures.

    You create `Statement` objects by calling the `Connection` object's `createStatement()`, `prepareStatement()`, or `prepareCall()` methods.

---

[1]JDBC 2.0 adds eight new interfaces and one new exception type.

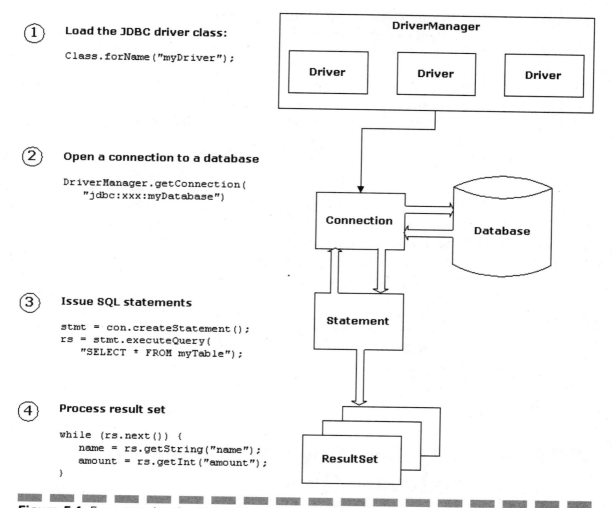

Figure 5-1 Four steps involved in database access with JDBC.

- ResultSet—An ordered list of the table rows returned by a SELECT statement or by calls to certain metadata functions. You iterate through the rows of a ResultSet using its next() method. Within the current row, you retrieve the column values individually with a getXXX() method, where XXX represents the Java data type to be returned.

■ DatabaseMetaData—A large collection of methods that describe the attributes and capabilities of the database. Use the Connection object's getMetaData() method to retrieve the DatabaseMetaData object.

■ ResultSetMetaData—An object that describes the columns in a particular result set. It provides methods that describe the number of columns, their names, types, display sizes, and precision. Not surprisingly, you get the ResultSetMetaData from a call to getMetaData() on a ResultSet object.

■ DriverManager—A class that controls the set of registered JDBC drives. All the methods in DriverManager are static; there is only one DriverManager in a virtual machine. The one method you will use most often is getConnection(), which binds to an active database session and returns a Connection object.

■ SQLException—A generic exception class for reporting database access problems. SQLException encapsulates the SQLSTATE value, an error message, and any vendor-specific error code. There can be more than one SQLException associated with an error. If this is the case, they are chained together in a linked list that can be navigated using the getNextException() method.

The remainder of this chapter illustrates how to use these classes from within a Java servlet.

5.1   Creating a Web Page from a Database Query

Problem

How do I query a database and show the results in a Web page?

Technique

Use a java.sql.Statement to execute an SQL SELECT, and extract the results a row at a time from the result set.

Discussion

A typical example of a Web page generated from a database is the department manager listing shown in Figure 5-2. The Internet Premium Food Market database contains two tables that together provide this information—the departments table, created with the SQL shown below[2]:

```
CREATE TABLE  departments (
   deptCode     CHAR(2),
   deptDesc     CHAR(40),
   deptMgrNo    CHAR(4)
)
```

and the employees table, created as follows:

```
CREATE TABLE  employees (
   empNo        CHAR(4),
   lname        CHAR(20),
   fname        CHAR(20),
   hireDate     DATE,
   isMgr        INT,
   deptNo       CHAR(2),
   title        CHAR(50),
   email        CHAR(32)
)
```

Our query needs the department description and the department manager's name, title, and email address. This information can be obtained by joining the two tables over the "manager number" field as follows:

```
SELECT    d.deptDesc, e.fname, e.lname, etitle, e.email
FROM      departments d, employees e
WHERE     d.deptMgrno = e.empno
ORDER  BY  d.deptDesc
```

The hard work is done; our servlet is easy to write. The complete listing is shown is Figure 5-3, but since this is the first example in this chapter, let's consider it in detail.

The program starts with the definitions of two constants that are specific to our database:

---

[2]Your own DBMS may use different keywords for the data types. This is an unfortunate divergence tolerated in the SQL standard. A later section in this chapter deals with generic coding techniques that can minimize the problem.

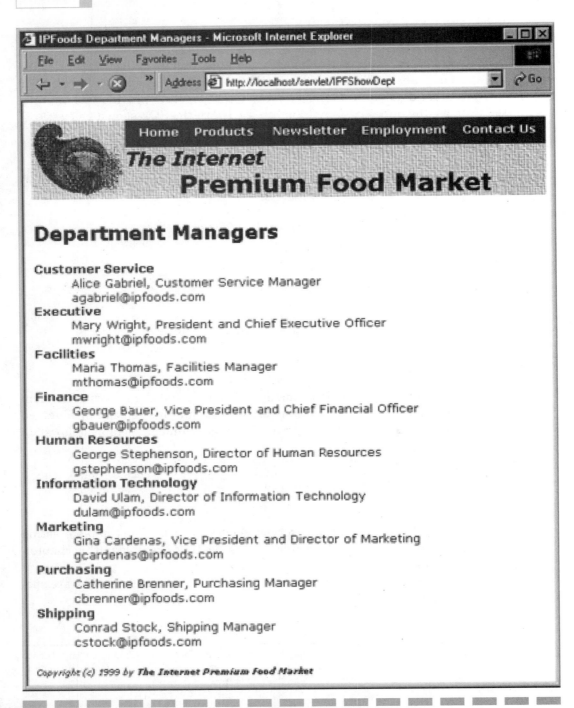

Figure 5-2 Results of a simple database query.

Figure 5-3

A servlet that creates the department manager listing.

```java
package ipfoods.about;

import java.io.*;
import java.net.*;
import java.sql.*;
import java.util.*;

import javax.servlet.*;
import javax.servlet.http.*;

/**
 * ShowDeptServlet
 */
public class ShowDeptServlet extends HttpServlet
{
    public static final String DRIVER = "jdbc.idbDriver";
    public static final String URL =
        "jdbc:idb:d:/book/ipfoods/database/database.prp";

    /**
     * Handles a GET request
     * @param request the servlet request object
     * @param response the servlet response object
     * @exception ServletException if a servlet exception occurs
     * @exception IOException if an I/O exception occurs
     */
    public void doGet(
            HttpServletRequest request,
            HttpServletResponse response)
        throws ServletException, IOException
    {
        PrintWriter out = response.getWriter();
        response.setContentType("text/raw-html");

        Connection con = null;
        try {

            // Load the driver

            Class.forName(DRIVER);

            // Connect to the database

            con = DriverManager.getConnection(URL);

            // Query the database for the list of
            // departments and their managers

            Statement stmt = con.createStatement();
            ResultSet rs = stmt.executeQuery(
                    "select"
                + "     d.deptDesc as DEPTNAME,"
                + "     e.fname as FNAME,"
                + "     e.lname as LNAME, "
                + "     e.title as TITLE,"
                + "     e.email as EMAIL"
                + " from      departments d, employees e"
```

Figure 5-3
(Continued)

```
                    + " where      (d.deptMgrno = e.empno)"
                    + " order by DEPTNAME"
            );

            // Format the results as a list

            out.println("<HTML>");
            out.println("<HEAD>");
            out.println("<TITLE>"
                + "IPFoods Department Managers</TITLE>");
            out.println("</HEAD>");
            out.println("<BODY>");
            out.println("<H2>Department Managers</H2>");
            out.println("<DL>");

            while (rs.next()) {

                // Get the fields from the current row
                // of the result set

                String deptName = rs.getString(1);
                String firstName = rs.getString(2);
                String lastName = rs.getString(3);
                String title = rs.getString(4);
                String email = rs.getString(5);

                // Write them as a list entry

                out.println("<DT><B>" + deptName + "</B></DT>");
                out.println("<DD>"
                    + firstName
                    + " " + lastName
                    + ", " + title + "<BR>");
                out.println("   " + email + "<BR>");
                out.println("</DD>");
            }

            // Finish the document

            out.println("</DL>");
            out.println("</BODY>");
            out.println("</HTML>");

        }
        catch (Exception e) {
            e.printStackTrace(new PrintWriter(out));
        }
        finally {

            // Always close the connection

            if (con != null) {
                try {
                    con.close();
                }
                catch (SQLException ignore) {}
            }
```

Figure 5-3
(Continued)

```
/**
 * Handles a POST request
 * @param request the servlet request object
 * @param response the servlet response object
 * @exception ServletException if a servlet exception occurs
 * @exception IOException if an I/O exception occurs
 */
public void doPost(
      HttpServletRequest request,
      HttpServletResponse response)
   throws ServletException, IOException
{
   doGet(request, response);
}
```

```
public static final String DRIVER = "jdbc.idbDriver";
public static final String URL =
   "jdbc:idb:d:/book/ipfoods/database/database.prp";
```

This example uses InstantDB as its database managment system.[3] InstantDB loads its database parameters from a properties file, which in this case is found in the `d:/book/ipfoods/database` directory. The database URL consists of three semicolon-separated fields as defined in the JDBC specification:

```
jdbc:<subprotocol>:<subname>
```

where

```
jdbc
```

is a fixed value that is the same for all URLs,

```
<subprotocol>
```

is a name for a group of drivers sharing some common access characteristics, and

```
<subname>
```

identifies the specific database. This field is defined entirely by the database driver vendor.

---

[3]InstantDB is freely available for noncommercial use from *http://www.instantdb.co.uk*.

Before attempting to connect to the database, we must ensure that the appropriate JDBC driver has been loaded. This is can be done by forcing the driver class to be loaded using the `Class.forName()` method. This operation is discussed in more detail in Section 5.5.

After loading the driver, we connect to the database by invoking a static method in `DriverManager`:

```
con = DriverManager.getConnection(URL);
```

When the driver manager is asked for a connection, it interrogates each registered driver to determine if the driver can connect to the specified URL. The first driver that volunteers is selected. If no suitable driver can be found, the driver manager throws an `SQLException`.

In order to execute SQL statements through the connection, we need a `Statement` object. A `Statement` is not instantiated directly with the `new` keyword but rather by invoking a method on the `Connection` object:

```
Statement stmt = con.createStatement();
```

The `Statement` object can then be used to issue a SELECT request to the database:

```
ResultSet rs = stmt.executeQuery(
   "select"
 + "    d.deptDesc as DEPTNAME,"
 + "    e.fname as FNAME,"
 + "    e.lname as LNAME, "
 + "    e.title as TITLE,"
 + "    e.email as EMAIL"
 + " from      departments d, employees e"
 + " where     (d.deptMgrno = e.empno)"
 + " order by DEPTNAME"
     );
```

At this point, we are ready to create the Web page. We will use a `<DL>...</DL>` block to list the entries in the result set:

```
while (rs.next()) {

   // Get the fields from the current row
   // of the result set
   String deptName = rs.getString(1);
   String firstName = rs.getString(2);
   String lastName = rs.getString(3);
   String title = rs.getString(4);
   String email = rs.getString(5);

   // Write them as a list entry
```

```
out.println("<DT><B>" + deptName + "</B></DT>");
out.println("<DD>"
        + firstName + " " + lastName
        + ", "
        + title + "<BR>");
out.println(" " + email + "<BR>");
out.println("</DD>");
}
```

When we are done, we need to close the database connection. To ensure that this is always done, no matter whether any intermediate code has failed and thrown an exception, we enclose the query in a try {...} catch (){...} block with a finally {...} section.

5.2 Connection Pooling

Problem

How can I reduce the time it takes for a servlet to connect to a database?

Technique

Use a connection pool that preallocates connections and recycles them when they are released.

Discussion

Connecting to a database is a time-consuming operation. If each request coming from a Web browser requires a new connection, response time can become unacceptably slow. However, the server has plenty of time to spare between requests; why not take advantage of this time to preallocate connections? An object that does this is known as a *connection pool*.

A Web search will show that there are quite a few products that do connection pooling and a great deal of interest in using them. In this section we shall develop a connection pool of our own.

The requirements are easy to determine. We need a ConnectionPool object that has a list of Connection objects, as illustrated in Figure 5-4. When asked for a connection, the pool needs to find an available connection, mark it as being in use, and pass it to the requester. The requester

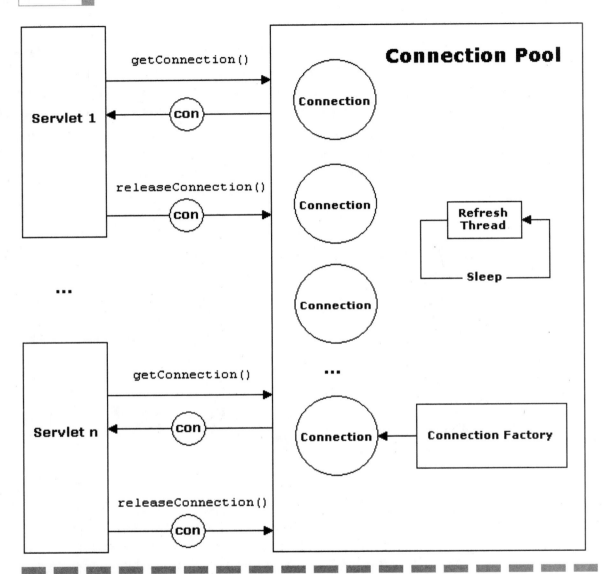

Figure 5-4 A database connection pool.

uses the connection to access the required data and then returns the connection to the pool for recycling. The pool needs to check periodically to determine whether any connections are invalid, too old, or overused, replacing these with new connections.

In order to make this work, we need the following components:

PoolEntry — A wrapper class that holds a connection. This class keeps track of the time the connection was created, the number of times it has been used, and its current allocation state (i.e., whether it is in use, available, or being recycled). The implementation of PoolEntry is shown in Figure 5-5.

ConnectionFactory — A Factory object that creates instances of a specific type of connection. The factory is associated with the connection pool in the pool's constructor. It turns out that this is the only component that needs to be customized for a specific database; so long as it returns a connection when asked, the connection pool does not need to get into the details. For this reason, we have designed ConnectionFactory as an interface, not a class (see Figure 5-6). It defines only one method: createInstance(), which returns a Connection object. A concrete class that implements this interface is OdbcConnectionFactory, shown in Figure 5-7.

ConnectionPool — An object that manages a set of connections that can be allocated and reused. The pool has several operating parameters that need to be configurable:

- The minimum number of entries in the pool at any given time
- The maximum number of entries
- The maximum number of times an entry can be reused
- The maximum age of an entry
- The frequency with which the pool is refreshed

A client of this class requests a connection by calling getConnection() and returns it to the pool with releaseConnection(). ConnectionPool is listed in Figure 5-8.

To monitor the status of its entries, the pool runs a background thread that periodically wakes up and tells the pool to refresh itself. This

Figure 5-5

Implementation of
the PoolEntry
class.

```java
package ijs.jdbc.pool;

import java.sql.*;
import java.text.*;
import java.util.Date;

/**
 * A wrapper class that holds a Connection.  This class
 * keeps track of the time the connection was created, how
 * often it has been used, and its current allocation state.
 * @see ConnectionPool
 * @see Connection
 */
public class PoolEntry
{
    private static int handleCounter = 0;
    public static final DateFormat timeFormat =
        new SimpleDateFormat("hh:mm:ss.SSS");

    /**
     * The initial state of an entry
     */
    public static final int CREATED = 0;

    /**
     * The state in which the entry is available for allocation
     */
    public static final int AVAILABLE = 1;

    /**
     * The state which an entry has when it is currently
     * allocated to a client.
     */
    public static final int IN_USE = 2;

    /**
     * A temporary state an entry has when it has been
     * released by a client but not yet refreshed by
     * the pool's <CODE>refresh()</CODE> method.
     */
    public static final int RECYCLING = 3;

    /**
     * A state that indicates the underlying resource
     * has been closed.
     */
    public static final int CLOSED = 4;

    private Connection con;
    private long creationTime;
    private int timesUsed;
    private int state;
    private int handle;

    /**
     * Creates a new pool entry containing the specified
     * connection
```

Figure 5-5
(Continued)

```
 * @param con the connection
 */
public PoolEntry(Connection con)
{
    this.con = con;
    this.creationTime = System.currentTimeMillis();
    this.timesUsed = 0;
    this.state = CREATED;
    this.handle = handleCounter++;
}

/**
 * Returns true if the connection is still valid
 */
public boolean isValid()
{
    boolean result = false;
    if (con != null) {
        try { result = !con.isClosed(); }
        catch (SQLException ignore) {}
    }
    return result;
}

/**
 * Returns the connection
 */
public Connection getConnection()
{
    return con;
}

/**
 * Returns the creation time in milliseconds
 */
public long getCreationTime()
{
    return creationTime;
}

/**
 * Returns the number of times the resource has been used
 */
public int getTimesUsed()
{
    return timesUsed;
}

/**
 * Changes the entry state to IN_USE and
 * increments the times used counter.
 */
public void allocate()
{
    state = IN_USE;
    timesUsed++;
}
```

Figure 5-5

(Continued)

```java
/**
 * Closes the underlying resource.
 */
public void close()
{
    state = CLOSED;
    if (con != null) {
        try { con.close(); }
        catch (SQLException ignore) {}
    }
}

/**
 * Returns the allocation state of the entry.
 */
public int getState()
{
    return state;
}

/**
 * Sets the entry's state
 */
public void setState(int newState)
{
    state = newState;
}

/**
 * Returns the entry's handle, which is a sequentially
 * assigned number that uniquely identifies this entry.
 */
public int getHandle()
{
    return handle;
}

/**
 * Returns the entry as a string
 */
public String toString()
{
    StringBuffer buffer = new StringBuffer();
    buffer.append(handle);
    buffer.append(":");
    buffer.append(con);
    buffer.append(",created=");
    buffer.append(timeFormat.format(
        new java.util.Date(creationTime)));
    buffer.append(",used=");
    buffer.append(timesUsed);
    buffer.append(",state=");
    switch (state) {
        case CREATED:   buffer.append("CREATED"); break;
        case AVAILABLE: buffer.append("AVAILABLE"); break;
        case IN_USE:    buffer.append("IN_USE"); break;
        case RECYCLING: buffer.append("RECYCLING"); break;
        case CLOSED:    buffer.append("CLOSED"); break;
    }
    return buffer.toString();
}
```

■■■ ■■■ ■■■ ■■■
Figure 5-6
The
Connection-
Factory
interface.

```java
package ijs.jdbc.pool;

import java.sql.*;

/**
 * A factory object that creates instances of a specific
 * <CODE>Connection</CODE> on demand.
 * @see java.sql.Connection
 */
public interface ConnectionFactory
{
    /**
     * Creates a new instance of the <CODE>Connection</CODE>
     */
    public Connection createInstance();
}
```

refresh operation is also invoked whenver a connection is returned to the pool.

Let's examine how the pool operates. Its constructor takes two parameters:

1. An object implementing the ConnectionFactory interface, which the pool will use to create new connections when it needs them

2. A Properties object containing the operating parameters

To make it simple for servlets to use our pool, we store default values for the parameters in a Properties file:

```java
Properties parms = new Properties();
InputStream propStream =
    getClass().getResourceAsStream("pool.properties");
...
parms.load(propStream);
```

The pool merges these defaults with whatever overriding values the user may have supplied and reads them into instance variables. The getResourceAsStream() method conveniently allows us to package the Properties file in the .jar file that contains our classes. We could have used static final variables for the default values, but with a large number of parameters, the code would have become more cluttered.

After creating the vector that will hold the connections, the pool calls its refresh() method. This has the effect of bringing the pool up to the minimum required size. Immediately thereafter, the pool starts a thread that causes refresh() to be called every 20 seconds (or however many seconds the Properties file specified for refreshFrequency).

Figure 5-7

A Connection-
Factory for
JDBC-ODBC
drivers.

```java
package ijs.jdbc.pool.odbc;

import java.io.*;
import java.sql.*;
import java.util.*;
import ijs.jdbc.pool.*;

/**
 * A ConnectionFactory for the JDBC-ODBC bridge.
 */
public class OdbcConnectionFactory implements ConnectionFactory
{
    protected String dsname;

    /**
     * Creates a new <CODE>OdbcConnectionFactory</CODE>
     * @dsname the data source name
     * @exception PoolException if the driver class
     * cannot be loaded
     */
    public OdbcConnectionFactory(String dsname)
        throws PoolException
    {
        this.dsname = dsname;
        try {
            Class.forName("sun.jdbc.odbc.JdbcOdbcDriver");
        }
        catch (Exception e) {
            throw new PoolException("Could not load ODBC driver");
        }
    }

    /**
     * Creates a connection
     * @return the connection object or null if it cannot
     * be created.
     */
    public Connection createInstance()
    {
        Connection con = null;
        try {
            con = DriverManager.getConnection("jdbc:odbc:" + dsname);
        }
        catch (SQLException ignore) {}

        return con;
    }
}
```

The `refresh()` method is marked as `synchronized` so that no
entries will be added to or removed from the pool while it is being
updated. The pool examines each connection according to its current
state:

Figure 5-8

Implementation
of the ConnectionPool class.

```java
package ijs.jdbc.pool;

import java.io.*;
import java.sql.*;
import java.util.*;

/**
 * A <CODE>ConnectionPool</CODE> manages a set of connections
 * that can be allocated and reused.
 * <P>
 * When created, a <CODE>ConnectionPool</CODE> is associated
 * with a specific <CODE>ConnectionFactory</CODE>,
 * which creates new connections when asked.
 * <P>
 * The pool has operating parameters that can be set
 * in its constructor by means of a <CODE>Properties</CODE>
 * object:
 * <UL>
 * <LI>minEntries - the minimum number of entries
 * the pool should contain at any time.
 * <LI>maxEntries - the maximum number of entries.
 * <LI>maxTimesUsed - the maximum number of times
 * an entry can be reused.
 * <LI>maxAge - the maximum number of seconds
 * a connection can be used before being considered
 * stale.
 * <LI>refreshFreqency - the interval in seconds
 * between times at which the pool is refreshed.
 * </UL>
 * <P>
 * A client of this class allocates a connection by calling
 * <CODE>getConnection()</CODE>.  A maximum wait time can
 * be specified on this call.  When the client is done
 * with the connection, the client calls
 * <CODE>releaseConnection(connection)</CODE>
 * <P>
 * Periodically, the pool is refreshed.  At this time,
 * the pool examines all its entries, closing any that
 * are too old or overused, recycling any entries that
 * have been released by clients, and bringing the pool
 * up to its minimum size.  The refresh event happens
 * automatically at the specified refreshFrequency
 * interval, and also any time a connection is released.
 * <P>
 * @see ConnectionFactory
 * @see Connection
 * @see PoolEntry
 */
public class ConnectionPool extends Thread
    implements Refreshable
{
    // ==============================================
    //      Instance data
    // ==============================================

    // The factory that creates new instances
    // of the pooled connection
```

Figure 5-8
(Continued)

```java
private ConnectionFactory factory;

// Operating parameters

private int minEntries;
private int maxEntries;
private int maxTimesUsed;
private int maxAge;
private int refreshFrequency;
private boolean closed;
private int nWaiting;
private boolean trace;

// The pool itself

private Vector pool;

// ================================================
//     Constructors
// ================================================

/**
 * Creates a connection pool with default properties
 * using the specified pooled connection factory
 * @param factory the factory class that creates
 * new instances of the pooled connection.
 * @exception PoolException if the pool cannot
 * be created.
 */
public ConnectionPool(ConnectionFactory factory)
   throws PoolException
{
   this(factory, new Properties());
}

/**
 * Creates a connection pool with specified properties
 * using the specified pooled connection factory
 * @param factory the factory class that creates
 * new instances of the pooled connection.
 * @param prop the operating parameters of the
 * connection pool:
 * @exception PoolException if the pool cannot
 * be created.
 */
public ConnectionPool(ConnectionFactory factory,
   Properties prop)
   throws PoolException
{
   this.factory = factory;

   // Load the default properties

   Properties parms = new Properties();
   InputStream propStream =
      getClass().getResourceAsStream("pool.properties");
```

Figure 5-8

(Continued)

```
if (propStream == null)
    throw new PoolException(
        "Could not find default pool properties file");
try {
    parms.load(propStream);
    propStream.close();
}
catch (IOException e) {
    throw new PoolException(e.getMessage());
}

// Make these the defaults for this pool

for (
    Enumeration names = prop.propertyNames();
    names.hasMoreElements(); )
{
    String name = (String) names.nextElement();
    parms.put(name, prop.getProperty(name));
}

// Get the parameters

minEntries          = getParameter(parms, "minEntries");
maxEntries          = getParameter(parms, "maxEntries");
maxTimesUsed        = getParameter(parms, "maxTimesUsed");
maxAge              = getParameter(parms, "maxAge");
refreshFrequency    = getParameter(
                            parms, "refreshFrequency");
String traceParm = parms.getProperty("trace", "false");
trace = Boolean.valueOf(traceParm).booleanValue();

// Create the pool

pool = new Vector();
closed = false;
setPriority(MIN_PRIORITY);
setDaemon(true);

log("Pool created");
log("minEntries=" + minEntries);
log("maxEntries=" + maxEntries);
log("maxTimesUsed=" + maxTimesUsed);
log("maxAge=" + maxAge);
log("refreshFrequency=" + refreshFrequency);

// Fill the pool to its minimum level

refresh();

log("Leaving constructor; starting thread");
start();
}

/**
 * Internal method that extracts a numeric parameter value
 * from a properties object
```

Figure 5-8
(Continued)

```java
 * @param parms the properties object
 * @param name the property name
 * @exception PoolException if the parameter value is
 * missing or not numeric.
 */
private static int getParameter(
    Properties parms, String name)
    throws PoolException
{
    String value = parms.getProperty(name);
    if (value == null)
        throw new PoolException
        (name + " property not found");

    try {
        return Integer.parseInt(value);
    }
    catch (NumberFormatException e) {
        throw new PoolException
        (name + " value [" + value + "] is not numeric");
    }
}


// ============================================
//     Instance methods
// ============================================

/**
 * Closes the pool, first closing all the unallocated entries
 */
public synchronized void close()
{
    log("close: entry");
    if (closed) {
        log("close: already closed");
        return;
    }
    closed = true;

    Vector tempPool = (Vector) pool.clone();
    pool = new Vector();

    Enumeration epool = tempPool.elements();
    while (epool.hasMoreElements()) {
        PoolEntry entry = (PoolEntry) epool.nextElement();
        if (entry.getState() == PoolEntry.IN_USE) {
            log("close: preserving entry "
                + entry.getHandle());
            pool.addElement(entry);
        }
        else {
            log("close: closing entry "
                + entry.getHandle());
            entry.close();
        }
    }
    log("close: exit");
```

Figure 5-8

(Continued)

```
}
/**
 * Allocates an entry from the pool, creating one
 * if necessary (if the pool is not at maximum
 * size).  If no entry is available, waits up to the
 * specified number of milliseconds for one to become
 * available.
 * <P>
 * @param timeout the maximum number of milliseconds
 * to wait before giving up.  A value of -1 means
 * to wait indefinitely.
 * @return the allocated underlying connection
 * or null if one cannot be allocated.
 */
public synchronized Connection getConnection(long timeout)
{
    log("getConnection: entry, timeout=" + timeout);

    if (closed) {
        log("getConnection: pool closed");
        return null;
    }

    Connection con = null;

    // Keep trying while there is still time

    while (timeout >= -1) {

        // Find the first available resource

        Enumeration epool = pool.elements();
        while (epool.hasMoreElements()) {
            PoolEntry entry = (PoolEntry) epool.nextElement();
            if (entry.getState() == PoolEntry.AVAILABLE) {

                // Found one

                log("getConnection: allocating entry "
                    + entry.getHandle());
                entry.allocate();
                return entry.getConnection();
            }
        }

        // No entries are available

        // If the pool is not at maximum size,
        // create a new entry and allocate it to
        // this client

        if (pool.size() != maxEntries) {
            con = factory.createInstance();
            if (con == null) {
                log("getConnection: could not create entry");
                return null;
```

Figure 5-8
(Continued)

```
        }

        PoolEntry entry = new PoolEntry(con);
        log("getConnection: created new entry " + entry);
        pool.addElement(entry);
        log("getConnection: allocating entry "
            + entry.getHandle());
        entry.allocate();
        return entry.getConnection();
    }

    // Otherwise, wait

    try {

        // Wait indefinitely if instructed

        if (timeout == -1) {
            log("getConnection: waiting indefinitely");
            nWaiting++;
            wait();
            nWaiting--;
            log("getConnection: waking up");
        }

        // Give up if time has expired

        else if (timeout <= 0) {
            log
            ("getConnection: not available; timing out");
            return null;
        }

        // Otherwise wait for up to the remaining
        // timeout value

        else {
            long stime = System.currentTimeMillis();
            log("getConnection: waiting up to "
                + timeout + " millliseconds");
            nWaiting++;
            wait(timeout);
            nWaiting--;
            log("getConnection: waking up");
            long etime = System.currentTimeMillis();

            timeout = etime - stime;
            if (timeout == -1)
                timeout = 0;
        }
    }
    catch (InterruptedException e) {
        log("Interrupted: " + e.getMessage());
        return null;
    }
}
```

```
        return null;
    }

    /**
     * Allocates an entry from the pool, creating one
     * if necessary (if the pool is not at maximum
     * size).  If no entry is available, waits
     * indefinitely for one to become available.
     * <P>
     * @return the allocated <CODE>Connection</CODE>,
     * or null if one cannot be allocated.
     */
    public synchronized Connection getConnection()
    {
        return getConnection(-1);
    }

    /**
     * Refreshes the entries in the pool.  This
     * involves:
     * <UL>
     * <LI>Removing any invalid recycled entries
     * <LI>Removing any overused recycled entries
     * <LI>Removing any available entries that are too old
     * <LI>Bringing the pool up to the minimum size
     * </UL>
     */
    public synchronized void refresh()
    {
        log("refresh: entry");

        // Examine each pool entry, removing
        // those that are no longer valid.

        Vector tempPool = (Vector) pool.clone();
        pool = new Vector();
        Vector recycledPool = new Vector();
        Enumeration epool = tempPool.elements();
        long now = System.currentTimeMillis();
        while (epool.hasMoreElements()) {
            PoolEntry entry = (PoolEntry) epool.nextElement();
            int age = (int) (now - entry.getCreationTime())/1000;
            log("refresh: examining " + entry);

            switch (entry.getState()) {

                case PoolEntry.AVAILABLE:

                    if (closed) {
                        log("refresh: deleting entry; pool closed");
                        entry.close();
                    }
                    else if (age > maxAge)
                    {
                        log("refresh: entry too old");
                        entry.close();
                    }
```

Figure 5-8

(Continued)

```
         else {
             log("refresh: still available");
             pool.addElement(entry);
         }
         break;

     case PoolEntry.IN_USE:

         log("refresh: entry in use");
         pool.addElement(entry);
         break;

     case PoolEntry.RECYCLING:

         if (closed) {
             log("refresh: deleting entry; pool closed");
             entry.close();
         }
         else if (!entry.isValid()) {
             log("refresh: entry not valid");
             entry.close();
         }
         else if (entry.getTimesUsed() > maxTimesUsed) {
             log("refresh: entry used too many times");
             entry.close();
         }
         else {
             log("refresh: recycling entry");
             entry.setState(PoolEntry.AVAILABLE);
             recycledPool.addElement(entry);
             notify();
         }
         break;
     }
}
for (int i = 0; i < recycledPool.size(); i++)
   pool.addElement(recycledPool.elementAt(i));
recycledPool = null;

// If the pool is closed, do not allocate any
// new entries.  Otherwise, bring the pool up to
// its minimum size.

if (closed) {
   log("refresh: pool closed; not adding entries");
}
else {
   int deficit = minEntries - pool.size();
   if (deficit > 0) {
      log("refresh: adding " + deficit + " entries");
      for (int i = 0; i < deficit; i++) {
         Connection con = factory.createInstance();
         log("refresh: " + i + " entry = " + con);
         if (con == null)
             continue;
         PoolEntry entry = new PoolEntry(con);
         entry.setState(PoolEntry.AVAILABLE);
```

Figure 5-8
(Continued)

```
                                    pool.addElement(entry);
                                    log("refresh: added entry " + entry);
                                    notify();
                                }
                            }
                        }

                    log("refresh: exit");
                }

                /**
                 * Releases a resource back to the pool
                 * @param con the underlying pooled con
                 */
                public synchronized void releaseConnection(Connection con)
                {
                    log("releaseConnection: entry, con=" + con);
                    Enumeration epool = pool.elements();
                    while (epool.hasMoreElements()) {
                        PoolEntry entry = (PoolEntry) epool.nextElement();
                        if (con.equals(entry.getConnection())) {
                            log("releaseConnection: recycling entry "
                                + entry.getHandle());
                            entry.setState(PoolEntry.RECYCLING);
                            new RefreshThread(this).start();
                            return;
                        }
                    }
                    log("releaseConnection: exit");
                }

                /**
                 * Periodically refreshes the pool
                 */
                public void run()
                {
                    log("run: entry");
                    long delay = (long) (refreshFrequency * 1000);
                    while (!closed) {
                        try {
                            log("run: sleeping");
                            sleep(delay);
                            log("run: waking up");
                            if (!closed) {
                                log("run: starting refresh thread");
                                new RefreshThread(this).start();
                            }
                        }
                        catch (InterruptedException e) {
                            log("run: interrupted: " + e.getMessage());
                            break;
                        }
                    }
                    log("run: exit");
                }

                /**
```

Figure 5-8

(Continued)

```
 * Returns the pool as a string
 */
public synchronized String toString()
{
    StringBuffer buffer = new StringBuffer();
    buffer.append("ConnectionPool");
    if (closed)
        buffer.append(" (closed)");
    buffer.append(" ");
    buffer.append(pool.size());
    buffer.append(" entries:");
    for (int i = 0; i < pool.size(); i++) {
        buffer.append("\n");
        buffer.append(pool.elementAt(i).toString());
    }
    buffer.append("\n");
    buffer.append(nWaiting);
    buffer.append(" thread(s) waiting for connections.");
    return buffer.toString();
}

/**
 * writes trace entries to System.out
 * @param msg the message to be written
 */
public void log(String msg)
{
    if (trace) {

        StringBuffer buffer = new StringBuffer();

        java.util.Date now =
            new java.util.Date(System.currentTimeMillis());
        buffer.append(PoolEntry.timeFormat.format(now));
        buffer.append(" ConnectionPool: ");
        buffer.append(msg);

        System.out.println(buffer.toString());
    }
}
}
```

1. AVAILABLE—Unused connections that are too old are closed and discarded. Connections are also discarded if the pool is closing down.

2. IN_USE—Any connection that is currently being used is retained unchanged.

3. RECYCLING—Connections that have just been returned to the pool are checked to see if they may have been closed or otherwise invalidated by the user. In this case, or in case the connection has been

used too many times, it is closed and deleted. This is also done if the pool itself is closing down.

After this examination of the pool entries is complete, the `refresh()` method creates any connections necessary to bring the number of entries in the pool up to the minimum size. This is not done if the pool is closing down.

The `getConnection()` method is also marked as `synchronized` to prevent two users from getting the same connection and to prevent the pool from changing state during the allocation operation.

When a user requests a connection, several procedures are tried in an attempt to satisfy the request. First, the connection vector is examined to find an available pool entry. If one exists, it is marked as "in use" and its underlying `Connection` object is returned to the caller:

```
Enumeration epool = pool.elements();
while (epool.hasMoreElements()) {
    PoolEntry entry = (PoolEntry) epool.nextElement();
    if (entry.getState() == PoolEntry.AVAILABLE) {
        entry.allocate();
        return entry.getConnection();
    }
}
```

If none of the entries in the pool are available and the pool size is not already at its maximum, the pool get a new connection from the `ConnectionFactory`, adds it to the pool, and returns it to the caller:

```
if (pool.size() != maxEntries) {
    con = factory.createInstance();
    if (con == null)
        return null;
    PoolEntry entry = new PoolEntry(con);
    pool.addElement(entry);
    entry.allocate();
    return entry.getConnection();
}
```

If neither of these methods supplies the necessary connection, the user has three options:

1. Wait indefinitely for a connection to become available
2. Wait for a user-specified time limit
3. Return a null connection to indicate failure

The user's choice is indicated by the value of the `timeout` parameter passed to `getConnection()`:

```
while (timeout >= -1) {
   ...
   if (timeout == -1)
      wait();
   else if (timeout <= 0)
      return null;
   else {
      long stime = System.currentTimeMillis();
      wait(timeout);
      long etime = System.currentTimeMillis();
      timeout = etime - stime;
      if (timeout == -1)
         timeout = 0;
   }
}
```

The `wait()` method causes the thread that is running `getConnection()` to release the synchronization lock and wait for some other thread to call `notify()` or `notifyAll()`. In our case, this is done by the `refresh()` method whenever it adds a new connection to the pool.

The `releaseConnection()` method is somewhat simpler. All that needs to be done is to search the pool vector for the appropriate entry and designate it for recycling:

```
public synchronized void releaseConnection(Connection con)
{
   Enumeration epool = pool.elements();
   while (epool.hasMoreElements()) {
      PoolEntry entry = (PoolEntry) epool.nextElement();
      if (con.equals(entry.getConnection())) {
         entry.setState(PoolEntry.RECYCLING);
         new RefreshThread(this).start();
         return;
      }
   }
}
```

We invoke `refresh()` indirectly in a background thread here because there is no reason to make the user wait (as long as the refresh operation does indeed get scheduled). Like checking books into a library, the user just dumps the used connection into the `releaseConnection` bin, and the librarian does the administrative work.

It is not terribly difficult to write your own connection pool, perhaps modeling it after the one presented in this section. You may wish to examine the `javax.sql` classes in the JDBC 2.0 Optional Package, which provides interfaces (but not implementations) for connection pooling, distributed transactions, and row sets. See *http://java.sun.com/j2ee/bulletin/jdbc_2/extension.html* for details.

5.3 Getting the Column Number Right

Problem

Operations on `ResultSet` or `ResultSetMetaData` objects refer to the columns as 1, 2,..., n, but array indexes in Java are 0, 1,..., $n - 1$. How do I keep from confusing them?

Technique

Use two different variables, one for the array index and one for the column number:

```
ResultSet rs = stmt.executeQuery("SELECT * FROM PRODUCTS");


// Get the column information

ResultSetMetaData rmd = rs.getMetaData();
int nColumns = rmd.getColumnCount();
int[] widths = new int[nColumns];
StringBuffer buffer = new StringBuffer();

// Print the column names

for (int i = 0; i < nColumns; i++) {
   int col = i+1;
   String name = rmd.getColumnName(col);
   int width = rmd.getColumnDisplaySize(col);
   while (name.length() < width)
      name += " ";
   widths[i] = name.length();
   buffer.append(name);
   buffer.append(" ");
}
System.out.println(buffer);
```

Discussion

As the first statement inside any loop over the columns in a `ResultSet`, create a variable named `col`, and set it equal to the array index plus one. If you have any parallel arrays (like the widths array in the example), index them with the loop variable. But use the `col` variable for any method that calls on the ResultSet. This technique may seem obvious, but it prevents you from being three levels deep in a subroutine stack with what could either be an array index or column number and that may or may not have already been adjusted for the index base.

5.4   The JDBC-ODBC Bridge

Problem

I do not have a database management system with a JDBC driver, but I do have Microsoft Access. How can I use JDBC with Access or other ODBC data sources?

Technique

Use the JDBC-ODBC bridge supplied with the Java Development Kit (JDK).

Discussion

Open Database Connectivity (ODBC) is an SQL-oriented application programming interface developed by Microsoft. Much like JDBC, ODBC is designed to isolate the details of accessing a particular vendor's database inside a single object (the ODBC driver). ODBC drivers are available for virtually all database management systems.

JavaSoft and Intersolv (now Merant) have leveraged the large ODBC installed base by developing a generic JDBC driver that interoperates with ODBC drivers. This driver (known as the *JDBC-ODBC bridge*) is distributed with the JDK and uses native methods to translate JDBC operations into their ODBC counterparts.

In order to use the bridge (or ODBC, for that matter), you need to have configured a data source. In this example, we shall connect to a copy of the U.S. Department of Agriculture's *Nutrient Database for Standard Reference*[4] on a Windows NT 4.0 system.

---

[4]This database can be freely downloaded from the USDA Nutrient Data Laboratory's Web site at *http://www.nal.usda.gov/fnic/foodcomp/ Data/SR12/dnload/sr12dnld.html*.

To configure the data source, first launch the ODBC Data Source Administrator from the Windows NT Control Panel (Start → Settings → Control Panel). You should see the dialog shown in Figure 5-9. Since the Web server is most likely running under some user ID other than yours, you will need to assign a system data source name, not a user data source name. Figure 5-10 shows what the System DSN tab looks like. Click on the "Add" button to begin creating a new data source. You should see the "Create New Data Source" dialog shown in Figure 5-11. Select Microsoft dBase Driver (*.dbf) from the list, and click "Finish." Next, the ODBC Data Source Administrator will prompt you for a name

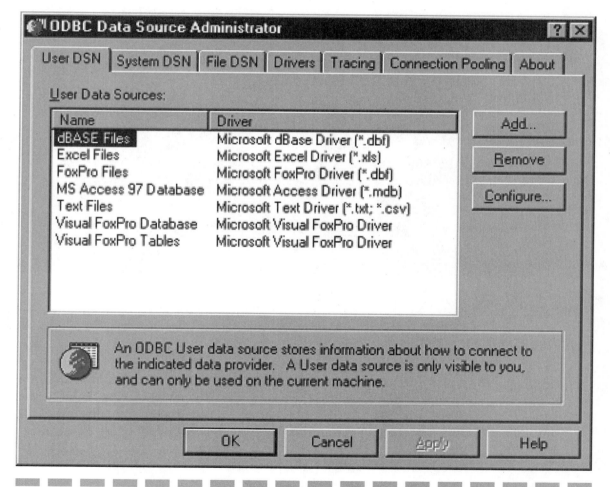

Figure 5-9 The ODBC Data Source Administrator.

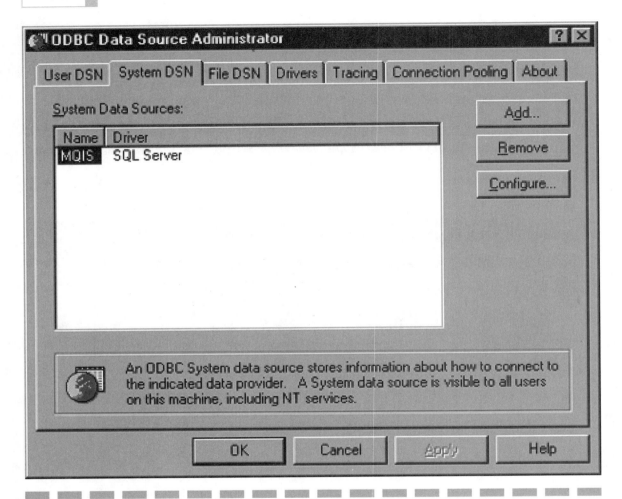

Figure 5-10 Configuring an ODBC system data source name.

and description for the data source, as shown in Figure 5-12. Enter "usda" for the data source name and "USDA Nutrient Database for Standard Reference" for the description. Then uncheck the "Use Current Directory" checkbox so that you can choose the specific directory that contains the USDA nutrient database. Select this directory in the dialog box shown in Figure 5-13. After clicking "OK," you should see the updated ODBC Data Source Administrator panel with the newly created USDA data source (see Figure 5-14).

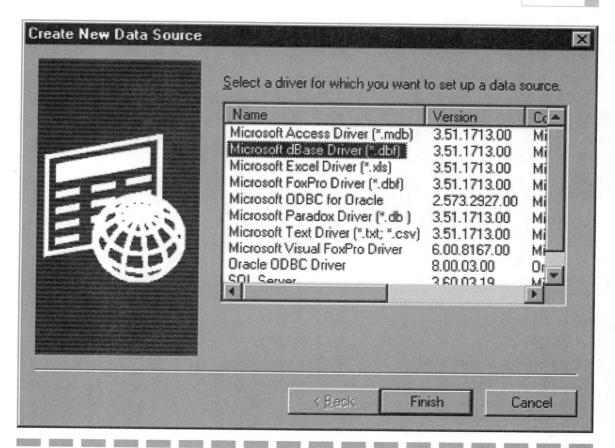

Figure 5-11 Selecting the driver for a new ODBC data source.

Figure 5-15 illustrates how the JDBC-ODBC bridge is used, which at this point is no different from any other JDBC driver. First, we ensure that the driver class has been loaded and registered with the driver manager:

```
Class.forName("sun.jdbc.odbc.JdbcOdbcDriver");
```

Then we establish the connection using a JDBC URL:

```
con = DriverManager.getConnection("jdbc:odbc:usda");
```

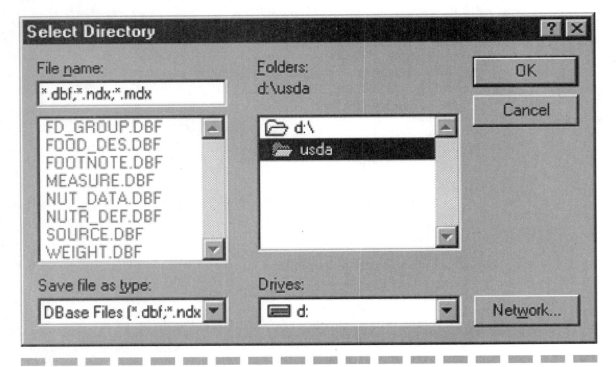

Figure 5-12 ODBC dBase data source setup.

Figure 5-13 Selecting the directory for an ODBC dBase data source.

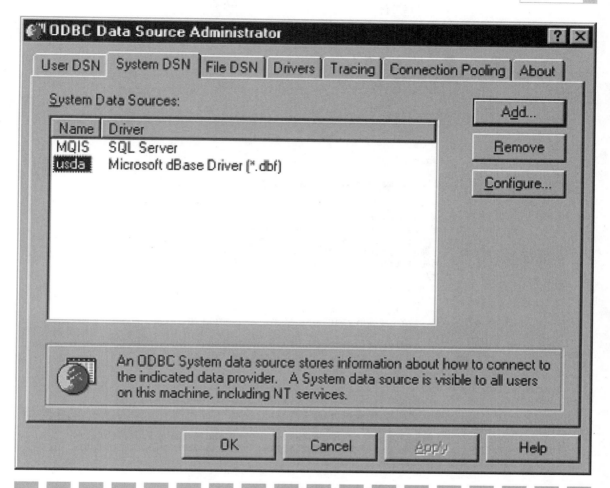

Figure 5-14 The completed ODBC dBase data source entry.

When the servlet is run, it produces the output shown in Figure 5-16.

The JDBC-ODBC bridge is of limited value in an applet environment because it requires the client to have ODBC software installed and properly configured. Moreover, the use of native code in untrusted applets is not allowed. In servlets, however, as we have seen, this is much less problematic because all the configuration happens on the server.

Figure 5-15

A servlet that uses
the JDBC-ODBC
bridge.

```java
package ijs.jdbc;

import java.io.*;
import java.net.*;
import java.sql.*;
import java.util.*;

import javax.servlet.*;
import javax.servlet.http.*;

/**
 * BananaBabyFoodsServlet
 */
public class BananaBabyFoodsServlet extends HttpServlet
{
    /**
     * Handles a GET request
     * @param request the servlet request object
     * @param response the servlet response object
     * @exception ServletException if a servlet exception occurs
     * @exception IOException if an I/O exception occurs
     */
    public void doGet(
            HttpServletRequest request,
            HttpServletResponse response)
        throws ServletException, IOException

    {
        response.setContentType("text/html");
        PrintWriter out = response.getWriter();

        out.println("<HTML>");
        out.println("<HEAD>");
        out.println("<TITLE>BananaBabyFoodsServlet</TITLE>");
        out.println("</HEAD>");
        out.println("<BODY>");
        out.println("<IMG SRC=\"/ijs/Chap05/banana.gif\">");
        out.println("<FONT SIZE=+2>Banana Baby Foods</FONT>");
        out.println("<P>");

        Connection con = null;
        Statement stmt = null;
        ResultSet rs = null;
        try {
            Class.forName("sun.jdbc.odbc.JdbcOdbcDriver");
            con = DriverManager.getConnection("jdbc:odbc:usda");
            stmt = con.createStatement();
            rs = stmt.executeQuery(""
                    + " SELECT    F.NDB_No as foodCode,"
                    + "           F.Desc as foodDesc"
                    + " FROM      FOOD_DES F, FD_GROUP G"
                    + " WHERE     F.FdGp_Cd = G.FdGp_Cd"
                    + " AND       F.Shrt_Desc LIKE '%BANANA%'"
                    + " AND       G.FdGp_Desc = 'Baby Foods'"
                    + " ORDER BY F.Desc"
                    );
            int nRows = 0;
            while (rs.next()) {
```

Figure 5-15

(Continued)

```
                        nRows++;
                        String foodCode = rs.getString("foodCode");
                        String foodDesc = rs.getString("foodDesc");
                        out.println("<B>" + foodCode + "</B>");
                        out.println(foodDesc);
                        out.println("<BR>");
                    }
                    out.println("<P>" + nRows
                        + " banana baby foods selected.<P>");
                }
            catch (Exception e) {
                out.println
                ("Could not connect to the nutrient database.<P>");
                out.println("The error message was");
                out.println("<PRE>");
                out.println(e.getMessage());
                out.println("</PRE>");
            }
            finally {
                if (rs != null) {
                    try { rs.close(); }
                    catch (SQLException ignore) {}
                }
                if (stmt != null) {
                    try { stmt.close(); }
                    catch (SQLException ignore) {}
                }
                if (con != null) {
                    try { con.close(); }
                    catch (SQLException ignore) {}
                }
            }

        out.println("</BODY>");
        out.println("</HTML>");
    }

    /**
     * Handles a POST request
     * @param request the servlet request object
     * @param response the servlet response object
     * @exception ServletException if a servlet exception occurs
     * @exception IOException if an I/O exception occurs
     */
    public void doPost(
            HttpServletRequest request,
            HttpServletResponse response)
        throws ServletException, IOException
    {
        doGet(request, response);
    }
```

Figure 5-16 The Web page produced by the BananaBabyFoods servlet.

5.5 Registering a JDBC Driver

Problem

I have a JDBC driver. How do I make it accessible to my servlet?

Technique

Register the class explicitly with `Class.forName(<driver class name>)` or by specifying it in the `jdbc.drivers` system property.

Discussion

A driver must be registered with the JDBC driver manager before it can be used. A properly written JDBC driver will do this automatically when its class is loaded. This means that all you should have to do is to load the class explicitly with the static `forName` method of `java.lang.Class`. For example, if the driver name is `com.ipfoods.jdbc.Driver`, it can be registered with

```
try {
    Class.forName("com.ipfoods.jdbc.Driver");
}
catch (ClassNotFoundException e) {
    // Handle the class not found exception
}
```

Alternatively, you can specify the driver class name in the system property `jdbc.drivers`. From a command line, this would be written as

```
java -Djdbc.drivers=com.ipfoods.jdbc.Driver <program name>
```

Some drivers incorrectly fail to do the registration step until their constructor is called. In this case, you will need to use the first method and actually call the constructor, as shown here:

```
try {
    Class.forName("com.ipfoods.jdbc.Driver").newInstance();
}
catch (ClassNotFoundException e) {
    // Handle the class not found exception
}
```

```
catch (InstantiationException e) {
   // Handle the instance creation exception
}
catch (IllegalAccessException e) {
   // Handle yet another exception
}
```

The JDBC driver manager maintains a list of drivers in the order in which they were registered. When it is asked for a connection to a particular database URL, it goes through each driver in the list asking it if it can connect to that URL. The first driver that responds positively is selected. If no driver volunteers, the driver manager throws an `SQLException` indicating that no suitable driver was found.

5.6 Using a `PreparedStatement`

Problem

How can I avoid problems with embedded apostrophes in search arguments?

Technique

Use a `PreparedStatement` to set a parameter with the search argument.

Discussion

A form like the one shown in Figure 5-17 is used frequently to prompt the user for keywords to be used in a database search. When the "Search" button is clicked, a JavaServer Page (JSP) is invoked to perform the database operation and generate an HTML table with the results.[5] In this case, with a search argument of "PIE," the results are as shown in Figure 5-18.

The servlet that performs the search extracts the value of the search argument from the HTTP request and substitutes it into an SQL statement character string as follows:

---

[5]JavaServer Pages are discussed at length in Chapter 13.

```
stmt = con.createStatement();
rs = stmt.executeQuery(""
    + " SELECT    itemCode, itemDesc"
    + " FROM      products"
    + " WHERE     itemDesc like '%" + searchArg + "%'"
    + " ORDER BY itemDesc"
);
```

Figure 5-17 A simple search of the product database.

Figure 5-18 Results of searching the product database for "PIE."

This appears to work well. However, if "JOHN'S PIES" is the search argument, the results consist of the nasty error message illustrated in Figure 5-19.

What happened? The error message complains about a syntax error:

```
Syntax error (missing operator) in query expression
'itemDesc alike '%JOHN'S PIES%' ORDER BY itemDesc'.
```

Figure 5-19 *Results of searching the product database for "JOHN'S PIES."*

Looking closely, we see the problem. The pattern used in the LIKE condition is `%JOHN'S PIES%`, which contains an embedded apostrophe. This causes the pattern to be interpreted as `%JOHN` followed by `S PIES%`, thoroughly confusing the SQL compiler.

Problems like this are quite unpleasant because they are usually not caught in routine testing. It takes an O'Brian or D'Artangnan to uncover the deficiency. One wonders how many Web sites have this bug lurking out there, waiting for a rogue search to bring down the server.

One solution is to filter the user input, subsituting the appropriate escape sequence for any apostrophes found. However, database products are not consistent in the syntax to be used for this purpose. Microsoft Access uses doubled apostrophes, while other products use the backslash character as a prefix.

The most reliable way to prevent this problem is to use a `java.sql.PreparedStatement` instead of a `java.sql.Statement`. Although prepared statements are used most often for performance reasons when repeatedly executing the same SQL operation, they offer the additional benefit of eliminating the quoted parameter problem. A `PreparedStatement` uses the question mark character as a placeholder for substitution parameters and allows you to specify the value to be used with a method call rather than a string concatenation. With a slight change to the servlet, this becomes

```
String sql = ""
    + " SELECT     itemCode, itemDesc"
    + " FROM       products"
    + " WHERE      itemDesc like ?"
    + " ORDER BY itemDesc"
;
PreparedStatement stmt = con.prepareStatement(sql);
stmt.setString(1, "%" + searchArg + "%");
rs = stmt.executeQuery();
```

The value to be inserted is specified by one of the `PreparedStatement` `setXXX()` methods, where `XXX` stands for the Java data type. In the preceding example, we are substituting % plus `searchArg` plus % for the first question mark in the prepared statement. Note that the question mark is used without any surrounding quotation marks or apostrophes, regardless of the data type involved.

SQL statements that have multiple substitution parameters should contain multiple question marks. These are referred to in subsequent `setXXX()` methods as parameter 1, parameter 2, and so on. For example, when loading the products database, we could use a `PreparedStatement` for the `INSERT` operation:

```
PreparedStatement pstmt = con.prepareStatement(
    "INSERT INTO products VALUES(?, ?)");
```

In the loop where we are reading from an input stream and writing to the database, we would use

```
for (;;) {
   String buffer = in.readLine();
   if (buffer == null)
      break;
   ...
   pstmt.setString(1, itemCode);
   pstmt.setString(2, itemDesc);
   pstmt.executeUpdate();
}
```

5.7 Handling Transactions with `Commit` and `Rollback`

Problem

How can I ensure that multiple database operations belonging to a transaction are completely applied or not applied?

Technique

Use the `java.sql.Connection commit()` and `rollback()` methods to surround logical transactions.

Discussion

Database operations frequently involve updating more than one table. For example, a funds transfer in an online banking application may consist of a withdrawal from one account followed by a deposit in another. Clearly, both parts of this logical transaction must happen consistently. If either one fails for any reason, the other must be reversed or negated.

Most database management systems and application servers have some means for handling these logical transactions. JDBC provides access to this mechanism with the `commit()` and `rollback()` methods of the `java.sql.Connection` object.

To make use of this feature, you first need to find out whether or not your JDBC driver supports transactions. This can be determined by calling a method in the `DatabaseMetaData` object:

```
Connection con = ...
DatabaseMetaData md = con.getMetaData();
if (md.supportsTransactions()) {
   // Yes, we can do transactions
}
else {
   // No, not supported
}
```

If the driver supports transactions, the next necessary step is to prevent the connection from committing changes automatically:

```
Connection con = ...
con.setAutoCommit(false);
```

The code that executes the update operation should be enclosed in a try...catch block, with commit() used at the end of the try block and rollback() coded in the catch block:

```
try {
   stmt.executeUpdate(""
      + " UPDATE    checking"
      + " SET       balance = balance - 100"
      + " WHERE     acctno = '0120'"
         );

   stmt.executeUpdate(""
      + " UPDATE    savings"
      + " SET       balance = balance + 100"
      + " WHERE     acctno = '0120'"
         );
   }

   con.commit();

catch (Exception e) {
   try {
      con.rollback();
   }
   catch (SQLException ignore) {}
}
```

5.8 Using `DatabaseMetaData` for Generic Code

Problem

I use more than one database management system. How can I discover what features each of them supports?

Technique

Open a connection to the database and call its `getMetaData()` method.
Interrogate the returned `DatabaseMetaData` object for the specifics of
supported features:

```
Connection con = DriverManager.getConnection(...);
DatabaseMetaData md = con.getMetaData();

// Get the desired metadata

String timeDateFunctions = md.getTimeDateFunctions();
ResultSet rs1 = md.getTableTypes();
...
```

Discussion

The `DatabaseMetaData` interface has more methods than any other
class in the JDK—149 in all. Using its methods, you can determine
ahead of time whether a particular feature is supported, gracefully
degrading if it is not.

A typical use for `DatabaseMetaData` is to find the data type names
employed by your database vendor. If you are writing a `CREATE TABLE`
statement, you may be dismayed to find out that what Microsoft Access
refers to as its `OleObject` data type is what InstantDB calls `BINARY`
and what Oracle calls `LONG RAW`, even though all these products adhere
to the SQL standard. Moreover, a numeric column may have zero, one, or
two creation parameters, depending on the vendor's implementation.

The metadata `getTypeInfo()` method will allow you to sort this out.
It creates a result set that maps JDBC data types to the database vendor's name(s) for the type. Figure 5-20 illustrates how this is done.

The `TypeMapper.jsp` JavaServer Page extracts a driver name and
database URL from its request parameters, which can be supplied by an
HTML form or by being appended to the query:

```
http://localhost/TypeMapper.jsp
   ?driverName=sun.jdbc.odbc.JdbcOdbcDriver
   &url=jdbc:odbc:dBASE+Files
```

NOTE *The URL shown above is split for clarity. It should be entered
as a single line.*

Figure 5-20
Mapping driver
data types into
JDBC data types.

```
<!DOCTYPE HTML PUBLIC "-//W3C//DTD HTML 4.0 Transitional//EN">
<HTML>

<HEAD>
<TITLE>Data Type Mapper</TITLE>
</HEAD>

<BODY>
<CENTER>
<H3>Type Mapping</H3>
<%@ page import="java.sql.*,ijs.jdbc.*" %>
    <TABLE BORDER=0 CELLPADDING=3>
<%
    Connection con = null;
    try {

        String driverName = request.getParameter("driverName");
        if (driverName == null)
            throw new SQLException("Driver name not specified");

        String url = request.getParameter("url");
        if (url == null)
            throw new SQLException("URL not specified");

        String userName = request.getParameter("userName");
        String password = request.getParameter("password");

        // Load the driver

        Class.forName(driverName);

        // Open the database connection and get the metadata

        if ((userName == null) && (password == null))
            con = DriverManager.getConnection(url);
        else
            con = DriverManager.getConnection(url,
                "admin", "admin");

        DatabaseMetaData md = con.getMetaData();

        String caption =
            md.getDriverName()
            + " "
            + md.getDriverVersion();

%>
    <CAPTION ALIGN=TOP> <%= caption %> </CAPTION>
    <TR>
    <TH ALIGN=CENTER VALIGN=MIDDLE>Type Name</TH>
    <TH ALIGN=CENTER VALIGN=MIDDLE>JDBC Name</TH>
    <TH ALIGN=CENTER VALIGN=MIDDLE>Precision</TH>
    </TR>
<%
        // Get the supported type info result set

        ResultSet rs = md.getTypeInfo();
```

```
    while (rs.next()) {

        // Get the individual fields

        String typeName = rs.getString("TYPE_NAME");
        int dataType = rs.getInt("DATA_TYPE");
        String jdbcTypeName = JDBCTypes.getName(dataType);
        int precision = rs.getInt("PRECISION");
%>
    <TR>
    <TD ALIGN=LEFT VALIGN=TOP><%= typeName %></TD>
    <TD ALIGN=LEFT VALIGN=TOP><%= jdbcTypeName %></TD>
    <TD ALIGN=RIGHT VALIGN=TOP><%= precision %></TD>
    </TR>
<%
    }
    }
    catch (Exception e) {
        e.printStackTrace(new PrintWriter(out));
    }
    finally {
        if (con != null) {
            try {
                con.close();
            } catch (SQLException ignore) {}
        }
%>
    </TABLE>
<%
    }
%>
</CENTER>
</BODY>

</HTML>
```

TypeMapper gets the DatabaseMetaData from the connection and calls its getTypeInfo() method. From the result set, it extracts the TYPE_NAME and DATA_TYPE columns. TYPE_NAME is the database vendor's term for the type, which is the value that should be used in the CREATE TABLE statement. DATA_TYPE is an integer that corresponds to one of the constants defined by the java.sql.Types class. DATA_TYPE can then be mapped to a JDBC type name by a static method in the ijs.jdbc.JDBCTypes class shown in Figure 5-21. JDBCTypes uses classes in the java.lang.reflect package to extract the names that correspond to the java.sql.Types constants.

The mapping generated by the JDBC-ODBC bridge driver reading dBase files is shown in Figure 5-22. The InstantDB driver mapping is shown in Figure 5-23. And an Oracle JDBC driver mapping is shown in Figure 5-24.

Figure 5-21
Translating a type
number into a type
name.

```java
package ijs.jdbc;

import java.lang.reflect.*;
import java.sql.*;

/**
 * A helper class that finds the names of JDBC data types
 */
public class JDBCTypes
{
    private static Object[][] typeNames;

    /**
     * Static method to initialize the type names array
     */
    static {
        Class cls = java.sql.Types.class;
        Field[] fields = cls.getDeclaredFields();
        typeNames = new Object[fields.length][2];
        for (int i = 0; i < fields.length; i++) {
            try {
                Field field = fields[i];
                typeNames[i][0] = new Integer
                    (field.getInt(field));
                typeNames[i][1] = field.getName();
            }
            catch (IllegalAccessException e) {
                e.printStackTrace();
            }
        }
    };

    /**
     * Returns a type name given a type number
     * @param type the type number
     */
    public static String getName(int type)
    {
        Integer itype = new Integer(type);
        for (int i = 0; i < typeNames.length; i++)
            if (typeNames[i][0].equals(itype))
                return (String) typeNames[i][1];
        return null;
    }
}
```

While it is theoretically possible to generate a CREATE TABLE
statement generically solely from metadata, it is far more work than you
probably want to do, unless you are developing a database interface
product. DatabaseMetaData is more useful as reference material.

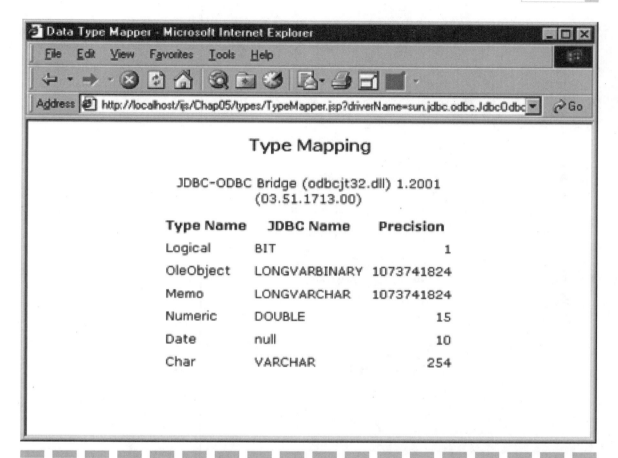

Figure 5-22 Type mapping of the ODBC dBase driver.

Figure 5-25 illustrates the output of a metadata explorer servlet that can be used to view this voluminous information from a Web page. `MetadataExplorerServlet` takes the same parameters as `TypeMapper.jsp`, a driver name and a database URL (Figure 5-26). It uses reflection to get a list of the methods declared by the driver's `DatabaseMetaData` object and invokes all the zero-parameter ones that return a `Boolean`, `String`, or `ResultSet` value.

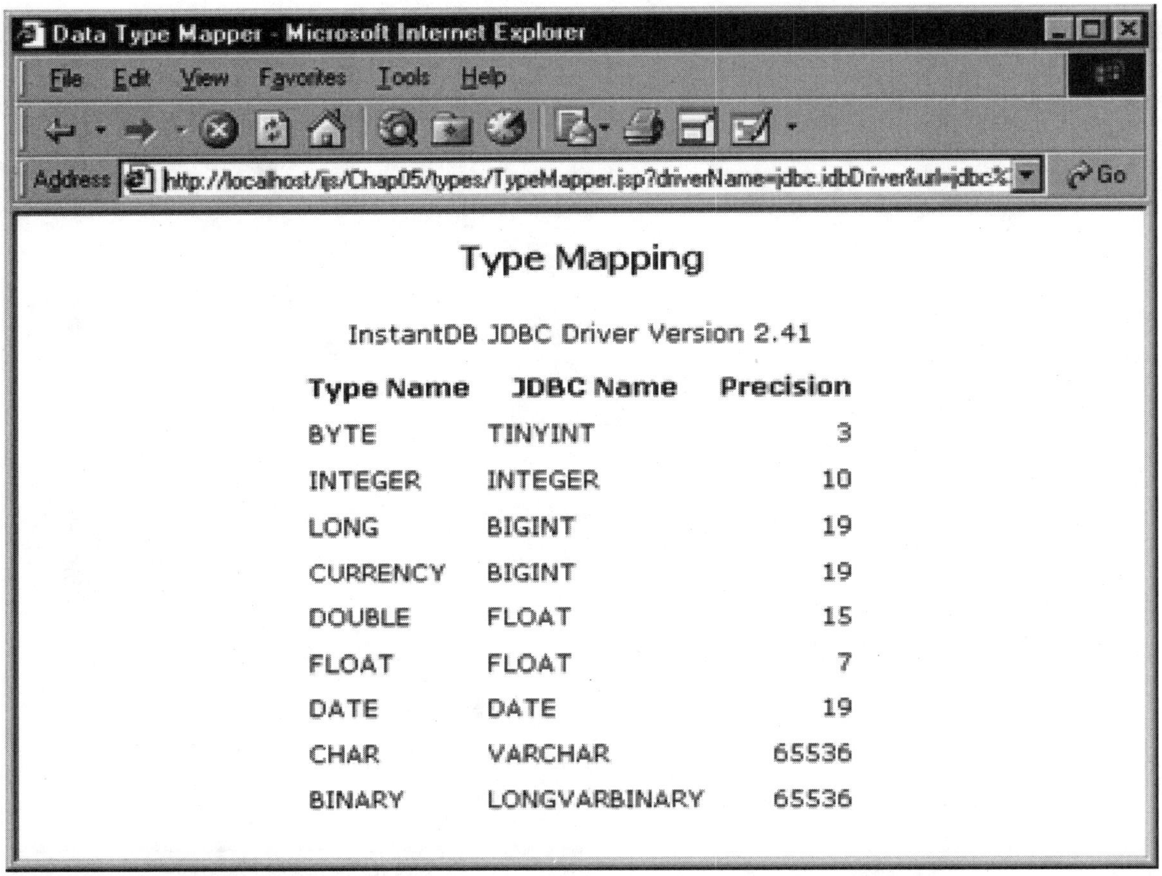

Type Name	JDBC Name	Precision
BYTE	TINYINT	3
INTEGER	INTEGER	10
LONG	BIGINT	19
CURRENCY	BIGINT	19
DOUBLE	FLOAT	15
FLOAT	FLOAT	7
DATE	DATE	19
CHAR	VARCHAR	65536
BINARY	LONGVARBINARY	65536

Figure 5-23 Type mapping of the InstantDB driver.

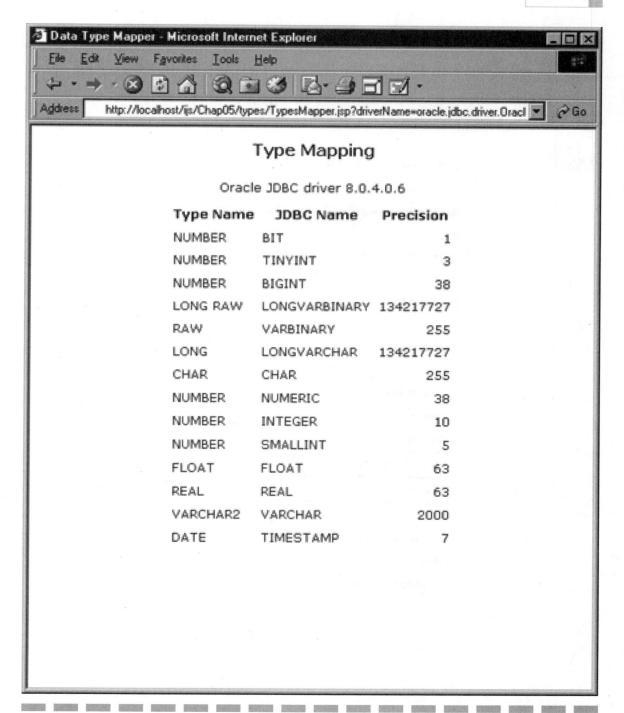

Figure 5-24 Type mapping of the Oracle driver.

Figure 5-25
Output of the
Metadata-
Explorer-
servlet.

Metadata Explorer Servlet

sun.jdbc.odbc.JdbcOdbcDriver jdbc:odbc:usda

allProceduresAreCallable

true

allTablesAreSelectable

true

dataDefinitionCausesTransactionCommit

false

dataDefinitionIgnoredInTransactions

false

doesMaxRowSizeIncludeBlobs

false

getCatalogSeparator

\

getCatalogTerm

Directory

getCatalogs

TABLE_QUALIFIER
D:\usda

getDatabaseProductName

DBASE

getDatabaseProductVersion

5.0

getDriverName

JDBC-ODBC Bridge (odbcjt32.dll)

Figure 5-25
(Continued)

getDriverVersion

1.2001 (03.51.1713.00)

getExtraNameCharacters

~@#$%^&*_-+=\}{";:?/><,

getIdentifierQuoteString

`

getNumericFunctions

ABS,ATAN,CEILING,COS,EXP,FLOOR,LOG,MOD,
POWER,RAND,SIGN,SIN,SQRT,TAN

getSQLKeywords

ALPHANUMERIC,AUTOINCREMENT,BINARY,BYTE,COUNTER,
CURRENCY,DATABASE,DATABASENAME,DATETIME,DISALLOW,
DISTINCTROW,DOUBLEFLOAT,FLOAT4,FLOAT8,GENERAL,IEEEDOUBLE,
IEEESINGLE,IGNORE,INT,INTEGER1,INTEGER2,INTEGER4,LEVEL,
LOGICAL,LOGICAL1,LONG,LONGBINARY,LONGCHAR,LONGTEXT,MEMO,
MONEY,NOTE,NUMBER,OLEOBJECT,OPTION,OWNERACCESS,PARAMETERS,
PERCENT,PIVOT,SHORT,SINGLE,SINGLEFLOAT,SMALLINT,STDEV,
STDEVP,STRING,TABLEID,TEXT,TOP,TRANSFORM,UNSIGNEDBYTE,
VALUES,VAR,VARBINARY,VARP,YESNO

getSchemaTerm

getSchemas

null

getSearchStringEscape

\

getStringFunctions

ASCII,CHAR,CONCAT,LCASE,LEFT,LENGTH,LOCATE,LOCATE_2,
LTRIM,RIGHT,RTRIM,SPACE,SUBSTRING,UCASE

getTableTypes

TABLE_TYPE
TABLE

getTimeDateFunctions

CURDATE,DAYOFMONTH,DAYOFWEEK,DAYOFYEAR,MONTH,WEEK,YEAR

Figure 5-25
(Continued)

getTypeInfo

TYPE_NAME	DATA_TYPE	PRECISION	LITERAL_PREFIX
Logical	-7	1	null
OleObject	-4	1073741824	0x
Memo	-1	1073741824	'
Numeric	8	15	null
Date	9	10	#
Char	12	254	'

TYPE_NAME	LITERAL_SUFFIX	CREATE_PARAMS	NULLABLE
Logical	null	null	1
OleObject	null	null	1
Memo	'	null	1
Numeric	null	null	1
Date	#	null	1
Char	'	MAX LENGTH	1

TYPE_NAME	UNSIGNED_ATTRIBUTE	MONEY	AUTO_INCREMENT
Logical	null	0	null
OleObject	null	0	null
Memo	null	0	null
Numeric	0	0	0
Date	null	0	null
Char	null	0	null

TYPE_NAME	MINIMUM_SCALE	MAXIMUM_SCALE

Figure 5-25
(Continued)

Logical	0	0
OleObject	null	null
Memo	null	null
Numeric	null	null
Date	null	null
Char	null	null

getURL

jdbc:odbc:usda

getUserName

isCatalogAtStart

true

isReadOnly

false

nullPlusNonNullIsNull

false

nullsAreSortedAtEnd

false

nullsAreSortedAtStart

false

nullsAreSortedHigh

false

nullsAreSortedLow

true

storesLowerCaseIdentifiers

false

storesLowerCaseQuotedIdentifiers

false

Figure 5-25
(Continued)

storesMixedCaseIdentifiers

false

storesMixedCaseQuotedIdentifiers

true

storesUpperCaseIdentifiers

true

storesUpperCaseQuotedIdentifiers

false

supportsANSI92EntryLevelSQL

true

supportsANSI92FullSQL

false

supportsANSI92IntermediateSQL

false

supportsAlterTableWithAddColumn

true

supportsAlterTableWithDropColumn

true

supportsBatchUpdates

null

supportsCatalogsInDataManipulation

true

supportsCatalogsInIndexDefinitions

true

supportsCatalogsInPrivilegeDefinitions

false

supportsCatalogsInProcedureCalls

true

supportsCatalogsInTableDefinitions

Figure 5-25
(Continued)

true

supportsColumnAliasing

true

supportsConvert

true

supportsCoreSQLGrammar

false

supportsCorrelatedSubqueries

true

supportsDataDefinitionAndDataManipulationTransactions

false

supportsDataManipulationTransactionsOnly

false

supportsDifferentTableCorrelationNames

false

supportsExpressionsInOrderBy

true

supportsExtendedSQLGrammar

false

supportsFullOuterJoins

false

supportsGroupBy

true

supportsGroupByBeyondSelect

true

supportsGroupByUnrelated

false

supportsIntegrityEnhancementFacility

false

Figure 5-25
(Continued)

supportsLikeEscapeClause

false

supportsLimitedOuterJoins

false

supportsMinimumSQLGrammar

true

supportsMixedCaseIdentifiers

true

supportsMixedCaseQuotedIdentifiers

true

supportsMultipleResultSets

false

supportsMultipleTransactions

false

supportsNonNullableColumns

false

supportsOpenCursorsAcrossCommit

false

supportsOpenCursorsAcrossRollback

false

supportsOpenStatementsAcrossCommit

true

supportsOpenStatementsAcrossRollback

true

supportsOrderByUnrelated

false

supportsOuterJoins

true

supportsPositionedDelete

Figure 5-25
(Continued)

false

supportsPositionedUpdate

false

supportsSchemasInDataManipulation

false

supportsSchemasInIndexDefinitions

false

supportsSchemasInPrivilegeDefinitions

false

supportsSchemasInProcedureCalls

false

supportsSchemasInTableDefinitions

false

supportsSelectForUpdate

false

supportsStoredProcedures

false

supportsSubqueriesInComparisons

true

supportsSubqueriesInExists

true

supportsSubqueriesInIns

true

supportsSubqueriesInQuantifieds

true

supportsTableCorrelationNames

true

supportsTransactions

false

Figure 5-25
(Continued)

supportsUnion

true

supportsUnionAll

true

usesLocalFilePerTable

true

usesLocalFiles

false

5.9 Analyzing the Columns in a `ResultSet`

Problem

I have a `ResultSet` that was returned by a `SELECT`. Where can I get information about the columns it contains?

Technique

Get name and type information for each column from the `ResultSetMetaData` object.

Discussion

If you have a `ResultSet` that was returned by this statement:

```
SELECT itemCode, itemDesc, price, onHand FROM products
```

then you obviously know the name and type of each column. On the other hand, if the `ResultSet` was generated by this statement:

```
SELECT * FROM products WHERE itemDesc LIKE '%BANANA%'
```

```
package ijs.jdbc;

import java.io.*;
import java.net.*;
import java.lang.reflect.*;
import java.sql.*;
import java.util.*;

import javax.servlet.*;
import javax.servlet.http.*;

/**
 * Metadata Explorer Servlet
 */
public class MetadataExplorerServlet extends HttpServlet
{
    /**
     * Inner class for passing parameters between methods
     */
    class Parameters {
        HttpServletRequest request;
        HttpServletResponse response;
        PrintWriter out;
        String driverName;
        String url;
        Connection con;
        DatabaseMetaData md;
        Class mdclass;
        Method method;
    }

    /**
     * Handles a GET request
     */
    public void doGet(
            HttpServletRequest request,
            HttpServletResponse response)
        throws ServletException, IOException
    {
        // Create the parameter structure
        // and store the objects we need

        Parameters parms = new Parameters();
        parms.request = request;
        parms.response = response;

        response.setContentType("text/html");
        PrintWriter out = response.getWriter();
        parms.out = out;

        // Connect to the database and write the document

        try {

            connect(parms);

            out.println("<HTML>");
```

Figure 5-26
(Continued)

```
         writeHead(parms);
         writeBody(parms);
         out.println("</HTML>");
      }

      // Close the database no matter what

      finally {
         Connection con = parms.con;
         if (con != null) {
            try {
               con.close();
            }
            catch (SQLException ignore) {}
         }
      }
   }

/**
 * Loads the driver and opens a connection to the database
 */
public void connect(Parameters parms)
   throws ServletException, IOException
{
   HttpServletRequest request = parms.request;

   // Get the driver name parameter

   String driverName = request.getParameter("driverName");
   if (driverName == null)
      throw new ServletException
         ("No driverName parameter specified");
   parms.driverName = driverName;

   // Get the database URL parameter

   String url = request.getParameter("url");
   if (url == null)
      throw new ServletException
         ("No url parameter specified");
   parms.url = url;

   // Load the driver class

   try {
      Class.forName(driverName);
   }
   catch (ClassNotFoundException e) {
      throw new ServletException
         ("Could not load driver class ["
         + driverName + "]");
   }

   // Connect to the database
   // and get the metadata

   try {
```

Figure 5-26
(Continued)

```
        Connection con = DriverManager.getConnection(url);
        parms.con = con;

        DatabaseMetaData md = con.getMetaData();
        parms.md = md;

        Class mdclass = md.getClass();
        parms.mdclass = mdclass;
    }
    catch (SQLException e) {
        throw new ServletException
            ("Could not connect to ["
            + url + "]"
            + " Error message is ["
            + e.getMessage() + "]");
    }
}

/**
 * Writes the HEAD section
 */
public void writeHead(Parameters parms)
    throws ServletException, IOException
{
    PrintWriter out = parms.out;

    out.println("<HEAD>");
    out.println("<TITLE>Metadata Explorer Servlet</TITLE>");
    out.println("</HEAD>");
}

/**
 * Writes the BODY section
 */
public void writeBody(Parameters parms)
    throws ServletException, IOException
{
    PrintWriter out = parms.out;
    String driverName = parms.driverName;
    String url = parms.url;

    out.println("<BODY>");
    out.println("<H2>Metadata Explorer Servlet</H2>");
    out.println("<H3>" + driverName + " " + url + "</H3>");

    writeMethodsTable(parms);

    out.println("</BODY>");
}

/**
 * Writes the methods table
 */
public void writeMethodsTable(Parameters parms)
    throws ServletException, IOException
{
    PrintWriter out = parms.out;
```

Figure 5-26
(Continued)

```
DatabaseMetaData md = parms.md;
Class mdclass = parms.mdclass;

// Get the list of methods.  Select only public
// methods that take no parameters and return
// either a boolean, a String, or a ResultSet

Method[] methods = mdclass.getDeclaredMethods();
Vector vm = new Vector();
for (int i = 0; i < methods.length; i++) {
   Method method = methods[i];

   if (!Modifier.isPublic(method.getModifiers()))
      continue;

   Class[] parmTypes = method.getParameterTypes();
   if (parmTypes.length > 0)
      continue;

   Class returnType = method.getReturnType();
   if (
      (!returnType.equals(java.lang.Boolean.TYPE)) &&
      (!returnType.equals(java.lang.String.class)) &&
      (!returnType.equals(java.sql.ResultSet.class)))
      continue;

   vm.addElement(method);
}
methods = new Method[vm.size()];
vm.copyInto(methods);

// Sort the list by method name

int n = methods.length;
int nm1 = n-1;
for (int i = 0; i < nm1; i++) {
   for (int j = i+1; j < n; j++) {
      String iname = methods[i].getName();
      String jname = methods[j].getName();
      if (iname.compareTo(jname) > 0) {
         Method temp = methods[i];
         methods[i] = methods[j];
         methods[j] = temp;
      }
   }
}

// Invoke each method and show the result

out.println("<DL>");

for (int i = 0; i < methods.length; i++) {
   Method method = methods[i];
   parms.method = method;
   String methodName = method.getName();

   out.println("<DT><B>" + methodName + "</B></DT>");
```

Figure 5-26
(Continued)

```
      out.println("<DD>");

      Class returnType = method.getReturnType();
      if (returnType.equals(java.lang.Boolean.TYPE))
         writeBooleanMethod(parms);
      else
      if (returnType.equals(java.lang.String.class))
         writeStringMethod(parms);
      else
      if (returnType.equals(java.sql.ResultSet.class))
         writeResultSetMethod(parms);

      out.println("</DD>");
      out.println("<P>");

   }

   out.println("</DL>");
}

/**
 * Writes a boolean method result to the table
 */
public void writeBooleanMethod(Parameters parms)
   throws ServletException, IOException
{
   PrintWriter out = parms.out;
   DatabaseMetaData md = parms.md;
   Method method = parms.method;

   try {
      Object[] nobody = new Object[0];
      Boolean value = (Boolean) method.invoke(md, nobody);
      out.println(value);
   }
   catch (Exception e) {
      out.println(e.getMessage());
   }
}

/**
 * Writes a String method result to the table
 */
public void writeStringMethod(Parameters parms)
   throws ServletException, IOException
{
   PrintWriter out = parms.out;
   DatabaseMetaData md = parms.md;
   Method method = parms.method;

   try {
      Object[] nobody = new Object[0];
      String value = (String) method.invoke(md, nobody);
      if (value == null)
         value = "";
      if (value.trim().equals(""))
         value = " ";
```

```
        out.println(value);
     }
     catch (Exception e) {
        out.println(e.getMessage());
     }
  }

  /**
   * Writes a ResultSet method result to the table
   */
  public void writeResultSetMethod(Parameters parms)
     throws ServletException, IOException
  {
     PrintWriter out = parms.out;
     DatabaseMetaData md = parms.md;
     Method method = parms.method;

     try {
        Object[] nobody = new Object[0];
        ResultSet value = (ResultSet) method.invoke(md, nobody);
        if (value == null)
           out.println("N/A");
        else
           out.println(new TableMaker(value).toString());
     }
     catch (Exception e) {
        out.println(e.getMessage());
     }
  }
}
```

you may not be so sure. The easiest way to find this out is to get the
ResultSetMetaData object. This can be obtained by calling the
ResultSet's getMetaData() method.

ResultSetMetaData provides a method that returns the number of
columns (appropriately named getColumnCount()) and 19 other methods that return information about individual columns.[6] Each of these column methods takes a single input parameter, the column number. The
first column is 1, the second is 2, and so on (unlike array indices, which
start with zero). Table 5-1 describes the more commonly used methods.

Armed with this useful class, you can handle a ResultSet generi-
cally. An obvious application is creating an HTML table from a
ResultSet. Figure 5-27 shows a class named TableMaker that uses the
ResultSetMetaData to do this.

TableMaker consists of a constructor and a single method—
toString(). The constructor takes a ResultSet as its argument and
stores it as a private instance variable. The toString() method uses

---

[6]JDBC 2.0 introduces an additional method—getColumnClassName().

TABLE 5-1

Method Name	Description
getColumnName(int column)	Returns the name of the column as it was specified in the CREATE TABLE statement.
getColumnType(int column)	Returns the SQL data type of this column. The value returned is one of the constants defined by the java.sql.Types class.
getColumnLabel(int column)	Returns the suggested column title. If none was specified in the CREATE TABLE statement, this method usually returns the column name.
getColumnDisplaySize(int column)	Returns the maximum width in characters of data in this column.
getPrecision(int column)	Returns the number of decimal digits in the column.
getScale(int column)	Returns the number of digits to the right of the decimal point.

the ResultSetMetaData object to extract the column information needed to generate appropriate headings and alignment values.

If we execute the SELECT statement shown at the beginning of this section, namely,

```
SELECT * FROM products WHERE itemDesc LIKE '%BANANA%'
```

and pass the results through the TableMaker object, we get the results shown in Figure 5-28.

5.10 Handling SQL Dates

Problem

How can I handle the SQL DATE, TIME, and TIMESTAMP data types?

Technique

Use the java.sql.Date, java.sql.Time, and java.sql.Timestamp classes for variables and SQL escape syntax in Statement objects.

Figure 5-27

Creating an HTML
table from a
ResultSet.

```java
package ijs.jdbc;

import java.io.*;
import java.net.*;
import java.sql.*;
import java.util.*;

/**
 * A class that creates an HTML table from a ResultSet
 */
public class TableMaker
{
    private ResultSet rs;

    /**
     * Creates a new TableMaker for the specified ResultSet
     * @param rs the result set
     * @exception SQLException if the result set cannot be read
     */
    public TableMaker(ResultSet rs) throws SQLException
    {
        this.rs = rs;
    }

    /**
     * Returns an HTML table corresponding to this result set
     */
    public String toString()
    {
        StringWriter sw = new StringWriter();
        PrintWriter out = new PrintWriter(sw);
        out.println("<TABLE BORDER=1 CELLPADDING=3>");
        try {
            ResultSetMetaData md = rs.getMetaData();

            // Create the headings row

            out.println("<TR>");
            int nColumns = md.getColumnCount();
            String[] align = new String[nColumns];
            for (int i = 0; i < nColumns; i++) {
                int col = i+1;

                // Get the column label.  Use the
                // column name if the label is not
                // available.

                String label = md.getColumnLabel(col);
                if (label == null)
                    label = md.getColumnName(col);

                // Left or right justify, depending on
                // the data type

                switch (md.getColumnType(col)) {
                    case Types.CHAR:
                    case Types.VARCHAR:
```

Figure 5-27
(Continued)

```
                        align[i] = "LEFT";
                        break;
                    default:
                        align[i] = "RIGHT";
                }
                out.println("<TH>" + label + "</TH>");
            }
            out.println("</TR>");

            // Create the detail rows

            while (rs.next()) {
                out.println("<TR>");
                for (int i = 0; i < nColumns; i++) {
                    int col = i+1;
                    String value = rs.getString(col);
                    StringBuffer buffer = new StringBuffer();

                    buffer.append("<TD ALIGN=\"");
                    buffer.append(align[i]);
                    buffer.append("\"");
                    buffer.append(" VALIGN=\"TOP\"");
                    buffer.append(">");
                    buffer.append(value);
                    buffer.append("</TD>");
                    out.println(buffer.toString());
                }
                out.println("</TR>");
            }
        }
        catch (SQLException e) {
            sw = new StringWriter();
            out = new PrintWriter(sw);
            out.println("<TABLE BORDER=0>");
            out.println("<TR><TD>"+e.getMessage()+"</TD></TR>");
        }
        finally {
            out.println("</TABLE>");
            sw.flush();
            return sw.toString();
        }
    }
}
```

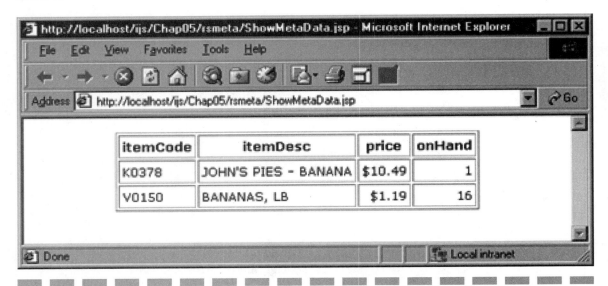

Figure 5-28 The `TableMaker` class illustrated.

Discussion

Database vendors' date and time data types vary significantly both in their internal and external representations. JDBC supports these types generically with three classes (Table 5-2).

TABLE 5-2

Class	Description
`java.sql.Date`	A subclass of `java.util.Date` that supports a (year, month, day) constructor. Can be used as the argument supplied to the `PreparedStatement setDate()` method and the `ResultSet getDate()` method. Note that if you import both the `java.sql.*` and `java.util.*` packages, you will need to fully qualify any reference to this class, since both packages have a class named `Date`.
`java.sql.Time`	A subclass of `java.util.Date` that supports an (hour, minute, second) constructor. Can be used as the argument supplied to the `PreparedStatement setTime()` method and the `ResultSet getTime()` method.
`java.sql.Timestamp`	A subclass of `java.util.Date` that keeps time to nanosecond precision. Can be used as the argument supplied to the `PreparedStatement setTimestamp()` method and the `ResultSet getTimestamp()` method.

JDBC also supports the ISO standard syntax for date and time literals used in `Statement` objects. They consist of a left curly brace, a keyword to identify the type involved, a string representation of the value, and a right curly brace (Table 5-3).

5.11   Reading Binary Objects from a Database

Problem

How can I retrieve large binary objects from a database in a servlet?

Technique

Use the `getBinaryStream()` or `getBytes()` methods of `java.sql.ResultSet`.

Discussion

Although we think of tables in relational databases as being rectangular, there is no reason why they cannot hold binary data of arbitrary length. Accessing these data with JDBC is no more complicated than retrieving strings or integers—you just need to specify the appropriate data type on the `ResultSet getXXX()` method.

A typical application would be using a database to store graphics images. Figure 5-29 illustrates the technique. First, we extract the desired graphics file name from the servlet `Request` object:

```
String name = request.getParameter("name");
```

TABLE 5-3

Literal Type	Syntax
DATE	`{d 'yyyy-mm-dd'}`
TIME	`{t 'hh:mm:ss'}`
TIMESTAMP	`{ts 'yyyy-mm-dd hh:mm:ss.ff...f'}`, where `ff...f` denotes the fractional seconds (an optional field).

```java
package ipfoods;

import java.io.*;
import java.net.*;
import java.sql.*;
import java.util.*;

import javax.servlet.*;
import javax.servlet.http.*;

/**
 * ImageRetrieverServlet
 */
public class ImageRetrieverServlet extends HttpServlet
{
    private Connection con;

    /**
     * Establishes the connection
     */
    public void init(ServletConfig config)
        throws ServletException
    {
        super.init(config);
        try {
            Class.forName("jdbc.idbDriver");
            con = DriverManager.getConnection(
                "jdbc.idb.d:/book/ipfoods/database/database.prp");
        }
        catch (Exception e) {
            throw new UnavailableException(this, e.getMessage());
        }
    }

    /**
     * Releases the connection
     */
    public void destroy()
    {
        if (con != null) {
            try {
                con.close();
            }
            catch (SQLException ignore) {}
        }
        super.destroy();
    }

    /**
     * Retrieves the image
     */
    public void doGet(
            HttpServletRequest request,
            HttpServletResponse response)
        throws ServletException, IOException
    {
        try {
```

Figure 5-29
(Continued)

```
// Get the image file name

String name = request.getParameter("name");

// Execute a query to find the binary data

String sql = "SELECT img FROM images WHERE name = ?";
PreparedStatement pstmt = con.prepareStatement(sql);
pstmt.setString(1, name);
ResultSet rs = pstmt.executeQuery();

if (rs.next()) {

    // Write the image data back to the requester

    response.setContentType("image/gif");
    InputStream in = rs.getBinaryStream(1);
    OutputStream out = response.getOutputStream();
    byte[] buffer = new byte[4096];
    for (;;) {
        int nBytes = in.read(buffer);
        if (nBytes == -1)
            break;
        out.write(buffer, 0, nBytes);
    }
    in.close();
    out.flush();
    out.close();
}
else {
    throw new SQLException(
        "image " + name + " not found");
}
}
catch (SQLException e) {
    e.printStackTrace();
}
}
}
```

Then we execute a database query to find the image data

```
String sql = "SELECT img FROM images WHERE name = ?";
PreparedStatement pstmt = con.prepareStatement(sql);
pstmt.setString(1, name);
ResultSet rs = pstmt.executeQuery();
```

Assuming that the file names are unique, we will get at most one row in the
ResultSet. We set the content type to the appropriate MIME type:

```
response.setContentType("image/gif");
```

and then create an input stream to receive the binary data:

```
InputStream in = rs.getBinaryStream(1);
```

At this point, it is simply a matter of copying the input stream to the servlet output stream:

```
OutputStream out = response.getOutputStream();
byte[] buffer = new byte[4096];
for (;;) {
    int nBytes = in.read(buffer);
    if (nBytes == -1)
        break;
    out.write(buffer, 0, nBytes);
}
```

The same technique can be used to handle character data, with `getAsciiStream()` or `getUnicodeStream()` taking the place of `getBinaryStream()`.

5.12   Logging JDBC Driver Activity

Problem

I have a bug somewhere in my database code, and I would like to get a detailed trace of the driver activity.

Technique

Use the `setLogStream()` method of the `java.sql.DriverManager` object:

```
// Turn on trace
DriverManager.setLogStream(System.out);
...
// Turn off trace
DriverManager.setLogStream(null);
```

Discussion

The driver manager will obligingly log all manner of messages to the specified print stream. In particular, the JDBC-ODBC driver will show the exact mapping of JDBC calls to their ODBC counterparts. Be advised, however, that

1. The log stream setting is global, affecting all drivers (not just the one you are debugging).
2. The volume of data can be overwhelming.

While using `System.out` as the log stream is convenient for console mode applications, it is probably more useful to log to a file:

```
PrintStream dblog =
   new PrintStream(
   new FileOutputStream("dblog.txt"));
DriverManager.setLogStream(dblog);
try {
...
}
finally {
   DriverManager.setLogStream(null);
   dblog.flush();
   dblog.close();
}
```

Be prepared for one minor annoyance—`setLogStream()` requires a `java.io.PrintStream`, which is now a deprecated class. Empower yourself to ignore the warning error.

5.13   Detecting Null Data

Problem

How do I know if a value in a `ResultSet` was null?

Technique

Read the column with `getXXX()`, and then test it with `wasNull()`:

```
rs.getNext();
...
String name = rs.getString(3);
if (rs.wasNull()) {
   // Handle the null value
}
```

Discussion

Yes, you can directly compare a `java.lang.String` to `null`, but this method will not work for primitive data types like `int`. `wasNull()` will work for any data type.

6

Debugging Servlets

Overview

Everyone makes programming errors. Whether it is because you are learning a new language or just because the project deadline is too short, you will rarely write a servlet (or any other program, for that matter) that compiles and runs properly the first time. For this reason, debugging skills are important. This chapter describes some tools and approaches that can be applied in solving problems related to debugging servlets.

Understanding the Framework

In order to write code that works correctly, you need a good mental model of how the servlet environment works. It is important to understand that

1. A Web browser creates GET or POST messages that consist of a request URI, zero or more request headers, and zero or more key/value parameter pairs.

2. A Web server listens for requests arriving at a particular port and handles the requests, returning a status code, zero or more response headers, and whatever content the request handler generated.

3. A servlet engine intercepts certain types of requests made to a Web server, interpreting those requests and creating the Web server's response.

Armed with a mental flowchart, you can identify how things ought to work and have some idea of where the problem might be if things go wrong.

A significant source of help is the fact that Sun Microsystems publishes the source code for the entire Java Servlet API. The time it takes you to read it will be repaid by the increased level of your understanding.

Design for Testability

Debugging is not (entirely) magic—it can be approached systematically. Rather than just trying to figure out what went wrong, you can plan for errors to occur and design your program so that it is easy to debug.

First, it is useful to write the program in stages, testing as you go. One way this can be done is by breaking down large tasks into subroutines. An example was given in Section 4.5 ("Structured HTML Generation"), where an output document was created with a hierarchy of routines (writeHead, writeBody, etc.) that can have skeleton implementations to begin with. This allows you to reduce the number of compilation errors and to get early warning if you are heading down a dead end.

It is also important to create natural stopping points where verification can be done. Java allows you to construct complex chains of method calls that can be written succinctly as a single line. For example,

```
int p = ((String) eList.nextElement()).substring(3).indexOf("<H1>");
```

is a compact expression that gets the next element from an Enumeration, casts it to the String type, and then finds the first occurrence of the substring <H1> that is at least 3 bytes from the beginning of the string. There is nothing wrong with code like this; however, if the results are not what you expect, you are not sure what the problem was. If the substring is not found, or if a null pointer exception occurs, it is not clear where the error occurred.

An alternative way to code this would be the following:

```
String s = (String) eList.nextElement();
String u = s.substring(3);
int p = u.indexOf("<H1>");
```

With these three individual expressions and suitable logging or breakpoint support, you can examine the intermediate results and quickly pinpoint the defect. Of course, this can be taken to unnecessary extremes, cluttering up your program with variables used only once. Use your own judgment to determine where you are most likely to need the finer granularity.

When Bad Things Happen to Good Programs

However, despite your best efforts, the unexpected still happens. When it does, there are two approaches you can take:

1. Add trace statements that document the program flow. You can use the ServletContext log() method to leave footprints before and after operations are performed, dumping the values of key variables.

2. Use a debugger and set breakpoints at critical sections. Even though you do not invoke a servlet from a command line, several tools are available that will let you use standard Java debuggers to step through your code line by line.

The remainder of this chapter illustrates how these techniques can be applied.

6.1   Checklist of Common Errors

Problem

Where do I start when debugging a servlet?

Technique

Consult the checklist in Table 6-1.

Discussion

If you have made a mistake before, you will probably make it again. Before resorting to more elaborate diagnostics, it sometimes helps to consult a frequently made errors list. Table 6-1 lists a few servlet-related errors that are encountered commonly; scribble more in the margins as you amass your own.

6.2   Understanding the Classpath

Problem

How do I determine where to put my classes?

Technique

Understand the difference between the user classpath, the servlet engine classpath, and the servlet engine servlet path, as described below.

Discussion

Configuring the servlet engine can be somewhat intimidating. Out of the box, the JRun 2.3.3 directory tree has no fewer than 263 files with an extension of .properties, out of which approximately 3 or 4 may need

TABLE 6-1

Symptom	Possible Cause
Servlet will not compile	Besides the usual Java language errors, there are a few servlet-specific reasons: 1. `javax.servlet.*` or `javax.servlet.http.*` not imported. 2. Class did not subclass `servlet` or one of its subclasses. 3. JSDK servlet classes (e.g., `servlet.jar`) not in the class path.
Servlet is not loaded	There are any number of reasons: 1. The wrong URL is used (e.g., /servlet is not specified). 2. The case is wrong. 3. The class is not in the servlet engine's servlet path. 4. Related classes are not in the servlet engine's classpath. 5. The servlet failed during initialization (see below). 6. The servlet engine is not running. 7. The Web server is not running.
Null parameter values	See whether `getParameter()` may have been used for a parameter with multiple values.
Null pointer exception	This could indicate failure to create a session before extracting values from it.
Wrong value for initial parameter	Make sure the parameter name is spelled exactly the same (including case) in the program and in the servlet properties.
Null initial parameters	`init()` method did not call `super.init(config)`.
Servlet engine hangs at shutdown	`destroy()` method did not call `super.destroy()`.
Wrong MIME type	Ensure that you call `setContentType()` before writing to the response output stream.
Corrupted data values	Verify that you are not using instance variables in unsynchronized methods. Remember, unless you explicitly implement `SingleThreadModel`, a single instance of your servlet can be run by multiple threads. If this is the case, any instance variables are shared by all threads.

to be modified.[1] ServletExec uses 6 properties files and requires some manual fiddling with the Web server configuration. Apache JServ is more parsimonious, with just 3 configuration files.

[1]The JRun 3.0 beta has reduced this number considerably—down to 2!

In most cases, you need to do very little to get the servlet engine working. One area that requires some thought, however, is the classpath.

The Java ClassPath   The class loader in a Java virtual machine consults a list of directories and class archives to find classes when they are first requested. This list is called the ClassPath. It consists of any number of the following:

1. Fully qualified directory names
2. Names of .jar files
3. Names of .zip files

Entries in this list are separated by colons in Unix environments or semicolons in the Microsoft Windows environment. An example would be

```
.:/usr/local/jdk1.1.7/lib/classes.zip:/u/home/java/classes
```

When the class loader is looking for a class named Parser, it would look first in the current directory (".") for a file named ./Parser.class. If this file did not exist, it would look in the /usr/local/jdk1.1.7/lib/classes.zip file for an entry named Parser.class. If it did not find the entry, it would check for the existence of /u/home/java/classes/Parser.class.[2]

For classes belonging to a package, the full package name is used. In the example given, if the Parser class were in the com.ipfoods.products package, the class names that would be searched for would be (in order)

```
./com/ipfoods/products/Parser.class
com/ipfoods/products/Parser.class in
/usr/local/jdk1.1.7/lib/classes.zip
/u/home/java/classes/com/ipfoods/products/Parser.class
```

The classpath is usually specified in an environment variable (called CLASSPATH) or passed to the Java interpreter on the command line.

The Servlet ClassPath   The situation is slightly more complicated for servlets. To begin with, the user account that is running the servlet

---

[2]JDK1.2 uses a slightly different approach for system classes, looking for them in the sun.boot.class.path system property rather than the user classpath.

engine is usually not your own. On a Windows NT 4.0 system using JRun or Apache JServ as an installed service, for example, the SYSTEM user is typically in control. The implication of this is that the environment variables in force are only those applicable to all users.

However, the classpath in this case is not even the one that belongs to the SYSTEM user. The servlet engine typically has a java.class.path parameter that it uses when it starts the virtual machine. In the case of JRun, this is found in the jsm.properties file.

In addition, the servlet engine maintains another list of class locations where it looks specifically for servlets. JRun, for example, looks in the jrun.properties file for a key named servletdir. The value of this key is a comma-delimited list of directories in which JRun will look for servlets when they are requested. ServletExec uses a ServletDirectory parameter on its Configure Virtual Servers administration Web page to specify the servlet classpath.

There is a subtle difference between these two classpath lists. Classes in the *servlet* classpath are dynamically reloaded whenever their .class file changes[3] (which happens all the time when you are developing a servlet). Classes in the *Java* classpath, however, are loaded only once during the lifetime of the Java virtual machine. This is probably the behavior that you want—you do not want •jar files scanned and supporting classes reloaded every time they are called.

The difference is small enough that you can write servlets for months and not be aware of it. However, when you come on an otherwise unexplainable ClassNotFoundException, it is helpful to have a mental model that accounts for it.

6.3 Intercepting Servlet Requests

Problem

How can I find out what values an HTML form is sending to a servlet?

---

[3]More precisely, whenever a servlet is requested and the .class file is newer than the one from which the running instance was loaded, the class is reloaded.

Technique

Substitute a debugging servlet that shows the request parameters. Instead of

```
<FORM ACTION="http://myserver/servlet/myservlet">
```

use

```
<FORM ACTION="/servlet/Echo">
```

where `Echo` is the servlet shown in Figure 6-1.

Discussion

A servlet-based Web application may involve two or three machines, several classes, and third-party software. It may work well with certain browsers but not others. For debugging purposes, it is important to be able to isolate each of these components and test them separately.

One way to do this is to use a proxy component—one that has the same interface as the real component but whose sole purpose is to capture information sent through the interface and display it. Figure 6-1 illustrates one such component, the `Echo` servlet.

`Echo` takes input from any servlet request and echoes it back to the browser in tabular format. Its output consists of five HTML tables:

1. *Form parameters.* The decoded key/value pairs that were sent by the HTML form. Multivalued parameters are shown on individual lines.

2. *Request headers.* Values that can be retrieved from the `HttpRequest` object. Most of these are generated by the HTTP request headers sent by the browser.

3. *Session attributes.* Information about the HTTP servlet session, including its creation time, last accessed time, maximum inactive interval limit, and any values that have been bound to the session.

4. *Servlet context.* Information about the servlet engine.

5. *System properties.* All the values that can be retrieved from the system properties object. This includes the Java classpath and library path, the Java home directory, the user name and home directory, and the current directory.

Figure 6-1

The Echo servlet.

```
package echo;

import java.io.*;
import java.net.*;
import java.util.*;

import javax.servlet.*;
import javax.servlet.http.*;

/**
 * EchoServlet
 */
public class EchoServlet extends HttpServlet
{
    public static final String TITLE = "Echo Servlet";

    /**
     * Inner class for passing parameters between methods
     */
    class Parameters {
        HttpServletRequest request;
        HttpServletResponse response;
        PrintWriter out;
        Hashtable entries;
        String title;
    }

    /**
     * Handles a GET request
     */
    public void doGet(
            HttpServletRequest request,
            HttpServletResponse response)
        throws ServletException, IOException
    {
        // Create local parameter structure

        Parameters parms = new Parameters();
        parms.request = request;
        parms.response = response;

        // Write the document

        response.setContentType("text/html");

        PrintWriter out = response.getWriter();
        parms.out = out;

        out.println("<HTML>");
        out.println("<HEAD>");
        out.println("<TITLE>" + TITLE + "</TITLE>");
        out.println("</HEAD>");
        out.println("<BODY>");
        out.println("<CENTER>");
        out.println("<H2>" + TITLE + "</H2>");

        writeForm(parms);
```

Figure 6-1
(Continued)

```java
    writeRequestHeaders(parms);
    writeSession(parms);
    writeServletContext(parms);
    writeSystemProperties(parms);

    out.println("</CENTER>");
    out.println("</BODY>");
    out.println("</HTML>");

    out.flush();
}

/**
 * Writes the form parameters section
 */
public void writeForm(Parameters parms)
    throws ServletException, IOException
{
    HttpServletRequest request = parms.request;
    parms.title = "Form Parameters";
    parms.entries = new Hashtable();

    Enumeration enames = request.getParameterNames();
    while (enames.hasMoreElements()) {
        String name = (String) enames.nextElement();
        String[] values = request.getParameterValues(name);
        if (values == null)
            continue;
        for (int i = 0; i < values.length; i++) {
            String value = values[i];
            if (value.trim().equals(""))
                value = " ";
            parms.entries.put(name, value);
        }
    }

    writeTable(parms);
}

/**
 * Writes the request headers section
 */
public void writeRequestHeaders(Parameters parms)
    throws ServletException, IOException
{
    HttpServletRequest request = parms.request;
    parms.title = "Request Headers";
    parms.entries = new Hashtable();

    Enumeration enames = request.getHeaderNames();
    while (enames.hasMoreElements()) {
        String name = (String) enames.nextElement();
        String value = parms.request.getHeader(name);
        if (value == null)
            value = "N/A";
        value = chopColons(value);
        if (value.trim().equals(""))
```

Figure 6-1
(Continued)

```
                value = " ";
            parms.entries.put(name, value);
        }
        writeTable(parms);
    }

    /**
     * Writes the session attributes section
     */
    public void writeSession(Parameters parms)
        throws ServletException, IOException
    {
        HttpServletRequest request = parms.request;
        HttpSession session = request.getSession(false);
        if (session == null)
            return;

        parms.title = "Session Attributes";
        parms.entries = new Hashtable();

        parms.entries.put("Creation Time",
            "" + new Date(session.getCreationTime()));
        parms.entries.put("ID", session.getId());
        parms.entries.put("Last Accessed Time",
            "" + new Date(session.getLastAccessedTime()));
        parms.entries.put("Max inactive interval (seconds)",
            "" + session.getMaxInactiveInterval());

        String[] valueNames = session.getValueNames();
        for (int i = 0; i < valueNames.length; i++) {
            String name = valueNames[i];
            String value = session.getValue(name).toString();
            parms.entries.put(name, value);
        }

        writeTable(parms);
    }

    /**
     * Writes the servlet context section
     */
    public void writeServletContext(Parameters parms)
        throws ServletException, IOException
    {
        HttpServletRequest request = parms.request;
        parms.title = "Servlet Context";
        parms.entries = new Hashtable();

        ServletContext context = getServletContext();

        Enumeration enames = context.getAttributeNames();
        while (enames.hasMoreElements()) {
            String name = (String) enames.nextElement();
            Object value = context.getAttribute(name);
            if (value != null)
                value = chopColons(value.toString());
            parms.entries.put(name, value);
```

```
    }

    parms.entries.put("Servlet API major version",
        "" + context.getMajorVersion());

    parms.entries.put("Servlet API minor version",
        "" + context.getMinorVersion());

    parms.entries.put("Server Info",
        context.getServerInfo());

    writeTable(parms);
}

/**
 * Writes the system properties section
 */
public void writeSystemProperties(Parameters parms)
    throws ServletException, IOException
{
    HttpServletRequest request = parms.request;
    parms.title = "System Properties";
    parms.entries = new Hashtable();

    Enumeration enames =
        System.getProperties().propertyNames();
    while (enames.hasMoreElements()) {
        String name = (String) enames.nextElement();
        String value = System.getProperty(name);
        value = chopColons(value);
        if (value.trim().equals(""))
            value = " ";
        parms.entries.put(name, value);
    }

    writeTable(parms);
}

/**
 * Writes key/value pairs as an HTML table
 */
public void writeTable(Parameters parms)
{
    PrintWriter out      = parms.out;
    String title         = parms.title;
    Hashtable entries    = parms.entries;

    StringBuffer buffer = new StringBuffer();

    // Table header

    buffer.append("<TABLE BORDER=1");
    buffer.append("        CELLPADDING=3");
    buffer.append("        CELLSPACING=0");
    buffer.append("        WIDTH=80%>");

    // Section title
```

Figure 6-1

(Continued)

```
buffer.append("<TR>");
buffer.append("</TR>");
buffer.append("<TD ALIGN=CENTER");
buffer.append("    VALIGN=MIDDLE");
buffer.append("    COLSPAN=2>");
buffer.append("<FONT SIZE=\"+1\">");
buffer.append("<B>");
buffer.append(title);
buffer.append("</B></FONT>");
buffer.append("</TD>");

// If there are no entries, say so

if (entries.size() == 0) {
   buffer.append("<TR>");
   buffer.append("<TD COLSPAN=2 ALIGN=CENTER>");
   buffer.append("None");
   buffer.append("</TD>");
   buffer.append("</TR>");
}
else {
   // Get an enumeration of the key names
   // in alphabetical order

   Vector v = new Vector();
   Enumeration enames = entries.keys();
   while (enames.hasMoreElements())
      v.addElement(enames.nextElement());
   enames = sortVector(v).elements();

   // Write each entry

   while (enames.hasMoreElements()) {
      String name = (String) enames.nextElement();
      String value = (String) parms.entries.get(name);

      buffer.append("<TR>");
      buffer.append("<TD ALIGN=LEFT");
      buffer.append("    VALIGN=TOP>");
      buffer.append(name);
      buffer.append("</TD>");
      buffer.append("<TD ALIGN=LEFT");
      buffer.append("    VALIGN=TOP>");
      buffer.append(value);
      buffer.append("</TD>");
      buffer.append("</TR>");
   }
}

// End of table

buffer.append("</TABLE><P>");

// Write the completed table to
// the servlet response output stream
```

Figure 6-1
(Continued)

```
        out.println(buffer.toString());
    }

    /**
     * Sorts the specified vector alphabetically
     */
    public static Vector sortVector(Vector v)
    {
        int n = v.size();
        for (int i = 0; i < n-1; i++) {
            for (int j = i+1; j < n; j++) {
                String iname = (String) v.elementAt(i);
                String jname = (String) v.elementAt(j);
                if (iname.compareTo(jname) > 0) {
                    v.setElementAt(iname, j);
                    v.setElementAt(jname, i);
                }
            }
        }
        return v;
    }

    /**
     * Replaces path separator characters
     * with HTML break tags
     */
    public static String chopColons(String s)
    {
        final char COLON = java.io.File.pathSeparatorChar;
        StringBuffer buffer = new StringBuffer();
        for (int i = 0; i < s.length(); i++) {
            char c = s.charAt(i);
            buffer.append(c);
            if (c == COLON)
                buffer.append("<BR>");
        }
        return buffer.toString();
    }

    /**
     * Handles a POST request
     */
    public void doPost(
            HttpServletRequest request,
            HttpServletResponse response)
        throws ServletException, IOException
    {
        doGet(request, response);
    }
}
```

Figure 6-2 shows an example of a form that can be debugged with the Echo servlet. Taken from the initial product search page of our hypothetical Internet Premium Food Market Web site, it contains three text fields, one select element, and two buttons.

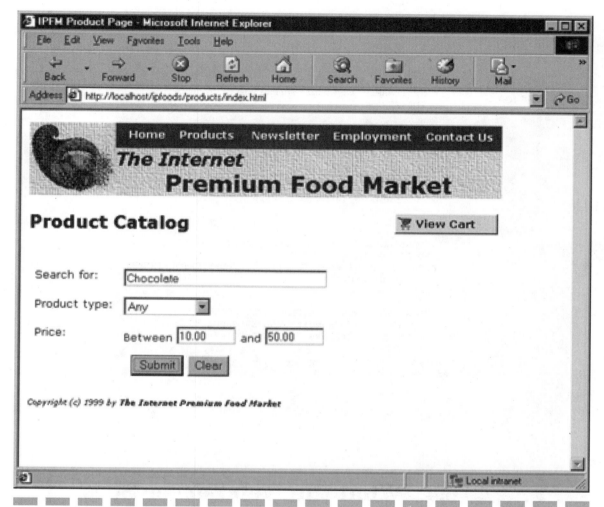

Figure 6-2 Input for the ProductSearch servlet.

Figure 6-3 shows the HTML that generates this form. The original target of the form (IPFProductSearch) is commented out, and in its place is the call to the Echo servlet. Part of the resulting diagnosing output is shown in Figure 6-4. We can see the value "Chocolate" in the keywords field, the code "A" (for "any") in the type field, and the 10.00 to 50.00 price range in the loPrice and hiPrice fields. Given this information, we can examine the source code of the ProductSearch servlet knowing exactly what input will be supplied in this test case.

Figure 6-3
HTML containing
the
`ProductSearch`
servlet input form.

```html
<!-- FORM METHOD="GET" ACTION="/servlet/IPFProductSearch" -->
<FORM METHOD="GET" ACTION="/servlet/Echo">
<TABLE BORDER=0 CELLPADDING=5>
<TR>
    <TD ALIGN=LEFT VALIGN=TOP>Search for:</TD>
    <TD ALIGN=LEFT VALIGN=TOP>
    <INPUT NAME="keywords" TYPE="TEXT" SIZE=32>
    </TD></TR>
<TR>
    <TD ALIGN=LEFT VALIGN=TOP>Product type:</TD>
    <TD ALIGN=LEFT VALIGN=TOP><SELECT NAME="type" SIZE=1>
        <OPTION VALUE="A">Any
        <OPTION VALUE="V">Produce
        <OPTION VALUE="G">Groceries
        <OPTION VALUE="P">Houseplants
        <OPTION VALUE="K">Gifts
    </SELECT>
    </TD></TR>
<TR>
    <TD ALIGN=LEFT VALIGN=TOP>Price:</TD>
    <TD ALIGN=LEFT VALIGN=TOP>
    Between <INPUT NAME="loPrice" TYPE="TEXT" SIZE=8>
    and <INPUT NAME="hiPrice" TYPE="TEXT" SIZE=8>
    </TD></TR>
<TR>
    <TD ALIGN=CENTER VALIGN=MIDDLE COLSPAN=2>
        <INPUT TYPE="submit" VALUE="Submit">
        <INPUT TYPE="reset"  VALUE="Clear">
    </TD></TR>
</TABLE>
</FORM>
```

6.4   What the Web Server Sees

Problem

I am not sure if my Web server and servlet engine is working properly. How can I find out exactly what input they are receiving?

Technique

Use a debugging client and/or server to capture the HTTP traffic and display it.

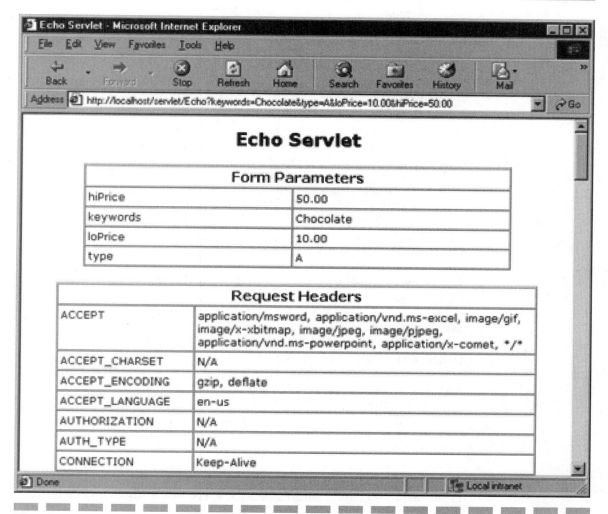

Figure 6-4 Output of the Echo servlet when used to debug Product/Search

Discussion

An HTTP request from a Web client may go through several stages before your servlet actually sees it. If a request involves authentication or redirection, there may be several back-and-forth exchanges between client and server, none of which are visible to the user. Consider the following example of calling

```
http://www.ipfoods.com/orgchart/main.html
```

which redirects the user to

```
/orgchart/main.jsp
```

in a directory protected with a `.htaccess` file. The original request that the Web browser program sends to the server looks like this:

```
GET /orgchart/main.html HTTP/1.0
```

The response sent back to the browser informs it of the redirection:

```
HTTP/1.1 302 Moved Temporarily
Date: Mon, 04 Oct 1999 06:02:10 GMT
Server: Apache/1.3.9 (Win32)
Location: http://www.ipfoods.com/orgchart/main.jsp
Connection: close
Content-Type: text/html
```

The browser picks up the new URL from the `Location:` header and issues a modified request:

```
GET /orgchart/main.jsp HTTP/1.0
```

to which the server responds:

```
HTTP/1.1 401 Authorization Required
Date: Mon, 04 Oct 1999 06:02:24 GMT
Server: Apache/1.3.9 (Win32)
WWW-Authenticate: Basic realm="ipfoods.com"
Connection: close
Content-Type: text/html
```

The browser then prompts for the user's name (which is `author`) and password (`goodness`) and reissues the request with the authorization header:

```
GET /orgchart/main.jsp HTTP/1.0
Authorization: Basic YXV0aG9yOmdvb2RuZXNz
```

which the server finally accepts, causing the `main.jsp` servlet to begin running. The only intermediate step of which the user would be aware would be the prompt for the user name and password. If the user had already entered this information for a previous request during the same browser session, even the password dialog would be skipped (the browser would remember the login credentials).

This is all very convenient, but obviously, things can go wrong anywhere along the way. In order to find out exactly what requests and responses are being sent, you can temporarily replace the Web server and/or browser with a debugging version that displays the headers. These are not difficult to write; they only need to listen on a socket connection for requests and write them to the console before responding.

Figure 6-5 contains a listing of a stub Web server that parses HTTP requests and echoes them back to the client and to a log. This can be useful if you suspect that the Web client is sending troublesome request headers.

DebugServer contains a stand-alone mainline that reads an optional port number from the command line and then creates an instance of the server class using this port. The constructor opens a java.net.ServerSocket over this port and starts listening for requests. When it accepts a request, the server starts a new HandlerThread for the requesting client. HandlerThread is an inner class that extends java.lang.Thread so that it can operate asynchronously while the server listens for other requests. In its run() method, HandlerThread does the following:

1. Opens an input stream over the client socket so that it can read the request

2. Opens an output stream over the client socket to which it will write a response

3. Sends back a status line indicating normal HTTP completion (HTTP/1.0 200 OK) followed by the document headings

4. Reads the request line and echoes it back to the client

5. Reads the request headers and echoes them back to the client

6. If a Content-Length header was supplied, reads and echoes the content

Although the DebugServer does not actually perform the requested action, it supplies all the necessary handshaking to elicit the details of the client request.

Let's use DebugServer to examine the same form we started debugging in the preceding section, the one shown in Figure 6-2. This time, we'll change the form's ACTION attribute to http://u25nv:8080/servlet/IPFProductSearch, which is a URL that will trigger our DebugServer. We reenter the search for chocolate products in the price range of $10 to $50 and click the "Submit" button. From Figure 6-6, we can determine that

1. The server accepts a GET request from our browser, which indicated that it is able to understand HTTP version 1.1.

■■■ ■■■ ■■■ ■■■
Figure 6-5
A stub Web server used for debugging requests.

```java
package ijs.web;

import java.io.*;
import java.net.*;
import java.text.*;
import java.util.*;

/**
 * A stub web server that shows the headers being sent
 */
public class DebugServer
{
    public static final int DEFAULT_PORT = 80;
    public static final DateFormat dateFmt =
        new SimpleDateFormat("HH:mm:ss.SSS");

    /**
     * Standalone mainline
     */
    public static void main(String[] args)
    {
        int port = DEFAULT_PORT;
        for (int i = 0; i < args.length; i++) {
            String arg = args[i];
            if (arg.equals("-port")) {
                i++;
                if (i < args.length) {
                    arg = args[i];
                    port = Integer.parseInt(arg);
                }
                break;
            }
        }
        try {
            new DebugServer(port);
        }
        catch (IOException e) {
            e.printStackTrace();
        }
    }

    /**
     * Instance variables
     */
    private ServerSocket server;

    /**
     * Constructor
     */
    public DebugServer(int port)
        throws IOException
    {
        server = new ServerSocket(port);
        log("Server listening on port " + port);
        for (;;) {
            Socket client = server.accept();
            log("Accepted request from "
```

Figure 6-5

(Continued)

```
                              + client.getInetAddress().getHostName());
              new HandlerThread(client).start();
          }
      }

      /**
       * Message logger
       */
      public void log(String msg)
      {
          StringBuffer buffer = new StringBuffer();
          buffer.append(dateFmt.format(new Date()));
          buffer.append(": ");
          buffer.append(msg);
          System.out.println(buffer.toString());
      }

      /**
       * Request handler thread
       */
      class HandlerThread extends Thread
      {
          private Socket client;

          /**
           * Creates a handler thread
           */
          public HandlerThread(Socket client)
          {
              this.client = client;
          }

          /**
           * Runs the handler thread
           */
          public void run()
          {
              try {

                  // Open streams for reading the client request
                  // and writing the response

                  DataInputStream in =
                      new DataInputStream(
                          client.getInputStream());

                  PrintWriter out =
                      new PrintWriter(
                      new OutputStreamWriter(
                          client.getOutputStream()));

                  // Start writing the output stream

                  out.println("HTTP/1.0 200 OK");
                  out.println("Content-type: text/html");
                  out.println();
                  out.println("<HTML>");
```

Figure 6-5
(Continued)

```
out.println("<HEAD>");
out.println("<TITLE>DebugServer</TITLE>");
out.println("</HEAD>");
out.println("<BODY>");

// Read the request line
// and echo it back to the client

String requestLine = in.readLine();
log(requestLine);

out.println("<H3>Request Line</H3>");
out.println("<PRE>");
out.println(requestLine);
out.println("</PRE>");

// Read the headers
// and echo them back to the client

int contentLength = 0;
out.println("<H3>Request Headers</H3>");
out.println("<PRE>");
for (;;) {
   String buffer = in.readLine();
   if (buffer == null)
      break;
   if (buffer.trim().equals(""))
      break;
   log(buffer);

   // Parse the header

   StringTokenizer st =
      new StringTokenizer(buffer, " :");
   String name = st.nextToken();
   String value = st.nextToken();

   // If content-length header is included,
   // save the length

   if (name.toUpperCase().
      equals("CONTENT-LENGTH"))
      contentLength = Integer.parseInt(value);

   // Write the header

   out.println(name + ": " + value);
}
out.println("</PRE>");

// If content-length was specified, read and
// echo the content

if (contentLength > 0) {
   byte[] content = new byte[contentLength];
   in.read(content);
   out.println("<H3>Content ("
```

Figure 6-5
(Continued)

```
                                      + contentLength + " bytes)</H3>");
                    out.println("<PRE>");
                    out.println(new String(content));
                    out.println("</PRE>");
                }

                // Finish the response document

                out.println("<P>");
                out.println("<HR>");
                out.println("<FONT SIZE=-1>");
                out.println("<I>");
                out.println("Generated by "
                    + DebugServer.this.getClass().getName()
                    + " at "
                    + new Date().toString());
                out.println("</I>");
                out.println("</FONT>");
                out.println("</BODY>");
                out.println("</HTML>");
                out.flush();
                client.close();

            }
            catch (Exception e) {
                e.printStackTrace();
            }
        }
    }
}
```

2. The browser is able to accept any content type in return (*/*).

3. The Web page initiating the request was http://u25nv/ ipfoods/products/index.html.

4. The browser prefers a response in English.

5. If the response is encoded, the browser prefers the gzip or deflate encoding method.

6. The browser is Microsoft Internet Explorer 5.0.

7. The host to which the request is directed is u25nv, port 8080.[4]

8. The browser will keep the connection alive until the server sends a Connection: close header.

A corresponding stub Web client is shown in Figure 6-7. It allows you to manually type in an HTTP request and its associated headers. You can use this to determine how the Web server responds to a given request.

---

[4]This is only meaningful if the server is running HTTP 1.1 with multiple hosts.

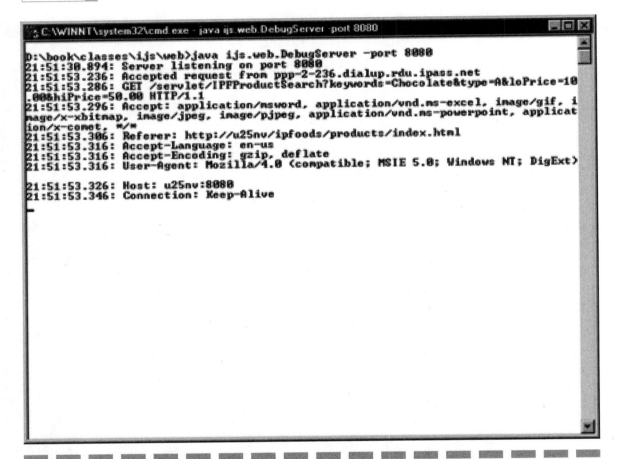

Figure 6-6 The debug Web server handling a ProductSearch servlet request.

DebugClient is quite simple. Like DebugServer, it contains a main-line that handles command-line parameters (in this case, the optional host name and port number) and then creates an instance of its class. The constructor does the following:

1. Opens a socket connection to the Web server

2. Opens input and output streams over the socket

3. Reads the HTTP request and headers that are typed into System.in, and echoes them to the socket output stream

Figure 6-7

A stub Web
browser used for
debugging
responses.

```java
package ijs.web;

import java.io.*;
import java.net.*;
import java.text.*;
import java.util.*;

/**
 * A stub web browser
 */
public class DebugClient
{
    public static final String DEFAULT_HOST = "localhost";
    public static final int DEFAULT_PORT = 80;

    /**
     * Displays calling syntax
     */
    public static void showUsage()
    {
        String[] text = {
            "usage: java ijs.web.DebugClient"
            + " [-host <hostname>] [-port <port>]"
        };
        for (int i = 0; i < text.length; i++)
            System.out.println(text[i]);
    }

    /**
     * Standalone mainline
     */
    public static void main(String[] args)
    {
        String host = DEFAULT_HOST;
        int port = DEFAULT_PORT;

        for (int i = 0; i < args.length; i++) {
            String arg = args[i];
            if (arg.equals("-host")) {
                if (++i < args.length)
                    host = args[i];
            }
            else if (arg.startsWith("-h")) {
                showUsage();
                return;
            }
            else if (arg.equals("-port")) {
                if (++i < args.length) {
                    arg = args[i];
                    port = Integer.parseInt(arg);
                }
            }
        }
        try {
            new DebugClient(host, port);
        }
        catch (IOException e) {
```

```java
            e.printStackTrace();
      }
   }

   /**
    * Constructor
    */
   public DebugClient(String host, int port)
      throws IOException
   {

      // Connect to the web server

      Socket socket = new Socket(host, port);

      BufferedReader in =
         new BufferedReader(
         new InputStreamReader(
         System.in));

      PrintWriter out =
         new PrintWriter(
         new OutputStreamWriter(
         socket.getOutputStream()));

      // Read HTTP request and request headers
      // from stdin and echo them to the web server

      while (true) {
         String buffer = in.readLine();
         if (buffer == null)
            break;
         if (buffer.trim().equals(""))
            break;
         out.println(buffer);
      }
      out.println();
      out.flush();
      in.close();

      // Read response and echo it to stdout

      in =
         new BufferedReader(
         new InputStreamReader(
         socket.getInputStream()));
      while (true) {
         String buffer = in.readLine();
         if (buffer == null)
            break;
         System.out.println(buffer);
      }

      socket.close();
   }
}
```

4. When a blank line is entered, sends it to the server and starts listening for the server's response

5. Reads and echoes the server output to System.out.

Since we know exactly what our HTML form is sending to the server, we can type it in manually and see exactly how the server responds, with us acting as a human proxy server. From Figure 6-8, we can see (among other things) that

1. The server accepted our request and redirected us to the ShowResults servlet.

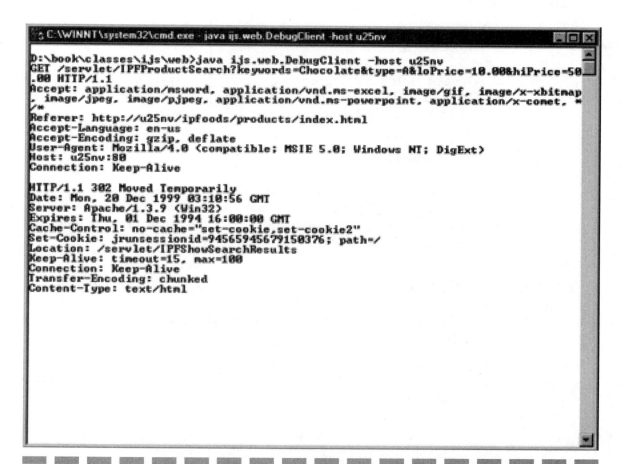

Figure 6-8 The debug Web client simulating a ProductSearch servlet request.

2. The server assigned a session ID of 94565945679150376, asking us to remember this and sending it back to us with subsequent requests to identify our particular session.

While this is usually far more information than we want to see, some problems are difficult to diagnose in any other way. Moreover, simply following the back-and-forth HTTP conversation will help build the mental flowchart of how forms and servlets interact.

6.5 Servlet Logs

Problem

I need to log debugging and trace information. I also write to `System.out` and `System.err`. How can I log messages from my servlet, and where do the logged statements go?

Technique

Use the `log(String msg)` method in either `ServletContext` or `HttpServlet`. The log output and the output from `stdout` and `stderr` go to one or more of the servlet logs. The location and format of these logs are specific to the servlet engine vendor.

Discussion

Debugging is largely a matter of verifying your assumptions. These assumptions fall into three categories:

Preconditions. Assertions about the state of the program before a given function is executed (e.g., "the input parameter is a nonnegative integer").

Postconditions. What you claim will always be true after the function is executed (e.g., "the database connection has been closed, even if an exception was thrown").

Invariants. What does not change while the function is executed (e.g., "the number of elements on the stack is always even").

If an error occurs, one or more of these assertions will be false. Debugging the problem, then, is a matter of identifying which assertion failed, which can be done by logging the state of the assertions at strategic places in the code.

There are several ways to do this. `System.out.println()` works in servlets as well as it does in a stand-alone application, and the `java.lang.Exception printStackTrace()` method writes to `System.err`. `HttpServlet` provides a slightly more useful `log()` method, which appends the class name and system time to messages. The output of these methods goes to vendor-specific log file locations. Here are some specifics for several leading servlet engines.

JRun 2.3.3 Output written with the `log()` method goes to the event log for the particular JRun service being used:

```
<JRunRoot>/jsm-default/services/<service>/logs/event.log
```

`System.out` and `System.err` output goes to a global location for all services:

```
<JRunRoot>/jsm-default/logs/stdout.log
<JRunRoot>/jsm-default/logs/stderr.log
```

ServletExec 2.2 `log()` output goes to

```
<ServletExecRoot>/Servlet Logs/Servlet.log
```

`System.out` and `System.err` output is intermingled in one file:

```
<ServletExecRoot>/ServletExec.log
```

Apache JServ 1.0 JServ uses the following file for `log()` output:

```
<ApacheJServRoot>/logs/jserv.log
```

but appears to ignore `System.out` and `System.err`. The location and nature of logged output are configured based on the contents of the `jserv.properties` file. Curiously enough, it does not seem to log anything in the `destroy()` method.

To see how logging can be used, consider the section of code shown below, from a servlet that lists employees hired during the 1970s. When the `DriverManager.getConnection(url)` statement is executed, it has two preconditions: the `url` parameter is nonnull, and the appropriate JDBC driver class has been loaded. Its postcondition is that a valid database connection has been established.

```
Connection con = null;
String driverName = request.getParameter("driverName");
String url = request.getParameter("url");
try {
    Class.forName(url);
    con = DriverManager.getConnection(url);
    Statement stmt = con.createStatement();
    ResultSet rs = stmt.executeQuery(""
        + " SELECT    lname, fname, hireDate"
        + " FROM      employees"
        + " WHERE     hireDate between"
        + "               {d '1970-01-01'} and"
        + "               {d '1979-12-31'} "
        + " ORDER BY hireDate"
        );
}
```

However, when we run the code with the URL

```
http://www.ipfoods.com/servlet/Get70Emps
    ?driverName=jdbc.idbDriver
    &url=jdbc:idb:database.prp
```

we get an exception saying that no suitable driver was found.[5] What happened?

We can use the `log()` method to find out:

```
Connection con = null;
String driverName = request.getParameter("driverName");
log("DEBUG: driverName = [" + driverName + "]");
String url = request.getParameter("url");
log("DEBUG: url = [" + url + "]");
try {
    log("DEBUG: About to load " + driverName + " driver");
    Class.forName(url);
    log("DEBUG: driverName + " driver loaded");
    con = DriverManager.getConnection(url);
    log("DEBUG: connected to [" + url + "]");
    Statement stmt = con.createStatement();
    ...
```

With JRun 2.3.3, this produces the following lines in `jsm-default/services/jse/logs/event.log`:

---

[5]The URL is split to make it easier to read. When it is entered in the browser "URL" field, it should be all one line.

```
Wed Oct 06 23:05:17 EDT 1999: jsp.ijs.Chap06.logs.Test:
DEBUG: driverName = [jdbc.idbDriver]
Wed Oct 06 23:05:17 EDT 1999: jsp.ijs.Chap06.logs.Test:
DEBUG: url = [jdbc:idb:D:/book/ipfoods/database/database.prp]
Wed Oct 06 23:05:17 EDT 1999: jsp.ijs.Chap06.logs.Test:
DEBUG: About to load jdbc.idbDriver driver
```

We note that the "driver loaded" message does not appear in the log, which directs our attention to the statement just before it:

```
Class.forName(url);
```

An exception must have been thrown here. We look in the `stderr` log `jsm-default/logs/stderr.log`:

```
java.lang.ClassNotFoundException:
dbc:idb:D:/book/ipfoods/database/database.prp
     at java.lang.Class.forName0(Native Method)
     at java.lang.Class.forName(Compiled Code)
```

and the error becomes obvious. We used the wrong parameter in the `forName()` method—`url` instead of `driverName`. A quick change to one line of code and we are done.

6.6   Using the Java Debugger

Problem

Is there any way to set breakpoints and step through Java code without using an integrated development environment (IDE)?

Technique

Use `jdb`, the Java command-line debugger, which is included in the JDK.

Discussion

Sometimes `System.out.println()` is not enough. If an exception is thrown, for example, you may need to explore the values of certain objects before execution is terminated. Likewise, if there are many places where an error potentially could occur, it is tedious to code line after line of logging methods, most of which will never indicate a problem. In cases like this, it is more convenient to use a debugger that allows you to set breakpoints and step through your code line by line.

Most commercial integrated development environments (IDEs) come with a fancy debugger. There is nothing wrong with these debuggers, but they are not available if you do not work with an IDE. For non-GUI types of programs like servlets, my own view is that IDEs are overkill. You can spend more time (and money) learning the IDE than learning the servlet API itself.

Fortunately, the JDK provides a simple command-line debugger called jdb. It is somewhat limited in functionality and ease of use, but it can handle most of the debugging you will ever need to do.

Invoking jdb   jdb is invoked from a command line with the same arguments as the Java interpreter. That is, if you normally start an application with

```
java com.mypackage.MyClass
```

you would start the debugger with

```
jdb com.mypackage.MyClass
```

Alternatively, you can start the debugger remotely and attach it to a running Java virtual machine. This takes a little more preparation. First, you must invoke the class to be debugged with debug options:

```
<JDK_HOME>/java -Djava.compiler=NONE -Xdebug com.mypackage.MyClass
```

When it loads the class, the Java interpreter will print a password that you will need when you launch the debugger.

Next, you need to provide some means of making the application wait until you start the debugger. Otherwise, your application will terminate before jdb has a chance to attach to it. If your application does not already provide a convenient stopping point, you can add one as follows:

```
System.out.println("Hit enter when ready...");
try { System.in.read(); } catch (IOException ignore) {}
```

Finally, when you launch the debugger, you must specify the host name on which the application is running and the password that it printed when it started:

```
jdb -host <hostname> -password <password>
```

At this point, you can set a breakpoint in the debugger and then hit the ENTER key in the remote application to start the debugging session.

jdb Commands   Table 6-2 lists all the commands that jdb provides.

A Sample jdb Session   To get a better understanding of how jdb works, let's debug a typical problem. The application listed in Figure 6-9 is intended to get a list of the employees of the Internet Premium Food Market that were hired in the 1970s. However, when it is run, it gets the following exception:

```
java.sql.SQLException: No suitable driver
        at java.sql.DriverManager.getConnection(Unknown Source)
        at java.sql.DriverManager.getConnection(Unknown Source)
        at ijs.debugging.Seventies.<init>(Seventies.java:37)
        at ijs.debugging.Seventies.main(Seventies.java:18)
```

There does not seem to be anything obviously wrong, so we are not sure where to put any logging statements. A better approach is to invoke the program through the debugger:

```
D:\book\classes\ijs\debugging>jdb ijs.debugging.Seventies
Initializing jdb...
0xae:class(ijs.debugging.Seventies)
>
```

We are now in the debugger, which is waiting for commands (indicated by the > prompt). The first thing we need to do is set a breakpoint somewhere so that we can start a line-by-line search for the bug. We could specify a breakpoint on a particular line number if we knew it, but it is probably easier to use the name of a method instead. To find out what methods our class implements, we use the methods command:

```
>methods ijs.debugging.Seventies
void main(java.lang.String[])
java.util.Properties loadProperties(java.lang.String)
void <init>(java.lang.String)
>
```

There are three methods—main, loadProperties, and <init>, which is the internal name for a constructor. Since we are not sure what we are looking for, we will be conservative and set a breakpoint at the beginning of the main method:

TABLE 6-2

Command	Operation
print <id> | [id's]	Displays the value of the indicated class, field, or thread. Threads can be specifed as t@nn, where nn is the thread number.
dump <id> | [id's]	Displays all information about the indicated class, field, or thread.
locals	Displays the values of all local variables, including the method arguments.
classes	Displays a list of all currently known classes.
methods <class id>	Displays the names of all the methods in the specified class.
threads [threadgroup]	Given a thread group name, displays the name and status of each thread in the group. If no thread group is specified, displays all threads.
thread <thread id>	Makes <thread id> the default thread.
suspend [thread id's]	Suspends all the listed threads. A suspended thread will perform no further activity until its resume() method has been invoked. If no thread IDs are specified, suspends all nonsystem threads.
resume [thread id's]	The counterpart of suspend. Causes the named threads (or all, if none are specified) to resume activity.
threadgroups	Displays the name and description of each active thread group.
threadgroup <name>	Sets the current thread group.
catch <class id>	Causes the debugger to break when the specified exception occurs.
ignore <class id>	Removes the specified exception from the list of exceptions the debugging is listening for. Note that this does not cause the debugger to ignore any arbitrary exception; it only removes an entry that was made with the catch command (see above).
cont	When specified during a breakpoint, resumes execution of the current thread.
step	Executes one source line and then breaks.
stepi	Executes one source instruction and then breaks. This is the same as step unless multiple statements are coded on one source line.
next	Executes the next source line but does not step into a method call.

TABLE 6-2

(Continued)

Command	Operation
`kill <thread ID>`	Kills the specified thread.
`where [thread id] | all`	Displays a stack trace of the indicated thread(s).
`wherei [thread id] | all`	Displays a stack trace of the indicated thread(s) that includes the value of the thread's program counter.
`up [n frames]`	Moves up the call stack the specified number of frames (default =1).
`down`	Moves down the call stack the specified number of frames (default =1).
`load <classname>`	Causes the debugger to find the specified class, loading it if it is not already loaded.
`run [<classname> [args]]`	Begins execution of the specified class. Be sure to set a breakpoint before issuing the `run` command; otherwise, you will not be able to stop execution.
`memory`	Shows the amount of free memory and total memory.
`gc`	Frees references to all objects except the current thread and the current thread group.
`stop`	Lists all the current breakpoints.
`stop in <classid>.<method>[(argtype,...)]`	Sets a breakpoint at the first executable statement in the specified method.
`stop at <classid>:<line>`	Sets a breakpoint at the specified line number. Note the colon delimiter.
`clear`	Lists all the current breakpoints.
`clear <classid>.<method>[(argtype,...)]`	Clears a breakpoint at the first executable statement in the specified method.
`clear <classid>:<line>`	Clears a breakpoint at the specified line number.
`list [<line>|<method>]`	Lists the source code for the current line, as well as the four previous and four next lines. You can specify the source location with the `use` command.
`use [<srcpath>]`	Specifies the locations in which to look for source code. Initialized to the value of `classpath`. When no argument is specified, shows the current value of the source path.
`help | ?`	Displays this list of commands.
`quit | exit`	Causes the debugger to stop and exit.

Figure 6-9

Program (with bug) to find employees hired in the 1970s.

```
package ijs.debugging;

import ijs.jdbc.*;
import java.io.*;
import java.sql.*;
import java.net.*;
import java.text.*;
import java.util.*;

public class Seventies
{
    public static void main(String[] args)
    {
        String fileName = "seventies.properties";
        if (args.length > 0)
            fileName = args[0];
        try {
            new Seventies(fileName);
        }
        catch (Exception e) {
            e.printStackTrace();
        }
    }

    public Seventies(String fileName)
        throws ClassNotFoundException, IOException
    {
        Properties prop = loadProperties(fileName);

        String driverName = prop.getProperty("driverName");
        String url = prop.getProperty("url");

        Class.forName(driverName);

        Connection con = null;
        try {
            con = DriverManager.getConnection(url);
            Statement stmt = con.createStatement();
            String sql = ""
                + " SELECT    lname, fname, hireDate"
                + " FROM      employees"
                + " WHERE     hireDate between"
                + "                {d '1970-01-01'} and"
                + "                {d '1979-12-31'}"
                + " ORDER BY hireDate"
                ;
            ResultSet rs = stmt.executeQuery(sql);
            RSViewer viewer = new RSViewer(rs);
            String table = viewer.toString();
            System.out.println(table);
        }
        catch (SQLException e) {
            e.printStackTrace();
        }
        finally {
            if (con != null) {
                try {
```

```
                                con.close();
                            }
                            catch (SQLException ignore){}
                    }
            }
    }

    public Properties loadProperties(String fileName)
        throws IOException
    {
        Properties prop = new Properties();
        InputStream propStream =
            getClass().getResourceAsStream(fileName);
        prop.load(propStream);
        propStream.close();
        return prop;
    }
}
```

```
> stop in Seventies.main
Breakpoint set in ijs.debugging.Seventies.main
>
```

If the class and method exist (which they do, in this case), the debugger informs us that the breakpoint was set. Notice that it is not necessary to specify the full package name once jdb has seen a fully qualified reference to it.

At this point, we can run the program:

```
> run
run ijs.debugging.Seventies
running ...
main[1]
Breakpoint hit: ijs.debugging.Seventies.main (Seventies:14)
main[1]
```

We have hit the breakpoint, so the debugger stops. The prompt has changed from > to main[1], which is the name and index number of the current thread (not the method containing the breakpoint, which by coincidence has the same name). To see the context of the line at which we are stopped, we ask the debugger to list the current source line:

```
main[1] list
Unable to find Seventies.java
```

The source file is in the current directory; why can't jdb find it? Where does jdb look for source files? Here is where the use command comes in:

```
main[1] use
d:\jdkl.2\jre\lib\rt.jar;d:\jdkl.2\jre\lib\il8n.jar;d:\jdkl.2\jre\
classes;.
main[1]
```

It turns out that jdb uses the full package name to determine the relative subdirectory structure to search for the class. In this case, this means that we need to add the grandparent directory ../.. to the source search path. We do this also with the use command, this time specifying a directory path. Since the path contains only the Java core libraries (with no source), we can get away with just specifying one directory:

```
main[1] use ../..
main[1]
```

Now the list command works:

```
main[1] list
10          public class Seventies
11          {
12              public static void main(String[] args)
13              {
14       =>         String fileName = "seventies.properties";
15                  if (args.length > 0)
16                      fileName = args[0];
17                  try {
18                      new Seventies(fileName);
main[1] list
```

We step through several lines and enter the constructor:

```
main[1]  step
main[1]
Breakpoint hit: ijs.debugging.Seventies.main (Seventies:15)
main[1] step
main[1]
Breakpoint hit: ijs.debugging.Seventies.main (Seventies:18)
main[1] step
main[1]
Breakpoint hit: ijs.debugging.Seventies.<init> (Seventies:27)
main[1] list
23              }
24
25          public Seventies(String fileName)
26              throws ClassNotFoundException, IOException
27       =>     {
28                  Properties prop = loadProperties(fileName);
29
30                  String driverName = prop.getProperty("driverName");
31                  String url = prop.getProperty("url");
main[1]
```

Stepping through several lines, we come to line 28. Before we try to load the properties, let's make sure of the file name:

```
main[1] print fileName
fileName = seventies.properties
main[1]
```

Just as we expect. We are pretty sure that the loadProperties method is working, so we step over the call using the next command:

```
main[1] next
main[1]
Breakpoint hit: ijs.debugging.Seventies.<init> (Seventies:30)
main[1] list
26                  throws ClassNotFoundException, IOException
27              {
28                  Properties prop = loadProperties(fileName);
29
30     =>           String driverName = prop.getProperty("driverName");
31                  String url = prop.getProperty("url");
32
33                  Class.forName(driverName);
34
main[1]
```

Let's step over the getProperty (driverName) line and examine the value it returns:

```
main[1] next
main[1]
Breakpoint hit: ijs.debugging.Seventies.<init> (Seventies:31)
main[1] print driverName
driverName = sun.jdbc.odbc.JdbcOdbcDriver
main[1]
```

It looks good. The spelling is correct, and we are sure the class exists. It ought to be a suitable driver. Let's continue, doing the same steps to get the database URL property:

```
main[1] next
main[1]
Breakpoint hit: ijs.debugging.Seventies.<init> (Seventies:33)
main[1] print url
url = ipfoods
main[1]
```

Aha! The URL contains an ODBC data source name, but not in the full JDBC URL format, which would be jdbc:odbc:ipfoods. This would explain the problem—the driver gets loaded, but it does not respond positively to the garbled URL. We exit from the debugger so that we can fix the problem.

```
main[1] quit
```

Fortunately, the URL is stored in a properties file, so it is easy to fix and does not even require that we recompile the program. Once we change it to the correct value and rerun the program, we get the following:

```
D:\book\classes\ijs\debugging>java ijs.debugging.Seventies
lname                  fname                  hireDate
_____                _____                _____

Hassinger              Samuel                 1974-06-16
Wendecker              Dorothy                1974-07-19
Strayer                Mathias                1975-02-08
Albright               Fred                   1975-04-04
Brenner                Catherine              1975-08-16
```

which is the expected result.

What Good Is a Command-Line Debugger? How does all this help with servlets, since you do not call them from a command line? This is the subject of the next two sections, which cover several commercial servlet debuggers. The approach they all take is basically the same— they provide a stub Web server that can handle servlet requests, which you then debug using your favorite debugging tool (which is jdb so far, right?).

6.7   Allaire's ServletDebugger

Problem

How do I use the ServletDebugger from Allaire Corporation?

Technique

Write a stub application that calls com.livesoftware.servletde-bugger.Debugger. Run the stub application with your favorite debugger.

Discussion

Allaire Corporation acquired Live Software, Inc., the developer of JRun, in June of 1999. Among the products that Live Software developed was ServletDebugger, a Java class library for testing and debugging servlets. For more details about ServletDebugger, refer to the JRun servlet add-on Website at *http://www.allaire.com/products/jrun/ServletAddOn.cfm.*

Installation ServletDebugger can be purchased from the Allaire Web site just noted. It is distributed as a zip file containing a `setup.exe` file. The installed components include `servletdebugger.jar`, documentation, and a sample program for debugging. The documentation describes how to install the debugger in various IDEs. Essentially, all you need is to have the `servletdebugger.jar` file accessible in your classpath.

How It Works ServletDebugger is not a stand-alone debugger but works in conjunction with third-party debugging tools (including `jdb`). It has two operating modes:

Normal. Creates a minimal servlet execution environment that writes all its output directly to `System.err`.

Server. Starts a special-purpose HTTP server that can accept servlet requests from a Web browser. Server mode operation also supports servlet stress testing.

In each case, you write an ordinary Java application that creates an instance of your servlet, builds certain parameter lists, and then invokes the `Debugger` class. Taking advantage of the fact that the debugger is a Java class that can itself be run in a debugger, you can set breakpoints and step into your own code.

Example Let's see how this would work in debugging the `Seventies` application from the preceding section. We have converted the application to a servlet and added a new bug (see Figure 6-10), which manifests itself in a null pointer exception. After reviewing the servlet logs, we determine that the error occurs on line 54 of `SeventiesServlet`, where the call to `loadProperties()` is made.

We write the required driver application, named `SeventiesServletDebugger`, as shown in Figure 6-11. The driver application uses server mode in this case because we would like to see the output rendered in HTML in a Web browser.

▬▬ ▬▬ ▬▬ ▬▬
Figure 6-10
Servlet (with
another bug)
to find 1970s
employees.

```
import ijs.jdbc.*;

import java.io.*;
import java.net.*;
import java.sql.*;
import java.text.*;
import java.util.*;

import javax.servlet.*;
import javax.servlet.http.*;

/**
 * SeventiesServlet
 */
public class SeventiesServlet extends HttpServlet
{
    /**
     * Performs servlet initialization
     * @exception ServletException if a servlet exception occurs
     */
    public void init(ServletConfig config)
        throws ServletException
    {
        super.init(config);
    }

    /**
     * Handles a GET request
     * @param request the servlet request object
     * @param response the servlet response object
     * @exception ServletException if a servlet exception occurs
     * @exception IOException if an I/O exception occurs
     */
    public void doGet(
            HttpServletRequest request,
            HttpServletResponse response)
        throws ServletException, IOException
    {
        // Start the document

        response.setContentType("text/html");
        PrintWriter out = response.getWriter();

        out.println("<HTML>");
        out.println("<HEAD>");
        out.println("<TITLE>SeventiesServlet</TITLE>");
        out.println("</HEAD>");
        out.println("<BODY>");
        out.println("<H3>Employees Hired in the 1970's</H3>");

        // Get the driver name and url properties

        String fileName = getInitParameter("fileName");
        Properties prop = loadProperties(fileName);

        String driverName = prop.getProperty("driverName");
        String url = prop.getProperty("url");
```

Figure 6-10

(Continued)

```
// Load the driver

try {
    Class.forName(driverName);
}
catch (ClassNotFoundException e) {
    throw new ServletException(e.getMessage());
}

// Run the query and print the results

Connection con = null;
try {
    con = DriverManager.getConnection(url);
    Statement stmt = con.createStatement();
    String sql = ""
        + " SELECT    lname, fname, hireDate"
        + " FROM      employees"
        + " WHERE     hireDate between"
        + "           {d '1970-01-01'} and"
        + "           {d '1979-12-31'}"
        + " ORDER BY hireDate"
        ;
    ResultSet rs = stmt.executeQuery(sql);
    TableMaker tm = new TableMaker(rs);
    String table = tm.toString();
    out.println(table);
}
catch (SQLException e) {
    throw new ServletException(e.getMessage());
}
finally {
    if (con != null) {
        try {
            con.close();
        }
        catch (SQLException ignore){}
    }
}

out.println("</BODY>");
out.println("</HTML>");




Handles a POST request
param request the servlet request object
param response the servlet response object
exception ServletException if a servlet exception occurs
exception IOException if an I/O exception occurs

lic void doPost(
    HttpServletRequest request,
    HttpServletResponse response)
throws ServletException, IOException
```

Figure 6-10
(Continued)

```
        doGet(request, response);
    }

    /**
     * Loads the servlet properties
     */
    public Properties loadProperties(String fileName)
        throws IOException
    {
        Properties prop = new Properties();
        InputStream propStream = new FileInputStream(fileName);
        prop.load(propStream);
        propStream.close();
        return prop;
    }
```

Figure 6-11

SeventiesServ-
letDebugger
driver.

```
import java.io.*;
import java.util.*;
import com.livesoftware.servletdebugger.*;

public class SeventiesServletDebugger
{
    public static void main(String[] args)
        throws Exception
    {
        String loggingDir = "logs";

        Hashtable initVals = new Hashtable();
        initVals.put("fileName", "seventies.properties");

        SeventiesServlet servlet = new SeventiesServlet();

        new Debugger(servlet, initVals, loggingDir, "8080");
    }
}
```

After ensuring that `servletdebugger.jar` is in our classpath, we invoke the driver through the command-line debugger:

```
D:\book\classes\ijs\debugging>jdb SeventiesServletDebugger
Initializing jdb...
0xad:class(SeventiesServletDebugger)
>
```

We set a breakpoint at line 54 of our servlet and start running the application:

```
> stop at SeventiesServlet:54
Breakpoint set at SeventiesServlet:54
> run
run SeventiesServletDebugger
running ...
```

```
main[1] Session timeout thread started, checking every 10s.
Server started.
```

The ServletDebugger control dialog pops up, informing us that the server is running on port 8080 (see Figure 6-12).

The debugging Web server is now waiting for servlet requests. We can invoke the servlet by starting a Web browser pointing at `http://localhost:8080`. The easiest way to do this is by clicking the Windows "Start" button, selecting the run option, and then entering the URL, as shown in Figure 6-13.

This causes the `doGet` method of the `SeventiesServlet` to be called, which triggers our breakpoint. We enter the `list` command to make sure we are where we think we are:

```
Breakpoint hit: SeventiesServlet.doGet (SeventiesServlet:54)
Thread-4[1] list
50
51                     // Get the driver name and url properties
52
53                     String fileName = getInitParameter("filename");
54      =>             Properties prop = loadProperties(fileName);
55
56                     String driverName = prop.getProperty("driverName");
57                     String url = prop.getProperty("url");
58
Thread-4[1]
```

Stepping into the `loadProperties` method, we execute the first two lines but then encounter a strange breakpoint:

Figure 6-12
The ServletDebugger control GUI.

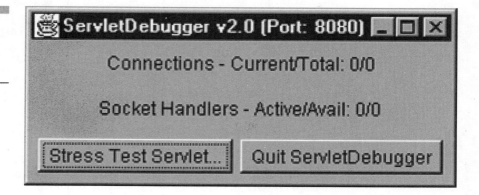

Figure 6-13
Launching the
`SeventiesServ-
let` from the Start
button.

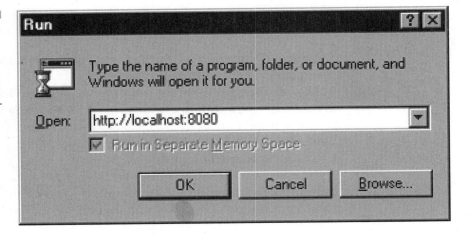

```
121             public Properties loadProperties(String
                fileName)
122                throws IOException
123             {
124                Properties prop = new Properties();
125      =>        InputStream propStream = new
                   FileInputStream(fileName);
126                prop.load(propStream);
127                propStream.close();
128                return prop;
129             }
Thread-3[1] next

Breakpoint hit: com.livesoftware.servletdebugger.Debugger.service (pc
22)
```

What happened? Obviously, we must have triggered an exception
when we executed line 125. Let's exit (by clicking the "Quit
ServletDebugger" button) and start over, this time setting a breakpoint
on line 125.

```
D:\book\classes\ijs\debugging>jdb SeventiesServletDebugger
Initializing jdb...
0xad:class(SeventiesServletDebugger)
> stop at SeventiesServlet:125
Breakpoint set at SeventiesServlet:125
> run
run SeventiesServletDebugger
running ...
main[1] Session timeout thread started, checking every 10s.
Server started.
```

After launching the Web browser request again, we hit the breakpoint at line 125. The only thing that could possibly be wrong on this line is the file name. We use the `print` command to see what it is:

```
Thread-3[1] print fileName
fileName = null
```

How could the file name be null? Let's back up again and see where it comes from. Looking at the source code, we see that it is retrieved from the initial parameter named `filename` (line 54). Checking our driver code, we verify that we specified it properly:

```
initVals.put("fileName", "seventies.properties");
```

The light bulb above our head now switches on. The parameter name is spelled differently—a lowercase n instead of an uppercase one. Thus the `getInitParameter()` method did not find a parameter by that name, returned a null, and we were lost.

The bug is easy to fix. We change the `getInitParameter()` line to use the correct name, recompile, and rerun the servlet. This time we get the results we were looking for, as shown in Figure 6-14.

A Generic Driver   It is not really necessary to write a custom debugging stub for each servlet. The same thing can be accomplished by writing a generic driver that reads its parameters from a properties file and instantiates the appropriate driver with `Class.forName()`. An implementation of approach this is the `DebuggerDriver` class listed in Figure 6-15.

`DebuggerDriver` contains a static `main()` method that interprets command line parameters, loads a properties file, and then creates an instance of its class using the specified mode and properties. By default, it operates in server mode, in which it launches an HTTP server to which servlet requests can be sent. It also can operate in what JRun calls *normal* mode, which runs the servlet and sends its output to `System.err`.

To run this generic driver for our example, we only need a properties file (named `debug70.properties`, perhaps) containing the following:

```
servletName=SeventiesServlet
initVals.fileName=seventies.properties
loggingDir=logs
port=8686
```

which can run from a command line as follows:

```
jdb DebuggerDriver -mode server -properties debug70.properties
```

Figure 6-14
Results of the
debugged
Seventies-
Servlet.

Employees Hired in the 1970's

lname	fname	hireDate
Hassinger	Samuel	1974-06-14
Wendecker	Dorothy	1974-07-19
Strayer	Mathias	1975-02-08
Albright	Fred	1975-04-04
Brenner	Catherine	1975-08-16

Figure 6-15

A generic driver for
ServletDebugger.

```java
import com.livesoftware.servletdebugger.*;
import java.io.*;
import java.util.*;
import javax.servlet.*;

/**
 * A generic driver for Allaire's ServletDebugger 2.0
 */
public class DebuggerDriver
{
    public static final int NORMAL = 0;
    public static final int SERVER = 1;

    /**
     * Mainline
     */
    public static void main(String[] args)
    {
        int mode = SERVER;
        Properties prop = null;

        // Process the command line

        try {
            for (int i = 0; i < args.length; i++) {
                String arg = args[i];

                // -mode <server|normal>

                if (arg.equals("-mode")) {
                    if (++i >= args.length)
                        throw new IllegalArgumentException
                        ("No mode specified after -mode");
                    arg = args[i];
                    if (arg.equalsIgnoreCase("SERVER"))
                        mode = SERVER;
                    else
                    if (arg.equalsIgnoreCase("NORMAL"))
                        mode = NORMAL;
                    else
                        throw new IllegalArgumentException
                        (arg + " is not a valid mode");
                }

                // -properties <fileName>

                if (arg.equals("-properties")) {
                    if (++i >= args.length)
                        throw new IllegalArgumentException
                        ("No name specified after -properties");
                    arg = args[i];
                    prop = new Properties();
                    prop.load(new FileInputStream(arg));
                }
            }

            // Verify that the properties were loaded
```

Figure 6-15
(Continued)

```
                                     \

                if (prop == null)
                    throw new RuntimeException
                    ("No properties were specified");
            }
            catch (Exception e) {
                System.out.println(e.getMessage());
                showUsage();
                System.exit(0);
            }

            // Invoke the debugger driver

            try {
                new DebuggerDriver(mode, prop);
            }
            catch (RuntimeException e) {
                System.out.println("Could not start the debugger:");
                System.out.println(e.getMessage());
                System.exit(1);
            }
        }

        /**
         * Displays calling syntax
         */
        public static void showUsage()
        {
            String[] text = {
                "usage: java DebuggerDriver"
                    + " [-mode <server|normal>]"
                    + " [-properties <fileName>]",
                "",
                "where: -mode server (default) Starts an HTTP server",
                "",
                "          -mode normal Runs the servlet and sends the",
                "                        output to System.err",
                "",
                "          <fileName>  is the name of a properties file",
                "                        that describes the servlet",
                "                        parameters",
            };
            for (int i = 0; i < text.length; i++)
                System.out.println(text[i]);
        }

        /**
         * Creates a new DebuggerDriver
         * @param mode the operating mode:
         * <UL>
         * <LI>SERVER - Server mode
         * <LI>NORMAL - Normal mode (no HTTP server)
         * </UL>
         * @param prop the servlet properties
         * <P>
         * The servlet properties can include the following:
         * <PRE>
```

Figure 6-15

(Continued)

```
 * servletName (required)
 * initVals.&lt;name&gt;=&lt;value&gt;
 * initVals.&lt;name&gt;=&lt;value&gt;
 * ...
 * initVals.&lt;name&gt;=&lt;value&gt;
 * formVals.&lt;name&gt;=&lt;value&gt;
 * formVals.&lt;name&gt;=&lt;value&gt;
 * ...
 * formVals.&lt;name&gt;=&lt;value&gt;
 * headerVals.&lt;name&gt;=&lt;value&gt;
 * headerVals.&lt;name&gt;=&lt;value&gt;
 * ...
 * headerVals.&lt;name&gt;=&lt;value&gt;
 * loggingDir
 * port (if server mode)
 * </PRE>
 */
public DebuggerDriver(int mode, Properties prop)
{
    /*
                Properties required in each mode

                        Normal   Server
        Servlet name       x        x
        Init vals          x        x
        Form vals          x        -
        Header vals        x        -
        Logging dir        x        x
        Port               -        x

    */

    String servletName;
    Servlet servlet;
    Hashtable initVals = null;
    Hashtable formVals = null;
    Hashtable headerVals = null;
    String loggingDir = null;
    String portString = null;

    // Load the servlet class

    servletName = prop.getProperty("servletName");
    if (servletName == null)
       throw new RuntimeException
          ("No servletName property found");
    try {
       Class cl = Class.forName(servletName);
       servlet = (Servlet) cl.newInstance();
    }
    catch (ClassNotFoundException e) {
       throw new RuntimeException
          ("Could not load class: [" + servletName + "]");
    }
    catch (InstantiationException e) {
       throw new RuntimeException
          (servletName + ": Instantiation exception");
```

Figure 6-15
(Continued)

```
        }
        catch (IllegalAccessException e) {
            throw new RuntimeException
                (servletName + ": Illegal access exception");
        }

        // Load properties specific to each mode
        // and start the debugger

        switch (mode) {

            // Normal mode - no HTTP server.  Loads the servlet
            // and writes output to System.err

            case NORMAL:
                initVals    = loadTable(prop, "initVals");
                formVals    = loadTable(prop, "formVals");
                headerVals  = loadTable(prop, "headerVals");
                loggingDir  = prop.getProperty
                            ("loggingDir", "logs");
                try {
                    Debugger d =
                        new Debugger(
                                servlet,
                                initVals,
                                formVals,
                                headerVals,
                                loggingDir
                                );
                }
                catch (Exception e) {
                    e.printStackTrace();
                    throw new RuntimeException(e.getMessage());
                }
                break;

            // Server mode - Starts an HTTP servlet

            case SERVER:
                initVals    = loadTable(prop, "initVals");
                portString  = prop.getProperty("port", "8080");
                loggingDir  = prop.getProperty
                            ("loggingDir", "logs");
                try {
                    Debugger d =
                        new Debugger(
                                servlet,
                                initVals,
                                loggingDir,
                                portString
                                );
                }
                catch (Exception e) {
                    e.printStackTrace();
                    throw new RuntimeException(e.getMessage());
                }
                break;
```

Figure 6-15
(Continued)

```java
        }
    }

    /**
     * Loads a hashtable with properties whose name
     * starts with the specified prefix
     * @param prop the properties object
     * @param prefix the key prefix (e.g., "initVals")
     * @return a hashtable with the selected properties
     * with the prefix stripped.
     */
    public static Hashtable loadTable
        (Properties prop, String prefix)
    {
        if (!prefix.endsWith("."))
            prefix += ".";

        Hashtable table = new Hashtable();

        Enumeration enames = prop.propertyNames();
        while (enames.hasMoreElements()) {
            String name = (String) enames.nextElement();
            if (name.startsWith(prefix)) {
                String value = prop.getProperty(name);
                name = name.substring(prefix.length());
                table.put(name, value);
            }
        }

        return table;
    }
```

6.8   Using New Atlanta's ServletExec Debugger

Problem

I have the ServletExec debugger from New Atlanta Communications. How do I debug my servlets with it?

Technique

Incorporate `ServletExecDebuggerMain` in your project and run it under your favorite debugger.

Discussion

New Atlanta Communications produces the ServletExec servlet engine and a companion ServletExec debugger. The servlet engine supports the Java Servlets 2.1 API, JSP 1.0, and is available for most major Web servers. The debugger is a simple Web server written in Java that includes the full ServletExec servlet engine. More details about these products can be found in the product section of New Atlanta's Web site at *http://www.newatlanta.com/products.html*.

Installation ServletExec debugger can be freely downloaded from the New Atlanta Web site just noted. The installed components include `ServletExecDebugger.jar`, documentation, and a sample program for debugging. The documentation includes comprehensive instructions for installing the debugger in various IDEs and a clearly written User's Guide that explains how to run it.

How It Works However, you do not need an IDE to use the debugger. All you really need to do is

1. Put the `ServletExecDebugger.jar` file in your classpath.
2. Run `ServletExecDebuggerMain.java` under the command-line debugger (`jdb`).

The debugger mainline allows you to specify the port number as well as the root directories for the debugger and your documents, but the defaults are usually sufficient.

In ordinary operation, you invoke the Web server by starting the main class from a command line:

```
D:\book\classes\ijs\debugging>java ServletExecDebuggerMain
New Atlanta ServletExec Debugger 2.1b3
    Copyright (c) 1997-1999 New Atlanta Communications, LLC.
    All rights reserved.    http://www.newatlanta.com/
ServletExec 2.1b3 initialized
ServletExec Debugger listening on port 8080
```

You can verify that the server is running by starting the *http://local-host:8080/servlet/admin* URL. This will bring up the administrative application in a Web browser, as shown in Figure 6-16.

To configure your servlet, enter the servlet name, class, and initialization parameters in the `Configure Servlets` frame, and then click the "Submit" button. This information is then stored in the `servlets.properties` file in the `./ServletExec Data/default` subdirectory.[6] You can test your servlet by invoking it as you normally would, specifying the debugger port number in the URL:

```
http://localhost:8080/servlet/<ServletName>
```

Debug Mode   To debug a servlet using a commercial IDE, follow the operating instructions in the User's Guide. However, if all you need to do is set breakpoints and step through your code, you can simply

[6]Yes, there is an embedded space in the directory name.

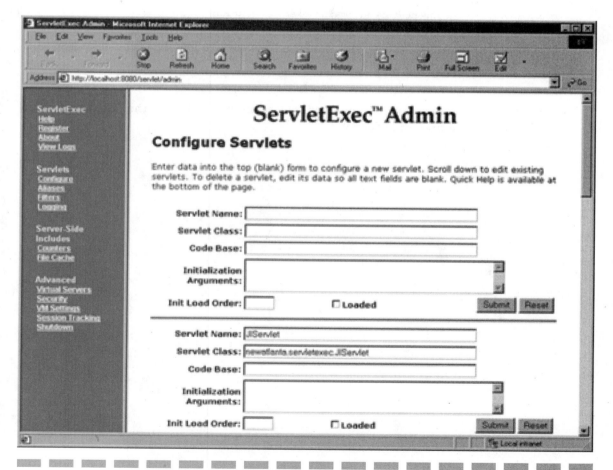

Figure 6-16 The ServletExec administrative application.

1. Invoke the Web server with jdb instead of java:

```
D:\book\classes\ijs\debugging>jdb ServletExecDebuggerMain
Initializing jdb...
0xae:class(ServletExecDebuggerMain)
```

2. Set breakpoints in your servlet, and start the debugger running:

```
> stop in SeventiesServlet.doGet
Breakpoint set in SeventiesServlet.doGet
> run
run ServletExecDebuggerMain
running ...
main[1] New Atlanta ServletExec Debugger 2.1b3
    Copyright (c) 1997-1999 New Atlanta Communications, LLC.
    All rights reserved.    http://www.newatlanta.com/
ServletExec 2.1b3 initialized

Current thread "main" died. Execution continuing...
> ServletExec Debugger listening on port 8080
```

3. Invoke the servlet from the Browser window using the debugger port number:

```
http://localhost:8080/servlet/SeventiesServlet
```

At this point, the debugging session is identical to the one described in the preceding section.

Session Management

Overview

HTTP is characterized as a *stateless* protocol, meaning that it does not remember from one request to another anything about previous requests. This is perfectly appropriate if all you are doing is serving up documents over the Internet. However, most applications require some back-and-forth exchange of information in order to do meaningful work. For example, a database search may involve entering

1. A user ID and password, and then, if the user ID is valid
2. Keywords that generate some search results, and finally
3. Forward or backward paging commands to view the selected records.

It would be cumbersome indeed to have to specify the user ID and password or to reenter the search criteria at each stage. To get around this restriction, clever programmers have devised various means of saving state information in the client application. Common Gateway Interface (CGI) programs often bundle these data into long, incomprehensible strings of hexadecimal characters that get appended to a rewritten URL. Other solutions involve using hidden fields in dynamically generated HTML forms or saving choice bits of information in HTTP cookies.[1]

These techniques work but may only solve half the problem. An application may involve creating complex objects that need to exist on the server for the duration of several client requests. In the database search example just described, it is not enough for the client to remember that it has seen records 3121 to 3140 of the current search—it is necessary for the server to keep the database connection open and the result set close at hand.

HTTP Sessions

To meet this need, the Java Servlet API defines an `HTTPSession` `object`. This object has the following desirable properties:

- It persists in an active process on the server between client requests.
- It is allocated on a per-user, per-browser session basis.
- It can hold named objects of any type.
- It is saved and restored if the Web server is brought down for maintenance.
- It can be deleted explicitly or automatically after a specified period of inactivity.

HTTP sessions are one of the most useful and distinguishing characteristics of the Servlet API and represent a key advantage over the use of CGI programs. The remainder of this chapter covers state-management issues in detail, describing how to set up HTTP sessions and how they can be used.

---

[1]See RFC 2109, "HTTP State Management Mechanism" at *http://www.cis.ohio-state.edu/htbin/rfc/rfc2109.html.*

7.1 Creating HTTP Sessions

Problem

How do I create and use an HTTP session?

Technique

Call the `getSession()` or `getSession(create)` methods of the `HttpServletRequest` object. Store objects with `HttpSession.putValue(name, object)` and retrieve them later with `HttpSession.getValue(name)`.[2] Close the session by calling `HttpSession.invalidate()`.

Discussion

Programming conversational Web applications is difficult in general, but fortunately, using sessions is not the difficult part. Typically, four steps are involved:

1. *Creating the session.* Inside your request handler, call the `HttpServletRequest getSession()` method. This will return the currently active session if there is one or create a new one if none exists. You also can call `getSession(true)` to perform exactly the same function or `getSession(false)` to access only an existing session, not a new one. `getSession(false)` will return `null` if there is no valid session.

2. *Storing objects in the session.* To store an object, call the `HttpSession putValue(name, value)` method. For example, to store a `java.lang.String` containing the user ID, write

   ```
   session.putValue("userID", userID);
   ```

---

[2]In the Servlet API 2.2 specification, `HttpSession.putValue()` and `HttpSession.getValue()` have been deprecated and replaced by `HttpSession.setAttribute()` and `HttpSession.getAttribute()`, respectively. Only the names have changed; the semantics remain the same.

The value can be any nonnull object but not a primitive type. To store a primitive type, use the appropriate `java.lang` wrapper object. For an integer, for example, write

```
session.putValue("count", new Integer(17));
```

In addition, the value object ought to be serializable, since sessions may be serialized and restored if the Web server is restarted. The name can be anything you like, but it helps to use something meaningful like the variable name (but see Section 7.7 on avoiding name space collisions).

3. *Retrieving objects from the session.* As you might expect, you retrieve stored objects with the `HttpSession getValue(name)` method. Much like a `Hashtable` or `Vector`, an `HttpSession` knows only that its contents are objects; it does not know their type. You must cast the values to the desired type when you retrieve them:

```
String userID = (String) session.getValue("userID");
Integer count = (Integer) session.getValue("count");
```

If there is no object stored in the session with the name you specify, `getValue()` returns null.

4. *Closing the session.* When you have finished using the session, you can close it with the `session.invalidate()` method, which unbinds all the objects stored in it and flags it as being invalid for further use. This is not strictly necessary, since the servlet engine will automatically invalidate the session after a certain period of inactivity. However, you may wish to do this explicitly to release resources used by the session.[3]

An Example Figure 7-1 is a simple illustration of how an `HttpSession` can be used. `RequestTracker` is a servlet that keeps track of each time it has been called during the current browser session.

---

[3]This raises a disagreeable point, however. There is only one session per user per browser at a time. This session may be shared by several different servlets. If you explicitly invalidate the session, it is invalidated for all servlets that may be using it. This may be fine for you, but what about the other servlet? What happens to the contents of the shopping cart?

Figure 7-1

A servlet that keeps
track of previous
requests.

```
package ijs.session;

import java.io.*;
import java.net.*;
import java.util.*;

import javax.servlet.*;
import javax.servlet.http.*;

/**
 * RequestTrackerServlet
 */
public class RequestTrackerServlet extends HttpServlet
{
    private static final String PREFIX = "ijs.session";
    private static final String REQLIST = PREFIX + ".reqList";

    /**
     * Handles a GET request
     * @param request the servlet request object
     * @param response the servlet response object
     * @exception ServletException if a servlet exception occurs
     * @exception IOException if an I/O exception occurs
     */
    public void doGet(
        HttpServletRequest request,
        HttpServletResponse response)
      throws ServletException, IOException
    {
        // Get the list of previous requests from the session.
        // Create a new list if one does not already exist.

        HttpSession session = request.getSession(true);

        Vector reqList = (Vector) session.getValue(REQLIST);

        if (reqList == null) {
            reqList = new Vector();
            session.putValue(REQLIST, reqList);
        }

        // Get information about this request and save it
        // as a string in the front of the vector.

        StringBuffer reqInfo = new StringBuffer();

        reqInfo.append("Request number: "
            + (reqList.size() + 1) + "\n");

        reqInfo.append("Request URL:     "
            + HttpUtils.getRequestURL(request) + "\n");

        reqInfo.append("Time:            "
            + new java.util.Date() + "\n");

        reqInfo.append("Session ID:      "
            + session.getId() + "\n");
```

Figure 7-1
(Continued)

```
        reqInfo.append("isNew():
            + session.isNew() + "\n");

    reqList.insertElementAt(reqInfo.toString(), 0);

    // Now echo the request vector back to the client

    StringBuffer buffer = new StringBuffer();

    buffer.append("<HTML>");
    buffer.append("<HEAD>");
    buffer.append("<TITLE>Request Tracker Servlet</TITLE>");
    buffer.append("</HEAD>");
    buffer.append("<BODY>");
    buffer.append("<H1>Request Tracker Servlet</H1>");
    buffer.append("You have made ");
    buffer.append(reqList.size());
    buffer.append(" request(s) to this servlet:");
    buffer.append("<P>");

    buffer.append("<PRE>\n");
    for (int i = 0; i < reqList.size(); i++) {
        String info = (String) reqList.elementAt(i);
        buffer.append(info);
        buffer.append("\n\n");
    }
    buffer.append("</PRE>\n");
    buffer.append("</BODY>");
    buffer.append("</HTML>");

    response.setContentType("text/html");
    PrintWriter out = response.getWriter();
    out.println(buffer.toString());
}


/**
 * Handles a POST request
 * @param request the servlet request object
 * @param response the servlet response object
 * @exception ServletException if a servlet exception occurs
 * @exception IOException if an I/O exception occurs
 */
public void doPost(
        HttpServletRequest request,
        HttpServletResponse response)
    throws ServletException, IOException
{
    doGet(request, response);
}
}
```

It displays its calling history from the most recent to the oldest request each time the browser reload button is clicked.

To begin with, it gets a reference to the current session or creates a new session if this is the first request:

```
HttpSession session = request.getSession(true);
```

It then gets the list of previous requests from the session or creates a new list (a `java.util.Vector` of strings) if required. If a new list is created, it is stored in the session under the name `<package-name>.reqList`:

```
private static final String PREFIX = "ijs.session";
private static final String REQLIST = PREFIX + ".reqList";
...
Vector reqList = (Vector) session.getValue(REQLIST);
if (reqList == null) {
   reqList = new Vector();
   session.putValue(REQLIST, reqList);
}
```

The information describing the current request includes the request number (how many times the servlet has been called), the URL with which it was called, the request time, the session ID, and whether the session was newly created for this request or not. All this information is concatenated into a string and stored in the `reqList` vector, which is already being tracked by the session. Finally, the servlet reads each entry in the vector and writes its contents to the HTML page being constructed. The results are as shown in Figure 7-2.

7.2 Controlling Application Sequence

Problem

My application consists of several servlets that must be accessed in a particular sequence. How do I prevent users from accessing them out of sequence?

Figure 7-2 The RequestTracker servlet in action.

Technique

Use `request.getSession(true)` in your first servlet and `request.getSession(false)` in all the others. Store your application objects in the session, and use them to determine where you are in the sequence, redirecting to the first servlet if necessary.

Discussion

Even though you may intend your users to start at a particular point in your application, there really is no way to ensure that they have not started from a bookmark for some intermediate point or hit the "Back" button on the browser by mistake. What you can do is determine whether the user has performed the preliminary steps that your application requires, redirecting him or her, if necessary, to the appropriate starting point. For example, if a user ID and password are required, and the user has not already been prompted for them, you can force the browser to go to your login servlet:

```
String userID = (String) session.getValue("userID");
String password = (String) session.getValue("password");
if ((userID == null) || (password == null)) {
    response.sendRedirect("/servlet/login");
    return;
}
```

When the browser receives the redirection header, it automatically switches to the specified URL and starts your application in the right place.

Sequence Control Example   To see this in action, let's examine a greatly simplified version of an online banking application. The ServletBank allows balance inquires and funds transfer over the Internet for customers with a valid account number and PIN code. The application consists of an HTML form and two servlets:

1. `GetAccountNumber.html`. As illustrated in Figure 7-3, this form prompts for the account number and PIN number and then posts this information to the PIN number validation servlet. The HTML is shown in Figure 7-4.

Figure 7-3 Output of `GetAccountNumber.html`.

2. `ValidatePIN`. This verifies that the numbers entered are valid.[4] If so, it stores them in a hashtable that it binds to the HTTP session under the name `ijs.session.login.account`. Then it displays the menu of banking transaction choices (Figure 7-5). The source code is found in Figure 7-6.

3. `BalanceInquiry`. This extracts the account object from the current session (see source code in Figure 7-8). If this object does not

---

[4]Apparently, 4311 is the only valid PIN number!

■■■■ ■■■■ ■■■■ ■■■■
Figure 7-4

*A prompt for the
account number.*

```
<HTML>

<HEAD>
<TITLE>Get Account Number</TITLE>
</HEAD>

<BODY>
<H3>Welcome to ServletBank</H3>
Enter your account number and PIN number below
to access your account.  The PIN number will
not be displayed.
<FORM METHOD=POST ACTION="/servlet/ValidatePIN">
<TABLE BORDER=0 CELLPADDING=3>
<TR>
    <TD>Account number:</TD>
    <TD><INPUT TYPE="TEXT" NAME="acctno" SIZE="16"></TD>
</TR>
<TR>
    <TD>PIN number:</TD>
    <TD><INPUT TYPE="PASSWORD" NAME="PIN" SIZE="4">
    <INPUT TYPE="SUBMIT" VALUE="OK">
    </TD>
</TR>
</TABLE>
</FORM>
</BODY>

</HTML>
```

exist, the user has entered the application out of sequence and must be redirected to the GetAccountNumber Web page. Otherwise, the current account balance is displayed (Figure 7-7).

It is instructive to see what happens when these servlets are accessed out of sequence. You can see for yourself by running the application but dragging bookmarks for each page to the desktop. When you try to reinvoke the second one (ValidatePIN) in a new browser session, you see an error message informing you that you have not entered an account number. When you try to go directly to the balance inquiry (BalanceInquiry), you do not even see an error message—you just see the initial account number entry page.

Figure 7-5 The ServletBank main menu.

Figure 7-6

A servlet to validate
the PIN number.

```java
package ijs.session.login;

import java.io.*;
import java.net.*;
import java.util.*;
import javax.servlet.*;
import javax.servlet.http.*;

/**
* A servlet that validates the user PIN number
*/
public class ValidatePINServlet extends HttpServlet
{
    public static final String PREFIX = "ijs.session.login";
    public static final String ACCOUNT = PREFIX + ".account";

    public void doGet(
            HttpServletRequest request,
            HttpServletResponse response)
        throws ServletException, IOException
    {
        PrintWriter out = response.getWriter();
        response.setContentType("text/html");

        HttpSession session = request.getSession(true);
        session.removeValue(ACCOUNT);
        try {

            // Get account number

            String acctno = request.getParameter("acctno");
            if (acctno == null)
                throw new RuntimeException
                ("No account number was specified");
            acctno = acctno.trim();
            if (acctno.equals(""))
                throw new RuntimeException
                ("Account number cannot be blank");

            // Get PIN number

            String PIN = request.getParameter("PIN");
            if (PIN == null)
                throw new RuntimeException
                ("No PIN number was specified");
            PIN = PIN.trim();
            if (PIN.equals(""))
                throw new RuntimeException
                ("PIN number cannot be blank");

            // Validate PIN number

            if (!PIN.equals("4311"))
                throw new RuntimeException
                ("Invalid PIN number");

            // Everything OK - proceed to main application
```

Figure 7-6
(Continued)

```
Hashtable account = new Hashtable();
account.put("acctno", acctno);
account.put("PIN", PIN);
session.putValue(ACCOUNT, account);

StringBuffer buffer = new StringBuffer();

buffer.append("<H3>Welcome to ServletBank</H3>");
buffer.append("Please select from");
buffer.append(" the following options:");
buffer.append("<OL>");
buffer.append("<LI>");
buffer.append("<A HREF=\"/servlet/BalanceInquiry\"");
buffer.append(">Balance Inquiry</A>");
buffer.append("<LI>Transfer Funds");
buffer.append("(not available at the moment)");
buffer.append("</OL>");

out.println(buffer.toString());
}
catch (RuntimeException e) {
    StringBuffer buffer = new StringBuffer();

buffer.append("<H3>Welcome to ServletBank</H3>");
buffer.append("<PRE>\n");
buffer.append(e.getMessage());
buffer.append("\n");
buffer.append("</PRE>");
buffer.append("<P>");
buffer.append("Click ");
buffer.append("<A HREF=\"");
buffer.append
("/ijs/Chap07/login/GetAccountNumber.html\"");
buffer.append(">here</A>");
buffer.append(" to enter your account number.");

out.println(buffer.toString());
}
finally {
    out.flush();
}
}

public void doPost(
    HttpServletRequest request,
    HttpServletResponse response)
  throws ServletException, IOException
{
  doGet(request, response);
}
```

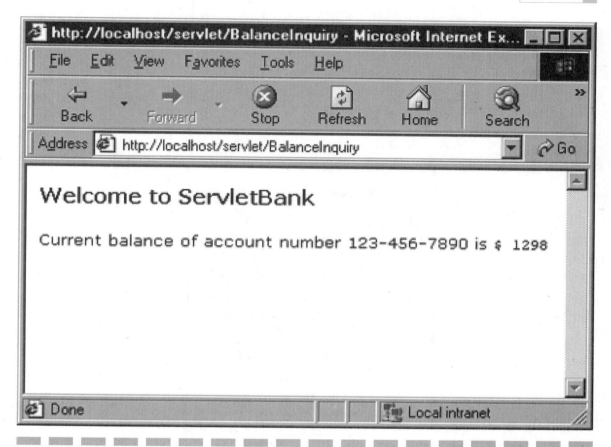

Figure 7-7 The ServletBank balance inquiry.

Figure 7-8

A servlet to get the account balance.

```java
package ijs.session.login;

import java.io.*;
import java.net.*;
import java.util.*;

import javax.servlet.*;
import javax.servlet.http.*;

/**
 * BalanceInquiryServlet
 */
public class BalanceInquiryServlet extends HttpServlet
{
    public static final String PREFIX = "ijs.session.login";
    public static final String ACCOUNT = PREFIX + ".account";

    /**
     * Handles a GET request
     */
    public void doGet(
            HttpServletRequest request,
            HttpServletResponse response)
        throws ServletException, IOException
    {
        response.setContentType("text/html");
        PrintWriter out = response.getWriter();

        HttpSession session = request.getSession(true);
        try {
            Object accountObject = session.getValue(ACCOUNT);

            // If no account object was put in the session, or
            // if one exists but it is not a hashtable, then
            // redirect the user to the original login page

            if (accountObject == null)
                throw new RuntimeException
                ("No account object");

            if (!(accountObject instanceof Hashtable))
                throw new RuntimeException
                ("Account object found but not hashtable");

            Hashtable account = (Hashtable) accountObject;
            String acctno = (String) account.get("acctno");

            int balance = (int) (Math.random() * 2000);
            String szBalance = "$ " + balance;
            out.println("<H3>Welcome to ServletBank</H3>");
            out.println("Current balance of account number ");
            out.println(acctno);
            out.println(" is <CODE>" + szBalance + "</CODE>");
        }
        catch (RuntimeException e) {
            log(e.getMessage());
            response.sendRedirect
```

Figure 7-8
(Continued)

```
                     ("/ijs/Chap07/login/GetAccountNumber.html");
                     return;
            }
    }

    /**
     * Handles a POST request
     */
    public void doPost(
            HttpServletRequest request,
            HttpServletResponse response)
        throws ServletException, IOException
    {
        doGet(request, response);
    }
```

7.3 Saving State in Hidden Fields

Problem

I have a simple application with a few fields that need to be remembered between requests. The application does not require a persistent server session. Is there a simple way to do this?

Technique

Use hidden fields in an HTML form.

Discussion

As handy as sessions are, there is no particular need to create them if something simpler will do. In general, you only need an HttpSession when all three of the following requirements are present:

1. Your application entails multiple HTTP requests.
2. You need to remember certain data between requests.
3. There is a server-side object that needs to persist between requests.

In particular, the third requirement determines whether an HttpSession is necessary. Even if you have a big, complicated server-side object, it needs to be a big, complicated server-side object that stays alive between requests before you to need an `HttpSession`.

For example, a database search requires a persistent connection between the Web server (your servlet) and a database. The initial request initializes a connection and supplies the search criteria. If there are several thousand records selected, the application only displays twenty or so and remembers a pointer to the last row displayed. Subsequent requests allow the user to page forward and backward or start a new search. Here, all three requirements are met:

1. The application consists of requests to initialize, search, page forward and backward, and quit.

2. The current record number and total number of records need to be tracked.

3. The opened database connection and the temporary result set need to persist between requests.

However, if you only have the first two requirements, you can manage simply by using hidden fields in an HTML form. Recall from Chapter 4 that a hidden field is a named HTML input element containing a fixed constant value that is invisible to the user. Hidden fields are passed back to the Web server in the query string or input stream in the same manner as text, option, or other input elements.

The format of a hidden field is as follows:

```
<INPUT TYPE="HIDDEN" NAME=name VALUE=value>
```

where

name   is the field name

value   is its constant value

You can hard-code hidden fields in an HTML document (e.g., to contain transaction codes or version numbers), but more frequently, you will generate them dynamically from a servlet. A simple example would be storing a user's language preference so that the servlet can generate messages, format dates, and currency notations in the appropriate manner:

```
// Save the user's language preference
out.println("<FORM METHOD=GET ACTION=/servlet/i18n>");
out.println("<INPUT TYPE=HIDDEN NAME=LOCALE VALUE="
  + locale.toString() + ">");
```

```
...
out.println("</FORM>");
```

It should be pointed out that this is hardly a new technique—mainframe transaction-processing systems have stored hidden fields in 80 × 24 black-and-green screen buffers for years. It also should be pointed out that the term *hidden* is a bit of a misnomer. All it means is that the contents of the field are not normally displayed by the browser. However, there is nothing to stop a curious user from viewing the HTML source of a form to retrieve or even modify the value of a hidden field. This implies a fourth criterion for when an HttpSession is appropriate:

4. The session state needs to be carefully controlled by the server.

An example where this is not the case is a game. Here, it is not critical that hidden fields are absolutely concealed; it is just more entertaining if they are.

A Complete Example   Let's look at just such an application for hidden fields. Consider the number-guessing game shown in Figure 7-9. When the game starts, the computer picks a four-digit random number. Each of the digits is an integer from one to eight, inclusive. There may be repeated digits. The player has ten guesses to figure out what the number is. After each guess, the computer reports back how many of the digits were guessed correctly, either a correct digit in the correct position (indicated by an X) or a correct digit in a wrong position (indicated by an O). The positions of the X and O markers do not mean anything, just the number of them. If the user fails to guess the answer in 10 tries, the computer reveals the solution. For example, in Figure 7-9, for the fifth guess (4618), the computer returns a value of "XO," meaning that one of the digits is correct and in the correct position, another digit is correct but in the wrong position, and the other two digits are wrong. By analyzing the results of each of the previous guesses and with a little deductive logic, the player usually can determine the correct answer.

In order for the game to work, the computer needs to keep track of the solution and each of the player's previous guesses. There is no particular need to keep this information on the server; the HTML form itself can maintain it in hidden fields. Figure 7-10 contains a listing of the servlet source code.

The same servlet is used to handle all aspects of the game, including generating the initial HTML page. The servlet figures out where it is in the game based on the contents of three hidden fields:

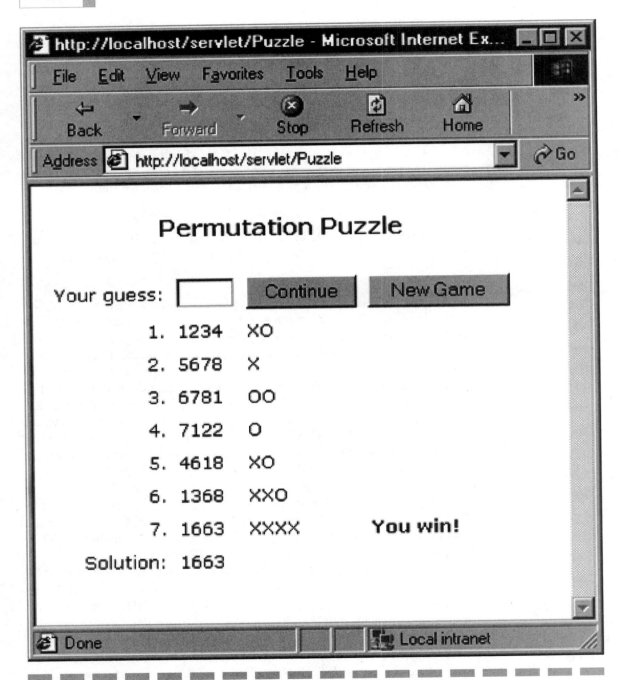

Figure 7-9 A number-guessing game that uses hidden fields to maintain state.

Figure 7-10

A listing of the permutation puzzle servlet.

```java
package ijs.session.hidden;

import java.io.*;
import java.net.*;
import java.util.*;

import javax.servlet.*;
import javax.servlet.http.*;

/**
 * PuzzleServlet
 */
public class PuzzleServlet extends HttpServlet
{
    public static final int LIMIT = 10;

    /**
     * Handles a GET request
     */
    public void doGet(
            HttpServletRequest request,
            HttpServletResponse response)
        throws ServletException, IOException
    {
        // Start the document

        response.setContentType("text/html");
        PrintWriter out = response.getWriter();

        out.println("<HTML>");
        out.println("<HEAD>");
        out.println("<TITLE>Puzzle</TITLE>");
        out.println("</HEAD>");
        out.println("<BODY>");

        // Start the form

        out.println("<FORM METHOD=POST ACTION=\""
            + request.getRequestURI() + "\">");

        // Start the table

        out.println("<TABLE BORDER=0 CELLPADDING=3>");
        out.println("<TR>");
        out.println("<TD ALIGN=CENTER COLSPAN=4>");
        out.println("<H3>Permutation Puzzle</H3>");
        out.println("</TD>");
        out.println("</TR>");

        // First row - prompt for the user's guess

        out.println("<TR>");
        out.println("<TD ALIGN=RIGHT>Your guess:</TD>");
        out.println("<TD ALIGN=LEFT>"
                + "<INPUT TYPE=TEXT NAME=\"guess\" SIZE=4>"
                + "</TD>");
        out.println("<TD>"
```

Figure 7-10
(Continued)

```
                              + "<INPUT TYPE=SUBMIT"
                              +      " NAME=\"btnContinue\""
                              +      " VALUE=\"Continue\""
                              + ">"
                              + "</TD>");
        out.println("<TD>"
                              + "<INPUT TYPE=SUBMIT"
                              +      " NAME=\"btnNewGame\""
                              +      " VALUE=\"New Game\""
                              + ">"
                              + "</TD>");
        out.println("</TR>");

        // Get the value of the new game button

        String btnNewGame = request.getParameter("btnNewGame");
        boolean newGame =
            (btnNewGame != null)
            && (btnNewGame.equals("New Game"));

        // See if the solution parameter exists.
        // If it does not, start a new game.

        String solution = request.getParameter("solution");
        if ((solution == null) || newGame) {

            // Create a new solution

            solution = "";
            for (int i = 0; i < 4; i++) {
                int n = 1 + (int) (Math.random() * 8);
                solution += Character.forDigit(n, 10);
            }

            // Write the solution as a hidden field

            out.println(
                "<INPUT TYPE=\"HIDDEN\""
                    + " NAME=\"solution\""
                    + " VALUE=\"" + solution + "\""
                    + ">");
        }
        else {

            // Extract all the previous guesses

            String parm = request.getParameter("nGuesses");
            if (parm == null)
                parm = "0";
            int nGuesses = Integer.parseInt(parm);
            Vector guesses = new Vector();
            for (int i = 0; i < nGuesses; i++)
                guesses.addElement
                (request.getParameter("guess." + i));

            // If the current guess is valid, add it to the list
```

```java
parm = request.getParameter("guess");
if (validGuess(parm))
    guesses.addElement(parm);

// Write the number of guesses as a hidden field

nGuesses = guesses.size();
out.println(
    "<INPUT TYPE=\"HIDDEN\""
        + " NAME=\"nGuesses\""
        + " VALUE=\"" + nGuesses + "\""
        + ">");

// Show the results of the previous guesses

boolean gameOver = (nGuesses >= LIMIT);

for (int i = 0; i < nGuesses; i++) {
    String guess = (String) guesses.elementAt(i);
    String match = getMatch(guess, solution);
    if (!gameOver)
        gameOver = match.equals("XXXX");

    out.println("<TR>");

    out.println("<TD ALIGN=RIGHT>");
    out.println((i+1) + ".");
    out.println("</TD>");

    out.println("<TD>");
    out.println(guess);

    // Rewrite the guess as a hidden field

    out.println(
        "<INPUT TYPE=\"HIDDEN\""
            + " NAME=\"guess." + i + "\""
            + " VALUE=\"" + guess + "\""
            + ">");

    out.println("</TD>");

    out.println("<TD>"
        + (match.equals("") ? " " : match)
        + "</TD>");

    out.println("<TD>"
        + (match.equals("XXXX")
            ? "<B>You win!</B>"
            : " ")
        + "</TD>");

    out.println("</TR>");
}

// If the game is over, show the solution
// otherwise write it as a hidden field
```

Figure 7-10
(Continued)

```
    if (gameOver) {
        out.println("<TR>");
        out.println("    <TD ALIGN=RIGHT>Solution:</TD>");
        out.println("    <TD>" + solution + "</TD>");
        out.println("    <TD> </TD>");
        out.println("    <TD> </TD>");
        out.println("</TR>");
    }
    else {
        out.println(
            "<INPUT TYPE=\"HIDDEN\""
                + " NAME=\"solution\""
                + " VALUE=\"" + .solution + "\""
                + ">");
    }
}


    // Finish the document

    out.println("</TABLE>");
    out.println("</FORM>");
    out.println("</BODY>");
    out.println("</HTML>");
}

/**
 * Returns true if the specified string is a
 * valid guess: exactly four digits, values 1-8
 */
public static final boolean validGuess(String s)
{
    if (s == null)
        return false;

    s = s.trim();
    if (s.length() != 4)
        return false;

    for (int i = 0; i < 4; i++) {
        char c = s.charAt(i);
        switch (c) {
            case '1': case '2': case '3': case '4':
            case '5': case '6': case '7': case '8':
                break;
            default:
                return false;
        }
    }

    return true;
}

/**
 * Returns an indication of how close the guess
 * is to the solution.  Each "X" indicates that
 * the guess contains a correct value in the
```

Figure 7-10
(Continued)

```
 * correct position.  Each "O" indicates that the
 * guess contains a correct value but that it is
 * in the wrong position.
 */
public static final String getMatch(
   String guess, String solution)
{
   StringBuffer result = new StringBuffer();
   StringBuffer guess2 = new StringBuffer();
   StringBuffer solution2 = new StringBuffer();

   for (int i = 0; i < 4; i++) {
      char cg = guess.charAt(i);
      char cs = solution.charAt(i);
      if (cg == cs)
         result.append("X");
      else {
         guess2.append(cg);
         solution2.append(cs);
      }
   }

   guess2.toString();
   solution2.toString();

   for (int i = 0; i < guess2.length(); i++) {
      char cg = guess2.charAt(i);
      for (int j = 0; j < solution2.length(); j++) {
         char cs = solution2.charAt(j);
         if (cg == cs) {
            result.append("O");
            solution2.setCharAt(j, (char) (0));
            break;
         }
      }
   }

   return result.toString();
}

/**
 * Handles a POST request
 */
public void doPost(
      HttpServletRequest request,
      HttpServletResponse response)
   throws ServletException, IOException
{
   doGet(request, response);
}
}
```

Field	Contents
solution	A string representing the 4-digit number the player is trying to guess.
nGuesses	The number of guesses the player has already made during this game.
guess.0,	The 4-digit guesses themselves.
guess.1,	
...,	
guess.<nGuesses-1>	

If the solution field is not present, the servlet knows that this must be the initial request of a new game. In this case, it randomly generates a new solution and stores it as a hidden field when it writes the form. Otherwise, the servlet retrieves the previous guesses from the other hidden fields: nGuesses to give the count and then guess.0, guess.1,...etc. for the guesses themselves. HTML has no notion of arrays of elements; we emulate an array by using numeric suffixes. If the current guess is valid (exactly four digits from one to eight), it is appended to the array. Then the array of guesses is printed and evaluated. If a solution is found, or if the number of entries exceeds the limit, the gameOver flag is set. At the end of the loop, if the gameOver flag is set, the solution is revealed. Otherwise, the solution is rewritten to the form as a hidden field

The advantage of hidden fields in this case is that the servlet engine is not required to keep track of the status of the game—the Web browser itself will do that. If there are hundreds of clients for an application, the performance implications may be significant.

Of course, as Figure 7-11 shows, the enterprising user need only invoke the View Source menu option to find the hidden fields and bring the game to a satisfying conclusion.

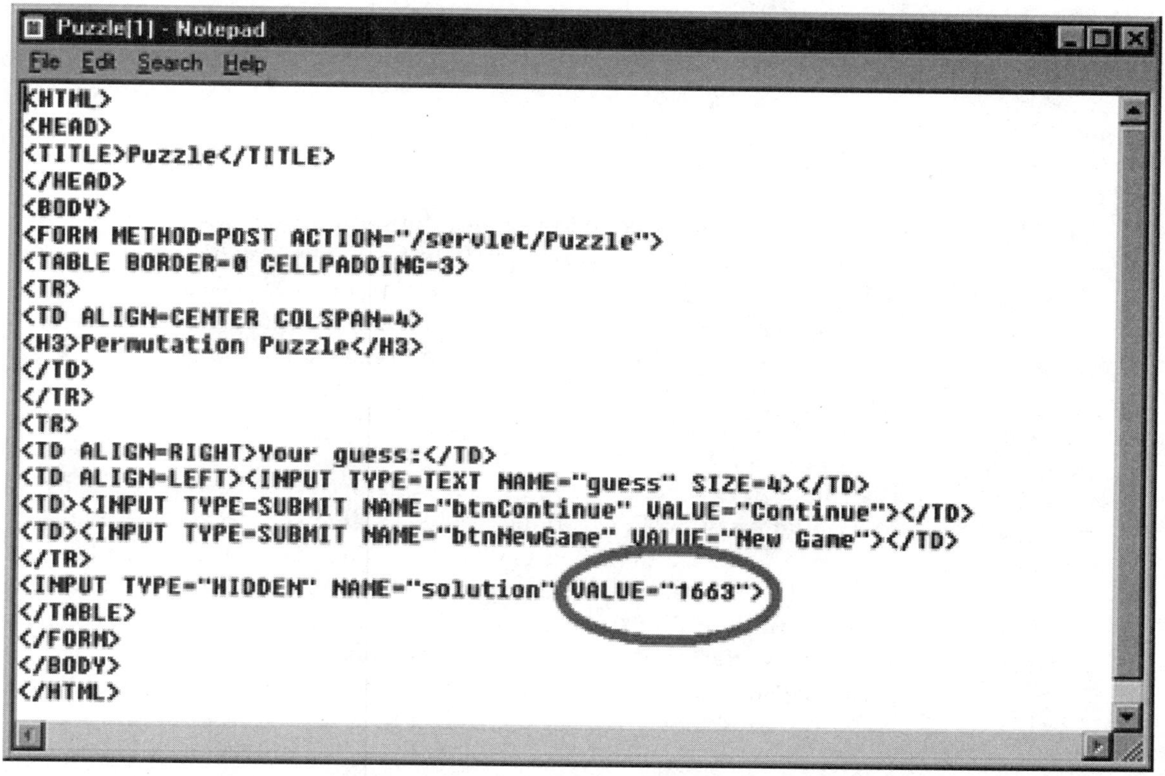

Figure 7-11 Cheating with View Source.

7.4 Saving State in Cookies

Problem

I need to save certain bits of information even after the user exits from the browser session so that I can access it the next time the user accesses my servlet. How can I do this?

Technique

Use the `HttpServletResponse addCookie()` method to tell the browser to store the information. When the user later accesses your Web site, you can read the cookie with the `HttpServletRequest` `getCookies()` method.

Discussion

A *cookie* is a small, named piece of information that is sent by the Web server and stored by the browser. It has a name, a value, an expiration date, and several optional fields. Every time the browser accesses the same Web site before the cookie's expiration date, it sends the name and value of the cookie back to the Web server. This is true even if the user has ended the browser session or even restarted the computer.

This is a very useful mechanism, but it is also a controversial one because of privacy considerations. Essentially, with cookies, a server has the capability of tracking the history of all access to its Web space by an individual browser. For example, the first time you access a Web site, it can assign you an identification number. Each time you access the site later, your browser will recognize the server address and send back the cookie with the identification number. Given this unique key, it can potentially maintain a database of the date and time of each access, what specific page you requested, the contents of any data entry fields, etc.

For this reason, some users decide to switch off the cookie-accepting mechanism in their browser. However, most users do not. Both Internet Explorer and Netscape Navigator accept cookies by default unless you turn off the capability (given that you can figure out how to do it!). The bottom line is that cookies usually work, but your application should handle the cases gracefully where they do not.

A Cookie Example   An example of where cookies can be useful is storing user preferences. If you have a multilingual front-end to your application, you may wish to allow users to select a preferred language. Later accesses to the front-end can detect the language preference and bypass the selection page. Figure 7-12 illustrates this technique.

When the user clicks a language selection button, the system knows to generate its subsequent messages in the selected language, as shown in Figure 7-13. If the user checks the "Remember This Selection" checkbox before clicking a language preference button, the servlet that processes the button click creates a new `javax.servlet.http.Cookie` and instructs your browser to store it:

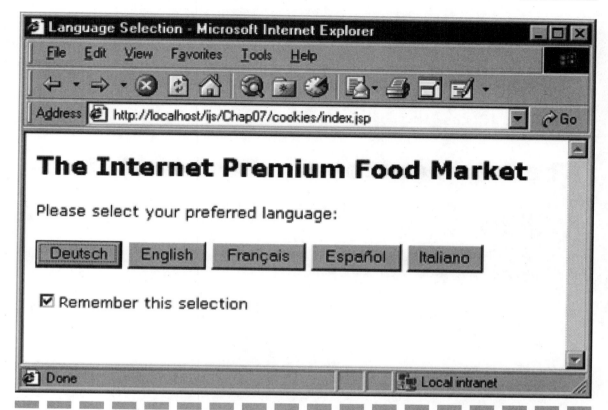

Figure 7-12 The language prompt in a multilanguage Web site.

```
String savePref = request.getParameter("savePref");
if (savePref != null) {
   if (savePref.equals("on")) {
      Cookie langPref = new Cookie("language", language);
      langPref.setMaxAge(120);
      response.addCookie(langPref);
   }
}
```

The HTTP header that the servlet generates looks like this:

```
Set-Cookie: language=Deutsch; expires=Mon, 18-Oct-1999 06:51:10 GMT
```

Later on, when the user again accesses the multilingual front-end, the browser sends the following HTTP header with the request

```
Cookie: language=Deutsch
```

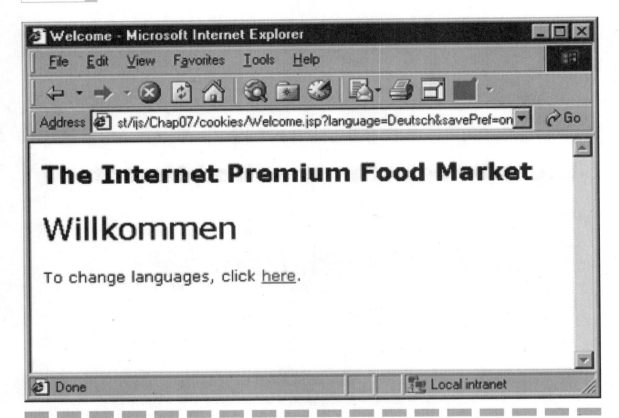

Figure 7-13 The German version of the welcome page.

The multilingual front-end servlet scans the request headers for a language cookie and redirects the browser to the appropriate page if it finds one.

```
Cookie[] cookies = request.getCookies();
if (cookies != null) {
    for (int i = 0; i < cookies.length; i++) {
        if (cookies[i].getName().equals("language")) {
            String language = cookies[i].getValue();
            response.sendRedirect(
                "/ijs/Chap07/cookies/Welcome.jsp"
                + "?language=" + URLEncoder.encode(language)
                );
            return;
        }
    }
}
```

All the user sees is the customized German language page.

It should be noted that this section deals with cookies that you create and use explicitly. Servlet engines also use cookies to save the session ID between requests, but this is ordinarily something that you do not need to concern yourself with.

See Also

The original Netscape specification for cookies can be found at *http://home.netscape.com/newsref/std/cookie_spec.html*. See also RFC2109 "HTTP State Management Mechanism" at *http://www.freesoft.org/CIE/RFC/Orig/rfc2109.txt*.

7.5 URL Rewriting

Problem

My application has to work with some browsers that do not support cookies. What can I do?

Technique

Use URL rewriting to pass the session ID back and forth. Pass all the URLs that you generate through the `HttpServletResponse` `encodeURL()` or `encodeRedirectURL()`.

Discussion

In terms of session management, the servlet engine does most of the work. After all, the `HttpSession` and all the objects it contains are Java objects, and you are ordinarily dealing with a non-Java client (namely, a Web browser). If there is any Java work to be done, it has to be done on the server.

Thus the Web server creates and maintains a hashtable of active sessions keyed by unique session IDs that it assigns. The only thing the client side of the application has to remember is its own session ID. As long as the client can pass back its session ID with each request, the server can do the rest.

There are two ways for the client to do this:

■ *In a cookie.* If there is an active session, the server sends a `Set-Cookie` header containing the session ID each time it sends an HTTP response. If the client accepts the cookie, it passes it back to the server with the each subsequent request until the cookie expires.

■ *In a request parameter.* Just like any other input element in a form, the session ID can be passed back in the query string. However, the client does not know that it has to do this. In order for this to work, the server (translation: you, the servlet programmer) has to embed the session ID parameter in each URL that a user might click.

Fortunately, the `HttpServletResponse` interface provides two methods[5] that make this all transparent to the programmer:

```
encodeURL(String url)
```

You should pass any URLs that you write to a document through `encodeURL()`, which will determine whether the URL needs to be modified or not. Servlet engines vary in how they implement this, but basically, the algorithm is this:

```
Return the URL unmodified if any of the following are true:

1. There is no current session.

2. The session ID came from a cookie. If the client has
   already indicated that it supports cookies, there is
   no need to pack the session ID into the URL.

3. The URL already contains the session ID key.

Otherwise, append ?<sessionIDkey>=<sessionID> to the URL
(using & instead of ? if the URL already has parameters).
encodeRedirectURL(String url).
```

---

[5]There are also two deprecated methods named `encodeUrl()` and `encodeRedirectUrl()`, whose sole transgression is that their names contain "Url" in mixed case. Most servlet engines implement them simply as one-line calls to `encodeURL()` and `encodeRedirectURL()`, respectively.

You should pass any URLs referenced in a `sendRedirect()` through `encodeRedirectURL()`. There are two different methods because the encoding rules are slightly different in this case:

```
Return the URL unmodified if either of the following are true:

1. There is no current session.

2. The URL does not contain the current server name.
   (If another web server will be handling the request,
   it won't know anything about our session, so what
   would it do with the session ID?

Otherwise, append ?<sessionIDkey>=<sessionID> to the URL
as described above.
```

7.6   HTTP Session Binding Events

Problem

My application allocates resources that need to be released when a user is no longer connected. How can I tell when a user has terminated a session?

Technique

Have your application resources implement the `HttpSession-BindingListener` interface. This will allow them to receive notification when they are bound or unbound from a session.

Discussion

This is a thorny problem in general. If you have a natural stopping point at which the user explicitly quits the application, you can release resources at that point. For example, a shopping cart application typically has a checkout page with a "Click Here to Place Your Order" button. After the "Thank you for your order" page, you can clear the shopping cart and remove it from the session.

However, if the user just wanders off to another Web site and never comes back, you need a way to be notified so that you can shut down the database connection. The only reasonable possibility is some kind of timeout. However, you cannot just check the time between requests if there never is another request. You could start a background timer thread, but this adds complexity to your application and consumes more resources.

The Servlet API provides a convenient means for handling this problem in a general way. When an object is added to an HttpSession (with the session.putValue() method[6]), the session checks to see whether the object implements the HttpSessionBindingListener interface. If so, the session calls the object's valueBound() method, passing it an HttpSessionBindingEvent object identifying the session and the object's name in the session, as shown below:

```
public class MyResource implements HttpSessionBindingListener
{
    ...
    public void valueBound(HttpSessionBindingEvent event)
    {
        // We now belong to a session. We can communicate
        // with other objects in the session by name

        HttpSession session = event.getSession();
        Object otherObject = session.getValue("otherObject");
        ...
    }
    public void valueUnbound(HttpSessionBindingEvent event)
    {
        // Time to shut down
    }
}
```

When the object is removed from a session, the object's valueUnbound() method is called. This can happen as a result of any of four events:

1. The object is explicitly unbound with session.removeValue().

2. The object is replaced by another session.putValue() with the same name.

3. The session is explicitly invalidated by the servlet calling session.invalidate().

---

[6]The putValue() and getValue() methods have been deprecated in Servlet API 2.2 in favor of two new setAttribute() and getAttribute() methods. This is only to establish more consistent naming conventions; the new methods do not change the functionality.

4. The session times out by exceeding its `MaxInactiveInterval` time value with no user requests.

Invalidating an entire session can have the undesirable side effect of corrupting another servlet application that happens to be sharing the session. Adding and removing individual objects that implement this interface presents a safer way to free resources.

A Complete Example   There is much valuable information that can be mined from session activity. For example, details about the time of day and length of time users spend in an application can be used to build statistical models that forecast server demand. Server logs keep some of this information, but at the wrong level of detail in this case. The logs keep track of HTTP requests but cannot group related requests into what we know are application sessions.

However, the servlet engine knows when sessions start and end. It also knows when objects are bound and unbound from sessions, sending `valueBound` and `valueUnbound` events to those objects which implement `HttpSessionBindingListener`. We can use this capability to develop a session monitor that keeps track of sessions and logs their characteristics.

Figure 7-14 contains the source listing of a `SessionMonitor` class that is designed for this purpose. A servlet voluntarily participates in the session monitoring by binding the monitor to its session at application start and unbinding it at application end. The monitor implements `HttpSessionBindingListener`, which means that its `valueBound()` method will be called when a servlet adds the monitor to a session. When this occurs, the `event` parameter passed to `valueBound()` allows the monitor to find the `HttpSession` that generated the event. The monitor stores the session in a hashtable keyed by the session ID. When the monitor is removed from a session, or when the session times out or is invalidated by a servlet, the monitor's `valueUnbound()` method is called. Again, the `event` parameter points to the session, allowing the monitor to remove the session from its tracking hashtable. At this point, the monitor can determine the time it was bound to the session and write this information to the log. A single instance of the `SessionMonitor` is created whenever its class is first loaded. This instance is made available through a static `newInstance()` method.

`SessionMonitor` is a background class that has no user interface. We can provide it with a Web-based interface using the `MonitorAdmin` servlet listed in Figure 7-15.

Figure 7-14
Source code for
the Session-
Monitor.

```java
package ijs.session.binding;

import java.io.*;
import java.net.*;
import java.text.*;
import java.util.*;

import javax.servlet.*;
import javax.servlet.http.*;

/**
 * The <CODE>SessionMonitor</CODE> is an object
 * that monitors HTTP sessions used by participating
 * servlets.  It keeps track of a list of active
 * sessions, and writes information about their
 * creation time and duration to a log.
 * <P>
 * Servlets must voluntarily participate in the
 * monitoring.  They do this by adding the
 * <CODE>SessionMonitor</CODE> to an HTTP session.
 * This results in <CODE>valueBound</CODE> and
 * <CODE>valueUnbound</CODE> events being sent to
 * the monitor for each session.
 * <P>
 * The session tracking log is started and stopped
 * by the <CODE>openLog()</CODE> and
 * <CODE>closeLog</CODE> methods, respectively.
 */
public class SessionMonitor
    implements HttpSessionBindingListener
{
    // =========================================
    //     Class methods
    // =========================================

    public static final SessionMonitor getInstance()
    {
        return instance;
    }

    // =========================================
    //     Class variables
    // =========================================

    /**
     * The single instance of SessionMonitor
     */
    private static final SessionMonitor instance
        = new SessionMonitor();

    private static final DateFormat datefmt
        = new SimpleDateFormat("yyyy/MM/dd HH:mm:ss:SSS");

    // =========================================
    //     Constructors
    // =========================================
```

Figure 7-14
(Continued)

```java
/**
 * The constructor is private because we want other
 * classes to use the getInstance() factory method.
 */
private SessionMonitor()
{
   sessions = new Hashtable();
}

// =============================================
//    Instance methods
// =============================================

/**
 * Adds a new session to the list
 */
public void valueBound(HttpSessionBindingEvent event)
{
   HttpSession session = event.getSession();
   String id = session.getId();

   synchronized(sessions) {
      sessions.put(id, session);
   }
}

/**
 * Removes a session from the list and
 * calculates its statistics
 */
public void valueUnbound(HttpSessionBindingEvent event)
{
   // Get the ID of the session to be unbound

   HttpSession session = event.getSession();
   String id = session.getId();
   HttpSession originalSession = null;

   synchronized(sessions) {

      // Retrieve the matching session object from
      // the sessions hashtable

      originalSession = (HttpSession) sessions.get(id);

      // Remove it

      sessions.remove(id);
   }

   // If the original session was found
   // and the log writer is active
   // then write a log record with the creation
   // time and total elasped time

   if ((originalSession != null) && (isLogging())) {
```

Figure 7-14
(Continued)

```java
        long create  = originalSession.getCreationTime();
        long now     = System.currentTimeMillis();
        double elapsed = (now - create) / 1000.0;

        Date createDate = new Date(create);
        String szCreateDate = datefmt.format(createDate);

        // Write the creation date and the elapsed time
        // in seconds to the log.

        logWriter.println(szCreateDate + "\t"
           + "session elapsed time: "
           + elapsed + " seconds");
        logWriter.flush();
     }
}

/**
 * Returns the number of active sessions
 */
public int getActiveSessionCount()
{
   return sessions.size();
}

/**
 * Returns a list of session ID's
 */
public Enumeration getIds()
{
   return sessions.keys();
}

/**
 * Returns the specified session
 */
public HttpSession getSession(String id)
{
   return (HttpSession) sessions.get(id);
}

/**
 * Opens the log writer
 */
public synchronized void openLog(String fileName)
   throws IOException
{
   // Reject the request if a log is already
   // active

   if (isLogging())
      throw new IOException
      ("Log already open");

   // Save the file name and assign the start time

   logFileName = fileName;
```

Figure 7-14
(Continued)

```java
    logStartTime = System.currentTimeMillis();

    // Format the date for printing in the log

    String szDate = datefmt.format(new Date(logStartTime));

    // Start the log writer and log the start message

    logWriter = new PrintWriter(new FileWriter(fileName));
    logWriter.println(szDate + "\tlog opened");
    logWriter.flush();
}

/**
* Closes the log writer
*/
public synchronized void closeLog()
    throws IOException
{
    // Ignore the request if logging is not active

    if (isLogging()) {

        // Assign the stop time and format it
        // for printing in the log

        long now = System.currentTimeMillis();
        double elapsed = (now - logStartTime) / 1000.0;
        String szDate = datefmt.format(new Date(now));

        // Log the elapsed time and the close message

        logWriter.println(szDate + "\t"
            + "log elapsed time: "
            + elapsed + " seconds");
        logWriter.println(szDate + "\tlog closed");

        // Close the log

        logWriter.flush();
        logWriter.close();

        // Reset the logging attributes

        logStartTime = 0;
        logWriter = null;
        logFileName = null;
    }
}

/**
* Returns true if the log is open
*/
public synchronized boolean isLogging()
{
    return (logWriter != null);
}
```

Figure 7-14
(Continued)

```
/**
 * Returns the log start time
 */
public long getLogStartTime()
{
    return logStartTime;
}


/**
 * Returns the log file name
 */
public String getLogFileName()
{
    return logFileName;
}



// ==============================================
//     Instance variables
// ==============================================

private Hashtable sessions;
private long logStartTime;
private PrintWriter logWriter;
private String logFileName;
}
```

The `MonitorAdmin` servlet shows the instance, status, and log file name of the `SessionMonitor`. It allows the user to open and close the log and to view the list of all active participating sessions. Figure 7-16 shows how it looks when it is first invoked.

After the file name is specified and the user clicks the "Open" button, the administrative servlet invokes the monitor's `openLog()` method and reports back on the monitor's status (Figure 7-17).

To provide sample input for the monitor, we can use the `Monitored` servlet listed in Figure 7-18. After starting a session, this servlet attaches the monitor with one line of code:

```
session.putValue("monitor", SessionMonitor.getInstance());
```

After performing whatever application-related work needs to be done, the servlet removes the monitor from its session as follows:

```
session.removeValue("monitor");
```

`MonitoredServlet` does not really do anything except this, but it illustrates the technique.

Figure 7-15

Source code for the Monitor-Admin servlet.

```java
package ijs.session.binding;

import java.io.*;
import java.util.*;
import javax.servlet.*;
import javax.servlet.http.*;

/**
 * A servlet that can be used to start or stop
 * the <CODE>SessionMonitor</CODE>.
 */
public class MonitorAdminServlet extends HttpServlet
{
    public void doGet(
        HttpServletRequest request,
        HttpServletResponse response)
        throws ServletException, IOException
    {
        // Start the output document

        response.setContentType("text/html");
        PrintWriter out = response.getWriter();

        out.println("<HTML>");
        out.println("<HEAD>");
        out.println("<TITLE>Session Monitor</TITLE>");
        out.println("</HEAD>");
        out.println("<BODY>");
        out.println("<FORM"
                    + " METHOD=GET"
                    + " ACTION=\""
                    + request.getRequestURI()
                    + "\""
                    + ">");

        // Start of first table

        out.println("<TABLE"
                    + " BORDER=0"
                    + " CELLPADDING=4"
                    + " CELLSPACING=2"
                    + " WIDTH=80%"
                    + ">");

        // Get a reference to the monitor, which is a single
        // instance accessed by a class method

        SessionMonitor monitor = SessionMonitor.getInstance();

        // Get the monitor status

        String status = "Closed";
        if (monitor.isLogging()) {
            status = "Open since "
                + new Date(monitor.getLogStartTime());
        }
```

Figure 7-15
(Continued)

```
// Perform requested action, if any

String action = request.getParameter("action");
String fileName = request.getParameter("fileName");
if (fileName != null)
    action = "open";

if (action != null) {

    // Start logging if requested

    if (!monitor.isLogging() && action.equals("open")) {
        if (fileName != null) {
            try {
                monitor.openLog(fileName);
                status = "Opened at "
                    + new Date(monitor.getLogStartTime());
            }
            catch (IOException e) {
                status = e.getMessage();
            }
        }
    }

    // Stop logging if requested

    else
    if (monitor.isLogging() && action.equals("close")) {
        monitor.closeLog();
        status = "Closed";
    }
}

// Generate the table

out.println("<TR>");
out.println("<TD"
            + " ALIGN=CENTER"
            + " COLSPAN=2"
            + " BGCOLOR="
            + COLORS[2]
            + ">");
out.println("<FONT SIZE=+1>");
out.println("<B>Session Monitor</B>");
out.println("</FONT>");
out.println("</TD>");
out.println("</TR>");
int row = 0;

// Instance name

out.println("<TR>");
out.println("<TD"
            + " ALIGN=RIGHT"
            + " BGCOLOR="
            + COLORS[row % 2]
            + ">");
```

Figure 7-15
(Continued)

```
out.println("Instance:");
out.println("</TD>");
out.println("<TD"
            + " ALIGN=LEFT"
            + " BGCOLOR="
            + COLORS[row % 2]
            + ">");
out.println("<B>" + monitor + "</B>");
out.println("</TD>");
out.println("</TR>");
row++;

// Status

out.println("<TR>");
out.println("<TD"
            + " ALIGN=RIGHT"
            + " BGCOLOR="
            + COLORS[row % 2]
            + ">");
out.println("Status:");
out.println("</TD>");
out.println("<TD"
            + " ALIGN=LEFT"
            + " BGCOLOR="
            + COLORS[row % 2]
            + ">");
out.println("<B>" + status + "</B>");
out.println("</TD>");
out.println("</TR>");
row++;

// Log file name

out.println("<TR>");
out.println("<TD"
            + " ALIGN=RIGHT"
            + " VALIGN=TOP"
            + " BGCOLOR="
            + COLORS[row % 2]
            + ">");
out.println("Log file name:");
out.println("</TD>");

// If the monitor is already logging,
// show the file name and allow the user
// to click the close button

if (monitor.isLogging()) {
   out.println("<TD"
            + " ALIGN=LEFT"
            + " BGCOLOR="
            + COLORS[row % 2]
            + ">");
   out.println("<B>");
   out.println(monitor.getLogFileName());
   out.println("</B>");
```

Figure 7-15
(Continued)

```
         out.println("<BR>");
         out.println("<INPUT"
                     + " TYPE=\"SUBMIT\""
                     + " NAME=\"action\""
                     + " VALUE=\"close\""
                     + ">");
         out.println("</TD>");
}

// Otherwise, prompt for the file name

else {
   out.println("<TD"
                     + " ALIGN=LEFT"
                     + " BGCOLOR="
                     + COLORS[row % 2]
                     + ">");
   out.println("<INPUT"
                     + " TYPE=\"TEXT\""
                     + " NAME=\"fileName\""
                     + " SIZE=32"
                     + ">");
   out.println("<BR>");
   out.println("<INPUT"
                     + " TYPE=\"SUBMIT\""
                     + " NAME=\"action\""
                     + " VALUE=\"open\""
                     + ">");
   out.println("</TD>");
}
out.println("</TR>");
row++;

// End of first table

out.println("</TABLE>");
out.println("<P>");

// Start of second table

out.println("<TABLE"
                     + " BORDER=0"
                     + " CELLPADDING=4"
                     + " CELLSPACING=2"
                     + " WIDTH=80%"
                     + ">");

out.println("<TR>");
out.println("<TD"
                     + " ALIGN=CENTER"
                     + " COLSPAN=2"
                     + " BGCOLOR="
                     + COLORS[2]
                     + ">");
out.println("<FONT SIZE=+1>");
out.println("<B>Active Sessions</B>");
out.println("</FONT>");
```

Figure 7-15
(Continued)

```
out.println("</TD>");
out.println("</TR>");

// Show the active sessions

int nActive = monitor.getActiveSessionCount();
if (nActive == 0) {
   out.println("<TR>");
   out.println("<TD"
               + " ALIGN=CENTER"
               + " BGCOLOR="
               + COLORS[0]
               + " COLSPAN=2"
               + ">");
   out.println("None");
   out.println("</TD>");
   out.println("</TR>");
}

else {
   out.println("<TR>");
   out.println("<TD"
               + " ALIGN=RIGHT"
               + " BGCOLOR="
               + COLORS[0]
               + ">");
   out.println("Count:");
   out.println("</TD>");
   out.println("<TD"
               + " ALIGN=LEFT"
               + " BGCOLOR="
               + COLORS[0]
               + ">");
   out.println("<B>" + nActive + "</B>");
   out.println("</TD>");
   out.println("</TR>");

   // Get an enumeration of the session ID's of
   // all active sessions

   Enumeration es = monitor.getIds();

   // Print each one:

   row = 1;
   while (es.hasMoreElements()) {

      // Extract the ID

      String id = (String) es.nextElement();

      // Retrieve the user session object

      HttpSession userSession = monitor.getSession(id);

      // Get the dates
```

Figure 7-15
(Continued)

```
Date creation = new Date(
    userSession.getCreationTime());
Date lastAccessed = new Date(
    userSession.getLastAccessedTime());

out.println("<TR>");

// Label

out.println("<TD"
            + " ALIGN=RIGHT"
            + " VALIGN=TOP"
            + " BGCOLOR="
            + COLORS[row % 2]
            + ">");
out.println(row);
out.println("</TD>");

// Details

out.println("<TD"
            + " ALIGN=LEFT"
            + " VALIGN=TOP"
            + " BGCOLOR="
            + COLORS[row % 2]
            + ">");
out.println(
    "<TABLE BORDER=0 CELLPADDING=3>"
    + "<TR>"
    + "<TD>ID:</TD>"
    + "<TD>" + id + "</TD>"
    + "</TR>"
    + "<TR>"
    + "<TD>Creation time:</TD>"
    + "<TD>" + creation + "</TD>"
    + "</TR>"
    + "<TR>"
    + "<TD>Last accessed time:</TD>"
    + "<TD>" + lastAccessed + "</TD>"
    + "</TR>"
    + "</TABLE>"
);
out.println("</TD>");

out.println("</TR>");
row++;
    }
}
row++;

// End of second table

out.println("</TABLE>");

// End of document

out.println("</FORM>");
```

Figure 7-15
(Continued)

```
        out.println("</BODY>");
        out.println("</HTML>");
    }

    public static final String[] COLORS = {
        "#F0F0F0", "#E0E0E0", "#C0C0C0", "#FFFFFF"
    };
}
```

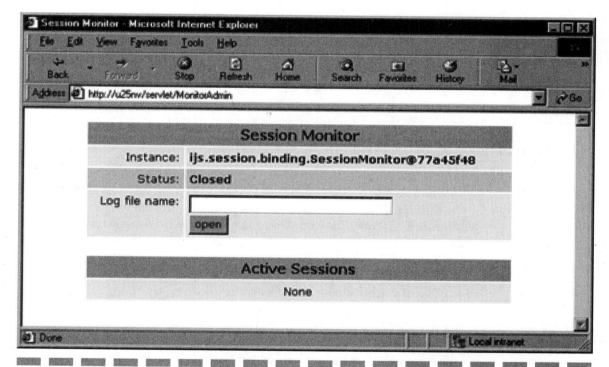

Figure 7-16 The MonitorAdmin servlet when it is first invoked.

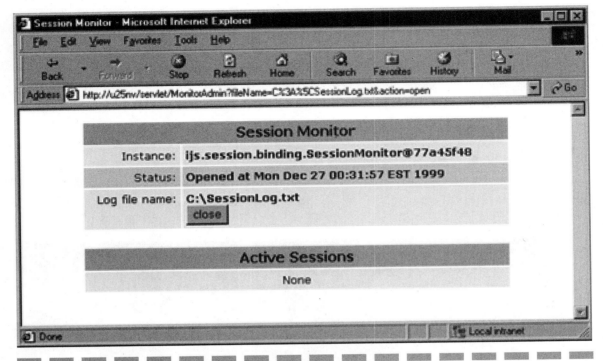

Figure 7-17 The `MonitorAdmin` servlet after the log is opened.

When `MonitoredServlet` is invoked (Figure 7-19), it reports back the session ID, which is 94627281611310043 in this case. If we click the browser's "Refresh" button where the administrative servlet is running, we see the new session listed (Figure 7-20). Note that the session has not yet been joined by the client, which results in last accessed time being zero.[7]

After the user clicks the "Continue" button, the `Monitored` servlet joins the session, as shown in Figure 7-21. When we refresh the administrative servlet, we see the updated access time (Figure 7-22).

If we invoke another instance of the `MonitoredServlet` (not shown here), we get a second session added to the list seen in Figure 7-23.

When the sessions are terminated and the monitor is shut down, the log file contains the information shown in Figure 7-24, which includes

---

[7]The creation time and last accessed time are reported as the number of milliseconds since January 1, 1970.

Figure 7-18

Source code for
the Monitored-
Servlet.

```java
package ijs.session.binding;

import java.io.*;
import java.net.*;
import java.util.*;

import javax.servlet.*;
import javax.servlet.http.*;

/**
* MonitoredServlet
* <P>
* Illustrates the use of the SessionMonitor
* <P>
* Starts a session, lets the user join it,
* then stop the session after the next request.
*/
public class MonitoredServlet extends HttpServlet
{
    public void doGet(
            HttpServletRequest request,
            HttpServletResponse response)
        throws ServletException, IOException
    {
        SessionMonitor monitor;
        int count;
        String parm;

        response.setContentType("text/html");
        PrintWriter out = response.getWriter();

        // Headings

        out.println(""
            + "<HTML>"
            + "<HEAD>"
            + "<TITLE>MonitoredServlet</TITLE>"
            + "</HEAD>"
            + "<BODY>"
            + "<H3>MonitoredServlet</H3>"
            + "<FORM ACTION=\"" + request.getRequestURI() + "\">"
            );

        // Access the current session (or create one)

        HttpSession session = request.getSession(true);

        // Get the click count

        count = 0;
        parm = request.getParameter("count");
        if (parm != null)
            count = Integer.parseInt(parm);

        // Perform the appropriate action

        switch (count) {
```

Figure 7-18
(Continued)

```
// First click - bind the monitor

case 0:
    monitor = SessionMonitor.getInstance();
    session.putValue("monitor", monitor);
    out.println (
        "New session "
        + session.getId()
        + " started");
    count = 1;
    break;

// Other clicks - perform some useful work

case 1:
    out.println("In session " + session.getId());
    count = 2;
    break;

// Finally - unbind the monitor

case 2:
    out.println("Leaving session " + session.getId());
    session.removeValue("monitor");
    session.invalidate();
    count = 0;
    break;
}

// End of page

out.println("<P>");
out.println("<INPUT TYPE=HIDDEN NAME=count VALUE="
    + count + ">");
out.println("<INPUT TYPE=SUBMIT VALUE=Continue>");
out.println("</FORM>");
out.println("</BODY></HTML>");
}
}
```

the starting time and elapsed time of each of the MonitoredServlet sessions. This log file can then be used as input to a data-mining application that can make use of the session information.

The example we have considered here tracks only the start time and elapsed time of each session. However, the monitor and its participating servlets can easily be extended to place other application-specific information in the session, such as product numbers or Web page URLs. This information can be extracted from the session by the monitor and added to the log file for more in-depth analysis.

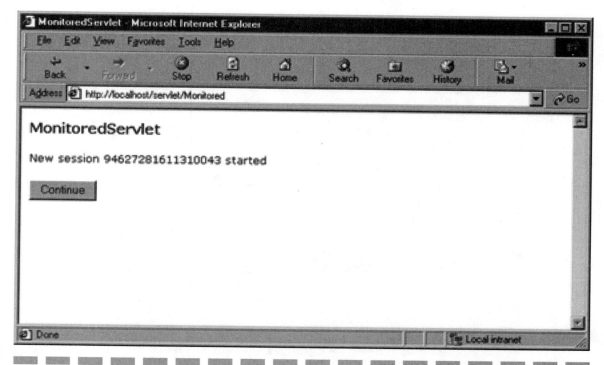

Figure 7-19 The monitored servlet when it is first invoked.

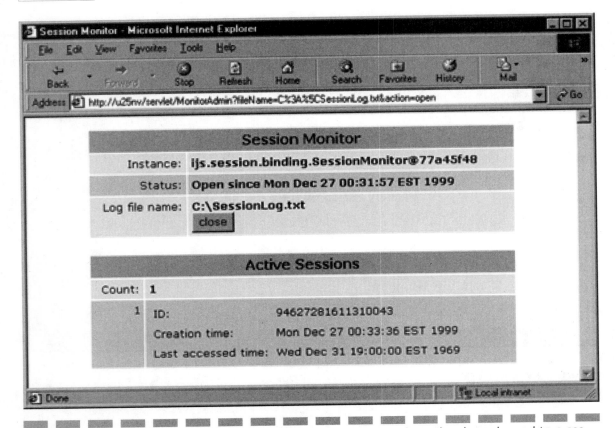

Figure 7-20 The MonitorAdmin servlet after the SessionMonitor has been bound to a session.

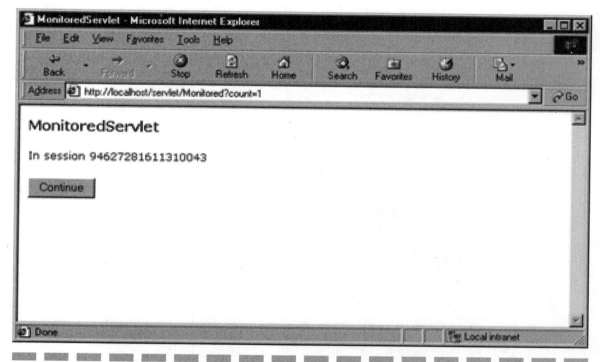

Figure 7-21 The monitored servlet after it joins the session.

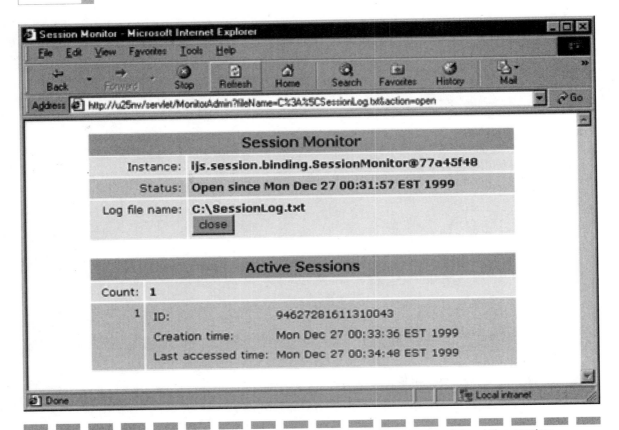

Figure 7-22 The `MonitorAdmin` servlet after the monitored servlet has joined the session.

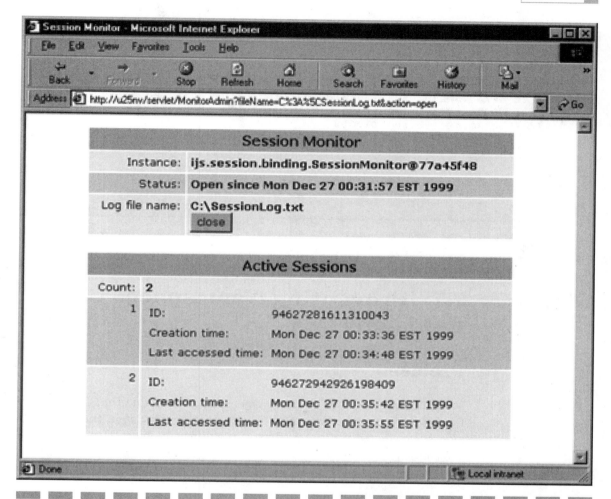

Figure 7-23 The `MonitorAdmin` servlet after a second monitored servlet has joined the session.

```
SessionLog.txt - Notepad
File  Edit  Search  Help
1999/12/27  00:31:57:552  log opened
1999/12/27  00:35:42:926  session elapsed time: 43.973 seconds
1999/12/27  00:33:36:113  session elapsed time: 176.905 seconds
1999/12/27  00:36:40:158  log elapsed time: 282.606 seconds
1999/12/27  00:36:40:158  log closed
```

Figure 7-24 The log produced by the `SessionMonitor`.

7.7 Preventing Namespace Collisions

Problem

My shopping cart servlet stores objects in a hashtable that I bind to an `HttpSession` under the name "cart." Another servlet in the same session, however, uses the name "cart" for a different object. How can I avoid the conflict?

Technique

Add the fully qualified package name of your servlet as a prefix to the names of all objects you store in a session.

Discussion

There is only one `HttpSession` object at a time per user per browser on a given Web server. If your Web site has multiple servlets that use sessions and the user happens to run them at the same time, it is possible that more than one servlet will use the same name for an object in the session. You can avoid this problem by making your object names unique. The most straightforward way of doing this is to prefix your names with the fully qualified package name of your servlet:

```
package ijs.session.demo;
...
public class DemoServlet extends HttpServlet
{
   public void doGet(
        HttpServletRequest request,
        HttpServletResponse response)
      throws ServletException, IOException
   {
      HttpSession session = request.getSession(true);
      ShoppingCart cart = new ShoppingCart();
      session.putValue("ijs.session.demo.cart", cart);
      ...
   }
}
```

This will work even if other servlets do not use the same naming convention (unless they go out of their way to use *your* names, of course!)

7.8   A Shopping Cart Application

Problem

How can I write a shopping cart application using servlets?

Technique

Develop a `ShoppingCart` object that holds items to be purchased, storing it in an HTTP session. Provide methods to add and delete items, to enumerate items, and to calculate order totals.

Discussion

We round out this chapter with a complete example, a shopping cart application. Figure 7-25 shows the data flow. In the diagram, the circles represent servlets, and the labeled rectangles represent the Web pages that they generate. Inside the rectangles are buttons for each function on the page with arrows showing which servlets get invoked.

Figure 7-25
Data flow diagram
of the shopping
cart application.

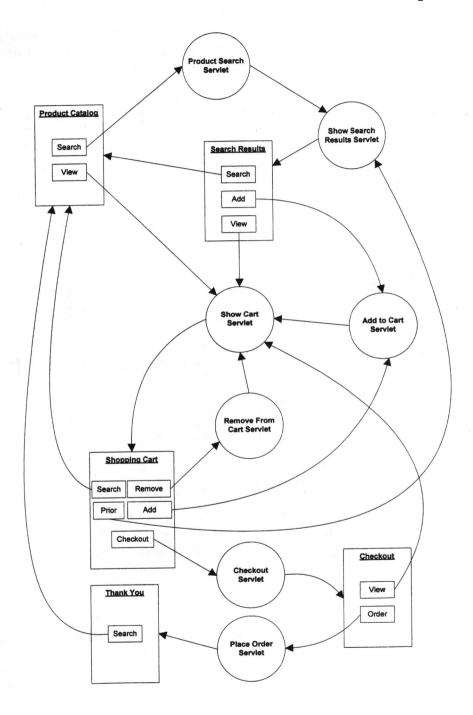

Figure 7-26 shows the starting point—a place for the user to enter search keywords, a product type, and a price range. The user can view the current contents of the shopping cart (which is empty at this point, although it may not be when the user later returns to this page) by clicking the "View Cart" button. Otherwise, the user clicks "Submit" to start the search.

Figure 7-27 lists the servlet that processes the request. After parsing the search criteria and running the database inquiry, it invokes the ShowSearchResults servlet, which produces the Web page shown in Figure 7-28. The ShowSearchResults servlet listing is found in Figure 7-29. It stores its search results in the session.

From the search results page, the user can either discard the results and perform a new search, view the current contents of the shopping cart (still empty at this point), or add one of the listed items to the cart. If the user clicks on the shopping cart icon to the right of the "Chocolate-Covered Strawberries" item, the AddToCart servlet is invoked (see source listing in Figure 7-30). This servlet has no visual component; it calls the shopping cart's put method to add the item and then redirects the browser to the ShowCart servlet (Figure 7-31). The resulting Web page is shown in Figure 7-32.

From ShowCart, the user can perform five different functions:

1. Return to the original product search page to search for a different product

2. Return to the most recent search results page to select another related item

3. Add to the quantity of an item

4. Subtract from the quantity of an item

5. Proceed to checkout

If the user chooses the last option (proceed to checkout), the Checkout servlet calculates the order total and displays the Web page shown in Figure 7-33. The source code for Checkout servlet is found in Figure 7-34.

Finally, the PlaceOrder servlet (not shown) performs the actual transaction and thanks the user for the order, as shown in Figure 7-35.

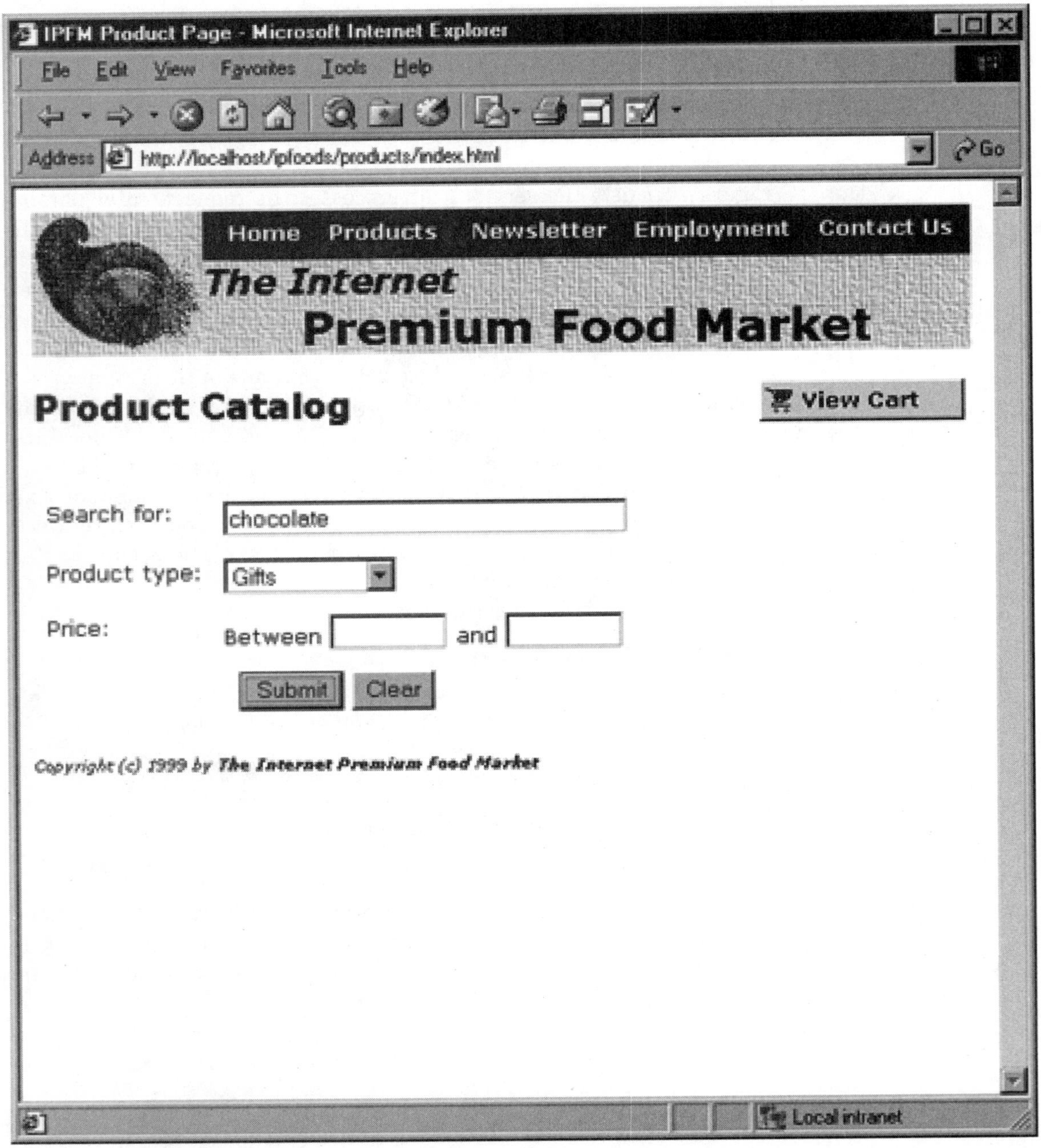

Figure 7-26 The product search page.

Figure 7-27

The product search servlet.

```java
package ipfoods;

import java.io.*;
import java.net.*;
import java.sql.*;
import java.text.*;
import java.util.*;

import javax.servlet.*;
import javax.servlet.http.*;

/**
 * ProductSearchServlet
 */
public class ProductSearchServlet extends HttpServlet
{
    /**
     * Given a search request, finds the set of products
     * that match the request and formats them as an HTML
     * table.
     *
     * @param request the servlet request object
     * @param response the servlet response object
     * @exception ServletException if a servlet exception occurs
     * @exception IOException if an I/O exception occurs
     */
    public void doGet(
            HttpServletRequest request,
            HttpServletResponse response)
        throws ServletException, IOException
    {
        try {

            // Get or create the session

            HttpSession session = request.getSession(true);

            // Get the catalog object from the session.

            Catalog catalog = (Catalog)
                session.getValue("catalog");

            if (catalog == null) {

                // If no catalog object exists in the session,
                // create a new one and store it in the session.
                // Note that this will create a database
                // connection.

                catalog = new Catalog();
                session.putValue("catalog", catalog);
            }

            // Build the query string based on the parameters
            // in the form

            String query = "";
```

Figure 7-27
(Continued)

```
int nbrAnds = 0;

// All types or one specific type

String type = request.getParameter("type");
if ((type != null) && (!type.equals("A"))) {
    nbrAnds++;
    if (nbrAnds > 1)
        query += " AND";
    query += " (itemCode like '" + type + "%')";
}

// All words in the search string

String keywords = request.getParameter("keywords");
StringTokenizer st =
    new StringTokenizer(keywords, " ");
nbrAnds++;
if (nbrAnds > 1)
    query += " AND";
query += " (";
int nbrOrs = 0;
while (st.hasMoreTokens()) {
    String token = st.nextToken().toUpperCase();
    token = Util.escape(token);
    nbrOrs++;
    if (nbrOrs > 1)
        query += " OR";
    query += " (itemDesc like '%" + token + "%')";
}
if (nbrOrs == 0)
    throw new RuntimeException
    ("No keywords were specified");
query += " )";

// Upper and lower bounds for the price

String priceString;
long loPrice = 0;
long hiPrice = 0;

// Low price

priceString = request.getParameter("loPrice");
if (priceString != null) {
    priceString = priceString.trim();
    if (!priceString.equals("")) {
        try {
            loPrice = Util.fromCurrencyString
                (priceString);
            nbrAnds++;
            if (nbrAnds > 1)
                query += " AND";
            query += " (price >= " + loPrice + ")";
        }
        catch (ParseException e) {
```

Figure 7-27

(Continued)

```
                                   throw new RuntimeException
                                   (priceString + " is not numeric");
                    }
                }
            }

            // High price

            priceString = request.getParameter("hiPrice");
            if (priceString != null) {
                priceString = priceString.trim();
                if (!priceString.equals("")) {
                    try {
                        hiPrice = Util.fromCurrencyString
                                   (priceString);
                        if (hiPrice < loPrice)
                            throw new RuntimeException
            ("The high price cannot be less than the low price");
                        nbrAnds++;
                        if (nbrAnds > 1)
                            query += " AND";
                        query += " (price <= " + hiPrice + ")";
                    }
                    catch (ParseException e) {
                        throw new RuntimeException
                        (priceString + " is not numeric");
                    }
                }
            }

            // Execute the query and store the results
            // in the session object, then redirect to
            // the ShowSearchResults servlet

            Vector results = catalog.getProducts(query);
            session.putValue("searchResults", results);
            response.sendRedirect
                ("/servlet/IPFShowSearchResults");
        }

        catch (RuntimeException e) {
            String msg = e.getMessage();
            String title = "Invalid Search";
            response.sendRedirect("/servlet/IPFError"
                + "?title="
                + URLEncoder.encode(title)
                + "&msg="
                + URLEncoder.encode(msg));
        }

        catch (Exception e) {
            String msg = e.getMessage();
            String title = "Error while searching the database";
            response.sendRedirect("/servlet/IPFError"
                + "?title="
                + URLEncoder.encode(title)
                + "&msg="
```

Figure 7-27
(Continued)

```
                                   + URLEncoder.encode(msg));
        }
    }

    /**
     * Handles a POST request
     * @param request the servlet request object
     * @param response the servlet response object
     * @exception ServletException if a servlet exception occurs
     * @exception IOException if an I/O exception occurs
     */
    public void doPost(
            HttpServletRequest request,
            HttpServletResponse response)
        throws ServletException, IOException
    {
        doGet(request, response);
    }
}
```

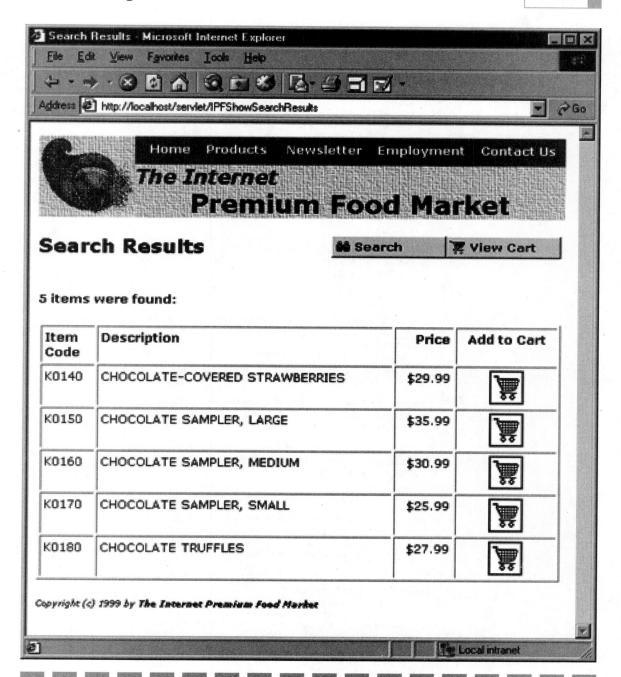

Figure 7-28 The product search results page.

■■ ■■ ■■ ■■
Figure 7-29
The
ShowSearchResu
lts servlet.

```java
package ipfoods;

import java.io.*;
import java.net.*;
import java.text.*;
import java.util.*;

import javax.servlet.*;
import javax.servlet.http.*;

/**
 * ShowSearchResultsServlet
 */
public class ShowSearchResultsServlet extends HttpServlet
{
    /**
     * Inner class for passing parameters between methods
     */
    class Parameters {
       HttpServletRequest request;
       HttpServletResponse response;
       ServletOutputStream out;
    }

    /**
     * Displays a table of the current search results.
     */
    public void doGet(
          HttpServletRequest request,
          HttpServletResponse response)
       throws ServletException, IOException
    {
       Parameters parms = new Parameters();
       parms.request = request;
       parms.response = response;

       // Set the content type to text/raw-html so that the
       // mime-based servlet chain will add the standard
       // headers and footers.

       response.setContentType("text/raw-html");

       ServletOutputStream out = response.getOutputStream();
       parms.out = out;

       // Get or create the session

       HttpSession session = request.getSession(true);
       Vector searchResults =
          (Vector) session.getValue("searchResults");
       if (searchResults == null) {
          sendError(parms, "There are no search results");
          return;
       }

       out.println("<HTML>");
       out.println("<HEAD>");
```

▬▬ ▬▬ ▬▬ ▬▬
Figure 7-29
(Continued)

```
out.println("<TITLE>Search Results</TITLE>");
out.println("</HEAD>");
out.println("<LINK REL=\"stylesheet\""
    + " HREF=\"/ipfoods/style.css\">");
out.println("<BODY>");

int nRows = searchResults.size();

// Write a table of the results

out.println("<P>");
out.println("<table border=0 cellpadding=0"
    + " cellspacing=0 width=546>");
out.println("<tr>");
out.println("<td><H2>Search Results</H2></td>");

out.println("<td width=120 valign=top>");
out.println
("<A HREF=\"/ipfoods/products/index.html\">");
out.println
("<img border=0 src=\"/ipfoods/images/search.gif\">");
out.println("</A>");
out.println("</td>");

out.println("<td width=120 valign=top>");
out.println("<A HREF=\"/servlet/IPFShowCart\">");
out.println
("<img border=0 src=\"/ipfoods/images/viewcart.gif\">");
out.println("</A>");
out.println("</td>");

out.println("</tr>");
out.println("</table>");

if (nRows == 0) {
   out.println("<H4>No items were found"
     + " that matched your search criteria</H4>");
}
else {
   out.println
   ("<H4> " + nRows + " items were found:</H4>");
   out.println
   ("<TABLE BORDER=1 CELLPADDING=3 WIDTH=546>");
   out.println("<TR>");
   out.println
   ("   <TH ALIGN=LEFT VALIGN=TOP>Item<BR>Code</TH>");
   out.println
   ("   <TH ALIGN=LEFT VALIGN=TOP>Description</TH>");
   out.println
   ("   <TH ALIGN=RIGHT VALIGN=TOP>Price</TH>");
   out.println
   ("   <TH ALIGN=CENTER VALIGN=TOP>Add to Cart</TH>");
   out.println("</TR>");

   Enumeration eProd = searchResults.elements();
   while (eProd.hasMoreElements()) {
      Product product = (Product) eProd.nextElement();
```

Figure 7-29
(Continued)

```java
            String itemCode = product.getItemCode();
            String itemDesc = product.getItemDesc();
            String price    =
               Util.toCurrencyString(product.getPrice());
            out.println("<TR>");
            out.println("<TD ALIGN=LEFT VALIGN=TOP>"
               + itemCode + "</TD>");
            out.println("<TD ALIGN=LEFT VALIGN=TOP>"
               + itemDesc + "</TD>");
            out.println("<TD ALIGN=RIGHT VALIGN=TOP>"
               + price + "</TD>");
            out.println("<TD ALIGN=CENTER VALIGN=TOP>"
               + "<A HREF=\""
               + "/servlet/IPFAddToCart?itemCode=" + itemCode
               + "\">"
               + "<IMG ALT=\"Cart\""
               + " SRC=\"/ipfoods/images/cart.gif\">"
               + "</A>"
               + "</TD>");
            out.println("</TR>");
         }

      out.println("</TABLE>");
      out.println("<P>");
      }
   out.println("</BODY>");
   out.println("</HTML>");
}

/**
 * Handles a POST request
 */
public void doPost(
      HttpServletRequest request,
      HttpServletResponse response)
   throws ServletException, IOException
{
   doGet(request, response);
}

/**
 * Redirects to an error page
 */
public void sendError(Parameters parms, String msg)
   throws IOException, ServletException
{
   HttpServletResponse response = parms.response;

   response.sendRedirect("/servlet/IPFError"
      + "?title="
      + URLEncoder.encode
      ("Error while showing search results")
      + "&msg="
      + URLEncoder.encode(msg));
}
```

▬▬ ▬▬ ▬▬ ▬▬

Figure 7-30

The `AddToCart`
servlet.

```java
package ipfoods;

import java.io.*;
import java.net.*;
import java.util.*;

import javax.servlet.*;
import javax.servlet.http.*;

/**
 * AddToCartServlet
 */
public class AddToCartServlet extends HttpServlet
{
    /**
     * Inner class for passing parameters between methods
     */
    class Parameters {
        HttpServletRequest request;
        HttpServletResponse response;
        PrintWriter out;
    }

    /**
     * This servlet adds an item to the shopping cart
     * then redirects the user to the ShowCart servlet
     */
    public void doGet(
            HttpServletRequest request,
            HttpServletResponse response)
        throws ServletException, IOException
    {
        Parameters parms = new Parameters();
        parms.request = request;
        parms.response = response;

        // Get or create the session

        HttpSession session = request.getSession(true);

        // Get or create the shopping cart

        ShoppingCart cart =
            (ShoppingCart) session.getValue("cart");
        if (cart == null) {
            cart = new ShoppingCart();
            session.putValue("cart", cart);
        }

        // Get the catalog

        Catalog catalog = (Catalog) session.getValue("catalog");
        if (catalog == null) {
            sendError(parms, "Could not find product catalog");
            return;
        }
```

Figure 7-30

(Continued)

```java
// Get the item code that the user selected

String[] itemCodes =
    request.getParameterValues("itemCode");
if ((itemCodes == null) || (itemCodes.length == 0)
    sendError(parms, "No item code specified");
    return;
}
String itemCode = itemCodes[0];

// See if the item already exists in the cart.
// If so, add to its quantity.
// Otherwise, create it with a quantity of one.

CartItem item = (CartItem) cart.get(itemCode);
if (item == null) {
    Product product = catalog.getProduct(itemCode);
    if (product == null) {
        sendError(parms,
            "Product "
            + itemCode
            + " not found in catalog");
        return;
    }
    item = new CartItem(product);
    item.setQuantity(1);
    cart.put(itemCode, item);
}
else {
    item.setQuantity(item.getQuantity() + 1);
}

// Redirect user to ShowCart page

response.sendRedirect("/servlet/IPFShowCart");
}

/**
 * Handles a POST request
 */
public void doPost(
        HttpServletRequest request,
        HttpServletResponse response)
    throws ServletException, IOException
{
    doGet(request, response);
}

/**
 * Redirects to an error page
 */
public void sendError(Parameters parms, String msg)
    throws IOException, ServletException
{
    HttpServletResponse response = parms.response;

    response.sendRedirect("/servlet/IPFError"
```

Figure 7-30
(Continued)

```
+ "?title="
+ URLEncoder.encode
("Error while adding items to the cart")
+ "&msg="
+ URLEncoder.encode(msg));
```

Figure 7-31

The ShowCart
servlet.

```java
package ipfoods;

import java.io.*;
import java.net.*;
import java.text.*;
import java.sql.*;
import java.util.*;

import javax.servlet.*;
import javax.servlet.http.*;

/**
 * ShowCartServlet
 */
public class ShowCartServlet extends HttpServlet
{
    /**
     * This servlet lists the items currently in the
     * shopping cart in tabular format.
     *
     * @param request the servlet request object
     * @param response the servlet response object
     * @exception ServletException if a servlet exception occurs
     * @exception IOException if an I/O exception occurs
     */
    public void doGet(
            HttpServletRequest request,
            HttpServletResponse response)
        throws ServletException, IOException

    {
        // Set content type to raw-html to invoke the servlet
        // chain that adds standard HTML header section.

        response.setContentType("text/raw-html");

        // Get or create the shopping cart

        HttpSession session = request.getSession(true);
        ShoppingCart cart =
            (ShoppingCart) session.getValue("cart");
        if (cart == null) {
            cart = new ShoppingCart();
            session.putValue("cart", cart);
        }

        // Start writing the HTML

        ServletOutputStream out = response.getOutputStream();
        out.println("<HTML>");
        out.println("<HEAD>");
        out.println("<TITLE>ShowCartServlet</TITLE>");
        out.println("<LINK REL=\"stylesheet\""
            + " HREF=\"/ipfoods/style.css\">");
        out.println("</HEAD>");
        out.println("<BODY>");

        // If there are no items, say just that
```

Figure 7-31

(Continued)

```java
int nItems = cart.getQuantity();

out.println("<P>");
out.println("<table border=0 cellpadding=0"
   + " cellspacing=0 width=546>");
out.println("<tr>");
out.println("<td><H2>Shopping Cart</H2></td>");
out.println("<td width=120 valign=top>");
out.println("<A HREF=\"/ipfoods/products/index.html\">");
out.println(
   "<img border=0 src=\"/ipfoods/images/search.gif\">");
out.println("</A>");
out.println("</td>");

Vector searchResults =
   (Vector) session.getValue("searchResults");
if (searchResults != null) {
   out.println("<td width=120 valign=top>");
   out.println(
      "<A HREF=\"/servlet/IPFShowSearchResults\">");
   out.println("<img border=0"
      + " src=\"/ipfoods/images/viewsearch.gif\">");
   out.println("</A>");
   out.println("</td>");
}

out.println("</tr>");
out.println("</table>");
out.println(
   "<H4>There are "
   + ((nItems == 0) ? " no" : ("" + nItems))
   + " items in your cart:</H4>");

if (nItems > 0) {

   out.println(
      "<TABLE BORDER=1 CELLPADDING=5 WIDTH=546>");
   out.println("<TR>");
   out.println("<TH ALIGN=CENTER VALIGN=MIDDLE>"
      + "Item<BR>Code</TH>");
   out.println("<TH ALIGN=CENTER VALIGN=MIDDLE>"
      + "Description</TH>");
   out.println("<TH ALIGN=CENTER VALIGN=MIDDLE>"
      + "Price</TH>");
   out.println("<TH ALIGN=CENTER VALIGN=MIDDLE>"
      + "Quantity</TH>");
   out.println("<TH ALIGN=CENTER VALIGN=MIDDLE>"
      + "Total</TH>");
   out.println("<TH ALIGN=CENTER VALIGN=MIDDLE>"
      + "Change<BR>Quantity</TH>");
   out.println("</TR>");

   // Get a list of the item codes of the items
   // in the cart

   Enumeration cartKeys = cart.keys();
```

Figure 7-31
(Continued)

```
while (cartKeys.hasMoreElements()) {

    // Get the item associated with this code

    String itemCode = (String) cartKeys.nextElement();
    CartItem item = (CartItem) cart.get(itemCode);
    Product product = item.getProduct();

    // Print a row for the item

    out.println("<TR>");
    out.println("<TD ALIGN=LEFT   VALIGN=TOP>"
        + itemCode + "</TD>");
    out.println("<TD ALIGN=LEFT   VALIGN=TOP>"
        + product.getItemDesc() + "</TD>");
    out.println("<TD ALIGN=RIGHT  VALIGN=TOP>"
        + Util.toCurrencyString(product.getPrice())
        + "</TD>");
    out.println("<TD ALIGN=RIGHT  VALIGN=TOP>"
        + item.getQuantity() + "</TD>");
    out.println("<TD ALIGN=RIGHT  VALIGN=TOP>"
        + Util.toCurrencyString(item.getExtendedPrice())
        + "</TD>");
    out.println("   <TD ALIGN=CENTER VALIGN=TOP>"

        + "<A HREF=\""
        + "/servlet/IPFAddToCart?itemCode="
        + itemCode
        + "\">"
        + "<IMG ALT=\"Cart\""
        + " SRC=\"/ipfoods/images/cart.gif\">"
        + "</A>"

        + "<A HREF=\""
        + "/servlet/IPFRemoveFromCart?itemCode="
        + itemCode
        + "\">"
        + "<IMG ALT=\"Cart\""
        + " SRC=\"/ipfoods/images/nocart.gif\">"
        + "</A>"

        + "</TD>");
    out.println("</TR>");
}

out.println("<TR>");
out.println("<TD ALIGN=LEFT   VALIGN=TOP>"
    + " </TD>");
out.println("<TD ALIGN=LEFT   VALIGN=TOP>"
    + "<B>Order Total</B></TD>");
out.println("<TD ALIGN=RIGHT  VALIGN=TOP>"
    + " </TD>");
out.println("<TD ALIGN=RIGHT  VALIGN=TOP>"
    + " </TD>");
out.println("<TD ALIGN=RIGHT  VALIGN=TOP>"
    + Util.toCurrencyString(cart.getExtendedPrice())
    + "</TD>");
```

Figure 7-31

(Continued)

```
                              out.println("<TD ALIGN=RIGHT  VALIGN=TOP>");
                              out.println("<A HREF=\"/servlet/IPFCheckout\">");
                              out.println("<img border=0"
                                 + " src=\"/ipfoods/images/checkout.gif\">");
                              out.println("</A>");
                              out.println("</TD>");
                              out.println("</TR>");
                              out.println("</TABLE>");
          }

          // Done

          out.println("</BODY>");
          out.println("</HTML>");

          out.flush();
          out.close();
      }

      /**
       * Handles a POST request
       * @param request the servlet request object
       * @param response the servlet response object
       * @exception ServletException if a servlet exception occurs
       * @exception IOException if an I/O exception occurs
       */
      public void doPost(
            HttpServletRequest request,
            HttpServletResponse response)
          throws ServletException, IOException
      {
          doGet(request, response);
      }
```

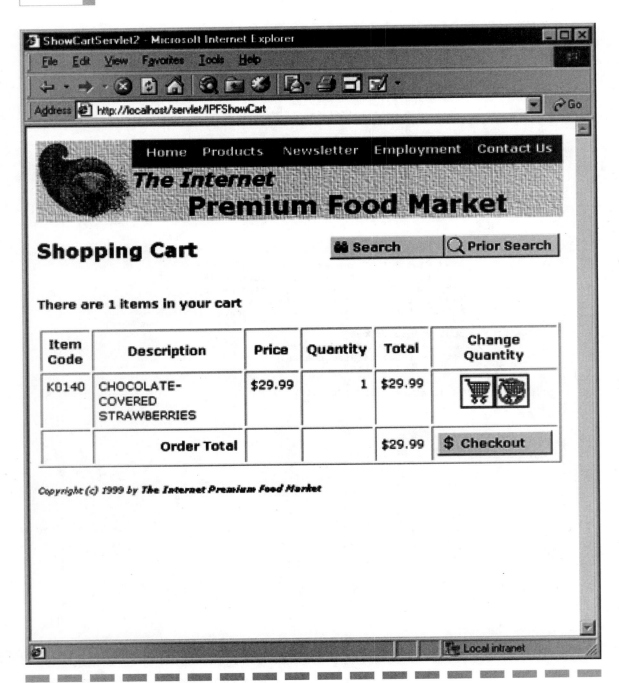

Figure 7-32 Output of the ShowCart servlet.

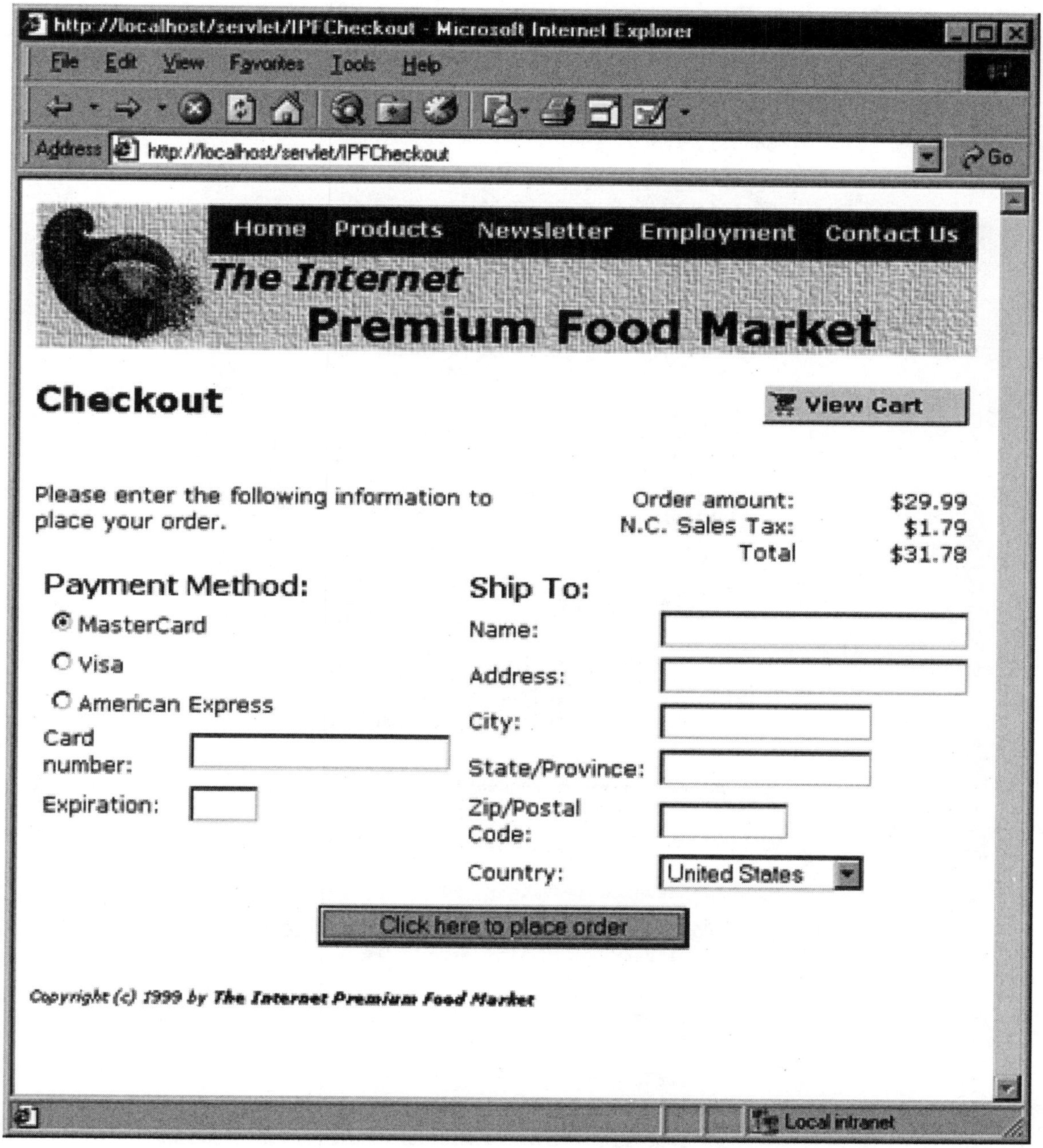

Figure 7-33 Output of the Checkout servlet.

```
package ipfoods;

import java.io.*;
import java.net.*;
import java.text.*;
import java.sql.*;
import java.util.*;

import javax.servlet.*;
import javax.servlet.http.*;

/**
 * CheckoutServlet
 */
public class CheckoutServlet extends HttpServlet
{
    /**
     * Inner class for passing parameters between methods
     */
    class Parameters {
        HttpServletRequest request;
        HttpServletResponse response;
        ServletOutputStream out;
        HttpSession session;
        ShoppingCart cart;
    }

    /**
     * This servlet lists the items currently
     * in the shopping cart in tabular format.
     */
    public void doGet(
            HttpServletRequest request,
            HttpServletResponse response)
        throws ServletException, IOException
    {
        Parameters parms = new Parameters();
        parms.request = request;
        parms.response = response;

        // Get the session

        HttpSession session = request.getSession(false);
        if (session == null) {
            response.sendRedirect("/ipfoods/product.html");
            return;
        }
        parms.session = session;

        // Get the shopping cart

        Object obj = session.getValue("cart");
        ShoppingCart cart = (ShoppingCart) obj;
        if (cart == null) {
            sendError(parms, "There are no items in your cart");
            return;
        }
```

Figure 7-34
(Continued)

```
      parms.cart = cart;

      // Access the servlet output stream

      ServletOutputStream out = response.getOutputStream();
      parms.out = out;

      // Write the document

      response.setContentType("text/raw-html");

      out.println("<HTML>");
      try {
         writeHead(parms);
         writeBody(parms);
      }
      catch (ServletException e) {
         sendError(parms, e.getMessage());
         return;
      }
      out.println("</HTML>");

      out.flush();
      out.close();
   }

   /**
    * Writes the HTML HEAD section
    */
   public void writeHead(Parameters parms)
      throws ServletException, IOException
   {
      ServletOutputStream out = parms.out;
      StringBuffer buffer = new StringBuffer();

      buffer.append("<HEAD>");
      buffer.append("<LINK REL=\"stylesheet\"");
      buffer.append(" HREF=\"/ipfoods/style.css\">");
      buffer.append("</HEAD>");

      out.println(buffer.toString());
   }

   /**
    * Writes the HTML BODY section
    */
   public void writeBody(Parameters parms)
      throws ServletException, IOException
   {
      ServletOutputStream out = parms.out;

      out.println("<BODY>");

      writeToolbar(parms);
      writeForm(parms);

      out.println("</BODY>");
```

Figure 7-34
(Continued)

```java
}
/**
* Writes the shopping cart toolbar
*/
public void writeToolbar(Parameters parms)
    throws ServletException, IOException
{
    ServletOutputStream out = parms.out;
    StringBuffer buffer = new StringBuffer();

    buffer.append("<P>");
    buffer.append("<TABLE BORDER=0 CELLPADDING=0");
    buffer.append("       CELLSPACING=0 WIDTH=546>");
    buffer.append("<TR>");
    buffer.append("<TD><H2>Checkout</H2></TD>");
    buffer.append("<TD WIDTH=120 VALIGN=TOP>");
    buffer.append("<A HREF=\"/servlet/IPFShowCart\">");
    buffer.append
    ("<IMG BORDER=0 SRC=\"/ipfoods/images/viewcart.gif\">");
    buffer.append("</A>");
    buffer.append("</TD>");
    buffer.append("</TR>");
    buffer.append("</TABLE>");

    out.println(buffer.toString());
}

/**
* Writes the main form
*/
public void writeForm(Parameters parms)
    throws ServletException, IOException
{
    ServletOutputStream out = parms.out;

    out.println("<FORM METHOD=\"GET\""
        + " ACTION=\"/ipfoods/products/thanks.html\">");

    writeOrderTotal(parms);

    out.println("<TABLE>");
    out.println("<TR>");

    writePaymentMethod(parms);
    writeShipTo(parms);

    out.println("</TR>");
    out.println("<TR>");

    writeButtons(parms);

    out.println("</TR>");
    out.println("</TABLE>");
    out.println("</FORM>");
}
```

Figure 7-34

(Continued)

```
/**
 * Writes the order total section
 */
public void writeOrderTotal(Parameters parms)
    throws ServletException, IOException
{
    ServletOutputStream out = parms.out;
    ShoppingCart cart = parms.cart;
    if (cart == null)
        throw new ServletException("No shopping cart found");

    // Write the individual items as hidden fields

    Enumeration keys = cart.keys();
    int nItems = 0;
    while (keys.hasMoreElements()) {
        String itemCode = (String) keys.nextElement();
        CartItem item = (CartItem) cart.get(itemCode);
        Product product = item.getProduct();
        int quantity = item.getQuantity();
        String buffer = quantity
            + ":" + itemCode
            + ":" + product.getPrice()
            + ":" + product.getItemDesc()
            ;
        writeHiddenField
        (parms, "cart.cartItem." + nItems, buffer);
        nItems++;
    }
    writeHiddenField
    (parms, "cart.itemCount", String.valueOf(nItems));

    // Write the summary

    long order = cart.getExtendedPrice();
    writeHiddenField(parms,
        "cart.orderAmount", String.valueOf(order));

    long tax = Util.getTax(order);
    writeHiddenField(parms,
        "cart.taxAmount", String.valueOf(tax));

    long total = order + tax;
    writeHiddenField(parms,
        "cart.totalAmount", String.valueOf(total));

    out.println(
        "<TABLE "
        + " BORDER=0"
        + " CELLPADDING=0"
        + " CELLSPACING=0"
        + " WIDTH=546>");

    out.println("<TR>");
    out.println("<TD ALIGN=LEFT VALIGN=TOP WIDTH=300 ROWSPAN=3>");
    out.println("Please enter the following information"
        + " to place your order.");
```

Figure 7-34

(Continued)

```
out.println("</TD>");

out.println("<TD ALIGN=RIGHT>");
out.println("Order amount:");
out.println("</TD>");

out.println("<TD ALIGN=RIGHT WIDTH=100>");
out.println(Util.toCurrencyString(order));
out.println("</TD>");
out.println("</TR>");

out.println("<TR>");
out.println("<TD ALIGN=RIGHT>");
out.println("N.C. Sales Tax:");
out.println("</TD>");

out.println("<TD ALIGN=RIGHT>");
out.println(Util.toCurrencyString(tax));
out.println("</TD>");
out.println("</TR>");

out.println("<TR>");
out.println("<TD ALIGN=RIGHT>");
out.println("Total");
out.println("</TD>");

out.println("<TD ALIGN=RIGHT>");
out.println(Util.toCurrencyString(total));
out.println("</TD>");
out.println("</TR>");

out.println("</TABLE>");
}

/**
 * Writes the payment method section
 */
public void writePaymentMethod(Parameters parms)
    throws ServletException, IOException
{
    ServletOutputStream out = parms.out;

    out.println("<!-- Payment method -->");
    out.println();
    out.println("<TD ALIGN=LEFT VALIGN=TOP>");
    out.println("<TABLE>");
    out.println("<TR>");
    out.println("<TD COLSPAN=2>");
    out.println
    ("<FONT SIZE=+1><B>Payment Method:</B></FONT>");
    out.println("</TD>");
    out.println("</TR>");

    out.println("<TR>");
    out.println("<TD COLSPAN=2>");
    out.println("<INPUT TYPE=RADIO");
    out.println("        NAME=\"creditCard\"");
```

Figure 7-34

(Continued)

```
    out.println("          VALUE=\"MC\"");
    out.println("          CHECKED>MasterCard");
    out.println("</TD>");
    out.println("</TR>");

    out.println("<TR>");
    out.println("<TD COLSPAN=2>");
    out.println("<INPUT TYPE=RADIO");
    out.println("          NAME=\"creditCard\"");
    out.println("          VALUE=\"VISA\">Visa");
    out.println("</TD>");
    out.println("</TR>");

    out.println("<TR>");
    out.println("<TD COLSPAN=2>");
    out.println("<INPUT TYPE=RADIO");
    out.println("          NAME=\"creditCard\"");
    out.println("          VALUE=\"AMEX\">American Express");
    out.println("</TD>");
    out.println("</TR>");

    out.println("<TR>");
    out.println("<TD>Card number:</TD>");
    out.println("<TD>");
    out.println("<INPUT TYPE=TEXT");
    out.println("          NAME=\"cardNumber\"");
    out.println("          SIZE=20>");
    out.println("</TD>");
    out.println("</TR>");

    out.println("<TR>");
    out.println("<TD>Expiration:</TD>");
    out.println("<TD>");
    out.println("<INPUT TYPE=TEXT");
    out.println("          NAME=\"expiration\"");
    out.println("          SIZE=4>");
    out.println("</TD>");
    out.println("</TR>");

    out.println("</TABLE>");
    out.println("</TD>");
}

/**
 * Writes the ship to section
 */
public void writeShipTo(Parameters parms)
    throws ServletException, IOException
{
    ServletOutputStream out = parms.out;

    out.println("<!-- Ship to-->");
    out.println();
    out.println("<TD ALIGN=LEFT VALIGN=TOP>");
    out.println("<TABLE>");
    out.println("<TR>"
        + "<TD COLSPAN=2>"
```

Figure 7-34
(Continued)

```
            + "<FONT SIZE=+1>"
            + "<B>Ship To:</B>"
            + "</FONT></TD></TR>");
        out.println("<TR>"
            + "<TD>Name:</TD>"
            + "<TD>"
            + "<INPUT TYPE=TEXT NAME=\"name\" SIZE=24>"
            + "</TD></TR>");
        out.println("<TR>"
            + "<TD>Address:</TD>"
            + "<TD>"
            + "<INPUT TYPE=TEXT NAME=\"addr\" SIZE=24>"
            + "</TD></TR>");
        out.println("<TR>"
            + "<TD>City:</TD>"
            + "<TD>"
            + "<INPUT TYPE=TEXT NAME=\"city\" SIZE=16>"
            + "</TD></TR>");
        out.println("<TR>"
            + "<TD>State/Province:</TD>"
            + "<TD>"
            + "<INPUT TYPE=TEXT NAME=\"state\" SIZE=16>"
            + "</TD></TR>");
        out.println("<TR>"
            + "<TD>Zip/Postal Code:</TD>"
            + "<TD>"
            + "<INPUT TYPE=TEXT NAME=\"zip\" SIZE=9>"
            + "</TD></TR>");
        out.println("<TR><TD>Country:</TD>");
        out.println("<TD>");
        out.println("<SELECT NAME=\"country\" SIZE=1>");
        out.println("<OPTION VALUE=\"US\">United States");
        out.println("<OPTION VALUE=\"CA\">Canada");
        out.println("<OPTION VALUE=\"UK\">United Kingdom");
        out.println("<OPTION VALUE=\"AU\">Australia");
        out.println("<OPTION VALUE=\"DE\">Germany");
        out.println("<OPTION VALUE=\"FR\">France");
        out.println("</SELECT>");
        out.println("</TD>");
        out.println("</TR>");
        out.println("</TABLE>");
        out.println("</TD>");
    }

    /**
    * Writes the buttons section
    */
    public void writeButtons(Parameters parms)
        throws ServletException, IOException
    {
        ServletOutputStream out = parms.out;

        out.println("<!-- Buttons -->");
        out.println();
        out.println("<TD ALIGN=CENTER VALIGN=MIDDLE COLSPAN=2>");
        out.println("<TABLE>");
        out.println("<TR><TD>");
```

Figure 7-34
(Continued)

```java
        out.println("<INPUT TYPE=SUBMIT");
        out.println(" VALUE=\"Click here to place order\">");
        out.println("</TD></TR>");
        out.println("</TABLE>");
        out.println("</TD>");
    }

    /**
     * Writes a hidden field
     */
    public void writeHiddenField(
        Parameters parms, String name, String value)
        throws ServletException, IOException
    {
        ServletOutputStream out = parms.out;

        out.println("<INPUT"
            + " TYPE=\"HIDDEN\""
            + " NAME=\"" + name + "\""
            + " VALUE=\"" + value + "\">");
    }

    /**
     * Handles a POST request
     */
    public void doPost(
        HttpServletRequest request,
        HttpServletResponse response)
        throws ServletException, IOException
    {
        doGet(request, response);
    }

    /**
     * Sends a page containing an error message
     */
    public void sendError(Parameters parms, String msg)
        throws ServletException, IOException
    {
        HttpServletResponse response = parms.response;

        response.sendRedirect("/servlet/IPFError"
            + "?title="
            + URLEncoder.encode("Error in CheckoutServlet")
            + "&msg="
            + URLEncoder.encode(msg));
    }
}
```

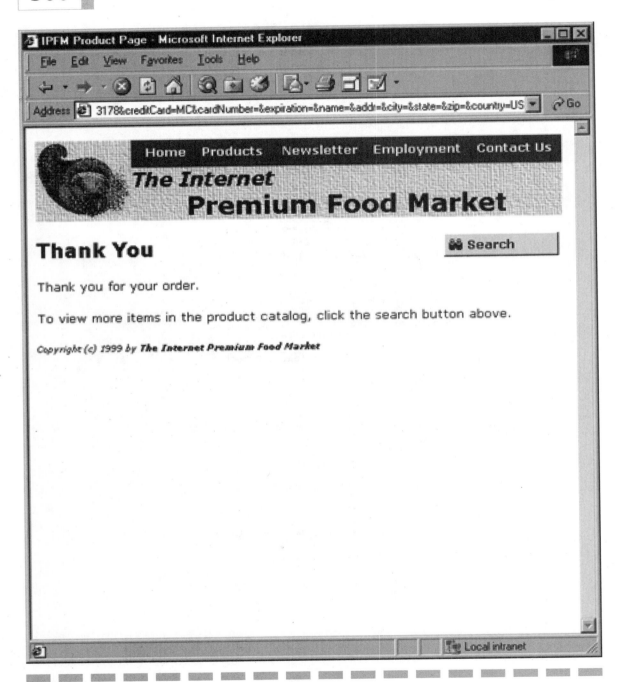

Figure 7-35 Output of the `PlaceOrder` servlet.

Servlet Life-Cycle Issues

Overview

In a traditional batch program, the logic starts at the top and flows to the bottom. Each step of the program is pretty much the result of other steps in the same program. Its life cycle can be traced as a continuous line.

This is not the case with event-driven programming. Programs like device drivers, graphic user interfaces, and (you guessed it) servlets consist of a set of individual functions that are called into action at unpredictable times, often in asynchronous threads. Rather than the program dictating its own order of events, an external force causes the appropriate sections of the program to be run when needed.

For example, a graphical user interface (GUI) may consist of a window that contains buttons, text fields, menus, and check boxes. The windowing system (such as AWT) does not control where the user types or clicks; it simply listens for specific events and invokes their corresponding event-handling functions.

In the same manner, servlets consist of individual functions that are called by a servlet engine in response to external events. Fortunately, this collection of events is small in size and completely straightforward. Better yet, you do not even have to handle an event if you do not have anything special to do; the class from which your servlet is derived provides default handlers for all events.[1]

The Servlet Life Cycle

There are essentially only three types of events in the life of a servlet:

1. Initialization
2. Request handling
3. Shutdown

Let's consider what each of these events means and what you can do when they happen.

Initialization   When a servlet is first loaded, the servlet engine calls its `init()` method, which has the following signature:

```
public void init(ServletConfig config) throws ServletException;
```

The servlet specification does not dictate exactly when this event occurs, only that the `init()` method is called exactly once when the servlet is

---

[1]Of course, if you let the parent class handle everything, your servlet will not do anything of interest except compile correctly.

loaded and that no requests will be serviced until the `init()` method completes successfully.

You can override `init()` to perform whatever initialization your servlet requires. For example, you may need to establish a database connection or create background threads. If there are any conditions that make the servlet unusable, such as the unavailability of some resource, you can throw an `UnavailableException`. This will conveniently prevent any further requests from being serviced.

The default function of `init()` is to store a reference to the `ServletConfig` object as an instance variable. Having access to this object will allow you to access the servlet context and any initialization parameters in other methods. If you override `init()`, you should ensure that this function is still performed by calling `super.init(config)` as the first statement in your method.

Request Handling Let's review the steps that happen when a user makes a request from a Web browser; in particular, a servlet request:

1. The user clicks a hyperlink in a Web page or types a URL in the browser's "location" field. For example, the URL for the product search application at the Internet Premium Food Market's Web site might look like the following:

   ```
   http://www.ipfoods.com/servlet/IPFProductSearch
   ```

2. The browser analyzes the URL, separating it into a protocol (`http`), a host name (`www.ipfoods.com`), and a file path (`/servlet/IPFProductSearch`).

3. The browser opens a socket connection to the host and sends several lines of text in the form of an HTTP request. This request may look similar to the following:

   ```
   GET /servlet/IPFProductSearch HTTP/1.0
   Accept: */*
   Accept-Language: en-us
   Accept-Encoding: gzip
   User-Agent: Mozilla/4.0
   ```

4. When the Web server at `www.ipfoods.com` receives the HTTP request, it determines whether it is a simple request for a document or whether special handling is involved. The mechanisms for indicating this depends on the specific Web server and servlet

engine involved, but in this case, the keyword `/servlet` indicates to the Web server that it needs to pass this request on to a servlet engine.

5. The servlet engine packages the request method, the document URL, the HTTP version, and all the headers into an `HttpServletRequest` object. Next, it determines whether there is an existing instance of the requested `IPFProductSearch` servlet or not. If one does not exist, the servlet engine creates a new instance and calls its `init()` method.

6. It then calls the servlet's `service()` method, passing it the servlet request object and a newly created servlet response object. `service()` looks at the first line of the request to determine the HTTP request method specified (i.e., `GET`, `POST`, `HEAD`, `PUT`, `OPTIONS`, `TRACE`, or `DELETE`), and then delegates the request to a method-specific function (`doGet()`, `doPost()`, etc.). In this case, since it is an HTTP `GET` request, the method called is `doGet()`.

7. The `doGet()` function does whatever is necessary to service the request, writing the results in HTML format to the servlet response output stream.

8. Finally, the Web browser receives the HTML and renders it visually in the browser window.

Thus several programs (a Web browser, a Web server, a servlet engine, and your servlet) cooperate to service an HTTP request, each one doing just its part. All you really need to do is respond to the `GET` or `POST` HTTP request event, filling in the `HttpServletResponse` object based on the contents of the `HttpServletRequest`.

Shutdown Once a servlet is loaded, it continues to exist in the Java virtual machine, servicing requests until it is explicitly unloaded by the servlet engine.[2] When the servlet engine shuts down, it goes through its list of active servlets and calls each one's `destroy()` method. You can

---

[2]The Java Servlet API Specification does not describe any particular means for shutting down individual servlets, leaving this instead entirely up to the servlet engine. The servlet engine is not required to keep a servlet in memory but may retire it at any time and reload it on demand. Some servlet engines provide an administrative interface that allows finer control of the process. New Atlanta's ServletExec, for example, provides a "Loaded" checkbox in its `admin` servlet. Checking or unchecking this checkbox will allow you to explicitly load or unload a servlet.

override the `destroy()` method to release any resources, stop any threads, or save the servlet state. If you do override the method, be sure to call `super.destroy()` at the end of your method. The `destroy()` method does not return until all threads running the `service()` method have exited or until a timeout period has elapsed.

The rest of this chapter discusses servlet life-cycle issues, including the servlet classpath, dynamic reloading, initialization parameters, the `init()` and `destroy()` methods, and servlet invocation.

8.1   The Servlet Classpath and Dynamic Reloading

Problem

Some of my classes get reloaded automatically when I recompile them, but some do not. Why is this, and what can I do about it?

Technique

Separate your classes into servlets and all other types; place servlets in the specifically designated servlets directory.

Discussion

Recall from Section 6.2 that with respect to a servlet engine, there are two[3] different classpaths involved:

1. The classpath for the virtual machine in which the servlet engine itself is running

2. The classpath used by the servlet engine to find servlets

The means for describing these paths to the servlet engine are entirely vendor-specific. Table 8-1 shows the places in which the paths are specified in several popular servlet engines:

---

[3]Actually, three, if you count the system classpath used by applications launched from the command line or a Web browser.

TABLE 8-1

Where to specify
the class path.

JRun 2.3.3

Servlets directory	`servletdir` **property in** `jsm-default/services/`**<service name>/properties/jrun.properties**
Classpath	`java.classpath` **property in** `jsm-default/properties/jsm.properties`

ServletExec 2.2

Servlets directory	`servletexec.default.servlets` **property in** `ServletExec/ServletExec Data/servers.properties`
Classpath	`-classpath` **parameter in the** `ServletExec <webserver-name>.bat file`

Apache JServ 1.0

Servlets directory	`repositories` **property in** `ApacheJServ/conf/zone.properties`
Classpath	`wrapper.classpath` **entries in** `ApacheJServ /conf/jserv.properties`

In each case, however, servlets actually can be loaded from either classpath, but the choice of classpath imparts different characteristics to the classes they contain, as we shall see.

Reloading Example   Consider the listing shown in Figure 8-1. The `ReloadTestServlet` displays the system classpath and information about three types of classes:

1. A servlet
2. A supporting class used by this servlet
3. A system class

Both the servlet and the supporting class (`other.Other`) have a static `VERSION` field that can be extracted with the `toString()` method. We have set `VERSION` equal to one in both classes.

It can be seen from the output shown in Figure 8-2 that different class loaders are used for each type of class.

Now increment the version number in each class and recompile. Leave the Web browser up, and click the "Reload" button to refresh the display. Figure 8-3 shows the results.

▪▪▪ ▪▪ ▪▪ ▪

Figure 8-1

A servlet that illustrates dynamic reloading.

```
package ijs.lifecycle;

import java.io.*;
import java.net.*;
import java.util.*;
import javax.servlet.*;
import javax.servlet.http.*;

/**
 * ReloadTestServlet
 */
public class ReloadTestServlet extends HttpServlet
{
    public static final int VERSION = 1;

    /**
     * Handles a GET request
     */
    public void doGet(
            HttpServletRequest request,
            HttpServletResponse response)
        throws ServletException, IOException
    {
        response.setContentType("text/html");
        PrintWriter out = response.getWriter();

        out.println("<HTML>"
            + "<HEAD>"
            + "<TITLE>Reload Test Servlet</TITLE>"
            + "</HEAD>"
            + "<BODY>"
            + "<H2>Reload Test Servlet</H2>"
        );

        showClassPath(out);
        showClassInfo
            (this, "This servlet", out);
        showClassInfo
            (new other.Other(), "A related class", out);
        showClassInfo
            (new java.util.BitSet(), "A system class", out);

        out.println("</BODY></HTML>");
    }

    /**
     * Shows the servlet engine classpath
     */
    protected void showClassPath(PrintWriter out)
        throws ServletException, IOException
    {
        out.println("<H3>Servlet Engine Class Path</H3>");

        StringBuffer buffer = new StringBuffer();
        String cp = System.getProperty("java.class.path");
        if (cp == null)
            buffer.append("Unknown<BR>");
```

Figure 8-1
(Continued)

```java
    else {
       StringTokenizer st = new StringTokenizer
          (cp, File.pathSeparator);
       while (st.hasMoreTokens()) {
          buffer.append(st.nextToken());
          buffer.append(' ');
       }
    }
    out.println(buffer.toString());
}

/**
 * Shows information about the specified class
 */
protected void showClassInfo(
     Object object,
     String label,
     PrintWriter out)
   throws ServletException, IOException
{
   out.println("<H3>" + label + "</H3>");

   Class cls = object.getClass();
   out.println("Class name is <CODE>"
      + cls.getName() + "</CODE><BR>");

   try {
      ClassLoader classLoader = cls.getClassLoader();
      out.println("Class loader is <CODE>"
         + classLoader + "</CODE><BR>");
   }
   catch (Exception e) {
      out.println
      ("Class loader is <CODE>unknown</CODE><BR>");
   }
   out.println("Value is <CODE>"
      + object.toString() + "</CODE><BR>");
}

/**
 * Returns the object as a formatted string
 */
public String toString()
{
   StringBuffer buffer = new StringBuffer();
   buffer.append(getClass().getName());
   buffer.append("[");
   buffer.append("version=");
   buffer.append(VERSION);
   buffer.append("]");
   return buffer.toString();
}
```

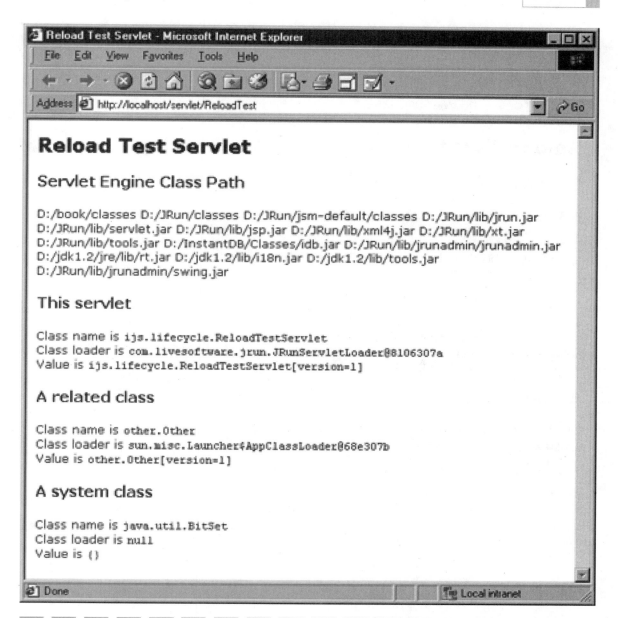

Figure 8-2 Output of the `ReloadTest` servlet.

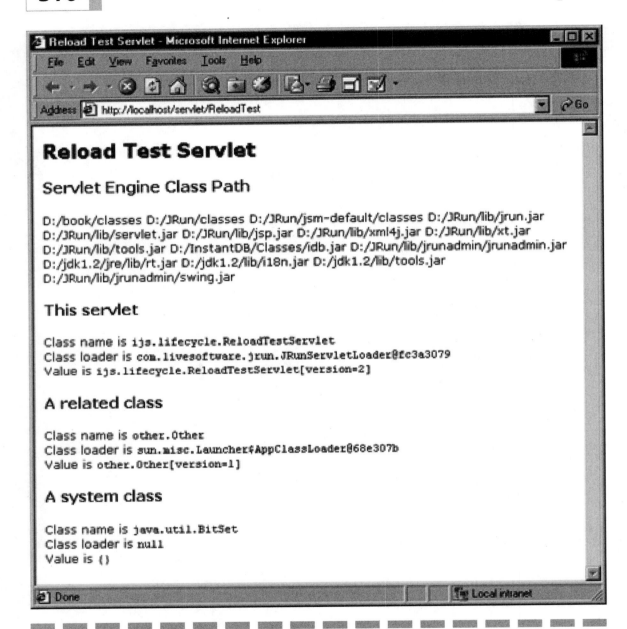

Figure 8-3 Output of the ReloadTest servlet after recompilation.

The version number for the servlet has changed, but not the version number for the supporting class. This indicates that a new version of the servlet has been loaded and a new instance created, which is desirable behavior during development. However, the instance of `other.Other` is still from the old class, still resident in the Java virtual machine. Clearly, this can lead to complications. Section 4.6 of the Java Servlet API 2.2 Specification describes this problem and prescribes that 2.2-compatible servlet containers must ensure that both servlets and the classes they may use are reloaded together.

8.2   Initialization Parameters

Problem

I have initialization parameters to pass to my servlet. Where do I put them, and how do I access them?

Technique

Place initialization parameters in the servlet properties file (see below). Access them with the `getInitParameterNames()` and `getInitParameter(name)` methods.

Discussion

In addition to the form parameters that are sent with each HTTP request, a servlet can have initialization parameters that are read when it is first loaded. This provides a convenient method of supplying the values of constants from outside the program so that it does not need to be recompiled when changes are necessary. Typical uses for these parameters could be

- The name of a JDBC driver
- The location of installation directory
- A locale identifier indicating the language in which messages are displayed

Most often, initialization parameters are used to customize the operation of a servlet to the environment in which it is deployed.

The means by which these parameters are set varies from servlet engine to servlet engine, but generally they are found in a properties file (usually the one in which servlet aliases are specified). Table 8-2 lists the location of this file for various servlet engines. The servlet engine vendor may supply a GUI or administrative servlet that allows you to modify these files, but it is often just as easy to edit the properties file directly with a text editor.

To access the value of a parameter at run time, you can use the `getInitParameter(String name)` method,[4] as shown below:

```
String jdbcDriverName = getInitParameter("jdbcDriverName");
if (jdbcDriverName == null)
    throw new UnavailableException(this, "No driver name specified");
```

You can access the parameter with this method at any time, in the `init()`, `service()`, or `destroy()` methods or methods that they call. Usually you know the name of the initialization parameter you want; if you need a list of them, use `getInitParameterNames()`:

TABLE 8-2

When initialization parameters are specified.

JRun 2.3.3

`servlet.<alias>.args` **property in** `jsm-default/services/<service name>/properties/servlets. properties`

ServletExec 2.2

`servlet.<alias>.initArgs` **property in** `ServletExec/ServletExec Data/<server name>/servlets.properties`

ApacheJServ 1.0

`servlet.<alias>.initArgs` **property in** `ApacheJServ/conf/zone.properties`

---

[4]`getInitParameter` **is a method in the** `ServletConfig` **interface, but there is a convenience method with the same name in the** `GenericServlet` **class that is inherited by** `HttpServlet` **and any of its subclasses. The convenience method simply calls** `getServletConfig().getInitParameter()`.

```
Enumeration enames = getInitParameterNames();
while (enames.hasMoreElements()) {
   String name = (String) enames.nextElement();
   String value = getInitParameter(name);
   // ... do something with the name and value
}
```

See Also

Section 8-3, "Specifying Multiple Initialization Parameters."

8.3 Specifying Multiple Initialization Parameters

Problem

I have more than one initialization parameter. How do I enter this in the properties file?

Technique

Use commas between `key=value` pairs, or use indirection to point to a properties file.

Discussion

There is only one property element in which initialization parameters can be specified, typically named `initArgs` or `args` depending on your servlet engine. Thus, if you have more than one parameter, you need to specify multiple parameters on one line. Put commas between the `key=value` pairs to indicate where one parameter stops and another starts, as illustrated below:

```
servlet.ShowInitParms.initArgs=parm1=value1,parm2=value2
```

You can retrieve these parameters individually by name using `getInitParameter(String name)` or get an enumeration of all of them with `getInitParameterNames()`, as shown here:

```
Enumeration enames = getInitParameterNames();
while (enames.hasMoreElements()) {
    String name = (String) enames.nextElement();
    String value = getInitParameter(name);
    out.println(name + " = " + value);
}
```

Ordinarily, this works fine, but if you have more than two or three parameters to specify, the line in the properties file gets very crowded. Worse, if you have a parameter value that contains a comma, you have to figure out some way to escape the comma or risk confusing the servlet engine. ServletExec handles this by allowing you to enclose the value in quotes, but neither JRun nor ApacheJServ provides an obvious way to do it.

A cleaner way to do this is to specify only one parameter, the name of a properties file that contains the real initialization parameters, that is,

```
servlet.ShowInitParmsIndirect.initArgs=properties=myprops.properties
```

which you would read simply with

```
String fileName = getInitParameter("properties");
Properties prop = new Properties();
prop.load(new FileInputStream(fileName));
```

The advantage of this indirect method is that properties can be edited (perhaps even by another process) without modifying the servlet engine configuration files.

8.4   Servicing Requests

Problem

How does the Web server route servlet requests to the servlet engine?

Technique

Based on a pattern match on the URL, the Web server determines if a request requires special handling. If so, the request is routed to the handler for the matched pattern. The handler may either be in-process or out-of-process (see below).

Discussion

Each servlet engine uses its own mechanism, but they all accomplish the same goal, which is to cause the Web server to

1. Filter incoming requests according to their URLs.
2. Divert those which it recognizes as servlet requests to the servlet engine.

Web servers with built-in servlet support generally use an in-process approach (Figure 8-4), in which the servlet engine shares a common address space with the main program.

Add-on servlet engines such as Allaire's JRun and New Atlanta's ServletExec use a more flexible out-of-process model (Figure 8-5), using

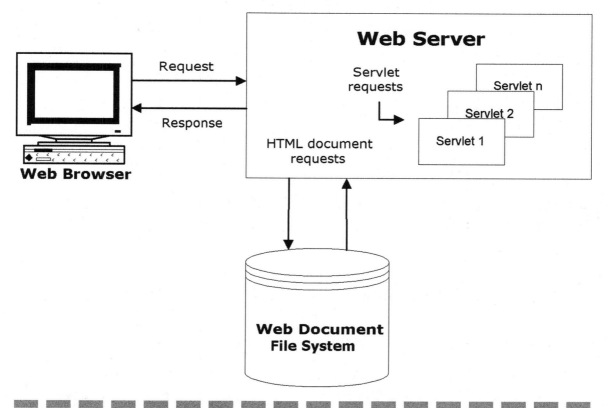

Figure 8-4 An in-process servlet engine.

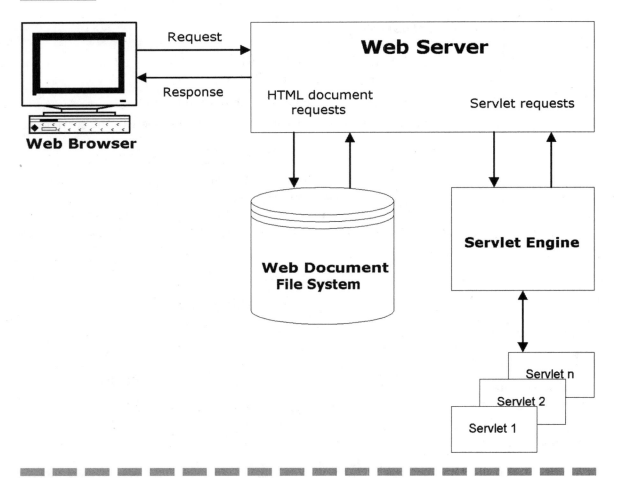

Figure 8-5 An out-of-process servlet engine.

socket connections to shuttle requests and responses between the Web server and the servlet engine. The out-of-process model provides several advantages. Since the servlet engine is not tied to the Web server's Java virtual machine (JVM), an installation can run multiple JVMs (even JVMs from different vendors), possibly with improved performance.

JRun, for example, installs a native handler called a *connector* in the Web server. The connector intercepts servlet requests and passes them on to the servlet engine through a socket connection to a connector proxy.

The proxy then communicates the request directly to the servlet engine, listens for its response, and passes the response back to the connector over the socket.

The connector and connector proxy communicate using a binary two-way protocol that sends requests, allows the proxy to ask for additional information, and pipes status and response data back to the Web server. For each command, the transmitting side sends an opcode preceded by a 32-bit length field, followed by any data that accompanies the command. Figure 8-6 is an annotated trace of how this protocol would handle a simple GET request.

The trace illustrates what happens when *http://localhost/servlet/ HelloWorldServlet* is processed by a Web server that has an embedded JRun connector. (Figure 8-6 uses mnemonics to represent the commands; the actual message exchange is purely binary.)

- The Web server opens a socket connection to the JRun connector proxy (JCP) and sends an initialization command (zero).
- Next, it sends the URI (that portion of the URL that comes after the protocol and host name) along with any HTTP headers that the client supplied.
- The connector then enters a command processing loop. JCP asks for the value of any additional variables it needs (using opcode 3). In this example, it asks for the query string, any cookies the client can supply, and the host name.
- After servicing the request, the JCP sends back the status (using opcode 6), the response headers (opcode 7), and the document content (opcode 8).
- The end of the response is signaled by opcode 9.

See Also

For details about specific servlet engine protocols, see the following references:

JRun 2.3.3	JRun User's Manual, Version 2.3, Chapter 1
ServletExec 2.2	ServletExec 2.2 User Guide
ApacheJServ 1.0	`/ApacheJServ/docs`, `/ApacheJServ/docs/ protocol`

Figure 8-6

An annotated trace
of the JRun con-
nector protocol.

```
#
# Initialize the connector proxy
#
SENDCOMMAND: 0
#
# Send URI and HTTP headers
#
SENDLENGTH:  73
SENDBYTES:   [URI: /servlet/HelloWorldServlet
REQUEST_METHOD: GET
CONTENT_LENGTH: 0
]
#
# Listen for commands from the connector proxy
#
#
# Command 3: Request for the value of a variable
#
RECVCMD:        3
COMMAND:        sendVar
RECVLENGTH:  12
RECVBYTES:      QUERY_STRING
SENDLENGTH:  0
SENDBYTES:      []
#
# Command 3: Request for the value of a variable
#
RECVCMD:        3
COMMAND:        sendVar
RECVLENGTH:  6
RECVBYTES:      COOKIE
SENDLENGTH:  0
SENDBYTES:      []
#
# Command 3: Request for the value of a variable
#
RECVCMD:        3
COMMAND:        sendVar
RECVLENGTH:  4
RECVBYTES:      HOST
SENDLENGTH:  0
SENDBYTES:      []
#
# Command 3: Request for the value of a variable
#
RECVCMD:        3
COMMAND:        sendVar
RECVLENGTH:  4
RECVBYTES:      HOST
SENDLENGTH:  0
SENDBYTES:      []
#
# Command 6: Status returned
#
RECVCMD:        6
COMMAND:        recvStatus
RECVSTATUS:  200
```

Figure 8-6
(Continued)

```
RECVLENGTH:   2
RECVBYTES:    OK
RECVCODESTR:  [OK]
#
# Command 7: Response headers returned
#
RECVCMD:      7
COMMAND:      echoHeaders
RECVLENGTH:   71
RECVBYTES:    Content-Length: 95
Connection: Keep-alive
Content-Type: text/html


#
# Command 8: Data returned
#
RECVCMD:      8
COMMAND:      echoData
RECVLENGTH:   95
RECVBYTES:    <html>
<head><title>Hello World</title></head>
<body>
<h1>Hello World</h1>
</body></html>

#
# Command 9: Done
#
RECVCMD:      9
```

8.5 Shutting Down Servlets

Problem

I have a servlet that does all its useful work in its init() method. I do not need it after that, and I would like to shut it down. How do I do it?

Technique

You probably cannot, but you probably do not need to.

Discussion

Other than by shutting down the servlet engine, the Java Servlet API Specification provides no means for doing this, although some servlet engines do make it possible from an administrative interface (notably New Atlanta's ServletExec). There is good reason for this. A container object like a servlet engine presumably needs exclusive control over what objects it contains. Otherwise, it could not be relied on to provide services that it claims to control.

Unless your servlet implements the `SingleThreadModel` interface, there is a single instance[5] of it that is owned by the servlet engine, which will unload it whenever the servlet engine wants to. You can no more unload yourself than elements can remove themselves from a `java.util.Hashtable`.

What if the servlet calls its own `destroy()` method? Isn't this what the servlet engine does during shutdown? The answer is yes, but all this accomplishes is whatever the `destroy()` method explicitly does. `GenericServlet`, which is probably your servlet's direct or indirect super class, simply writes "destroy" to the servlet log. You can verify this with the servlet shown in Figure 8-7.

`TestDestroyServlet` increments a counter each time it is called. In addition, it looks for a parameter named "command" with a value of "destroy." If it exists, the servlet saves the current value of the counter in an `HttpSession` as `destroyReq` and calls `destroy()`. The output generated by the servlet includes the current value of the counter and its value when `destroy()` was last called. If you run the servlet and click the "Reload" button three times, you see the message "This Is Request Number 4." Modify the URL to be

```
http://localhost/servlet/TestDestroy?command=destroy
```

and see what happens. As Figure 8-8 shows, the servlet reports that on request number 5, the `destroy()` method was scheduled to be called. But if you take the `?command=destroy` command out of the URL and reload the page, you will see that the servlet continues to exist after `destroy()` (Figure 8-9).

This should not really be a problem, however. If you allocate resources in `init()` and do not intend to service requests, you can simply release the resources at the end of `init()`. The mere existence of an instance of your servlet, so long as it is not active, uses very little in the way of resources. You can force the servlet refuse to handle requests by throwing an `UnavailableException`, but this is somewhat brutal and

[5]Actually, there is one instance per alias, if the servlet is loaded under several aliases.

Figure 8-7

What destroy ()
does not do.

```
package ijs.lifecycle;

import java.io.*;
import java.net.*;
import java.util.*;

import javax.servlet.*;
import javax.servlet.http.*;

/**
 * TestDestroyServlet - demonstrates what
 * the destroy() method doesn't do.
 */
public class TestDestroyServlet extends HttpServlet
{
    public void doGet(
        HttpServletRequest request,
        HttpServletResponse response)
        throws ServletException, IOException
    {
        // Get the request count

        HttpSession session = request.getSession(true);
        Integer count = (Integer) session.getValue
            ("ijs.lifecycle.TestDestroyServlet.count");
        if (count == null)
            count = new Integer(0);

        count = new Integer(count.intValue() + 1);
        session.putValue
        ("ijs.lifecycle.TestDestroyServlet.count", count);

        // See if "destroy" has already been called.
        // If it has been, then destroyReq will contain
        // the request number during which destroy was
        // called.

        Integer destroyReq = (Integer) session.getValue
            ("ijs.lifecycle.TestDestroyServlet.destroyReq");

        String command = request.getParameter("command");

        // See if the "destroy" command was specified
        // on this request

        boolean doDestroy = false;
        if ((command != null) && (command.equals("destroy")))
            doDestroy = true;

        // Set up for output

        response.setContentType("text/html");
        PrintWriter out = response.getWriter();

        out.println(""
            + "<HTML>"
            + "<BODY>"
```

Figure 8-7

(Continued)

```
        + "<H1>Test Destroy Servlet</H1>"
        + "This is request number "
        + count.toString()
        + "<P>"
        );

    if (doDestroy)
        out.println(""
            + "The destroy() method is about to be called"
            + "<P>"
            );

    if (destroyReq != null)
        out.println(""
            + "The destroy() method was called in request "
            + destroyReq.toString()
            + "<P>"
            );

    out.println(""
        + "</BODY>"
        + "</HTML>"
        );

    // Call destroy if requested

    if (doDestroy) {
        session.putValue
        ("ijs.lifecycle.TestDestroyServlet.destroyReq",
        count);

        this.destroy();
    }
}
```

intended more to signal unexpected error conditions. A more elegant solution would be to handle the shutdown request by calling a synchronized method that sets an instance variable and then interrogating this variable to determine if requests can be handled.

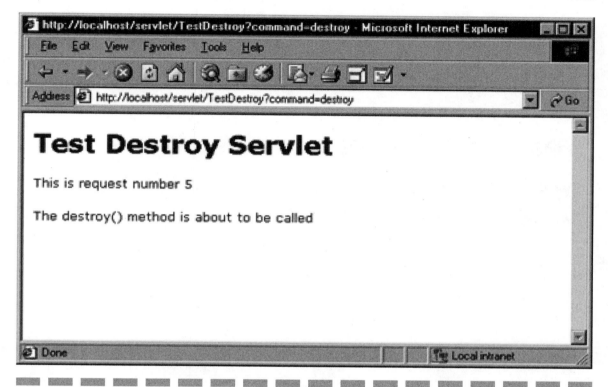

Figure 8-8 The destroy() method is about to be called.

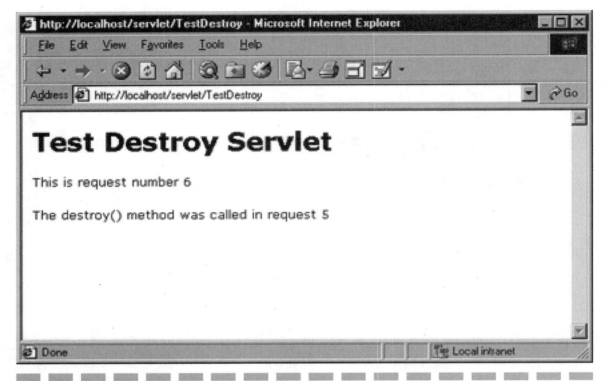

Figure 8-9 Servlet life after destruction.

8.6   Saving State Between Invocations

Problem

My servlet contains complex objects that need to be saved when the servlet engine is shut down and restored when it comes back up. How can I do this?

Technique

Override the `init()` and `destroy()` methods. In `destroy()`, open an `ObjectOutputStream` and save objects to it using `writeObject()`. In `init()`, check for the existence of the saved object file. If it exists, restore it using an `ObjectInputStream` and `readObject()`.

Discussion

The Servlet API provides convenient hooks for saving and restoring state. The `init()` method is guaranteed to execute before any requests are serviced, and the `destroy()` method is guaranteed to be called whenever the servlet is shut down (barring any unpleasant occurrences that bring down the entire servlet engine). Figure 8-10 illustrates how a chess-playing servlet can save the configuration of the board when the servlet is shut down and restore it when the servlet is restored.

In this case, the chess board is stored in the servlet context as long as the servlet is running. When the `destroy()` method is called, the servlet checks to see if there is an active game. If so, it creates an `ObjectOutputStream` over an ordinary `FileOutputStream` and serializes the `board` object. Later, when the servlet engine starts up again[6] and the `init()` method is called, the servlet checks for the existence of the saved file. If it finds the file, it creates an `ObjectInputStream` over a `FileInputStream` and reconstitutes the board with `readObject()`.

If you use serialization, be sure to indicate that each of the objects you save implements either the `java.io.Serializable` interface or the `java.io.Externalizable` interface, or else mark them as `transient` and provide your own code to save and restore them.

See Also

The "Object Serialization" topic in the JDK documentation.

---

[6]Even on a different machine, if you move the serialized file appropriately.

Figure 8-10
Saving and restor-
ing servlet state.

```java
package ijs.lifecycle;

import ijs.lifecycle.chess.*;

import java.io.*;
import java.net.*;
import java.util.*;

import javax.servlet.*;
import javax.servlet.http.*;

/**
 * ChessServlet
 */
public class ChessServlet extends HttpServlet
{
    /**
     * The name of the file to which the game
     * will be serialized between servlet
     * invocations.
     */
    public static final String SAVE_FILE
        = "D:/book/Chap08/chess/game.ser";

    /**
     * The name of the attribute in the servlet context
     * that represents the current chess board.
     */ servlet exception
    public static final String ATTR_NAME
        = "ijs.lifecycle.chess.board";

    /**
     * Performs servlet initialization
     * @exception ServletException if a occurs
     */
    public void init(ServletConfig config)
        throws ServletException
    {
        super.init(config);
        try {
            Board board = null;
            File file = new File(SAVE_FILE);

            // If there is a game in progress, restore it.
            // Otherwise, create a new one.

            if (file.exists()) {
                FileInputStream s = new FileInputStream(file);
                ObjectInputStream in = new ObjectInputStream(s);
                board = (Board) in.readObject();
                s.close();
            }
            else
                board = new Board();

            ServletContext context = getServletContext();
```

Figure 8-10
(Continued)

```
                    context.setAttribute(ATTR_NAME, board);
        }
        catch (Exception e) {
            throw new UnavailableException
                (this, e.getMessage());
        }
    }

    /**
     * Saves servlet state before being destroyed
     */
    public void destroy()
    {
        try {
            ServletContext context = getServletContext();
            Board board = (Board) context.getAttribute(ATTR_NAME);
            if (board != null) {
                File file = new File(SAVE_FILE);
                FileOutputStream s = new
FileOutputStream(file);
                ObjectOutputStream out = new ObjectOutputStream(s);
                out.writeObject(board);
                out.flush();
                s.close();
            }
        }
        catch (Exception e) {
            log(e.getMessage());
        }
        super.destroy();
    }

    /**
     * Handles a GET request
     * @param request the servlet request object
     * @param response the servlet response object
     * @exception ServletException if a servlet exception occurs
     * @exception IOException if an I/O exception occurs
     */
    public void doGet(
            HttpServletRequest request,
            HttpServletResponse response)
        throws ServletException, IOException
    {
        ServletContext context = getServletContext();
        Board board = (Board) context.getAttribute(ATTR_NAME);

        // ... interact with player making moves (not shown) ...
    }
}
```

8.7   Preloading Servlets

Problem

My servlet performs some lengthy initialization, and I do not want the first user to pay the performance penalty.

Technique

Preload the servlet according to the method provided by your servlet engine (see Table 8-3).

Discussion

Most servlet engines provide a way to preload servlets, even though this is not strictly required by the servlet specification. Table 8-3 lists the methods used by several popular servlet engines.

TABLE 8-3

Properties File Where Preload Attribute is Specified

JRun 2.3.3

`servlet.<alias>.preload=true` **property in** `jsm-default/services/<service name>/properties/servlets.properties`

ServletExec 2.2

Specify the servlet alias in the `servlets.startup` property in `ServletExec/ ServletExec Data/<server name>/servlets.properties` **or, using the** admin servlet, specify a nonzero entry in the servlet's `Init Load Order` parameter.

ApacheJServ 1.0

Add the servlet alias to the `servlets.startup` **property in** `ApacheJServ/conf/ zone.properties`

9

Threading Issues

Overview

A key advantage of Java servlets over Common Gateway Interface (CGI) programs is performance. CGI programs typically handle a single HTTP request and then terminate. This works reasonably well, but it injects the overhead of creating a new process for every request, which can result in noticeable delays when traffic is heavy. Servlets, on the other hand, can handle any number of requests during their lifetime, even servicing multiple requests simultaneously. Servlet engines accomplish this by creating a single persistent instance of each servlet when it is first requested, maintaining a pool of threads, and then dispatching HTTP requests to servlet instances using the next available thread.

As beneficial as this is, it introduces difficulties that do not exist in simpler models. For example, instance variables are shared among all threads. If you call another method from inside a servlet, you cannot rely on the value of an instance variable being the same as it was in the calling routine. Similarly, in a servlet that uses an external resource such as a database, it is possible for the read and update operations of two threads to overlap if nothing is done to prevent it.

Fortunately, Java provides efficient means for handling multiple threads and synchronizing their operation. This chapter presents two different threading models that can be used, pointing out the advantages and disadvantages of each. To begin with, however, let's define our terms and review some concepts that relate to threads.

Threading Basics

Thread A *thread* is a single sequential flow of control, sometimes referred to as a *lightweight process*. A thread has its own stack and program counter and is able to operate independently with respect to other threads in the same process. Programs with multiple threads appear to be doing more than one thing at a time. Java is somewhat unique among programming languages in that it has built-in support for multiple-threaded programs both in the core libraries and in the language itself. Threads are represented as instances of the `java.lang.Thread` class.

Instance An *instance* of a class is an executable number of the class with its own state and behavior. An instance has a unique identity and occupies a specific memory location. Once a class is loaded in the Java virtual machine, any number of instances of the class can be created. In the case of servlet classes, the servlet engine takes care of creating and destroying instances of the class.

Start and Run A `java.lang.Thread` exists as an object as soon as it is created, but it is not active (i.e., not assigned to an actual thread) until its `run()` method is started. This allows methods to be called to set the thread's priority and other characteristics before it begins running. For example:

```
Thread t = new SubclassOfThread();
t.setName("ProgressMeter");
t.setPriority(Thread.MIN_PRIORITY);
t.start();
```

Note that you do not ordinarily call the run() method directly. There is nothing to prevent you from doing this, but it would mean simply that the run() method would be executed in the same thread as the one calling run(). There is not actually a second thread running until the Java virtual machine starts it, which you trigger by calling the start() method.

Two techniques are available for creating threads. The first is to subclass java.lang.Thread, overriding its run() method to perform useful work. Instances of this subclass can then be created and started and will run in their own threads. Figure 9-1 shows an example of this usage. It defines a class named SubThread that extends Thread. The constructor of the main class creates and starts an instance of SubThread, and then both objects run a short loop, pausing a random amount of time between iterations. After each iteration, they print the elapsed time in seconds and their thread name. The output is shown in Figure 9-2.

The other technique is to declare that your class implements the Runnable interface. In this case, you provide a run() method and create a java.lang.Thread, passing it a reference to your class in the constructor. When you invoke the thread's start() method, it will run your run() method while you perform other tasks. Figure 9-3 shows how this is done, using the same example as Figure 9-1. Here, RunnableDemo declares that it implements Runnable. It creates and starts an instance of Thread itself, passing a reference to the RunnableDemo instance in the constructor. As before, both classes run a short loop and print the elapsed time in seconds and their thread name. The output is shown in Figure 9-4.

Each technique has its advantages. Subclassing java.util.Thread allows you to create more than one additional thread, but it prevents you from subclassing anything else (Java does not support multiple inheritance). Implementing Runnable is somewhat simpler, since you only need to write a run() method, and the technique can be used for classes that already extend to some other class. However, you can only implement one run() method, so you are restricted to one additional thread.

Synchronization The synchronized keyword is used to denote a method or block of statements that can be executed only by a single thread at a time. For example, when the following code is executed, that is,

```
synchronized (obj) {
    // ... single threaded code here
}
```

Figure 9-1

A class that
demonstrates how
to subclass
Thread to run an
additional thread.

```java
import java.text.*;

public class ThreadDemo
{
    public static final long DELAY = 150;
    public static final int LIMIT = 10;
    public static final DecimalFormat fmt
        = new DecimalFormat("#0.000");

    private long startTime;

    /**
     * Mainline
     */
    public static void main(String[] args)
    {
        new ThreadDemo();
    }

    /**
     * Constructor which runs the demo
     */
    public ThreadDemo()
    {
        System.out.println();
        System.out.println("Elapsed\tThread");
        System.out.println("Time\tName");
        System.out.println("----\t----");
        startTime = System.currentTimeMillis();

        // Start another thread that will use
        // the run method in this class

        SubThread other = new SubThread(this);
        other.start();

        // While the other thread is running,
        // continue printing the count in this thread

        for (int i = 0; i < LIMIT; i++) {
            long delay = (long) (DELAY + Math.random() * 50);
            try {
                Thread.sleep(delay);
            }
            catch (InterruptedException ignore) {}
            print(Thread.currentThread().getName());
        }
    }

    /**
     * Prints the elapsed time and thread name
     */
    public synchronized void print(String name)
    {
        long now = System.currentTimeMillis();
        double elapsed = (now - startTime) / 1000.0;
        System.out.println(fmt.format(elapsed) + "\t" + name);
```

Figure 9-1
Continued)

```
        }
    }

/**
 * A separate class that subclasses <CODE>Thread</CODE>.
 */
class SubThread extends Thread
{
    private ThreadDemo parent;

    /**
     * Creates a new <CODE>SubThread</CODE>
     */
    public SubThread(ThreadDemo parent)
    {
        this.parent = parent;
    }

    /**
     * Counts down to zero
     */
    public void run()
    {
        long LIMIT = ThreadDemo.LIMIT;
        long DELAY = ThreadDemo.DELAY;

        for (int i = 0; i < LIMIT; i++) {
            long delay = (long) (DELAY + Math.random() * 50);
            try {
                Thread.sleep(delay);
            }
            catch (InterruptedException ignore) {}
            parent.print(Thread.currentThread().getName());
        }
    }
}
```

the current thread attempts to acquire a lock on the object specified inside the parentheses (obj). When the lock is acquired, the statements inside the block are executed, and then the lock is released. If some other thread already has the object locked, the current thread waits until the lock is available. This ensures that only one thread at a time can execute the instructions inside the block. Entire methods can be synchronized by specifying the synchronized keyword on the method declaration, as we saw in the print() method of RunnableDemo:

```
public synchronized void print(String name)
{
    // ...
}
```

## Chapter 9

Figure 9-2

The output of
ThreadDemo.

Elapsed Time	Thread Name
----	----
0.171	Thread-0
0.261	main
0.421	main
0.441	Thread-0
0.591	Thread-0
0.611	main
0.751	Thread-0
0.802	main
0.922	Thread-0
0.992	main
1.112	Thread-0
1.182	main
1.302	Thread-0
1.332	main
1.473	Thread-0
1.513	main
1.653	Thread-0
1.693	main
1.803	Thread-0
1.873	main

which is equivalent to

```
public void print(String name)
{
    synchronized(this) {
      // ...
    }
}
```

Synchronized blocks are sometimes referred to as *critical sections*. It is good to keep these sections as small as possible to avoid degrading performance.

Wait and Notify When two or more threads must cooperate to accomplish a task, they can synchronize their operations using the wait and notify methods they inherit from java.lang.Object. When a thread running inside a synchronized block calls wait,[1] it relinquishes the object lock and waits until another thread calls notify or notifyAll on the same object lock.[2] We used this technique in the ConnectionPool

---

[1] Or the related wait(long timeout) or wait(long timeout, int nanos) methods, which provide for timeout.
[2] Notify wakes up a single thread arbitrarily chosen from among those waiting for the object lock. notifyAll wakes up all threads waiting for the lock.

Figure 9-3

Figure 9-3

A class that
demonstrates how
to implement
Runnable to run
an additional
thread.

```java
import java.text.*;

public class RunnableDemo implements Runnable
{
    public static final long DELAY = 150;
    public static final int LIMIT = 10;
    public static final DecimalFormat fmt
        = new DecimalFormat("#0.000");

    private long startTime;

    /**
     * Mainline
     */
    public static void main(String[] args)
    {
        new RunnableDemo();
    }

    /**
     * Constructor which runs the demo
     */
    public RunnableDemo()
    {
        System.out.println();
        System.out.println("Elapsed\tThread");
        System.out.println("Time\tName");
        System.out.println("----\t----");
        startTime = System.currentTimeMillis();

        // Start another thread that will use
        // the run method in this class

        Thread other = new Thread(this);
        other.start();

        // While the other thread is running,
        // continue printing the count in this thread

        for (int i = 0; i < LIMIT; i++) {
            long delay = (long) (DELAY + Math.random() * 50);
            try {
                Thread.sleep(delay);
            }
            catch (InterruptedException ignore) {}
            print(Thread.currentThread().getName());
        }
    }

    /**
     * This method will be run by another thread
     */
    public void run()
    {
        for (int i = 0; i < LIMIT; i++) {
            long delay = (long) (DELAY + Math.random() * 50);
            try {
```

```
                              Thread.sleep(delay);
                }
                catch (InterruptedException ignore) {}
                print(Thread.currentThread().getName());
            }
        }

        /**
         * Prints the elapsed time and thread name
         */
        public synchronized void print(String name)
        {
            long now = System.currentTimeMillis();
            double elapsed = (now - startTime) / 1000.0;
            System.out.println(fmt.format(elapsed) + "\t" + name);
        }
    }
```

```
Elapsed Thread
Time    Name
----    ----
0.200   main
0.280   Thread-0
0.471   main
0.471   Thread-0
0.641   main
0.641   Thread-0
0.831   Thread-0
0.831   main
1.012   Thread-0
1.022   main
1.202   Thread-0
1.212   main
1.372   main
1.392   Thread-0
1.532   main
1.572   Thread-0
1.703   main
1.733   Thread-0
1.883   main
1.913   Thread-0
```

class shown in Figure 5-8. The getConnection() method is synchronized to prevent more than one client from allocating the same resource. If no connection is available, however, it waits at most for a specified length of time for one to be returned to the pool, releasing the object lock while it waits. When the synchronized refresh() method makes a connection available, it calls notify() to wake up one waiting thread and allow it to get the resource. This ensures that getConnection() does not have to wait for a lengthy fixed interval, since it is notified as soon as possible.

The Servlet Threading Model

The servlet engine controls the life cycle of a servlet using one of two models:

1. A single multithreaded instance of the servlet
2. A pool of instances run by a single thread each

The first model is used by default. When a servlet is first loaded, its `init()` method is called. The servlet engine guarantees that no requests will be run until the `init()` method completes successfully. Each request subsequently processed by the servlet is assigned to a separate thread. The thread may be newly created, or it may be recycled from a pool of threads. The single instance of the servlet remains available for use until the servlet engine unloads it. When all threads running the servlet's `service()` method have terminated, the servlet's `destroy()` method is called, and the class is unloaded.

The second model, which is much less common in practice, uses a pool of instances of the same servlet. Incoming requests are run in the next available instance, with at most one thread active in a single instance at one time. This ensures that instance variables cannot be overwritten when multiple requests are processed. You indicate that this model should be used by declaring that your servlet class implements the `SingleThreadModel` interface. As we shall see later on, this does not accomplish everything you might think it does.

The remainder of this chapter examines servlet threading issues, paying particular attention to the problems that can arise and discussing techniques for solving them.

9.1   Thread Safety

Problem

I get strange results when two or more people run my servlet at the same time. This does not happen when the requests are run one at a time. What is happening, and what can I do about it?

Technique

Recall that the servlet engine by default creates just one instance of a servlet with multiple threads to handle requests. If the servlet uses instance variables, multiple threads may be overwriting them simultaneously. Move all the instance variables into an inner class, create an instance of that class as a local variable, and pass that variable to all subroutines.

Discussion

Threading problems are particularly difficult to debug because they are so hard to reproduce. We'll use the example of a search engine servlet because its run time is long enough to induce interference between requests.

Consider the first attempt, shown in Figure 9-5. `Unsafe-SearchServlet`[3] accepts a search string as a request parameter and finds HTML files in the server's document tree that contain the string. The output is a list of hyperlinks containing the names of matching documents followed by the number of hits.

The heart of the program is the `search(String path)` method. Given a directory name, it gets a list of all the directory's entries, processing each one in turn. If an entry is a subdirectory, the `search` method is called recursively to process that subdirectory and anything below it. If an entry is a file with a name ending in `.html`, the program examines its contents looking for the search string. If it finds the string, it writes a hyperlink containing the file name to the output stream and increments the counter.

Figures 9-6 and 9-7 show the output of typical requests processed by the servlet, first with a search string of `HttpSessionBindingListener` (which finds 13 matching documents) and then with `GenericServlet` (which matches 21). Everything appears to be working as expected. But let's see what happens when we run these two searches at the same time. Figure 9-8 shows garbled results from the search for `HttpSessionBindingListener`. The document count is 26 this time. Closer inspection shows that each document is listed twice, but interleaved somewhat. The `GenericServlet` search in Figure 9-9 is even

---

[3]You would think that the program name alone should have been enough to warn the programmer that there was a problem!

■■■ ■■■ ■■■ ■■■

Figure 9-5

*Unsafe search
servlet.*

```
package ijs.threads;

import java.io.*;
import java.net.*;
import java.util.*;

import javax.servlet.*;
import javax.servlet.http.*;

/**
 * UnsafeSearchServlet - does not work properly!
 */
public class UnsafeSearchServlet extends HttpServlet
{
    private HttpServletRequest request;
    private HttpServletResponse response;
    private PrintWriter out;
    private String rootURL;
    private String rootPath;
    private String search;
    private int count;

    /**
     * Handles a GET request
     * @param request the servlet request object
     * @param response the servlet response object
     * @exception ServletException if a servlet exception occurs
     * @exception IOException if an I/O exception occurs
     */
    public void doGet(
          HttpServletRequest request,
          HttpServletResponse response)
        throws ServletException, IOException
    {
        response.setContentType("text/html");
        PrintWriter out = response.getWriter();

        this.request = request;
        this.response = response;
        this.out = out;

        // Start the output document

        out.println(""
            + "<HTML>"
            + "<HEAD>"
            + "<TITLE>UnsafeSearchServlet</TITLE>"
            + "</HEAD>"
            );

        try {

            // Get the search string

            search = request.getParameter("search");
            if (search == null)
                throw new RuntimeException
```

Figure 9-5
(Continued)

```
                   ("No search string specified");

                // Get the root URL

                rootURL = getInitParameter("rootURL");
                if (rootURL == null)
                    throw new RuntimeException("No URL specified");
                rootPath = getServletContext().getRealPath(rootURL);

                // Start the search

                out.println
                ("<BODY LINK=\"#0000FF\" VLINK=\"#0000FF\">");
                out.println("<H3>Matching Documents</H3>");
                out.println("<OL>");

                count = 0;
                search(rootPath);

                out.println("</OL>");
                out.println("<P>");
                out.println(count +
                    " documents contained [" + search + "]");

                out.println("</BODY>");
                out.println("</HTML>");
            }
        catch (RuntimeException e) {
            StringWriter sw = new StringWriter();
            PrintWriter pw = new PrintWriter(sw);
            pw.println("<BODY>");
            pw.println("<H3>Error:</H3>");
            pw.println("<PRE>");
            e.printStackTrace(pw);
            pw.println("</PRE>");
            pw.println("</BODY>");
            pw.println("</HTML>");
            pw.flush();
            out.println(sw.toString());
        }
    }


/**
 * Searches recursively for documents containing
 * the specified search string
 * @param path the URL of the directory to be searched
 */
protected void search(String path)
    throws IOException
{
    // Get the list of entries in this directory

    File dir = new File(path);
    String[] entries = dir.list();

    for (int i = 0; i < entries.length; i++) {
        String fileName = entries[i];
```

Figure 9-5

(Continued)

```
File entry = new File(dir, fileName);

// If this entry is a subdirectory,
// call search recursively

if (entry.isDirectory()) {
    search(entry.getPath());
    continue;
}

// Ignore everything but HTML files

if (!fileName.endsWith(".html"))
    continue;

// Open the file and scan it for
// the search string

BufferedReader in =
    new BufferedReader(
    new FileReader(entry));

while (true) {
    String buffer = in.readLine();
    if (buffer == null)
        break;
    if (buffer.indexOf(search) >= 0) {
        count++;
        String subPath = entry.getPath();

        // Make a URL out of the absolute path

        subPath = rootURL
            + subPath.substring(rootPath.length());
        subPath = subPath.replace('\\', '/');

        String subPathFull = "http://"
            + request.getServerName()
            + ":"
            + request.getServerPort()
            + subPath;

        // Create a hyperlink

        out.println("<LI>"
            + "<A HREF=\""
            + subPathFull
            + "\">"
            + subPath
            + "</A>");
        break;
    }
}
in.close();
}
}
}
```

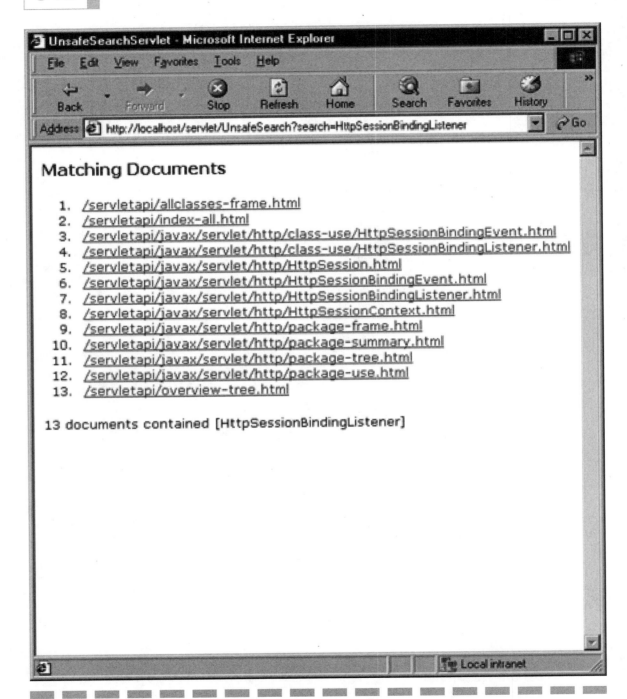

Figure 9-6 Results of search for `HttpSessionBindingListener`.

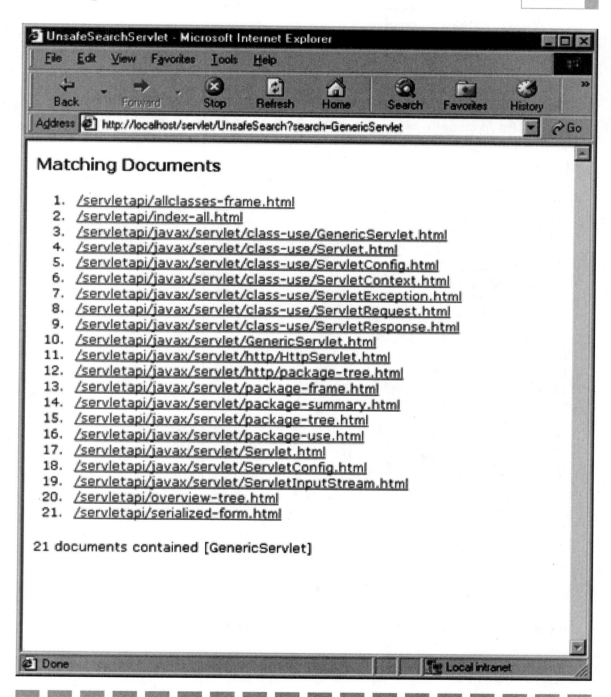

Figure 9-7 Results of search for GenericServlet.

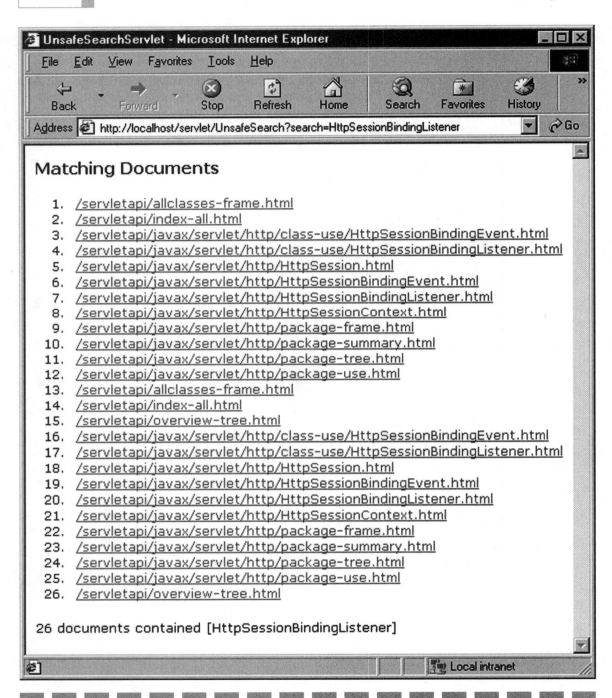

Figure 9-8 Results of simultaneous search for `HttpSessionBindingListener`.

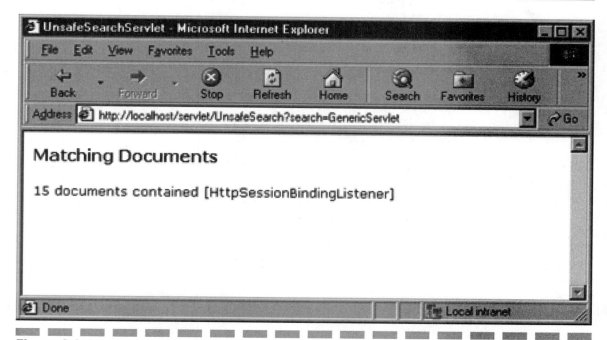

Figure 9-9 Results of simultaneous search for `GenericServlet`.

worse—a document count of 15, the wrong search string, and nothing else! The explanation lies in the unsynchronized use of instance variables. The search for `GenericServlet` was just underway when the `HttpSessionBindingListener` search started. The second request overlaid the `search` instance variable so that both requests were now searching for `HttpSessionBindingListener` and writing their results to the second request's output stream. When the first request finished, it took a snapshot of the `count` instance variable, which was 15 at that point, and printed that as its total.

Clearly, this is an undesirable situation. It can easily be fixed, however, by avoiding the use of instance variables, using local variables on the stack instead. Figure 9-10 shows an improved version of the servlet

Figure 9-10
(Continued)

```
package ijs.threads;

import java.io.*;
import java.net.*;
import java.util.*;

import javax.servlet.*;
import javax.servlet.http.*;

/**
 * Thread safe search servlet
 */
public class SafeSearchServlet extends HttpServlet
{
    /**
     * Inner class for passing parameters between methods
     */
    class Parameters {
        HttpServletRequest request;
        HttpServletResponse response;
        PrintWriter out;
        String rootURL;
        String rootPath;
        String search;
        int count;
    }

    /**
     * Handles a GET request
     * @param request the servlet request object
     * @param response the servlet response object
     * @exception ServletException if a servlet exception occurs
     * @exception IOException if an I/O exception occurs
     */
    public void doGet(
            HttpServletRequest request,
            HttpServletResponse response)
        throws ServletException, IOException
    {
        Parameters parms = new Parameters();
        parms.request = request;
        parms.response = response;

        response.setContentType("text/html");
        PrintWriter out = response.getWriter();
        parms.out = out;

        // Start the output document

        out.println(""
            + "<HTML>"
            + "<HEAD>"
            + "<TITLE>SafeSearchServlet</TITLE>"
            + "</HEAD>"
            );

        try {
```

Figure 9-10
(Continued)

```java
    // Get the search string

    String search = request.getParameter("search");
    if (search == null)
        throw new RuntimeException
        ("No search string specified");
    parms.search = search;

    // Get the root URL

    String rootURL = getInitParameter("rootURL");
    if (rootURL == null)
        throw new RuntimeException("No URL specified");
    parms.rootURL = rootURL;
    String rootPath =
        getServletContext().getRealPath(rootURL);
    parms.rootPath = rootPath;

    // Start the search

    out.println
    ("<BODY LINK=\"#0000FF\" VLINK=\"#0000FF\">");
    out.println("<H3>Matching Documents</H3>");
    out.println("<OL>");

    search(parms, rootPath);

    out.println("</OL>");
    out.println("<P>");
    out.println(parms.count +
        " documents contained [" + search + "]");

    out.println("</BODY>");
    out.println("</HTML>");
  }
  catch (RuntimeException e) {
    StringWriter sw = new StringWriter();
    PrintWriter pw = new PrintWriter(sw);
    pw.println("<BODY>");
    pw.println("<H3>Error:</H3>");
    pw.println("<PRE>");
    e.printStackTrace(pw);
    pw.println("</PRE>");
    pw.println("</BODY>");
    pw.println("</HTML>");
    pw.flush();
    out.println(sw.toString());
  }
}

/**
 * Searches recursively for documents containing
 * the specified search string
 * @param parms the local parameter object
 * @param path the URL of the directory to be searched
 */
```

Figure 9-10
(Continued)

```
protected void search(Parameters parms, String path)
    throws IOException
{
    // Get the list of entries in this directory

    File dir = new File(path);
    String[] entries = dir.list();

    for (int i = 0; i < entries.length; i++) {
        String fileName = entries[i];
        File entry = new File(dir, fileName);

        // If this entry is a subdirectory,
        // call search recursively

        if (entry.isDirectory()) {
            search(parms, entry.getPath());
            continue;
        }

        // Ignore everything but HTML files

        if (!fileName.endsWith(".html"))
            continue;

        // Open the file and scan it for
        // the search string

        BufferedReader in =
            new BufferedReader(
            new FileReader(entry));

        while (true) {
            String buffer = in.readLine();
            if (buffer == null)
                break;
            if (buffer.indexOf(parms.search) >= 0) {
                parms.count++;
                String subPath = entry.getPath();

                // Make a URL out of the absolute path

                subPath = parms.rootURL
                    + subPath.substring
                        (parms.rootPath.length());

                subPath = subPath.replace('\\', '/');

                String subPathFull = "http://"
                    + parms.request.getServerName()
                    + ":"
                    + parms.request.getServerPort()
                    + subPath;

                // Create a hyperlink

                parms.out.println("<LI>"
```

```
                              + "<A HREF=\""
                              + subPathFull
                              + "\">"
                              + subPath
                              + "</A>");
                  break;
            }
        }
        in.close();
    }
```

that uses this technique. `SafeSearchServlet` uses an inner class to hold the servlet parameters:

```
/**
 * Inner class for passing parameters between methods
 */
class Parameters {
    HttpServletRequest request;
    HttpServletResponse response;
    PrintWriter out;
    String rootURL;
    String rootPath;
    String search;
    int count;
}
```

The `doGet()` method instantiates a `Parameters` object as a local variable, initializing it with the object references that need to be kept separate for each request. This `Parameters` object is then passed as an argument to the `search()` method. This allows the `search()` method to distinguish between the `search`, `count`, and `out` variables that belong to each request. The result is that `SafeSearchServlet` gives the same output for a given request regardless of whether it is run at the same time as another request or not.

▰▰ ▰▰ 9.2 SingleThreadModel

Problem

My servlet accesses an external resource that has no locking mechanism. I have tried implementing `SingleThreadModel` to prevent simultaneous updates, but I still see multiple requests interfering with each other. How can I prevent this problem?

Technique

Define a class variable (not an instance variable), and synchronize all access to the external resource on this variable. For example:

```
private static Object dbLock = new Object();
public void doGet(
      HttpServletRequest request,
      HttpServletResponse response)
   throws ServletException, IOException
{
   ...
   synchronized(dbLock) {
      // ... single threaded operations here
   }
}
```

Discussion

First, let's review the two servlet models. Figure 9-11 illustrates the default model. A single instance of the servlet is loaded by the servlet engine.[4] When requests for the servlet are received, they are assigned to a thread, either newly created or from a pool of recycled threads. Note that the requests can overlap inside the servlet's service() method (or the doGet() and doPost() methods it usually calls). Since each thread

Figure 9-11

Default threading model—one instance with multiple threads.

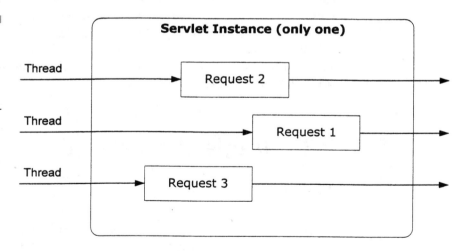

---

[4]Usually this happens in response to the first request for the servlet, but servlet engines typically make provision for preloading servlets. All that you know for certain is that the servlet's init() method has been called and has completed successfully.

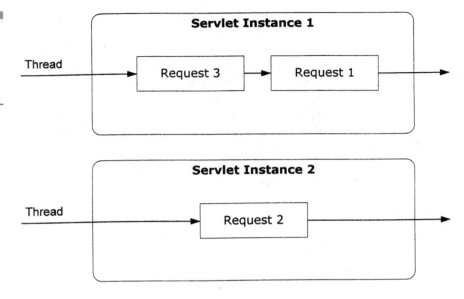

has its own instruction pointer and its own stack on which local variables are allocated, this does not usually present a problem. Figure 9-12 shows the SingleThreadModel in action. There are in this example two instances of the same servlet each running in their own thread. Requests within a single instance are handled one at a time. Note, however, that request 2 still overlaps requests 1 and 3.

This brings us to the heart of the problem. The SingleThreadModel interface is frequently misunderstood. True, it guarantees that within the service() method of an instance of the servlet, only one thread at a time can be active. What is commonly overlooked, however, is that the servlet engine typically creates multiple instances of Single-ThreadModel servlets to maintain acceptable performance. These multiple instances are thread-safe in themselves but not with respect to each other. From the standpoint of an external resource, there is no difference between being accessed by a multithreaded single instance or multiple instances running in their own threads.

If you really need to ensure that exactly one access to an external resource is made by your servlet, you need to control it through a common object that is known to all instances of the servlet and all threads running the instances. The easiest way to do this is to create a static object (of any kind) and synchronize all external access on this object. It is common to all instances of the class because it is static, and it is respected by all threads because it is the target of a synchronize block.

So what good is `SingleThreadModel`, then? Its main benefit is that it allows you to use instance variables to store objects while the `service()` method is executing. For example, if you take a structured approach to generating a complex HTML document, you may have a hierarchy of methods that generate the `<HEAD>` section, the `<BODY>` section, tables within the body, etc. In this case, it might be convenient to store the response object's `PrintWriter` object in an instance variable so that it can be used without being passed as a parameter. However, the same thing can be accomplished by using an inner class or `Hashtable` that is passed to all subroutines. The decision of which technique to use is essentially a matter of personal preference.

9.3 A Multithreaded Application

Problem

How can I have my servlet perform useful work between requests so that individual clients do not incur a performance penalty?

Technique

Delegate the work to an object running in another thread. Create the object during your `init()` method, store it in the servlet context so that it can be accessed by request service routines, and terminate it in your `destroy()` method.

Discussion

In this section we will begin developing an application that will be extended later in Chapter 11. The application is a news headlines ticker that gets its input by periodically scanning a specific Web page for headlines and extracting their URLs. For now, we will just display the output as a Web page. Later on, we will see how this can be embedded in an applet for a more compact and useful presentation.

The Application   Quite a number of Web sites are devoted to news and current events. These sites frequently have a main page containing brief references to their top stories, each of which has a URL that points to the full story on some other Web page. Of course, anything a Web browser can read a Java program can read as well, so it should be possible to design a servlet application that dynamically collects this information (possibly even from several sources) and presents a digest in some convenient form. The steps involved would be

1. Open a URL connection to a fixed Web site.
2. Scan the returned HTML (which must be in a known format) for the headlines and their URLs.
3. Make a collection of headline objects from the results.
4. Provide these objects to clients when prompted by a servlet request.
5. Refresh the headline collection by repeating steps 1 to 4 on a periodic basis.

It certainly would be possible to do all this without multithreading simply by extracting the information only when it is requested. However, if there are hundreds of clients accessing the servlet on an intranet, it would be quite wasteful to access the source Web site and parse its headlines for every request. The servlet provides a convenient place to cache the headlines. All we need to do is provide it with the capability of updating itself as necessary between requests. A low-priority background thread is the solution.

Class Design To begin with, we need a simple data structure to represent an individual headline. Figure 9-13 defines a `Headline` class that keeps track of a news headline and its associated URL. Its only operations are `get` and `set` methods for each of its fields.

Next, we need some means of collecting a group of `Headline` objects and periodically refreshing them. For testing purposes and maximum flexibility, we will make this an interface rather than a concrete class. This also allows us to concentrate on the operations it needs to perform rather than the details of how to do them. Figure 9-14 shows this interface, which we will call `HeadlineSource`.

Classes that implement `HeadlineSource` agree to provide four methods:

- `getHeadlines()`—which returns the current array of headline objects
- `getLastRefreshTime()`—which informs the client how old the data is

Figure 9-13

The news headline
object.

```java
package ijs.news;

import java.io.*;
import java.net.*;

/**
 * A news headline and its URL at a news website
 */
public class Headline implements Serializable
{
    private String title;
    private URL url;

    /**
     * Returns the title
     */
    public String toString()
    {
        return title;
    }

    /**
     * Returns the title
     */
    public String getTitle()
    {
        return title;
    }

    /**
     * Sets the title
     * @param title the new title
     */
    public void setTitle(String title)
    {
        this.title = title;
    }

    /**
     * Returns the URL
     */
    public URL getURL()
    {
        return url;
    }

    /**
     * Sets the URL from a URL
     * @param url the URL
     */
    public void setURL(URL url)
    {
        this.url = url;
    }

    /**
     * Sets the URL from a string
```

Figure 9-13

(Continued)

```
 * @param url the URL
 */
public void setURL(String url)
    throws MalformedURLException
{
    this.url = new URL(url);
}

/**
 * True if this object is the same as another specified
 * object.
 * @param other the other object
 */
public boolean equals(Object other)
{
    if (other == null)
        return false;
    if (other instanceof Headline) {
        Headline that = (Headline) other;
        return (
            this.title.equals(that.title) &&
            this.url.equals(that.url)
            );
    }
    return false;
}

/**
 * Returns the hash code
 */
public int hashCode()
{
    return title.hashCode() + url.hashCode();
}
```

- `start()`—which will start the periodic refresh thread
- `stop()`—which will stop the thread

We may choose to get news headlines from several different sources, perhaps switching between them or even combining them, depending on network availability and user preference. For each source, we need to have a class that implements `HeadlineSource`. However, their implementations will no doubt have a lot in common. They all need to open URL connections, read and parse HTML, manage a refresh thread, and so on. The only thing unique to a particular source is likely to be the format of its HTML. It makes sense, then, to use a base class from which specific `HeadlineSource` classes can be derived. We will call this base class `HeadlineSourceImpl` (**Figure 9-15**). `HeadlineSourceImpl` defines instance variables in which it stores the current headline array, the date and time it was last updated, and the refresh thread. It imple-

Figure 9-14

An interface defining a source of headlines.

```
package ijs.news;

import java.util.*;

/**
 * A source of headline objects
 */
public interface HeadlineSource
{
    /**
     * Starts the headline refresh thread
     */
    public void start();

    /**
     * Stops the headline refresh thread
     */
    public void stop();

    /**
     * Returns the current array of headline objects
     */
    public Headline[] getHeadlines();

    /**
     * Returns the date the headlines were last updated
     */
    public Date getLastRefreshTime();
}
```

ments each of the four methods of `HeadlineSource`. We are most interested in `start()` and `stop()`.

After first ensuring that it has not already been called, `start()` creates the refresh thread, sets it to a low priority so that it does not overuse the CPU, sets its daemon attribute so that the Java virtual machine can shut down without waiting for it to complete, and then calls its `start()` method. This in turn causes the virtual machine to create a new thread and invoke its `run()` method. `run()` does nothing but call a `refresh()` method in a loop, sleeping for a fixed interval[5] between iterations. The loop is terminated when the refresh thread reference is set to `null`, which is done by the `stop()` method. We have defined `HeadlineSourceImpl` to be an abstract class to force subclasses to implement the `refresh()` method.

Note that after starting the refresh thread, `start()` invokes the `wait()` method. The reason this is necessary is to allow the newly cre-

---

[5]We have hard-coded a 3-minute interval here. In a production implementation, this should be a configurable parameter.

Figure 9-15

The base implemen-
tation of
HeadlineSource.

```
package ijs.news;

import java.io.*;
import java.net.*;
import java.util.*;

/**
 * The base class for implementations of HeadlineSource.
 */
public abstract class HeadlineSourceImpl
    implements HeadlineSource, Runnable
{
    protected Date lastRefreshTime;
    protected Headline[] headlines;
    protected transient Thread refreshThread;

    // ===============================================
    //      Instance methods
    // ===============================================

    /**
     * Refreshes the list of headlines.  Subclasses
     * must override this method.
     */
    protected abstract void refresh()
        throws IOException;

    // ===============================================
    //      Implementation of Runnable
    // ===============================================

    /**
     * Periodically refreshes the list of headlines
     */
    public void run()
    {
        try {
            while (refreshThread != null) {
                refresh();
                Thread.sleep(3*60*1000);
            }
        }
        catch (Exception e) {
            headlines = null;
            e.printStackTrace();
            return;
        }
    }


    // ===============================================
    //      Implementation of HeadlineSource
    // ===============================================

    /**
     * Returns a copy of the headlines array
     */
    public Headline[] getHeadlines()
```

Figure 9-15
(Continued)

```
{
    Headline[] copy = null;
    if (headlines != null) {
        copy = new Headline[headlines.length];
        System.arraycopy(
            headlines, 0, copy, 0, headlines.length);
    }
    return copy;
}

/**
 * Returns the last update time
 */
public Date getLastRefreshTime()
{
    return lastRefreshTime;
}

/**
 * Starts the refresh thread
 */
public void start()
{
    if (refreshThread == null) {

        // Start the refresh thread

        synchronized (this) {
            refreshThread = new Thread(this);
            refreshThread.setPriority(Thread.MIN_PRIORITY);
            refreshThread.setDaemon(true);
            refreshThread.start();
            try {
                wait();
            }
            catch (InterruptedException ignore) {}
        }
    }
}

/**
 * Stops the refresh thread
 */
public void stop()
{
    if (refreshThread != null) {
        refreshThread = null;
    }
}

public static String stripMarkup(String s)
{
    int state = 0;
    StringBuffer buffer = new StringBuffer();
    for (int i = 0; i < s.length(); i++) {
        char c = s.charAt(i);
        switch (state) {
```

```
                    case 0:
                        if (c == '<')
                            state = 1;
                        else
                            buffer.append(c);
                        break;
                    case 1:
                        if (c == '>')
                            state = 0;
                        break;
                }
            }
        return buffer.toString();
    }
```

ated thread to complete its first call to `refresh()` before a servlet request tries to retrieve its results. The `refresh()` method should call `notify()` or `notifyAll()` at its end to wake up the waiting thread and indicate that data are available.

News Sources   At this point, we are ready to choose a particular Web site from which to read headlines. Most of the major news organizations have such Web sites, and it turns out that most of them appear to generate their HTML programmatically so that it is easy to parse. For the purposes of this exercise, we will return to our hypothetical Internet Premium Food Market Web site, which conveniently provides a Web page that is ideal for our use. While not completely realistic, it is enough to illustrate the technique. You should have no trouble defining your own `HeadlineSource` classes after understanding how one works.

The Internet Premium Food Market publishes a newsletter with product and company announcements. The HTML for the relevant section of the Web page looks like this:

```
<H2>NewsLetter</H2>
What's new at the Internet Premium Food Market?
<!— news —>
<H3><A HREF="/ipfoods/newsletter/VideoShopping.html">
    IPFM to offer video shopping</A></H3>
<H3><A HREF="/ipfoods/newsletter/Board.html">
    Bauer, Cardenas named to IPFM board</A></H3>
<H3><A HREF="/ipfoods/newsletter/Schech.html">
    Schechs honored for Hunger Project work</A></H3>

<!— /news —>
```

The news item section is contained between the <!— news —> and <!— /news —> comment lines. Our parser, then, needs to look for these two markers and extract any <A HREF="url">title</A> lines it finds between them.

Figure 9-16 is a listing of the implementation of IPFHeadline-Source, a subclass of HeadlineSourceImpl containing a refresh() method that reads and parses the Internet Premium Food Market newsletter. Using the appropriate URL, it calls the openStream() method to get access to the contents of the Web page. The parsing logic accumulates Headline objects in a java.util.Vector until the end of the news item section is found. It then copies the contents of the vector to the headlines array, updates the last refresh time, and calls notifyAll() to indicate to any waiting threads that the update is complete.

The Servlet Finally, we need a host class of some kind to launch the HeadlineSource object and relay its results to requesting clients. We will call this TickerServlet (Figure 9-17).

TickerServlet ties the whole application together. In its init() method, it instantiates the IPFHeadlineSource, starts it running, and stores a reference to it in the servlet context. For each HTTP client request, the doGet() method interrogates the HeadlineSource for its array of Headline objects and creates a Web page to display them. When the servlet engine shuts down TickerServlet, the destroy() method calls the HeadlineSource stop() method to cause the refresh thread to shut down as well.

In Chapter 11 we will develop a new client for this servlet, a Java applet that cycles through the headlines and allows the user to click for further information.

Figure 9-16

"The Internet
Premium Food
Market" *headline
source class.*

```java
package ijs.news;

import java.io.*;
import java.net.*;
import java.util.*;

/**
 * A HeadlineSource over the IPF web site
 */
public class IPFHeadlineSource extends HeadlineSourceImpl
{
    public static final String URL =
        "http://localhost/ipfoods/newsletter/index.html";

    // Constants used to indicate parsing state

    private static final int BEFORE_NEWS = 1;
    private static final int READING_NEWS = 2;

    // Markers encountered in the HTML input

    private static final String START_NEWS = "<!-- news -->";
    private static final String END_NEWS   = "<!-- /news -->";
    private static final String LINKSTART = "<A HREF=\"";
    private static final String URLEND    = "\">";
    private static final String LINKEND = "</A>";

    // Parsing state

    private int state;

    // =========================================
    //     Constructors
    // =========================================

    public IPFHeadlineSource()
    {
        super();
        state = BEFORE_NEWS;
    }

    // =========================================
    //     Instance methods
    // =========================================

    /**
     * Updates the list of headlines
     */
    protected synchronized void refresh() throws IOException
    {
        String href;
        String title;
        Vector v = new Vector();

        URL baseURL = new URL(URL);

        BufferedReader in =
```

```
                        new BufferedReader(
                        new InputStreamReader(
                        baseURL.openStream())));

                state = BEFORE_NEWS;
                main: while (true) {
                    String line = ((BufferedReader) in).readLine();
                    if (line == null)
                        break;

                    switch (state) {

                        // Look for start of news section

                        case BEFORE_NEWS:
                            if (line.startsWith(START_NEWS))
                                state = READING_NEWS;
                            break;

                        // Extracting URL's until end of
                        // the news section

                        case READING_NEWS:
                            if (line.startsWith(END_NEWS))
                                break main;
                            else {

                                // Look for URL's

                                String uline = line.toUpperCase();

                                // Start with <A HREF=

                                int p = uline.indexOf(LINKSTART);
                                if (p > -1) {
                                    p += LINKSTART.length();

                                    // HREF ends with >

                                    int q = uline.indexOf(URLEND, p);
                                    if (q > -1) {

                                        href = line.substring(p, q).trim();
                                        try {
                                            URL url = new URL(baseURL, href);
                                            href = url.toString();
                                        }
                                        catch (MalformedURLException e) {
                                            break;
                                        }

                                        // Title starts after URL

                                        p = q + URLEND.length();
                                        q = uline.indexOf(LINKEND);
                                        if (q > -1) {
```

```
                                    title = line.substring(p, q).trim();
                                    if (title.equals(""))
                                        break;

                                    // Create a new headline object and
                                    // add it to the vector

                                    Headline headline = new Headline();
                                    headline.setURL(href);
                                    headline.setTitle(title);

                                    v.addElement(headline);
                                }
                            }
                        }
                    }
                    break;
                }
            }

            in.close();

            // Update last refresh time

            lastRefreshTime = new Date();

            // Copy the vector into the headlines array

            headlines = new Headline[v.size()];
            v.copyInto(headlines);

            // Let waiting threads know that the update is complete

            notifyAll();
        }
    }
```

Figure 9-17
A basic servlet
reading from the
headline source.

```
package ijs.news;

import java.io.*;
import java.net.*;
import java.util.*;

import javax.servlet.*;
import javax.servlet.http.*;

/**
 * TickerServlet
 */
public class TickerServlet extends HttpServlet
{
    /**
     * Starts the headline source
     */
    public void init(ServletConfig config)
        throws ServletException
    {
        super.init(config);

        // Get the headline source class

        String className = getInitParameter("className");
        if (className == null)
            throw new UnavailableException
            (this, "No className parameter");

        Object sourceObject = null;
        try {
            sourceObject = Class.forName(className).newInstance();
        }
        catch (Exception e) {
            throw new UnavailableException
            (this, e.getMessage());
        }

        // Start the news source thread

        HeadlineSource source = (HeadlineSource) sourceObject;
        source.start();

        // Save it in the servlet context

        String name = getClass().getName() + ".source";
        getServletContext().setAttribute(name, source);
    }

    /**
     * Stops the headline source
     */
    public void destroy()
    {
        // Get the headline source object

        String name = getClass().getName() + ".source";
```

Figure 9-17
(Continued)

```
        HeadlineSource source = (HeadlineSource)
            getServletContext().getAttribute(name);

        // If it exists, stop it

        if (source != null)
            source.stop();

        super.destroy();
    }

    /**
     * Handles a GET request
     */
    public void doGet(
            HttpServletRequest request,
            HttpServletResponse response)
        throws ServletException, IOException
    {
        // Get the headline source object from the
        // servlet context

        String name = getClass().getName() + ".source";
        HeadlineSource source = (HeadlineSource)
            getServletContext().getAttribute(name);

        // Retrieve the latest headlines

        Date lastRefreshTime = source.getLastRefreshTime();
        Headline[] headlines = source.getHeadlines();

        // Write them to the web page

        response.setContentType("text/html");
        PrintWriter out = response.getWriter();

        out.println(""
            + "<HTML>"
            + "<HEAD>"
            + "<TITLE>Headlines</TITLE>"
            + "</HEAD>"
            + "<BODY>"
            + "<H3>Headlines</H3>"
            );

        out.println("<H4>Last update: "
            + lastRefreshTime + "</H4>");

        if (headlines == null)
            out.println("<PRE>"
            + "Headlines not available"
            + "</PRE>"
            );
        else {
            for (int i = 0; i < headlines.length; i++) {
                out.println(
                    "<A HREF=\""
```

Figure 9-17
(Continued)

```
                            + headlines[i].getURL()
                            + "\">"
                            + headlines[i].getTitle()
                            + "</A><BR>"
                            );
                }
            }

            out.println(""
                + "</BODY>"
                + "</HTML>"
                );
        }
    }
```

10

Interservlet Communication

Overview

One of the organizing principles around which the Unix operating system is designed is the idea of small, modular tools. Programs such as `sort`, `cut`, `paste`, `diff`, `uniq`, and others can be combined in a pipeline to perform complex tasks. This provides for a significant amount of code reuse and cuts development time dramatically. Entire batch applications often can be written in a few lines of shell script code.

Servlets also can be used in this manner. Rather than generating a Web page intended for direct viewing, a servlet can cooperate with other servlets to produce a more complex result. There are several ways this can be done:

Servlet Chaining A servlet can send its output to another general-purpose servlet for postprocessing, possibly to be filtered even further before being rendered in a browser. Chains can be constructed either explicitly or by use of specialized MIME types that trigger post-processing.

Redirection The HTTP protocol provides a means for indicating that a document has been moved from its original location. The redirection is handled automatically by Web browsers so that users are unaware of the forwarding. It turns out that this technique makes it possible for a servlet to trigger another using the browser as the control point. Frequently, this is done to cause error pages to be displayed, but it also can be used to construct multiservlet applications with both visible and invisible components. The shopping cart application described in Section 7.8 includes several servlets (`AddToCart`, `RemoveFromCart`, `ProductSearch`) that perform behind-the-scenes work and then call other servlets to render their results.

Request Dispatching Version 2.1 of the Java Servlet API Specification added `RequestDispatcher` to the API. A `RequestDispatcher` provides programmed access to another Web-based object (usually a servlet), essentially allowing you to construct on-the-fly servlet chains under program control. Requests can be forwarded to a `RequestDispatcher` for completion, or the `RequestDispatcher` can produce output that is included in the current servlet's response.

HTTP Requests Like any other Java program, a servlet can open a `Socket` or `URLConnection` object and make HTTP requests. This means that the program can request and read Web pages, including those generated by other servlets. While similar functionality is provided by the other techniques just described, this method offers certain advantages, notably the ability to access programmatic content from other environments such as CGI, ASP, or servlets running in other Web servers. Chapter 12 describes this technique further.

Direct Calls Earlier versions of the Java Servlet API Specification provided `ServletContext` methods to access other servlets running in the same context. There are several problems with these methods, however, including lack of security and the difficulty of controlling access by servlets in other threads. For this reason and others, these methods have been deprecated and should not be used.

Although there is no general means by which you can access all active servlets, you can have servlets voluntarily register themselves as attributes in the servlet context, as shown below:

```
getServletContext().setAttribute("<servlet class name>", this);
```

Then, in another servlet in the same context, you can use

```
<servlet class name> firstServlet = (<servlet class name>)
    getServletContext().getAttribute("<servlet class name>");
```

to get a reference to the instance of the first servlet. Note that the servlet reference has to be cast into the appropriate class, since `getAttribute()` returns only a `java.lang.Object`.

The remainder of this chapter covers these techniques in more detail, providing complete examples of how they can be used and discussing their relative merits.

10.1   Servlet Chaining

Problem

How can I put together a chain of servlets to handle a single request?

Technique

There are no changes required to the first servlet in the chain. Each subsequent servlet should

1. Copy the request headers to the response object (modifying them where necessary).
2. Read from the request objects input stream.
3. Transform the input stream as required.
4. Write the results to the response output stream.

The mechanism used to invoke the chain depends on the particular servlet engine being used.

Discussion

Servlet chains can be used to apply general-purpose transformations to servlet-generated output. This can simplify coding and enable you to develop a toolkit of useful filters. For example, you may wish to generate raw data in one servlet, sort it in another, format it as an HTML table in a third, and add standard headers and footers in a fourth.

The example we will develop in this section is a table of contents generator. It reads an HTML document that was created by another servlet and constructs an outline based on text appearing between the <H1> through <H6> tags. From each line of text, it constructs a hyperlink outline entry to the associated <Hn> tag and inserts the entry at the top of the document, indented as appropriate. After constructing the table of contents and writing it to the response output stream, it writes the main text of the document, modified to include the hyperlink target tags.

In a servlet chain, the response object created by one servlet is used to create the request object for the next. Any HTTP headers created by the first servlet need to be passed on through the second servlet's response object so that they are delivered to the servlet chain's final destination. This can be done as follows:

```
Enumeration en = request.getHeaderNames();
while (en.hasMoreElements()) {
   String name = (String) en.nextElement();
   if (name.equalsIgnoreCase("Content-Length"))
      continue;
   String value = request.getHeader(name);
   response.setHeader(name, value);
}
```

We make an exception for the Content-Length header in our case because we know we will be creating additional text.

The actual contents of the Web page can be read from the request object's input stream. The table of contents servlet will use a BufferedReader constructed over the input stream to read the text a line at a time:

```
BufferedReader in =
   new BufferedReader(
   new InputStreamReader(
   request.getInputStream()));
```

The first problem we face is that generating the table of contents requires making a complete pass of the input stream, during which we would ordinarily be writing lines to the output stream. Unfortunately, we can make only one pass through the input stream. In order to write the contents section at the beginning of the document, we need to temporarily store the output lines we generate and write them after the contents section is complete. An easy way to do this is with a `java.io.StringWriter`, which stores its output in memory and can be accessed as a string:

```
StringWriter sw = new StringWriter();
PrintWriter out = new PrintWriter(sw);
```

Wrapping the `StringWriter` in a `PrintWriter` makes it possible to use the `println()` methods, making it easier to switch back to ordinary output if later versions of the servlet require it.

As the text is read, it is scanned for `<H1>` through `<H6>` tags. In this example, we will make the simplifying assumption that the beginning and ending `<Hn>` tags are written on the same line. More sophisticated parsers could be used, but this is sufficient to illustrate the technique.

```
String uBuffer = buffer.toUpperCase();
int p = uBuffer.indexOf("<H");
if (p == -1) {
    out.println(buffer);
    continue;
}

char level = buffer.charAt(p+2);
if ((level < '1') || (level > '6')) {
    out.println(buffer);
    continue;
}

int q = uBuffer.indexOf("</H" + level, p+1);
if (q == -1) {
    out.println(buffer);
    continue;
}
```

We make an uppercase copy of the input line so that the search for the beginning and ending tags can be case-insensitive.

Once we have located a heading tag, we increment a counter used to create unique hyperlink names and generate a table of contents entry, indented according to the heading level:[1]

---

[1] In this example, a `java.util.Vector` is used to hold the generated table of contents entries. This is necessary because the completed table of contents does not actually appear at the very top of the file but rather after the `<BODY>` tag.

```
int linkNumber = toc.size() + 1;

String text = buffer.substring(p+4, q).trim();
text = "<A HREF=\"#TOC" + linkNumber + "\">" + text + "</A>";
int indent = Character.digit(level, 10);
text = indents[indent] + text;
toc.addElement(text);
```

We insert a corresponding <A NAME="TOCnnn">...</A> tag into the document where the heading tag occurs and write the line to the output buffer:

```
buffer = buffer.substring(0, p)
    + "<A NAME=\"TOC" + linkNumber + "\"></A>"
    + buffer.substring(p);

out.println(buffer);
```

After processing the entire document generated by the previous servlet, we extract the generated Web page from StringWriter and write it and the table of contents to the response output stream. The complete servlet listing appears in Figure 10-1.

Figure 10-2 shows an example of input to the table of contents servlet, in this case the Constitution of the United States. The input is assumed to have been generated by a previous servlet, possibly one that converted it from XML to HTML.[2]

The HTML behind Figure 10-2 looks in part like this:

```
<H1>United States Constitution</H1>
We the People of the United States, in Order to form a more
perfect Union, establish Justice, insure domestic Tranquility,
provide for the common defence, promote the general Welfare, and
secure the Blessings of Liberty to ourselves and our Posterity,
do ordain and establish this Constitution for the United States
of America.
<H2>Article I - Legislative Branch</H2>
<H3>Section 1 - How Constituted</H3>
<P>All legislative Powers herein granted shall be vested in a Congress
of the
United States, which shall consist of a Senate and House of
Representatives.
<H3>Section 2 - House of Representatives</H3>
```

---

[2]In this case, it was simply copied from an external HTML file, which is why the previous servlet was called cat (after the Unix command).

```
package ijs.interserv;

import java.io.*;
import java.net.*;
import java.util.*;

import javax.servlet.*;
import javax.servlet.http.*;

/**
 * A filter that generates a table of contents from the H1-H6
 * tags in an HTML document.
 */
public class TOCGeneratorServlet extends HttpServlet
{
    private static final int MAX_INDENTS = 8;
    private static String[] indents;

    /**
     * Initializes the servlet
     */
    public void init(ServletConfig config)
    {
        indents = new String[MAX_INDENTS];
        StringBuffer buffer = new StringBuffer();
        for (int i = 0; i < MAX_INDENTS; i++) {
            indents[i] = buffer.toString();
            buffer.append("   ");
        }
    }

    /**
     * Handles a GET request
     */
    public void doGet(
            HttpServletRequest request,
            HttpServletResponse response)
        throws ServletException, IOException
    {
        // Echo headers except Content-Length

        Enumeration en = request.getHeaderNames();
        while (en.hasMoreElements()) {
            String name = (String) en.nextElement();
            if (name.equalsIgnoreCase("Content-Length"))
                continue;
            String value = request.getHeader(name);
            response.setHeader(name, value);
        }

        // Read input stream and build table of contents

        BufferedReader in =
            new BufferedReader(
            new InputStreamReader(
            request.getInputStream()));
```

Figure 10-1
(Continued)

```
// Write output to a buffer so that table of contents
// can be written first

Vector toc = new Vector();
StringWriter sw = new StringWriter();
PrintWriter out = new PrintWriter(sw);
for (
   String buffer = in.readLine();
   buffer != null;
   buffer = in.readLine())
{
   // Look for a <Hn> tag

   // For simplicity, we will assume that the beginning
   // and ending tags are written on the same line.

   String uBuffer = buffer.toUpperCase();
   int p = uBuffer.indexOf("<H");
   if (p == -1) {
      out.println(buffer);
      continue;
   }

   char level = buffer.charAt(p+2);
   if ((level < '1') || (level > '6')) {
      out.println(buffer);
      continue;
   }

   // Look for its ending tag

   int q = uBuffer.indexOf("</H" + level, p+1);
   if (q == -1) {
      out.println(buffer);
      continue;
   }

   // Generate the link number and attach it

   int linkNumber = toc.size() + 1;

   // Extract the text between the tags and
   // store it in the table of contents vector

   String text = buffer.substring(p+4, q).trim();
   text = "<A HREF=\"#TOC"
      + linkNumber + "\">"
      + text + "</A>";
   int indent = Character.digit(level, 10);
   text = indents[indent] + text;
   toc.addElement(text);

   // Attach the link number to the <Hn> tag

   buffer = buffer.substring(0, p)
      + "<A NAME=\"TOC" + linkNumber + "\"></A>"
      + buffer.substring(p);
```

Figure 10-1
(Continued)

```
    out.println(buffer);
}
in.close();

// Now write the real document, inserting the table
// of contents immediately after the BODY tag.

out.flush();
sw.flush();
String webpage = sw.toString();
out.close();

out = response.getWriter();

int p = webpage.indexOf("<BODY");
int q = webpage.indexOf(">", p);

out.println(webpage.substring(0, q+1));
out.println("<H3>Table of Contents</H3>");
out.println("<FONT SIZE=-1>");
for (int i = 0; i < toc.size(); i++) {
    String s = (String) toc.elementAt(i);
    out.println(s + "<BR>");
}
out.println("</FONT>");
out.println("<P><HR><P>");
out.println(webpage.substring(q+2));
out.flush();
```

With the generated hyperlinks added after the table of contents servlet postprocesses the text, the HTML looks like this:

```
<A NAME="TOC1"></A><H1>United States Constitution</H1>
<P>
We the People of the United States, in Order to form a more
perfect Union, establish Justice, insure domestic Tranquility,
provide for the common defence, promote the general Welfare, and
secure the Blessings of Liberty to ourselves and our Posterity,
do ordain and establish this Constitution for the United States
of America.
<A NAME="TOC2"></A><H2>Article I - Legislative Branch</H2>
<A NAME="TOC3"></A><H3>Section 1 - How Constituted</H3>
<P>All legislative Powers herein granted shall be vested in a Congress
of the
United States, which shall consist of a Senate and House of
Representatives.
<A NAME="TOC4"></A><H3>Section 2 - House of Representatives</H3>
```

The HTML in the generated table of contents is

```
   <A HREF="#TOC1">United States Constitution</A><BR>
     <A HREF="#TOC2">
Article I - Legislative Branch</A><BR>
        <A HREF="#TOC3">
Section 1 - How Constituted</A><BR>
```

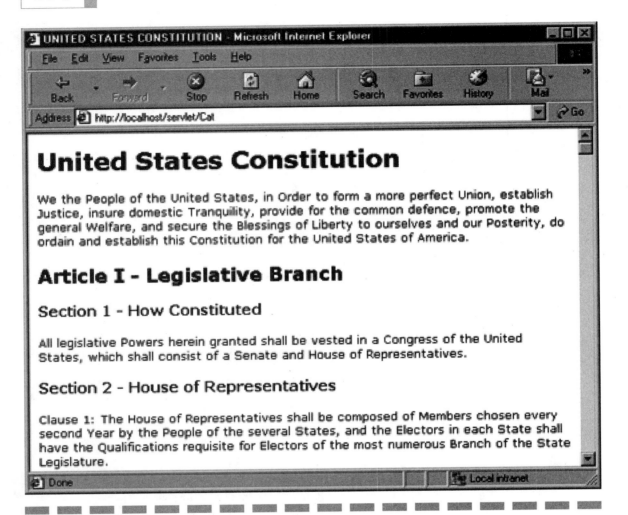

Figure 10-2 Input to the Table of Contents servlet.

```
         <A HREF="#TOC4">
Section 2 - House of Representatives</A><BR>
```

Figure 10-3 shows the finished product as rendered by the Web browser.

Servlet engines differ in the means they provide for configuring servlet chains. In some cases, they support being called directly from a URL containing multiple servlet names separated by commas, for example:

```
http://localhost/servlet/Cat,TOCGenerator
```

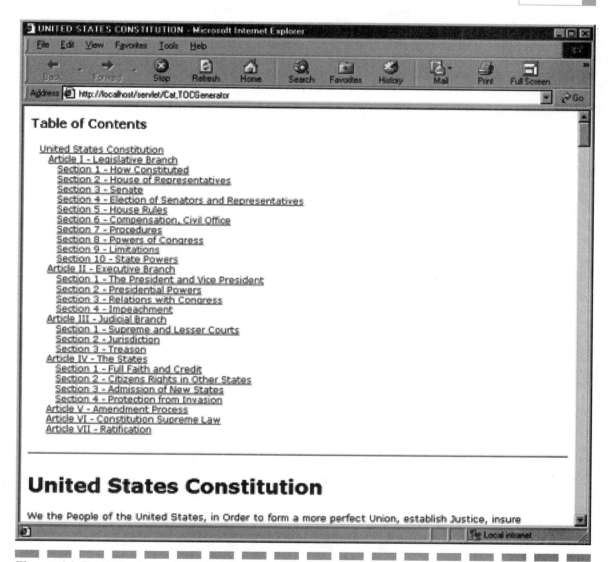

Figure 10-3 HTML document with a generated table of contents.

More commonly, aliases are used to represent servlet chains. Sections 10.3 and 10.4 describe how this can be done with several popular servlet engines.

10.2   Servlet Chaining Using MIME Types

Problem

I have a servlet that adds standard headers and footers to every Web page. I do not want to create explicit servlet chains for every servlet that should be postprocessed in this manner. What can I use instead?

Technique

Create a MIME type that can be tied to a particular postprocessing servlet.

Discussion

MIME-type servlet chains are easy to construct. The servlet engine can be configured to invoke a utility servlet (such as one that adds standard headers and footers) whenever it produces servlet output that has a specific `Content-Type` header. The utility servlet is then called automatically whenever that content type is encountered.

Our example will be a servlet that checks for invalid or out-of-date hyperlinks in documents generated by other servlets. It uses the following approach:

1. Parses an HTML document generated by another servlet looking for `<A HREF="`*`some url`*`">...</A>` links.

2. For each link, open a URL connection to the target host and issue an HTTP `HEAD` request for the specified resource. Recall from Chapter 2 that the `HEAD` method works like `GET` but only requests headers to be sent, not the document content.

3. If the URL connection returns a "Not Found" status code, the link is removed from the document, and its HREF is shown in italics.

4. Valid links and all other text are returned unmodified.

The link-validating servlet will be invoked automatically whenever the servlet engine encounters a MIME type of text/html-unverified.

As in Section 10.1, we first need to echo any HTTP headers that the previous servlet generated:

```
Enumeration en = request.getHeaderNames();
while (en.hasMoreElements()) {
   String name = (String) en.nextElement();
   if (name.equalsIgnoreCase("Content-Length"))
      continue;
   String value = request.getHeader(name);
   response.setHeader(name, value);
}
```

We make an exception for the Content-Length header because we know we will generate additional text if we encounter any bad links.

In order to analyze relative URLs correctly, we need the base URL of the document that generated them. We can extract this from the request object:

```
URL baseURL = new URL(HttpUtils.getRequestURL(request).toString());
```

The document is scanned for HTML anchor tags, again with the simplifying assumptions that the beginning and ending tags are on the same line and that there is at most one anchor per line:

```
int p1 = buffer.indexOf("<A HREF=");
if (p1 == -1)
   out.println(buffer);
else {
   int p2 = p1 + "<A HREF=".length();
   int p3 = buffer.indexOf(">", p2);
   String href = buffer.substring(p2, p3);
   if (href.startsWith("\""))
      href = href.substring(1);
   if (href.endsWith("\""))
      href = href.substring(0, href.length()-1);
}
```

If there are leading and trailing quotation marks in the HREF, these are stripped away before the URL is extracted.

Once we have a link to examine, we open an HttpURLConnection over its URL and issue a HEAD request:

```
URL url = null;
try {
   url = new URL(baseURL, href);
}
catch (MalformedURLException ex) {
   throw new RuntimeException(href);
}
HttpURLConnection con = (HttpURLConnection) url.openConnection();
con.setUseCaches(false);
con.setFollowRedirects(false);
con.setRequestMethod("HEAD");
con.connect();
```

If the return code is 2xx or 3xx, we know that the link is valid:

```
int rc = con.getResponseCode();
int firstDigit = rc / 100;
if ((firstDigit < 2) || (firstDigit > 3))
   throw new RuntimeException(href);
out.println(buffer);
```

The URL validation code is surrounded by a `try...catch` block. If the URL connection fails, or if the status code indicates that the document was not found, we replace the link with an italicized error message:

```
int p4 = buffer.indexOf("</A>", p3);
buffer = buffer.substring(0, p1)
   + "<I>Bad link: "
   + href
   + "</I> "
   + buffer.substring(p3+1, p4)
   + buffer.substring(p4+4);
out.println(buffer);
```

Figure 10-4 shows the complete source code for the `LinkValidator` servlet.

Figure 10-5 shows an example of a servlet that uses MIME-type chaining to invoke `LinkValidator`. The sole change made in the sample code to get it to invoke the servlet chain was the line setting the content type to `text/html-unverified`.

`BadLinkServlet` simply generates a list of five document names, each enclosed in HTML hyperlink tags. In our example, we delete one of the files to see what happens. We can see in Figure 10-6 that the bad link (`link4.html`) is detected and modified.

The means used to configure MIME-type servlet chains differ according to the servlet engine used. This topic is covered in the next two sections.

Figure 10-4

The LinkValidator
servlet.

```
package ijs.interserv;

import java.io.*;
import java.net.*;
import java.util.*;

import javax.servlet.*;
import javax.servlet.http.*;

/**
 * A filter that verifies that links are valid
 * when an HTML document is generated.
 */
public class LinkValidatorServlet extends HttpServlet
{
    /**
     * Handles a GET request
     */
    public void doGet(
            HttpServletRequest request,
            HttpServletResponse response)
        throws ServletException, IOException
    {

        response.setContentType("text/html");

        // Echo headers except Content-Length

        Enumeration en = request.getHeaderNames();
        while (en.hasMoreElements()) {
            String name = (String) en.nextElement();
            if (name.equalsIgnoreCase("Content-Length"))
                continue;
            String value = request.getHeader(name);
            response.setHeader(name, value);
        }

        // Read and echo input stream, validating
        // anchor tags as they are encountered

        URL baseURL =
            new URL(HttpUtils.getRequestURL(request).toString());
        BufferedReader in =
            new BufferedReader(
            new InputStreamReader(
            request.getInputStream()));
        PrintWriter out = response.getWriter();
        for (;;) {
            String buffer = in.readLine();
            if (buffer == null)
                break;

            // For the sake of simplicity, we will assume that
            // anchor tags begin and end on the same line
            // and that there is only one anchor on a line.

            int p1 = buffer.indexOf("<A HREF=");
            if (p1 == -1)
```

```
            out.println(buffer);
        else {
            int p2 = p1 + "<A HREF=".length();
            int p3 = buffer.indexOf(">", p2);
            String href = buffer.substring(p2, p3);
            if (href.startsWith("\""))
                href = href.substring(1);
            if (href.endsWith("\""))
                href = href.substring(0, href.length()-1);

            // Validate the URL

            try {
                URL url = null;
                try {
                    url = new URL(baseURL, href);
                }
                catch (MalformedURLException ex) {
                    throw new RuntimeException(href);
                }
                HttpURLConnection con =
                    (HttpURLConnection) url.openConnection();
                con.setUseCaches(false);
                con.setFollowRedirects(false);
                con.setRequestMethod("HEAD");
                con.connect();
                int rc = con.getResponseCode();
                int firstDigit = rc / 100;
                if ((firstDigit < 2) || (firstDigit > 3))
                    throw new RuntimeException(href);

                // If we get this far, the link is good

                out.println(buffer);
            }
            catch (Exception e) {

                // Remove the HREF
                // and italicize the text

                int p4 = buffer.indexOf("</A>", p3);
                buffer = buffer.substring(0, p1)
                    + "<I>Bad link: "
                    + href
                    + "</I> "
                    + buffer.substring(p3+1, p4)
                    + buffer.substring(p4+4);
                out.println(buffer);
            }
        }
    }
    in.close();
    }
}
```

Figure 10-5

A servlet that triggers the LinkValidator chain.

```
package ijs.interserv;

import java.io.*;
import java.net.*;
import java.util.*;

import javax.servlet.*;
import javax.servlet.http.*;

/**
 * BadLinkServlet
 */
public class BadLinkServlet extends HttpServlet
{
    /**
     * Handles a GET request
     */
    public void doGet(
            HttpServletRequest request,
            HttpServletResponse response)
        throws ServletException, IOException
    {
        response.setContentType("text/html-unverified");
        PrintWriter out = response.getWriter();

        out.println(""
            + "<HTML>"
            + "<HEAD>"
            + "<TITLE>BadLinkServlet</TITLE>"
            + "</HEAD>"
            + "<BODY>"
            + "<H3>Some Good and Bad Links</H3>"
            + "<UL>"
            );
        String prefix = "/ijs/Chap10/links";
        for (int i = 1; i <= 5; i++) {
            String anchor = "<A HREF=\""
                + prefix + "/link" + i + ".html"
                + "\">Link " + i + "</A>";
            out.println("<LI>" + anchor);
        }
        out.println(""
            + "</UL>"
            + "</BODY>"
            + "</HTML>"
            );
    }
}
```

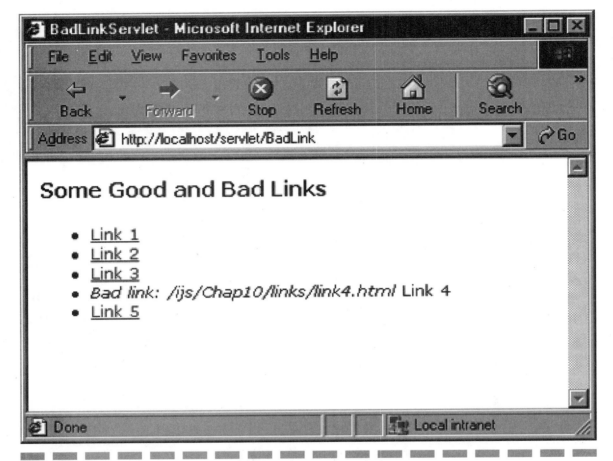

Figure 10-6 Output generated by the `LinkValidator` chain.

10.3 Configuring Servlet Chains with JRun

Problem

How do I configure servlet chain aliases and MIME-type servlet chains with JRun?

Technique

Add entries to

```
jsm-default/services/jse/properties/rules.properties
```

for servlet chain aliases or

```
jsm-default/services/jse/properties/mimeservlets.properties
```

for MIME-type servlet chains.

Discussion

Ordinary servlet chains can be specified directly in the URL by concatenating several names after the /servlet portion of the URL, separating the names with commas. It is more convenient, however, to assign an alias for the servlet chain. For the example in Section 10.1, which used the Cat and TOCGenerator servlets, the URL would look like this:

```
http://localhost/servlet/Cat,TOCGenerator
```

It may be more convenient, however, to assign a mapping for the servlet chain. These mappings should be entered in the rules.properties file, which is located in the *<JRun root>*/jsm-default/services/jse/properties directory. With the table of contents servlet chain added, this file looks similar to the following:

```
/servlet/=invoker
*.jrun=invoker
*.shtml=ssifilter
*.jsp=com.livesoftware.jsp.JSPServlet
*.thtml=template
/jws/=file
/TOCChain=Cat,TOCGenerator
```

JRun also provides a GUI administration application that can be used to modify the appropriate property files. Figure 10-7 shows the panel that corresponds to the rules.properties file.

For the LinkValidator chain described in Section 10.2, we used MIME-type chaining. This involves adding an entry to the mimeservlets.properties file in the same directory. The entry is simply a type=name **pair:**

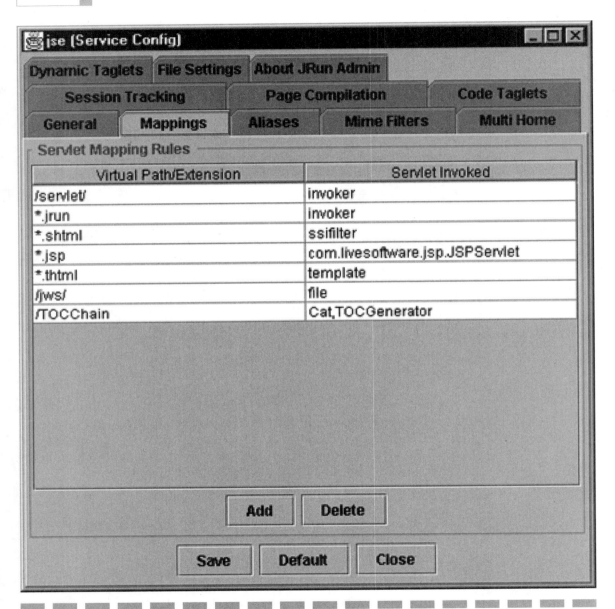

Figure 10-7 The JRun GUI panel for configuring servlet chain mappings.

```
text/html-unverified=LinkValidator
```

The JRun administrator GUI panel that corresponds to the mime-servlets.properties file is shown in Figure 10-8.

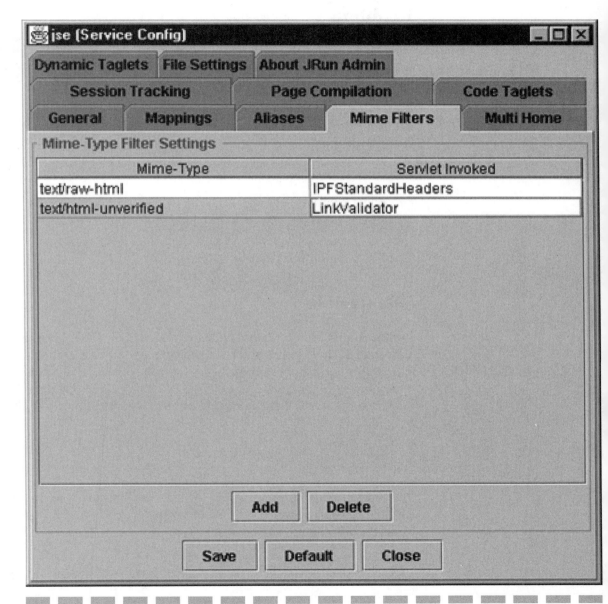

Figure 10-8 The JRun GUI panel for configuring MIME-type servlet chains.

10.4 Configuring Servlet Chains with ServletExec

Problem

How do I configure servlet chain aliases and MIME-type servlet chains with New Atlanta's ServletExec?

Technique

Add entries to

`<ServletExecRoot>/ServletExec Data/default/rules.properties`

for servlet chain aliases or

`<ServletExecRoot>/ServletExec Data/default/mimeservlets.properties`

for MIME-type servlet chains.

Discussion

Servlet chains are configured by being assigned an alias. For the example in Section 10.1, which used the `Cat` and `TOCGenerator` servlets, the alias mapping would be entered in the `rules.properties` file located in the `<ServletExecRoot>/ServletExec Data/default` directory. With the table of contents servlet chain added, this file looks in part like this:

```
/TOCChain=Cat,TOCGenerator
*.oldjsp=JSPServlet
*.jhtml=JIServlet
*.shtml=SSIServlet
```

In addition, depending on which Web server you use, you may need to modify the Web server's configuration to recognize the new alias. For Apache 1.3.9, this means adding

```
<Location <prefix alias>
   SetHandler servlet-exec
</Location>
```

to the `httpd.conf` file and restarting the Web server.

Ser/letExec also provides a Web-based administration application that can be used to modify the appropriate property files. Figure 10-9 shows the page that corresponds to the `rules.properties` file. The manual Web server modifications also need to be made in this case.

For the `LinkValidator` chain described in Section 10.2, we used MIME-type chaining. This involves adding an entry to the `mime-servlets.properties` file in the same directory. The entry is simply a `type=name` pair:

```
text/html-unverified=LinkValidator
```

The administrator Web page that corresponds to the `mimeserv-lets.properties` file is shown in Figure 10-10. Note that only the last servlet in a chain can be mapped to a MIME type.

Figure 10-9 The ServletExec Web page for configuring servlet chain mappings.

Figure 10-10 The ServletExec Web page for configuring MIME-type servlet chains.

10.5 HTTP Redirection

Problem

My application consists of a group of related servlets. How do I control the sequence in which they are presented?

Technique

Use `response.sendRedirect()` to cause the browser to request the appropriate servlet.

Discussion

HTTP requests do not always simply succeed or fail; they may require additional action on the part of the client. A `3xx` status code in response to a `GET` request, for example, indicates that the requested document has moved, either temporarily or permanently. Most Web browsers are programmed to handle this response by extracting the new location from the returned headers and requesting the document again using the new URL. This redirection is usually automatic, without the user even being aware of it.

For example, if user requests a document named `/newsletter/ ek0205.html` that has been moved to an archive, the HTTP request-and-response conversation looks like this:

```
Client:
      GET /newsletter/ek0205.html HTTP/1.0

Server:
      HTTP/1.1 302 Moved Temporarily
      Date: Tue, 07 Mar 2000 01:47:40 GMT
      Server: Apache/1.3.9 (Win32)
      Location: /archive/ek0205.html
      Connection: close
      Content-Type: text/html
```

The Web browser extracts the document's new URL from the `Location` header and formulates a new request:

```
Client:
      GET /archive/ek0205.html

Server:
      HTTP/1.1 200 OK
      Date: Tue, 07 Mar 2000 01:47:41 GMT
      Server: Apache/1.3.9 (Win32)
      Connection: close
      Content-Type: text/html

      (document contents)
```

Servlets can take advantage of this feature, using the browser to manage the sequence in which other servlets are requested. The

`HttpServletResponse` object has a `sendRedirect(String url)` method that returns the appropriate status code and includes the expected `Location` header. If you need to invoke another servlet, you simply call `sendRedirect()` with the new servlet's URL and then return from the `service()` method. This is usually done to produce an error message page, but it can be used to call any type of HTTP-accessible resource.

Figure 10-11 shows an application that uses this technique. The application consists of an HTML form and two servlets that prompt for an order number, perform a database query, and present a Web page showing the order details. If any errors occur, an error page is generated. The flow of control between the servlets and the HTML form is controlled with HTTP redirection.

To begin with, the user brings up the HTML form (see the source in Figure 10-12), which prompts for the order number. Figure 10-13 shows the form with a valid order number entered. The HTML form contains one input element, a text field named `orderNumber`. The form's `action` attribute contains the URL of a servlet that performs the database query. This servlet, `ShowOrderDetail`, is listed in Figure 10-14.

When `ShowOrderDetail` is invoked, it extracts the order number parameter that was entered in the form. If the order number is null, it means that `ShowOrderDetail` was requested from somewhere other than the HTML form.[3] If it is blank, it means that the user just clicked the "Show Detail" button without entering anything. In either case, the user is redirected back to the HTML form. Otherwise, a database query is run, and the results are formatted in an HTML table (Figure 10-15).

The database operations are done in a `try...catch` block so that any exceptions can be funneled through a single exit point. This exit point uses HTTP redirection to point to an error message servlet (listed in Figure 10-16), passing it the error message as one of its request parameters. If, for example, the order number is not found, the servlet throws a `java.lang.RuntimeException` with the appropriate error message. The resulting error page is shown in Figure 10-17.

---

[3]This happens more often than you might think. Any Web page that is displayed in a browser can be bookmarked, added to the favorites folder, or emailed to another user. If the Web page is one of several that must be called in a particular sequence, this sequence is not preserved when the bookmark is captured.

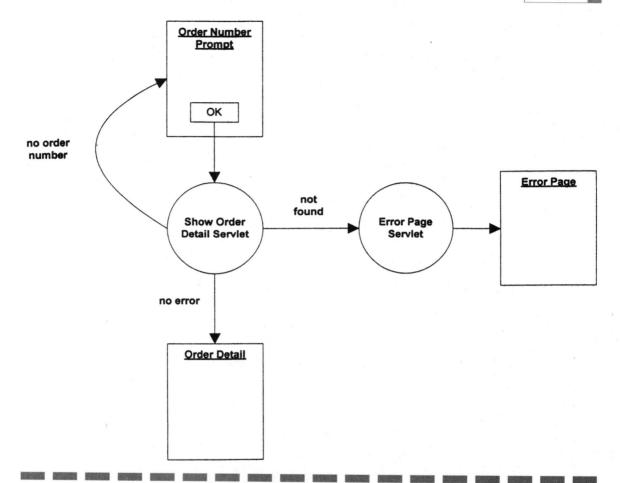

Figure 10-11 Diagram of an application using HTTP redirection to control program flow.

It should be noted that no HttpSession object was created in this example, because no object state needed to be preserved between requests. More complex applications with persistent server-side objects may need to use the session management techniques described in Chapter 7.

Figure 10-12
HTML for the order
number prompt.

```
<HTML>

<HEAD>
<TITLE>Order Number Prompt</TITLE>
</HEAD>

<BODY>
<H3>Order Detail Inquiry</H3>
<FORM METHOD="POST" ACTION="/servlet/RedirShowOrderDetail">
<TABLE BORDER="0" CELLPADDING="3">
    <TR>
        <TD>Order number:</TD>
        <TD><INPUT TYPE="TEXT" NAME="orderNumber" SIZE="8"></TD>
        <TD><INPUT TYPE="SUBMIT" VALUE="Show Detail"></TD>
    </TR>
</TABLE>
</FORM>
</BODY>

</HTML>
```

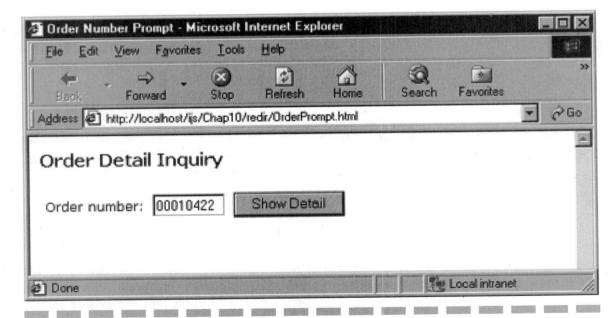

Figure 10-13 The order number prompt.

Figure 10-14

A servlet that creates the order detail page.

```
package ijs.interserv;

import ipfoods.*;
import java.io.*;
import java.net.*;
import java.sql.*;
import java.util.*;
import javax.servlet.*;
import javax.servlet.http.*;

/**
 * A servlet that displays the details of an order.
 * Uses HTTP redirection to control application flow.
 */
public class ShowOrderDetailServlet extends HttpServlet
{
    // Document constants

    public static final String DOCROOT
        = "/ijs/Chap10/redir";

    public static final String ORDER_PROMPT
        = DOCROOT + "/OrderPrompt.html";

    public static final String ERROR_PAGE
        = "/servlet/RedirErrorPage";

    public static final String DBURL
        = "jdbc:idb:/book/ipfoods/database/database.prp";

    public static final String DRIVER_NAME
        = "jdbc.idbDriver";

    /**
     * Handles a GET request
     */
    public void doGet(
            HttpServletRequest request,
            HttpServletResponse response)
        throws ServletException, IOException
    {
        PrintWriter out = response.getWriter();
        response.setContentType("text/html");

        // Get order number parameter.  If not specified
        // then return to order number prompt

        String orderNumber =
            request.getParameter("orderNumber");
        if (orderNumber == null)
            orderNumber = "";
        orderNumber = orderNumber.trim();
        if (orderNumber.equals("")) {
            response.sendRedirect(ORDER_PROMPT);
            return;
        }
```

Figure 10-14
(Continued)

```java
Connection con = null;

try {

    // Load JDBC driver

    Class.forName(DRIVER_NAME);

    // Open a database connection

    con = DriverManager.getConnection(DBURL);

    // Look up the order

    java.util.Date orderDate = null;
    String customerNumber = null;

    PreparedStatement stmt = con.prepareStatement(
        "SELECT orderDate, customerNumber"
        + " FROM orders WHERE orderNumber = ?");

    stmt.setString(1, orderNumber);
    ResultSet rs = stmt.executeQuery();

    if (rs.next()) {
        orderDate = rs.getDate(1);
        customerNumber = rs.getString(2);
    }
    else
        throw new RuntimeException
        ("Order number " + orderNumber + " not found");

    rs.close();
    stmt.close();

    // Generate the document heading

    String[] lines = {
        "<HTML>",
        "<HEAD>",
        "<TITLE>Show Order Detail</TITLE>",
        "</HEAD>",
        "<BODY>",
        "<CENTER><H3>Order Detail</H3></CENTER>",
        "<TABLE BORDER=0 CELLPADDING=3>",
        "<TR>",
        "    <TD><B>Order number:</B></TD>",
        "    <TD ALIGN=RIGHT>" + orderNumber + "</TD>",
        "</TR>",
        "<TR>",
        "    <TD><B>Order date:</B></TD>",
        "    <TD ALIGN=RIGHT>" + orderDate + "</TD>",
        "</TR>",
        "<TR>",
        "    <TD><B>Customer number:</B></TD>",
        "    <TD ALIGN=RIGHT>" + customerNumber + "</TD>",
        "</TR>",
```

Figure 10-14
(Continued)

```
                          "</TABLE>",
                          "<P>",
                          "<TABLE BORDER=1 CELLPADDING=5>",
                          "<TR>",
                          "    <TH>Item<BR>Code</TH>",
                          "    <TH>Description</TH>",
                          "    <TH ALIGN=RIGHT>Price</TH>",
                          "    <TH ALIGN=RIGHT>Quantity</TH>",
                          "    <TH ALIGN=RIGHT>Extended<BR>Price</TH>",
                          "</TR>",
                      };
                      for (int i = 0; i < lines.length; i++)
                          out.println(lines[i]);

                      // Show details

                      stmt = con.prepareStatement(
                          "   SELECT    P.itemCode,"
                          + "            P.itemDesc,"
                          + "            P.price,"
                          + "            D.qty"
                          + "   FROM     products P, orderDetail D"
                          + "   WHERE    D.orderNumber = ?"
                          + "   AND      P.itemCode = D.itemCode"
                          );
                      stmt.setString(1, orderNumber);
                      rs = stmt.executeQuery();
                      while (rs.next()) {
                          String itemCode = rs.getString(1);
                          String itemDesc = rs.getString(2);
                          long price = rs.getLong(3);
                          String priceString = Util.toCurrencyString(price);
                          int qty = rs.getInt(4);
                          long extPrice = price * qty;
                          String extPriceString =
                              Util.toCurrencyString(extPrice);
                          lines = new String[] {
                              "<TR>",
                              "<TD>" + itemCode + "</TD>",
                              "<TD>" + itemDesc + "</TD>",
                              "<TD ALIGN=RIGHT>" + priceString + "</TD>",
                              "<TD ALIGN=RIGHT>" + qty + "</TD>",
                              "<TD ALIGN=RIGHT>" + extPriceString + "</TD>",
                              "</TR>",
                          };
                          for (int i = 0; i < lines.length; i++)
                              out.println(lines[i]);
                      }
                      rs.close();
                      stmt.close();
                      out.println("</TABLE></BODY></HTML>");
                  }
                  catch (Exception e) {
                      response.sendRedirect(
                          ERROR_PAGE
                          + "?errmsg="
                          + URLEncoder.encode(e.getMessage())
```

Figure 10-14
(Continued)

```
            );
        return;
    }
    finally {
        if (con != null) {
            try {
                con.close();
            }
            catch (SQLException ignore){}
        }
    }
}

/**
 * Handles a POST request
 */
public void doPost(
        HttpServletRequest request,
        HttpServletResponse response)
    throws ServletException, IOException
{
    doGet(request, response);
}
}
```

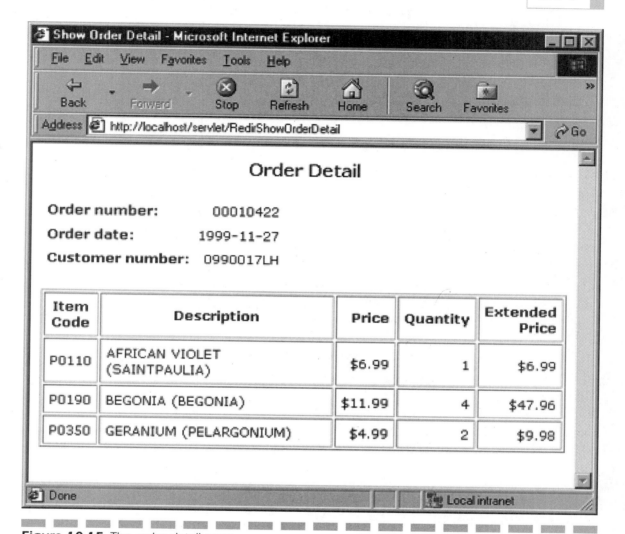

Figure 10-15 The order detail page.

Figure 10-16
A servlet that gen-
erates an error
message page.

```java
package ijs.interserv;

import java.io.*;
import java.net.*;
import java.util.*;

import javax.servlet.*;
import javax.servlet.http.*;

/**
 * ErrorPageServlet
 */
public class ErrorPageServlet extends HttpServlet
{
    /**
     * Handles a GET request
     */
    public void doGet(
            HttpServletRequest request,
            HttpServletResponse response)
        throws ServletException, IOException
    {
        response.setContentType("text/html");
        PrintWriter out = response.getWriter();
        String message = request.getParameter("errmsg");
        out.println(""
            + "<HTML>"
            + "<BODY>"
            + "<H3>Application Error</H3>"
            + "The following error occurred:"
            + "<PRE>"
            + message
            + "</PRE>"
            + "</BODY>"
            + "</HTML>"
        );
    }
}
```

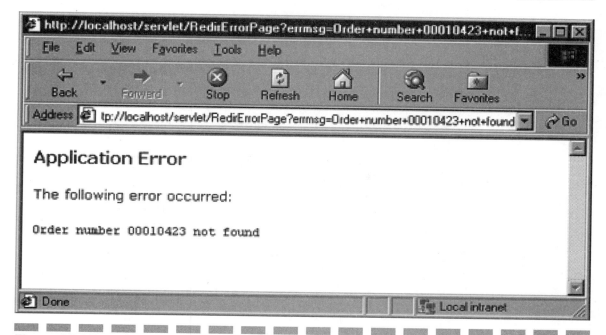

Figure 10-17 An example of the error message page.

10.6   Forwarding Requests

Problem

What technique can I use to efficiently separate the content of a servlet from its presentation?

Technique

Write two servlets, one to create the contents of the Web page, and one to format the page and write it to the servlet output stream. Create a `RequestDispatcher` for the formatting servlet using the `getRequest-`

Dispatcher() method of ServletContext.[4] Call the dispatcher's forward() method to forward the request to the formatting servlet.

Discussion

RequestDispatcher is a new feature of the Java Servlet API in Version 2.1. Among other things, it allows you to forward a request to another servlet. This can be used to cleanly separate the parts of an application that create content and the parts that format and present it.

We anticipated this technique in Section 7.8, where ProductSearch ran the SQL query and ShowSearchResults created the output Web page, using HTTP redirection to link the two. This can be converted to use request dispatching by changing one line in ProductSearch. Near the end of the doGet() method, just before the catch blocks, there is a section of code that stores the search results in an HTTP session and calls sendRedirect(). We need to replace the last line with the following:

```
ServletContext context = getServletContext();
RequestDispatcher rd = context.getRequestDispatcher
    ("/servlet/IPFShowSearchResults");
rd.forward(request, response);
```

The advantage of using a RequestDispatcher instead of redirection is that it does not require an additional request from the client. Rather, it executes the service() method of the other servlet in the same thread and returns to the calling servlet. In some cases, this may result in a performance improvement.

You cannot just split a servlet at an arbitrary point, however. The RequestDispatcher's forward() method can only be used before the servlet response output stream has been accessed, when no output has yet been written. This makes sense from the standpoint of dividing content and presentation.

---

[4] The Java Servlet API Version 2.2 introduces two related methods— ServletContext.getNamedDispatcher(), which returns a RequestDispatcher for a servlet with a specific name, rather than for a resource in the Web server's document space, and ServletRequest.getRequestDispatcher(), which is similar to the servlet context's method but uses URLs relative to the request, not the context.

10.7   Including Output from Other Servlets

Problem

How can I include standard headers and footers in the HTML that my servlet generates?

Technique

Create a `RequestDispatcher` and call its `include(ServletRequest request, ServletResponse response)` method.

Discussion

We introduced `RequestDispatcher` in the preceding section. In addition to its `forward()` method, it also has an `include()` method, which pulls in content generated by another servlet and merges it with the current servlet output stream.

An obvious application for this feature is using it to include standard headers and footers. Figure 10-18 lists the source code for a plain login servlet.[5] Its output is shown in Figure 10-19.

To include the standard header, all we need to do is create a request dispatcher and invoke its `include()` method. The modified source code is listed in Figure 10-20. The standard header (Figure 10-21) copies HTML content (in this case a logo image, the company name, and a clickable image map) from an external file. The standard footer differs only in that it uses a different file for input (one containing a copyright notice). The result is a distinct improvement (Figure 10-22).

---

[5]Paradoxically named `PlainLoginServlet`

Figure 10-18

A plain login
servlet.

```java
package ijs.interserv;

import java.io.*;
import java.net.*;
import java.util.*;

import javax.servlet.*;
import javax.servlet.http.*;

/**
 * PlainLoginServlet
 */
public class PlainLoginServlet extends HttpServlet
{
    /**
     * Handles a GET request
     */
    public void doGet(
            HttpServletRequest request,
            HttpServletResponse response)
        throws ServletException, IOException
    {
        response.setContentType("text/html");
        PrintWriter out = response.getWriter();
        out.println("<HTML>");
        out.println("<BODY>");
        out.println("<CENTER>");
        out.println("<H3>Please login:</H3>");
        out.println("<TABLE BORDER=0 CELLPADDING=5>");
        out.println("<TR>");
        out.println("   <TD>User ID:</TD>");
        out.println("   <TD><INPUT NAME=USERID"
                            + " TYPE=TEXT"
                            + " SIZE=8></TD>");
        out.println("</TR>");
        out.println("<TR>");
        out.println("   <TD>Password:</TD>");
        out.println("   <TD><INPUT NAME=PASSWORD"
                            + " TYPE=PASSWORD"
                            + " SIZE=8></TD>");
        out.println("</TR>");
        out.println("<TR>");
        out.println("   <TD> </TD>");
        out.println("   <TD><INPUT TYPE=SUBMIT VALUE=OK></TD>");
        out.println("</TR>");
        out.println("</TABLE>");
        out.println("</CENTER>");
        out.println("</BODY>");
        out.println("</HTML>");
    }
}
```

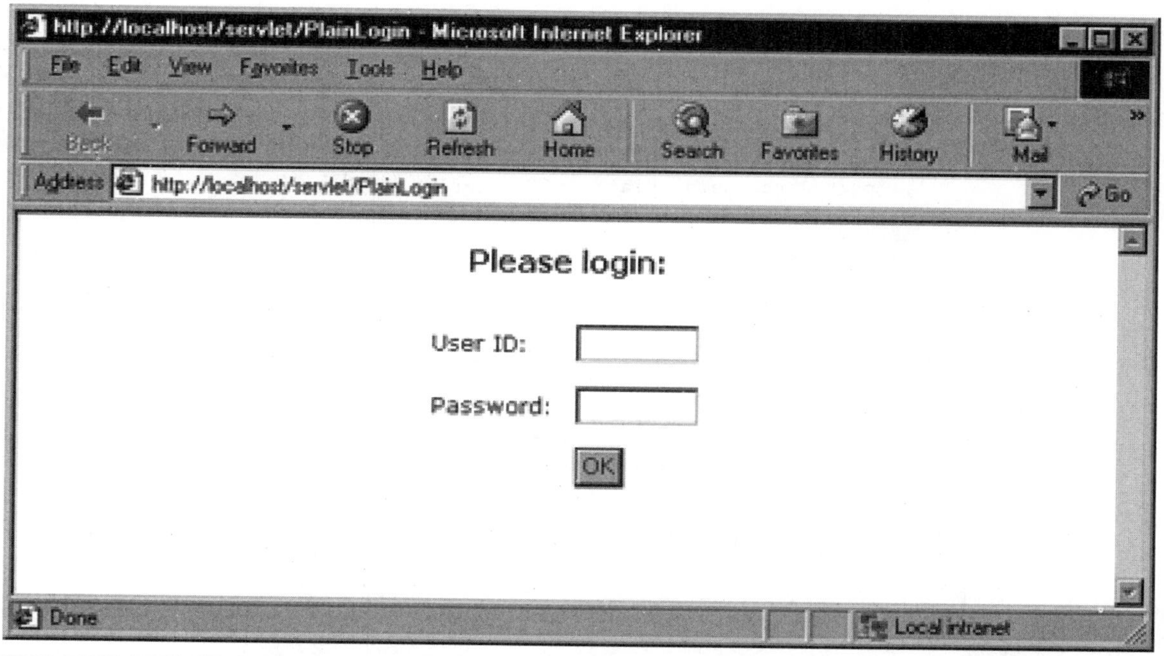

Figure 10-19 *Output of the plain login servlet.*

Figure 10-20

A login servlet that includes the standard headers and footers.

```
package ijs.interserv;

import java.io.*;
import java.net.*;
import java.util.*;

import javax.servlet.*;
import javax.servlet.http.*;

/**
* ImprovedLoginServlet
*/
public class ImprovedLoginServlet extends HttpServlet
{
    /**
    * Handles a GET request
    */
    public void doGet(
            HttpServletRequest request,
            HttpServletResponse response)
        throws ServletException, IOException
    {
        response.setContentType("text/html");
        PrintWriter out = response.getWriter();
        out.println("<HTML>");
        out.println("<BODY>");
        out.println("<CENTER>");

        // Include the standard header

        ServletContext context = getServletContext();
        RequestDispatcher rd =
            context.getRequestDispatcher("/servlet/Ch10Header");
        rd.include(request, response);

        out.println("<H3>Please login:</H3>");
        out.println("<TABLE BORDER=0 CELLPADDING=5>");
        out.println("<TR>");
        out.println("   <TD>User ID:</TD>");
        out.println("   <TD><INPUT NAME=USERID"
                            + " TYPE=TEXT"
                            + " SIZE=8></TD>");
        out.println("</TR>");
        out.println("<TR>");
        out.println("   <TD>Password:</TD>");
        out.println("   <TD><INPUT NAME=PASSWORD"
                            + " TYPE=PASSWORD"
                            + " SIZE=8></TD>");
        out.println("</TR>");
        out.println("<TR>");
        out.println("   <TD> </TD>");
        out.println("   <TD><INPUT TYPE=SUBMIT VALUE=OK></TD>");
        out.println("</TR>");
        out.println("</TABLE>");

        // Include the standard footer
```

Figure 10-20

(Continued)

```
                          context = getServletContext();
                          rd = context.getRequestDispatcher("/servlet/Ch10Footer");
                          rd.include(request, response);

                          out.println("</CENTER>");
                          out.println("</BODY>");
                          out.println("</HTML>");
                     }
                 }
```

Figure 10-21

The standard
header servlet.

```
package ijs.interserv;

import java.io.*;
import java.net.*;
import java.util.*;

import javax.servlet.*;
import javax.servlet.http.*;

/**
 * StandardHeaderServlet
 */
public class StandardHeaderServlet extends HttpServlet
{
    /**
     * Handles a GET request
     */
    public void doGet(
         HttpServletRequest request,
         HttpServletResponse response)
       throws ServletException, IOException
    {
       PrintWriter out = response.getWriter();
       BufferedReader in =
          new BufferedReader(
          new FileReader(
          "/book/ipfoods/public_html/header.html"));
       for (;;) {
          String line = in.readLine();
          if (line == null)
             break;
          out.println(line);
       }
       in.close();
       out.flush();
    }
}
```

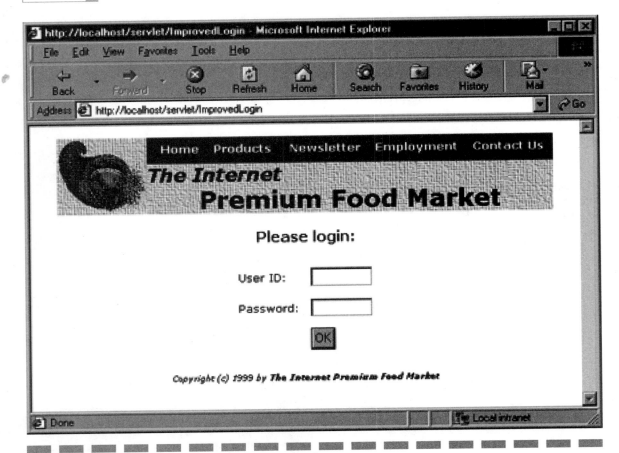

Figure 10-22 Output of the improved login servlet.

11

Other Clients

Overview

While Web browsers are the most common servlet clients, any network-enabled environment can be used. In this chapter we will see how Java applets, Perl scripts, and stand-alone Java applications can interact with servlets, in most cases more easily than they can communicate with each other.

There are problems to overcome, however. To begin with, these clients do not operate in the same virtual machine as the servlet. This introduces timing and synchronization issues. In addition, it means that they cannot call the servlet's methods directly but must do all their communication using network I/O. Furthermore, the client and server sides must be able to read and write a common data format.

HTTP to the Rescue The Hypertext Transfer Protocol (HTTP) solves each of these problems. It provides an input-output (I/O) channel that synchronizes data transfer and furnishes return codes. It has a well-documented set of request and response headers, which convey instructions separate from the application data path. If a client can open sockets in a TCP/IP network, it can send HTTP requests and appear to be no different from a Web browser. Likewise, to the client, the servlet can appear to be an input stream.

The key consideration is the choice of a data format, which must be the same on both sides. As long as the `Content-Type` and `Content-Length` headers are set correctly, any format can be used:

- *Plain text*. In the simplest of cases, the servlet simply can write lines of output as ASCII text. The client can read the text as if it were coming from an ordinary file.

- *Serialized objects*. For Java clients, either applets or applications, a servlet can transform objects into a stream of bytes that is sent as the response output and reconstituted at the other end. This requires that the client and server use a compatible version of the Java runtime environment. If used bidirectionally to share objects whose methods can be called on either side, this technique is called *HTTP tunneling*.[1]

- *XML or other specialized formats*. Given the explosion of interest in Extensible Markup Language (XML), it is significant that a servlet can produce XML output, making it instantly compatible as a data source for current and future applications. Other specialized formats, both binary or text-based, are also available.

The remainder of the chapter will provide complete examples of each of these approaches.

11.1 Applet-to-Servlet Communication

Problem

How can I invoke a servlet from a Java applet running in a Web browser?

---

[1] For a comprehensive look at HTTP tunneling, refer to *Java Servlets*, 2d ed., by Karl Moss (New York: Computing McGraw-Hill, ISBN: 0071351884, 1999).

Technique

Create a URL using the `URL(URL url, String path)` constructor, where

`url`   is the applet's code base

`path` is `/servlet/<servletname>`

With the URL that is returned, invoke its `openStream()` method, and read the resulting input stream.

Discussion

In Section 9.3 we developed the server side of an application that scanned a Web site for news headlines and monitored it for updates. The news ticker servlet managed the updates and provided the headlines to requester in a simple HTML format.

In this section we will develop a more interesting client—a Java applet that cycles through the headlines every 5 seconds or so and allows the user to scan forward and backward in the list and to view the full Web page that corresponds to the headline.

Modifications to the Servlet   First, we need to replace the HTML output that the servlet produces with serialized objects that the applet can reconstitute. We will subclass the servlet, overriding only its `doGet()` method. Figure 11-1 shows the source code for the new servlet.

The essential difference is that we do not need all the HTML headings and tables, just a binary copy of three serialized objects:

1. A `boolean` flag that indicates whether it is followed by valid data. Our headline source may be offline at times, and we need to be able to distinguish this from the case where there are simply no headlines.[2]

2. A `java.util.Date` indicating the date and time at which the headline source was refreshed.

---

[2]Another variation would be to drop the boolean flag and use an error response code (e.g., 404—Not found) to indicate errors in retrieving headlines. The client in that case would open a `URLConnection` to the servlet URL and examine its response headers.

Figure 11-1 An
Updated
NewsTicker
Servlet That
Returns
Serialized
Objects.

```java
package ijs.news;

import java.io.*;
import java.util.*;
import javax.servlet.*;
import javax.servlet.http.*;

/**
 * A subclass of <CODE>TickerServlet</CODE> that returns its
 * contents as a serialized array of <CODE>Headline</CODE>
 * objects.
 */
public class TickerObjectServlet extends TickerServlet
{
    public void doGet(
        HttpServletRequest request,
        HttpServletResponse response)
      throws ServletException, IOException
    {
        // Get the headline source object from the
        // servlet context

        String name = getClass().getName() + ".source";
        HeadlineSource source = (HeadlineSource)
            getServletContext().getAttribute(name);

        // Retrieve the latest headlines

        Date lastRefreshTime = source.getLastRefreshTime();
        Headline[] headlines = source.getHeadlines();

        // Serialize them

        ByteArrayOutputStream baos = new ByteArrayOutputStream();
        ObjectOutputStream oos = new ObjectOutputStream(baos);

        if (headlines == null)
            oos.writeBoolean(false);
        else {
            oos.writeBoolean(true);
            oos.writeObject(lastRefreshTime);
            oos.writeObject(headlines);
        }
        oos.flush();
        byte[] buffer = baos.toByteArray();
        oos.close();

        // Write them to the web page

        response.setContentType("application/octet-stream");
        response.setContentLength(buffer.length);
        ServletOutputStream out = response.getOutputStream();
        out.write(buffer);
        out.flush();
        out.close();
    }
}
```

3. An array of `ijs.news.Headline` objects, each of which contain the text of a headline and its URL.

We do not write the serialized data directly to the response output stream, because we need to know how many bytes we have generated and send that value in the `Content-Length` header. A `ByteArrayOutputStream` makes this easy.

How the Applet Works   Figure 11-2 is a screenshot of the applet. It is a compact 500 × 20 pixel rectangle with buttons on the left and a cycling set of news headlines on the right. The applet takes up very little space and can be embedded easily in other Web pages.

The four buttons operate as follows:

`refresh`   Forces an immediate refresh of the headlines from the server

`back`   Moves back to the previous headline

`pause`   Stops the display cycle at the current headline

`forward` Moves forward to the next headline

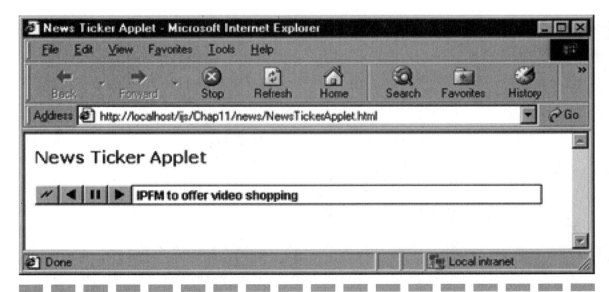

Figure 11-2 The `NewsTicker` Applet in Action.

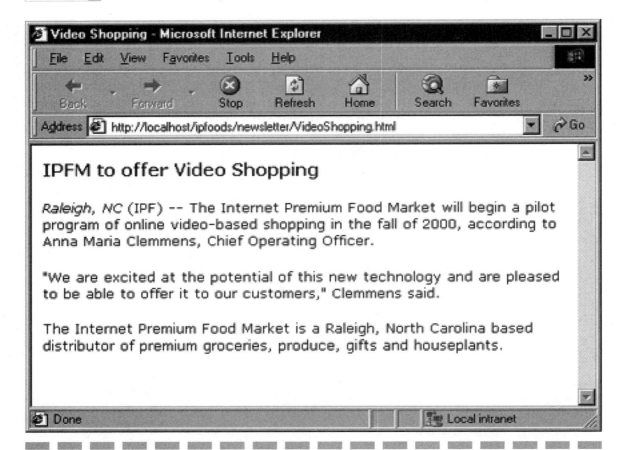

Figure 11-3 Details of the Selected Headline.

When the user clicks on the headline itself, the applet looks up the corresponding URL and displays its full contents in a new browser window (see the example in Figure 11-3).

Structure of the Applet   In the init() method of the applet, we load the button image file, determine the cycler frequency, and set up a MouseListener to handle mouse clicks. The paint() method displays the buttons and the current headline. At the heart of the applet are the start(), stop(), run(), and refresh() methods that control the background thread that updates the display. Finally, there are the doBack(), doForward(), doPause(), and doOpen() methods that handle the mouse clicks. The complete applet is listed in Figure 11-4.

Figure 11-4

Source Code for
the
NewsTicker
Applet.

```java
import ijs.news.*;
import java.applet.*;
import java.awt.*;
import java.awt.event.*;
import java.io.*;
import java.net.*;
import java.util.*;

/**
 * An applet that cycles through a list of headline objects.
 * Methods are provided to refresh the list, to pause the
 * display, to move to the previous and next headline, and
 * to view the web page behind a headline.
 */
public class NewsTickerApplet extends Applet
    implements Runnable
{
    // Button image

    private Image imgButtons;

    // Cycling objects

    private int cyclerFrequency;
    private Thread cyclerThread;
    private int cycleCount;
    private int currentIndex;
    private boolean paused;

    // Headlines objects

    private Date lastRefreshTime;
    private Headline[] headlines;

    /**
     * Initializes the objects used in the applet
     */
    public void init()
    {
        // Load the button image

        imgButtons = getImage
            (getCodeBase(), "images/buttons.gif");

        // Get the number of seconds between cycles

        String parm = getParameter("freq");
        cyclerFrequency = (parm == null)
            ? 5 : Integer.parseInt(parm);

        // Listen for mouse clicks

        addMouseListener(new MouseAdapter() {
            public void mouseClicked(MouseEvent event)
            {
                int x = event.getX();
                if (x < 24)        refresh();
```

Figure 11-4

(Continued)

```
                        else if (x < 48) doBack();
                        else if (x < 72) doPause();
                        else if (x < 96) doForward();
                        else             doOpen();
                }
        });
}

/**
 * Paints the buttons and the headline text
 */
public void paint(Graphics g)
{
    Headline headline = null;
    synchronized (this) {
        if (headlines != null)
            headline = headlines[currentIndex];
    }

    // Return if no headlines are available

    if (headline == null) {
        g.setColor(Color.black);
        g.setFont(new Font ("SansSerif", Font.ITALIC, 12));
        g.drawString("No headlines available", 5, 15);
        return;
    }

    // Draw the buttons and current headline

    g.setColor(Color.white);
    g.fillRect(0, 0, 500, 20);
    g.setColor(Color.black);
    g.drawRect(0, 0, 500-1, 20-1);
    g.setFont(new Font ("SansSerif", Font.BOLD, 12));
    g.drawString(headline.getTitle(), 5 + 96, 15);
    if (imgButtons != null)
        g.drawImage(imgButtons, 0, 0, this);
}

// =========================================
//     Cycler thread methods
// =========================================

/**
 * Starts the cycler thread
 */
public void start()
{
    if (cyclerThread == null) {
        refresh();
        cyclerThread = new Thread(this);
        cyclerThread.start();
    }
}

/**
```

Figure 11-4
(Continued)

```
 * Stops the cycler thread
 */
public void stop()
{
    if (cyclerThread != null) {
        cyclerThread = null;
    }
}

/**
 * Runs the cycler
 */
public void run()
{
    try {

        while (cyclerThread != null) {

            // Schedule a repaint of the screen

            repaint();

            // Wait a while

            Thread.sleep(cyclerFrequency * 1000);

            // If not paused, advance to the next headline

            if (!paused) {

                // Every ten cycles, refresh the data

                cycleCount++;
                if (cycleCount >= 10) {
                    cycleCount = 0;
                    refresh();
                }

                // Update the headline index

                if (headlines != null)
                    currentIndex = (currentIndex + 1)
                        % headlines.length;
            }

        }
    }
    catch (InterruptedException e) {
        return;
    }
}

/**
 * Updates the headlines array
 */
public synchronized void refresh()
{
```

Figure 11-4

(Continued)

```
try {

    // Get the latest headlines object from the
    // news ticker servlet

    URL url = new URL(getCodeBase(),
        "/servlet/NewsTickerObject");
    ObjectInputStream ois =
        new ObjectInputStream(url.openStream());
    boolean hasValidData = ois.readBoolean();
    if (!hasValidData) {
        lastRefreshTime = null;
        headlines = null;
        return;
    }

    // Check the server's last refresh time.  If the data
    // has not changed, there is no need to go further

    Date lrt = (Date) ois.readObject();
    if (lrt.equals(lastRefreshTime))
        return;
    lastRefreshTime = lrt;

    // Get the headlines from the object input stream

    headlines = (Headline[]) ois.readObject();

    // Start the current index at the first headline

    currentIndex = 0;

    // Done with the input stream

    ois.close();
}
catch (IOException e) {
    e.printStackTrace();
}
catch (ClassNotFoundException e) {
    e.printStackTrace();
}

    // Repaint the screen

    repaint();
}

// ============================================
//    Mouse click handling methods
// ============================================

/**
 * Handles the back button
 */
public void doBack()
{
```

Figure 11-4
(Continued)

```
      paused = false;
      synchronized (this) {
         if (headlines != null) {
            currentIndex--;
            if (currentIndex < 0)
               currentIndex = headlines.length - 1;
         }
      }
      repaint();
   }

   /**
    * Handles the forward button
    */
   public void doForward()
   {
      paused = false;
      synchronized (this) {
         if (headlines != null) {
            currentIndex++;
            if (currentIndex >= headlines.length)
               currentIndex = 0;
         }
      }
      repaint();
   }

   /**
    * Handles the pause button
    */
   public void doPause()
   {
      paused = !paused;
      repaint();
   }

   /**
    * Handles the headline click event.
    */
   public void doOpen()
   {
      paused = false;
      if (headlines != null) {
         URL url = headlines[currentIndex].getURL();
         getAppletContext().showDocument(url, "_blank");
      }
   }
```

11.2 Extending Applet Capabilities

Problem

Security restrictions make applets difficult to work with. How can I use
servlets to provide capabilities that applets do not have by default?

Technique

Use a servlet as a proxy for operations that the applet cannot do.

Discussion

Java's applet security model gives users a substantial degree of protection against damage from malicious programs. In this respect, it differs significantly from other distributed-object schemes that can give unlimited access to rogue components. Among other things, an applet[3] cannot

- *Open a network connection to an arbitrary host.* The only host to which an applet can open a socket is the one from which its class was loaded. If this were not true, an applet could be designed to upload information from your applet context to a system of its choice without your knowledge.

- *Read or write files on the local file system.* Obviously, since an applet can be downloaded from anywhere, you do not want it to be able to destroy data on your system.

- *Start programs on the local host.* This is prohibited for similar reasons.

Unfortunately, to prevent a small number of malicious applets from doing damage, the default applet environment has to curtail privileges for all applets. This limits their usefulness—there is only so much you can do without persistent input and output or without free access to the network.

Proxy Servlets Servlets provide a solution to these problems. An applet can send data to them and read back results, either with the high-level HTTP or directly with sockets. The servlet can then perform operations on behalf of the applet, sending the results back through the socket.

Figure 11-5 illustrates how this technique can be used to handle the first problem—inability to access arbitrary network connections. The applet opens a URL connection to the servlet, passing it the name and port number of the remote host, as well as any request data required by

---

[3]JDK 1.1.x, 1.2, and the Java PlugIn provide much finer-grained security for applets. Unfortunately, browsers differ significantly in their support for these models. In this section we are discussing ordinary applets running in the common default environment.

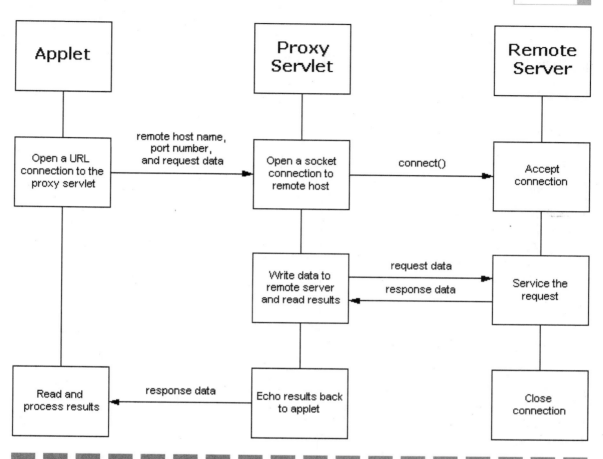

Figure 11-5 Using a Proxy Servlet to Perform Remote Socket Operations.

the socket application to be performed. For example, if the proxy servlet is designed to act as a client for the Unix `rexec` facility, the applet would supply the host name, user ID, password, and command to be executed. The servlet would then open a socket connection to the remote host, write the data required by the protocol, and then read the results and echo them back to the applet in the servlet response output stream.

Similarly, a proxy servlet can be used to upload file data to the server's file system. Figure 11-6 shows how this can be done. Here, the file name and content length are sent as request parameters, with the file data being sent using the POST method. The servlet writes the file on behalf of the applet and sends status information back with the servlet

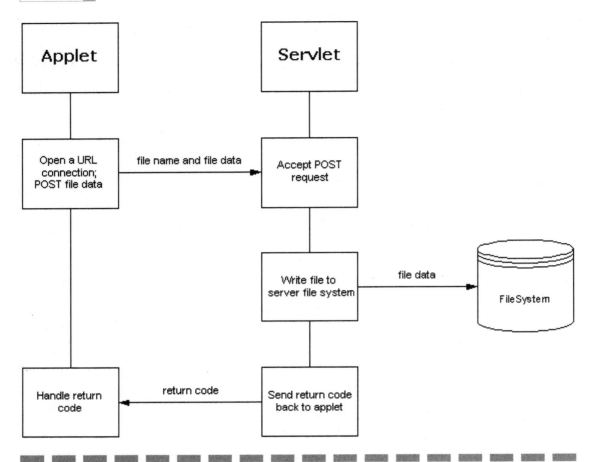

Figure 11-6 Using a Proxy Servlet to Write a File on the Server.

response. The file system to which the file is written does not have to be in the server's Web directory tree; a servlet is a Java application, not an applet, and therefore can read and write files using whatever means are made available to it.

A proxy servlet can be used to run any kind of noninteractive command or program, not just socket-based ones. Figure 11-7 illustrates how a servlet can accept a program name and parameters from an applet, execute the command using `java.lang.Runtime.exec(String cmd)`, and return the results through the servlet response. In this case, it is important to consider the length of time the command is expected to take. Very long running commands would better be handled by:

1. Launching a separate thread to run the command.
2. Returning an identifier that represents the thread.
3. Allowing the applet some means of monitoring the progress of the thread, retrieving its results, or canceling it.

Security Considerations But the applet security model is there for a reason—doesn't the use of proxy servlets just move the problem from one place to another? Not really. The key thing to remember is that applets can be downloaded from anywhere, but servlets are installed in a secure

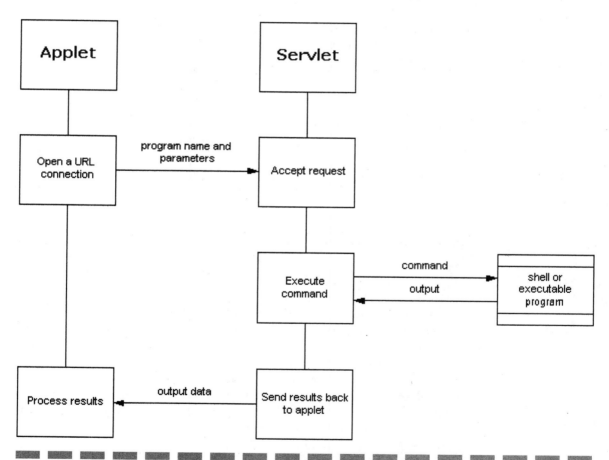

Figure 11-7 Using a Proxy Servlet to Execute a Command Remotely.

environment entirely under the control of the Web administrator. As long as access to the servlet is appropriately controlled, it is possible to provide significantly more functionality to applets without compromising security.

11.3   Perl Clients

Problem

I have a number of applications written in Perl, and I would like to access servlet functions from within them. How can I call a servlet from a Perl script?

Technique

Open a socket to the Web server, write an HTTP request, and read the results.

Discussion

Perl is an interpreted scripting language widely used in the Unix environment. It has excellent text-handling capabilities, which has made it popular for system administration tasks. Like Java, it also has built-in networking support, which has made it the dominant language for CGI applications. Since it supports sockets,[4] it can read and write HTTP requests, which makes it easy to communicate with servlets, as we shall see.

Why would we want to call a servlet from a Perl script? One obvious application is database connectivity. Recall from Chapter 5 that because of the JDBC-ODBC bridge, virtually all database systems are accessible from Java, probably more so than from Perl. Given the Perl-to-Java communication channel that HTTP provides, we can use servlets as middleware for Perl database access.

---

[4]Other higher-level networking mechanisms are available, notably the LWP package.

The Application   In this section we will develop an application that illustrates this technique. The application consists of two components:

1. A general-purpose database query servlet. The servlet will accept HTTP requests that contain a JDBC driver name, a database URL, and an SQL SELECT statement. It will run the query and send the results back to the requester as a tab-delimited data string, including a row of column names so that the client program can identify the fields in the result set.

2. A Perl script that sends a database query to the servlet and prints the results.

The Servlet   The servlet is listed in Figure 11-8. We enclose the code in the doGet() method in a try...catch...finally block for two reasons:

1. To simplify the error handling. We want all error conditions to return an error message with a 404 status code so that the client can determine whether the operation was successful.

2. To ensure that the database connection is closed in all cases, even if an exception is thrown.

First extracting the DRIVER, URL, and QUERY parameters and performing some preliminary validation, the servlet loads the driver class and opens the database connection. It uses a PreparedStatement to avoid problems with embedded quotes and to allow for an exception to be thrown if there is a syntax error. When the query is run, a ResultSet is produced, with column names supplied by the ResultSetMetadata object. A row of headings is then written to the response output stream, followed by each data row in the result set.

In this example, we chose application/x-www-form-urlencoded as the content type to simplify parsing by the client. Comma-separated-values would be another good choice, although slightly complicated by the need to quote strings that happen to contain commas.

The Perl Script   Before we dive into the Perl client, it is good to note that Perl is a highly idiomatic language. There are at least as many ways to write a program as there are programmers available to write it. Throughout the program, there are coding alternatives—many of which basically come down to a matter of style. Feel free to experiment.

Figure 11-8 A
General-Purpose
Database Select
Servlet.

```
package ijs.jdbc;

import java.io.*;
import java.net.*;
import java.sql.*;
import java.util.*;

import javax.servlet.*;
import javax.servlet.http.*;

/**
 * A general-purpose database select server.
 * Accepts an HTTP request with three parameters:
 * <UL>
 * <LI>DRIVER - the JDBC driver class name
 * <LI>URL - the JDBC database URL
 * <LI>QUERY - a SELECT statement to be executed
 * </UL>
 * The results are written in tab-separated-values
 * format, with the column names in the first row.
 */
public class SQLSelectServlet extends HttpServlet
{
    /**
     * Handles a GET request
     */
    public void doGet(
          HttpServletRequest request,
          HttpServletResponse response)
        throws ServletException, IOException
    {
        Connection con = null;
        try {

            // Get the driver name and database URL parameters

            String driver = request.getParameter("DRIVER");
            if (driver == null)
               throw new RuntimeException
               ("No driver class name specified");

            String url = request.getParameter("URL");
            if (url == null)
               throw new RuntimeException
               ("No url class name specified");

            // Get the SELECT statement to be executed

            String query = request.getParameter("QUERY");
            if (query == null)
               throw new RuntimeException
               ("No QUERY parameter specified");

            // Verify that it is a SELECT statement

            query = query.trim();
            if (!query.toUpperCase().startsWith("SELECT"))
```

Figure 11-8

(Continued)

```
            throw new RuntimeException
                ("Only SELECT statements are valid");

        // Make sure the driver is loaded

        Class.forName(driver);

        // Open the connection

        con = DriverManager.getConnection(url);

        // Compile the query statement.  If it is invalid,
        // a SQLException will be thrown.

        PreparedStatement stmt = con.prepareStatement(query);

        // Execute the query

        ResultSet rs = stmt.executeQuery();

        // Write the column headings

        response.setContentType("text/tab-separated-values");
        PrintWriter out = response.getWriter();

        ResultSetMetaData rmd = rs.getMetaData();
        int nColumns = rmd.getColumnCount();
        StringBuffer buffer = new StringBuffer();
        for (int i = 0; i < nColumns; i++) {
            int col = i+1;
            if (i > 0)
                buffer.append("\t");
            buffer.append(rmd.getColumnName(col));
        }
        out.println(buffer.toString());

        // Write the data from the result set

        while (rs.next()) {
            buffer = new StringBuffer();
            for (int i = 0; i < nColumns; i++) {
                int col = i+1;
                if (i > 0)
                    buffer.append("\t");
                buffer.append(rs.getString(col));
            }
            out.println(buffer.toString());
        }

        // Done

        rs.close();
        stmt.close();
    }
    catch (Exception e) {

        // If any errors occur, send back a "not found"
```

Figure 11-8
(Continued)

```
                // error indication

        response.getWriter().println(e.getMessage());
        response.setStatus(404);
    }
    finally {
        if (con != null) {
            try {
                con.close();
            }
            catch (SQLException ignore){}
        }
    }
}

/**
 * Handles a POST request
 */
public void doPost(
        HttpServletRequest request,
        HttpServletResponse response)
    throws ServletException, IOException
{
    doGet(request, response);
}
}
```

The Perl script will access a local mirror of the U.S. Department of Agriculture (USDA) nutrient database,[5] selecting an alphabetical list of food groups and printing the list to standard output. A listing of the script is found in Figure 11-9. The first two noncomment lines turn on the Perl interpreter's strict error-checking mode and import the socket-handling module. The first executable code is a call to the IO::Socket::INET constructor, passing it the host name and port number and specifying the tcp protocol. Before accessing the socket, we turn on autoflush mode so that the full HTTP request will be written to the server before we try to read the results.

Next, we create the list of parameters to be sent. These are

■ DRIVER. The name of the JDBC driver class.

■ URL. The database URL.

■ QUERY. The select statement to be run.

---

[5]Source: U.S. Department of Agriculture, Agricultural Research Service. USDA Nutrient Database for Standard Reference, Release 13, 1999. Nutrient Data Laboratory Home Page, *http://www.nal.usda.gov/fnic/foodcomp.*

Figure 11-9 A
Perl Client for the
Database Select
Servlet.

```perl
#! perl -w

# ================================================
# Program:        GetFoodGroups
#
# Description:
#
#     Sample Perl script that sends a database
#     query to the SQLSelect servlet.
# ================================================

use strict;
use IO::Socket;

my $hostName = "u25nv";
my $hostPort = "80";

# Open a socket to the host

my $socket = new IO::Socket::INET(
     PeerAddr => $hostName,
     PeerPort => $hostPort,
     Proto    => "tcp"
     );

# Set autoflush on

my $saveSelect = select $socket;
$| = 1;
select $saveSelect;

# Create the command

my $cmd = "";
$cmd .= "DRIVER=" . encode("sun.jdbc.odbc.JdbcOdbcDriver");
$cmd .= "&URL="   . encode("jdbc:odbc:usda");
$cmd .= "&QUERY=" . encode(<<EOF);
SELECT    *
FROM      FD_GROUP
ORDER BY FDGP_DESC
EOF

my $cmdLength = length($cmd);

# Send the HTTP request

print $socket (<<EOF);
POST /servlet/SQLSelect HTTP/1.0
Content-Type: application/x-www-form-urlencoded
Content-Length: $cmdLength

$cmd
EOF

# Read back the status code

my $line = <$socket>;
```

Figure 11-9
(Continued)

```
my ($httpVersion, $status) = split(/\s+/, $line);
if ($status != 200) {

    #  Handle the error ...

}
else {

    #  Skip the rest of the headers and display the results.
    #  End of headers is signalled by a blank line.

    my $inData = 0;
    while (<$socket>) {
        chomp;

        ($inData == 0) && do {
            $inData = 1 unless (/\S/);
            next;
        };

        ($inData == 1) && do {
            print "$_\n";
            next;
        };
    }
}

#  Done

$socket->close();

#  Subroutine to URL-encode a parameter string

sub encode {
    my $s = shift;
    $s =~ s/([^A-Za-z0-9 ])/"%" . sprintf("%02X", ord($1))/eg;
    $s =~ s/ /+/g;
    return $s;
}
```

The parameter values are URL-encoded, meaning that spaces are converted to plus signs and special characters are replaced with their hexadecimal values. This is necessary to avoid confusing the HTTP server that handles the request.

At this point, the script is ready to send the request. It uses the POST method to avoid query string length restrictions and sends the content type and content length as headers. After sending a blank line to indicate the end of the headers, it sends the encoded parameter list and begins reading the response. The first line of the response contains the return code in its second field. A return code of 200 indicates success; 404 indicates failure. If the request is successful, the script skips the rest of the headers, echoes the remaining data lines to standard output, and closes the socket.

It is worth noting that Perl scripts can be used not only as clients of Java servlets but also as servers to Java clients. We will examine this in more detail in Chapter 12.

11.4 XML Clients

Problem

How can I use XML to develop a more full-featured client?

Technique

Use sockets to communicate client requests to a servlet. In the servlet, generate XML output and send it back to the client over the socket. Use an XML parser in the client to recreate the full object.

Discussion

Extensible Markup Language (XML) has emerged as a promising standard for representing complex objects in a portable format. Using markup tags that you define in a document type definition (DTD), you can store data and complete information about data relationships in ordinary text files. There are an abundance of tools available to read, write, validate, and transform XML into just about any other data format. If your application can produce and understand XML documents, its interoperability with other applications increases substantially. A full treatment of XML is beyond the scope of this book; a popular reference work is *Building XML Applications*, by Simon St. Laurent (New York: Computing McGraw-Hill, June 1999, ISBN 0071341161). The official reference specification (available at *http://www.w3.org/TR/REC-xml*) is also helpful.

In this section we will develop a stand-alone Java client that gets XML-formatted data from a servlet. The application we will return to is the NewsTicker, for which we have developed several other clients. We will modify the NewsTicker servlet to produce XML output. Our GUI environment will be the Java Foundation Classes, commonly referred to as *Swing*.

The XML Document   Figure 11-10 shows the XML document that we need to generate. The document consists of three parts:

1. A processing instruction `<?xml version="1.0"?>` to indicate that this is an XML document. If we wanted to use an encoding mechanism other than ASCII, we could indicate this in this instruction. All valid XML documents must begin with this line.

2. A `<!DOCTYPE>` element with an internal document type definition (DTD). The DTD describes the structure of the document, which make it possible for tools to validate and process it. In this case, the DTD says that the document consists of a `<HEADLINES>` element containing zero or more `<HEADLINE>` elements. It specifies that the `<HEADLINES>` tag has an optional DATE attribute and that the `<HEADLINE>` tags require both a TITLE and an HREF attribute. DTDs can be either internal (embedded in the document itself, as shown here) or external, pointed to in the `<!DOCTYPE>` element using the SYSTEM or PUBLIC keyword.

3. The headlines data. In this case, there are three `<HEADLINE>` elements representing three stories from our *Internet Premium Food Market* news source.

The `NewsTickerXML` Servlet   As we did in Section 11.1 with the Java applet client, we need to update `TickerServlet` to generate XML out-

Figure 11-10

The NewsTicker Output as an XML Document with an Internal DTD.

```
<?xml version="1.0" ?>
<!DOCTYPE HEADLINES [
<!ELEMENT    HEADLINES      (HEADLINE)*>
<!ATTLIST    HEADLINES
   DATE      CDATA          #IMPLIED
   >
<!ELEMENT    HEADLINE       (#PCDATA)>
<!ATTLIST    HEADLINE
   TITLE     CDATA          #REQUIRED
   HREF      CDATA          #REQUIRED
   >
]>
<HEADLINES DATE="Sat Dec 04 13:26:26 EST 1999">
<HEADLINE
   TITLE="IPFM to offer video shopping"
   HREF="http://ipfoods.com/newsletter/VideoShopping.html"/>
<HEADLINE
   TITLE="Bauer, Cardenas named to IPFM board"
   HREF="http://ipfoods.com/newsletter/Board.html"/>
<HEADLINE
   TITLE="Schechs honored for Hunger Project work"
   HREF="http://ipfoods.com/newsletter/Schech.html"/>
</HEADLINES>
```

put instead of plain text. Taking advantage of Java's object orientation, we can just subclass `TickerServlet` to produce `TickerXMLServlet`, overriding only the `doGet()` method. Figure 11-11 shows how the `ijs.news.Headline` object array can be written as XML. Note that the content type is set to `text/xml`. The servlet can be tested simply by calling it from a Web browser. Microsoft Internet Explorer versions 5.0 and later will recognize the output as XML and display it in a color-highlighted clickable tree format.

The XML Client Application   Our JFC client, `ijs.news.viewer.ViewerFrame`, will bring up a frame window with a menu and toolbar. Either from the menu or the toolbar, the user can open a news source. We could provide a choice of several; for this example, we will just use the default *Internet Premium Food Market* news source. Figure 11-12 shows how the frame will look after the XML document is loaded in a tree view.

At this point, the user can select a story to be read or click the "Close" button to close the news source. Once an item has been selected (see Figure 11-13), the "read" and "print" toolbar buttons are enabled. Figure 11-14 shows the results of clicking the "Read" button. The window is split into a left half containing the list of headlines and a right half in which the story is displayed.

The GUI Code   The JFC code starts with a two-line `public static void main(String args[])` method, which simply calls the `ViewerFrame` constructor and makes the resulting frame visible:

```
JFrame frame = new ViewerFrame();
frame.setVisible(true);
```

The constructor has a lot to do, so we make it strictly a mainline that calls internal methods:

```
public ViewerFrame()
{
    super();
    initWindow();
    createActions();
    createToolBar();
}
```

GUI programs frequently have a lot of maintenance, with menu options being added and deleted. Unless this is planned for in the code design, it can quickly result in methods that are several pages long.

▬▬ ▬▬ ▬▬ ▬▬
Figure 11-11
An Updated
`NewsTicker`
Servlet That
Creates XML
Output.

```java
package ijs.news;

import java.io.*;
import java.net.*;
import java.util.*;

import javax.servlet.*;
import javax.servlet.http.*;

/**
 * TickerXMLServlet
 */
public class TickerXMLServlet extends TickerServlet
{
    /**
     * Handles a GET request
     */
    public void doGet(
            HttpServletRequest request,
            HttpServletResponse response)
        throws ServletException, IOException
    {
        // Get the headline source object from the
        // servlet context

        String name = getClass().getName() + ".source";
        HeadlineSource source = (HeadlineSource)
            getServletContext().getAttribute(name);

        // Retrieve the latest headlines

        Date lastRefreshTime = source.getLastRefreshTime();
        Headline[] headlines = source.getHeadlines();

        // Initialize for XML output

        response.setContentType("text/xml");
        PrintWriter out = response.getWriter();

        // Write the DTD

        out.println("<?xml version=\"1.0\" ?>");
        out.println("<!DOCTYPE HEADLINES [");
        out.println("<!ELEMENT   HEADLINES    (HEADLINE)*>");
        out.println("<!ATTLIST   HEADLINES");
        out.println("    DATE      CDATA       #IMPLIED");
        out.println("    >");
        out.println("<!ELEMENT   HEADLINE     (#PCDATA)>");
        out.println("<!ATTLIST   HEADLINE");
        out.println("    TITLE     CDATA       #REQUIRED");
        out.println("    HREF      CDATA       #REQUIRED");
        out.println("    >");
        out.println("]>");

        // Write the document header

        if (lastRefreshTime == null)
```

Figure 11-11
(Continued)

```
            out.println("<HEADLINES>");
        else
            out.println("<HEADLINES DATE=\""
                + lastRefreshTime.toString() + "\">");

        // Write the headlines

        if (headlines != null) {
            for (int i = 0; i < headlines.length; i++) {
                Headline headline = headlines[i];
                StringBuffer buffer = new StringBuffer();
                buffer.append("<HEADLINE");
                buffer.append(" TITLE=\"");
                buffer.append(headline.getTitle());
                buffer.append("\"");
                buffer.append(" HREF=\"");
                buffer.append(headline.getURL().toString());
                buffer.append("\"");
                buffer.append("/>");
                out.println(buffer.toString());
            }
        }

        // Write the document footer

        out.println("</HEADLINES>");

        out.flush();
        out.close();
    }
}
```

After the frame is made visible, it waits for events generated by user actions, either from menu items or toolbar buttons. These events are handled by the `actionPerformed()` methods of the action listeners defined for each function:

- *Open.* When the "Open" button is clicked, the program opens an input stream from the servlet and passes the input stream to an XML parser.[6] The parser constructs the document object model (DOM) for the document and provides an industry-standard interface for navigating through its structure. Using `getAttribute()` to extract the date and `getChildNodes()` to scan the document, we can create `Headline` objects from the XML elements:

---

[6]IBM freely distributes a popular XML parser for Java from its *http://www.alphaworks.ibm.com* Web site. Sun Microsystems and other vendors also produce freely available implementations of parsers that conform to the W3C document object model.

Figure 11-12 ViewerFrame Window after the News Source Has Been Opened.

```
Headline headline = new Headline();
String title = element.getAttribute("TITLE");
String href = element.getAttribute("HREF");
headline.setTitle(title);
headline.setURL(href);
```

We will render the document in a `javax.swing.JTree` component, using `DefaultMutableTreeNode` components to wrap each
`Headline` object:

```
DefaultMutableTreeNode hnode =
  new DefaultMutableTreeNode(headline);
top.add(hnode);
```

After the `JTree` is constructed and added to the layout, we create a
`TreeSelectionListener` to listen for user selections made in the
tree. When the selected headline changes, the corresponding
`Headline` object is stored in the `currentHeadline` instance
variable.

Figure 11-13 ViewerFrame Window after a Headline Has Been Selected.

- *Close.* When the user clicks the "Close" button, the split pane is removed from the layout, and the container is revalidated.
- *Read.* When a news headline is selected, the corresponding URL is used to create a `javax.swing.JEditorPane` that acts as a mini-Web browser, loading the URL contents into a scroll pane. This scroll pane and the XML outline are combined in a split pane that displays the two panels side by side.
- *Print.* Code can be added here to print or otherwise process the selected URL content.
- *Exit.* When the "Exit menu" option is selected, the window is closed, and `System.exit()` is called.

Figure 11-15 contains the complete listing.

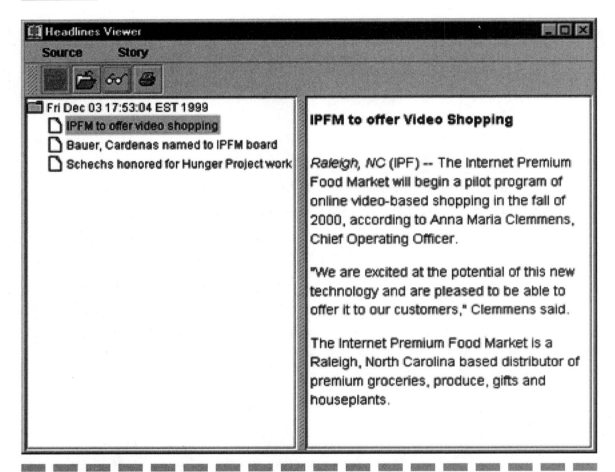

Figure 11-14 Split Screen Showing the Outline Tree and the Selected Story.

Figure 11-15

A Stand-alone JFC
Headlines Client.

```java
package ijs.news.viewer;

import com.ibm.xml.parsers.*;
import org.w3c.dom.*;
import org.xml.sax.*;
import ijs.news.*;
import java.awt.*;
import java.awt.event.*;
import java.io.*;
import java.net.*;
import java.util.*;
import javax.swing.*;
import javax.swing.tree.*;
import javax.swing.event.*;

/**
 * A headlines viewer that reads XML headline objects
 * from a servlet.
 */
public class ViewerFrame extends JFrame
{
    // =============================================
    //       Class methods
    // =============================================

    /**
     * Standalone mainline
     */
    public static void main(String[] args)
    {
        JFrame frame = new ViewerFrame();
        frame.setVisible(true);
    }


    // =============================================
    //       Class variables
    // =============================================

    public static final String TITLE = "Headlines Viewer";
    public static final int WIDTH = 600;
    public static final int HEIGHT = 400;

    public static final int STATE_CLOSED = 0;
    public static final int STATE_OPEN = 1;
    public static final int STATE_SELECTED = 2;

    // =============================================
    //       Constructors
    // =============================================

    /**
     * Creates a new ViewerFrame frame
     */
    public ViewerFrame()
    {
        super();
        initWindow();
```

Figure 11-15

(Continued)

```java
      createActions();
      createMenus();
      createToolBar();
   }


   // ===============================================
   //    Instance methods
   // ===============================================

   /**
    * Initializes the window
    */
   public void initWindow()
   {
      setTitle(TITLE);
      setSize(WIDTH, HEIGHT);

      // Set the icon image for the frame

      Class myClass = getClass();
      URL myURL = myClass.getResource("images/newspaper.gif");
      ImageIcon myIcon = new ImageIcon(myURL);
      Image myImage = myIcon.getImage();
      setIconImage(myImage);

      // Create the main interior panel

      pnlMain = new JPanel();
      pnlMain.setLayout(new BorderLayout());
      getContentPane().add(pnlMain, BorderLayout.CENTER);

      // Listen for window closing events

      addWindowListener(new WindowAdapter() {
         public void windowClosing(WindowEvent event) {
            doExit();
         }
      });
   }

   /**
    * Creates the abstract actions that are used for both
    * the menus and the toolbar
    */
   public void createActions()
   {

      actExit = new AbstractAction() {
         public void actionPerformed(ActionEvent event) {
            doExit();
         }
      };

      actOpen = new AbstractAction() {
         public void actionPerformed(ActionEvent event) {
            doOpen();
         }
```

Figure 11-15
(Continued)

```
      };

      actClose = new AbstractAction() {
         public void actionPerformed(ActionEvent event) {
            doClose();
         }
      };

      actRead = new AbstractAction() {
         public void actionPerformed(ActionEvent event) {
            doRead();
         }
      };

      actPrint = new AbstractAction() {
         public void actionPerformed(ActionEvent event) {
            doPrint();
         }
      };

      // Enable actions appropriately

      setState(STATE_CLOSED);
   }

   /**
   * Sets the application state so that buttons and menu items
   * can be set properly.
   * <PRE>
   * 0 - No open source
   * 1 - open source
   * </PRE>
   * @param state the new state
   */
   public void setState(int state)
   {
      this.state = state;

      switch (state) {
         case STATE_CLOSED:
            actOpen.setEnabled(true);
            actClose.setEnabled(false);
            actRead.setEnabled(false);
            actPrint.setEnabled(false);
            break;
         case STATE_OPEN:
            actOpen.setEnabled(false);
            actClose.setEnabled(true);
            actRead.setEnabled(false);
            actPrint.setEnabled(false);
            break;
         case STATE_SELECTED:
            actOpen.setEnabled(false);
            actClose.setEnabled(true);
            actRead.setEnabled(true);
            actPrint.setEnabled(true);
            break;
```

Figure 11-15
(Continued)

```
        }
    }

    /**
     * Creates the menus
     */
    public void createMenus()
    {
        JMenuBar mb = new JMenuBar();
        setJMenuBar(mb);

        // News source menu

        JMenu mnuSource = new JMenu("Source");
        mb.add(mnuSource);

        JMenuItem mnuOpen = mnuSource.add(actOpen);
        mnuOpen.setText("Open");

        JMenuItem mnuClose = mnuSource.add(actClose);
        mnuClose.setText("Close");

        mnuSource.addSeparator();

        JMenuItem mnuExit = mnuSource.add(actExit);
        mnuExit.setText("Exit");

        // Story menu

        JMenu mnuStory = new JMenu("Story");
        mb.add(mnuStory);

        JMenuItem mnuRead = mnuStory.add(actRead);
        mnuRead.setText("Read");

        JMenuItem mnuPrint = mnuStory.add(actPrint);
        mnuPrint.setText("Print");
    }

    /**
     * Creates the toolbar
     */
    public void createToolBar()
    {
        JToolBar tb = new JToolBar();
        Insets zeroInsets = new Insets(0, 0, 0, 0);

        // Open button

        JButton btnOpen = tb.add(actOpen);
        Icon imgOpen = new ImageIcon(
            getClass().getResource("images/open.gif"));
        btnOpen.setIcon(imgOpen);
        btnOpen.setToolTipText("Opens a news source");
        btnOpen.setMargin(zeroInsets);

        // Close button
```

Figure 11-15
(Continued)

```
    JButton btnClose = tb.add(actClose);
    Icon imgClose = new ImageIcon(
        getClass().getResource("images/close.gif"));
    btnClose.setIcon(imgClose);
    btnClose.setToolTipText("Closes a news source");
    btnClose.setMargin(zeroInsets);

    // Read button

    JButton btnRead = tb.add(actRead);
    Icon imgRead = new ImageIcon(
        getClass().getResource("images/read.gif"));
    btnRead.setIcon(imgRead);
    btnRead.setToolTipText("Reads a news source");
    btnRead.setMargin(zeroInsets);

    // Print button

    JButton btnPrint = tb.add(actPrint);
    Icon imgPrint = new ImageIcon(
        getClass().getResource("images/print.gif"));
    btnPrint.setIcon(imgPrint);
    btnPrint.setToolTipText("Prints a news source");
    btnPrint.setMargin(zeroInsets);

    // Add the toolbar to the content pane

    getContentPane().add(tb, BorderLayout.NORTH);
}

// ============================================
//      Event handlers
// ============================================

/**
 * Handles the window close event
 */
public void doExit()
{
    dispose();
    System.exit(0);
}

/**
 * Handles the news source open event
 */
public void doOpen()
{
    setState(STATE_OPEN);
    treePanel = null;

    try {

        // Open the XML input stream

        URL servletURL =
```

Figure 11-15
(Continued)

```
          new URL("http://localhost/servlet/NewsTickerXML");

// Parse the XML headlines document

InputSource is =
    new InputSource(servletURL.openStream());
DOMParser parser = new DOMParser();
parser.parse(is);

// Get the <HEADLINES> element

Document doc = parser.getDocument();
Element root = doc.getDocumentElement();

// Get its DATE attribute

String dateString = root.getAttribute("DATE");
DefaultMutableTreeNode top =
    new DefaultMutableTreeNode(dateString);

// Traverse the list of all children

NodeList children = root.getChildNodes();
for (int i = 0; i < children.getLength(); i++) {

    // Get element nodes only

    Node child = children.item(i);
    if (child.getNodeType() != Node.ELEMENT_NODE)
        continue;
    Element element = (Element) child;

    // Get the <HEADLINE> element

    if (!element.getTagName().equals("HEADLINE"))
        continue;

    Headline headline = new Headline();

    String title = element.getAttribute("TITLE");
    String href = element.getAttribute("HREF");

    headline.setTitle(title);
    headline.setURL(href);
    DefaultMutableTreeNode hnode =
        new DefaultMutableTreeNode(headline);
    top.add(hnode);
}

// Create the tree

tree = new JTree(top);
treePanel = new JScrollPane(tree);

// Add the selection listener

tree.getSelectionModel().setSelectionMode
```

Figure 11-15
(Continued)

```
                                   (TreeSelectionModel.SINGLE_TREE_SELECTION);

            tree.addTreeSelectionListener
               (new TreeSelectionListener() {
               public void valueChanged(TreeSelectionEvent e)
               {
                   DefaultMutableTreeNode node =
                      (DefaultMutableTreeNode)
                      tree.getLastSelectedPathComponent();
                   currentHeadline = null;
                   if (node == null) {
                       setState(STATE_OPEN);
                       return;
                   }
                   currentHeadline =
                      (Headline) node.getUserObject();
                   setState(STATE_SELECTED);
               }
            });
            pnlMain.removeAll();
            pnlMain.add(treePanel, BorderLayout.CENTER);
            validate();
            repaint();
        }
        catch (Exception e) {
            e.printStackTrace();
        }
    }

    /**
     * Handles the news source close event
     */
    public void doClose()
    {
        pnlMain.removeAll();
        validate();
        repaint();
        setState(STATE_CLOSED);
    }

    /**
     * Creates the split pane.  The left pane is a tree view of
     * the XML document.  The right pane is an HTML view of the
     * contents of the selected item.
     */
    public void doRead()
    {
        // Create the HTML editor pane

        JEditorPane htmlPanelInner = new JEditorPane();
        htmlPanelInner.setEditable(false);
        try {
            htmlPanelInner.setPage(currentHeadline.getURL());
        }
        catch (IOException e) {
            e.printStackTrace();
        }
```

```java
        htmlPanel = new JScrollPane(htmlPanelInner);

        // Create the split pane and add it to the main panel

        splitPane = new JSplitPane(
            JSplitPane.HORIZONTAL_SPLIT,
            true,
            treePanel,
            htmlPanel
            );

        pnlMain.removeAll();
        pnlMain.add(splitPane, BorderLayout.CENTER);
        validate();
        repaint();
    }

    /**
     * Handles the news story print event
     */
    public void doPrint()
    {
        // ... place code here to print the story
    }

    // ===============================================
    //      Instance variables
    // ===============================================

    private int state;

    private Action actOpen;
    private Action actClose;
    private Action actRead;
    private Action actPrint;
    private Action actExit;

    private JPanel pnlMain;
    private JSplitPane splitPane;
    private JScrollPane treePanel;
    private JScrollPane htmlPanel;
    private JTree tree;
    private Headline currentHeadline;
```

Other Servers

Overview

In the preceding chapter we learned that servlets can act as the server-side component for clients other than just HTML forms. The same is true in the other direction—servlets can act as clients to many other applications and services. This versatility makes servlets ideal middleware, linking Java components to other applications, to legacy systems, and to new protocols. This chapter demonstrates techniques that can be used for this purpose. We shall explore the following areas:

- *File upload.* Servlets can be used to securely transfer files from a client to a server or a server-side application. This can be done with the Hypertext Transfer Protocol (HTTP) PUT method or with the more flexible multipart/form-data encoding technique.

- *Native methods.* Servlets can gain access to platform-specific features and possibly optimize performance using calls to C or C++ routines. The Java Native Interface (JNI) makes this possible.

- *Access to Web data in other forms.* Servlets can invoke other server-oriented protocols such as Common Gateway Interface (CGI) and Active Server Pages (ASP). Subsets of data selected using these protocols can be reformatted and incorporated into other client or server applications.

- *Extending the functionality of applets.* By acting as a proxy to other applications and protocols, a servlet can enhance the usefulness of applets as application front-ends. Servlets can enable applets to access File Transfer Protocol (FTP) data and to communicate with RMI or CORBA objects in a distributed system.

The central idea is that all these distributed application functions can be made to look like static (but intelligent) Web documents. Servlets, besides being useful in their own right, can be the glue that makes this possible.

12.1   File Upload with HTTP PUT

Problem

I would like to allow users to upload files to the server. How can I do this with a servlet?

Technique

Use HTTP PUT to send the file data. In your servlet, override doPut() to receive the data and write it to a secure location.

Discussion

HTTP is used most often as a protocol for downloading files, but it also makes provision for uploading them. There are two different mechanisms that can be used: the HTTP PUT method and multipart/form-data encoding. In this section we shall consider the first approach. Section 12.2 deals with the second.

The HTTP PUT Method   In addition to GET and POST, the HTTP defines five other methods: OPTIONS, HEAD, PUT, DELETE, and TRACE. The PUT method is similar to POST in that file data are included in the body of the request. However, rather than containing the name of a resource that will handle the request (i.e., a servlet or CGI program), the request URI on the first line of a PUT request is an identifier for the file itself. The processing program can use this URI as a file name, for example.

There are several restrictions that make HTTP PUT less often used than other approaches. To begin with, there is no built-in mechanism in HTML to act as the client for the request. HTML forms are limited to METHOD=GET or METHOD=POST. This means that a custom application or applet must be written to submit the request. Second, the implementation of HTTP PUT is always specific to the Web server. To understand why this is so, consider the URI used to invoke a PUT request. It contains not the servlet name but rather the name of the file to be uploaded. This being the case, how does the servlet engine (or the Web server, for that matter) know how to handle the request? The answer is that the Web server configuration must be involved.

The Apache Web server uses a Script directive to identify the handler for PUT requests. For example, to associate a servlet named Put with the PUT method, the following block should be added to the httpd.conf file:

```
<Limit PUT>
  Script PUT "/servlet/Put"
</Limit>
```

If this is done, then whenever PUT requests are received, the Web server will invoke the /servlet/Put URL to handle them.

The Server-Side Handler Figure 12-1 is a listing of a servlet that can be used to handle HTTP PUT requests. It extracts the file name from the request object and converts it to a name in the server's file system that is reserved for uploads. To comply with the HTTP/1.1 specification for PUT requests,[1] it uses a return code of 200 (OK) for existing files, 201 (CREATED) for new ones, or 501 (NOT IMPLEMENTED) if there are any Content-* headers besides Content-Type and Content-Length. After reading the headers and assigning the file name, PutServlet starts copying the file data, first creating any intermediate directories that may be required. After flushing and closing the output stream, it returns the appropriate status code.

The Client As we observed, HTML forms make no direct provision for the PUT method. However, the java.net.HttpURLConnection class recognizes it and can be used in either an application or an applet to handle the client side of the request. Figure 12-2 lists a stand-alone client application that uses this approach.

PutClient accepts a server name and file name as parameters to its constructor. After verifying that the file exists, it transforms the name into a format that can be incorporated into a URL (i.e., no drive letters or backward slashes). It then opens an HttpUrlConnection and sets the request method to PUT and the content length to the number of bytes to be sent. After this, it begins copying data to the connection's output stream. The server returns the response code, which the client echoes to System.out.

See also Section 12-2.

---

[1]See RFC2068 at *http://www.freesoft.org/CIE/RFC/2068/index.htm.*

Figure 12-1
A Servlet That
Implements HTTP
PUT.

```
package ijs.servers;

import java.io.*;
import java.net.*;
import java.util.*;

import javax.servlet.*;
import javax.servlet.http.*;

/**
 * PutServlet
 */
public class PutServlet extends HttpServlet
{
    /**
     * Handles a PUT request
     */
    public void doPut(
            HttpServletRequest request,
            HttpServletResponse response)
        throws ServletException, IOException
    {
        // Hope for the best

        int status = response.SC_OK;

        // Get the file name from the request

        String name = request.getPathInfo();
        if (name == null)
            throw new ServletException
            ("No file name specified");

        // Assign the server-relative file name

        String baseName = getInitParameter("baseName");
        if (baseName == null)
            throw new ServletException
            ("No baseName init parameter found");

        name = baseName + "/" + name;

        // Determine whether this is a new file
        // or an existing one

        File file = new File(name);
        if (!file.exists())
            status = response.SC_CREATED;

        // Verify that no unimplemented Content-* headers
        // were sent

        Enumeration enames = request.getHeaderNames();
        while (enames.hasMoreElements()) {
            String uname = (String) enames.nextElement();
            uname = uname.toUpperCase();
            if (uname.startsWith("CONTENT-")) {
```

Figure 12-1

(Continued)

```
            if (uname.startsWith("CONTENT-TYPE"))
                continue;
            if (uname.startsWith("CONTENT-LENGTH"))
                continue;
            status = response.SC_NOT_IMPLEMENTED;
            response.setStatus(status);
            return;
        }
    }

    // Open the output file, making any intermediate
    // directories that may be required

    String parentName = file.getParent();
    if (parentName != null) {
        File parent = new File(parentName);
        if (!parent.exists()) {
            boolean dirsOK = parent.mkdirs();
            if (!dirsOK)
                throw new ServletException
                    ("Could not make directories for " + name);
        }
    }

    BufferedOutputStream fileOut =
        new BufferedOutputStream(
        new FileOutputStream(file));

    // Write the file data

    InputStream in = request.getInputStream();
    byte[] buffer = new byte[4096];
    while (true) {
        int nBytes = in.read(buffer);
        if (nBytes == -1)
            break;
        fileOut.write(buffer, 0, nBytes);
    }
    fileOut.flush();
    fileOut.close();

    // Send the response

    response.setStatus(status);
    return;
    }
}
```

Figure 12-2

A Standalone
Client That
Uploads a File with
HTTP PUT.

```java
package ijs.servers;

import java.io.*;
import java.net.*;
import java.util.*;

/**
 * An example of using the HTTP PUT method to upload a file.
 */
public class PutClient
{
    /**
     * Uploads a file to the specified HTTP server
     * @param host the server name
     * @param fileName the file name
     */
    public PutClient(String host, String fileName)
        throws IOException
    {
        // Verify that the file exists

        File file = new File(fileName);

        if (!file.exists())
            throw new IOException
                (fileName + " does not exist");

        if (!file.canRead())
            throw new IOException
                (fileName + " is not readable");

        // Open the input file

        InputStream fileIn =
            new BufferedInputStream(
            new FileInputStream(file));

        // Transform the file name into one
        // that is acceptable to the server

        fileName = fileName.replace('\\', '/');
        int p = fileName.indexOf(":");
        if (p > -1)
            fileName = fileName.substring(p+1);
        if (!fileName.startsWith("/"))
            fileName = "/" + fileName;

        // Form the URL

        URL url = new URL("http", host, fileName);

        // Open an HTTP URL connection

        HttpURLConnection con = (HttpURLConnection)
            url.openConnection();

        // Set the headers of interest:
```

Figure 12-2
(Continued)

```
con.setRequestMethod("PUT");
con.setUseCaches(false);
con.setDoOutput(true);
con.setRequestProperty(
    "Content-length",
    String.valueOf(file.length()));

// Write the file contents to the URL output stream

OutputStream urlOut =
    new BufferedOutputStream(
    con.getOutputStream());

byte[] buffer = new byte[4096];
for (;;) {
    int nBytes = fileIn.read(buffer);
    if (nBytes == -1)
        break;
    urlOut.write(buffer, 0, nBytes);
}
fileIn.close();
urlOut.flush();

// Echo the return code

int status = con.getResponseCode();
String message = con.getResponseMessage();
System.out.println(status + " " + message);

// Close the connection

con.disconnect();
}

/**
 * Standalone mainline
 */
public static void main(String[] args)
{
    if (args.length != 2) {
        showUsage();
        return;
    }

    String host = args[0];
    String fileName = args[1];
    try {
        new PutClient(host, fileName);
    }
    catch (IOException e) {
        e.printStackTrace();
    }
}

/**
 * Displays calling syntax
```

Figure 12-2

(Continued)

```
*/
public static void showUsage()
{
    String[] text = {
        "usage: java ijs.servers.PutClient"
            + " <server> <filename>",
        "where: server   is the web server name",
        "       filename is the file to be uploaded",
    };
    for (int i = 0; i < text.length; i++)
        System.out.println(text[i]);
}
}
```

12.2   File Upload with `multipart/form-data`

Problem

I would like to use an HTML form to upload files to the server. How can I handle the server side of the upload?

Technique

Use `ENCTYPE="multipart/form-data"` in the HTML `FORM` tag and an input element with `TYPE="FILE"` to specify the file. In the servlet, parse the boundary markers to find each field. The file data will be included in the request and should be copied to the server's file system.

Discussion

As we saw in the preceding section, files can be uploaded with HTTP requests that use the `PUT` method. However, the HTTP `PUT` technique requires server-specific configuration changes and cannot be initiated by an HTML form. Another approach that does not have these drawbacks is the use of `multipart/form-data` encoding.

This technique, which is documented in RFC1867 and RFC2388, differs from the default form encoding (`x-www-form-urlencoded`) in that each field is transmitted in its own block, delimited by boundary markers. Each block can have its own HTTP headers, particularly `Content-`

`Type` and `Content-Disposition`. The block delimiter is a pseudorandom string chosen by the client application and is sent in the `Content-Type` header's `boundary` attribute. Each block starts with the boundary string and is terminated by the next block's starting boundary string. The final block is terminated by the boundary string followed by two hyphen characters.

A Complete Example   The Internet Premium Food Market sells menu-planning software, for which it provides Web-based technical support. One of the technical support Web pages provides an area for customers to upload error log files. Figure 12-3 shows a stack trace generated by an application. The stack trace has been saved in a file named `MenuPlanner.txt`.

The technical support Web page (see Figure 12-4) prompts the user for a product serial number and the name of a file to be uploaded. The Web browser automatically provides a "Browse" button that can be used to navigate the local file system for the desired file.

When the "Submit" button is clicked, the file is uploaded and processed by a server-side application. A confirmation number is returned for the customer's reference (see Figure 12-5).

Figure 12-6 shows the HTML necessary to perform this operation. There are two input elements: a `TEXT` field for the product serial number and a `FILE` element for the file to be uploaded. The only difference between this and an ordinary HTML form is the use of the `ENCTYPE="multipart/form-data` attribute in the `<FORM>` tag.[2]

The resulting HTTP request (which we captured with the `DebugServer` servlet developed in Chapter 6) is shown in Figure 12-7. It begins with a request line that specifies the `POST` method, the name of the servlet (`IPFTechnicalSupport`), and the HTTP version number. Other headers specify information about the browser, such as the user agent, the original form name, the desired language, etc.

The `Content-Type` header indicates that `multipart/form-data` encoding is used and that the boundary string is ----------- `7cf1781378b801ae`. The two form fields follow in their own sections, delimited by the boundary string. Inside each section is a `Content-Disposition` header in which the field name is specified. After the headers in each section, the data follow. We see that the `serial` field contains the product serial number `081619RJ` and that the `logData`

---

[2]The `FILE` element can be used with `x-www-form-urlencoded` forms as well, but it only sends the file name, not the contents of the file.

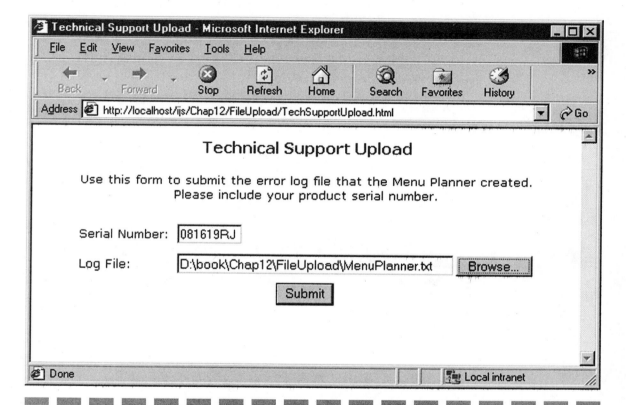

Figure 12-3
A Stack Trace
Generated by an
Application Error.

```
java.io.FileNotFoundException: ipfoods.ini
    (The system cannot find the file specified)
    at java.io.FileInputStream.open(Native Method)
    at java.io.FileInputStream.<init>(FileInputStream.java;68)
    at ijs.servers.MenuPlanner.init(MenuPlanner.java:36)
    at ijs.servers.MenuPlanner.<init>(MenuPlanner.java;28)
    at ijs.servers.MenuPlanner.main(MenuPlanner.java:18)
```

Figure 12-4 A Form for Uploading Error Log Files to a Defect-Tracking System.

field holds the contents of the uploaded file. The final boundary marker
has two additional hyphen characters to indicate that there are no more
fields.

A Servlet That Handles the Uploaded File   Figure 12-8 contains the
source listing for the TechSupportServlet, which interprets and
processes the HTTP request. The servlet examines the Content-Type

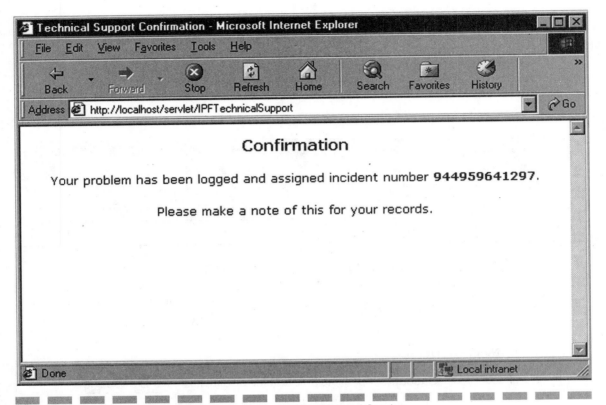

Figure 12-5 The Confirmation Returned by the File Upload Servlet.

header to get the boundary string. It then reads the request input stream, parsing the individual sections to get their names and values. Finally, it calls the `reportDefect` method to process the file data and generates a confirmation page.

In our example, `reportDefect` is just a stub method that simulates processing the uploaded data. Later, in Section 12.7, we will develop an implementation of this method.

Figure 12-6 An HTML Form That Supports File Upload.

```
<HTML>

<HEAD>
<TITLE>Technical Support Upload</TITLE>
</HEAD>

<BODY>
<!-- ACTION="/servlet/IPFTechnicalSupport" -->

<CENTER>
<H3>Technical Support Upload</H3>
<FORM
    METHOD="POST"
    ACTION="http://u25nv:4284/servlet/IPFTechnicalSupport"
    ENCTYPE="multipart/form-data"
    >
Use this form to submit the error log file
that the Menu Planner created.
<BR>
Please include your product serial number.
<P>

<TABLE BORDER=0 CELLPADDING=3>
<TR>
    <TD>Serial Number:</TD>
    <TD><INPUT TYPE="TEXT" NAME="serial" SIZE=8></TD>
</TR>
<TR>
    <TD>Log File:</TD>
    <TD><INPUT TYPE="FILE" NAME="logData" SIZE=40></TD>
</TR>
<TR>
    <TD COLSPAN=2 ALIGN=CENTER>
    <INPUT TYPE="SUBMIT" VALUE="Submit">
    </TD>
</TR>
</TABLE>
</FORM>
</CENTER>
</BODY>

</HTML>
```

Figure 12-7

Multipart Form
Data Generated
by the
TechSupportUp-
load Form.

```
POST /servlet/IPFTechnicalSupport HTTP/1.1
Accept: application/msword, application/vnd.ms-excel,
        image/gif, image/x-xbitmap, image/jpeg, image/pjpeg,
        application/vnd.ms-powerpoint, application/x-comet,
        */*
Referer: http://u25nv/TechSupportUpload.html
Accept-Language: en-us
Content-Type: multipart/form-data;
        boundary=---------------------------7cf1781378b801ae
Accept-Encoding: gzip, deflate
User-Agent: Mozilla/4.0
        (compatible; MSIE 5.0; Windows NT; DigExt)
Host: u25nv:4284
Content-Length: 713
Connection: Keep-Alive

---------------------------7cf1781378b801ae
Content-Disposition: form-data; name="serial"

081619RJ
---------------------------7cf1781378b801ae
Content-Disposition: form-data; name="logData";
    filename="D:\book\Chap12\FileUpload\MenuPlanner.txt"
Content-Type: text/plain

java.io.FileNotFoundException: ipfoods.ini
    (The system cannot find the file specified)
    at java.io.FileInputStream.open(Native Method)
    at java.io.FileInputStream.<init>(FileInputStream.java:68)
    at ijs.servers.MenuPlanner.init(MenuPlanner.java:36)
    at ijs.servers.MenuPlanner.<init>(MenuPlanner.java:28)
    at ijs.servers.MenuPlanner.main(MenuPlanner.java:18)

---------------------------7cf1781378b801ae--
```

Figure 12-8

A File Upload
Servlet That
Handles multi-
part/form-data
Content

```
package ijs.servers;

import java.io.*;
import java.net.*;
import java.util.*;

import javax.servlet.*;
import javax.servlet.http.*;

/**
 * TechSupportServlet
 */
public class TechSupportServlet extends HttpServlet
{
  /**
   * Handles a POST request
   */
  public void doPost(
      HttpServletRequest request,
      HttpServletResponse response)
    throws ServletException, IOException
  {
    PrintWriter out = response.getWriter();
    response.setContentType("text/html");
    try {

      // Verify the content type

      String ct = request.getContentType();
      if (!ct.startsWith("multipart/form-data"))
        throw new RuntimeException
        ("Invalid content type");

      // Get the boundary string

      int p = ct.indexOf("boundary=");
      if (p == -1)
        throw new RuntimeException
        ("No boundary string found");

      p += "boundary=".length();
      String boundary = "--" + ct.substring(p);
      String finalBoundary = boundary + "--";

      // We'll parse the multipart/form-data
      // with a finite state machine

      // Define names for the parser states

      final int INIT = 0;
      final int READING_HEADERS = 1;
      final int READING_DATA = 2;

      int state = INIT;

      // Read and extract the fields
```

Figure 12-8

(Continued)

```
Hashtable fields = new Hashtable();
String name = null;
String value = null;

BufferedReader in = request.getReader();
main: for (;;) {
    String line = in.readLine();
    if (line == null)
        break;

    switch (state) {

        // State 0: Ignoring everything before
        // the first boundary

        case INIT:
            if (line.startsWith(finalBoundary))
                break main;
            if (line.startsWith(boundary)) {
                state = READING_HEADERS;
                name = "";
                value = "";
            }
            break;

        // State 1: Parsing the headers

        case READING_HEADERS:
            if (line.length() == 0)
                state = READING_DATA;
            else {

                // We are only interested in the
                // Content-Disposition headers

                p = line.indexOf("Content-Disposition");
                if (p == -1)
                    break;
                p += "Content-Disposition".length();

                // Get the field name

                p = line.indexOf("name=\"", p);
                if (p == -1)
                    break;
                p += "name=\"".length();

                // ... up to the closing quote.

                int q = line.indexOf("\"", p);
                if (q == -1)
                    break;
                name = line.substring(p, q);
                value = "";
            }
            break;
```

Figure 12-8
(Continued)

```
// State 2: Reading the data

case READING_DATA:
    if (line.startsWith(finalBoundary)) {
        fields.put(name, value);
        break main;
    }
    if (line.startsWith(boundary)) {
        fields.put(name, value);
        state = READING_HEADERS;
    }
    else {
        if (value.length() > 0)
            value += "\n";
        value += line;
    }
    break;
    }
}

// Done parsing form - invoke the defect reporting
// application and get the incident number

String serial = (String) fields.get("serial");
if (serial == null || serial.trim().equals(""))
    throw new RuntimeException
    ("No product serial number was entered");

String logData = (String) fields.get("logData");
if (logData == null || logData.trim().equals(""))
    throw new RuntimeException
    ("No log data was found");

String inbr = reportDefect(serial, logData);

// Report the incident number back to the client

String[] text = {
    "<HTML>",
    "<HEAD>",
    "<TITLE>Technical Support Confirmation</TITLE>",
    "</HEAD>",
    "<BODY>",
    "<CENTER>",
    "<H3>Confirmation</H3>",
    "Your problem has been logged and assigned",
    "incident number <B>" + inbr + "</B>.",
    "<P>",
    "Please make a note of this for your records.",
    "</CENTER>",
    "</BODY>",
    "</HTML>",
};
for (int i = 0; i < text.length; i++)
    out.println(text[i]);
}
```

Figure 12-8
(Continued)

```
catch (Exception e) {

    // Write the exception message

    out.println("<H3>Error:</H3>");
    out.println("<PRE>");
    out.println(e.getMessage());
    out.println("</PRE>");
  }
  finally {
    out.flush();
  }
}

/**
 * Reports the problem to the defect tracking
 * application (not shown.  All we will do
 * here is make up an incident number).
 */
public String reportDefect(String serial, String logData)
{
    return String.valueOf(System.currentTimeMillis());
  }
}
```

12.3   Using Native Methods in a Servlet

Problem

I have a library of C-language mathematical routines that I would like to call from within a Web application. How can I access the routines from a servlet?

Technique

Use the Java Native Interface (JNI).

Discussion

Native methods are methods that are implemented outside the Java virtual machine, usually in C or C++. They are declared using the native keyword and have a body consisting of just a semicolon rather than a block of code. There are four principal reasons why native methods are used:

1. They provide access to platform-specific functions such as the Win32 API.

2. They may improve performance in numerically intensive calculations. Most of the `java.lang.Math` functions have native implementations.

3. They can be used to make subroutine libraries or legacy applications accessible as Java objects.

4. They can obfuscate proprietary code. A compiled C++ function is harder to disassemble than a Java method.[3]

While native methods are necessarily system-specific, the JNI provides a standardized programming interface for implementing them. JNI allows Java classes to call native functions and allows these native functions to call back into the Java virtual machine. In addition, JNI enables native executables to create a new Java virtual machine and run Java applications.

There are drawbacks, of course. The developer must provide implementations for all platforms on which the application runs. Native methods are also hard to debug, since they cannot be called easily from outside the Java virtual machine. They can introduce security problems and cause the virtual machine to crash. Moreover, they cannot be called from applets generally, at least not from ordinary applets running in typical browser environments.

This is where servlets can be helpful. Servlets can use native methods beneficially for the same four reasons listed above, but in particular, they can act as proxies to make external functions available to applets.

A Complete Example In this section we will develop a servlet that uses a native method to calculate the determinant[4] of a matrix passed by an applet. There are over 100 functions in the JNI; we will discuss only a few here, just enough to develop a working example. For a complete discussion of JNI, see the official specification at *http://java.sun.com/products/jdk/1.2/docs/guide/jni/spec/jniTOC.doc.html* or the JNI tutorial at *http://java.sun.com/docs/books/tutorial/native1.1/index.html*.

---

[3]This is relative, of course. Given enough time and motivation, a determined programmer can reconstruct almost anything.

[4]The determinant is an important matrix function used in linear algebra. We are not concerned here with its definition, nor with finding the most efficient algorithm for calculating it. We use it only as an example of the kind of function that may be implemented with a native method.

Figure 12-9 shows the source code for a minimal `Matrix` class. It has a constructor that accepts an array of integers and a `toString()` method that returns a string representation. It also declares a native method that returns the determinant of the matrix:

```
public native int det();
```

To make it possible to access the `det()` method, the `Matrix` class uses a static initializer that loads its external implementation:

```
static {
    System.loadLibrary("MatrixImpl");
}
```

It would be useful to add a stand-alone `main()` function to `Matrix.java` to simplify debugging.

Figure 12-10 shows the makefile used to create the application in a Win32 environment. It compiles the Java class first, using an ordinary `javac` compiler invocation. Next, it uses the `javah`[5] tool to generate the header file `ijs_servers_jni_Matrix.h` that contains the native method's C-language function prototype. It then compiles the C-language implementation file `MatrixImpl.c`, using two additional `include` directories that contain the `jni` header files. Finally, it packages the `MatrixImpl` object file as a dynamically linked library named `MatrixImpl.dll`.

The generated header file `ijs_servers_jni_Matrix.h` is shown in Figure 12-11. It contains the function prototype that will be the starting point for the implementation:

```
JNIEXPORT jint JNICALL Java_ijs_servers_jni_Matrix_det
    (JNIEnv *, jobject);
```

It uses the package name and method name concatenated with underscores as the C function name. The function has two arguments: a pointer to the JNI and a pointer to the `Matrix` object (equivalent to `this` in Java).

---

[5]`javah` is distributed with the Java Development Kit (JDK).

Figure 12-9

A Matrix Class
with a Native
Method.

```java
package ijs.servers.jni;

import java.io.*;
import java.util.*;

/**
 * An example of calling native methods using
 * the Java Native Interface (JNI)
 */
public class Matrix
{
   /**
    * Static initializer - loads the native
    * method library
    */
   static {
      System.loadLibrary("MatrixImpl");
   }

   private int[] x;
   private int nRows;
   private int nCols;

   /**
    * Creates a new matrix
    */
   public Matrix(int[] values)
   {
      // Calculate the number of rows and columns

      nRows = 0;
      while (nRows * nRows < values.length)
         nRows++;
      if (nRows * nRows > values.length)
         throw new RuntimeException
         ("Not a square matrix");
      nCols = nRows;

      // Store the matrix elements

      x = new int[values.length];
      System.arraycopy(values, 0, x, 0, values.length);
   }

   /**
    * Creates a string representation of the matrix
    */
   public String toString()
   {
      StringBuffer buffer = new StringBuffer();
      int widest = 0;
      for (int i = 0; i < x.length; i++) {
         int value = x[i];
         int len = String.valueOf(value).length();
         if (len > widest)
            widest = len;
      }
```

Figure 12-9
(Continued)

```
    widest += 2;
    int k = 0;
    for (int i = 0; i < nRows; i++) {
        for (int j = 0; j < nCols; j++) {
            if (j > 0)
                buffer.append("  ");
            buffer.append(x[k++]);
        }
        buffer.append("\n");
    }
    return buffer.toString();
}

/**
 * Native method to calculate the determinant
 */
public native int det();
```

Figure 12-10

The Makefile Used to Compile the JNI Application.

```
!include <win32.mak>

JCC = javac
JFLAGS = -g
cflags=$(cflags) -I$(JDK_HOME)\include -I$(JDK_HOME)\include\win32

.SUFFIXES : .class .java

.java.class :
        $(JCC) $(JFLAGS) $<

all : Matrix.class ijs_servers_jni_Matrix.h MatrixImpl.dll

ijs_servers_jni_Matrix.h : Matrix.java
        javah -jni ijs.servers.jni.Matrix

MatrixImpl.dll : MatrixImpl.obj
        $(link) /PDB:NONE /DLL $** $(dlllibs)

MatrixImpl.obj : MatrixImpl.c ijs_servers_jni_Matrix.h
    $(cc) $(cflags) $(cvars) MatrixImpl.c

clean:
        if exist Matrix.class del Matrix.class
        if exist MatrixImpl.obj del MatrixImpl.obj
        if exist MatrixImpl.dll del MatrixImpl.dll
```

Figure 12-12 lists the native method implementation file, `MatrixImpl.c`. The steps needed to access the internal fields of the `Matrix` class are as follows:

1. Get the `Matrix` class object by calling the JNI `GetObjectClass()` function. The class object reference is an index within an object table in the Java virtual machine.

Figure 12-11

The Header File
Generated by
javah.

```
/* DO NOT EDIT THIS FILE - it is machine generated */
#include <jni.h>
/* Header for class ijs_servers_jni_Matrix */

#ifndef _Included_ijs_servers_jni_Matrix
#define _Included_ijs_servers_jni_Matrix
#ifdef __cplusplus
extern "C" {
#endif
/*
 * Class:     ijs_servers_jni_Matrix
 * Method:    det
 * Signature: ()I
 */
JNIEXPORT jint JNICALL Java_ijs_servers_jni_Matrix_det
  (JNIEnv *, jobject);

#ifdef __cplusplus
}
#endif
#endif
```

2. Call `GetFieldID()` to get the field ID of the "x" array field within the class object.

3. Call `GetObjectField()` to get a reference to the array itself.

4. Ensure that the array elements are in contiguous storage locations by calling `GetIntArrayElements()`. This is referred to as *pinning* the array. JNI may need to copy the array elements to accomplish this, but you will be unaware of it (except that you need to release the copy, as described in step 7).

5. Get the number of array elements by calling `GetArrayLength()`.[6]

6. Invoke the internal `det()` function to calculate the determinant.

7. Release the array that was pinned in step 4 by calling `ReleaseIntArrayElements()`. Again, this may result in JNI copying the modified array elements back to their original location, if they were not contiguous to begin with.

8. Return the calculated value.

Here again, for debugging purposes, it would be useful to add a stand-alone mainline to this file, possibly controlled by `#ifdef DEBUG`.

---

[6]Wouldn't it be nice if C could do this in general? If it could figure out the number of elements in any array, it would simplify the argument lists of many functions and prevent quite a few memory access exceptions.

Figure 12-12

The C Language
Implementation of
the det() Native
Method.

```c
#include <jni.h>
#include <stdlib.h>
#include "ijs_servers_jni_Matrix.h"

/**
 * Local function prototype
 */
static int det(int *pX, int size);

/**
 * Implementation of the determinant function
 */
JNIEXPORT jint JNICALL
  Java_ijs_servers_jni_Matrix_det(
      JNIEnv *env,
      jobject matrix)
{
  jclass      Matrix;
  jfieldID    fidX;
  jintArray   objX;
  jboolean    isCopy;
  jsize       size;
  int         *pX;
  int         d;

  /* Get a pointer to the Matrix class object */

  Matrix = (*env)->GetObjectClass(env, matrix);
  if (Matrix == 0) {
     fprintf
     (stderr, "Could not get the Matrix class object\n");
     exit(1);
  }

  /* Get a pointer to the int[] x array field ID */

  fidX = (*env)->GetFieldID(env, Matrix, "x", "[I");
  if (fidX == 0) {
     fprintf
     (stderr, "Could not get the x array field ID\n");
     exit(1);
  }

  /* Get the array itself */

  objX = (*env)->GetObjectField(env, matrix, fidX);
  if (objX == 0) {
     fprintf
     (stderr, "Could not get the x array object field\n");
     exit(1);
  }

  /* Get a local pointer to the array */

  pX = (*env)->GetIntArrayElements(env, objX, &isCopy);
  if (pX == 0) {
     fprintf
```

Figure 12-12
(Continued)

```
                                   (stderr, "Could not pin the x array\n");
                                   exit(1);
                               }

                           /* Get the array length */

                           size = (*env)->GetArrayLength(env, objX);

                           /* Calculate the determinant */

                           d = det(pX, size);

                           /* Release the local pointer */

                           (*env)->ReleaseIntArrayElements(env, objX, pX, JNI_ABORT);

                           /* Return the calculated value */

                           return d;
                       }

/**
 * Local function that calculates the determinant
 * of the specified 3 x 3 integer matrix
 */
static int det(int *x, int size)
{
   int sum = 0;

   if (size != 9) {
      fprintf(stderr, "DEBUG: I only handle 3x3 matrices\n");
      return 86;
   }

   sum += x[0] * ((x[4]*x[8]) - (x[7]*x[5]));
   sum -= x[1] * ((x[3]*x[8]) - (x[6]*x[5]));
   sum += x[2] * ((x[3]*x[7]) - (x[6]*x[4]));

   return sum;
}
```

The servlet that accesses the Matrix class and calls the native method requires no special treatment. It exists solely as the "glue" that makes the Matrix class accessible to HTTP clients (in our case, a Java applet). Figure 12-13 is a listing of DeterminantServlet.java, which simply extracts the matrix elements from a request parameter, creates the Matrix object, calls its det() method, and returns the result in the response output stream.

Figure 12-14 shows how to access this servlet from a Java applet. The applet has a 3 × 3 array of text fields in which the matrix elements can be entered. When the "Calculate" button is clicked, the applet extracts the matrix elements from the text fields, packages them as a comma-separated list, and appends them to the URL of the servlet. It then opens the URL input stream, which causes the request to be sent to the server and the response to be sent back. The function value (-90 in this case) is displayed on the status line at the bottom of the browser window, as shown in Figure 12-15.

▬▬ ▬▬ ▬▬ ▬▬
Figure 12-13

A Servlet That Calls
a Native Method
on Behalf of an
Applet.

```
package ijs.servers.jni;

import java.io.*;
import java.net.*;
import java.util.*;

import javax.servlet.*;
import javax.servlet.http.*;

/**
 * A servlet that calls a native method to
 * calculate the determinant of a matrix.
 */
public class DeterminantServlet extends HttpServlet
{
    public void doGet(
            HttpServletRequest request,
            HttpServletResponse response)
        throws ServletException, IOException
    {
        // Get the input matrix.  It should be
        // comma-separated list of nine integer

        String values = request.getParameter("n
        if (values == null)
            throw new ServletException
            ("No matrix parameter specified");

        // Verify the number of elements

        StringTokenizer st = new StringTokenize
        int n = st.countTokens();
        if (n != 9)
            throw new ServletException
            ("Expected 9 values.  Found " + n);

        // Convert to an array of integers

        int[] x = new int[n];
        for (int i = 0; i < n; i++) {
            String token = st.nextToken();
            try {
                x[i] = Integer.parseInt(token);
            }
            catch (NumberFormatException e) {
                throw new ServletException
                ("[" + token + "] is not numeric");
            }
        }

        // Create the matrix object

        Matrix mat = new Matrix(x);

        // Calculate the determinant

        int d = mat.det();
```

Figure 12-13
(Continued)

```
                              // Write the determinant back to the client

                              response.setContentType("text/plain");
                              PrintWriter out = response.getWriter();
                              out.println(d);
                              out.flush();
                              out.close();
                        }
                    }
```

Figure 12-14

*An Applet That
Calls a Native
Method Indirectly
Through a Servlet.*

```
import java.applet.*;
import java.awt.*;
import java.awt.event.*;
import java.io.*;
import java.net.*;
import java.util.*;

/**
 * An applet that calls a servlet which uses native methods.
 * The servlet has a Matrix class that calculates its
 * determinant using a native method written in C.
 */
public class DeterminantClient extends Applet
    implements ActionListener
{
    /**
     * Sets up the GUI
     */
    public void init()
    {
        setLayout(new BorderLayout());

        // Create the label at the top

        Label banner = new Label("Deter
        banner.setAlignment(Label.CENTE
        banner.setBackground(Color.blac
        banner.setFont(new Font("Dialog'
        banner.setForeground(Color.white
        add(banner, BorderLayout.NORTH);

        // Create the matrix data entry

        Panel pnlCenter = new Panel();
        pnlCenter.setLayout(new GridLayou
        tx = new TextField[3][3];
        for (int i = 0; i < 3; i++) {
            for (int j = 0; j < 3; j++) {
                String value = (i == j) ? "1" : "0";
                tx[i][j] = new TextField(value);
                pnlCenter.add(tx[i][j]);
            }
        }
        add(pnlCenter, BorderLayout.CENTER);

        // Create the button row

        Panel pnlBottom = new Panel();

        btnCalc = new Button("Calculate");
        btnCalc.addActionListener(this);
        pnlBottom.add(btnCalc);

        add(pnlBottom, BorderLayout.SOUTH);
    }

    /**
```

Figure 12-14

(Continued)

```java
 * Handles action events
 */
public void actionPerformed(ActionEvent event)
{
    if (event.getSource() == btnCalc)
        doDet();
}

/**
 * Handles the Determinant button click event
 */
public void doDet()
{
    try {

        // Get the matrix values

        StringBuffer buffer = new StringBuffer();
        int k = 0;
        for (int i = 0; i < 3; i++) {
            for (int j = 0; j < 3; j++) {
                k++;
                if (k > 1)
                    buffer.append(",");
                buffer.append(tx[i][j].getText().trim());
            }
        }
        String matrix = buffer.toString();

        // Create a URL passing the matrix to
        // the Determinant servlet

        String urlString = "/servlet/Determinant"
            + "?matrix=" + URLEncoder.encode(matrix);
        URL url = new URL(getCodeBase(), urlString);

        // Connect to the servlet and open an input
        // stream for the output it generates

        BufferedReader in =
            new BufferedReader(
            new InputStreamReader(
            url.openStream()));

        // Read the determinant

        String determinant = in.readLine();
        showStatus("Determinant = " + determinant);
    }
    catch (IOException e) {
        showStatus(e.getMessage());
    }
}

private Button btnCalc;
private TextField[][] tx;
```

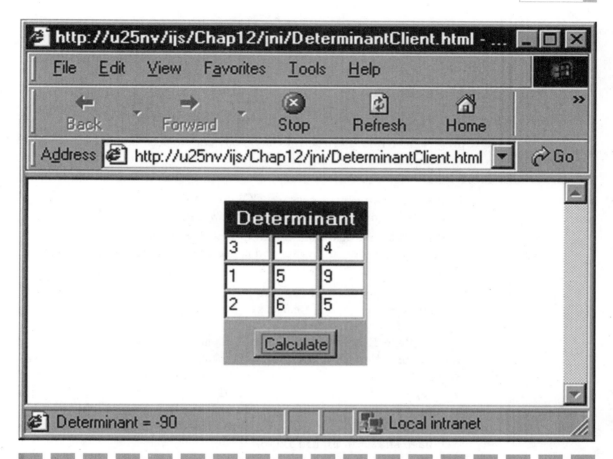

Figure 12-15 The Output of the `DeterminantClient` Applet.

12.4   Getting Data from CGI Scripts

Problem

How can I use a servlet to access a CGI script?

Technique

In the servlet's `doGet()` method, create a URL that refers to the CGI script and passes any necessary parameters. Use the

`URL.openStream()` method to read the CGI output and postprocess it as required.

Discussion

There is a vast amount of dynamic Web content that is served up by CGI programs. While these scripts obviously can be accessed directly by Web browsers, there are several reasons why you may want to use a servlet as a middleware layer:

1. A servlet can postprocess the CGI output data, selecting a subset of interest and reformatting it for new and different uses.

2. A servlet can start a background thread that accesses the CGI script at periodic intervals and collects an ongoing set of observations.

Servlets can access CGI content easily using networking support provided by the `java.net.*` classes.

A Complete Example   A typical application for dynamic Web content is the publication of weather data. The National Center for Atmospheric Research in Boulder, Colorado, for example, samples the temperature, wind speed, barometric pressure, and other variables at its Foothills Laboratory every 5 minutes and makes the readings available over the Internet by means of a CGI program.[7] The CGI program produces the Web page shown in Figure 12-16.

Like most Web pages, this snapshot of weather conditions is intended for human viewing. However, since it is written in HTML, it can be read by a program (a servlet, in this case), and its information can be extracted for postprocessing. Figure 12-17 lists the source code for a servlet that will access the Web page, extract the current readings, and reformat them into XML.

The servlet creates a URL for the CGI script and then accesses its input stream using the `URL.openStream()` method. It passes the input stream to a `WeatherParser` object (an inner class in the servlet), which extracts the current weather readings from the HTML table. It then gen-

---

[7]The URL is *http://www.atd.ucar.edu/cgi-bin/temperature*.

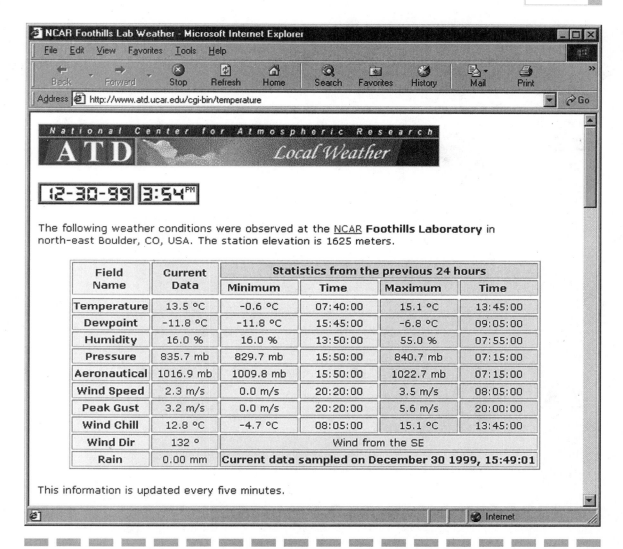

Figure 12-16 Weather Data from the National Center for Atmospheric Research.

erates an XML document using the `WeatherParser` object's `toXML()` method.

The resulting XML document (shown in Figure 12-18) can then be used as standardized input into systems that process the weather data.

```java
package ijs.servers.cgi;

import java.io.*;
import java.net.*;
import java.util.*;

import javax.servlet.*;
import javax.servlet.http.*;

/**
 * NCARWeatherServlet downloads weather data from
 * the National Center for Atmospheric Research
 * Foothills Lab in Boulder, Colorado.
 * <P>
 * Source: http://www.atd.ucar.edu/cgi-bin/temperature
 */
public class NCARWeatherServlet extends HttpServlet
{
    /**
     * Handles a GET request
     */
    public void doGet(
            HttpServletRequest request,
            HttpServletResponse response)
        throws ServletException, IOException
    {
        // Open a URL connection to the CGI website

        URL url = new URL
        ("http://www.atd.ucar.edu/cgi-bin/temperature");

        InputStream stream =
            new BufferedInputStream(url.openStream());

        // Parse the CGI output

        WeatherParser parser = new WeatherParser();
        parser.parse(stream);

        // Write XML back to the requester

        response.setContentType("text/xml");
        PrintWriter out = response.getWriter();
        out.println(parser.toXML());

        out.flush();
        out.close();
    }

    /**
     * Inner class for parsing the web page
     */
    class WeatherParser
    {
        private Hashtable values;
        private String date = null;
```

Figure 12-17

(Continued)

```
/**
 * Creates a new parser
 */
public WeatherParser()
{
    values = new Hashtable();
}

/**
 * Parses the URL input stream
 */
public void parse(InputStream stream)
    throws IOException
{
    // Constants to represent the state
    // of the parser

    final int BEFORE_TABLE = 0;
    final int IN_TABLE = 1;
    final int CAPTURING_DATA = 2;

    // Current parser state

    int state = BEFORE_TABLE;

    // Read the input stream a line at a time

    BufferedReader in =
        new BufferedReader(
        new InputStreamReader(stream));

    // Main parsing loop

    main: for (;;) {
        String line = in.readLine();
        if (line == null)
            break;

        switch (state) {

            // Look for the beginning of the table

            case BEFORE_TABLE:
                if (line.startsWith("<table"))
                    state = IN_TABLE;
                break;

            // Once in the table, look for the beginning
            // of the cells we want to capture

            case IN_TABLE:
                if (line.startsWith("<tr")) {
                    TableRow tr = new TableRow(line);
                    String[] cells = tr.getCells();
                    if (cells.length >= 2) {
                        if (cells[0].equals("Temperature")) {
                            String token = cells[1];
```

Figure 12-17
(Continued)

```
                                    int p = token.indexOf(" ");
                                    if (p > -1)
                                        token = token.substring(0, p);
                                    values.put(cells[0], token);
                                    state = CAPTURING_DATA;
                                }
                            }
                        }
                        else if (line.startsWith("</table"))
                            break main;
                        break;

                // Parse individual table rows for the
                // weather data of interest

                case CAPTURING_DATA:
                    if (line.startsWith("<tr")) {
                        TableRow tr = new TableRow(line);
                        String[] cells = tr.getCells();
                        if (cells.length >= 2) {
                            String token = cells[1];
                            int p = token.indexOf(" ");
                            if (p > -1)
                                token = token.substring(0, p);
                            values.put(cells[0], token);
                            if (cells.length > 2) {
                                token = cells[2];
                                if (token.startsWith
                                ("Current data sampled on ")) {
                                    date =
                                    token.substring(24).trim();
                                }
                            }
                        }
                    }
                    else if (line.startsWith("</table"))
                        break main;
                    break;
            }
        }

        in.close();
    }

    /**
     * Returns the parsed data as XML
     */
    public String toXML()
    {
        final String CRLF = "\r\n";

        StringBuffer buffer = new StringBuffer();

        buffer.append("<?xml version=\"1.0\"?>");
        buffer.append(CRLF);

        buffer.append("<WEATHER");
```

Figure 12-17

(Continued)

```
            buffer.append(" STATION=\"");
            buffer.append("NCAR Foothills Lab");
            buffer.append("\"");
            buffer.append(" DATE=\"" + date + "\"");
            buffer.append(">");
            buffer.append(CRLF);

            Enumeration keys = values.keys();
            while (keys.hasMoreElements()) {
                String key = (String) keys.nextElement();
                String value = (String) values.get(key);

                key = key.replace(' ', '_');

                buffer.append("<");
                buffer.append(key);
                buffer.append(">");

                buffer.append(value);

                buffer.append("</");
                buffer.append(key);
                buffer.append(">");

                buffer.append(CRLF);
            }
            buffer.append("</WEATHER>");
            return buffer.toString();
        }
    }

/**
 * Inner class for parsing an individual table row
 */
class TableRow
{
    private String[] cells;

    /**
     * Parses a table row
     */
    public TableRow(String s)
    {
        // Tokenize the input string using
        // "<" and ">" as delimiters.

        StringTokenizer st =
            new StringTokenizer(s, "><", true);
        Vector v = new Vector();
        int state = 0;
        while (st.hasMoreTokens()) {
            String token = st.nextToken();
            switch (state) {
                case 0:  // Outside of markup
                    if (token.equals("<"))
                        state = 1;
                    else
```

Figure 12-17
(Continued)

```
                                v.addElement(token);
                          break;
                     case 1:  // Inside markup
                          if (token.equals(">"))
                               state = 0;
                          break;
               }
          }

          // Copy parsed tokens into a string array

          cells = new String[v.size()];
          v.copyInto(cells);
     }

     /**
      * Returns the cells in this row
      */
     public String[] getCells()
     {
          return cells;
     }
}
}
```

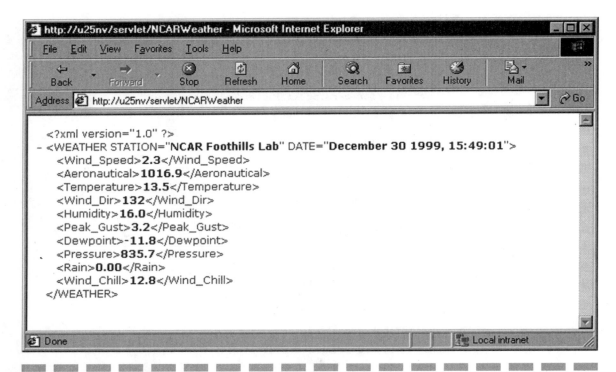

```
<?xml version="1.0" ?>
- <WEATHER STATION="NCAR Foothills Lab" DATE="December 30 1999, 15:49:01">
    <Wind_Speed>2.3</Wind_Speed>
    <Aeronautical>1016.9</Aeronautical>
    <Temperature>13.5</Temperature>
    <Wind_Dir>132</Wind_Dir>
    <Humidity>16.0</Humidity>
    <Peak_Gust>3.2</Peak_Gust>
    <Dewpoint>-11.8</Dewpoint>
    <Pressure>835.7</Pressure>
    <Rain>0.00</Rain>
    <Wind_Chill>12.8</Wind_Chill>
  </WEATHER>
```

Figure 12-18 Weather Data Converted to XML.

12.5 Invoking Active Server Pages (ASPs)

Problem

How can I extract information from an Active Server Page (ASP) at another Web server?

Technique

Open a URL connection, pass an HTTP request for the Active Server Page (ASP), and parse the resulting input stream.

Discussion

Active Server Pages (ASPs) are components of a Microsoft Web programming environment that allow developers to intermingle HTML and scripting commands to produce dynamic content. ASPs work in conjunction with Microsoft Web servers and operating systems. This section does not discuss how to develop ASPs, only how to invoke them. A complete discussion of ASPs can be found in *Instant ASP Scripts,* by Greg Buzcek (New York: McGraw-Hill, 1999, ISBN 0071352058).

Since ASP documents are designed to be accessed as Web pages, using them in a servlet is simply a matter of creating a URL with the appropriate parameters, sending a request, and parsing the HTML that is generated. The process is no different in this respect from reading the output of a CGI script or from reading an ordinary Web page for that matter. So why bother to use a servlet as the middleware? There are three reasons:

1. You can subset and reformat the data before returning them to your requester.
2. You can merge the data with other servlet-accessible resources.
3. You can make it possible for a Java applet to access ASPs on a different Web server.

Here's an example that illustrates the technique.

Converting ASP Output to XML   Our hypothetical Internet Premium Food Market has a shipping system with an ASP inquiry component. The system was installed on a departmental Web server running under Windows NT 4.0. The `OrderStatus.asp` script will prompt for an order number if one is not already supplied, look up the order in a Microsoft Access database, and then generate an HTML table showing each event in the order's history (see Figure 12-19). We would like to invoke this ASP and convert its output to XML.

If we use the ViewSource menu option in the Web browser, we can see the HTML that was generated (see Figure 12-20). As is typical of HTML that is generated by a program, it is quite regular and fairly easy to parse.[8] Each event in the order history is preceded by a comment line containing a record key (presumably one that identifies this item in the database). This is followed by a line with the `<TR>` table row start tag and then two lines containing data of interest, the date, and the event description.

Figure 12-21 shows the servlet that parses the ASP output and converts it to XML. The servlet performs the following steps:

1. Gets the order number parameter from the servlet request object.

2. Forms a URL that consists of the ASP URL with the order number parameter appended.

3. Opens the URL input stream. This causes the request to be sent to the Web server, which invokes the ASP and sends back its output to the servlet.

4. Reads the ASP output, extracts the order history events, and writes them as XML elements.

The resulting XML document is shown in Figure 12-22. This can be viewed with Internet Explorer directly or saved as an XML file and passed to other systems.

---

[8]We should point out that every ASP is different. The means you will use to parse documents will differ from URL to URL. If the output is not particularly regular, you may need to consult the original ASP source code, if you have access to it. Of course, if you are writing both the ASP and the servlet, you can ensure that you provide the appropriate markers.

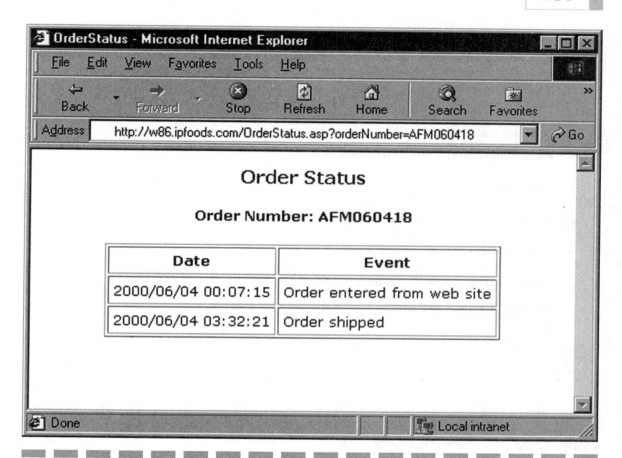

Figure 12-19 The Original ASP Order Status Inquiry.

```
┌─────────────────────────────────────────────────────────────────────────┐
│ ▤ OrderStatus.asp.out - Notepad                                   _ □ ×  │
├─────────────────────────────────────────────────────────────────────────┤
│ File Edit Search Help                                                     │
├─────────────────────────────────────────────────────────────────────────┤
│ <HTML>                                                                ▲   │
│ <HEAD>                                                                    │
│ <TITLE>OrderStatus</TITLE>                                                │
│ </HEAD>                                                                   │
│ <BODY>                                                                    │
│ <CENTER>                                                                  │
│ <H3>Order Status</H3>                                                     │
│ <H4>Order Number: AFM060418</H4>                                          │
│ <TABLE BORDER=1 CELLPADDING=4 CELLSPACING=2>                              │
│ <TR>                                                                      │
│    <TH>Date</TH>                                                          │
│    <TH>Event</TH>                                                         │
│ </TR>                                                                     │
│                                                                          │
│    <!-- Record key 960091635322AFM060418 -->                             │
│    <TR>                                                                   │
│       <TD>2000/06/04 00:07:15</TD>                                        │
│       <TD>Order entered from web site</TD>                                │
│    </TR>                                                                  │
│                                                                          │
│    <!-- Record key 960103941322AFM060418 -->                             │
│    <TR>                                                                   │
│       <TD>2000/06/04 03:32:21</TD>                                        │
│       <TD>Order shipped</TD>                                              │
│    </TR>                                                                  │
│                                                                          │
│ </TABLE>                                                                  │
│ </CENTER>                                                                 │
│ </BODY>                                                               ▼   │
│ </HTML>                                                                   │
├─────────────────────────────────────────────────────────────────────────┤
│ ◄                                                                   ►     │
└─────────────────────────────────────────────────────────────────────────┘
```

Figure 12-20 HTML Generated by the Order Status ASP.

Figure 12-21

A Servlet That
Makes an ASP
Request and
Converts Its Output
to XML.

```
package ijs.servers.asp;

import java.io.*;
import java.net.*;
import java.util.*;

import javax.servlet.*;
import javax.servlet.http.*;

/**
 * This servlet reads an Active Server Page containing
 * order status and converts it to XML.
 */
public class OrderStatusServlet extends HttpServlet
{
    /**
     * Handles a GET request
     */
    public void doGet(
            HttpServletRequest request,
            HttpServletResponse response)
        throws ServletException, IOException
    {
        // Get the order number parameter

        String orderNumber =
            request.getParameter("orderNumber");
        if (orderNumber == null)
            throw new ServletException
            ("No order number specified");

        // Form the URL and append the order number parameter

        String urlString =
            "http://w86.ipfoods.com/OrderStatus.asp"
            + "?orderNumber="
            + URLEncoder.encode(orderNumber);
        URL url = new URL(urlString);

        // Send the ASP request by opening the URL input stream

        InputStream aspStream = url.openStream();

        BufferedReader in =
            new BufferedReader(
            new InputStreamReader(aspStream));

        // Read and parse the results and write the XML version

        response.setContentType("text/xml");
        PrintWriter out = response.getWriter();

        // XML header

        out.println("<?xml version=\"1.0\" ?>");
        out.println("<order number=\"" + orderNumber + "\">");
```

Figure 12-21

(Continued)

```
int p = 0;
int q = 0;
String date = null;
String description = null;

// Use a finite state machine to parse the HTML

int state = 0;

while (true) {
   String line = in.readLine();
   if (line == null)
      break;

   switch (state) {

      case 0:  // Looking for new table row
         if (line.indexOf("<!-- Record key") > -1)
            state = 1;
         break;

      case 1:  // The <TR> tag
         state = 2;
         break;

      case 2:  // The date line
         p = line.indexOf("<TD>");
         if (p == -1)
            break;
         p += "<TD>".length();
         q = line.indexOf("</TD>", p);
         if (q == -1)
            break;
         date = line.substring(p, q);
         state = 3;
         break;

      case 3:  // The event line
         p = line.indexOf("<TD>");
         if (p == -1)
            break;
         p += "<TD>".length();
         q = line.indexOf("</TD>", p);
         if (q == -1)
            break;
         description = line.substring(p, q);

         // Write the observation

         out.println("<event>");
         out.println("<date>" + date + "</date>");
         out.println("<description>"
                     + description + "</description>");
         out.println("</event>");

         // Start looking for another block
```

Figure 12-21
(Continued)

```
                                     state = 0;
                                     break;
                    }
            }

            // End of document

            out.println("</order>");
            out.flush();
            in.close();
        }
    }
```

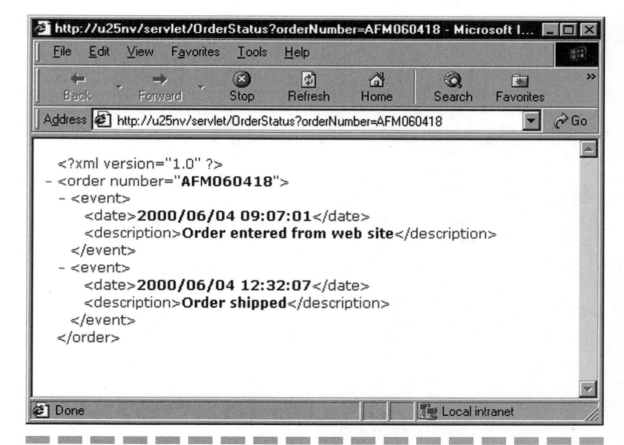

Figure 12-22 The XML Output of the OrderStatus Servlet.

12.6 Using a Servlet as an FTP Proxy

Problem

How can an applet download files from an FTP server?

Technique

Send a request to a servlet that handles the FTP connection and performs the download. Read the file data from the servlet's response output stream.

Discussion

File Transfer Protocol (FTP) is a widely used system for distributing files over a network. It is typically used from a command line to download programs and data files from a central repository. Before HTTP and Web browsers became popular, FTP was the dominant means for file transfer along the Internet, and extensive resources are still stored in FTP servers. In most cases, these servers accept anonymous logins with the user's email address serving as the password, although in an intranet environment, a genuine user ID and password are required.

How It Works   The FTP, which is documented in RFC959,[9] is somewhat more involved than HTTP because two socket connections are required: one for commands and one for data transfer. An FTP client reads commands from a user interactively or from a batch script and manages both sockets to perform the required operations. A typical FTP session involves the following steps:

■ *Authentication.* The FTP client opens a socket connection to an FTP server, usually on port 21. After receiving a positive acknowledgment, the client sends the user ID and password with the USER and PASS commands, respectively. The server validates the credentials and passes back a positive response or an error code.

---

[9]See *http://www.freesoft.org/CIE/RFC/959/index.htm.*

■ *Directory navigation.* Based on user commands, the FTP client indicates to the server the directory in which the desired file(s) are found.

■ *File transfer.* To transfer the contents of a file or a directory listing, the FTP client opens a server socket, informs the FTP server of the IP address and port number, and then waits to be contacted. The FTP server (acting as a client in this case) opens the connection and writes (to download) or reads (to upload) the requested data.

■ *Termination.* After all data transfer operations are complete, the FTP client sends a QUIT command.

How a Servlet Can Help FTP is fairly well supported by Web browsers, but only in anonymous mode. Java applications can easily perform all the socket I/O using the networking support classes in the JDK, but Java applets typically are restricted from connecting to servers other than the one from which their classes were loaded. These two constraints make it difficult to integrate FTP seamlessly into Web applications. Using a servlet as a proxy client, however, solves both problems.

A servlet can act as an FTP client to handle all the networking operations required to transfer files. An applet can then treat the servlet as if it were simply a static Web page that happens to contain the required file data. The applet can open a URL connection to the servlet, supply host and file name information as request parameters, and pass the user ID and password using HTTP basic authentication.[10] The user ID and password also could be sent as request parameters, but using the architected HTTP authentication scheme means that the same servlet can be used for both applet and HTML clients, for which the Web browser can cache the credentials.

A Complete Example In this section we will develop a servlet that can act as an FTP proxy for HTTP clients. We also will cover how to encode and decode the user ID and password for HTTP basic authentication and how to access the proxy with an applet client.

To begin with, we need a Java class that handles the FTP protocol. It is helpful to separate this function from the main servlet for ease of testing and debugging. Figure 12-23 shows a simple implementation. The

---

[10]Basic authentication is not particularly secure, but it is still widely used. See RFC1945 at *http://www.freesoft.org/CIE/RFC/1945/index.htm* for details. Of course, any password encryption scheme can be used as long as both the client and server can support it.

Figure 12-23
A Simple FTP
Client.

```java
package ijs.net.ftp;

import java.io.*;
import java.net.*;
import java.util.*;

/**
 * A class that acts as a requester to an FTP server.
 * Intended as a simple illustration of the protocol.
 * Does not implement any error checking and is not
 * optimized for performance.
 */
public class FTPClient
{
    private String host;
    private Socket control;
    private BufferedReader cmdin;
    private PrintWriter cmdout;
    private boolean verbose;

    /**
     * Creates a new FTPClient for the specified host
     * @param host the host name
     */
    public FTPClient(String host)
    {
        this.host = host;
    }

    /**
     * Opens the control socket
     */
    public void open() throws IOException
    {
        if (control == null) {
            control = new Socket(host, 21);
            cmdin =
                new BufferedReader(
                new InputStreamReader(
                control.getInputStream()));
            cmdout =
                new PrintWriter(
                new OutputStreamWriter(
                control.getOutputStream()));
            if (verbose) {
                System.out.println("S: " + receive());
                System.out.flush();
            }
        }
    }

    /**
     * Closes the control socket
     */
    public void close() throws IOException
    {
        if (control != null) {
```

`FTPClient` class includes methods that open and close the control socket, issue commands, and read responses. Its `getFileData()` method opens a server socket and waits to be contacted by the FTP server, which writes the requested file data to the socket. The data are returned as a `java.lang.String`.[11]

Figure 12-24 lists the `FTPDownload` servlet. Its sole function is to accept HTTP requests that include a host name and file name, create an `FTPClient` to handle the request, and relay the output to the requester.

The implementation of HTTP basic authentication for handling the user ID and password requires a little explanation. Figure 12-25 illustrates the standard protocol. First, a document is requested with no user ID or password specified. If the document is not password-protected, the Web server simply returns its contents. Otherwise, the Web server checks to see if the user ID and password were supplied. If not, or if the credentials were invalid, the server returns a `401 Not Authorized` response, including a `WWW-Authenticate` header indicating the type of authentication (basic) and the authentication realm. In a Web browser environment, the browser typically will check to see if this information already has been supplied for the specified realm. If not, the browser prompts the user for a user ID and password and stores them in memory for the duration of the session so that repeated prompts are not required. The browser then requests the same document again, this time sending an additional `Authorization` header with the encoded user ID and password. The server verifies the credentials again, and this time passes back the document contents.

The encoding scheme used by HTTP basic authentication is called *base64 encoding*.[12] It involves mapping groups of 3-byte chunks into four ASCII characters. The user ID and password are concatenated with a colon in the middle, and the resulting string is base64-encoded and transmitted in the `Authorization` header. Figures 12-26 and 12-27 show classes that encode and decode strings using this mechanism.[13]

---

[11]In this example, we consider only text files. Binary files such as images or program executables can be downloaded in the same manner.

[12]Base64 encoding is documented in RFC1521, available at *http://www.freesoft.org/CIE/RFC/1521/index.htm.*

[13]Sun Microsystems also supplies the `sun.misc.BASE64Encoder` and `sun.misc.BASE64Decoder` classes with the JDK but cautions against their use because they are not part of the core Java libraries and are not guaranteed to be supported in the future.

Figure 12-23
(Continued)

```
        cmdout.flush();
        cmdout.close();
        cmdin.close();
        control.close();
        control = null;
    }
}

/**
 * Logs in with the specified user ID
 * and password
 */
public void login(String user, String pass)
    throws IOException
{
    if (control == null)
        throw new IOException
        ("Control socket never opened");

    send("USER " + user);
    send("PASS " + pass);
}

/**
 * Sends a command to the server
 */
public void send(String cmd) throws IOException
{
    if (verbose) {
        System.out.println("C: " + cmd);
        System.out.flush();
    }
    cmdout.println(cmd);
    cmdout.flush();
    String response = receive();
    if (response.startsWith("5"))
        throw new IOException(response);

    if (verbose) {
        System.out.println("S: " + response);
        System.out.flush();
    }
}

/**
 * Receives a server response
 */
public String receive() throws IOException
{
    return cmdin.readLine();
}

/**
 * Changes to the specified directory
 */
public void chdir(String dirName) throws IOException
{
```

Figure 12-23
(Continued)

```
      send("CWD " + dirName);
   }

/**
 * Receives a file and returns its contents
 * as a string.
 * @param fileName the file to be retrieved
 */
public String getFileData(String fileName)
   throws IOException
{
   if (verbose) {
      System.out.println
      ("C: Entering getFileData for " + fileName);
      System.out.flush();
   }

   // Change to the appropriate directory

   fileName = fileName.replace('\\', '/');
   int p = fileName.lastIndexOf("/");
   if (p >= 0) {
      String dirName = fileName.substring(0, p);
      if (verbose) {
         System.out.println
         ("C: Changing directory to " + dirName);
         System.out.flush();
      }
      chdir(dirName);
      fileName = fileName.substring(p+1);
      if (verbose) {
         System.out.println
         ("C: base file name is " + fileName);
         System.out.flush();
      }
   }

   // Open a server socket on any available port

   ServerSocket server = new ServerSocket(0);

   // Get the local host address and the port
   // number of the server socket we just opened.

   String addr =
      InetAddress.getLocalHost().getHostAddress();
   addr = addr.replace('.', ',');

   int port = server.getLocalPort();
   int portHi = port / 256;
   int portLo = port % 256;
   addr += "," + portHi + "," + portLo;

   // Send the addresses with a PORT command.

   send("PORT " + addr);
```

Figure 12-23
(Continued)

```java
// Now send the RETR command

send("RETR " + fileName);

// Wait for the FTP server to contact us on our
// server port.

Socket client = server.accept();

// We are done with the server port

server.close();

// Open the client socket and read its data

StringBuffer buffer = new StringBuffer();
BufferedInputStream in =
    new BufferedInputStream(client.getInputStream());
for (;;) {
    int c = in.read();
    if (c == -1)
        break;
    buffer.append((char) c);
}
in.close();

// Return the file data

return buffer.toString();
    }

/**
 * Sets the verbose flag
 */
public void setVerbose(boolean yesno)
{
    verbose = yesno;
}
}
```

Figure 12-24

A Servlet for
Downloading FTP
Data.

```
package ijs.servers.ftp;

import ijs.net.ftp.*;
import ijs.secure.*;
import java.io.*;
import java.net.*;
import java.util.*;
import javax.servlet.*;
import javax.servlet.http.*;

/**
 * FTPDownloadServlet
 */
public class FTPDownloadServlet extends HttpServlet
{
    /**
     * Handles a GET request
     */
    public void doGet(
            HttpServletRequest request,
            HttpServletResponse response)
        throws ServletException, IOException
    {
        try {

            // Get the host and file name parameters

            String host = request.getParameter("host");
            if ((host == null) ||
                (host.trim().equals("")))
            {
                throw new ServletException
                ("No host name specified");
            }

            String fileName = request.getParameter("fileName");
            if ((fileName == null) ||
                (fileName.trim().equals("")))
            {
                throw new ServletException
                ("No file name specified");
            }

            // Verify that the user ID and password for this
            // host have been specified

            String credentials =
                request.getHeader("Authorization");
            if ((credentials == null) ||
                (credentials.trim().equals("")))
            {
                response.setStatus(401);
                response.setHeader("WWW-Authenticate",
                    "Basic realm=ftp." + host);
                return;
            }
```

Figure 12-24
(Continued)

```
// Decode the credentials

int p = credentials.indexOf(" ");
String userPass = credentials.substring(p).trim();
userPass = new String(Base64Decoder.decode(userPass));

p = userPass.indexOf(":");
String user = userPass.substring(0, p);
String pass = userPass.substring(p+1);
if (user.equals("") || pass.equals("")) {
    response.setStatus(401);
    response.setHeader("WWW-Authenticate",
        "Basic realm=ftp." + host);
    return;
}

// Log on using the FTP client

FTPClient ftpClient = new FTPClient(host);
ftpClient.setVerbose(true);
ftpClient.open();
ftpClient.login(user, pass);

// Retrieve the specified file

String fileData = ftpClient.getFileData(fileName);

// Close the FTP connection

ftpClient.close();

// Write the file data back to the client

response.setContentType("application/octet-stream");
ServletOutputStream out = response.getOutputStream();
out.write(fileData.getBytes());
out.flush();
out.close();
}

// If any uncaught exceptions occur, send
// and error message back to the client

catch (Exception e) {
    response.setContentType("text/plain");
    PrintWriter out = response.getWriter();
    out.println(e.getMessage());
    e.printStackTrace();
}
}
```

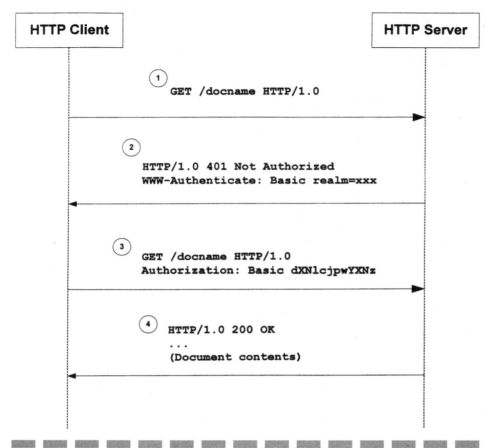

Figure 12-25 HTTP Basic Authentication Protocol.

Equipped with this authorization-handling mechanism, which is understood and automatically handled by Web browsers, the FTPDownload servlet can be called directly from an HTML form or hyperlink. Figure 12-28 shows a simple example of a clickable reference to the servlet that is created using HTML similar to the following:

```
Click
<A HREF="http://.../servlet/FTPDownload?host=xxx&file=xxx">
here
</A>
to download "SimpleGifts.txt"
```

Figure 12-26

A Class that
Encodes
Authentication
Strings Using the
Base64 Algorithm.

```
package ijs.secure;

/**
 * A class providing a static function for encoding
 * binary data using the Base64 algorithm.
 * <P>
 * The details of Base64 encoding can be found in RFC 1521,
 * section 5.2.  The basic idea is this:
 * <P>
 * <PRE>
 * ---------------|---------------|---------------|
 * 0 1 2 3 4 5 6 7 0 1 2 3 4 5 6 7 0 1 2 3 4 5 6 7
 * -----------|-----------|-----------|-----------|
 * </PRE>
 * <UL>
 * <LI>Split each three bytes of input into four 6-bit
 * integers
 * <LI>Use each integer as an index into a table of
 * printable characters
 * <LI>Output the four characters thus selected.
 * </UL>
 * <P>
 * If the number of bytes of input is not evenly
 * divisible by three, use zero bits on the right
 * to flush any remaining input, then pad the output
 * with "=" characters as follows:
 * <PRE>
 * Input Length
 *    Mod 3
 *      0            No padding
 *      1            Pad with two "="
 *      2            Pad with one "="
 * </PRE>
 * The translation table consists of the uppercase
 * alphabetic characters, followed by the lowercase
 * alphabetic characters, followed by the digits 0
 * through 9, and finally "+" and "/":
 * <PRE>
 *  0 A          16 Q          32 g          48 w
 *  1 B          17 R          33 h          49 x
 *  2 C          18 S          34 i          50 y
 *  3 D          19 T          35 j          51 z
 *  4 E          20 U          36 k          52 0
 *  5 F          21 V          37 l          53 1
 *  6 G          22 W          38 m          54 2
 *  7 H          23 X          39 n          55 3
 *  8 I          24 Y          40 o          56 4
 *  9 J          25 Z          41 p          57 5
 * 10 K          26 a          42 q          58 6
 * 11 L          27 b          43 r          59 7
 * 12 M          28 c          44 s          60 8
 * 13 N          29 d          45 t          61 9
 * 14 O          30 e          46 u          62 +
 * 15 P          31 f          47 v          63 /
 * </PRE>
 */
public class Base64Encoder
```

Figure 12-26

(Continued)

```java
{
/**
 * The translation table
 */
public static final String base64Table =
    "ABCDEFGHIJKLMNOPQRSTUVWXYZ" +
    "abcdefghijklmnopqrstuvwxyz" +
    "0123456789" +
    "+/";

/**
 * Encodes the given byte buffer
 * @param buffer the byte buffer
 * @return the encoded string
 */
public static String encode(byte[] buffer)
{
    StringBuffer result = new StringBuffer();
    int state = 0;
    int n = buffer.length;
    int index = 0;

    for (int i = 0; i < n; i++) {
        int c = buffer[i] & 0xFF;

        // Take three bytes of input = 24 bits
        // Split it into 4 chunks of six bits each
        // Treat these chunks as indices into the
        // base64 table above.

        switch (state) {

            case 0:
                index = (c >> 2) & 0x3F;
                result.append(base64Table.charAt(index));
                index = (c << 4) & 0x30;
                break;

            case 1:
                index |= (c >> 4) & 0x0F;
                result.append(base64Table.charAt(index));
                index = (c << 2) & 0x3C;
                break;

            case 2:
                index |= (c >> 6) & 0x03;
                result.append(base64Table.charAt(index));
                index = c & 0x3F;
                result.append(base64Table.charAt(index));
                break;
        }
        state = (state + 1) % 3;
    }

    // Complete the string with zero bits
    // and pad with "=" characters as necessary
```

Figure 12-26
(Continued)

```
    switch (state) {
        case 0:
            // No padding necessary
            break;
        case 1:
            result.append(base64Table.charAt(index));
            result.append('=');
            result.append('=');
            break;
        case 2:
            result.append(base64Table.charAt(index));
            result.append('=');
            break;
    }

    return result.toString();
  }
}
```

When the hyperlink is clicked, the Web browser (Internet Explorer 5.0 in this case) prompts the user for the login credentials with the dialog box shown in Figure 12-29, and then the specified text file is downloaded and displayed (see Figure 12-30).

The same servlet can be invoked as a general-purpose proxy by the Java applet listed in Figure 12-31. The applet has input fields for the host name, file name, user ID, and password. When the "Download" button is clicked, the credentials string is created by base64-encoding the user ID and password:

```
ijs.secure.Base64Encoder encoder =
    new ijs.secure.Base64Encoder();
String credentials = encoder.encode(
    (userID + ":" + password).getBytes());
```

A URL pointing to the `FTPDownload` servlet is created, and the host name and file name are appended to it as parameters. The applet then opens a `java.net.URLConnection` from the URL and sets the `Authorization` header with the encoded credentials. At this point, the URL input stream can be opened and read into the text area line by line. The results are shown in Figure 12-32.

Figure 12-27

A Class that
Decodes Base64-
Encoded
Authentication
Strings.

```java
package ijs.secure;

import java.io.*;
import java.util.*;

/**
 * A class providing a static function for decoding
 * binary data using the Base64 algorithm.
 * <P>
 * @see ijs.secure.Base64Encoder
 */
public class Base64Decoder
{
    /**
     * The translation table
     */
    public static final String base64Table =
        "ABCDEFGHIJKLMNOPQRSTUVWXYZ" +
        "abcdefghijklmnopqrstuvwxyz" +
        "0123456789" +
        "+/";

    /**
     * Decodes the given string buffer
     * @param buffer the string to be decoded
     * @return the decoded byte array
     * @exception java.io.IOException if the buffer
     * contains invalid data
     */
    public static byte[] decode(String buffer)
        throws IOException
    {
        if ((buffer.length() % 4) != 0)
            throw new IOException
            ("Buffer length not a multiple of four");

        int state = 0;
        int ch = 0;
        Vector result = new Vector();
        for (int i = 0; i < buffer.length(); i++) {
            int b = buffer.charAt(i);
            int p = base64Table.indexOf(b);
            if (p == -1)
                if (b == '=')
                    p = 0;
                else
                    throw new IOException
                    ("Invalid character in input");

            switch (state) {

                case 0:
                    ch = (p << 2) & 0xFC;
                    break;

                case 1:
                    ch |= ((p >> 4) & 0x03);
```

Figure 12-27

A Class that Decodes Base64-Encoded Authentication Strings.

```
                result.addElement(new Integer(ch));
                ch = (p << 4) & 0xF0;
                break;

            case 2:
                ch |= ((p >> 2) & 0x0F);
                result.addElement(new Integer(ch));
                ch = (p << 6) & 0xC0;
                break;

            case 3:
                ch |= (p & 0x3F);
                result.addElement(new Integer(ch));
                break;
            }
            state = (state + 1) % 4;
        }

        // Remove the trailing nulls

        int nPad = 0;
        for (int i = buffer.length()-1; i >= 0; i--) {
            char c = buffer.charAt(i);
            if (c == '=')
                nPad++;
            else break;
        }
        int n = result.size() - nPad;
        if (n < 0)
            n = 0;

        // Return the byte array

        byte[] bytes = new byte[n];
        for (int i = 0; i < n; i++)
            bytes[i] =
                ((Integer) result.elementAt(i)).byteValue();

        return bytes;
    }
}
```

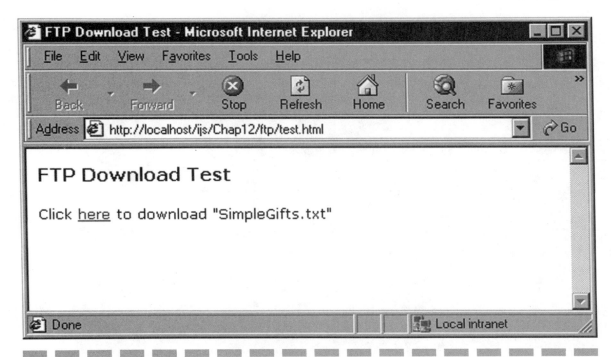

Figure 12-28 A Web Page with a Password-Protected FTP Link.

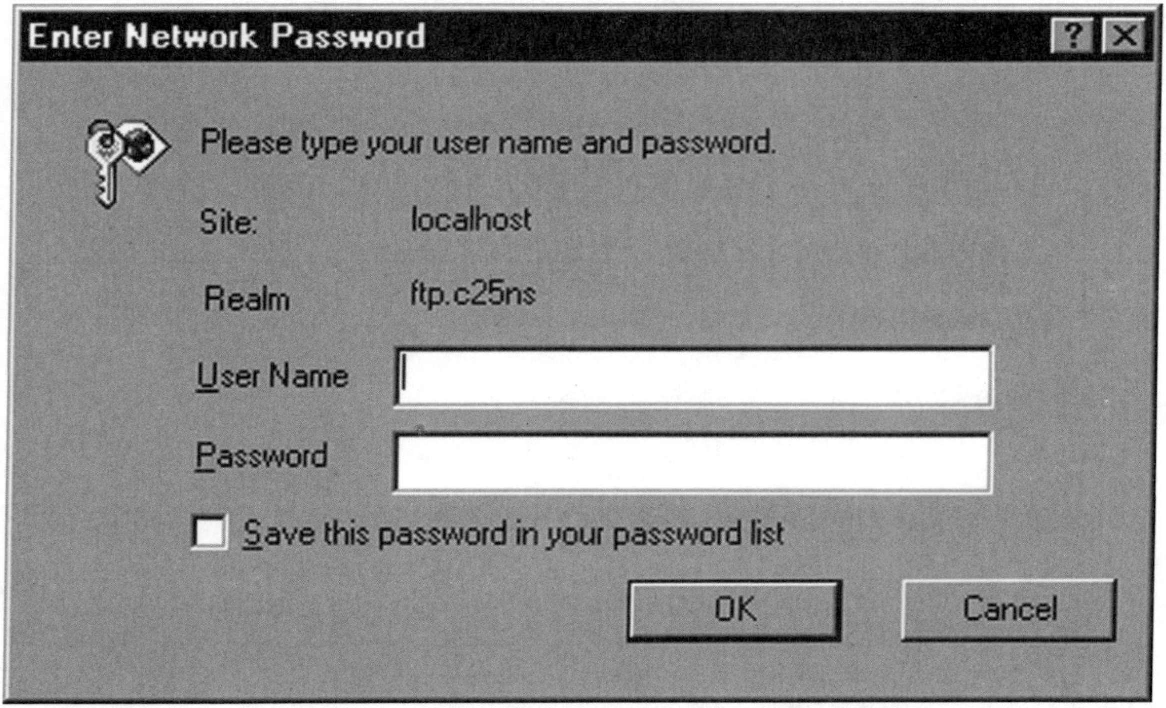

Figure 12-29 The Authentication Prompt Used to Supply Credentials to the FTP Client.

Figure 12-30
Output Returned
by Invoking the
FTP Client from a
Browser.

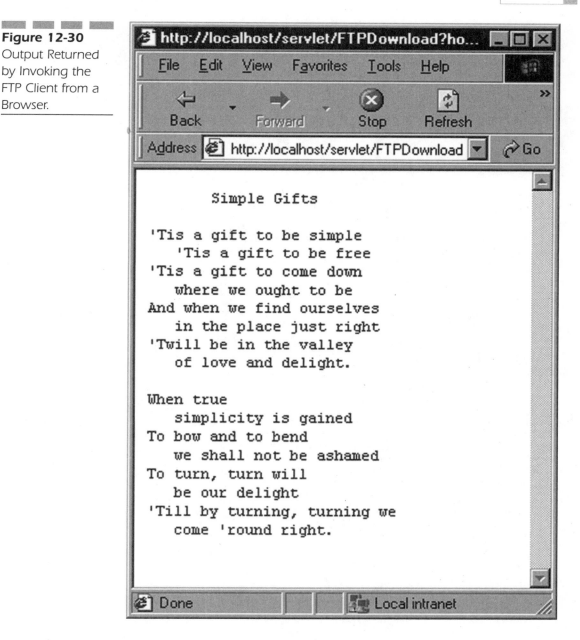

Figure 12-31

An Applet That
Uses the
FTPDownload
Servlet.

```java
import java.applet.*;
import java.awt.*;
import java.awt.event.*;
import java.io.*;
import java.net.*;
import java.util.*;

/**
 * This applet is designed to demonstrate how the
 * FTPDownloadServlet can be used to allow applets
 * to communicate with FTP servers
 */
public class FTPDemoApplet extends Applet
    implements ActionListener
{
    private Button btnDownload;
    private TextField txtHost;
    private TextField txtFileName;
    private TextField txtUserID;
    private TextField txtPassword;
    private TextArea txtOutput;

    /**
     * Creates the GUI elements
     */
    public void init()
    {
        setLayout(new GridBagLayout());
        GridBagConstraints c;

        // Banner

        Label lblBanner = new Label("FTP Demo Applet");
        lblBanner.setFont(new Font("Serif", Font.BOLD, 18));
        c = new GridBagConstraints();
        c.gridwidth = c.REMAINDER;
        c.insets = new Insets(5, 5, 5, 5);
        c.weightx = 1.0;
        add(lblBanner, c);

        // Prompt for host name

        Label lblHost = new Label("Host:");
        c = new GridBagConstraints();
        c.anchor = c.WEST;
        c.insets = new Insets(5, 5, 0, 0);
        add(lblHost, c);

        txtHost = new TextField(16);
        c = new GridBagConstraints();
        c.anchor = c.WEST;
        c.gridwidth = c.REMAINDER;
        c.insets = new Insets(5, 5, 0, 5);
        c.weightx = 1.0;
        add(txtHost, c);

        // Prompt for file name
```

Figure 12-31
(Continued)

```
Label lblFileName = new Label("File name:");
c = new GridBagConstraints();
c.anchor = c.WEST;
c.insets = new Insets(5, 5, 0, 0);
add(lblFileName, c);

txtFileName = new TextField(48);
c = new GridBagConstraints();
c.anchor = c.WEST;
c.gridwidth = c.REMAINDER;
c.insets = new Insets(5, 5, 0, 5);
c.weightx = 1.0;
add(txtFileName, c);

// Prompt for user ID

Label lblUserID = new Label("User ID:");
c = new GridBagConstraints();
c.anchor = c.WEST;
c.insets = new Insets(5, 5, 0, 0);
add(lblUserID, c);

txtUserID = new TextField(8);
c = new GridBagConstraints();
c.anchor = c.WEST;
c.gridwidth = c.REMAINDER;
c.insets = new Insets(5, 5, 0, 5);
c.weightx = 1.0;
add(txtUserID, c);

// Prompt for password

Label lblPassword = new Label("Password:");
c = new GridBagConstraints();
c.anchor = c.WEST;
c.insets = new Insets(5, 5, 0, 0);
add(lblPassword, c);

txtPassword = new TextField(24);
txtPassword.setEchoChar('*');
c = new GridBagConstraints();
c.anchor = c.WEST;
c.gridwidth = c.REMAINDER;
c.insets = new Insets(5, 5, 0, 5);
c.weightx = 1.0;
add(txtPassword, c);

// Button to start download

Panel pnlDownload = new Panel();

btnDownload = new Button("Download");
btnDownload.addActionListener(this);
pnlDownload.add(btnDownload);

Label lblDownload = new Label
```

Figure 12-31

(Continued)

```
        ("Click to download selected file");
    pnlDownload.add(lblDownload);

    c = new GridBagConstraints();
    c.anchor = c.WEST;
    c.gridwidth = c.REMAINDER;
    add(pnlDownload, c);

    // Output text area

    txtOutput = new TextArea(20, 48);
    txtOutput.setFont(
        new Font("Monospaced", Font.PLAIN, 12));
    c = new GridBagConstraints();
    c.fill = c.BOTH;
    c.gridheight = c.REMAINDER;
    c.gridwidth = c.REMAINDER;
    c.insets = new Insets(5, 5, 5, 5);
    c.weightx = 1.0;
    c.weighty = 1.0;
    add(txtOutput, c);
}

/**
 * Handles action events
 */
public void actionPerformed(ActionEvent event)
{
    if (event.getSource() == btnDownload)
        new DownloadThread().start();
}

/**
 * Enables or disables GUI components.
 * Used to prevent double submissions while
 * background thread is running.
 */
public void enableGUI(boolean enable)
{
    Component[] list = {
        txtHost,
        txtFileName,
        txtUserID,
        txtPassword,
        btnDownload,
    };

    for (int i = 0; i < list.length; i++) {
        Component comp = list[i];
        comp.setEnabled(enable);
    }
    setCursor(enable
        ? Cursor.getPredefinedCursor(Cursor.DEFAULT_CURSOR)
        : Cursor.getPredefinedCursor(Cursor.WAIT_CURSOR)
        );
}
```

Figure 12-31

(Continued)

```
/**
 * Inner class to handle download
 */
public class DownloadThread extends Thread
{
    public DownloadThread()
    {
        setPriority(Thread.MIN_PRIORITY);
        setDaemon(true);
        enableGUI(false);
    }

    public void run()
    {
        try {
            // Get the host, file name, user ID, and password

            String host = txtHost.getText().trim();
            String fileName = txtFileName.getText().trim();
            String userID = txtUserID.getText().trim();
            String password = txtPassword.getText().trim();

            // Build the credentials string

            ijs.secure.Base64Encoder encoder =
                new ijs.secure.Base64Encoder();

            String credentials = encoder.encode(
                (userID + ":" + password).getBytes());

            // Create the base URL

            URL url = new URL
                (getDocumentBase(),
                "/servlet/FTPDownload");

            // Append the host and file name parameters

            String urlString =
                url.toString()
                + "?host=" + URLEncoder.encode(host)
                + "&fileName=" + URLEncoder.encode(fileName);
            url = new URL(urlString);

            // Open a URL connection and pass the
            // authorization string

            URLConnection con = url.openConnection();
            con.setRequestProperty(
                "Authorization",
                "Basic " + credentials
                );

            // Send the request and read the output
            // back into the text area

            BufferedReader in =
```

```
                        new BufferedReader(
                        new InputStreamReader(
                        con.getInputStream())));

            txtOutput.setText("");
            for (;;) {
                String line = in.readLine();
                if (line == null)
                    break;
                txtOutput.append(line + "\n");
            }
        }
        catch (Exception e) {
            StringWriter sw = new StringWriter();
            PrintWriter pw = new PrintWriter(sw);
            e.printStackTrace(pw);
            pw.flush();
            txtOutput.setText(sw.toString());
        }
        finally {
            enableGUI(true);
        }
    }
}
```

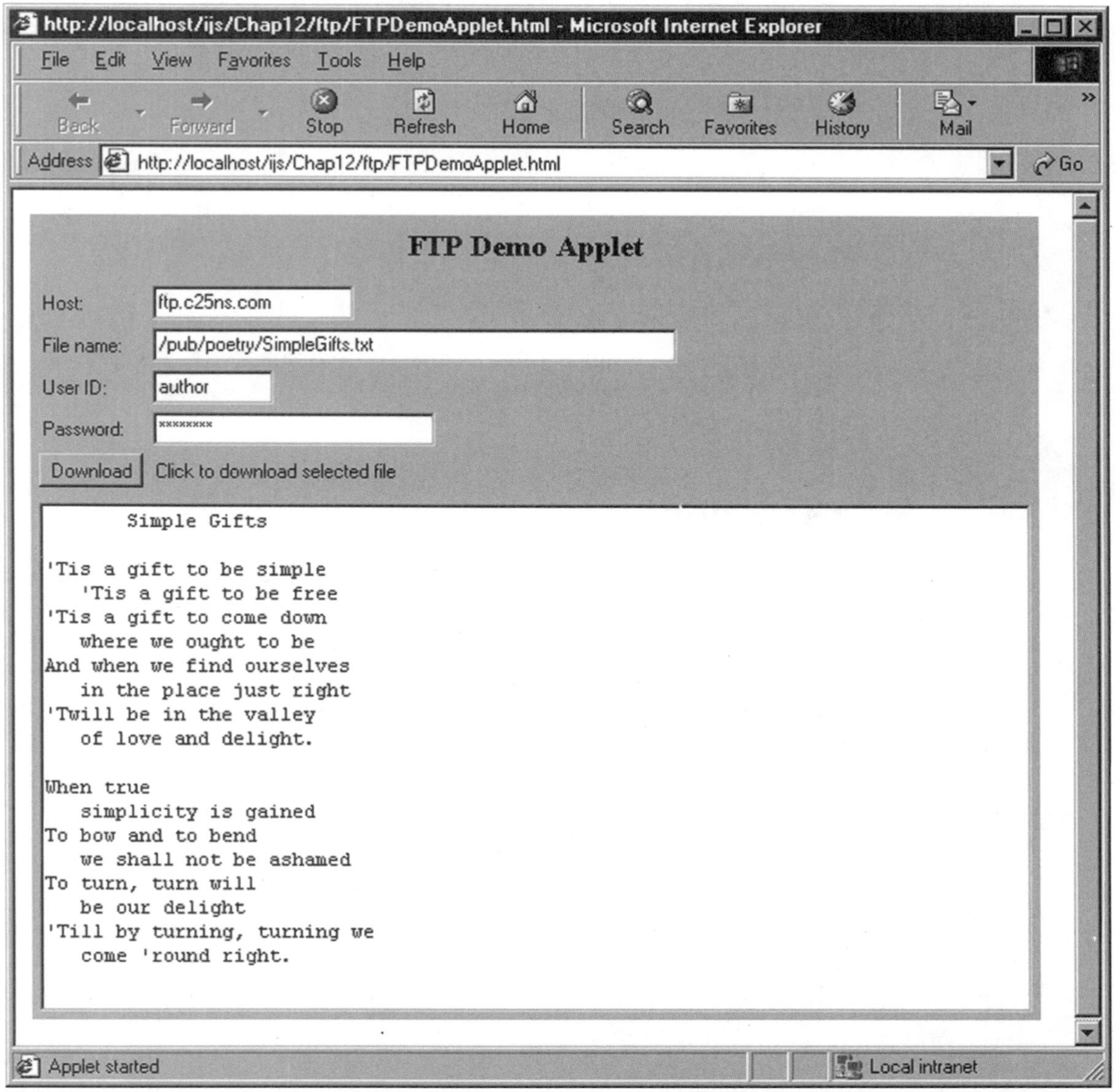

Figure 12-32 Output Returned by Invoking the FTP Client Indirectly from an Applet.

12.7   Servlets as CORBA Clients

Problem

How can I get a servlet to act as a client to a CORBA-based application?

Technique

Have the servlet create and initialize an object request broker (ORB). Use the ORB to obtain a reference to the name service. Use the name service to resolve a reference to the desired service, whose methods will then be accessible.

Discussion

CORBA (Common Object Request Broker Architecture) is an industry standard system for distributed object interoperability. Objects can be implemented in Java, C, C++, COBOL, Smalltalk, or Ada, and systems can contain any combination of these language mappings. CORBA-based systems use interfaces as their basic programming unit, so the individual components of a system do not have to know where the other components are located or even what programming language they are written in. Components use local proxies that implement the required interfaces, and object request brokers (ORBs) handle the details of communicating method calls to the remote objects that implement the interfaces and return their results.

The amount of documentation, tutorial, and reference material about CORBA is voluminous. We will not attempt to go into any details of how to develop an entire CORBA system; we are only concerned with how to use interfaces that are already part of a functioning system. Good starting points for learning about CORBA are the Object Management Group's Web site at *http://www.omg.org* and the Java IDL tutorial at *http://java.sun.com/docs/books/tutorial/idl/index.html*.

IPFTechnicalSupport Revisited   In Section 12.2 we developed a technical support file upload servlet that allowed software customers of the Internet Premium Food Market to submit stack traces and other files as part of a defect tracking system. We concentrated on the mechanics of uploading the file data, using a stub `reportDefect()` method that just made up an incident number. In this section we will implement that method in a CORBA environment.

Figure 12-33 shows our entry point into the defect-tracking system, the `DefectTracker` interface definition. This is written in CORBA

Figure 12-33

The
`DefectTracker`
Interface
Definition.

```
// Nested modules are used to create the desired
// Java package structure: ijs.servers.corba

module ijs {
    module servers {
        module corba {

            // The module has one interface: DefectTracker

            interface DefectTracker {

                // Exception thrown if a defect
                // cannot be logged for some reason

                exception CouldNotLogException {
                    string reason;
                };

                // Exception thrown if a previously
                // logged defect cannot be retrieved

                exception NotFoundException {
                    string reason;
                };

                // Given a product serial number and the
                // contents of a stack trace, this method
                // will create an incident in the defect
                // tracking system.  The incident number
                // is returned.

                string reportDefect(
                        in string serial,
                        in string data
                        )
                    raises (CouldNotLogException);

                // Given an incident number, retrieves the
                // incident data

                string getDefect(
                        in string incidentNumber
                        )
                    raises (NotFoundException);
            };
        };
    };
};
```

Interface Definition Language (IDL), which should be fairly readable to a Java or C++ programmer. The interface consists of two methods:

```
string reportDefect(in string serial, in string data)
    raises (CouldNotLogException);
string getDefect(in string incidentNumber)
    raises (NotFoundException);
```

The `reportDefect()` method accepts a product serial number and the contents of a stack trace, enters the data in the defect-tracking system, and returns the assigned incident number. If the defect cannot be logged for some reason, the method raises (throws) a `CouldNotLogException`. Its counterpart is the `getDefect()` method, which takes a previously entered incident number and returns the data that were logged.

When the `DefectTracker.idl` file is processed with the `idltojava` compiler, it creates Java source code for the equivalent Java interface, for the server-side implementation base class, and for a number of CORBA support classes.

After the interface and implementation base class have been generated, we can write the actual implementation of the two methods. Figure 12-34 shows the `DefectTrackerServant` class, which subclasses the generated implementation base class. To accomplish `reportDefect()`, we will do three things:

1. Assign an incident number that consists of the current time in milliseconds.

2. Write the log data as an XML document in a fixed directory location.

3. Return the incident number.

`getDefect()` will perform the complementary task of looking up the XML file that corresponds to a given incident number.

In order to make `DefectTrackerServant` accessible to CORBA clients, we need a mainline that creates an instance and registers it with a CORBA naming service. This mainline could be included in the service class itself, but it is a little clearer to put it in a class of its own. Figure 12-35 is a listing of this class. It creates and initializes an object request broker (ORB), creates an instance of the service, registers it with the ORB, and then binds the service to a CORBA naming service.

It should be emphasized that none of the preceding steps needed to be implemented in Java. As we said at the beginning of this section, the only part of the system we are concerned with here is the client interface;

Figure 12-34

An Implementation
of the
`DefectTracker`
Interface.

```java
package ijs.servers.corba;

import java.io.*;
import java.net.*;
import java.util.*;
import ijs.servers.corba.DefectTrackerPackage.*;

/**
 * A class that implements the defect tracking service
 */
public class DefectTrackerServant
    extends _DefectTrackerImplBase
{
    private String dirName;

    /**
     * Creates a new DefectTrackerServant
     */
    public DefectTrackerServant(String dirName)
    {
        this.dirName = dirName;
    }

    /**
     * Creates a new problem and assigns it an incident number.
     * Returns the incident number.
     * @param serial the product serial number
     * @param data the data to be logged
     * @return the incident number
     * @exception CouldNotLogException if the problem
     * could not be logged for any reason
     */
    public String reportDefect(String serial, String data)
        throws CouldNotLogException
    {
        // Assign the incident number

        String incidentNumber =
            String.valueOf(System.currentTimeMillis());

        // Write the data as an XML document

        try {
            File dir = new File(dirName);
            File logFile =
                new File(dir, incidentNumber + ".xml");

            PrintWriter out =
                new PrintWriter(new FileWriter(logFile));

            String[] lines = {
            "<?xml version=\"1.0\" ?>",
            "<INCIDENT NUMBER=\"" + incidentNumber + "\">",
            "<SERIAL>" + serial + "</SERIAL>",
            "<LOGDATA>"
                + "<![CDATA[" + data + "]]>"
                + "</LOGDATA>",
```

Figure 12-34

(Continued)

```
            "</INCIDENT>",
        };

        for (int i = 0; i < lines.length; i++)
            out.println(lines[i]);

        out.flush();
        out.close();
    }
    catch (IOException e) {
        throw new CouldNotLogException(e.getMessage());
    }

    // Returns the incident number

    return incidentNumber;
}

/**
 * Looks up the log file associated with
 * an incident number.  Returns the associated
 * data.
 * @param incidentNumber the incident number
 * @return the XML data written for this incident
 * @exception NotFoundException if the log data
 * could not be read
 */
public String getDefect(String incidentNumber)
    throws NotFoundException
{
    try {

        File dir = new File(dirName);

        // Read the data

        File logFile =
            new File(dir, incidentNumber + ".xml");
        int nBytes = (int) logFile.length();
        byte[] buffer = new byte[nBytes];
        FileInputStream in = new FileInputStream(logFile);
        in.read(buffer);
        in.close();

        // Return the data

        return new String(buffer);
    }
    catch (IOException e) {
        throw new NotFoundException(e.getMessage());
    }
}
}
```

we are assuming that the other side is already developed and operational. However, it is helpful to have at least a basic implementation of the server side of our CORBA application so that we can actually see it in operation in a demonstration environment.

At this point we are ready to write the client servlet. We already have a basic servlet that does the file upload; all we need to do is override the `reportDefect()` method. Figure 12-36 contains the source code for our servlet subclass, which is named `CorbaTechSupportServlet`. Its `reportDefect()` method performs the following steps:

1. Initialize an object request broker (ORB).
2. Get a reference to the naming service.
3. Use the naming service to get a reference to the `DefectTracker` service.
4. Invoke the `DefectTracker` service's own `reportDefect()` method.
5. Return the assigned incident number.

All the pieces are in place. We start the naming service and the `DefectTracker` server as follows[14]:

```
tnameserv -ORBInitialPort 1050
java ijs.servers.corba.DefectTracker -ORBInitialPort 1050 <dirname>
```

We can now rerun the `TechnicalSupportUpload` Web page and submit a stack trace, as shown in Figure 12-37. The incident is logged and the confirmation page (Figure 12-38) is returned.

The resulting XML data used by the defect tracking system are shown in Figure 12-39.

---

[14]In a production CORBA environment, we would assume that these services are already running. The steps we show here are only necessary in our demonstration environment.

Figure 12-35

A Wrapper Class
That Initializes the
`DefectTracker`
Service.

```java
package ijs.servers.corba;

import java.io.*;
import java.net.*;
import java.util.*;

import org.omg.CORBA.*;
import org.omg.CosNaming.*;
import org.omg.CosNaming.NamingContextPackage.*;

/**
 * Creates an ORB and registers a new DefectTracker
 * with a naming service
 */
public class DefectTrackerServer
{
    /**
     * Mainline
     */
    public static void main(String[] args)
    {
        boolean verbose = false;

        try {

            // Get the directory name from the command line

            String dirName = null;

            for (int i = 0; i < args.length; i++) {
                String arg = args[i];

                if (arg.startsWith("-v")) {
                    verbose = true;
                    continue;
                }

                if (arg.startsWith("-")) {
                    i++;
                    continue;
                }

                dirName = arg;
                break;
            }

            if (dirName == null)
                throw new RuntimeException
                ("No directory name specified");

            // Initialize the object request broker (ORB).
            // The port number can be supplied in
            // the command line argument -ORBInitialPort

            ORB orb = ORB.init(args, null);
            if (verbose)
                System.out.println
```

Figure 12-35

(Continued)

```java
            ("ORB registered");

      // Create the defect tracker service

      DefectTrackerServant servant =
         new DefectTrackerServant(dirName);
      if (verbose)
         System.out.println
         ("DefectTrackerServant created");

      // Register the service with the ORB

      orb.connect(servant);
      if (verbose)
         System.out.println
         ("Servant connected to ORB");

      // Get the naming context

      NamingContext namingContext =
         NamingContextHelper.narrow(
            orb.resolve_initial_references
            ("NameService")
            );

      // Bind the object reference

      NameComponent[] path = {
         new NameComponent("DefectTracker", "")
      };
      namingContext.rebind(path, servant);
      if (verbose)
         System.out.println
         ("Servant rebound");

      // Sit back and wait for client invocations

      java.lang.Object waitObject = new java.lang.Object();
      synchronized(waitObject) {
         if (verbose)
            System.out.println
            ("Waiting for client invocations");
         waitObject.wait();
      }
   }
   catch (Exception e) {
      e.printStackTrace();
   }
  }
}
```

Figure 12-36

A Subclass of
TechSupport-
Servlet That
Uses the CORBA-
Based Defect
Tracking
System.

```java
package ijs.servers.corba;

import ijs.servers.*;

import java.io.*;
import java.net.*;
import java.util.*;

import javax.servlet.*;
import javax.servlet.http.*;

import org.omg.CORBA.*;
import org.omg.CosNaming.*;
import org.omg.CosNaming.NamingContextPackage.*;

/**
 * CorbaTechSupportServlet
 */
public class CorbaTechSupportServlet extends TechSupportServlet
{
    /**
     * Reports the problem to the CORBA-based defect tracking
     * application.
     */
    public String reportDefect(String serial, String logData)
    {
        String incidentNumber = null;
        try {

            // Initialize the object request broker (ORB)

            String[] args = {
                "-ORBInitialPort", "1050",
                };
            ORB orb = ORB.init(args, null);

            // Get the naming context from which we can find
            // the defect tracking service

            NamingContext namingContext =
                NamingContextHelper.narrow(
                    orb.resolve_initial_references("NameService"));

            // Get a reference to the defect tracker
            // from the name service

            NameComponent[] path = {
                new NameComponent("DefectTracker", "")
            };

            DefectTracker dt =
                DefectTrackerHelper.narrow(
                    namingContext.resolve(path));

            // Call the reportDefect method
            // and return the incident number

            incidentNumber = dt.reportDefect(serial, logData);
        }
        catch (org.omg.CORBA.UserException e) {
            throw new RuntimeException(e.getMessage());
        }

        return incidentNumber;
    }
}
```

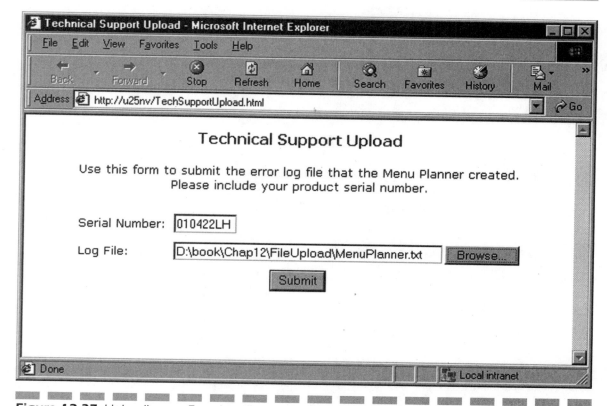

Figure 12-37 Uploading an Error Log File to the CORBA-Based Defect-Tracking System.

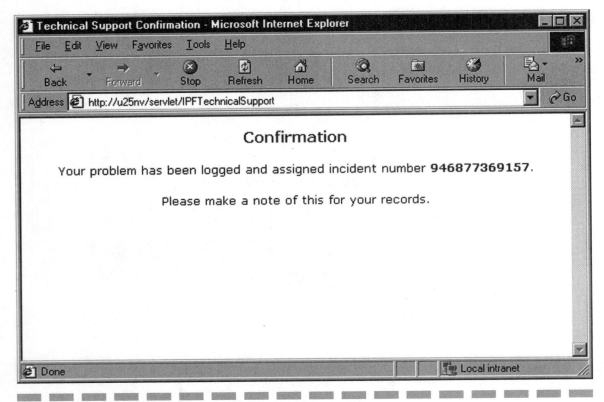

Figure 12-38 The Confirmation Returned by `CorbaTechSupportServlet`.

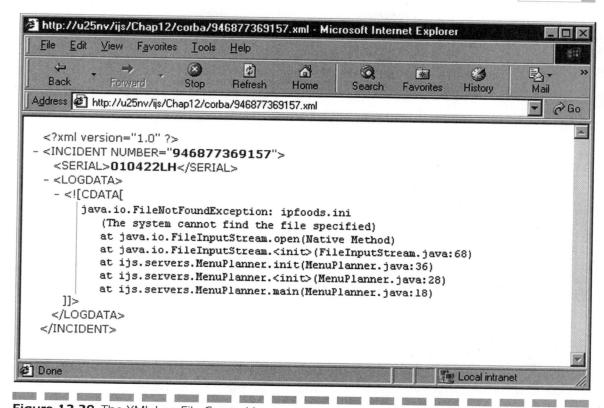

Figure 12-39 The XML Log File Created by `CorbaTechSupportServlet`.

JavaServer
Pages

Overview

As powerful as servlets are, sometimes they can be a bit cumbersome when it comes to generating complex HTML. Take, for example, this line of code that generates the beginning of an HTML table:

```
out.println("<table border=\"1\" cellpadding=\"4\""
            + " cellspacing=\"2\" width=\"75%\">");
```

It works, true, but can you tell at a glance whether all the quotes are closed? Compare that with the clarity of the HTML that you would write manually:

```
<table border="1" cellpadding="4" cellspacing="2" width="75%">
```

Most servlets contain a little code that handles application logic and a lot more code that handles output formatting. This can make it difficult to separate and reuse portions of the code when a different output format is needed (like XML, for example). For these and other reasons, many developers are turning to JavaServer Pages (JSP) as their preferred servlet environment.

What Is JSP? JavaServer Pages (JSP) is a server-side scripting environment that allows you to combine Java language statements and HTML to produce dynamic content. Starting with an ordinary HTML document, you use a simple set of tags to mark the beginning and ending of sections of Java code, as shown in the following example:

```
<HTML>
<BODY>
<%
   Date now = new Date();
   java.text.DateFormat fmt =
     new java.text.SimpleDateFormat("hh:mm:ss aa zzz");
   String formattedDate = fmt.format(now);
%>
The current time is <%= formattedDate %>
</BODY>
</HTML>
```

When this JSP page is invoked, it outputs the HTML exactly as it was entered but executes the Java code to produce the rest of the document:

```
<HTML>
<BODY>
The current time is 08:40:38 PM EST
</BODY>
</HTML>
```

How It Works   Unlike JavaScript, which is interpreted in the Web browser, JSP pages are translated into Java servlets and execute in the servlet engine. All the work is done on the server, and all the browser sees is ordinary HTML.[1] Here are the steps involved:

1. A JSP page is written and stored in the document tree of a Web server, usually as a file with name ending in .jsp.

2. The Web server receives a request for the document. Since the name ends in .jsp, it forwards the request to the servlet engine.

3. The servlet engine passes the request on to the JSP engine, which is typically a servlet itself.

4. The JSP engine determines whether the .jsp file is newer than the servlet class that implements it. If this is the case, it parses the .jsp file and creates Java source code for the equivalent servlet. It then compiles the servlet and causes the servlet engine to load and execute it.

The creation and compilation of the Java servlet described in step 4 is only necessary the first time the file is requested after it is initially created or later modified. In a production environment, this means that JSP pages typically are ready to run when requested.

The JSP environment is directly supported by the JRun and ServletExec servlet engines. For ApacheJServ and other systems, there is a third-party JSP implementation called GNUJSP. Sun Microsystems produced an early reference implementation called the JavaServer Web Development Kit (JSWDK), which was intended for development and testing purposes. More recently, Sun has joined forces with the Apache Software Foundation on the Tomcat project, which is the combined JSP

---

[1]Sometimes this can be a drawback. Microsoft Internet Explorer by default will substitute an error page of its own making if your servlet generates a ServletException or anything else that returns a 500 status code. This generally obscures any helpful error messages that you might want. You can disable this behavior by bringing up the Tools→Internet Options dialog Advanced tab and deselecting "Show friendly HTTP error messages."

1.1 and Servlets 2.2 reference implementation.[2] JSP and Java servlets are key elements of the Java 2 Enterprise Edition.

Features and Advantages   JSP pages have all the advantages of servlets (after all, they *are* servlets in another guise) as well as unique features of their own:

- *Ease of use.* JSP pages are installed simply as Web pages, using the natural package structure of the Web server's document tree. They are complied automatically the first time they are requested and recompiled whenever their source changes.

- *Platform independence.* As a server-side scripting environment, JSP runs on virtually any platform that supports Java servlets. In addition, the fact that it generates ordinary HTML makes it naturally compatible with any Web browser. In this respect, it is a more attractive choice than Active Server Pages or JavaScript, requiring neither a specific Web server nor any special configuration of the browser.

- *Separate content and presentation.* With its seamless support for JavaBeans, JSP allows a developer to place application logic into pure processing classes that can be developed and tested outside the Web environment and reused in contexts other than HTML generation.

Given the ease with which Web applications can be developed and deployed in the Internet environment, it is entirely possible that JSP could become the most widely used environment for Java programming.

This chapter discusses the more commonly used JSP elements, their syntax, and how they are used. We will provide working examples of JSP pages that incorporate each of these elements. The focus here is on getting started with working code. If you would like to explore how a particular element works in greater detail, the JavaServer Pages Specification document[3] is the best place to look. It also can be quite instructive simply to use the element and then look at the generated Java source code itself. Table 13-1 lists the locations in which several popular JSP environments store their generated servlets.

---

[2]More information about Tomcat can be found at *http://jakarta.apache.org/tomcat/index.html*.

[3]Available at *http://java.sun.com/products/jsp/download.html*.

JSP Engine	Generated Servlet Location
JRun 2.3.3	Relative to first directory listed in `servletdir` **property** in `jsm-default/services/<service name>/properties/jrun.properties`
ServletExec 2.2	Relative to the `<ServletExecRoot>/servlets/pagecompile` **directory**
ApacheJServ with GNUJSP	In the directory specified in the `GNUJSP` **servlet** -`scratchpath` **parameter.**

13.1   Expressions

Syntax

```
<%= expression %>
```

Description

Expressions are the simplest JSP elements. An *expression* can consist of any Java code that returns a value. The expression is evaluated, converted to a string, and substituted into the document, replacing the `<%=...%>` tags. No semicolon should be used at the end of the expression.

Examples

Figure 13-1 lists three simple examples of JSP expressions, in each case showing the original JSP source code and then the HTML that results when the expression is evaluated. The first one uses the static `sqrt()` method of `java.lang.Math` to calculate the square root of 2. The second shows how to access system properties, for example, the `java.home` property. The last one uses the implicit `request` object to get the name of the current script (see Section 13.3). `request` is equivalent to the `HttpServletRequest` object that is passed to the `service()` method

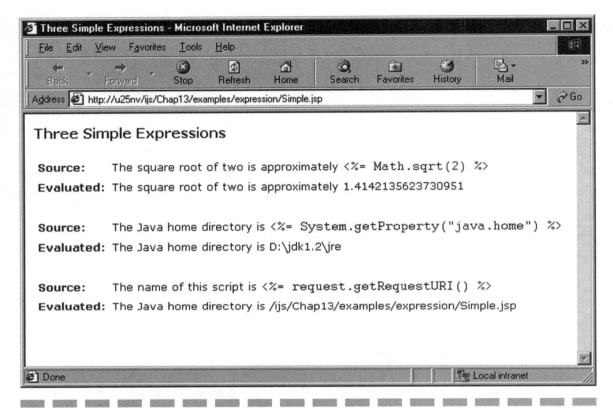

Figure 13-1 Simple Examples of JSP Expressions

of the underlying servlet. The JSP page used for these three examples is found in Figure 13-2.

13.2 Scriptlets

Syntax

```
<% statements %>
```

Description

A *scriptlet* consists of one or more valid Java statements. These can be any kinds of statements as long as they make sense when used inside a

Figure 13-2

The JSP Source for the Three Simple Expressions Example

```
<HTML>
<BODY>
<H3>Three Simple Expressions</H3>
<TABLE BORDER=0 CELLPADDING=3>
    <TR>
        <TD><B>Source:</B></TD>
        <TD>
            The square root of two is approximately
            <FONT FACE="Courier" SIZE="+1">
            &lt;%= Math.sqrt(2) %&gt;
            </FONT>
        </TD>
    </TR>
    <TR>
        <TD><B>Evaluated:</B></TD>
        <TD>The square root of two is approximately
            <%= Math.sqrt(2) %>
        </TD>
    </TR>
    <TR><TD COLSPAN=2> </TD></TR>
    <TR>
        <TD><B>Source:</B></TD>
        <TD>
            The Java home directory is
            <FONT FACE="Courier" SIZE="+1">
            &lt;%= System.getProperty("java.home") %&gt;
            </FONT>
        </TD>
    </TR>
    <TR>
        <TD><B>Evaluated:</B></TD>
        <TD>
            The Java home directory is
            <%= System.getProperty("java.home") %>
        </TD>
    </TR>
    <TR><TD COLSPAN=2> </TD></TR>
    <TR>
        <TD><B>Source:</B></TD>
        <TD>
            The name of this script is
            <FONT FACE="Courier" SIZE="+1">
            &lt;%= request.getRequestURI() %&gt;
            </FONT>
        </TD>
    </TR>
    <TR>
        <TD><B>Evaluated:</B></TD>
        <TD>
            The Java home directory is
            <%= request.getRequestURI() %>
        </TD>
    </TR>
</TABLE>
</BODY>
</HTML>
```

single method. The JSP compiler will insert all the scriptlet statements found in a JSP page into the _jspService() method of the generated servlet in the order in which they are coded.

Examples

HelloTime.jsp (see Figure 13-3) shows how scriptlets can be used to create different output depending on the time of day. It accesses the system time and then uses a three-part IF-THEN-ELSE statement to display either Good Morning, Good Afternoon, or Good Evening.

Details of the JSP Source Code   Let's walk through the details of HelloTime. It begins with two lines of HTML markup that typically would be found at the beginning of a Web page:

```
<HTML>
<BODY>
```

These lines will be written directly to the output Web page. The next line contains <% to mark the beginning of a scriptlet. Everything that follows

Figure 13-3

A JSP Page That Illustrates How to Use Scriptlets

```
<HTML>
<BODY>
<%
    java.util.Calendar now = java.util.Calendar.getInstance();
    int hour = now.get(java.util.Calendar.HOUR_OF_DAY);
    if (hour < 12) {
%>
    <H3>Good Morning</H3>
<%
    }
    else if (hour < 18) {
%>
    <H3>Good Afternoon</H3>
<%
    }
    else {
%>
    <H3>Good Evening</H3>
<%
    }
%>
</BODY>
</HTML>
```

this until the first occurrence of %> is treated as Java code. There are three lines in the scriptlet:

```
<%
    java.util.Calendar now = java.util.Calendar.getInstance();
    int hour = now.get(java.util.Calendar.HOUR_OF_DAY);
    if (hour < 12) {
%>
```

Notice that the opening brace after the if statement is not closed in this scriptlet. This is so because we are switching back into HTML to write some output that is conditioned by (hour < 12):

```
<H3>Good Morning</H3>
```

Immediately after the <H3> line, we switch back into Java mode:

```
<%
    }
    else if (hour < 18) {
%>
```

This second scriptlet closes the if statement and tests the second condition, again leaving an open brace so that we can include some HTML that is conditioned by (hour < 18):

```
<H3>Good Afternoon</H3>
```

Again we switch into Java mode for the third scriptlet, which closes the second if statement and begins the default else case:

```
<%
    }
    else {
%>
    <H3>Good Evening</H3>
```

One last scriptlet is required to close the else case:

```
<%
    }
%>
```

And finally, the page ends with the closing HTML document tags:

```
</BODY>
</HTML>
```

How the JSP Is Processed When `HelloTime.jsp` is first requested from a Web browser, the JSP engine compares its timestamp with the timestamp on the generated servlet class. If the class is older (or nonexistent), the JSP engine creates the Java source code for a servlet and compiles it. The generated class is then loaded as any other servlet would be. When it is executed (at 11:52 P.M., for example), it produces HTML that looks like this:

```
<HTML>
<BODY>
   <H3>Good Evening</H3>
</BODY>
</HTML>
```

The Generated Java Servlet JSP pages exhibit the helpful property of leaving their generated Java source code behind for inspection. If there is any aspect of a particular JSP page that you do not understand, you can examine the actual Java code that the JSP engine created and probably figure it out. Figures 13-4, 13-5, and 13-6 show the servlet code that JRun, ServletExec, and GNUJSP generate for `HelloTime.jsp`.[4]

All three versions accomplish the same result, although by slightly different means. What they have in common is the following:

1. They all implement `javax.servlet.jsp.HttpJspPage`, either directly or indirectly.
2. They call the static `JspFactory.getDefaultFactory()` method to create a `JspFactory`.
3. Using the `JspFactory`, they create a `PageContext` object. `PageContext` is an implementation-dependent wrapper for the attributes, request, response, and context objects that a JSP uses.
4. They concatenate all the scriptlets in a page to form the body of the `_jspService()` method. For any HTML code found between scriptlets, they generate corresponding `out.print()` statements. The GNUJSP version inserts comments in the generated Java code to cross-reference generated `out.print()` statements to the line numbers in the original JSP source.

A Complete Example Almost any servlet can be converted into a JSP. Consider the `BananaBabyFoods` servlet from Section 5.4. This is a

---

[4]The source code has been re-formatted slightly for readability.

Figure 13-4

The JRun Servlet
Equivalent of
`HelloTime.jsp`

```
// Generated by JRun, do not edit

package jsp;
import java.io.*;
import java.util.*;
import java.net.*;
import java.beans.*;
import javax.servlet.*;
import javax.servlet.http.*;
import javax.servlet.jsp.*;
import com.livesoftware.jsp.*;
import com.livesoftware.scripting.*;

public class HelloTime extends HttpJSPServlet
    implements JRunJspPage
{
    public void _jspService(
        HttpServletRequest request,
        HttpServletResponse response)
      throws ServletException, IOException
    {
      ServletConfig config = getServletConfig();
      ServletContext application = config.getServletContext();

      Object page = (Object) this;
      PageContext pageContext =
        JspFactory.getDefaultFactory().getPageContext
        (this, request, response,  null, true,8192, true);
      JspWriter out = pageContext.getOut();
      HttpSession session = request.getSession(true);
      response.setContentType("text/html");

      out.print("<HTML>\r\n<BODY>\r\n");
      java.util.Calendar now
        = java.util.Calendar.getInstance();
      int hour = now.get(java.util.Calendar.HOUR_OF_DAY);
      if (hour < 12) {
        out.print("\r\n    <H3>Good Morning</H3>\r\n");
      }
      else if (hour < 18) {
        out.print("\r\n    <H3>Good Afternoon</H3>\r\n");
      }
      else {
        out.print("\r\n    <H3>Good Evening</H3>\r\n");
      }
      out.print("\r\n</BODY>\r\n</HTML>\r\n");
      out.flush();
    }

    private static final String[] __dependencies__ = {""};

    public String[] __getDependencies()
    {
      return __dependencies__;
    }
}
```

Figure 13-5
The ServletExec
Servlet Equivalent
of `Hello-`
`Time.jsp`

```java
package pagecompile;

import java.io.*;
import java.util.*;
import javax.servlet.*;
import javax.servlet.http.*;
import javax.servlet.jsp.*;
import java.beans.Beans;
import newatlanta.servletexec.JSP10HttpJspPage;
import newatlanta.servletexec.JSP10Servlet;

public final class _HelloTime_xjsp extends JSP10HttpJspPage
{
    public void _jspService(
            HttpServletRequest request,
            HttpServletResponse response)
        throws ServletException, IOException
    {

        response.setContentType("text/html; charset=iso-8859-1");

        JspFactory na_jsp_factory
            = JspFactory.getDefaultFactory();
        PageContext pageContext
            = na_jsp_factory.getPageContext
                (this, request, response, "null", true, 8, true);
        ServletConfig config = pageContext.getServletConfig();
        ServletContext application
            = pageContext.getServletContext();
        Object page = this;
        JspWriter out = pageContext.getOut();
        HttpSession session = pageContext.getSession();

        try {
            out.print( "<HTML>\r\n<BODY>\r\n" );
            java.util.Calendar now
                = java.util.Calendar.getInstance();
            int hour = now.get(java.util.Calendar.HOUR_OF_DAY);
            if (hour < 12) {
                out.print("\r\n    <H3>Good Morning</H3>\r\n");
            }
            else if (hour < 18) {
                out.print("\r\n    <H3>Good Afternoon</H3>\r\n");
            }
            else {
                out.print("\r\n    <H3>Good Evening</H3>\r\n");
            }
            out.print("\r\n</BODY>\r\n</HTML>\r\n");
        }
        catch (Exception e) {
            pageContext.handlePageException(e);
        }
        finally {
            out.flush();
            na_jsp_factory.releasePageContext(pageContext);
        }
    }
}
```

Figure 13-6

The GNUJSP
Servlet Equivalent
of Hello-
Time.jsp

```
/*
    Generated by JavaEmitter on Thu Jan 20 21:53:47 EST 2000
    Please do not modify.
*/

import java.io.IOException;
import javax.servlet.*;
import javax.servlet.http.*;
import javax.servlet.jsp.*;

public class jsp___2fHelloTime_2ejsp
   extends org.gjt.jsp.HttpJspPageImpl
{
   public final long _gnujspGetTimestamp()
   {
      return 948423227036L;
   }

   private static final String[] _gnujspDeps =
      new String[] { "/HelloTime.jsp" };

   public final String[] _gnujspGetDeps()
   {
      return _gnujspDeps;
   }

   public final long _gnujspGetCompilerVersion()
   {
      return 1999101701L;
   }

   public void _jspService(
       HttpServletRequest request,
       HttpServletResponse response)
      throws ServletException, IOException
   {
      response.setContentType("text/html");
      JspFactory factory = JspFactory.getDefaultFactory();
      PageContext pageContext = factory.getPageContext
         (this, request, response, null, true, 8192, true);
      HttpSession session = pageContext.getSession ();
      ServletContext application =
         pageContext.getServletConfig().getServletContext();
      JspWriter out = pageContext.getOut();
      ServletConfig config = pageContext.getServletConfig();
      Object page = this;

      try {

         // line:/HelloTime.jsp:1
         out.print("<HTML>\n<BODY>\n");

         // line:/HelloTime.jsp:4
         java.util.Calendar now =
            java.util.Calendar.getInstance();
         int hour = now.get(java.util.Calendar.HOUR_OF_DAY);
         if (hour < 12) {
```

Figure 13-6
(Continued)

```
// line:/HelloTime.jsp:8
out.print("\n    <H3>Good Morning</H3>\n");

// line:/HelloTime.jsp:10
}
else if (hour < 18) {

// line:/HelloTime.jsp:13
out.print("\n    <H3>Good Afternoon</H3>\n");

// line:/HelloTime.jsp:15
}
else {

// line:/HelloTime.jsp:18
out.print("\n    <H3>Good Evening</H3>\n");

// line:/HelloTime.jsp:20
}

// line:/HelloTime.jsp:22
out.print("\n</BODY>\n</HTML>\n");
}
catch (Exception e) {
   out.clearBuffer();
   pageContext.handlePageException(e);
}
finally {
   out.close();
   factory.releasePageContext(pageContext);
}
  }
}
```

servlet that uses JDBC to access a nutrient database for a list of baby foods that contain bananas. The servlet source code, which is listed in Figure 5-15, contains both the database access logic and code to generate the HTML that presents the results. The corresponding JSP (see Figure 13-7) converts all the formatting code into ordinary HTML, leaving the database code inside four scriptlets. The same output (see Figure 13-8) is produced.

One of the benefits of JSP is that it allows you to separate processing logic from presentation logic. In this example, the separation is mainly visual, with Java code in one section and HTML in another. We will see later on in the section about JSP and JavaBeans that virtually all the processing logic can be abstracted away, resulting not only in a much simpler JSP but also in a reusable bean component as well.

```
<%@ page import="java.io.*,java.sql.*,java.util.*" %>
<HTML>
<HEAD>
<TITLE>Banana Baby Foods JSP</TITLE>
</HEAD>
<BODY>
<IMG SRC="/ijs/Chap05/banana.gif">
<FONT SIZE="+2">Banana Baby Foods (Using JSP)</FONT>
<P>
<%
    Connection con = null;
    Statement stmt = null;
    ResultSet rs = null;
    try {
        Class.forName("sun.jdbc.odbc.JdbcOdbcDriver");
        con = DriverManager.getConnection("jdbc:odbc:usda");
        stmt = con.createStatement();
        rs = stmt.executeQuery(""
            + " SELECT    F.NDB_No as foodCode,"
            + "           F.Desc as foodDesc"
            + " FROM      FOOD_DES F, FD_GROUP G"
            + " WHERE     F.FdGp_Cd = G.FdGp_Cd"
            + " AND       F.Shrt_Desc LIKE '%BANANA%'"
            + " AND       G.FdGp_Desc = 'Baby Foods'"
            + " ORDER BY F.Desc"
            );
        int nRows = 0;
        while (rs.next()) {
            nRows++;
            String foodCode = rs.getString("foodCode");
            String foodDesc = rs.getString("foodDesc");
%>
<B><%= foodCode %></B>
<%= foodDesc %><BR>
<%
        }
%>
<P>
<%= nRows %> banana baby foods selected<P>
<%
    }
    catch (Exception e) {
%>
Could not connect to the nutrient database.<P>
The error message was
<PRE>
<%= e.getMessage() %>
</PRE>
<%
    }
    finally {
        if (rs != null) {
            try { rs.close(); }
            catch (SQLException ignore) {}
        }
        if (stmt != null) {
            try { stmt.close(); }
```

Figure 13-7

(Continued)

```
            catch (SQLException ignore) {}
        }
    if (con != null) {
        try { con.close(); }
        catch (SQLException ignore) {}
    }
  }
}
%>
</BODY>
</HTML>
```

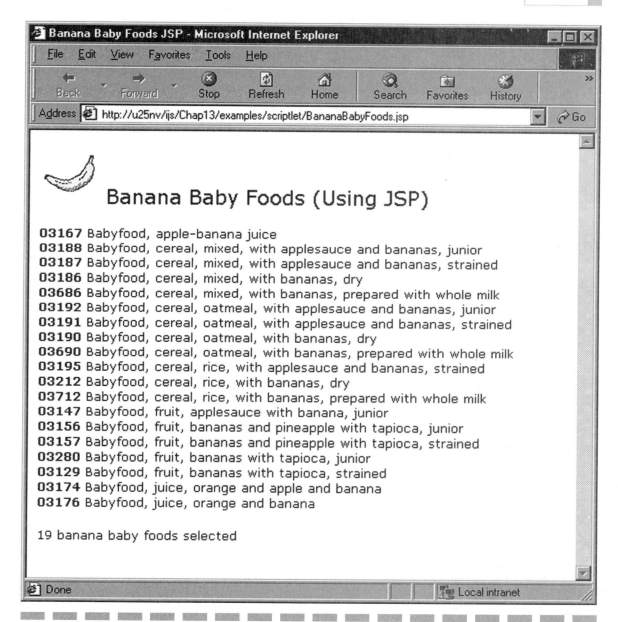

Figure 13-8 Output of the `BananaBabyFoods` JSP Page

13.3 Implicit Objects

All the scriptlets in a JSP page are concatenated and placed inside the generated servlet's `_jspService()` method. At the beginning of this method, before the user code, the JSP translator generates statements that create references to various useful objects. You can access these objects without having to declare them. For this reason, they are sometimes referred to as *implicit objects*. Table 13-2 presents a list of these objects.

Note that implicit objects are only available inside scriptlets or JSP expressions, not declarations. This is so because declaration code is generated outside the `_jspService()` method. If you need access to one of these objects inside a declaration, you must explicitly pass it as a parameter.

TABLE 13-2

Variable Name	Type	Notes
request	javax.servlet.http.HttpServletRequest	
response	javax.servlet.http.HttpServletResponse	
pageContext	javax.servlet.jsp.PageContext	
session	javax.servlet.http.HttpSession	All JSPs have a session allocated by default.
application	javax.servlet.ServletContext	
out	javax.jsp.JspWriter	
config	javax.servlet.ServletConfig	
page	java.lang.Object	
exception	java.lang.Throwable	Only available if the page directive's errorPage="yes" attribute is specified.

13.4 Declarations

Syntax

```
<%! statements %>
```

Description

A *declaration* consists of one or more valid Java statements that are intended to be placed outside the generated servlet's _jspService() method. These statements can include variable declarations as well as method definitions. This makes it possible to override servlet life-cycle methods, for example. It also makes it possible to define inner classes.

Unlike scriptlets, declaration sections do not have access to JSP implicit objects (see Section 13.3). If you need access to the request object, for example, you need to explicitly pass it as a parameter.

Examples

There are three main uses for declaration sections: variable declarations, method definitions, and inner class definitions. We will give examples of each.

Variable Declarations   Declaration sections can be used to define constants, as shown below:

```
<%! public static final int MAX_ITERATIONS = 5; %>
<%
   for (int i = 0; i < MAX_ITERATIONS; i++) {
%>
Iteration <%= (i+1) %> of <%= MAX_ITERATIONS %><BR>
<%
   }
%>
```

The first line, in which MAX_ITERATIONS is defined, is enclosed in the opening and closing declaration tags <%! ... %>. The for loop is coded as a scriptlet <% ... %>, with its output line written in HTML with two JSP expressions. The for loop's ending curly brace is coded in its own <%

. . . `%>` scriptlet section. Figure 13-9 shows how a JSP container might translate this into servlet code. We see that the two scriptlets and the `out.print()` statements that generate the HTML have been concatenated and placed inside the `_jspService()` method, whereas the contents of the declaration section (the definition of `MAX_ITERATIONS`) has been moved outside the method, where the other static variables and method declarations are located.

A typical use of declarations would be to provide a place for all the string constants used by a program to be gathered into one maintainable section:

```
<%! public static final String
        TITLE            = "Baby Foods Containing Bananas",
        DRIVER_NAME      = "sun.jdbc.odbc.JdbcOdbcDriver",
        URL              = "jdbc:odbc:usda"
    ;
%>
```

Method Definitions   Figure 13-10 is a more involved example of declaration sections, demonstrating how they can be used to declare methods. This example creates a database connection in a `jspInit()` method and closes it in `jspDestroy()`. A reference to the connection object is stored in the servlet context where it can be retrieved quickly by the JSP when it services HTTP requests.

When a request is made of the JSP, it checks to see if a `searchString` parameter was specified. This parameter will be used as the argument of an SQL `LIKE` predicate when the database query is executed. If no parameter is found, the JSP uses `%` as the default, since this will match any value. After getting the parameter value, the JSP retrieves the connection object from the servlet context. If the `jspInit()` method fails to create a connection, this value will be `null`, and an appropriate error message will be produced. Otherwise, the JSP will execute the query and create an HTML table with the results, as shown in Figure 13-11.

The database connection remains open,[5] however, so the next time a request is made (with a search string of `Products`, perhaps), the response time is almost immediate, producing the output shown in Figure 13-12.

---

[5]This is not intended as a particularly efficient database connection strategy. Using a connection pool as described in Chapter 5 would be better.

Figure 13-9

The Generated
Servlet
Corresponding to
MaxIterations.
jsp

```java
// Generated by JRun, do not edit

package jsp.ijs.Chap13.examples.declaration;

import java.io.*;
import java.util.*;
import java.net.*;
import java.beans.*;
import javax.servlet.*;
import javax.servlet.http.*;
import javax.servlet.jsp.*;
import com.livesoftware.jsp.*;
import com.livesoftware.scripting.*;

public class MaxIterations extends HttpJSPServlet
    implements JRunJspPage
{
    public void _jspService(
        HttpServletRequest request,
        HttpServletResponse response)
      throws ServletException, IOException
    {
        ServletConfig config = getServletConfig();
        ServletContext application = config.getServletContext();

        Object page = (Object) this;
        PageContext pageContext = JspFactory.getDefaultFactory()
          .getPageContext(
              this, request, response,  null, true, 8192, true);
        JspWriter out = pageContext.getOut();

        HttpSession session = request.getSession(true);
        response.setContentType("text/html");

        for (int i = 0; i < MAX_ITERATIONS; i++) {
           out.print("\r\nIteration ");
           out.print((i+1) );
           out.print(" of ");
           out.print(MAX_ITERATIONS );
           out.print("<BR>\r\n");
        }
        out.flush();
    }

    public static final int MAX_ITERATIONS = 5;

    private static final String[] __dependencies__ = {""};

    public String[] __getDependencies()
    {
       return __dependencies__;
    }
}
```

Figure 13-10

A JSP Page That
Uses a Preinitialized
Database
Connection

```jsp
<%@ page import="java.sql.*" %>
<%!

    public final String
        CON = getClass().getName() + ".con",
        DRIVER_NAME = "sun.jdbc.odbc.JdbcOdbcDriver",
        URL = "jdbc:odbc:usda",
        COLORS[] = {"#F0F0F0", "#E0E0E0", "#C0C0C0"}
        ;

    /**
     * Create database connection when JSP
     * is first loaded.
     */
    public void jspInit()
    {
        Connection con = null;
        try {
            Class.forName(DRIVER_NAME);
            con = DriverManager.getConnection(URL);
            getServletContext().setAttribute(CON, con);
        }
        catch (Exception e) {
            log(e.getMessage());
        }
    }

    /**
     * Close database connection when JSP
     * is unloaded.
     */
    public void jspDestroy()
    {
        Connection con = (Connection)
            getServletContext().getAttribute(CON);
        if (con != null) {
            try {
                con.close();
            }
            catch (SQLException ignore) {}
        }
    }
%>
<%
    String searchString = request.getParameter("searchString");
    if (searchString == null)
        searchString = "%";

    // Get database connection, if it exists

    Connection con = (Connection)
        getServletContext().getAttribute(CON);
    if (con == null) {
%>
<H3>Error: No database connection available</H3>
<%
    }
```

Figure 13-10

(Continued)

```
else {
   try {
      synchronized(con) {
         String sql =
            " SELECT * FROM FD_GROUP"
            + " WHERE FDGP_DESC LIKE "
            + "'%" + searchString + "%'"
            + " ORDER BY FDGP_DESC"
            ;
         Statement stmt = con.createStatement();
         ResultSet rs = stmt.executeQuery(sql);
         int row = 0;
%>
   <CENTER>
   <H3><%=
      searchString.equals("%")
         ? "All Food Groups"
         : "Food Groups Containing \"" + searchString + "\""
       %>
   </H3>
   <TABLE BORDER=0 CELLPADDING=2>
   <TR ALIGN="LEFT">
      <TH BGCOLOR="<%= COLORS[2] %>">Code</TH>
      <TH BGCOLOR="<%= COLORS[2] %>">Description</TH>
   </TR>
<%
            while (rs.next()) {
               row++;
               String code = rs.getString(1);
               String desc = rs.getString(2);
%>
   <TR>
      <TD BGCOLOR="<%= COLORS[row % 2] %>"><%= code %></TD>
      <TD BGCOLOR="<%= COLORS[row % 2] %>"><%= desc %></TD>
   </TR>
<%
            }
%>
   </TABLE>
   </CENTER>
<%
            rs.close();
            stmt.close();
         }
      }
      catch (SQLException e) {
%>
<H3>Error: <%= e.getMessage() %></H3>
<%
      }
   }
%>
```

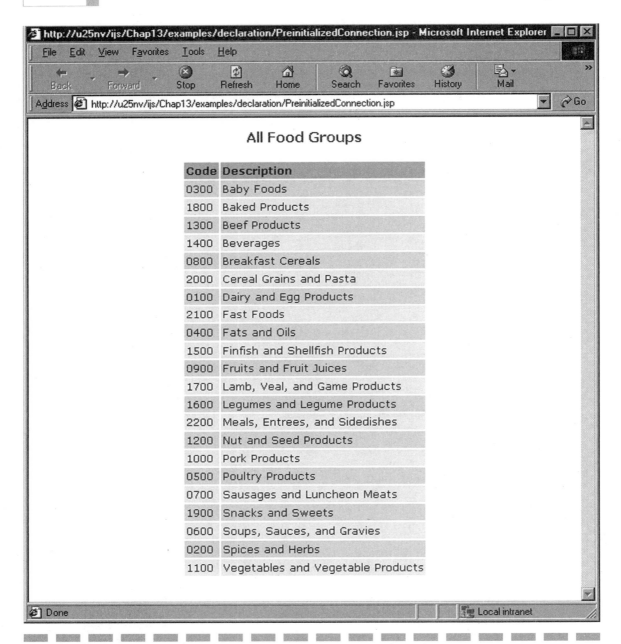

Figure 13-11 Default Output of `PreinitializedConnection.jsp`

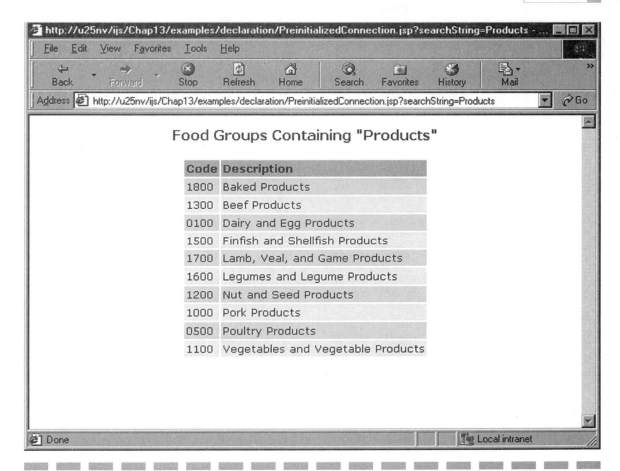

Figure 13-12 Output of `PreinitializedConnection.jsp` with a Search String

Inner Classes Figure 13-13 features all three uses of declaration sections: variable declarations, method definitions, and inner classes. The task of this JSP is the search for prime number pairs. A *prime number* is an integer that has exactly two distinct divisors, namely, one and the number itself. A curious fact about prime numbers is that they tend to occur in pairs—11 and 13, 71 and 73, 173357 and 173359, and so on. It is not known whether there are infinitely many prime number pairs. We will use a class running in a background thread to search for these pairs.

Figure 13-13

A JSP Page That
Uses a Background
Thread to Search
for Prime Number
Pairs

```
<%!
    public static SearchThread pps = null;

    /**
     * Starts the background thread when the JSP
     * is first loaded.
     */
    public void jspInit()
    {
        if (pps == null) {
            pps = new SearchThread();
            pps.start();
        }
    }

    /**
     * Stops the background thread when the JSP is
     * unloaded.
     */
    public void jspDestroy()
    {
        if (pps != null)
            pps.stop();
    }

    /**
     * An inner class that runs a background thread
     * to search for prime number pairs
     */
    class SearchThread implements Runnable
    {
        /**
         * Internal thread
         */
        private Thread kicker;

        /**
         * List of the last ten prime pairs found
         */
        private long[] last10 = {
            3, 5, 11, 17, 29, 41, 59, 71, 101, 107
        };

        /**
         * Current integer being evaluated
         */
        private long n;

        /**
         * Starts the thread if it is not already
         * running.
         */
        public void start()
        {
            if (kicker == null) {
                kicker = new Thread(this);
                kicker.setPriority(Thread.MIN_PRIORITY);
```

```
                    kicker.setDaemon(true);
                    kicker.start();
            }
    }

    /**
     * Stops the thread
     */
    public void stop()
    {
        if (kicker != null)
            kicker = null;
    }

    /**
     * Runs the prime pair search thread
     */
    public void run()
    {
        int N = last10.length;
        n = last10[N-1];
        while (kicker != null) {
            n += 2;
            if (isPrime(n) && isPrime(n+2)) {
                synchronized(last10) {
                    for (int i = 1; i < N; i++)
                        last10[i-1] = last10[i];
                    last10[N-1] = n;
                }
            }
        }
    }

    /**
     * Returns the list of the last ten primes
     */
    public synchronized long[] getLast10()
    {
        long[] list = new long[last10.length];
        System.arraycopy(last10, 0, list, 0, last10.length);
        return list;
    }

    /**
     * Returns the list as a string
     */
    public String toString()
    {
        long[] list = getLast10();
        StringBuffer buffer = new StringBuffer();
        buffer.append("<TABLE BORDER=0 CELLPADDING=3>");
        for (int i = 0; i < list.length; i++) {
            buffer.append("<TR>");
            buffer.append("<TD>");
            buffer.append(list[i]);
            buffer.append("</TD>");
            buffer.append("<TD>");
```

Figure 13-13

(Continued)

```java
            buffer.append(list[i] + 2);
            buffer.append("</TD>");
            buffer.append("</TR>");
        }
        buffer.append("</TABLE>");
        return buffer.toString();
    }

    /**
     * Returns the current integer being evaluated
     */
    public long getNumber()
    {
        return n;
    }

    /**
     * Returns true if the specified integer is prime
     */
    public boolean isPrime(long n)
    {
        final long[] list = {
            2, 3, 5, 7, 11, 13, 17, 19, 23, 29,
        };
        long divisor = 1;

        for (int i = 0; i < list.length; i++) {
            divisor = list[i];
            if (n < divisor) return false;
            if (n == divisor) return true;
            if ((n % divisor) == 0) return false;
        }

        for (;;) {
            divisor += 2;
            long remainder = n % divisor;
            if (divisor != n)
                if (remainder == 0)
                    return false;
            long quotient = n / divisor;
            if (divisor > quotient)
                return true;
        }
    }
}
%>
<CENTER>
<%
    // Check for start request

    String start = request.getParameter("start");
    if (start != null) {
        synchronized(this) {
            if (pps == null) {
                pps = new SearchThread();
                pps.start();
            }
```

Figure 13-13
(Continued)

```
        }
    }

    // Check for stop request
    String stop = request.getParameter("stop");
    if (stop != null) {
        pps.stop();
        long lastN = pps.getNumber();
        pps = null;
%>
<H3>Prime Pairs Search Cancelled
    at <%= lastN %></H3>
<%
    }
    else if (pps == null) {
%>
<H3>Prime Pairs Search Not Running</H3>
<%
    }
    else {
%>
<H3>Last Ten Prime Pairs Found:</H3>
<%= pps %>
</CENTER>
<%
    }
%>
```

PrimePairSearcher.jsp partitions the task into work for two classes: the JSP itself and a static SearchThread object. SearchThread is an inner class defined in a declaration section. It performs the actual prime pair search, always maintaining a list of the last 10 prime pairs it has found. The JSP, on the other hand, simply creates and starts the SearchThread during JSP initialization, reports its progress when requested (see Figure 13-14), and stops it when the JSP is unloaded. It also can accept START and STOP commands as parameters in an HTTP request (see Figure 13-15).

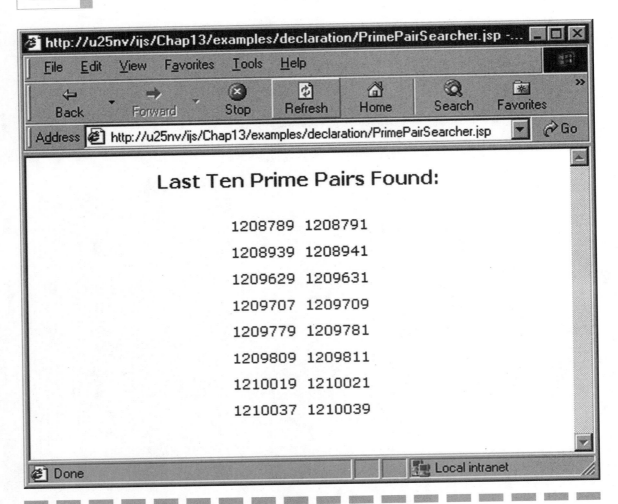

Figure 13-14 A Snapshot of the Progress of the Prime Pairs Search

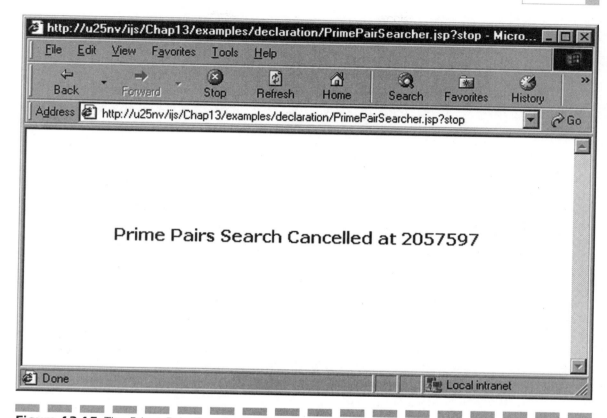

Figure 13-15 *The Prime Pairs Search after Being Cancelled*

13.5 Comments

Syntax

```
<%- Hidden comments -%>
```

Description

In addition to the ordinary comments `<!- comment ->` used in HTML, JSP makes provision for hidden comments. These are comments that are intended for the JSP source code alone and not for the generated HTML. The comments and their enclosing brackets do not appear in the generated HTML document.

A side effect of using this comment format is that no code between the opening <%– and ending –%> is interpreted. This can be used to temporarily disable (comment out) JSP code. Beware, however, that hidden comments do not nest. If you have one section of code commented out, you cannot comment out a larger section that contains it.

Thus, when would you use one comment style or another? It makes sense to use hidden comments to document the compilation aspects of the JSP page itself, such as special instructions for the JSP author or information about JavaBeans or other dependencies. Ordinary HTML comments are better suited for marking sections of the generated document that may be postprocessed by other programs. For example, <SCRIPT> or <STYLE> sections typically use HTML comments to prevent their contents from being misinterpreted by older Web browsers that do not handle JavaScript or stylesheets. Of course, within a scriptlet or declaration section, you also can use the regular Java comment styles, the same as you would in any other Java program.

Examples

Here are both types of comments:

```
<!– This comment will be visible in the HTML source –>
<%– but this one will not –%>
```

and here is an example of the use of the hidden comment syntax to temporarily disable code:

```
<%–
<%
   doSomethingReallyDangerous();
%>
–%>
```

Code interpretation is suppressed inside hidden comments but not HTML comments. This allows you to generate dynamic content inside HTML comments. A typical use would be to save information about the compilation date and time for debugging purposes, as shown below.

```
<!–
   JSP name:          <%= this.getClass().getName() %>
   Servlet engine:    <%= application.getServerInfo() %>
   Date produced:     <%= new java.util.Date() %>
–>
```

```
<HTML>
<BODY>
Use the <CODE>view source</CODE> menu option
to see the generated comments.
</BODY>
</HTML>
```

When the JSP is requested, it produces HTML like that shown below:

```
<!--
    JSP name:         jsp.ijs.Chap13.examples.comments.InsertDate
    Servlet engine:   JRun/2.3.3 build 153
    Date produced:    Mon Jan 24 13:23:45 EST 2000
-->
<HTML>
<BODY>
Use the <CODE>view source</CODE> menu option
to see the generated comments.
</BODY>
</HTML>
```

13.6   Including Files

Syntax

```
<%@ include file="name" %>
<jsp:include page="name" flush="true" />
```

Description

It is quite convenient to be able to include the contents of other files into a JSP page. This makes it easier to use standard HTML headers and footers or to share common code among multiple JSP pages. The JavaServer Pages specification provides two different means to accomplish this:

1. The `<%@ include %>` directive for static content. This directive includes the contents of the specified URL into the Java source file at the time it is first compiled. This is not a run-time operation—it only includes whatever were the contents of the URL at compile time.

2. The `<jsp:include>` action for either static or dynamic content. This action includes the contents of the specified URL into the

Java source file at run time. The URL may refer either to a static resource such as an HTML document or to a dynamic resource such as a servlet or another JSP page. Note that `<jsp:include>` is an XML tag and so must be terminated with `/>` or with an ending `</jsp:include>` tag.

Examples

A typical use for included files might be legal disclaimers that show up as footnotes in other documents. Since these disclaimers may be used in a number of places, it may be useful to keep them in a separate document.

The `<%@ include %>` Directive   Figure 13-16 shows a fragment of a JSP page used in a marketing Web page. The JSP page has two footnotes and uses the `<%@ include %>` directive to include another JSP page that actually generates the footnote text, as listed in Figure 13-17. When the two documents are merged, they produce the appropriately disclaimed output shown in Figure 13-18.

To see exactly how this is accomplished, let's look at the source code for the generated servlet,[6] shown in Figure 13-19. The JSP translator generates `out.print()` statements to write the text from the main JSP page. Then, when it encounters the `<%@ include %>` directive, it reads and translates the `Disclaimers.jsp` file, copying its scriptlet code verbatim and replacing its HTML with `out.print()` statements. If you check the JSP scratch directory where the translated source code is kept, you will not find `Disclaimers.java`. This is so because it is not treated as an individual compilation unit; its contents are simply merged into the overall JSP source code and translated with its including JSP page. In this respect, it is very similar to the `#include` C preprocessor directive.

---

[6]This is the GNUJSP version. The source code has been re-formatted slightly for readability.

Figure 13-16

A JSP That Uses a Static `include` Directive

```
Old Carpet Soda<sup><font size="-1">1</font></sup>
contains nothing but the finest
natural ingredients<sup><font size="-1">2</font></sup>.
<%@ include file="Disclaimers.jsp" %>
```

Figure 13-17

The Included JSP

```
<BR>
<HR ALIGN=LEFT WIDTH=200>
<%
    String[] text = {
        "This is not an offering to sell,"
            + " which may only be made by prospectus.",
        "Some traces of polyvinylchloride remain"
            + " after purification process.",
    };
    for (int i = 0; i < text.length; i++) {
        int footnoteNumber = i+1;
%>
<EM>
<FONT SIZE="-1">
<SUP><%= footnoteNumber %></SUP> <%= text[i] %>
</FONT>
</EM>
<BR>
<%
    }
%>
```

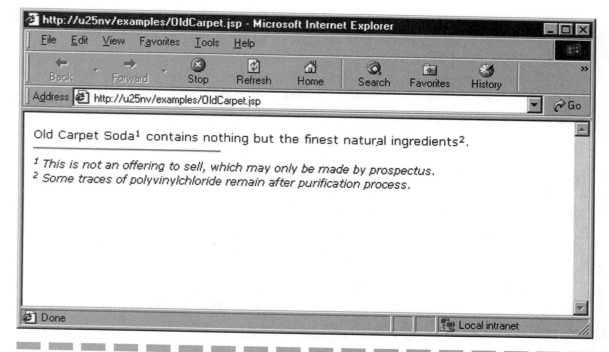

Figure 13-18 `OldCarpet.jsp` with Disclaimers Included

Figure 13-19
A Servlet
Generated for a
JSP Page with a
Static include
Action

```
/*
    Generated by JavaEmitter on Sun Jan 23 14:47:48 EST 2000
    Please do not modify.
 */
import java.io.IOException;
import javax.servlet.*;
import javax.servlet.http.*;
import javax.servlet.jsp.*;

public class jsp___2fexamples_2fOldCarpet_2ejsp
    extends org.gjt.jsp.HttpJspPageImpl
{
    public final long _gnujspGetTimestamp()
    {
        return 948656868543L;
    }

    private static final String[] _gnujspDeps = new String[]
    {"/examples/OldCarpet.jsp", "/examples/Disclaimers.jsp"};

    public final String[] _gnujspGetDeps()
    {
        return _gnujspDeps;
    }

    public final long _gnujspGetCompilerVersion()
    {
        return 1999101701L;
    }

    public void _jspService(
            HttpServletRequest request,
            HttpServletResponse response)
        throws ServletException, IOException
    {
        response.setContentType("text/html");
        JspFactory factory = JspFactory.getDefaultFactory();
        PageContext pageContext = factory.getPageContext
            (this, request, response, null, true, 8192, true);
        HttpSession session = pageContext.getSession();
        ServletContext application =
            pageContext.getServletConfig().getServletContext();
        JspWriter out = pageContext.getOut();
        ServletConfig config = pageContext.getServletConfig();
        Object page = this;

        try {

            // line:/examples/OldCarpet.jsp:1

            out.print("Old Carpet Soda<sup><font size=\"-1\">"
                + "1</font></sup>\ncontains nothing but the"
                + " finest\nnatural ingredients<sup><font"
                + " size=\"-1\">2</font></sup>.\n");

            // line:/examples/Disclaimers.jsp:1
```

```
                    out.print ("<BR>\n<HR ALIGN=LEFT WIDTH=200>\n");

                    // line:/examples/Disclaimers.jsp:4

                    String[] text = {
                       "This is not an offering to sell,"
                       + " which may only be made by prospectus.",
                       "Some traces of polyvinylchloride remain"
                       + " after purification process.",
                    };

                    for (int i = 0; i < text.length; i++) {
                       int footnoteNumber = i+1;

                       // line:/examples/Disclaimers.jsp:13

                       out.print ("\n<EM>\n<FONT SIZE=\"-1\">\n<SUP>");

                       // line:/examples/Disclaimers.jsp:15

                       out.print ( footnoteNumber );

                       // line:/examples/Disclaimers.jsp:15

                       out.print ("</SUP> ");

                       // line:/examples/Disclaimers.jsp:15

                       out.print ( text[i] );

                       // line:/examples/Disclaimers.jsp:16

                       out.print ("\n</FONT>\n</EM>\n<BR>\n");

                       // line:/examples/Disclaimers.jsp:20

                    }

                    // line:/examples/Disclaimers.jsp:22

                    out.print ("\n\n");
                 }
                 catch (Exception e) {
                    out.clearBuffer ();
                    pageContext.handlePageException (e);
                 }
                 finally {
                    out.close ();
                    factory.releasePageContext (pageContext);
                 }
              }
           }
```

The `<jsp:include>` Action   A quite different effect is produced by the `<jsp:include>` action. Whereas the `<%@ include %>` directive is evaluated just once, at translation time, the `<jsp:include>` action is evaluated dynamically each time a request is made to the including JSP page. If the file to be included is a JSP page, it will be invoked, and its output will be merged with the output of the including JSP page. Figure 13-20 shows a version of the `OldCarpet.jsp` page that uses this dynamic include capability.

Figure 13-21 lists the source code for the generated servlet. This time, we see that in evaluating the `<jsp:include>` action, the JSP translator simply writes a line invoking the `pageContext.include()` method. If we track down the source code for the JSP translator object that implements the `javax.servlet.jsp.PageContext` interface,[7] we see that this is handled by creating a `RequestDispatcher` for the file to be included and calling its `include()` method. The included file does not even have to exist until it is called.

Which Approach to Use   So which method should you use? If all you are doing is including standard text, the `<%@ include %>` directive is more efficient, since it incorporates everything it needs into the calling file at JSP translation time. On the other hand, if the content of the included file changes depending on the context in which it is called, you need to use the `<jsp:include>` action. As you always suspected, this is how automated customer service wait times are calculated:

```
CallWaiting.jsp:
Your call will be answered in approximately
<jsp:include page="random.jsp" flush="true" /> hours and
<jsp:include page="random.jsp" flush="true" /> minutes.
Please stay on the line.

random.jsp:
<%= (int)(Math.random() * 60) %>
```

---

[7]Which is `org.gjt.jsp.PageContextImpl` in this case.

Figure 13-20

`OldCarpet.jsp` with a Dynamic include Action

```
Old Carpet Soda<sup><font size="-1">1</font></sup>
contains nothing but the finest
natural ingredients<sup><font size="-1">2</font></sup>.
<jsp:include page="Disclaimers.jsp" flush="true"/>
```

Figure 13-21

A Servlet
Generated for a
JSP Page with a
Dynamic include
Action

```
/*
    Generated by JavaEmitter on Sun Jan 23 15:50:14 EST 2000
    Please do not modify.
 */

import java.io.IOException;
import javax.servlet.*;
import javax.servlet.http.*;
import javax.servlet.jsp.*;

public class jsp___2fexamples_2fDynamicOldCarpet_2ejsp
    extends org.gjt.jsp.HttpJspPageImpl
{
    public final long _gnujspGetTimestamp()
    {
        return 948660614269L;
    }

    private static final String[] _gnujspDeps = new String[]
        {"/examples/DynamicOldCarpet.jsp"};

    public final String[] _gnujspGetDeps()
    {
        return _gnujspDeps;
    }

    public final long _gnujspGetCompilerVersion()
    {
        return 1999101701L;
    }

    public void _jspService (
            HttpServletRequest request,
            HttpServletResponse response)
        throws ServletException, IOException
    {
        response.setContentType("text/html");
        JspFactory factory = JspFactory.getDefaultFactory();
        PageContext pageContext = factory.getPageContext
            (this, request, response, null, true, 8192, true);
        HttpSession session = pageContext.getSession ();
        ServletContext application =
            pageContext.getServletConfig().getServletContext();
        JspWriter out = pageContext.getOut();
        ServletConfig config = pageContext.getServletConfig();
        Object page = this;
        try {

            // line:/examples/DynamicOldCarpet.jsp:1

            out.print ("Old Carpet Soda<sup><font size=\"-1\">"
                + "1</font></sup>\ncontains nothing but the"
                + " finest\nnatural ingredients<sup><font"
                + " size=\"-1\">2</font></sup>.\n");

            // line:/examples/DynamicOldCarpet.jsp:4
```

Figure 13-21
(Continued)

```
        pageContext.include ("Disclaimers.jsp");

        // line:/examples/DynamicOldCarpet.jsp:5

        out.print ("\n");

    }
    catch (Exception e) {
        out.clearBuffer ();
        pageContext.handlePageException (e);
    }
    finally {
        out.close ();
        factory.releasePageContext (pageContext);
    }
  }
}
```

13.7 Forwarding Requests

Syntax

```
<jsp:forward page="url"/>
```

Description

The `<jsp:forward>` action forwards an HTTP request to another file to be handled. The URL can refer to another JSP page, a servlet, or an HTML file and can be either relative to the current document URL or absolute. After the request is forwarded, the JSP engine does no further processing in the current JSP page. A typical use of `<jsp:forward>` might be in a JSP page that queries a database and saves its results in an intermediate object that is rendered by another JSP page that creates an HTML table. Note that `<jsp:forward>` is an XML tag and so must be terminated with `/>`.

Examples

Request forwarding can be used to make a clean separation between processing logic and presentation logic. Figure 13-22 shows an example of a JSP page that does only calculation. Its input and output are handled by other Web resources; the input comes from an HTML page, and the output is rendered by another JSP page.

Figure 13-22

A JSP Page That
Uses the
`<jsp:forward>`
Action

```
<%@ page import="java.util.*" %>
<%
    String number = request.getParameter("number");
    if (number == null) {
%>
<jsp:forward page="NumberPrompt.html"/>
<%
        return;
    }
    int n = Integer.parseInt(number);
    Vector v = new Vector();
    for (int base = 2; base <= n; base++) {
        int exp = 0;
        while ((n % base) == 0) {
            exp++;
            n /= base;
        }
        if (exp > 0) {
            v.addElement(new Integer(base));
            v.addElement(new Integer(exp));
        }
    }
    request.setAttribute("factors", v);
%>
<jsp:forward page="ShowFactors.jsp"/>
```

PrimeFactors.jsp looks for a request parameter called number. If it does not find one, it forwards the request to NumberPrompt.html, which uses the HTML form shown in Figure 13-23 to prompt for the desired parameter. The action attribute of the form refers back to the PrimeFactors.jsp page. Once the JSP page is invoked with a suitable number (see Figure 13-24), it calculates the number's prime factors, saving them in a java.util.Vector. The vector itself is stored as an attribute of the request, which is then forwarded to ShowFactors.jsp.

Again, it is useful to look at the generated servlet (shown in Figure 13-25) to see exactly how the `<jsp:forward>` actions are handled. In both cases, the JSP translator invokes the pageContext.forward() method, which itself uses the RequestDispatcher forward() method to handle the request.

Figure 13-23

HTML Used to
Supply the
Number to
PrimeFactors.
jsp

```
<HTML>
<BODY>
<H3>Prime Factors</H3>
<FORM ACTION="PrimeFactors.jsp">
Number to be factored:
<INPUT TYPE="text" NAME="number" SIZE="8">
<INPUT TYPE="submit" VALUE="Go">
</FORM>
</BODY>
</HTML>
```

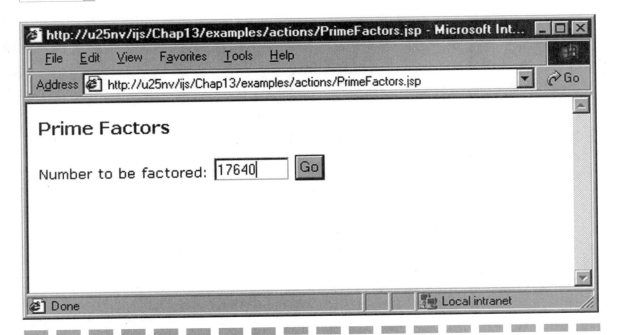

Figure 13-24 The Number Prompt for `PrimeFactors.jsp`

When it receives the request, `ShowFactors.jsp` (listed in Figure 13-26) retrieves the number with `request.getParameter()` and the vector with `request.getAttribute()`. Using this information, it is able to create HTML that displays the prime factorization of the number, as shown in Figure 13-27.

Figure 13-25
The Servlet
Generated for
PrimeFactors.j
sp

```java
// Generated by JRun, do not edit

package jsp.ijs.Chap13.examples.actions;

import java.io.*;
import java.util.*;
import java.net.*;
import java.beans.*;

import javax.servlet.*;
import javax.servlet.http.*;
import javax.servlet.jsp.*;

import com.livesoftware.jsp.*;
import com.livesoftware.scripting.*;

import java.util.*;

public class PrimeFactors extends HttpJSPServlet
    implements JRunJspPage
{
    public void _jspService(
        HttpServletRequest request,
        HttpServletResponse response)
      throws ServletException, IOException
    {
        ServletConfig config = getServletConfig();
        ServletContext application = config.getServletContext();

        Object page = (Object) this;
        PageContext pageContext =
            JspFactory.getDefaultFactory().getPageContext
            (this, request, response,  null, true, 8192, true);
        JspWriter out = pageContext.getOut();

        HttpSession session = request.getSession(true);
        response.setContentType("text/html");

        String number = request.getParameter("number");
        if (number == null) {
            pageContext.forward("NumberPrompt.html");
            return;
        }

        int n = Integer.parseInt(number);
        Vector v = new Vector();
        for (int base = 2; base <= n; base++) {
            int exp = 0;
            while ((n % base) == 0) {
                exp++;
                n /= base;
            }
            if (exp > 0) {
                v.addElement(new Integer(base));
                v.addElement(new Integer(exp));
            }
        }
```

```
        request.setAttribute("factors", v);
        pageContext.forward("ShowFactors.jsp");
        out.flush();
    }

    private static final String[] __dependencies__ = {""};

    public String[] __getDependencies()
    {
        return __dependencies__;
    }
}
```

```
<%@ page import="java.util.*" %>
<BODY>
<H3>Prime Factors</H3>
<%= request.getParameter("number") %>
=
<%
    Vector v = (Vector) request.getAttribute("factors");
    for (int i = 0; i < v.size(); i += 2) {
        int base = ((Integer) v.elementAt(i)).intValue();
        int exp  = ((Integer) v.elementAt(i+1)).intValue();
        if (i > 0)
            out.print(" times ");
        out.print(base);
        if (exp > 1)
            out.print("<sup>" + exp + "</sup>");
    }
%>
</BODY>
```

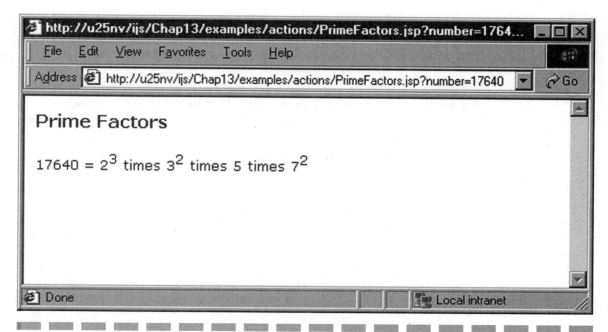

Figure 13-27 The Prime Factorization of 17640

13.8 The Page Directive

Syntax

```
<%@ page
      [language="java" ]
      [extends="className" ]
      [import=package.*,package.*,..."]
      [session="true|false" ]
      [buffer="none|8kb|sizekb" ]
      [autoFlush="true|false" ]
      [isThreadSafe="true|false" ]
      [info="text" ]
      [errorPage="url" ]
      [contentType="mimeType" [;charset=charSet" ]
      [isErrorPage="true|false" ]
%>
```

Description

The page directive sets the attributes of the JSP page as a whole, including any files that are included with the <%@ include %> directive. All the `page` directive's attributes are optional and may be specified only once, with the exception of the `import` attribute. The following subsections will discuss each of the attributes and how they are used.

language   The `language` attribute specifies the language used in scriptlets, declarations, and expressions. Currently, the only valid value is `java`, although, in principle, other languages may be supported later. According to the JavaServer Pages specification, any future scripting language must support the Java Runtime Environment, implicit variables, JavaBeans component properties, and public methods, so it is a little difficult to imagine something terribly different from Java emerging anytime soon.

extends   JSP pages normally extend a superclass chosen by the JSP container. You can create your own superclass, however, and specify its fully qualified name in the `page` directive's `extends` attribute. This superclass must implement the `javax.servlet.jsp.HttpJspPage` interface, which by inheritance requires classes to implement the `javax.servlet.jsp.JSPPage` and `javax.servlet.Servlet` interfaces as well. This means that the JSP base class must provide implementations for the ordinary servlet methods as well as the `jspInit()` and `jspDestroy()` methods for startup and shutdown. When the JSP container creates a servlet from your `.jsp` file, it generates a `_jspService()` method for handling requests.

For pages created by the JRun JSP container, the default superclass is `com.livesoftware.jsp.HttpJSPServlet`, which itself extends `GenericServlet`. ServletExec subclasses New Atlanta's `JSP10HttpJspPage` class, which implements all the interface methods directly. GNUJSP's `org.gjt.jsp.HttpJspPageImpl` extends the standard `HttpServlet` class, calling the `jspInit()`, `jspDestroy()`, and `_jspService()` methods from within its `init()`, `destroy()`, and `service()` methods.

Why would you want to use a different base class?[8] For one thing, this allows you to add debugging and trace information, providing breakpoint targets for a servlet debugger. In addition, you can supply additional functionality to your subclasses in your `init()` and `destroy()` methods. For example, you could have a base class that automatically allo-

---

[8]Especially since the JavaServer Pages specification warns you not to try this unless you know what you are doing.

cates a database connection when it is loaded and deallocates it when unloaded. Figure 13-28 shows an abstract JSP base class that does this.

This base class (ijs.jsp.ConnectedPage) automatically connects to the U.S. Department of Agriculture ((USDA) nutrient database in its init() method and disconnects in its destroy() method. It stores a reference to the connection object in a protected variable. Any JSP page can take advantage of this connection simply by specifying extends="ijs.jsp.ConnectedPage" in its page directive. Figure 13-29 demonstrates this, using the FoodGroups JSP example described in Section 13.4.

Since FoodGroups.jsp is a subclass of ijs.jsp.ConnectedPage, it can directly access the database connection in the protected variable con much the same as any other implicit object. It uses the connection object to perform an Structured Query Language (SQL) query, displaying the results in an HTML table, as shown in Figure 13-30.

import Like any other Java class, a JSP page can import class definitions. In order for the Java compiler to resolve these definitions, the JSP page's generated Java source code must have import statements. You provide these statements using the import attribute of the page directive. You can specify multiple classes or packages by separating them with commas, like this:

```
<%@page import="java.sql.*,ijs.jdbc.*,mypackage.MyClass" %>
```

or commas and whitespace, like this:

```
<%@page import="
   java.sql.*,
   ijs.jdbc.*,
   mypackage.MyClass" %>
```

or by specifying multiple page directives, like this:

```
<%@page import="java.sql.*" %>
<%@page import="ijs.jdbc.*" %>
<%@page import="mypackage.MyClass" %>
```

All three methods produce the same functional result in your generated code:

```
import java.sql.*;
import ijs.jdbc.*;
import mypackage.MyClass;
```

Figure 13-28

A JSP Base Class
That Automatically
Provides a
Database
Connection

```java
package ijs.jsp;

import java.io.*;
import java.net *;
import java.sql.*;
import java.util.*;
import javax.servlet.*;
import javax.servlet.http.*;
import javax.servlet.jsp.*;

/**
 * A abstract JSP base class that automatically
 * connects to the USDA nutrient database when
 * first loaded and disconnects when unloaded.
 */
public abstract class ConnectedPage implements HttpJspPage
{
    /**
     * JDBC driver name
     */
    private static final String DRIVER_NAME =
        "sun.jdbc.odbc.JdbcOdbcDriver";

    /**
     * Nutrient database URL
     */
    private static final String URL = "jdbc:odbc:usda";

    /**
     * The servlet configuration object.
     */
    private ServletConfig config;

    /**
     * The database connection object
     */
    protected Connection con;

    /**
     * Performs any initialization that must be done
     * when the JSP is first loaded.
     */
    public void jspInit()
    {
    }

    /**
     * Performs any tasks that must be done when the
     * JSP is unloaded.
     */
    public void jspDestroy()
    {
    }

    /**
     * Initializes the JSP by saving the <CODE>config</CODE>
     * object, creating a database connection, and then
```

Figure 13-28

(Continued)

```
   *  calling <CODE>jspInit()</CODE>.
   */
   public void init(ServletConfig config)
      throws ServletException
   {
      this.config = config;
      ServletContext context = config.getServletContext();

      // Open the implicit database connection

      context.log("Connecting to database");
      try {
         Class.forName(DRIVER_NAME);
         con = DriverManager.getConnection(URL);
      }
      catch (Exception e) {
         context.log("Connection failed");
         throw new ServletException
         (e.getMessage());
      }
      context.log("Connected");


      // and then call jspInit

      jspInit();
   }

   /**
    * Returns a reference to the servlet configuration
    * object.
    */
   public ServletConfig getServletConfig()
   {
      return config;
   }

   /**
    * Handles servlet requests by calling the
    * <CODE>_jspService()</CODE> method
    */
   public void service(
         ServletRequest request,
         ServletResponse response)
      throws ServletException, IOException
   {
      _jspService(
         (HttpServletRequest) request,
         (HttpServletResponse) response);
   }

   /**
    * Returns information about the servlet
    */
   public String getServletInfo()
   {
      return "ConnectedPage";
```

Figure 13-28
(Continued)

```
    }

/**
 * Calls <CODE>jspDestroy</CODE> when
 * the JSP is unloaded.
 */
public void destroy()
{
    jspDestroy();

    // Close the implicit database connection

    ServletContext context = config.getServletContext();
    if (con == null) {
        context.log("No connection to close");
    }
    else {
        try {
            context.log("Closing connection");
            con.close();
            con = null;
            context.log("Connection closed");
        }
        catch (SQLException e) {
            context.log("Closing failed: " + e.getMessage());
        }
    }
}
```

JSP pages automatically import `java.lang.*`, `javax.servlet.*`, `javax.servlet.http.*`, and `javax.servlet.jsp.*`. Some JSP containers import more than this, but you cannot count on it. If you want your JSP page to be portable, you should explicitly import any other packages you need besides those listed above.

session By default, JSP pages automatically use an `HttpSession` object, creating a new one if necessary. You access the session simply by using the implicit `session` variable. If you do not need to use session features, you can inhibit this behavior by specifying `session="false"` in the `page` directive. Doing so will save memory by not creating unnecessary sessions. See Chapter 7 for details about HTTP sessions.

buffer and `autoFlush` The JavaServer Pages specification gives you a certain amount of control over how and when your output is written based on the values specified for the `buffer` and `autoFlush` attributes of the `page` directive. Table 13-3 describes the effects of specifying various values for each. If you do not specify otherwise, an 8-kb buffer will be used, and output will be autoflushed.

Figure 13-29
A JSP Page That
Accesses the
Automatic
Database
Connection

```
<%@ page extends="ijs.jsp.ConnectedPage"
        import="java.sql.*" %>
<%!
    public final String COLORS[] = {
        "#F0F0F0", "#E0E0E0", "#C0C0C0"
    };
%>
<%
    try {
        synchronized(con) {
            String sql =
                " SELECT * FROM FD_GROUP"
                + " WHERE FDGP_CD LIKE '1%'"
                + " ORDER BY FDGP_CD"
                ;
            Statement stmt = con.createStatement();
            ResultSet rs = stmt.executeQuery(sql);
            int row = 0;
%>
    <CENTER>
    <H3>Food Groups in the 1000 Series</H3>
    <EM>Powered by <B>ConnectedPage.java</B></EM><P>
    <TABLE BORDER=0 CELLPADDING=2>
    <TR ALIGN="LEFT">
        <TH BGCOLOR="<%= COLORS[2] %>">Code</TH>
        <TH BGCOLOR="<%= COLORS[2] %>">Description</TH>
    </TR>
<%
        while (rs.next()) {
            row++;
            String code = rs.getString(1);
            String desc = rs.getString(2);
%>
    <TR>
        <TD BGCOLOR="<%= COLORS[row % 2] %>"><%= code %></TD>
        <TD BGCOLOR="<%= COLORS[row % 2] %>"><%= desc %></TD>
    </TR>
<%
        }
%>
    </TABLE>
    </CENTER>
<%
        rs.close();
        stmt.close();
        }
    }
    catch (SQLException e) {
%>
<H3>Error: <%= e.getMessage() %></H3>
<%
    }
%>
```

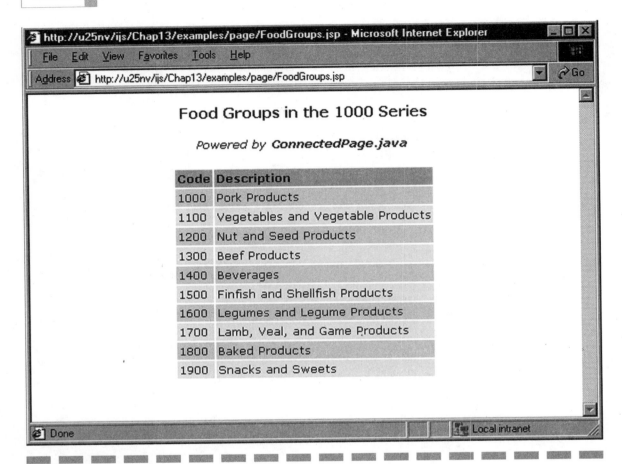

Figure 13-30 Output of FoodGroups.jsp

isThreadSafe Unless you specify isThreadSafe="false" in the page directive, your JSP page will adopt the standard servlet threading model, which means that there will be one instance of your JSP class running with each request running in a separate thread. You can cause the JSP page to use the other approach (SingleThreadModel) by specifying isThreadSafe="false". See Chapter 9 for a discussion of the two threading models and their implications.

info The javax.http.Servlet interface, which all JSP pages must implement, provides for a method called getServletInfo(), which can be used by a GUI administrative application that manages the servlet

TABLE 13-3

buffer	autoFlush	action
none	true	Characters are written directly to the response object's writer object.
none	false	Illegal; should cause a compile error, but this requirement is widely ignored.
8kb	true	(Default setting) An 8192-byte buffer is used. When it is full, it is written to the response object's writer object, and the buffer is cleared.
8kb	false	An 8192-byte buffer is used. When it is full, a java.io.Exception is thrown.
*size*kb	true	A buffer of the specified number of kilobytes is used. When it is full, it is written to the response object's writer object, and the buffer is cleared.
*size*kb	false	A buffer of the specified number of kilobytes is used. When it is full, a java.io.Exception is thrown.

engine. When called, this method should return a string containing identifying information about the JSP page. Rather than implementing this method directly, you should specify the info="text" attribute in the page directive, and the JSP translator will create a getServletInfo() method for you.

contentType If you do not specify otherwise, your JSP page will set the content type of the response object's writer to text/html. You can indicate that a different content type should be used by specifying it in the contentType attribute of the page directive. Although the JavaServer Pages specification does not explicitly mention it, this content type must be character-based, not binary. The reason for this is that the _jspService() method automatically creates a javax.servlet.jsp.JspWriter object and initializes it by calling the response object's getWriter() method. The JspWriter is a direct subclass of java.io.Writer and has no methods for writing binary data. Since the getWriter() method has already been called before you can do anything about it, you cannot legally[9] call getOutputStream() to get a byte-oriented output stream. When you need to generate binary data—to send image data, for example—a servlet is a better choice than a JSP page.

---

[9]It seems to work anyway with JRun, but you cannot count on this behavior.

errorPage and isErrorPage The `errorPage` attribute is a very handy way to specify the name of another JSP page that should be invoked if the current page throws any unhandled exceptions. If you do this, then you do not need to enclose your scriptlet code in `try` ... `catch` blocks. The error page will be invoked automatically if an exception is thrown, and it will be able to access the implicit `exception` object. The `ErrorPage` JSP page must specify `isErrorPage="true"` for it to be able to access `exception`.

Figure 13-31 shows how a JSP page can benefit from this feature. This JSP page is used to calculate a loan monthly payment from a principal amount, an annual interest rate, and a term in years. It expects these values to be passed as parameters. If any of them are omitted or not numeric, an error message should be displayed. The combination of the `if` ... `then` ... `else` logic and the `try` ... `catch` blocks makes the code hard to follow.

This can be tidied up nicely using an error page. Figure 13-32 shows the same JSP page with the error messages produced by throwing run-time exceptions. Taking advantage of the fact that execution of a Java method terminates after an exception is thrown, the amortization JSP page can do away with the `if` ... `then` ... `else`. The `ErrorPage` JSP page (see Figure 13-33) is invoked whenever an exception occurs (either these deliberately thrown exceptions or any unanticipated ones that the JSP page may throw).

Figure 13-34 shows the output of the simple error page. In this case, all we do is write one line with the text of the exception. It is quite easy, however, to add a stack trace and detailed context information, making the error page an easy-to-add debugging tool.

Figure 13-35 lists an error page that does all this. It uses a set of radio buttons with which the user can select various diagnostic information, much like a tabbed dialog. The available diagnostics include a stack trace, information about the servlet request, the form parameters, the servlet context, and the HTTP session. Associated with each radio button is a two-character code that serves as the panel ID. When a button is clicked, the JavaScript `onClick` event is triggered, which is handled with `this.form.submit()`. The panel ID code becomes available as a form parameter. Based on this code, the appropriate panel is generated.

Figure 13-36 shows the stack trace diagnostic panel. The information for this panel is generated by a call to the `printStackTrace()` method of the implicit `exception` object, bracketed with `<PRE>` and `</PRE>` tags. This is similar to the common use of `printStackTrace()` in a catch block, except here a `PrintWriter` object is required, since the out-

Figure 13-31

A JSP Page That
Calculates a Loan
Monthly Payment

```jsp
<%@ page
       import="java.text.*"
%>
<%
   String parm,
   double p = 0;
   double i = 0;
   int n = 0;

   // Get principal amount

   parm = request.getParameter("p");
   if (parm == null) {
%>
<H3>Error: No principal amount specified</H3>
<%
   }
   else {
      try {
         p = Double.valueOf(parm).doubleValue();

         // Get interest rate

         parm = request.getParameter("i");
         if (parm == null) {
%>
<H3>Error: No interest rate specified</H3>
<%
         }
         else {
            try {
               i = Double.valueOf(parm).doubleValue();

               // Get term in months

               parm = request.getParameter("n");
               if (parm == null) {
%>
<H3>Error: No term specified</H3>
<%
               }
               else {
                  try {
                     n = Integer.parseInt(parm);

                     // Convert to monthly

                     i /= 1200;
                     n *= 12;

                     // Calculate monthly payment

                     double fv =
                        Math.pow((1 + i), (double) n);
                     double pmt = p * i * fv / (fv - 1);
                     DecimalFormat fmt =
                        new DecimalFormat("#####.00");
```

Figure 13-31

(Continued)

```
%>
<H3>Monthly payment = <%= fmt.format(pmt) %></H3>
<%
                    }
                        catch (NumberFormatException e) {
%>
<H3>Error: Term not numeric</H3>
<%
                    }
                }
            }
            catch (NumberFormatException e) {
%>
<H3>Error: Interest not numeric</H3>
<%
                }
            }
        }
        catch (NumberFormatException e) {
%>
<H3>Error: Principal not numeric</H3>
<%
            }
    }
%>
```

put is not going to `System.err`. We cannot use the implicit `out` object directly because `JspWriter` is not a subclass of `PrintWriter`.

The servlet request diagnostic panel is shown in Figure 13-37. The code that produces this panel uses parallel `java.util.Vector` objects to store the names and values of the request attributes.[10] The code walks through the `getAttributeNames()` and `getHeaderNames()` enumerations and stores their name-value pairs in the two vectors. Additionally, it calls the explicit `getXXX()` methods of `HttpServletRequest` and its superclass, `ServletRequest`. The name and value vectors are sorted before being written to the output stream.

Figure 13-38 shows the form parameters panel. This code is slightly more complicated because the original parameters are replaced the first time you click a radio button to switch to a different view. The program gets around this by saving the original values in a hashtable, which is then stored in the HTTP session.

The servlet context panel is useful if your servlet engine supports the 2.1 API or higher. ApacheJServ 1.1 does not, so there are several servlet

---

[10]This could be done more easily with a `java.util.SortedMap` if your server environment is entirely JDK 1.2 or later.

Figure 13-32

The Same JSP Page Using an Error Page

```
<%@ page
        import="java.text.*"
        errorPage="ErrorPage.jsp"
%>
<%
    String parm;
    double p = 0;
    double i = 0;
    int n = 0;

    // Get principal amount

    parm = request.getParameter("p");
    if (parm == null)
        throw new RuntimeException
        ("No principal amount specified");
    try {
        p = Double.valueOf(parm).doubleValue();
    }
    catch (NumberFormatException e) {
        throw new RuntimeException
        ("Principal is not numeric");
    }

    // Get interest rate

    parm = request.getParameter("i");
    if (parm == null)
        throw new RuntimeException
        ("No interest rate specified");
    try {
        i = Double.valueOf(parm).doubleValue();
    }
    catch (NumberFormatException e) {
        throw new RuntimeException
        ("Interest is not numeric");
    }

    // Get term in months

    parm = request.getParameter("n");
    if (parm == null)
        throw new RuntimeException
        ("No term specified");
    try {
        n = Integer.parseInt(parm);
    }
    catch (NumberFormatException e) {
        throw new RuntimeException
        ("Term is not numeric");
    }

    // Convert to monthly

    i /= 1200;
    n *= 12;

    // Calculate montnly payment

    double fv = Math.pow((1 + i), (double) n);
    double pmt = p * i * fv / (fv - 1);
    DecimalFormat fmt = new DecimalFormat("#####.00");
%>
<H3>Monthly payment = <%= fmt.format(pmt) %></H3>
```

Figure 13-33
A Simple Error
Page

```
<%@ page isErrorPage="true" %>
<H3>Error: <%= exception.getMessage() %></H3>
```

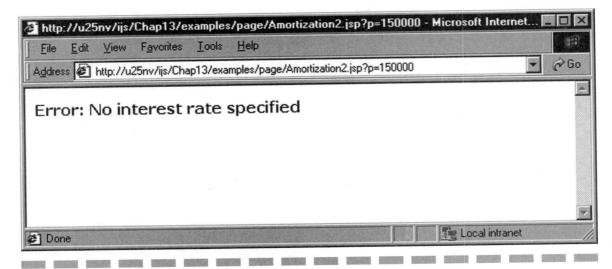

Figure 13-34 Output of the Simple Error Page

context methods it does not support. If you are using JRun or ServletExec, you can uncomment the code that accesses some of these methods. Figure 13-39 shows the typical contents of this panel.

Figure 13-40 shows the final panel, the one for the HTTP session. The table in this panel will include the session creation time, last accessed time, the session ID, and any attributes that have been stored in the session.

Figure 13-35

A Debugging Error Page

```jsp
<%@ page isErrorPage="true" %>
<%@ page import="java.io.*" %>
<%@ page import="java.util.*" %>
<HTML>
<HEAD>
<TITLE>Debugging Error Page</TITLE>
<STYLE>
TD {
    font-size:  8pt;
};
</STYLE>
</HEAD>
<BODY>

<%
    String prefix = getClass().getName();
    if (exception == null)
        exception = (Exception)
            session.getValue(prefix + ".exception");
    else
        session.putValue(prefix + ".exception", exception);
%>

<H3>Error: <%= exception.getMessage() %></H3>

<%-- Diagnostics section below --%>

<%!
    public static final String[] TAB_NAMES = {
        "STStack Trace",
        "RERequest",
        "PMParameters",
        "CTContext",
        "SESession",
    };
%>
<FORM ACTION="<%= request.getRequestURI() %>">

<%-- Outer table consists of a header cell
     and the main body cell.  The header cell
     contains radio buttons that are used to
     switch between sections in the manner of
     a tabbed dialog.  --%>

<TABLE BORDER="0" CELLPADDING="0" CELLSPACING="4" WIDTH="700">

<%-- Header row --%>
<TR>
<%
    String selectedTab = request.getParameter("selectedTab");
    String selectedLabel = null;
    if (selectedTab == null) {

        // This is the first request.

        // Choose the first tab name in the array as the
        // default value.
```

```
    selectedTab = TAB_NAMES[0].substring(0, 2);
    selectedLabel = TAB_NAMES[0].substring(2);

    // Save the form parameters, since they will be
    // lost when this form is resubmitted (which
    // happens when any other tab is selected)

    Hashtable parms = new Hashtable();
    Enumeration eparms = request.getParameterNames();
    while (eparms.hasMoreElements()) {
        String name = (String) eparms.nextElement();
        String[] values = request.getParameterValues(name);
        parms.put(name, values);
    }
    session.putValue(prefix + ".parms", parms);
}

%><TH ALIGN="LEFT"><%

    for (int i = 0; i < TAB_NAMES.length; i++) {
        String tabName = TAB_NAMES[i];
        String code = tabName.substring(0, 2);
        String label = tabName.substring(2);
        String CHECKED = "";
        if (code.equals(selectedTab)) {
            CHECKED = "CHECKED";
            selectedLabel = label;
        }
%><INPUT
        TYPE="radio"
        NAME="selectedTab"
        VALUE="<%= code %>"
        <%= CHECKED %>
        onClick="this.form.submit()"
    >
    <%= label %>
<%
    }
%>
</TH>
</TR>
<%-- End of header row --%>

<%-- Main body row --%>
<TR>
<TD>

<%-- Inner table.  Displays the specified
     object properties as key=value pairs --%>

<TABLE BORDER=1 CELLPADDING=5 CELLSPACING=0 WIDTH="100%">
<%
    // ============================================
    //    Stack trace
    // ============================================
```

Figure 13-35
(Continued)

```java
        if (selectedTab.equals("ST")) {
            out.println("<PRE>");
            exception.printStackTrace(new PrintWriter(out));
            out.println("</PRE>");
        }

        // ================================================
        //     Form parameters
        // ================================================

        else
        if (selectedTab.equals("PM")) {
            Vector names = new Vector();
            Vector values = new Vector();

            // Retrieve the saved parameters

            Hashtable parms = (Hashtable) session.getValue
                (prefix + ".parms");

            Enumeration eparms = parms.keys();
            while (eparms.hasMoreElements()) {
                String name = (String) eparms.nextElement();
                String[] pvalues = (String[]) parms.get(name);
                for (int i = 0; i < pvalues.length; i++) {
                    String value = pvalues[i];
                    names.addElement(name);
                    values.addElement(value);
                }
            }

            sortVectors(names, values);

            int n = names.size();
            for (int i = 0; i < n; i++) {
                String name = (String) names.elementAt(i);
                String value = values.elementAt(i).toString();
%>
    <TR>
        <TD ALIGN="RIGHT"><%= name %></TD>
        <TD ALIGN="LEFT"><B><%= value %></B></TD>
    </TR>
<%
            }
        }

        // ================================================
        //     Request
        // ================================================

        else
        if (selectedTab.equals("RE")) {
            Vector names = new Vector();
            Vector values = new Vector();

            Enumeration enames;
```

Figure 13-35
(Continued)

```
/*

Uncomment this code if your servlet engine version
is 2.1 or higher (ApacheJServ is not, at this
writing).

enames = request.getAttributeNames();
while (enames.hasMoreElements()) {
   String name = (String) enames.nextElement();
   String value = request.getAttribute(name).toString();
   if (value != null) {
      names.addElement(name);
      values.addElement(value);
   }
}

*/

enames = request.getHeaderNames();
while (enames.hasMoreElements()) {
   String name = (String) enames.nextElement();
   String value = request.getHeader(name);
   if (value != null) {
      names.addElement(name);
      values.addElement(value);
   }
}

String parm;

parm = request.getAuthType();
if (parm != null) {
   names.addElement("getAuthType()");
   values.addElement(parm);
}

parm = request.getMethod();
if (parm != null) {
   names.addElement("getMethod()");
   values.addElement(parm);
}

parm = request.getPathInfo();
if (parm != null) {
   names.addElement("getPathInfo()");
   values.addElement(parm);
}

parm = request.getPathTranslated();
if (parm != null) {
   names.addElement("getPathTranslated()");
   values.addElement(parm);
}

parm = request.getQueryString();
if (parm != null) {
   names.addElement("getQueryString()");
```

Figure 13-35
(Continued)

```
            values.addElement(parm);
        }

        parm = request.getRemoteUser();
        if (parm != null) {
            names.addElement("getRemoteUser()");
            values.addElement(parm);
        }

        parm = request.getRequestedSessionId();
        if (parm != null) {
            names.addElement("getRequestedSessionId()");
            values.addElement(parm);
        }

        parm = request.getRequestURI();
        if (parm != null) {
            names.addElement("getRequestURI()");
            values.addElement(parm);
        }

        parm = request.getServletPath();
        if (parm != null) {
            names.addElement("getServletPath()");
            values.addElement(parm);
        }

        parm = request.getCharacterEncoding();
        if (parm != null) {
            names.addElement("getCharacterEncoding()");
            values.addElement(parm);
        }

        int len = request.getContentLength();
        names.addElement("getContentLength()");
        values.addElement("" + len);

        parm = request.getContentType();
        if (parm != null) {
            names.addElement("getContentType()");
            values.addElement(parm);
        }

        parm = request.getProtocol();
        if (parm != null) {
            names.addElement("getProtocol()");
            values.addElement(parm);
        }

        parm = request.getRemoteAddr();
        if (parm != null) {
            names.addElement("getRemoteAddr()");
            values.addElement(parm);
        }

        parm = request.getRemoteHost();
        if (parm != null) {
```

Figure 13-35
(Continued)

```
                                    names.addElement("getRemoteHost()");
                                    values.addElement(parm);
                                }

                            parm = request.getScheme();
                            if (parm != null) {
                                names.addElement("getScheme()");
                                values.addElement(parm);
                            }

                            parm = request.getServerName();
                            if (parm != null) {
                                names.addElement("getServerName()");
                                values.addElement(parm);
                            }

                            names.addElement("getServerPort()");
                            values.addElement("" + request.getServerPort());

                            sortVectors(names, values);

                            int n = names.size();
                            for (int i = 0; i < n; i++) {
                                String name = (String) names.elementAt(i);
                                String value = values.elementAt(i).toString();
%>
        <TR>
            <TD ALIGN="RIGHT"><%= name %></TD>
            <TD ALIGN="LEFT"><B><%= value %></B></TD>
        </TR>
<%
                            }
                        }

                        // ============================================
                        //      Servlet context
                        // ============================================

                        else
                        if (selectedTab.equals("CT")) {
                            Vector names = new Vector();
                            Vector values = new Vector();

                            /*

                            Uncomment this code if your servlet engine version
                            is 2.1 or higher (ApacheJServ is not, at this
                            writing).

                            Enumeration enames = application.getAttributeNames();
                            while (enames.hasMoreElements()) {
                                String name = (String) enames.nextElement();
                                Object value = application.getAttribute(name);
                                names.addElement(name);
                                values.addElement(value);
                            }
```

```
                                  */
                        names.addElement("getServerInfo()");
                        values.addElement(application.getServerInfo());

                        sortVectors(names, values);

                        int n = names.size();
                        for (int i = 0; i < n; i++) {
                            String name = (String) names.elementAt(i);
                            String value = values.elementAt(i).toString();
%>
    <TR>
        <TD ALIGN="RIGHT"><%= name %></TD>
        <TD ALIGN="LEFT"><B><%= value %></B></TD>
    </TR>
<%
                        }
                    }

                    // ============================================
                    //     Session
                    // ============================================

                    else
                    if (selectedTab.equals("SE")) {
                        Vector names = new Vector();
                        Vector values = new Vector();

                        String[] enames = session.getValueNames();
                        for (int i = 0; i < enames.length; i++) {
                            String name = enames[i];
                            if (name.startsWith(prefix))
                                continue;
                            Object value = session.getValue(name);
                            names.addElement(name);
                            values.addElement(value);
                        }

                        names.addElement("getCreationTime()");
                        values.addElement(
                            new Date(session.getCreationTime()).toString());

                        names.addElement("getId()");
                        values.addElement(session.getId());

                        names.addElement("getLastAccessedTime()");
                        values.addElement(
                            new Date(session.getLastAccessedTime()).toString());

                        sortVectors(names, values);

                        int n = names.size();
                        for (int i = 0; i < n; i++) {
                            String name = (String) names.elementAt(i);
                            String value = values.elementAt(i).toString();
%>
```

Figure 13-35
(Continued)

```
    <TR>
        <TD ALIGN="RIGHT"><%= name %></TD>
        <TD ALIGN="LEFT"><B><%= value %></B></TD>
    </TR>
<%
        }
    }
%>
<%-- End of inner table --%>
</TABLE>
</TD>

<%-- End of main body row --%>
</TR>

<%-- End of outer table --%>
</TABLE>
</FORM>

<%-- Sort routine --%>
<%!
    private static void sortVectors(Vector v1, Vector v2)
    {
        int n = v1.size();
        for (int i = 0; i < n-1; i++) {
            for (int j = i+1; j < n; j++) {
                String istr = (String) v1.elementAt(i);
                String jstr = (String) v1.elementAt(j);
                if (istr.compareTo(jstr) > 0) {

                    Object temp = v1.elementAt(i);
                    v1.setElementAt(v1.elementAt(j), i);
                    v1.setElementAt(temp, j);

                    temp = v2.elementAt(i);
                    v2.setElementAt(v2.elementAt(j), i);
                    v2.setElementAt(temp, j);
                }
            }
        }
    }
%>
</BODY>
</HTML>
```

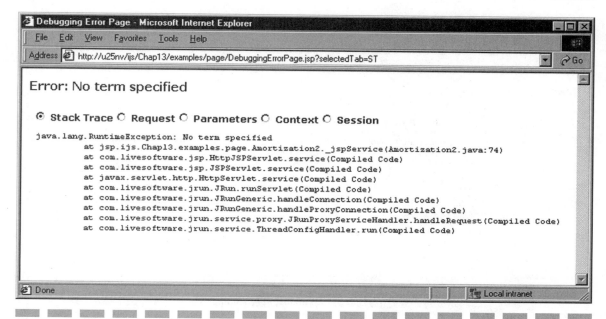

Figure 13-36 The Debugging Error Page Stack Trace Panel

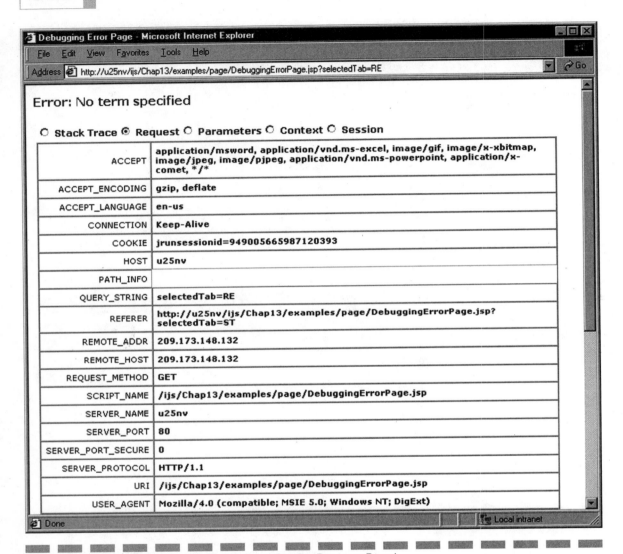

Figure 13-37 The Debugging Error Page Servlet Request Panel

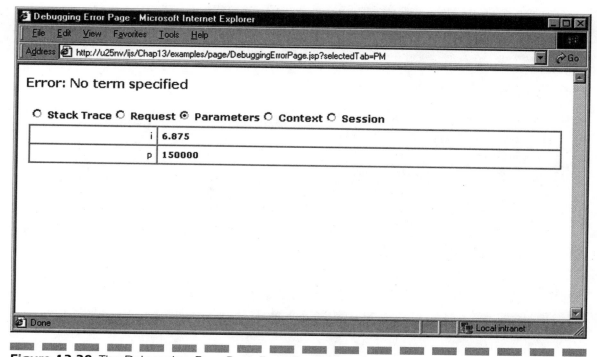

Figure 13-38 The Debugging Error Page Form Parameters Panel

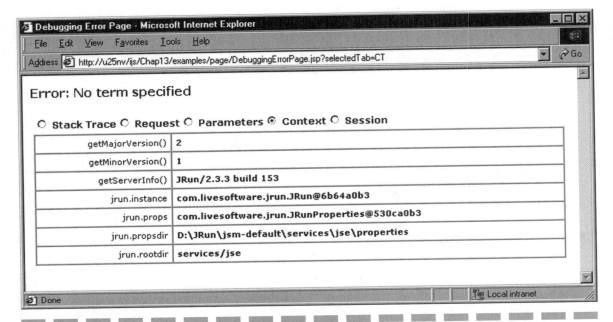

Figure 13-39 The Debugging Error Page Servlet Context Panel

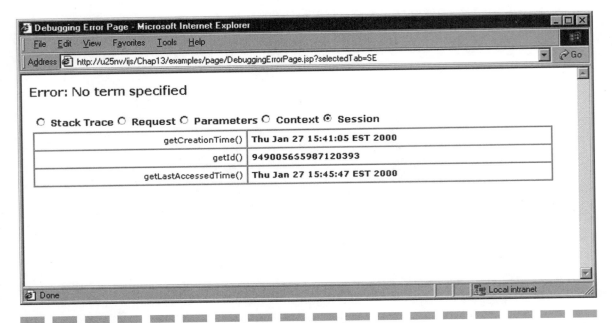

Figure 13-40 The Debugging Error Page Session Panel

13.9   Using JavaBeans with JSP

Syntax

```
<jsp:useBean
        id="beanInstanceName"
        [ scope="page|request|session|application" ]
        [ class=className" ]
        [ type="className" ]
        [ beanName="name|<%= expression %>" ]
    other tags
        </jsp:useBean>¹¹
<jsp:setProperty
        name="beanInstanceName"
        {
            property="*" |
            property="propertyName" [ param="parmName" ] |
            property="propertyName" value="value"
        }
        />
<jsp:getProperty
        name="beanInstanceName"
        property="propertyName"
        />
```

Description

The JavaBeans component model makes it easy to develop reusable classes that can be deployed in more than one environment. Properly designed, the same bean can be used in a Java applet, a stand-alone Java application, and (you guessed it) a JSP page. This allows Web applications to be separated cleanly into content and presentation, using JavaBeans to do the heavy lifting and HTML to show the results.

JavaBeans are ordinary Java classes that adhere to a fairly minimal set of requirements. For an object to be a bean, it should[12] do the following:

1. It should be serializable.

---

[11]If no other tags are included in the body of the `<jsp:useBean>` tag, the ending `</jsp:useBean>` can be omitted as long as the `<jsp:useBean>` tag is closed with `/>`.

[12]*Should* instead of *must* because there are exceptions to each of these rules. The property naming convention, for example, provides a standard means for bean container environments such as IDEs to determine the properties that a bean supports. A bean may use property descriptors instead, but this would limit its usefulness in many environments (including JSP).

2. It should provide a public zero-argument constructor.

3. For each property xyz, it should provide a getXyx() method.

4. For each non-read-only property xyz, it should provide a setXyx() method.

The JavaServer Pages specification provides three bean-related scripting actions: <jsp:useBean> to declare the bean, <jsp:setProperty> to set its properties, and <jsp:getProperty> to retrieve them.

<jsp:useBean> Before a bean can be used, it must be declared. The <jsp:useBean> action creates an instance of the specified bean (or uses an existing one, if one having the same ID exists in the specified scope) and associates it with a variable name. This variable can then be used in scriptlets and expressions in the current block[13] like any other object reference.

The scope of the bean refers to the context in which it exists. There are four possible choices:

page   The bean is available as long as the page is active servicing the current request. This is the default value of the scope attribute.

request   The bean is available while this page or the target of any <jsp:forward> or <jsp:include> action is active servicing the current request.

session   The bean is accessible from any JSP page participating in the same HTTP session. If the user closes the browser session, the bean is no longer available.

application   The bean can be accessed from any JSP page in the same servlet context. This means that the bean persists even if the user closes the browser session and later starts a new one as long as the servlet has not been unloaded.

In addition to the id="name" attribute, the bean's class must be declared. This can be done by specifying any of the following attribute combinations:

class="className"   If an object with a matching ID exists in the specified scope, it is cast into the speci-

---

[13]Recall that scriptlets are concatenated and placed inside the _jspService() method of the generated servlet.

	fied class. Otherwise, the class constructor is invoked to create a new bean.
`type="className"`	An object with a matching ID must exist in the specified scope. The object is cast into the specified type. This choice is most useful when a bean implements several types (interfaces).
`class="className"` `type="className"`	If an object with a matching ID exists in the specified scope, it is cast into the specified type. Otherwise, the class constructor is invoked to create a new bean.
`type="className"` `beanName=` *"name*`|<%=`**expression**`%>"`	If an object with a matching ID exists in in the specified scope, it is cast into the specified type. Otherwise, the `java.beans.Beans.instantiate()` method is called to create a new bean (or deserialize one if the bean name refers to a serialized object).

The flowchart in Figure 13-41 shows in more detail how the `<jsp:useBean>` action works. Note that either the `class` or `type` attribute must be specified but that only `type` is valid when `beanName` is also specified. In addition, note that the body of the `<jsp:useBean>` ... `</jsp:useBean>` block (if any) is only evaluated if a new bean is created. Most often, the body of this block is used to initialize the bean with `<jsp:setProperty>`. If the body is empty, the standard XML `<jsp:useBean attr="value" attr="value" />` syntax can be used, with the ending `</jsp:useBean>` tag omitted.

`<jsp:setProperty>` Once a bean is loaded, its properties can be set with the `<jsp:setProperty>` action. This action operates in one of two ways, taking its values either from parameters in the `request` object or from values specified as scriptlet expressions or string constants.

The first usage, assigning properties from parameter values in the `request` object, can either set all available properties at once

```
<jsp:setProperty name="beanID" property="*" />
```

or individually

```
<jsp:setProperty name="beanID" property="name" />
<jsp:setProperty name="beanID" property="address" />
<jsp:setProperty name="beanID" property="phoneNumber" />
```

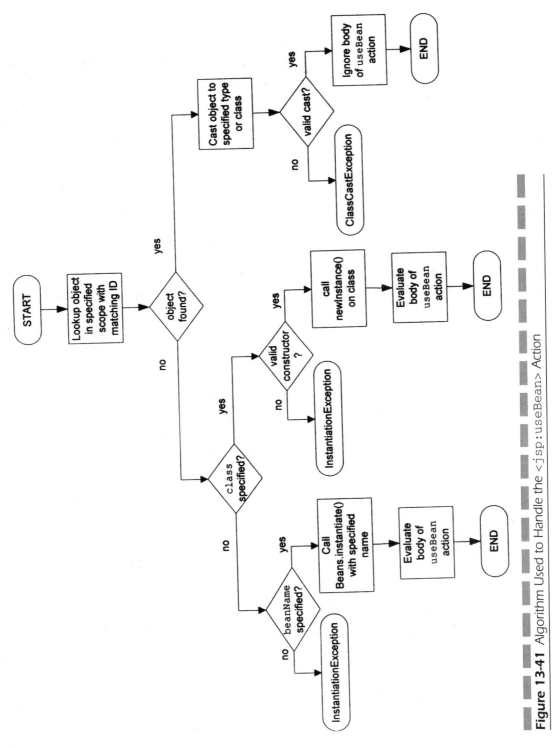

Figure 13-41 Algorithm Used to Handle the <jsp:useBean> Action

In these cases, the JSP engine goes through the list of nonblank request parameters, trying to match them up to bean property names. If the parameter names are not the same as the desired bean property names, the param attribute can be used:

```
<jsp:setProperty name="beanID" property="name" param="userName"/>
<jsp:setProperty name="beanID" property="address" />
<jsp:setProperty name="beanID" property="phoneNumber" />
```

The other way to set bean properties with <jsp:setProperty> is to use the value attribute. The value can come either from an expression

```
<jsp:setProperty
    name="beanID"
    property="lastUpdate"
    value="<%= new java.util.Date().toString()"/>
```

or from a string constant:

```
<jsp:setProperty name="beanID" property="count" value="0"/>
```

The param and value attributes are mutually exclusive.

It should be noted that in addition to their role as JSP page components, beans continue to be ordinary Java objects whose properties can be set using method calls inside of scriptlets:

```
<%
    beanID.setName("Fred");
    beanID.setAddress("Bedrock");
    beanID.setPhoneNumber(request.getParameter("phone"));
%>
```

<jsp:getProperty> Retrieving bean properties is even simpler than setting them. If a bean is declared with a variable name of myBean and has a method named getPhoneNumber(), its value can be accessed as shown in this example:

```
<UL>
<LI>Phone number is <jsp:getProperty name="myBean"
property="phoneNumber"/>
</UL>
```

The <jsp:getProperty> tag may be coded anywhere in the HTML of a JSP page. The JSP engine will call the bean's getPhoneNumber() method and convert the returned value to a string. The string will then be substituted for the entire <jsp:getProperty ... /> tag.

As was the case with <jsp:setProperty>, bean properties also can be retrieved with accessor methods in scriptlets or expressions:

```
<UL>
<LI>Phone number is <%= myBean.getPhoneNumber() %>
</UL>
```

Examples

In this section we will cover four complete examples of using JavaBeans in JSP pages:

1. The ultimate version of the `BananaBabyFoods` servlet, which accesses the database through a JDBC bean

2. A JSP page that determines which Web server a given URL uses, illustrating the use of `<jsp:getProperty>` and `<jsp:setProperty>`

3. A loan amortization calculator that shows how to access indexed properties

4. A latitude and longitude distance calculator, which uses JSP pages and JavaBeans with no Java code at all

`Accessing JDBC from a Bean` So far we have developed two versions of the servlet that queries the nutrient database to find baby foods that contain bananas: a pure servlet version in Section 5.4 (the JDBC-ODBC bridge) and a JSP version in Section 13.2. The JSP version was simpler because all the HTML could be written directly as HTML, but the database logic was still necessary. In this version, we will see how JavaBeans can separate content generation (accessing the database) from presentation entirely.

Figure 13-42 lists a JavaBean class that handles all the database logic. It has a `foodName` property that is used in the SQL `SELECT` statement to extract the desired subset of the nutrient database. It also has a `getMatchingFoods()` method that returns an array of strings describing foods that matched the criteria. Each string contains the five-digit food code and the food description, with the two fields separated by a single space.

With all these details taken care of, all the JSP page has to do is declare the bean, give it a food name, and display the resulting string array. Even lavishly decorated with whitespace, the source code (see Figure 13-43) is only 33 lines long. The resulting Web page is shown in Figure 13-44.

Figure 13-42

A JavaBean That
Provides Access to
the Nutrient
Database

```
package ijs.beans.jdbc;

import java.io.*;
import java.net.*;
import java.sql.*;
import java.util.*;

/**
 * A class that looks up baby foods in the USDA nutrient
 * database.
 */
public class NutrientLookupBean
{
    private String foodName;
    private Vector matchingFoods;

    /**
     * Creates a new NutrientLookupBean
     */
    public NutrientLookupBean()
    {
        foodName = null;
        matchingFoods = null;
    }

    /**
     * Returns the foodName.
     */
    public String getFoodName()
    {
        return foodName;
    }

    /**
     * Sets the foodName and creates the result set.
     * @param foodName the foodName.
     */
    public void setFoodName(String foodName)
        throws IOException
    {
        this.foodName = foodName;

        Connection con = null;
        Statement stmt = null;
        ResultSet rs = null;
        try {
            Class.forName("sun.jdbc.odbc.JdbcOdbcDriver");
            con = DriverManager.getConnection("jdbc:odbc:usda");
            stmt = con.createStatement();
            String sql = ""
                    + " SELECT    F.NDB_No as foodCode,"
                    + "           F.Desc as foodDesc"
                    + " FROM      FOOD_DES F, FD_GROUP G"
                    + " WHERE     F.FdGp_Cd = G.FdGp_Cd"
                    + " AND       F.Shrt_Desc LIKE "
                    +             "'%" + foodName + "%'"
                    + " AND       G.FdGp_Desc = 'Baby Foods'"
```

Figure 13-42

(Continued)

```java
                    + " ORDER BY F.Desc"
                    ;
            rs = stmt.executeQuery(sql);
            matchingFoods = new Vector();
            while (rs.next()) {
                String foodCode = rs.getString("foodCode");
                String foodDesc = rs.getString("foodDesc");
                String matchingFood = foodCode + " " + foodDesc;
                matchingFoods.addElement(matchingFood);
            }
        }
        catch (Exception e) {
            throw new IOException(e.getMessage());
        }
        finally {
            if (rs != null) {
                try { rs.close(); }
                catch (SQLException ignore) {}
            }
            if (stmt != null) {
                try { stmt.close(); }
                catch (SQLException ignore) {}
            }
            if (con != null) {
                try { con.close(); }
                catch (SQLException ignore) {}
            }
        } .
    }


    /**
     * Returns the matchingFoods.
     */
    public String[] getMatchingFoods()
    {
        String[] list = null;

        if (matchingFoods == null) {
            list = new String[0];
        }
        else {
            int n = matchingFoods.size();
            list = new String[n];
            matchingFoods.copyInto(list);
        }
        return list;
    }
```

Figure 13-43

The
BananaBabyFood
s Servlet Using JSP
and JavaBeans

```
<%@ page
       errorPage="ErrorPage.jsp"
       import="java.io.*,java.util.*,ijs.jdbc.*"
%>

<jsp:useBean
    id="foods"
    class="ijs.beans.jdbc.NutrientLookupBean"/>

<HTML>

<HEAD>
<TITLE>Banana Baby Foods JSP</TITLE>
</HEAD>

<BODY>
<IMG SRC="/ijs/Chap05/banana.gif">
<FONT SIZE="+2">Banana Baby Foods (using JSP+JavaBeans)</FONT>
<P>
<%
    foods.setFoodName("BANANA");
    String[] matchingFoods = foods.getMatchingFoods();
    for (int i = 0; i < matchingFoods.length; i++) {
        String record = matchingFoods[i];
        int p = record.indexOf(" ");
        String foodCode = record.substring(0, p);
        String foodDesc = record.substring(p+1);
%> <B><%= foodCode %></B> <%= foodDesc %><BR><%
    }
%>
<P><%= matchingFoods.length %> banana baby foods selected<P>
</BODY>
</HTML>
```

Using setProperty and getProperty Among the headers normally returned by a Web server in response to any HTTP request is the `Server` header. For example, when a request is made to `http://www.ipfoods.com`, it returns the following headers:

```
HTTP/1.1 200 OK
Server: Netscape-Enterprise/3.6 SP1
Date: Mon, 31 Jan 2000 06:07:35 GMT
Content-type: text/html
Connection: close
```

It is a simple matter in a Java class to open a URL connection and extract this header.[14] Figure 13-45 shows a JavaBean that does this. The bean has a `URL` property and a read-only `server` property.

---

[14]It is interesting to run this JSP page for the Web sites of all the Fortune 500 companies. The results may not be what you expect. At the time of this writing, among the largest of these companies, especially the top 100, the dominant choice for a Web server is not Apache or Microsoft IIS but Netscape Enterprise.

Figure 13-44 The Output of the JSP + JavaBeans Version of the BananaBabyFoods Servlet

Figure 13-45

A Bean That
Determines the
Web Server Used
by a Given URL

```java
package ijs.beans.server;

import java.io.*;
import java.net.*;
import java.util.*;

/**
 * A bean that extracts information about a web server
 */
public class ServerInfoBean implements Serializable
{
    public static final int DEFAULT_PORT = 80;

    private String urlString;

    /**
     * Returns the URL.
     */
    public String getURL()
    {
        return urlString;
    }

    /**
     * Sets the URL.
     * @param urlString the URL.
     */
    public void setURL(String urlString)
    {
        if (!urlString.startsWith("http://"))
            urlString = "http://" + urlString;
        this.urlString = urlString;
    }

    /**
     * Returns the server type
     */
    public String getServer() throws IOException
    {
        URL url = new URL(getURL());
        URLConnection con = url.openConnection();
        String server = con.getHeaderField("server");
        if (server == null)
            server = "unknown";

        return server;
    }
}
```

A JSP page that uses this bean is listed in Figure 13-46.
ServerInfo.jsp performs its task in two steps: It displays an HTML
form, prompting for the URL of the Web server to be analyzed, and then
it presents the results after the "Submit" button is clicked. It can tell the
difference between these two steps by checking for the existence of a
hidden field named state. If the field exists, it means that the user has

Figure 13-46
A JSP Page That
Uses Properties of
`ServerInfoBean`

```jsp
<%@ page import="java.io.*,ijs.beans.server.*" %>

<%-- Declare a server information bean --%>

<jsp:useBean
     id="serverInfo"
     class="ijs.beans.server.ServerInfoBean" />

<%-- Load properties from the request into the bean --%>

<jsp:setProperty name="serverInfo" property="*" />

<%-- Determine if the form has already been shown --%>

<% boolean first = (request.getParameter("state") == null); %>

<HTML>
<BODY>
<H3>Which Web Server Do They Use?</H3>
<FORM>

<%-- Use a hidden "state" field to determine whether
     the user has already seen the form --%>

<INPUT TYPE="hidden" NAME="state" VALUE="1">
<TABLE BORDER="0" CELLPADDING="3" CELLSPACING="0">

<%-- Prompt for the URL, showing its previous value
     if this is not the first request --%>

<TR>
   <TD>URL:</TD>
   <TD>
       <INPUT TYPE="TEXT"
              NAME="URL"
              SIZE="48"

<% if (!first) { %>

VALUE=<jsp:getProperty name="serverInfo" property="URL"/>

<% } %>
       >
       <INPUT
           TYPE="SUBMIT"
           VALUE="submit">
   </TD>
</TR>

<%-- If the user has entered a URL, get its server
     information from the bean  --%>

<% if (!first) { %>

<TR>
   <TD COLSPAN="2">
      Web server is
       <jsp:getProperty name="serverInfo" property="server"/>
   </TD>
</TR>

<% } %>

</TABLE>
</FORM>
</BODY>
</HTML>
```

clicked the "Submit" button and this is the second time through the page.

`ServerInfo.jsp` declares an instance of the bean using the `<jsp:useBean>` action and then sets all its properties (in this case, there is only one—the URL property) using the "set all" approach:

```
<jsp:setProperty name="serverInfo" property="*"/>
```

The first time through the page, all the request parameters are null, so no properties are set. When the user fills in the form and clicks the "Submit" button, the page is entered again, and the URL property is automatically set. This time the `state` variable is detected, causing the server name to be extracted and displayed:

```
Web server is <jsp:getProperty name="serverInfo" property="server"/>
```

The results are shown in Figure 13-47.

Accessing Indexed Properties   In addition to simple scalar properties, JavaBeans can have properties whose values are arrays. Known as

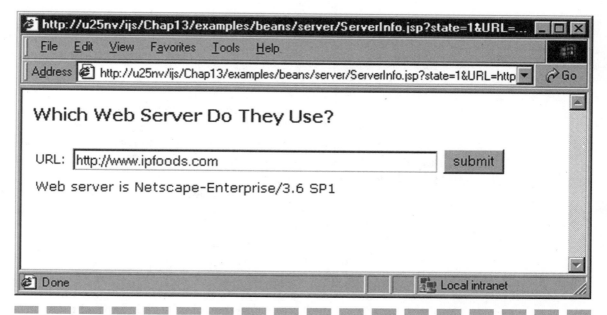

Figure 13-47 The `ServerInfo` JSP Page in Action

indexed properties, these values can be accessed using an additional index parameter in the method calls. For example, if `temperature` is a bean property that is maintained for each of 12 months, then its value in March can be set using

```
aBean.setTemperature(2, value);
```

and retrieved using

```
double value = aBean.getTemperature(2);
```

The index value for the month of March is 2 in this case because Java arrays are zero-based. Values for an entire year can be set with

```
double[] values = ...;
aBean.setTemperature(values);
```

and retrieved using

```
double[] value = aBean.getTemperature();
```

The JavaServer Page specification describes setting indexed properties using the following syntax:

```
<% double[] values = ...; %>
<jsp:setProperty
   name="aBean"
   property="temperature"
   value="<%= values %>" />
```

but as of this writing, support is buggy in several JSP engines.

The example we will use to demonstrate indexed properties is a loan amortization calculator. `LoanBean` is a class that stores the loan parameters and calculates the payment information. It has the properties shown in Table 13-4.

The implementation of `LoanBean` is shown in Figure 13-48. The heart of the class is the `recalculate()` method, which calculates the monthly payment and the monthly allocations of the payment to interest and principal. This method is called only when one of the calculated properties is requested and only if one or more of the input parameters has changed. The `get` and `set` method indices are one-based rather than zero-based because it is more natural to relate them to payment numbers than to Java array indices. The class includes a static method for round-

TABLE 13-4

Property Name	Indexed	Read-Only	Description
principal	No	No	Original amount of the loan.
interestRate	No	No	Annual interest rate as a percent (8.5% is stored as 8.5, not 0.085).
term	No	No	Number of years for which the loan is made.
monthlyPayment	No	Yes	Amount required each month to pay off the principal and interest in the specified number of years. This value is calculated by the bean from the principal, interestRate, and term properties.
numberOfPayments	No	Yes	Number of years times 12. The size of each of the arrays described below.
interestAmount	Yes	Yes	An array of doubles, one for each payment, showing the amount of the monthly payment that is used to pay that month's interest on the outstanding loan balance.
principalAmount	Yes	Yes	An array of doubles, one for each payment, showing the amount remaining in the monthly payment after interest is paid. This is the amount by which the loan balance is reduced.
totalPayment	Yes	Yes	The total payment (interest + principal) for each month.
balance	Yes	Yes	The remaining balance at the end of each month.

ing doubles to the nearest 1/100 of the currency unit so that calculations can be exact.

The user interface is handled by Loan.jsp, listed in Figure 13-49. It prompts for the principal amount, the annual interest rate, and the term in years (see Figure 13-50). Like ServerInfo.jsp, it uses a hidden field to distinguish whether it is being called with the form already submitted or not.

When the "Submit" button is clicked, the parameters are validated by a JavaScript function (see Figure 13-51). All three fields must be present,

Figure 13-48
A Bean That
Calculates a Loan
Amortization
Schedule

```java
package ijs.beans.loan;

import java.io.*;
import java.net.*;
import java.text.*;
import java.util.*;

/**
 * A bean that calculates a loan amortization schedule.
 */
public class LoanBean implements Serializable
{
    public static final NumberFormat fmt
        = NumberFormat.getCurrencyInstance();

    // ==========================================
    //    Instance variables
    // ==========================================

    private double principal;
    private double interestRate;
    private int term;
    private double monthlyPayment;
    private double[] interestAmount;
    private double[] principalAmount;
    private double[] totalPayment;
    private double[] balance;
    private boolean needToRecalculate;

    // ==========================================
    //    Constructors
    // ==========================================

    /**
     * Creates a new loan with default values
     */
    public LoanBean()
    {
        needToRecalculate = true;
    }

    // ==========================================
    //    Instance methods
    // ==========================================

    /**
     * Calculates the monthly payment and the
     * amortization schedule.
     */
    private void recalculate()
    {
        // Calculate the monthly payment

        double p = round(principal);
        double i = interestRate / 1200.0;
        int n = getNumberOfPayments();
```

```java
            double fv = Math.pow((1 + i), (double) n);
            monthlyPayment =
                round(principal * i * fv / (fv - 1.0));

            // Calculate the amortization schedule

            interestAmount  = new double[n];
            principalAmount = new double[n];
            totalPayment    = new double[n];
            balance         = new double[n];

            // First payment

            interestAmount[0]  = round(p * i);
            principalAmount[0] = monthlyPayment - interestAmount[0];
            totalPayment[0]    = monthlyPayment;
            balance[0]         = p - principalAmount[0];

            // Every payment but the last

            for (int k = 1; k < n-1; k++) {
                interestAmount[k]  = round(balance[k-1] * i);
                principalAmount[k] =
                    monthlyPayment - interestAmount[k];
                totalPayment[k]    = monthlyPayment;
                balance[k]         =
                    balance[k-1] - principalAmount[k];
            }

            // Last payment

            interestAmount[n-1]  = round(balance[n-2] * i);
            principalAmount[n-1] = balance[n-2];
            totalPayment[n-1]    =
                interestAmount[n-1] + principalAmount[n-1];
            balance[n-1]         =
                balance[n-2] - principalAmount[n-1];

            // Done

            needToRecalculate = false;
        }

    /**
     * Returns the principal amount.
     */
    public double getPrincipal()
    {
        return principal;
    }

    /**
     * Sets the principal amount.
     * @param principal the principal.
     */
    public void setPrincipal(double principal)
    {
```

Figure 13-48

(Continued)

```
        this.principal = principal;
        needToRecalculate = true;
    }

    /**
     * Returns the annual interest rate.
     */
    public double getInterestRate()
    {
        return interestRate;
    }

    /**
     * Sets the annual interest rate.
     * The rate should be entered as a percentage,
     * that is, 8.5 percent is 8.5, not 0.085
     * @param interestRate the interest rate
     */
    public void setInterestRate(double interestRate)
    {
        if (interestRate <= 0)
            throw new IllegalArgumentException
            ("Interest rate must be postive");

        this.interestRate = interestRate;
        needToRecalculate = true;
    }

    /**
     * Returns the term in years.
     */
    public int getTerm()
    {
        return term;
    }

    /**
     * Sets the term in years.
     * @param term the term.
     */
    public void setTerm(int term)
    {
        if (term <= 0)
            throw new IllegalArgumentException
            ("Term in years must be positive");

        this.term = term;
        needToRecalculate = true;
    }

    /**
     * Returns the monthlyPayment.
     */
    public double getMonthlyPayment()
    {
        if (needToRecalculate)
            recalculate();
```

Figure 13-48
(Continued)

```
      return monthlyPayment;
   }

   /**
    * Returns the number of payments (term * 12)
    */
   public int getNumberOfPayments()
   {
      return term * 12;
   }

   /**
    * Returns the interest amount in the kth period.
    * Periods are numbered 1, 2, ..., n
    */
   public double getInterestAmount(int k)
   {
      if (needToRecalculate)
         recalculate();

      int n = getNumberOfPayments();

      if ((k < 1) || (k > n))
         throw new IllegalArgumentException
         ("Period number must be from 1 to " + n);

      return interestAmount[k-1];
   }

   /**
    * Returns the principal amount in the kth period.
    * Periods are numbered 1, 2, ..., n
    */
   public double getPrincipalAmount(int k)
   {
      if (needToRecalculate)
         recalculate();

      int n = getNumberOfPayments();

      if ((k < 1) || (k > n))
         throw new IllegalArgumentException
         ("Period number must be from 1 to " + n);

      return principalAmount[k-1];
   }

   /**
    * Returns the total payment amount in the kth period.
    * Periods are numbered 1, 2, ..., n
    */
   public double getTotalPayment(int k)
   {
      if (needToRecalculate)
         recalculate();

      int n = getNumberOfPayments();
```

Figure 13-48

(Continued)

```
   if ((k <_1) || (k > n))
      throw new IllegalArgumentException
      ("Period number must be from 1 to " + n);

   return totalPayment[k-1];
}

/**
 * Returns the balance at the end of the kth period.
 * Periods are numbered 1, 2, ..., n
 */
public double getBalance(int k)
{
   if (needToRecalculate)
      recalculate();

   int n = getNumberOfPayments();

   if ((k < 1) || (k > n))
      throw new IllegalArgumentException
      ("Period number must be from 1 to " + n);

   return balance[k-1];
}

// ==============================================
// ` Class methods
// ==============================================

/**
 * Rounds the specified number to two decimal places
 * @param x the number to be rounded
 */
public static double round(double x)
{
   long lx = (long) (x * 100.0 + 0.5);
   double dx = (double) lx;
   return dx / 100.0;
}

/**
 * Formats the specified number as a currency amount
 * @param x the number to be formatted
 */
public static String format(double x)
{
   return fmt.format(x);
}
```

and the interest rate and term must be greater than zero. The JavaScript function is included with the static `<%@ include %>` directive.

After the form is submitted, the monthly payment and amortization arrays are available. Since there can be hundreds of payments in a typi-

Figure 13-49

A JSP Page That
Uses LoanBean
Interactively

```
<%@ page
     errorPage="/ErrorPage.jsp"
     import="java.io.*,ijs.beans.loan.*"
%>

<%-- Create a LoanBean to store the principal, interest
     rate, and term.  The bean will calculate the monthly
     payment and an amortization schedule.  --%>

<jsp:useBean
   id="loan"
   class="ijs.beans.loan.LoanBean"
   scope="session"/>

<%-- Document header --%>

<html>
<head>
<title>Loan Calculator</title>
<script language="JavaScript">
<%@ include file="CheckParms.js" %>
</script>
</head>

<%-- Document body --%>

<body>
<center>

<%-- Check the state parameter to determine if this is
     the first time through this page.  If so, display
     the input form.  --%>

<% if (request.getParameter("state") == null) { %>

<form method="post" onSubmit="return checkParms(this);">
<input type="hidden" name="state" value="1">
<table border="0" cellpadding="3">
   <tr>
      <td align="center" colspan="2">
      <h3>Loan Calculator</h3>
      </td>
   </tr>
   <tr>
      <td>Principal amount:</td>
      <td>
      <input name="principal"
              type="text"
              size="16"
              align="right">
      </td>
   </tr>
   <tr>
      <td>Interest rate:</td>
      <td>
      <input name="interestRate"
              type="text"
```

Figure 13-49

(Continued)

```
                        size="8"
                        align="right">
              (e.g. 6.875)
              </td>
      </tr>
      <tr>
         <td>Term:</td>
         <td>
         <input name="term"
                type="text"
                size="8"
                align="right">
         (in years)
         </td>
      </tr>
      <tr>
         <td> </td>
         <td>
         <input type="submit" value="submit">
         <input type="reset"  value="clear">
         </td>
      </tr>
   </table>
   </form>

<%-- After the parameters have been entered, the bean can
     calculate the monthly payment and the amortization
     schedule.  --%>

<% } else if (request.getParameter("state").equals("1")) { %>

<%-- Use <jsp:setProperty> to assign the value of
     each request parameter to its corresponding
     bean parameter.  --%>

<jsp:setProperty name="loan" property="*"/>

<%
         String sy = request.getParameter("year");
         if (sy == null)
            sy = "1";
         int year = Integer.parseInt(sy);
         String yearButton =
            request.getParameter("yearButton");
         if (yearButton != null) {
            if (yearButton.equals("First"))
               year = 1;
            else if (yearButton.equals("Prev"))
               year--;
            else if (yearButton.equals("Next"))
               year++;
            else if (yearButton.equals("Last"))
               year = loan.getTerm();
         }
         if (year < 1)
            year = 1;
         if (year > loan.getTerm())
```

Figure 13-49
(Continued)

```
                               year = loan.getTerm();
     %>

     <%--  Show the amortization schedule, first listing
           the principal, interest rate, term in years,
           and calculated monthly payment.  --%>

     <table border="1" cellpadding="3" cellspacing="0">

        <tr>
           <td colspan="5" align="center">
           <h3>Amortization Schedule</h3>
           </td>
        </tr>

        <tr>
           <td colspan="4">Principal amount:</td>
           <td align="right">
           <%= loan.format(loan.getPrincipal()) %>
           </td>
        </tr>

        <tr>
           <td colspan="4">Annual interest rate:</td>
           <td align="right">
           <%= loan.getInterestRate() %> %
           </td>
        </tr>

        <tr>
           <td colspan="4">Term:</td>
           <td align="right">
           <%= loan.getTerm() %> years
           </td>
        </tr>

        <tr>
           <td colspan="4">Monthly payment:</td>
           <td align="right">
           <%= loan.format(loan.getMonthlyPayment()) %>
           </td>
        </tr>

     <%--  Show the year number and the scrolling buttons --%>

     <%
           int n = loan.getNumberOfPayments();
           int lo = (year - 1) * 12 + 1;
           int hi = lo + 12 - 1;
     %>
        <tr>
           <td align="center" valign="middle" colspan="5">
           <form method="POST">
           <input type="hidden" name="year" value="<%= year %>">
           <input type="hidden" name="state" value="1">
           <B>Year <%= year %> of <%= loan.getTerm() %></B>
                 
```

Figure 13-49

(Continued)

```
            <input type="submit" value="First" name="yearButton">
            <input type="submit" value="Prev"  name="yearButton">
            <input type="submit" value="Next"  name="yearButton">
            <input type="submit" value="Last"  name="yearButton">
          </form>
          </td>
        </tr>

    <%-- Show the column headings --%>

        <tr>
          <th width="100">Payment<br>Number</th>
          <th width="100">Interest<br>Amount</th>
          <th width="100">Principal<br>Amount</th>
          <th width="100">Total<br>Payment</th>
          <th width="100">Remaining<br>Balance</th>
        </tr>

    <%-- Show twelve months of payments --%>

    <%    for (int pmtnbr = lo; pmtnbr <= hi; pmtnbr++) { %>

        <tr>
          <td align="right"><%= pmtnbr %></td>
          <td align="right">
            <%= loan.format(loan.getInterestAmount(pmtnbr)) %>
          </td>
          <td align="right">
            <%= loan.format(loan.getPrincipalAmount(pmtnbr)) %>
          </td>
          <td align="right">
            <%= loan.format(loan.getTotalPayment(pmtnbr)) %>
          </td>
          <td align="right">
            <%= loan.format(loan.getBalance(pmtnbr)) %>
          </td>
        </tr>

    <%    } %>

    </table>

    <% } %>

    <%-- Document footer --%>

    </center>
    </body>
    </html>
```

cal loan, it usually is not possible to show the whole schedule on one page
without scrolling. The Loan.jsp handles this by showing only one year
at a time, with buttons that allow the user to go to the first, last, previous, and next years. Each time a year is requested, the beginning and
ending payment numbers are determined and used as the bounds of a

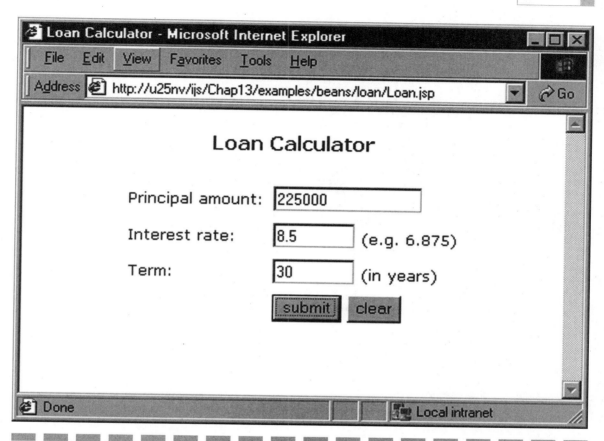

Figure 13-50 Typical Parameters for Loan.jsp

loop. For each iteration of the loop, the values of interest amount, principal amount, total payment, and balance are extracted from the appropriate indexed properties and written to an HTML table row. As can be seen in Figure 13-52, the first few payments are allocated almost entirely to pay interest.

JSP for HTML Authors The final example in this chapter will demonstrate how JavaBeans make it possible to write useful JSP pages that have no Java code at all. The application is a calculator that finds the surface distance between any two points on earth given their latitude and longitude. There are two bean classes involved: LocationBean, which represents a named surface point with its latitude and longitude,

```
// This JavaScript function is intended for use as
// an "onSubmit" event handler for Loan.jsp.  It
// verifies that:
//
// 1. The principal amount is specified
// 2. The interest rate is positive
// 3. The term is positive

function checkParms(frm)
{
    var errors = false;
    var msg = "";
    if (frm.principal.value == "") {
        msg += "\nPrincipal amount must be specified";
        errors = true;
    }
    if ((frm.interestRate.value == "") ||
        !(frm.interestRate.value > 0)) {
        msg += "\nPositive interest rate must be specified";
        errors = true;
    }
    if ((frm.term.value == "") ||
        !(frm.term.value > 0)) {
        msg += "\nPositive term must be specified";
        errors = true;
    }
    if (errors)
        alert(msg);
    return !errors;
}
```

and `DistanceBean`, which contains two `LocationBeans` and calculates the distance between them. The user interface consists of an HTML form and a JSP page. The JSP page accepts the two locations as form parameters and uses the beans to calculate the distance between them.

Figure 13-53 lists the `LocationBean` source code. It has a `name` property and two coordinate properties, one for latitude and one for longitude. The coordinates are stored as decimal degrees, with latitude from −90° (the South Pole) to 90° (the North Pole), and longitude from 0° to 180° west of Greenwich to 0° to −180° east of Greenwich, England. Coordinates can be set directly or as three individual fields (degrees, minutes, seconds). The bean takes care of converting the individual fields back into decimal degrees.

The `DistanceBean` (shown in Figure 13-54) has two `LocationBean` properties and a read-only `distance` property. The distance is also presented as `distanceInKilometers` and `distanceInMiles`, which

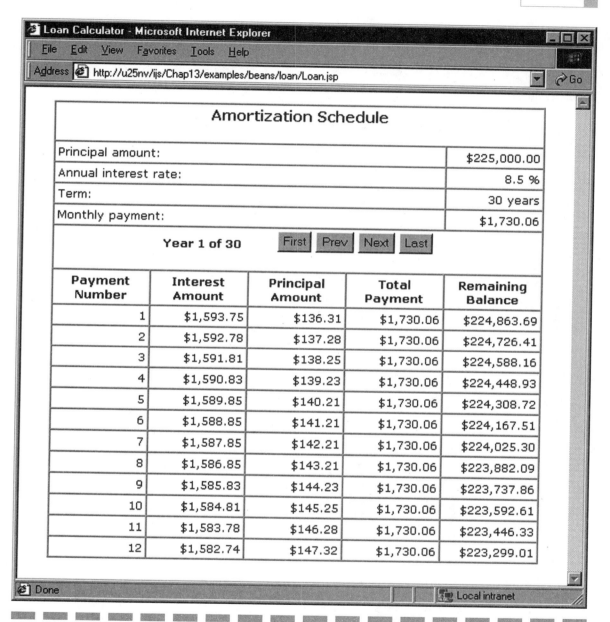

Figure 13-52 Allocation of Principal and Interest for the First 12 Loan Payments

Figure 13-53

A Bean That
Represents the
Name, Latitude,
and Longitude of a
Point on the Earth's
Surface

```java
package ijs.beans.distance;

import java.io.*;
import java.net.*;
import java.util.*;

/**
 * A bean that stores information about
 * a point on the earth's surface.
 */
public class LocationBean implements Serializable
{
    // ==========================================
    //     Instance variables
    // ==========================================

    private String name;

    private double latitude;
    private int latitudeDegrees;
    private int latitudeMinutes;
    private int latitudeSeconds;

    private double longitude;
    private int longitudeDegrees;
    private int longitudeMinutes;
    private int longitudeSeconds;

    // ==========================================
    //     Instance methods
    // ==========================================

    /**
     * Returns the name.
     */
    public String getName()
    {
        return name;
    }

    /**
     * Sets the name.
     * @param name the name.
     */
    public void setName(String name)
    {
        this.name = name;
    }

    /**
     * Returns the latitude.
     */
    public double getLatitude()
    {
        return latitude;
    }
```

Figure 13-53

(Continued)

```java
/**
 * Sets the latitude.
 * @param latitude the latitude.
 */
public void setLatitude(double latitude)
{
    this.latitude = latitude;
}

/**
 * Returns the latitudeDegrees.
 */
public int getLatitudeDegrees()
{
    return latitudeDegrees;
}

/**
 * Sets the latitudeDegrees.
 * @param latitudeDegrees the latitudeDegrees.
 */
public void setLatitudeDegrees(int latitudeDegrees)
{
    this.latitudeDegrees = latitudeDegrees;
    recalculateLatitude();
}

/**
 * Returns the latitudeMinutes.
 */
public int getLatitudeMinutes()
{
    return latitudeMinutes;
}

/**
 * Sets the latitudeMinutes.
 * @param latitudeMinutes the latitudeMinutes.
 */
public void setLatitudeMinutes(int latitudeMinutes)
{
    this.latitudeMinutes = latitudeMinutes;
    recalculateLatitude();
}

/**
 * Returns the latitudeSeconds.
 */
public int getLatitudeSeconds()
{
    return latitudeSeconds;
}

/**
 * Sets the latitudeSeconds.
 * @param latitudeSeconds the latitudeSeconds.
 */
```

Figure 13-53
(Continued)

```java
public void setLatitudeSeconds(int latitudeSeconds)
{
    this.latitudeSeconds = latitudeSeconds;
    recalculateLatitude();
}

/**
 * Returns the longitude.
 */
public double getLongitude()
{
    return longitude;
}

/**
 * Sets the longitude.
 * @param longitude the longitude.
 */
public void setLongitude(double longitude)
{
    this.longitude = longitude;
}

/**
 * Returns the longitudeDegrees.
 */
public int getLongitudeDegrees()
{
    return longitudeDegrees;
}

/**
 * Sets the longitudeDegrees.
 * @param longitudeDegrees the longitudeDegrees.
 */
public void setLongitudeDegrees(int longitudeDegrees)
{
    this.longitudeDegrees = longitudeDegrees;
    recalculateLongitude();
}

/**
 * Returns the longitudeMinutes.
 */
public int getLongitudeMinutes()
{
    return longitudeMinutes;
}

/**
 * Sets the longitudeMinutes.
 * @param longitudeMinutes the longitudeMinutes.
 */
public void setLongitudeMinutes(int longitudeMinutes)
{
    this.longitudeMinutes = longitudeMinutes;
    recalculateLongitude();
```

Figure 13-53
(Continued)

```
/**
 * Returns the longitudeSeconds.
 */
public int getLongitudeSeconds()
{
    return longitudeSeconds;
}

/**
 * Sets the longitudeSeconds.
 * @param longitudeSeconds the longitudeSeconds.
 */
public void setLongitudeSeconds(int longitudeSeconds)
{
    this.longitudeSeconds = longitudeSeconds;
    recalculateLongitude();
}

/**
 * Recalculates latitude from degrees, minutes, seconds
 */
private void recalculateLatitude()
{
    int seconds = latitudeDegrees * 3600
                + latitudeMinutes * 60
                + latitudeSeconds;
    latitude = ((double) seconds) / 3600.0;
}

/**
 * Recalculates longitude from degrees, minutes, seconds
 */
private void recalculateLongitude()
{
    int seconds = longitudeDegrees * 3600
                + longitudeMinutes * 60
                + longitudeSeconds;
    longitude = ((double) seconds) / 3600.0;
}
```

round the value to the nearest integer value[15] in the appropriate units. The key method is getDistance(). It converts the locations from polar to rectangular coordinates (x, y, z) so that the straight-line distance between them (the distance directly through the earth) can be calculated. From this, the angle formed by the two points and the earth's center can be found, from which the distance along the earth's surface can be calculated.

---

[15]There is little point in calculating fractional miles or kilometers, since the values are approximate anyway. The earth is not perfectly spherical, and the radius differs somewhat between the poles and the equator.

Figure 13-54

A Bean That
Calculates the
Surface Distance
Between Two
Points on the
Earth's Surface

```java
package ijs.beans.distance;

import java.io.*;
import java.net.*;
import java.util.*;

/**
 * A class that computes the distance between
 * two points on the earth's surface.
 */
public class DistanceBean implements Serializable
{
    /**
     * Mean radius of the earth in kilometers
     */
    public static final double RADIUS = 6371.22;

    /**
     * Degree to radians conversion constant
     */
    public static final double D2R = Math.PI / 180.0;

    /**
     * km to miles conversion constant
     */
    public static final double KM2M =
        (2.54 * 12 * 5280) / 100000.0;

    // =========================================
    //      Instance variables
    // =========================================

    private LocationBean point1;
    private LocationBean point2;

    // =========================================
    //      Constructors
    // =========================================

    /**
     * Creates a new DistanceBean
     */
    public DistanceBean()
    {
        point1 = new LocationBean();
        point2 = new LocationBean();
    }

    // =========================================
    //      Instance methods
    // =========================================

    /**
     * Returns the first point.
     */
    public LocationBean getPoint1()
    {
```

Figure 13-54
(Continued)

```
      return point1;
}
/**
 * Sets the first point.
 * @param point1 the first point
 */
public void setPoint1(LocationBean point1)
{
    this.point1 = point1;
}

/**
 * Returns the second point.
 */
public LocationBean getPoint2()
{
    return point2;
}

/**
 * Sets the second point.
 * @param point2 the second point
 */
public void setPoint2(LocationBean point2)
{
    this.point2 = point2;
}

/**
 * Returns the distance in kilometers
 * between points 1 and 2 along the surface
 * of the earth.
 */

public double getDistance()
{
    double[] lat = new double[2];
    double[] lon = new double[2];

    lat[0] = point1.getLatitude();
    lat[1] = point2.getLatitude();

    lon[0] = point1.getLongitude();
    lon[1] = point2.getLongitude();

    double[] x = new double[2];
    double[] y = new double[2];
    double[] z = new double[2];

    for (int i = 0; i < 2; i++) {
        double phi = D2R * lat[i];
        double theta = D2R * (lon[i] + 360);
        x[i] = RADIUS * Math.cos(phi) * Math.cos(theta);
        y[i] = RADIUS * Math.cos(phi) * Math.sin(theta);
        z[i] = RADIUS * Math.sin(phi);
    }
```

Figure 13-54
(Continued)

```java
        double dx = x[0] - x[1];
        double dy = y[0] - y[1];
        double dz = z[0] - z[1];

        double sld = Math.sqrt(dx*dx + dy*dy + dz*dz);

        double d = 2 * RADIUS * Math.asin(sld / (2*RADIUS));

        return d;
    }

    /**
     * Returns the distance rounded
     * to the nearest whole kilometer
     */
    public int getDistanceInKilometers()
    {
        return (int) (getDistance() + 0.5);
    }

    /**
     * Returns the distance rounded
     * to the nearest whole mile
     */
    public int getDistanceInMiles()
    {
        return (int) (toMiles(getDistance()) + 0.5);
    }

    // ============================================
    //      Class methods
    // ============================================

    /**
     * Converts kilometers to miles
     */
    public static final double toMiles(double km)
    {
        return km / KM2M;
    }

    /**
     * Converts miles to kilometers
     */
    public static final double toKilometers(double miles)
    {
        return miles * KM2M;
    }
```

The HTML form that prompts for the values is shown in Figure 13-55. For each of the two locations, it has input fields for the name, latitude (degrees, minutes, seconds), and longitude (degrees, minutes, seconds). The form's ACTION attribute specifies the name of the JSP page that will display the results.

Figure 13-55

A Form That
Prompts for the
Location
Parameters

```
<HTML>

<HEAD>
<TITLE>Distance between Two Places on Earth</TITLE>
</HEAD>

<BODY>
<CENTER>
<H3>Distance between Two Places on Earth</H3>

<FORM METHOD="POST" ACTION="DistanceResults.jsp">
<TABLE BORDER="0" CELLPADDING="3" CELLSPACING="0">
    <TR>
        <TH WIDTH="250">Place Name</TH>
        <TH WIDTH="150" COLSPAN="3">Latitude<BR>(DD MM SS)</TH>
        <TH WIDTH="150" COLSPAN="3">Longitude<BR>(DD MM SS)</TH>
    </TR>
    <TR>
        <TD><INPUT TYPE="TEXT" NAME="city1"  SIZE="32"></TD>
        <TD><INPUT TYPE="TEXT" NAME="latdd1" SIZE="3"></TD>
        <TD><INPUT TYPE="TEXT" NAME="latmm1" SIZE="3"></TD>
        <TD><INPUT TYPE="TEXT" NAME="latss1" SIZE="3"></TD>
        <TD><INPUT TYPE="TEXT" NAME="londd1" SIZE="3"></TD>
        <TD><INPUT TYPE="TEXT" NAME="lonmm1" SIZE="3"></TD>
        <TD><INPUT TYPE="TEXT" NAME="lonss1" SIZE="3"></TD>
    </TR>
    <TR>
        <TD><INPUT TYPE="TEXT" NAME="city2"  SIZE="32"></TD>
        <TD><INPUT TYPE="TEXT" NAME="latdd2" SIZE="3"></TD>
        <TD><INPUT TYPE="TEXT" NAME="latmm2" SIZE="3"></TD>
        <TD><INPUT TYPE="TEXT" NAME="latss2" SIZE="3"></TD>
        <TD><INPUT TYPE="TEXT" NAME="londd2" SIZE="3"></TD>
        <TD><INPUT TYPE="TEXT" NAME="lonmm2" SIZE="3"></TD>
        <TD><INPUT TYPE="TEXT" NAME="lonss2" SIZE="3"></TD>
    </TR>
    <TR>
        <TD COLSPAN="7" ALIGN="CENTER">
            <INPUT TYPE="SUBMIT" VALUE="Submit">
            <INPUT TYPE="RESET"  VALUE="Clear">
        </TD>
    </TR>
</TABLE>
</FORM>
</CENTER>
</BODY>
</HTML>
```

DistanceResults.jsp (see Figure 13-56) declares three beans: one DistanceBean and its two associated LocationBeans. It sets the LocationBean properties from the corresponding request parameters and then sets the DistanceBean point1 and point2 properties. The distance values are then extracted and displayed. All this is done entirely with <jsp:useBean>, <jsp:setProperty>, and <jsp:getProperty>, with no Java scriptlets or declarations.

Figure 13-56

A JSP Page
That Uses
DistanceBean
to Calculate the
Distance Between
the Two Locations

```jsp
<%@ page import="ijs.beans.distance.*" %>

<%-- Get an instance of the Distance bean --%>

<jsp:useBean
     id="dist"
     class="ijs.beans.distance.DistanceBean"
     />

<%-- and two Location beans --%>

<jsp:useBean
     id="point1"
     class="ijs.beans.distance.LocationBean"
     />

<jsp:useBean
     id="point2"
     class="ijs.beans.distance.LocationBean"
     />

<HTML>

<HEAD>
<TITLE>Distance between Two Places on Earth</TITLE>
</HEAD>

<BODY>
<CENTER>
<H3>Distance between Two Places on Earth</H3>

<%-- Point 1 --%>

<jsp:setProperty name="point1"
                   property="name"
                   param="city1"/>
<jsp:setProperty name="point1"
                   property="latitudeDegrees"
                   param="latdd1"/>
<jsp:setProperty name="point1"
                   property="latitudeMinutes"
                   param="latmm1"/>
<jsp:setProperty name="point1"
                   property="latitudeSeconds"
                   param="latss1"/>
<jsp:setProperty name="point1"
                   property="longitudeDegrees"
                   param="londd1"/>
<jsp:setProperty name="point1"
                   property="longitudeMinutes"
                   param="lonmm1"/>
<jsp:setProperty name="point1"
                   property="longitudeSeconds"
                   param="lonss1"/>

<%-- Point 2 --%>
```

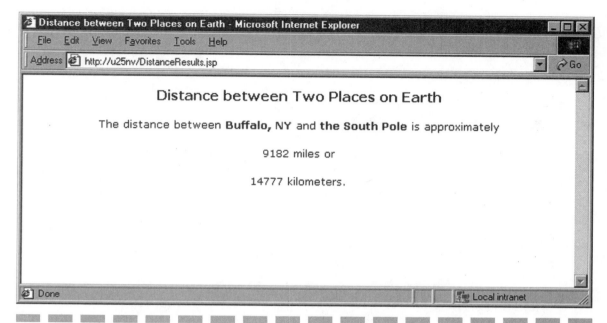

Figure 13-58 Results Calculated by the `DistanceBean`

Applications

Overview

Throughout our examination of what servlets can do, we have found that there is very little that they cannot do. Servlets prove to be ideal middleware, providing the glue that makes a wide range of data sources and processing tools work together.

Up to this point, we have focused mainly on techniques—how to access a database, how to handle sessions and threads, how to interface with other servers and clients. In this final chapter we will take a look at several different types of applications in which servlets can be useful:

- Serving up images
- Creating spreadsheets
- Sending and receiving mail
- Systems administration
- And of course, games

Some of these are complete applications, but others are intended as starting points for your own exploration. Almost all the servlets in this book also could be written as JavaServer Pages (JSPs). You may find it instructive to convert them. Many of the techniques we have covered involve low-level interfaces such as sockets; there are higher-level alternatives such as Enterprise Java Beans for robust, scalable transaction handling, JNDI (Java Naming and Directory Interface) for directory server access, Java Data Objects for OODBMS, and the JavaMail API. You can experiment with communicating through different layers; servlets can be used with all of them.

14.1 Supporting New Image Types

As the Web has evolved, not all technologies have moved at the same pace. Images, for example, exist in a wide variety of formats. They can be included in HTML pages using the <IMG> tag, but there is no universally accepted standard for the format in which the images can be represented. Even the official HTML 4.01 specification says only that "...examples of widely recognized image formats include GIF, JPEG, and PNG."[1] The result is that browsers differ in their list of supported for-

---

[1] See *http://www.w3.org/TR/html4/struct/objects.html#h-13.2.*

mats. Java applets (as of JDK 1.1.x, the default version in most browsers) support only GIF and JPEG.

Class Libraries That Can Translate Image Formats

The problem is not intrinsically difficult to solve. Graphics tools such as Jasc PaintShop Pro, Adobe PhotoShop, and Microsoft Photo Editor easily convert one format to another. There are Java class libraries for automated conversion as well. The Java Advanced Imaging API can handle most types of image I/O and conversion in the JDK 1.2 environment. According to Sun, a standard extension for image I/O is currently being developed.

A simple package that works well in the JDK 1.1.x environment is the Jimi class library. Jimi was developed originally by Activated Intelligence, LLC, of Cary, North Carolina, but was purchased by Sun Microsystems and is freely available for download at *http://java.sun.com/products/jimi*. Jimi supports a wide variety of graphics formats and allows developers to extend its capabilities by adding new format handlers. Images can be loaded from files, generic input streams, or `java.awt.Image` objects.

Servlets Integrate Translation Software and the Web

In line with their role as an enabling technology, servlets can be used to bring together the image files, the translation software, and the browser environment. Figure 14-1 shows a servlet that can read image data in a variety of formats and use Jimi to translate it to JPEG. The resulting image stream is written to the servlet response output stream.

The servlet accepts a `url` parameter from the HTTP request, which must be an absolute path relative to the Web server document root. From this parameter, the servlet context's `getRealPath()` method is invoked to get an absolute file name. The servlet then uses a static method in the main Jimi class to get a `java.awt.ImageProducer` object:

```
ImageProducer producer = Jimi.getImageProducer(fileName);
```

■■■ ■■ ■■ ■■
Figure 14-1
A Servlet That Uses
Jimi to Convert
Image Formats

```
package ijs.app.image;

import com.sun.jimi.core.*;
import java.awt.image.*;
import java.io.*;
import java.net.*;
import java.util.*;
import javax.servlet.*;

/**
 * A servlet that reads an image file in a number of different
 * formats and uses JIMI converts it to a JPEG data stream.
 */
public class ImageViewerServlet extends GenericServlet
{
    public void service(
            ServletRequest request,
            ServletResponse response)
        throws ServletException, IOException
    {
        // Get URL of the image file

        String urlString = request.getParameter("url");
        if (urlString == null)
            throw new ServletException
            ("No URL specified");

        // From the URL, get the real file name

        ServletContext application = getServletContext();
        String fileName = application.getRealPath(urlString);

        // Use Jimi to get an ImageProducer for the file

        ImageProducer producer =
            Jimi.getImageProducer(fileName);

        // Write the image to the output stream

        ServletOutputStream out = response.getOutputStream();
        try {
            Jimi.putImage("image/jpeg", producer, out);
        }
        catch (JimiException e) {
            throw new IOException(e.getMessage());
        }
        out.flush();
        out.close();
    }
}
```

Once the `ImageProducer` is created, the servlet opens the servlet output stream, sets its content type to image/jpeg, and writes the image data:

```
Jimi.putImage("image/jpeg", producer, out);
```

Using the ImageViewer Servlet

The image translation servlet can be used wherever any ordinary URL is used. In a Web page, for example, the <IMG> tag accepts a URL in its SRC attribute. This URL ordinarily refers to a static image file, but a call to the servlet can be placed here just as well. The JimiProClasses.zip file needs to be added to the servlet engine's class path, but no special environment in the browser is required. Figure 14-2 illustrates the use of ImageViewer to display a TIFF file in a Web page. In the example, the <IMG> tag has an SRC attribute that points to the servlet:

```
SRC="/servlet/ImageViewer?url=/ijs/Chap14/image/fig12-15.tif"
```

The image being translated is Figure 12-15 from this book. It was captured originally as a screen shot using Paint Shop Pro 5 from Jasc Software and saved in TIFF format for high-resolution output. If you try to display it directly, the browser balks and displays an image placeholder instead. However, when it is filtered through the ImageViewer servlet, it becomes the JPEG image stream shown in Figure 14-3.

Figure 14-2

A Demonstration of the ImageViewer Servlet

```
<HTML>

<HEAD>
<TITLE>A Demonstration of the ImageViewer Servlet</TITLE>
</HEAD>

<BODY>
<H3>A Demonstration of the ImageViewer Servlet</H3>

This web page uses the ImageViewer servlet
to display an image that is in TIFF format.
The image being displayed is the original source
for Figure 12-15.

<P>
<IMG SRC=
"/servlet/ImageViewer?url=/ijs/Chap14/image/fig12-15.tif">
</BODY>

</HTML>
```

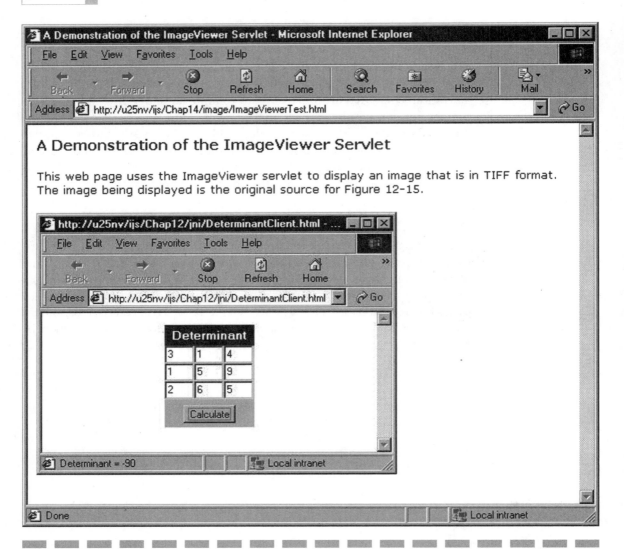

Figure 14-3 Output of the Demonstration

14.2 Downloading Data as a Spreadsheet

Spreadsheet programs such as Microsoft Excel or Lotus 1-2-3 are the natural destinations for tabular data. Users are familiar with them, their graphics capabilities are very good, and they can read and write most data formats. Although much Web output is organized in HTML tables, and spreadsheet programs may be able to read HTML, there is a missing step in the middle. HTML documents cannot be imported directly from the Web into the spreadsheet program; usually they must be downloaded as files and then imported.

Fortunately, you need not rely on the spreadsheet program to provide an explicit means of importing a Web page—most spreadsheet programs can be registered as external viewers for data in a form you can easily produce. Microsoft Excel in the Windows environment, for example, can be associated with a file extension so that when a file of that type is downloaded, Excel will be used to open it. If the file is contained in a folder in the local file system, and the file's icon is double-clicked, Windows starts a copy of Excel that loads the data. The same is true for URLs opened in a Web browser, although the situation is more complicated, as we will see.

MIME Types and CSV

It is not necessary to use the native internal worksheet format—Excel will comfortably handle any of several standard data-exchange formats. The easiest to produce is an ASCII text file with comma-separated values (CSVs). This is a very simple format, consisting of a row of column headings followed by any number of data rows. The values in each of these rows are separated by commas. If there are any commas in a data field, it is written as a quoted string to avoid confusing the parser. Files of this type typically have the extension `.csv`.

Curiously enough, there is no MIME type officially[2] assigned to the comma-separated values format. Moreover, the two major Web browsers differ considerably in how they handle downloaded CSV files, depending on the HTTP headers and the form of the URL. The variables involved are these:

■ *MIME type.* This is sent in the `Content-Type` header. Common choices are `application/octet-stream` and `application/vnd.ms-excel`. If neither is specified, the browser assumes `text/html` or `text/plain`, neither of which will work for this purpose.

---

[2]The Internet Architecture Board (IAB) has designated the Internet Assigned Numbers Authority (IANA) as the official repository of MIME types and other protocol numbers. The list can be found at *http://www.isi.edu/in-notes/iana/assignments/media-types/*.

■ *Content disposition*. As is the case with an email attachment, a file name can be suggested for the downloaded data. This is specified in a `Content-Disposition` header as follows:

```
Content-Disposition: attachment; filename="name"
```

■ *URL*. The URL used to refer to the file may have additional path information consisting of a file name with a `.csv` extension.

Servlets and CGI programs can be found that use all combinations of these variables, with varying degrees of success. In the example below, we will show how a servlet can make the best choice, depending on the user's browser environment.

Servlets Bridge the Gap

In this section we will revisit the loan amortization calculator from Section 13-8, this time downloading the results as an Excel spreadsheet instead of an HTML table. The advantage of this approach is that the data can be further manipulated by the user and integrated into other applications. Figure 14-4 shows the revised HTML form that collects the loan parameters. An example of the filled-out form is shown in Figure 14-5. It has three input fields: `principal`, `interestRate`, and `term`. When the user clicks the "Submit" button, the fields are validated and then passed to the `LoanDownload` servlet. The URL for this servlet has additional path information appended to it in the form of a file name—`loan.csv`.

The servlet we will use is `LoanDownload`, shown in Figure 14-6. The JavaBean we developed in Chapter 13 that performs the actual calculation (`ijs.beans.loan.LoanBean`) can be reused unchanged, although this time it will be called directly from within the servlet.

The servlet performs the expected operations of retrieving the input parameters, creating the bean, setting its properties, and then rendering its output (which is simple—just column values with commas in between). The only twist is that the browser environment will be taken into account in generating the `Content-Disposition` header. Netscape can launch Excel as a separate application and send the `.csv` file to it. Internet Explorer can do the same, but it also can invoke Excel directly in the browser window. Its two behaviors are triggered by the presence or absence of a file name in a `Content-Disposition` header. If there is a

Figure   14-4
The HTML Form
That Invokes the
Loan Calculation
Servlet

```
<HTML>

<HEAD>
<TITLE>Loan Calculator</TITLE>
<SCRIPT LANGUAGE="JavaScript" SRC="CheckParms.js">
</SCRIPT>
</HEAD>

<BODY>
<CENTER>
<FORM METHOD="POST" ACTION="/servlet/LoanDownload/loan.csv"
   onSubmit="return checkParms(this);">
<TABLE BORDER="0" CELLPADDING="3">

    <TR><TD ALIGN="CENTER" COLSPAN="2">
        <H3>Loan Calculator</H3>
        </TD></TR>

    <TR><TD>Principal amount:</TD>
        <TD><INPUT NAME="principal" TYPE="text" SIZE="16"
                ALIGN="right"></TD></TR>

    <TR><TD>Interest rate:</TD>
        <TD><INPUT NAME="interestRate" TYPE="text" SIZE="8"
                ALIGN="right"> (e.g. 6.875)</TD></TR>

    <TR><TD>Term:</TD>
        <TD><INPUT NAME="term" TYPE="text" SIZE="8"
                ALIGN="right"> (in years)</TD></TR>

    <TR><TD> </TD>
        <TD><INPUT TYPE="SUBMIT" VALUE="submit">
            <INPUT TYPE="RESET"  VALUE="clear"></TD></TR>

</TABLE>
</FORM>
</CENTER>
</BODY>
</HTML>
```

file name, Internet Explorer downloads it to an external instance of Excel. If not, it starts Excel in the browser window, which is the preferred behavior in our case.

The browser identification can be found in the USER_AGENT header, but rather than specifically limiting ourselves to a particular browser (there may be others that have the behavior we want), we will take the more direct approach of checking the ACCEPT header. An HTTP client sends an ACCEPT header to indicate the MIME types it is equipped to handle. If it contains application/vnd.ms-excel, we can expect it to handle our CSV data directly within the browser. To force this behavior, we do not send a file name in the Content-Disposition header.

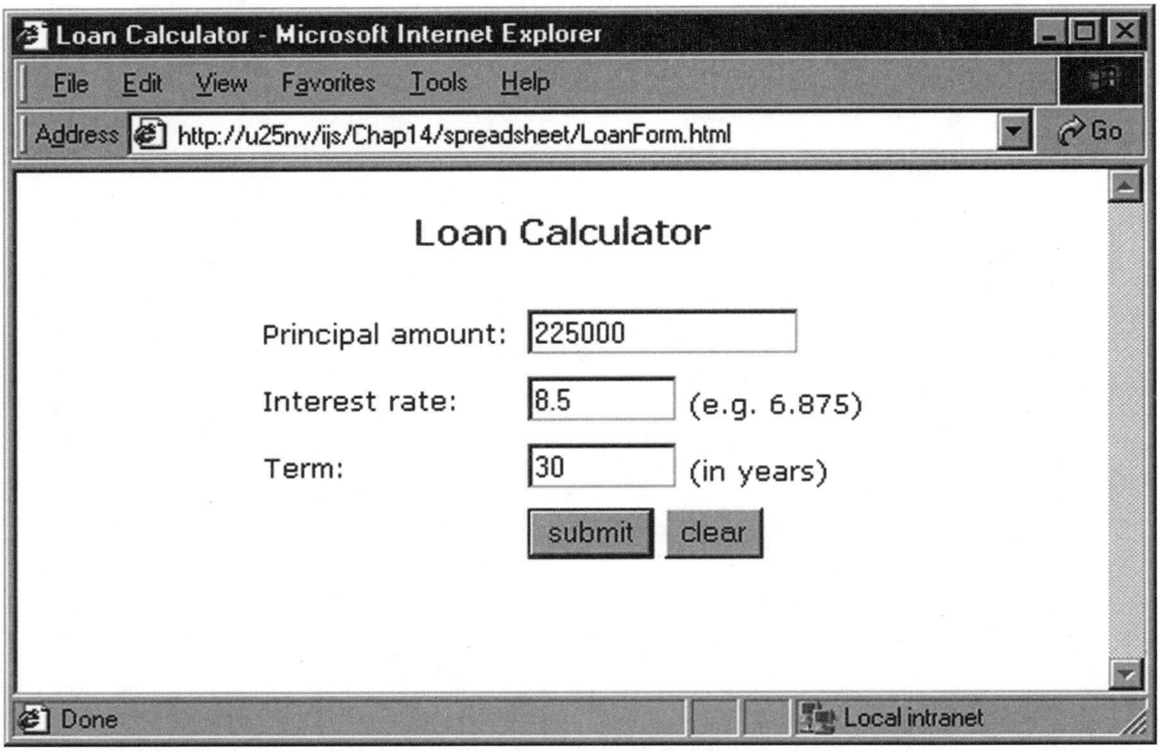

Figure 14-5 Input for the Loan Calculation

Figure 14-7 shows the text data stream produced. The first row consists of the five column labels, quoted and separated by commas. The remaining rows have the numeric values of the five fields, again separated by commas.

If all goes well, the browser will launch Excel in the browser window and show the results, as seen in Figure 14-8. The user now can save the file locally, create graphs and charts, and integrate the results into other applications.

Figure 14-6

A Servlet That
Creates
Spreadsheet
Output

```java
package ijs.app.spreadsheet;

import ijs.beans.loan.*;
import java.io.*;
import java.net.*;
import java.text.*;
import java.util.*;
import javax.servlet.*;
import javax.servlet.http.*;

/**
* A class that downloads a loan amortization schedule
* as a Microsoft Excel spreadsheet
*/
public class LoanDownloadServlet extends HttpServlet
{
    public void doPost(
        HttpServletRequest request,
        HttpServletResponse response)
      throws ServletException, IOException
    {
        PrintWriter out = response.getWriter();

        // Check the ACCEPT header to determine if the
        // web browser will handle Excel-formatted
        // data directly

        boolean InternetExplorer = false;
        String accept = request.getHeader("ACCEPT");
        if (accept != null) {
            accept = accept.toLowerCase();
            int p = accept.indexOf("application/vnd.ms-excel");
            InternetExplorer = (p != -1);
        }

        // Set the content type

        response.setContentType("application/vnd.ms-excel");

        if (!InternetExplorer) {

            // The browser does not handle Excel data
            // directly - it needs to download it and
            // spawn an external viewer.  In this case,
            // we need to specify a file name.
            //
            // We will use loanxxxx.csv, where
            // xxxx is a random 4-digit number

            int number = (int)
                ((241 * System.currentTimeMillis()) % 9973);

            String fileName = "0000" + number;
            fileName = fileName.substring
                (fileName.length() - 4);
            fileName = "loan" + fileName + ".csv";
            String contentDisposition = "attachment"
```

```
                                    + ";filename=\"" + fileName + "\"";

            response.setHeader
               ("Content-Disposition", contentDisposition);
        }

        // Get the request parameters

        double principal;
        double interestRate;
        int term;

        String parm;

        // Principal

        parm = request.getParameter("principal");
        if (parm == null)
           throw new ServletException
           ("Principal was not specified");
        principal = Double.valueOf(parm).doubleValue();

        // Interest rate

        parm = request.getParameter("interestRate");
        if (parm == null)
           throw new ServletException
           ("Interest rate was not specified");
        interestRate = Double.valueOf(parm).doubleValue();

        // Term

        parm = request.getParameter("term");
        if (parm == null)
           throw new ServletException
           ("Term was not specified");
        term = Integer.parseInt(parm);

        // Create the bean that calculates the loan

        LoanBean loan = new LoanBean();

        loan.setPrincipal(principal);
        loan.setInterestRate(interestRate);
        loan.setTerm(term);

        // Calculate the monthly payment

        double monthlyPayment = loan.getMonthlyPayment();

        // Write the column headings

        out.println("\"Payment\","
           + "\"Interest\","
           + "\"Principal\","
           + "\"Total\","
           + "\"Balance\""
```

Figure 14-6
(Continued)

```
            );

   // Write each payment

   DecimalFormat fmt = new DecimalFormat("########0.00");

   int n = loan.getNumberOfPayments();
   for (int i = 0; i < n; i++) {
      int pmtnbr = i+1;
      double intamt = loan.getInterestAmount(pmtnbr);
      double priamt = loan.getPrincipalAmount(pmtnbr);
      double totpmt = loan.getTotalPayment(pmtnbr);
      double balance = loan.getBalance(pmtnbr);
      out.println(pmtnbr
         + "," + fmt.format(intamt)
         + "," + fmt.format(priamt)
         + "," + fmt.format(totpmt)
         + "," + fmt.format(balance)
         );
   }

   out.flush();
   out.close();
}
```

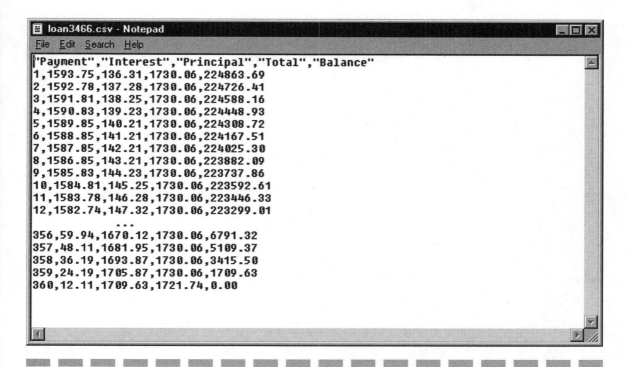

Figure 14-7 Comma-Separated Values Data Generated by the LoanDownload Servlet

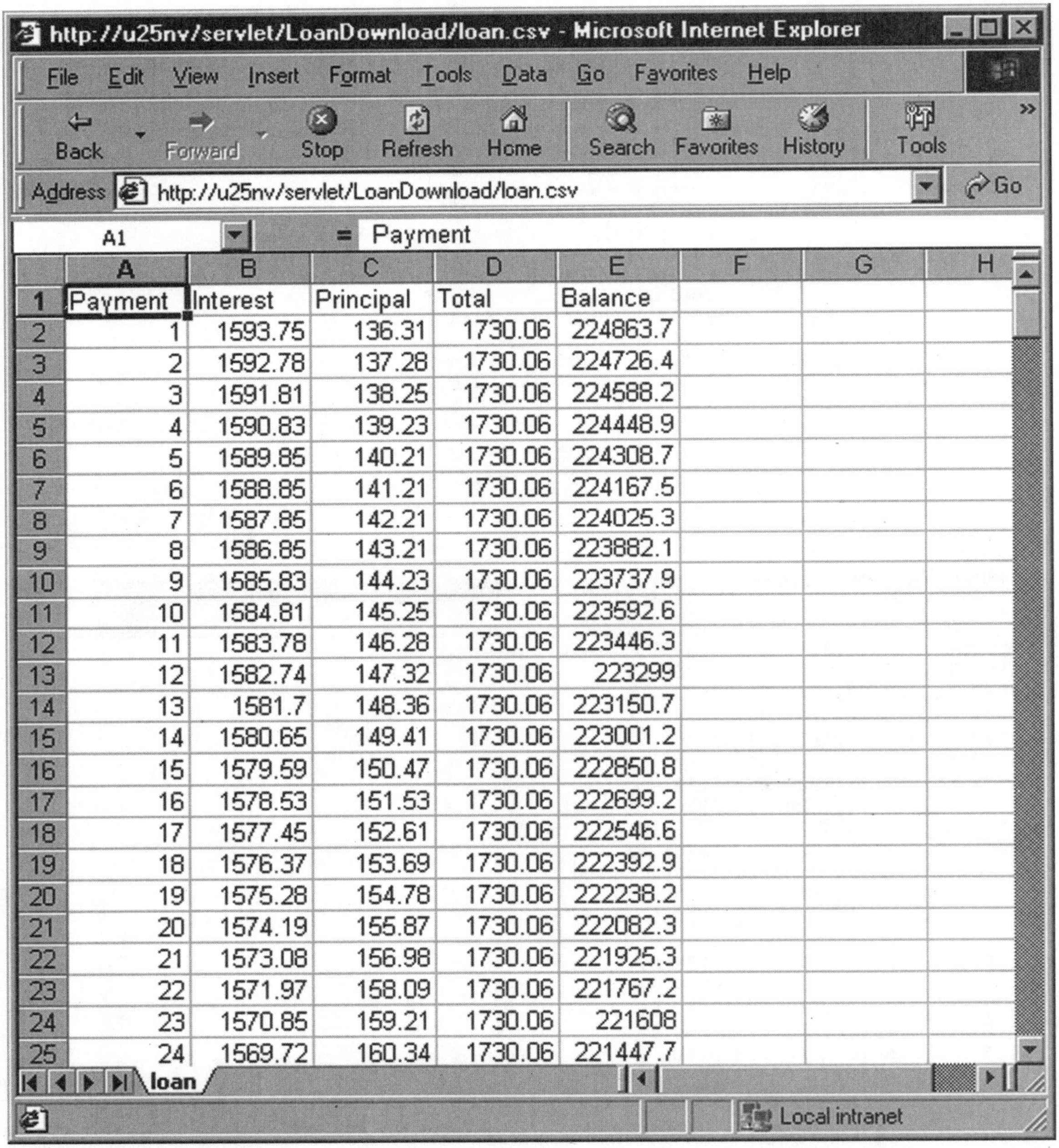

	A	B	C	D	E	F	G	H
1	Payment	Interest	Principal	Total	Balance			
2	1	1593.75	136.31	1730.06	224863.7			
3	2	1592.78	137.28	1730.06	224726.4			
4	3	1591.81	138.25	1730.06	224588.2			
5	4	1590.83	139.23	1730.06	224448.9			
6	5	1589.85	140.21	1730.06	224308.7			
7	6	1588.85	141.21	1730.06	224167.5			
8	7	1587.85	142.21	1730.06	224025.3			
9	8	1586.85	143.21	1730.06	223882.1			
10	9	1585.83	144.23	1730.06	223737.9			
11	10	1584.81	145.25	1730.06	223592.6			
12	11	1583.78	146.28	1730.06	223446.3			
13	12	1582.74	147.32	1730.06	223299			
14	13	1581.7	148.36	1730.06	223150.7			
15	14	1580.65	149.41	1730.06	223001.2			
16	15	1579.59	150.47	1730.06	222850.8			
17	16	1578.53	151.53	1730.06	222699.2			
18	17	1577.45	152.61	1730.06	222546.6			
19	18	1576.37	153.69	1730.06	222392.9			
20	19	1575.28	154.78	1730.06	222238.2			
21	20	1574.19	155.87	1730.06	222082.3			
22	21	1573.08	156.98	1730.06	221925.3			
23	22	1571.97	158.09	1730.06	221767.2			
24	23	1570.85	159.21	1730.06	221608			
25	24	1569.72	160.34	1730.06	221447.7			

Figure 14-8 Loan Amortization Schedule after Being Downloaded to Microsoft Excel

14.3 Sending Mail

As business comes to rely more and more on email, the ability to send mail from within an application becomes important. Besides the traditional human-to-human email systems, we see

- *Human to computer.* Subscriptions to LISTSERV's, registering for classes, requesting documents, and other applications use email as a front-end to a program listening for messages.
- *Computer to human.* Batch systems that basically run unattended can use email to notify responsible parties when exceptions occur.
- *Computer to computer.* List servers can use email as both a source of commands and a means of delivering output to subscribers.

Although email may be slow and bulky compared with other networking architectures, it has two key advantages:

1. It runs well in a completely heterogeneous environment that includes mainframes, department servers, and personal computers.
2. It does not require both parties to be available at the same time—messages are queued up and handled when the receiving party is ready.

This section and the next will provide an overview of simple ways to send and receive email from within a Java program, with complete working examples in both cases. These are not robust, industrial-strength implementations—in particular, there is no security and only rudimentary error checking—but they are intended to illustrate the protocols and techniques. Your particular security and error-handling environment will dictate what you need to do to adapt them to your use.

Java Mail Packages

There are several choices available for sending mail from Java. Sun provides a JavaMail API as a Java platform standard extension. The API is a set of abstract classes and interfaces for mail and messaging applications, allowing for service providers to plug in their own implementations of the core protocols. Sun also ships a reference implementation of the basic package, which also requires the JavaBeans Activation Framework to be installed.

JavaMail works well, but it may be overkill for some applications. If all you need is basic computer-generated transmission of ordinary email messages, the Simple Mail Transfer Protocol (SMTP) is easy to use directly. All you need is the standard `java.net.*` classes and a network connection on which you can use sockets.

Simple Mail Transfer Protocol

SMTP is a well-established protocol for sending mail across a network. It is fully documented in RFC 821, which can be downloaded from *http://www.freesoft.org/CIE/RFC/821/index.htm*. Its basic operations involve little more than

1. Opening a socket for communicating with the SMTP mail host.
2. Verifying the domain name with the HELO command.
3. Specifying the sender with the MAIL from:*<user>* command.
4. Specifying the receiver(s) with one or more RCPT to:*<user>* commands.
5. Sending data with the DATA command.
6. Issuing the QUIT command and closing the socket.

After each command is issued, the mail host responds with a three-digit reply code that indicates the success or failure of the operation.

A Working Example

In this section we will develop a working version of a JavaServer Page (JSP) that sends email using SMTP. Figure 14-9 shows an HTML form that captures all the fields we need—the mail host, the sender and receiver names, the subject, and the message text. Figure 14-10 shows the HTML used to produce the form.

To process the form, the JSP page reads and validates each of the input parameters, throwing a RuntimeException if any are missing or invalid. It then opens a socket connection to the mail host and begins issuing commands. The commands and responses are written to a log file that is displayed in the browser when the session is completed. In the log, commands sent from the client (the Web browser) are prefixed with C:. Responses from the server (the mail host) are prefixed with S:.

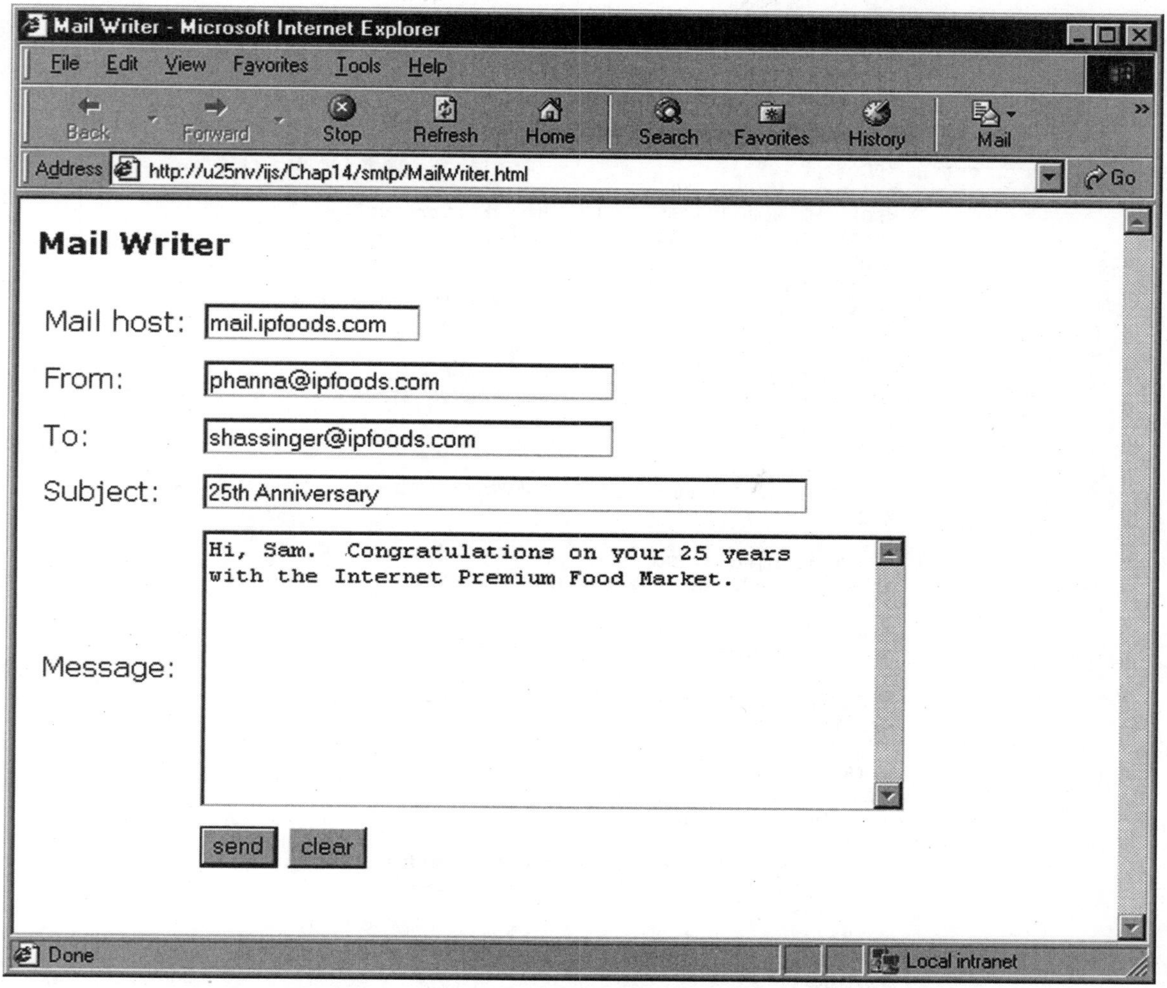

Figure 14-9 MailWriter Input Form

The JSP page uses two local methods called sendCommand() and sendData() to simplify the program flow. When sendCommand() is called, it echoes its command to the log page and then sends it to the mail host. The response coming back is also echoed to the log page. The complete JSP listing is found in Figure 14-11, and the log page is shown in Figure 14-12.

Figure 14-10
HTML for the
MailWriter
Input Form

```
<HTML>

<HEAD>
<TITLE>Mail Writer</TITLE>
</HEAD>

<BODY>
<H3>Mail Writer</H3>
<FORM METHOD="POST" ACTION="MailWriter.jsp">
<TABLE BORDER=0 CELLPADDING=5 CELLSPACING=0>
<TR>
    <TD>Mail host:</TD>
    <TD><INPUT NAME="mailHost" TYPE="TEXT" SIZE=16></TD>
</TR>
<TR>
    <TD>From:</TD>
    <TD><INPUT NAME="from" TYPE="TEXT" SIZE=32></TD>
</TR>
<TR>
    <TD>To:</TD>
    <TD><INPUT NAME="to" TYPE="TEXT" SIZE=32></TD>
</TR>
<TR>
    <TD>Subject:</TD>
    <TD><INPUT NAME="subject" TYPE="TEXT" SIZE=48></TD>
</TR>
<TR>
    <TD>Message:</TD>
    <TD>
<TEXTAREA NAME="message" ROWS=10 COLS=48>
</TEXTAREA>
    </TD>
</TR>
<TR>
    <TD> </TD>
    <TD>
        <INPUT TYPE="SUBMIT" VALUE="send">
        <INPUT TYPE="RESET"  VALUE="clear">
    </TD>
</TR>
</TABLE>
</FORM>
</BODY>

</HTML>
```

Figure 14-11

A JSP Page That
Sends Mail Using
SMTP

```jsp
<%@ page
      errorPage="/ErrorPage.jsp"
      import="java.io.*,java.net.*,java.util.*"
%>
<%!
    /**
     * Inner class for passing parameters
     * between methods.
     */
    class Parameters
    {
        JspWriter out;
        Socket socket;
        PrintWriter mailOut;
        BufferedReader mailIn;
    }

    /**
     * Sends a command to the host and echoes
     * the response to the web page.  Does no
     * error handling.
     */
    void sendCommand(Parameters parms, String cmd)
        throws IOException
    {
        parms.out.println("C: " + cmd);
        parms.mailOut.print(cmd + "\r\n");
        parms.mailOut.flush();
        String line = parms.mailIn.readLine();
        parms.out.println("S: " + line);
    }

    /**
     * Sends data to the host.
     * Does no error handling.
     */
    void sendData(
            Parameters parms,
            String to,
            String subject,
            String message)
        throws IOException
    {
        message = "to: " + to + "\r\n" + message;
        message = "subject: " + subject + "\r\n" + message;
        parms.out.println(message);
        parms.mailOut.print(message);
        parms.mailOut.print("\r\n.\r\n");
        parms.mailOut.flush();
        String line = parms.mailIn.readLine();
        parms.out.println("S: " + line);
    }
%>
<%
    // Get form parameters

    String mailHost = request.getParameter("mailHost");
```

Figure 14-11
(Continued)

```
if ((mailHost == null) || (mailHost.trim().equals("")))
   throw new RuntimeException
   ("No mailHost parameter specified");

String from = request.getParameter("from");
if ((from == null) || (from.trim().equals("")))
   throw new RuntimeException
   ("No from parameter specified");

String to = request.getParameter("to");
if ((to == null) || (to.trim().equals("")))
   throw new RuntimeException
   ("No to parameter specified");

String subject = request.getParameter("subject");
if ((subject == null) || (subject.trim().equals("")))
   throw new RuntimeException
   ("No subject parameter specified");

String message = request.getParameter("message");
if ((message == null) || (message.trim().equals("")))
   throw new RuntimeException
   ("No message parameter specified");

// Open a socket connection to the SMTP host
// and prepare the input and output streams

out.println("<H3>Mail Writer Log</H3>");
out.println("<PRE>");
Parameters parms = new Parameters();
parms.out = out;
parms.socket = new Socket(mailHost, 25);

parms.mailOut =
   new PrintWriter(parms.socket.getOutputStream(), true);

parms.mailIn =
   new BufferedReader(
   new InputStreamReader(
   parms.socket.getInputStream()));

// Read the greeting from the SMTP host

String line = parms.mailIn.readLine();
parms.out.println("S: " + line);

sendCommand(parms, "HELO " + mailHost);
sendCommand(parms, "MAIL from:" + from);
sendCommand(parms, "RCPT to:" + to);
sendCommand(parms, "DATA");
sendData(parms, to, subject, message);
sendCommand(parms, "QUIT");

parms.socket.close();
out.println("</PRE>");
```

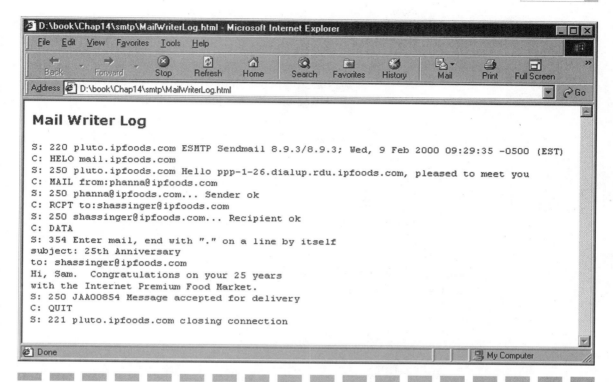

Figure 14-12 The `MailWriter` Log

14.4 Receiving Mail

The preceding section dealt with sending mail from within a Java application. This section deals with the other side—receiving mail. As is the case with sending mail, the JavaMail API provides classes and interfaces for handling incoming mail. Again, however, for simple applications, you can access the mail system directly using the Post Office Protocol (POP3), which is documented in RFC 1725, available at *http://www.freesoft.org/CIE/RFC/1725/index.htm.*

Like SMTP, POP3 uses a simple set of commands and positive or negative responses, all sent in ordinary ASCII format in lines terminated with a CR+LF. We will use just the following:

user <username>   Identifies the user.

pass <password>   Sends the user's password to the server.

list   Causes the server to send a list of message numbers and their lengths. The list is terminated with a line containing just a period.

retr <index>   Retrieves the data for the specified message number. The data are terminated with a line containing just a period.

dele <index>   Deletes the specified message.

quit   Closes the server session.

Receiving mail is somewhat more complicated because of the variety of formats that messages and attachments can take. In our example, we will simply download each mail message in its ordinary ASCII form with all its headers intact. This is well suited for postprocessing applications that simply read the text.

A Working Example

Figure 14-13 shows the login form that specifies the necessary parameters—the mail host, the user ID, and the user's password. The HTML that generates the form is listed in Figure 14-14. The ACTION parameter in its <FORM> tag identifies the JSP page that will process the form (MailReader.jsp).

MailReader.jsp validates the parameters as before and then opens a socket to the mail host. We will again use a sendCommand() subroutine to issue all the commands and log both sides of the transmission in a log page. The login credentials are sent with the USER and PASS commands and then the list of message numbers is retrieved with the LIST command. For each message, the getMessage() subroutine issues a RETR command. This returns a line containing the reply code (+OK) and the message length in bytes, followed by the message headers and data lines, terminated with a line consisting of a single period. The complete message is written to a file named mail**xxx** where xxx is the message number. After it is downloaded, it is deleted from the mail server with the DELE command. After the last message is retrieved, the program issues a QUIT command and closes the socket.

A complete listing of MailReader.jsp can be found in Figure 14-15, and the log it generates is shown in Figure 14-16.

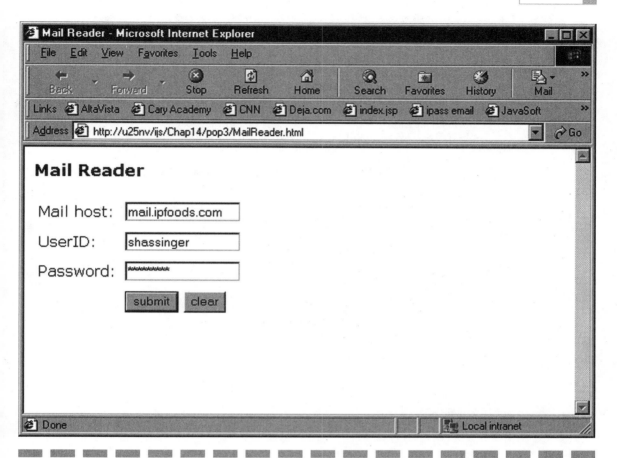

Figure 14-13 MailReader Input Form

Figure 14-14
HTML for the
MailReader
Input Form

```html
<HTML>

<HEAD>
<TITLE>Mail Reader</TITLE>
</HEAD>

<BODY>
<H3>Mail Reader</H3>
<FORM METHOD="POST" ACTION="MailReader.jsp">
<TABLE BORDER=0 CELLPADDING=5 CELLSPACING=0>
   <TR>
      <TD>Mail host:</TD>
      <TD><INPUT NAME="mailHost" TYPE="TEXT" SIZE=16</TD>
   </TR>
   <TR>
      <TD>UserID:</TD>
      <TD><INPUT NAME="userID" TYPE="TEXT" SIZE=16</TD>
   </TR>
   <TR>
      <TD>Password:</TD>
      <TD><INPUT NAME="password" TYPE="PASSWORD" SIZE=16</TD>
   </TR>
   <TR>
      <TD> </TD>
      <TD>
         <INPUT TYPE="SUBMIT" VALUE="submit">
         <INPUT TYPE="RESET" VALUE="clear">
      </TD>
   </TR>
</TABLE>
</FORM>
</BODY>

</HTML>
```

Figure 14-15
A JSP Page That
Reads Mail Using
POP3

```
<%@ page
    contentType="text/plain"
    errorPage="/ErrorPage.jsp"
    import="java.io.*,java.net.*,java.util.*"
%>
<%!
    /**
     * Inner class for storing parameters
     * between methods.
     */
    class Parameters
    {
        HttpServletRequest request;
        JspWriter out;
        Socket socket;
        PrintWriter mailOut;
        BufferedReader mailIn;
    }

    /**
     * Sends a command to the host and echoes
     * the response to the web page.  Does no
     * error handling.
     */
    void sendCommand(Parameters parms, String cmd)
        throws IOException
    {
        parms.out.println("C: " + cmd);
        parms.mailOut.print(cmd + "\r\n");
        parms.mailOut.flush();
        String line = parms.mailIn.readLine();
        parms.out.println("S: " + line);
    }

    /**
     * Retrieves a message from the mailbox
     */
    void getMessage(Parameters parms, int msg)
        throws IOException
    {
        // Send the RETR to retrieve the message

        parms.out.println("Retrieving " + msg);
        sendCommand(parms, "RETR " + msg);

        // This program simply saves each message
        // as a file.  See RFC 822 for the format.

        String thisURI = parms.request.getRequestURI();
        String thisPath = parms.request.getRealPath(thisURI);
        File thisFile = new File(thisPath);
        String fileName =
            thisFile.getParent() + "/mail" + msg + ".eml";
        PrintWriter fileOut =
            new PrintWriter(new FileWriter(fileName));
        for (;;) {
            String line = parms.mailIn.readLine();
```

Figure 14-15
(Continued)

```
                          if (line.startsWith("."))
                              break;
                          fileOut.println(line);
                      }
                  fileOut.flush();
                  fileOut.close();
              }
          %>
          <%
             // Get form parameters

             String mailHost = request.getParameter("mailHost");
             if ((mailHost == null) || (mailHost.trim().equals("")))
                throw new RuntimeException
                ("No mail host specified");

             String userID = request.getParameter("userID");
             if ((userID == null) || (userID.trim().equals("")))
                throw new RuntimeException
                ("No userID specified");

             String password = request.getParameter("password");
             if ((password == null) || (password.trim().equals("")))
                throw new RuntimeException
                ("No password specified");

             // Open a socket to the mail host
             // and get its input and output streams

             out.println("<H3>Mail Reader Log</H3>");
             out.println("<PRE>");
             Parameters parms = new Parameters();
             parms.request = request;
             parms.out = out;
             parms.socket = new Socket(mailHost, 110);

             parms.mailOut =
                new PrintWriter(parms.socket.getOutputStream());

             parms.mailIn =
                new BufferedReader(
                new InputStreamReader(parms.socket.getInputStream()));

             // Read the hello message sent by the mail host

             String line = parms.mailIn.readLine();
             out.println(line);

             // Login to the host

             sendCommand(parms, "USER " + userID);
             sendCommand(parms, "PASS " + password);

             // Get the list of messages

             sendCommand(parms, "LIST");
             Vector messageList = new Vector();
```

Figure 14-15
A JSP Page That
Reads Mail Using
POP3

```
for (;;) {
    line = parms.mailIn.readLine();
    if (line.startsWith("."))
        break;
    messageList.addElement(line);
}

// Retrieve each message

int n = messageList.size();
for (int i = 0; i < n; i++) {
    int msg = i+1;
    getMessage(parms, msg);
    sendCommand(parms, "DELE " + msg);
}

// Hang up

sendCommand(parms, "QUIT");
parms.socket.close();
out.println("</PRE>");
%>
```

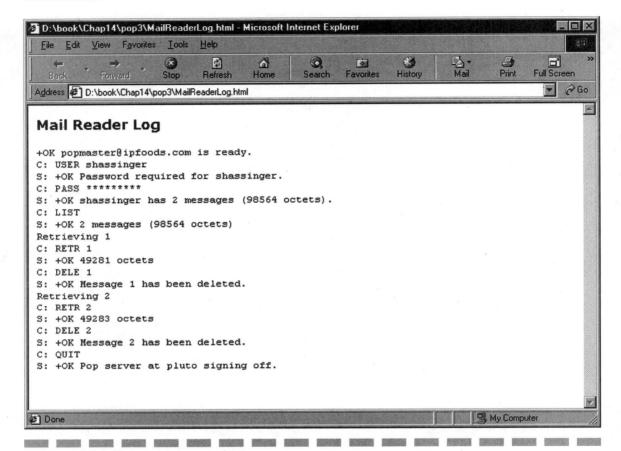

Figure 14-16 The MailReader Log

14.5 Converting Servlets to JSP (LogViewer)

Almost anything a servlet can do, a JavaServer Page can do, which is not surprising, since JSP pages are implemented as servlets. It is therefore possible to convert almost any servlet to an equivalent JSP page. Why would this be desirable? For HTML-intensive servlets, JSP is an easier environment with which to work.

- HTML can be entered directly as template text.
- Logic can be abstracted away into beans, promoting modularity and reuse.

- The `ErrorPage` feature makes it possible to remove `try ... catch` logic.
- No explicit compilation is required.
- The Web directory structure maps into a natural package structure.

In this section we will convert the `LogViewer` servlet from Section 4.8 into a JSP page.

The `LogViewer` Servlet

The servlet engine and Web server create a number of logs scattered about in various directories. These can be viewed with a text editor, but remembering their full path names taxes the frontal lobes. The `LogViewer` servlet introduced in Section 4.8 makes this simpler by presenting a list of files in a table of contents frame and showing their contents in another frame. We will improve this further by converting the servlet (actually, it was three servlets: one for the frameset, one for the list of files, and one to display the data) to a JSP page.

The first improvement we will make is to make the list of log files a properties file rather than a servlet initialization parameter. Figure 14-17 shows an example of such a properties file. It consists of two sections—an index of the categories of files to be viewed and then detailed information about each category. In this example, the file describes two categories—the JRun servlet engine and the Apache Web server. The `category.0` and `category.1` fields contain the names of the JRun and Apache sections to follow. Within each of these sections, the individual files are described. Each file is represented by a `<category>.<index>.file` property giving its absolute path and a `<category>.<index>.label` property containing a short on-screen description of the file. This is the second improvement—path names are too long and uninformative as table of contents entries.

The third improvement we can make is to combine all three servlets into one JSP page. None of them can exist on their own anyway, so we do not sacrifice any reusability. The resulting JSP page (shown in Figure 14-18) is 205 lines long, whereas the original servlets had a combined length of 319 lines. HTTP requests for each of the frames will be handled by the same JSP page, which tells the difference by means of a new request parameter named `frame`.

The main logic of the servlet does not change when incorporated into a JSP page, with the exception of the use of a properties file. It is con-

Figure 14-17

The Properties File
Describing the Log
Files to Be Viewed

```
#   This is the index section, which contains the names of
#   the other sections that describe the individual log
#   files.
#
#   Set category.max equal to the maximum number of log file
#   categories that are in this file.  The actual number may
#   be less, but never more.  The program interpreting this
#   number will perform a loop from 0 to (category.max - 1)
#   looking for the actual categories.  This allows you to
#   comment out categories without renumbering all the
#   others.
#
category.max=2
category.0=JRun
category.1=Apache
#
#   Same numbering scheme applies to each category.  Set
#   .max equal to the upper limit of the entries you include
#   in this file.
#
#
#   There are two entries for each file:
#
#   <category>.<index>.file    the absolute file name
#   <category>.<index>.label   short on-screen description
#

JRun.max=5
JRun.0.file=d:/JRun/jsm-default/logs/event.log
JRun.0.label=Global event log
JRun.1.file=d:/JRun/jsm-default/logs/stdout.log
JRun.1.label=Global stdout log
JRun.2.file=d:/JRun/jsm-default/logs/stderr.log
JRun.2.label=Global stderr log
JRun.3.file=d:/JRun/jsm-default/services/jse/logs/event.log
JRun.3.label=JSE event log
JRun.4.file=d:/JRun/jsm-default/services/jse/logs/error.log
JRun.4.label=JSE error log

Apache.max=2
Apache.0.file=d:/apache1/logs/access.log
Apache.0.label=Access log
Apache.1.file=d:/apache1/logs/error.log
Apache.1.label=Error log
```

venient to locate this file in the same place as the JSP page, although it takes a little work to find the name of the directory. The request itself holds the necessary information. With its getRequestURI() method, we can get the URL of the JSP file, which we can convert to an absolute path using the servlet context's getRealPath() method. Once we know this, we can use methods in java.io.File to get the parent directory and to construct the name of the properties file. The resulting JSP page produces the handy navigator shown in Figure 14-19.

Figure 14-18
The LogViewer
Servlet as a
JavaServer Page

```jsp
<%@ page
     errorPage="ErrorPage.jsp"
     import="java.io.*,java.net.*,java.util.*" %>
<%--

     This JSP uses is displayed in two frames:

     1. A narrow table of contents frame on the left
     2. The main data frame on the right

     The same JSP is used for both frame as well as
     for the FRAMESET that drives them.  The JSP
     tells the difference between requests for each
     frame by means of a "frame" parameter.

--%>
<%
   String frame = request.getParameter("frame");
   if (frame == null) {
%>
<%--

     ==========================================
          FRAMESET request
     ==========================================
--%>
<FRAMESET COLS="200,*">
   <FRAME NAME="LIST" SRC="index.jsp?frame=list">
   <FRAME NAME="DATA" SRC="index.jsp?frame=data">
</FRAMESET>
<%--

     ==========================================
          LIST frame request
     ==========================================
--%>
<% } else if (frame.equals("list")) { %>

<HTML>
<HEAD>
<STYLE>
body, td {
   color: #FFFFC0;
   background-color: Navy;
   font-family: Verdana,Arial,sans-serif;
   font-size: 9pt;
}
a:link { color: #E0E0E0; }
a:visited { color: #E0E0E0; }
</STYLE>
</HEAD>
<BODY>
<H3>Log Files</H3>
<%
   // Load the properties file

   Properties prop = new Properties();
   try {
      String uri = request.getRequestURI();
```

```
        String uriPath =
           getServletContext().getRealPath(uri);
        File docFile = new File(uriPath);
        File pfl = new File
           (docFile.getParent(), "logviewer.properties");
        prop.load(new FileInputStream(pfl));
}
catch (IOException e) {
   throw new RuntimeException
   ("Could not load properties file: "
      + e.getMessage());
}

// Get the max number of categories

String catKey = "category";
int maxCategories =
   Integer.parseInt
      (prop.getProperty(catKey + ".max", "0"));
for (int i = 0; i < maxCategories; i++) {
   String catKeyIndex = catKey + "." + i;
   String category = prop.getProperty(catKeyIndex);
   if (category == null)
      continue;

   %> <H4><%= category %></H4> <%

   // Get the file names in this category

   int max =
      Integer.parseInt
         (prop.getProperty(category + ".max", "0"));

   for (int j = 0; j < max; j++) {

      // Get the file name

      String fileKeyIndex =
         category + "." + j + ".file";

      String name = prop.getProperty(fileKeyIndex);
      if (name == null)
         continue;
      name = name.trim();

      // Get the file label

      String labelKeyIndex =
         category + "." + j + ".label";

      String label = prop.getProperty(labelKeyIndex);
      if (label == null)
         continue;
      label = label.trim();

      File logFile = new File(name);
      String url = "index.jsp"
```

```
                               +  "?frame=data"
                               +  "&name="
                               +  URLEncoder.encode(logFile.getPath())
                               .
%>
    <A HREF="<%= url %>" TARGET="DATA"><%= label %></A><BR>
<%
        }
    }
%>
</BODY>
</HTML>
<%--
        ============================================
            DATA frame request
        ============================================
--%>
<% } else if (frame.equals("data")) { %>

<HTML>
<HEAD>
<STYLE>
.small {
    font-family: Lucida Console;
    font-size: 8pt;
}
</STYLE>
</HEAD>
<BODY>
<%
    // If no name parameter exists, prompt for it

    String name = request.getParameter("name");
    if (name == null)
        name = "";
    name = name.trim();
    if (name.equals("")) {
%><H3>Select log file name at left</H3><%
    }
    else {

        // Verify that the log file exists

        File logFile = new File(name);
        if (!logFile.exists())
            throw new RuntimeException
            (logFile.getPath() + " does not exist");

        // Clear the file if requested

        String command = request.getParameter("command");
        if (command != null) {
            if (command.equals("Clear")) {
                try {
                    new FileOutputStream(logFile).close();
                }
                catch (IOException e) {
```

```
                                throw new RuntimeException
                                ("Exception in clearFile for "
                                + logFile.getPath());
                    }
                }
            }
%>
<H3><%= logFile.getPath() %></H3>

<FORM METHOD="GET" ACTION="index.jsp">
    <INPUT TYPE="HIDDEN" NAME="frame" VALUE="data">
    <INPUT TYPE="HIDDEN" NAME="name"
        VALUE="<%= logFile.getPath() %>">
    <INPUT TYPE="SUBMIT" NAME="refresh" VALUE="Refresh">
    <INPUT TYPE="SUBMIT" NAME="command" VALUE="Clear">
    <P>
    <TEXTAREA ROWS=32 COLS=96 CLASS="small">
<%
        BufferedReader in =
            new BufferedReader(new FileReader(name));
        for (;;) {
            String buffer = in.readLine();
            if (buffer == null)
                break;
            out.println(buffer);
        }
        in.close();
%>
    </TEXTAREA>
</FORM>
<%
    }
}
%>
```

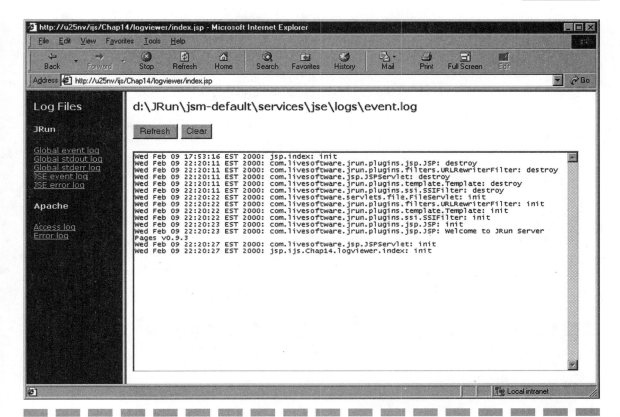

Figure 14-19 The `LogViewer` JSP Page in Action

14.6 A Web-Based Class Browser

Like the `java.sql` package and other APIs, the servlet and JavaServer Page API consists mainly of interfaces and abstract classes. The servlet engine vendor provides concrete implementations of the classes. This provides a standard common framework for application developers while allowing vendors to provide commercial products with superior implementations. These implementations are usually shipped as class libraries in binary form.

It can be difficult sometimes to determine exactly which class is being used to implement an interface or abstract class. For debugging purposes, it is useful to know, for example, which level of an API is implemented or whether a particular JAR file is being loaded correctly. For this reason, an online class browser that can examine its own Java virtual machine can be useful.

A JSP Page for Examining Classes

In this section we will describe a Web-based class browser that uses the Java Reflection API to determine the contents and structure of all the classes that are accessible from the servlet engine's class path. Figure 14-20 shows the first screen of the class browser. It has three levels of navigation:

1. The class to be analyzed can be specified directly in an input field.

2. For a particular class, the category of information (class, constructors, methods, or fields) can be selected by means of a set of radio buttons. These buttons act like the tabs in a tabbed dialog—only one panel is active and visible at any given time.

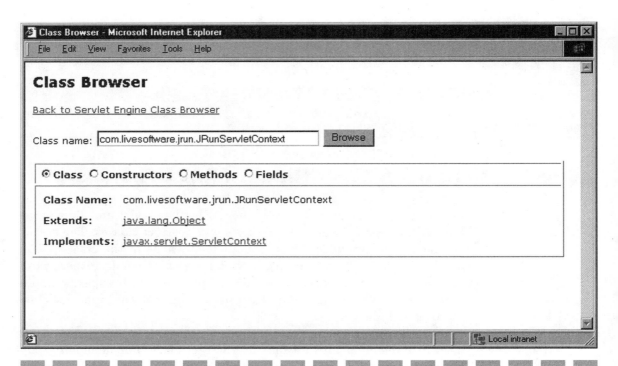

Figure 14-20 The `ClassBrowser` Class Tab

3. Any class or interface to which the class refers is shown as an active hyperlink.

The JRun class com.livesoftware.jrun.JRunServletContext is shown in this example. Figures 14-21, 14-22, and 14-23 show the Constructor, Methods, and Fields tabs, respectively. The JSP page that drives the class browser illustrates two techniques:

1. Using radio buttons to simulate a tabbed dialog

2. Using the Java Reflection API to explore class and method structure

Figure 14-24 is a source listing of ClassBrowser.jsp. The code is rather lengthy, so lets examine it a piece at a time. The basic structure is an HTML form with an input field to specify the class name and radio

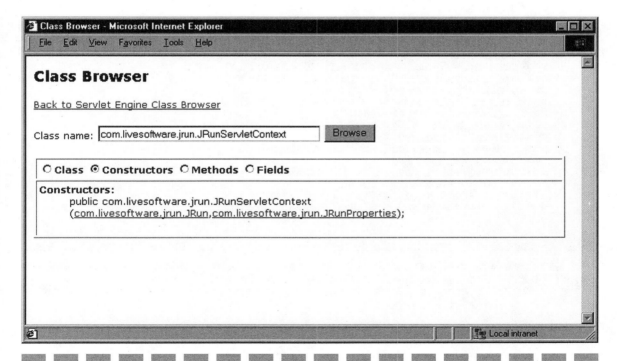

Figure 14-21 The ClassBrowser Constructors Tab

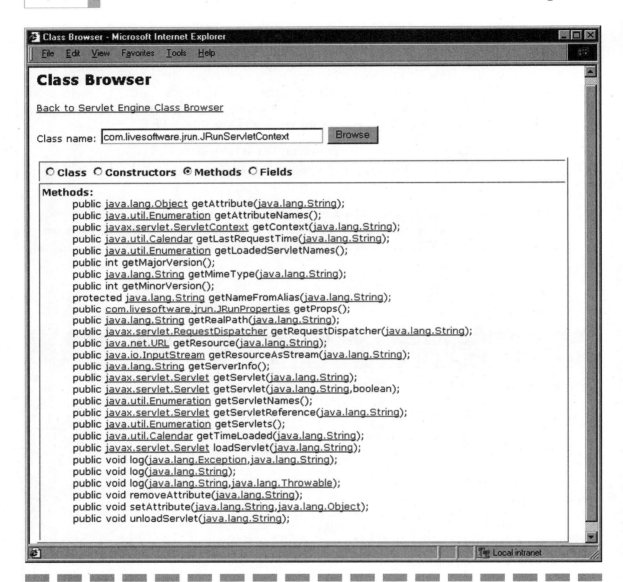

Figure 14-22 The ClassBrowser Methods Tab

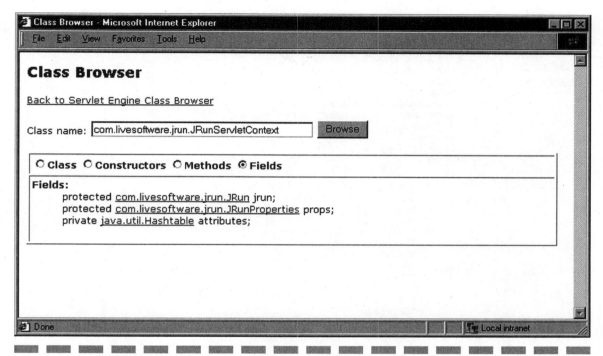

Figure 14-23 The ClassBrowser Fields Tab

Figure 14-24 A
JSP Page for a
Web-Based Class
Browser

```
<%@ page errorPage="ErrorPage.jsp" %>
<%@ page import="java.io.*" %>
<%@ page import="java.util.*" %>
<%@ page import="java.net.*" %>
<%@ page import="java.lang.reflect.*" %>
<HTML>
<HEAD>
<TITLE>Class Browser</TITLE>
<LINK REL="stylesheet" HREF="style.jsp">
</HEAD>
<BODY>
<H2>Class Browser</H2>
<FORM>
<%
    String prevClassName = null;
    String className = null;
    Class cls = null;

    String[] classTabNames = {
        "Class",
        "Constructors",
        "Methods",
        "Fields",
    };
    String[] interfaceTabNames = {
        "Interface",
        "Methods",
        "Fields",
    };
    String[] tabNames = null;
    int selectedIndex = 0;

    // Get the previous class name
    // so that we can determine if this is a new class

    prevClassName = request.getParameter("prevClassName");
    if (prevClassName == null)
        prevClassName = "";

    // Get the class name that the user entered in
    // the input text field.  If nothing was entered,
    // use the default starting class.

    className = request.getParameter("className");
    if ((className == null) || (className.trim().equals("")))
        className = "java.lang.Object";
%>
    <INPUT
        TYPE="HIDDEN"
        NAME="prevClassName"
        VALUE="<%= className %>">
<%

    // Load the class if it is not already loaded

    try {
        cls = Class.forName(className);
```

Figure 14-24
(Continued)

```
    }
    catch (ClassNotFoundException e) {
        throw new RuntimeException
        (className + " class not found");
    }

    // Set the list of tab names, depending on whether
    // the class is an interface or a class

    tabNames = cls.isInterface()
        ? interfaceTabNames
        : classTabNames;

    // Get the selected tab index number

    if (prevClassName.equals(className)) {
        String parm = request.getParameter("selectedIndex");
        if (parm == null)
            parm = "0";
        selectedIndex = Integer.parseInt(parm);
    }
    else {

        // New class - force index to be zero

        selectedIndex = 0;
    }
%>
<A HREF="ServletEngineClassBrowser.jsp">
Back to Servlet Engine Class Browser
</A>
<P>
Class name:
<INPUT TYPE="TEXT" NAME="className" SIZE="40"
    VALUE="<%= className %>">
<INPUT TYPE=SUBMIT VALUE="Browse">
<P>
<TABLE BORDER="1" CELLPADDING="3" WIDTH="700">

<!-- Headings row -->

<TR>
<TH ALIGN="LEFT">
<%
    for (int i = 0; i < tabNames.length; i++) {
        String tabName = tabNames[i];
%>
    <INPUT
        TYPE="RADIO"
        NAME="selectedIndex"
        ONCLICK="this.form.submit()"
        VALUE="<%= i %>"
        <%= (i == selectedIndex) ? "CHECKED" : "" %>
        ><%= tabName %>
<%
    }
%>
```

Figure 14-24

(Continued)

```
</TH>
</TR>

<!-- Main body of table -->

<TR>
<TD ALIGN="LEFT" VALIGN="TOP">
<%
    // Tab name "Class"

    if (tabNames[selectedIndex].equals("Class")) {
%> <%= makeClassTab(cls) %> <%
    }

    // Tab name "Interface"

    else
    if (tabNames[selectedIndex].equals("Interface")) {
%> <%= makeClassTab(cls) %> <%
    }

    // Tab name "Constructors"

    else
    if (tabNames[selectedIndex].equals("Constructors")) {
%> <%= makeConstructorsTab(cls) %> <%
    }

    // Tab name "Methods"

    else
    if (tabNames[selectedIndex].equals("Methods")) {
%> <%= makeMethodsTab(cls) %> <%
    }

    // Tab name "Fields"

    else
    if (tabNames[selectedIndex].equals("Fields")) {
%> <%= makeFieldsTab(cls) %> <%
    }

%>
</TD>
</TR>

<!-- End of table -->

</TABLE>
</FORM>
</BODY>
</HTML>
<%!
    /**
     * Creates a string that represents the class,
     * possibly with a hyperlink to the class name.
     * @param cl the class
```

Figure 14-24
(Continued)

```java
*/
public String formatClass(Class cl)
{
    if (cl.isPrimitive())
        return cl.toString();

    if (cl.isArray())
        return formatClass(cl.getComponentType()) + "[]";

    String name = cl.getName();
    StringBuffer buffer = new StringBuffer();
    buffer.append("<A HREF=\"");
    buffer.append("ClassBrowser.jsp?className=");
    buffer.append(URLEncoder.encode(name));
    buffer.append("&selectedIndex=0");
    buffer.append("\"");
    buffer.append(">");
    buffer.append(name);
    buffer.append("</A>");
    return buffer.toString();
}

/**
 * Creates a string that represents a constructor
 * @param ctor the constructor
 */
public String formatConstructor(Constructor ctor)
{
    StringBuffer buffer = new StringBuffer();
    buffer.append(Modifier.toString(ctor.getModifiers()));
    buffer.append(" ");
    buffer.append(ctor.getName());
    Class[] parms = ctor.getParameterTypes();
    if (parms.length == 0) {
        buffer.append("()");
    }
    else {
        buffer.append("(");
        for (int i = 0; i < parms.length; i++) {
            if (i > 0)
                buffer.append(",");
            Class parm = parms[i];
            buffer.append(formatClass(parm));
        }
        buffer.append(")");
    }
    buffer.append(";");
    return buffer.toString();
}

/**
 * Creates a string that represents a field
 * @param fld the field
 */
public String formatField(Field fld)
{
    StringBuffer buffer = new StringBuffer();
```

Figure 14-24
(Continued)

```java
        buffer.append(Modifier.toString(fld.getModifiers()));
        buffer.append(" ");
        Class fldType = fld.getType();
        buffer.append(formatClass(fldType));
        buffer.append(" ");
        buffer.append(fld.getName());
        buffer.append(";");
        return buffer.toString();
    }

    /**
    * Creates a string that represents a method
    * @param method the method
    */
    public String formatMethod(Method method)
    {
        StringBuffer buffer = new StringBuffer();
        buffer.append
            (Modifier.toString(method.getModifiers()));
        buffer.append(" ");
        Class returnType = method.getReturnType();
        buffer.append(formatClass(returnType));
        buffer.append(" ");
        buffer.append(method.getName());
        Class[] parms = method.getParameterTypes();
        if (parms.length == 0) {
            buffer.append("()");
        }
        else {
            buffer.append("(");
            for (int i = 0; i < parms.length; i++) {
                if (i > 0)
                    buffer.append(",");
                Class parm = parms[i];
                buffer.append(formatClass(parm));
            }
            buffer.append(")");
        }
        buffer.append(";");
        return buffer.toString();
    }

    /**
    * Creates the "Class" tab
    */
    public String makeClassTab(Class cl)
    {
        boolean isInterface = cl.isInterface();
        boolean isClass = !isInterface;

        StringBuffer buffer = new StringBuffer();
        buffer.append("<TABLE BORDER=0 CELLPADDING=5>");

        // Class name

        buffer.append("<TR>");
        buffer.append("<TD ALIGN=LEFT VALIGN=TOP>");
```

Figure 14-24
(Continued)

```java
    if (isInterface)
        buffer.append("<B>Interface Name:</B>");
    else
        buffer.append("<B>Class Name:</B>");
    buffer.append("</TD>");
    buffer.append("<TD>" + cl.getName() + "</TD>");
    buffer.append("</TR>");

    // Extends

    if (isClass) {
        buffer.append("<TR>");
        buffer.append("<TD ALIGN=LEFT VALIGN=TOP>");
        buffer.append("<B>Extends:</B>");
        buffer.append("</TD>");
        buffer.append("<TD>");
        if (cl.getSuperclass() == null)
            buffer.append("none");
        else {
            buffer.append(formatClass(cl.getSuperclass()));
            buffer.append("<BR>");
        }
        buffer.append("</TD>");
        buffer.append("</TR>");
    }

    // Implements

    buffer.append("<TR>");
    buffer.append("<TD ALIGN=LEFT VALIGN=TOP>");
    buffer.append(
        isClass
            ? "<B>Implements:</B>"
            : "<B>Extends:</B>");
    buffer.append("</TD>");
    buffer.append("<TD>");
    Class[] ifaces = cl.getInterfaces();
    if ((ifaces == null) || (ifaces.length == 0))
        buffer.append("Nothing");
    else {
        for (int i = 0; i < ifaces.length; i++) {
            buffer.append(formatClass(ifaces[i]));
            buffer.append("<BR>");
        }
    }
    buffer.append("</TD>");
    buffer.append("</TR>");

    // Return the created HTML

    buffer.append("</TABLE>");
    return buffer.toString();
}

/**
 * Creates the "Constructors" tab
 */
```

Figure 14-24

(Continued)

```
public String makeConstructorsTab(Class cl)
{
    boolean isInterface = cl.isInterface();
    boolean isClass = !isInterface;

    StringBuffer buffer = new StringBuffer();
    buffer.append("<DL>");

    // Constructors

    buffer.append("<DT><B>Constructors:</B></DT>");
    buffer.append("<DD>");
    Constructor[] ctors = cl.getDeclaredConstructors();
    if (ctors.length == 0)
       buffer.append("None");
    else {
       for (int i = 0; i < ctors.length; i++) {
          Constructor ctor = ctors[i];
          buffer.append(formatConstructor(ctor));
          buffer.append("<BR>");
       }
    }
    buffer.append("</DD>");

    // Return the created HTML

    buffer.append("</DL>");
    return buffer.toString();
}

/**
 * Creates the "Fields" tab
 */
public String makeFieldsTab(Class cl)
{
    boolean isInterface = cl.isInterface();
    boolean isClass = !isInterface;

    StringBuffer buffer = new StringBuffer();
    buffer.append("<DL>");

    // Fields

    buffer.append("<DT><B>Fields:</B></DT>");
    buffer.append("<DD>");
    Field[] fields = cl.getDeclaredFields();
    if (fields.length == 0)
       buffer.append("None");
    else {
       for (int i = 0; i < fields.length; i++) {
          Field field = fields[i];
          buffer.append(formatField(field));
          buffer.append("<BR>");
       }
    }
    buffer.append("</DD>");
```

Figure 14-24
(Continued)

```
    // Return the created HTML

    buffer.append("</DL>");
    return buffer.toString();
}

/**
 * Creates the "Methods" tab
 */
public String makeMethodsTab(Class cl)
{
    boolean isInterface = cl.isInterface();
    boolean isClass = !isInterface;

    StringBuffer buffer = new StringBuffer();
    buffer.append("<DL>");

    // Methods

    buffer.append("<DT><B>Methods:</B></DT>");
    buffer.append("<DD>");
    Method[] methods = cl.getDeclaredMethods();
    if (methods.length == 0)
        buffer.append("None");
    else {
        for (int i = 0; i < methods.length; i++) {
            Method method = methods[i];
            buffer.append(formatMethod(method));
            buffer.append("<BR>");
        }
    }
    buffer.append("</DD>");

    // Return the created HTML

    buffer.append("</DL>");
    return buffer.toString();
}
```

buttons to select the panel to be viewed. The radio buttons are generated based on an array of tab names:

```
String[] classTabNames = {
    "Class",
    "Constructors",
    "Methods",
    "Fields",
};
```

If the class is actually an interface, a different set of tab names is used. The value of each radio button corresponds to an index into this array. The buttons are generated in a loop over the array:

```
<% for (int i = 0; i < tabNames.length; i++) { %>
<INPUT TYPE="RADIO" NAME="selectedIndex"
       ONCLICK="this.form.submit()" VALUE="<%= i %>"
       <%= (i == selectedIndex) ? "CHECKED" : "" %>
   ><%= tabNames[i] %>
<% } %>
```

The `ONCLICK` attribute provides the necessary action that submits the form and switches tabs.

When the form is processed, the value of the current radio button setting (the `selectedIndex` request parameter) provides the array index. Based on this index, the program selects among functions that handle the particular request:

```
<% if (tabNames[selectedIndex].equals("Class")) {
%> <%= makeClassTab(cls) %> <% }
else if (tabNames[selectedIndex].equals("Constructors")) {
%> <%= makeConstructorsTab(cls) %> <% }
else if (tabNames[selectedIndex].equals("Methods")) {
%> <%= makeMethodsTab(cls) %> <% }
   ...
}%>
```

The individual functions use the Java Reflection API to construct their output. The `makeMethods()` function, for example, calls the `getDeclaredMethods()` method of the current class to get an array of `java.lang.reflect.Method` objects. There is one entry in this array for each method the class declares (but not inherited methods). The string describing the method is created by the `formatMethod()` function using methods supplied by the `java.lang.reflect.Method` class. For each of the method's arguments, a hyperlink is generated for the argument's class. The form uses a hidden field to keep track of the class name. If it changes, the tab index is automatically set back to 0 so that the Class tab is displayed.

The result is a compact and easy-to-navigate Web page describing any class the servlet engine knows about. A style sheet (shown in Figure 14-25) is used to control the appearance.

Browsing the JSP Classes

JSP engines define nine implicit objects, most of which are declared using interface types. A useful application for the class browser is to show the concrete implementations of each of these interfaces. Figure

14-26 shows a front-end Web page that lists these classes and contains hyperlinks to the class browser that have the full class name specified. The simple JSP page that produces this form is shown in Figure 14-27.

Figure 14-25

The Stylesheet
Used by the Class
Browser

```
<%@ page contentType="text/css" %>
body, td {
    background-color: #FEFEF2;
    font-family: Verdana,Arial,sans-serif;
    font-size: 10pt;
}
h2{
    background-color: #FEFEF2;
    font-family: Verdana,Arial,sans-serif;
    font-size: 14pt;
}
a:link { color: #0000FF; }
a:visited { color: #0000FF; }
```

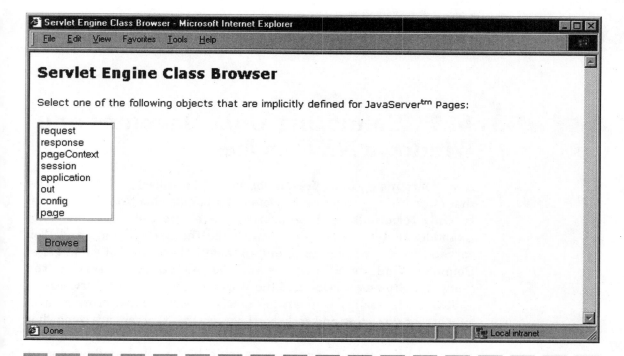

Figure 14-26 The Servlet Engine Class Browser Selection Screen

Figure 14-27
A Front-End to
`ClassBrowser.j`
`sp` That Introspects
the JSP
Environment Itself

```
<%@ page errorPage="ErrorPage.jsp" %>
<HTML>
<HEAD>
<TITLE>Servlet Engine Class Browser</TITLE>
<LINK REL="stylesheet" HREF="style.jsp">
</HEAD>
<BODY>
<H2>Servlet Engine Class Browser</H2>
<FORM METHOD="POST" ACTION="ClassBrowser.jsp">
Select one of the following objects that are
implicitly defined for JavaServer<SUP>tm</SUP> Pages:
<P>
<SELECT NAME="className" SIZE=8>
<OPTION VALUE="<%= request.getClass().getName() %>">request
<OPTION VALUE="<%= response.getClass().getName() %>">response
<OPTION VALUE=
        "<%= pageContext.getClass().getName() %>" >pageContext
<OPTION VALUE="<%= session.getClass().getName() %>">session
<OPTION VALUE=
   "<%= application.getClass().getName() %>" >application
<OPTION VALUE="<%= out.getClass().getName() %>">out
<OPTION VALUE="<%= config.getClass().getName() %>">config
<OPTION VALUE="<%= page.getClass().getName() %>">page
</SELECT>
<P>
<INPUT TYPE="SUBMIT" VALUE="Browse">
</FORM>
</BODY>
</HTML>
```

14.7 Emulating Unix Daemons and Windows NT Services

Most operating systems provide for system-level background processes that start when the system is booted and handle client/server requests. In Unix terminology, these processes are referred to as *daemons*. Examples include `telnetd`, `ftpd`, and the `smtp`, `pop`, and Web servers. In the Windows NT environment, these are called *services*. Common Windows NT services include the Event Log service, the Computer Browser service, and the Workstation and Server services.

Java lends itself well to writing server classes because of its built-in support for threading and sockets. However, these servers are somewhat limited in value if they have to be started manually by a logged-in user. It would be useful if Java classes could be handled as daemons or Windows NT services. Unfortunately, the operating system does not always cooperate. Windows NT, for example, despite its positioning as a server operating system, makes no straightforward provision for treating arbitrary executables as services.[3]

A Servlet Solution

Once again, servlets can be used as the enabling technology. In this section we will develop a `ServiceManager` servlet that launches services in background threads from its `init()` method. The `ServiceManager` will be set up as an autostart (sometimes referred to as *preloaded*) servlet so that it does not require a user to log in and make a request of it before it starts.

In order to do this in a general way, we will define a `Service` interface that all our services must implement (see Figure 14-28). The interface defines a minimal set of three methods—`start()`, `stop()`, and `isRunning()`. These methods allow the `ServiceManager` to control the execution of the service and to determine its current state, and they are the only points of contact the `ServiceManager` needs.

Figure 14-29 shows a service that implements the interface `QotdService` (the standard Unix "quote of the day" service). It also implements the `Runnable` interface so that it can operate in a background thread.[4] In its `start()` method, it opens a server socket, sets the quote to be used,[5] and then creates and starts a thread that runs the service. In the `run()` method, the service listens for socket connections. When it accepts a connection, the service opens the client socket's output stream and writes the quote to it. It could start another thread to handle the request, but since `QotdService` writes only one line and then quits, it does not adversely affect performance to handle requests inline. The `stop()` method simply closes the server socket and sets the thread reference to `null`. While `QotdService` was fairly simple, more complex services can be implemented in the same manner as long as they implement the `Service` interface by providing the three necessary methods.

In order to be registered with the `ServiceManager`, service descriptions are entered in a `services.properties` file, shown in Figure

---

[3]There is an add-on program in the Windows NT Resource Kit called SRVANY.EXE that will do this, but it is not part of the standard Windows NT system.

[4]Another alternative would be for the service to extend `java.lang.Thread`. See Chapter 9 for a discussion of both approaches.

[5]The quote is hard-coded here. In real life, it probably would be selected randomly from a file.

Figure 14-28

The Interface
That Services
Must Implement

```
package ijs.app.services;

import java.io.*;

/**
 * An interface for services designed to run
 * under the control of the ServiceManager servlet.
 */
public interface Service
{
    /**
     * Starts the service.
     * @exception IOException if the service
     * cannot be started for some reason
     */
    public void start() throws IOException;

    /**
     * Stops the service
     * @exception IOException if the service
     * cannot be stopped for some reason
     */
    public void stop() throws java.io.IOException;

    /**
     * Returns true if the service is currently
     * running, false otherwise.
     */
    public boolean isRunning();
}
```

14-30. This file consists of a `services` key, which is a comma-separated master list of service key prefixes referred to elsewhere in the file. For each entry in the list, there are three keys that describe the service:

name   The name displayed by the `ServiceManager` for this service

class   The name of the Java class that implements the service

start   "Automatic," "Manual," or "Disabled," indicating how the service is started

In the example shown in Figure 14-30, there are two services listed: the `Hello` service, which is run by the `ijs.app.services.HelloService` class and must be started manually, and the `Qotd` service we just described, which is implemented by `ijs.app.services.QotdService` and starts automatically whenever the `ServiceManager` starts.

This brings us to the `ServiceManager` itself, which is listed in Figure 14-31. In its `init()` method, the `ServiceManager` servlet parses the `service.properties` file. For each service description it finds, it does the following:

Figure 14-29

The Quote of the
Day Service

```java
package ijs.app.services;

import java.io.*;
import java.net.*;
import java.util.*;

/**
 * A service that returns the quote of the day.
 * See RFC 865 for details.
 */
public class QotdService implements Service, Runnable
{
    // ===============================================
    //      Instance variables
    // ===============================================

    private Thread thread;
    private ServerSocket server;
    private String quote;

    // ===============================================
    //      Constants
    // ===============================================

    /**
     * Port on which the service listens
     */
    public static final int PORT = 17;

    // ===============================================
    //      Implementation of the Service interface
    // ===============================================

    /**
     * Returns true if the service is running,
     * false otherwise.
     */
    public boolean isRunning()
    {
        return (thread != null);
    }

    /**
     * Starts the service
     * @exception IOException if the service
     * cannot be started for some reason.
     */
    public void start() throws IOException
    {
        if (thread == null) {

            // Load the quote
            // (Hard coded in this example - Could
            //    be loaded from a file.)

            setQuote(
"You can lead a horse to water but you can't make him drink"
```

```java
        );

        // Start the server socket

        server = new ServerSocket(PORT);

        // Start the server thread

        thread = new Thread(this);
        thread.setPriority(Thread.MIN_PRIORITY);
        thread.setDaemon(true);
        thread.start();
    }
}

/**
 * Stops the service
 * @exception IOException if the service
 * cannot be stopped for some reason.
 */
public void stop() throws IOException
{
    if (thread != null) {
        thread = null;
        try {
            server.close();
        }
        catch (Exception ignore) {}
    }
}

// ===============================================
//      Implementation of the Runnable interface
// ===============================================

/**
 * Runs the service.
 */
public void run()
{
    try {

        // Wait for socket connections

        while (thread != null) {
            Socket client = null;
            try {
                client = server.accept();
            }
            catch (Exception ignore) {
                break;
            }

            // Write the quote back to the client

            PrintWriter out =
                new PrintWriter(client.getOutputStream());
```

```
                out.println(getQuote());

                out.flush();
                out.close();
                client.close();
            }
        }
        catch (Exception e) {
            e.printStackTrace();
        }
        finally {
            thread = null;
        }
    }

    // ==============================================
    //    Methods to get and set the quote
    // ==============================================

    /**
     * Returns the quote.
     */
    public String getQuote()
    {
        return quote;
    }

    /**
     * Sets the quote.
     * @param quote the quote.
     */
    public void setQuote(String quote)
    {
        this.quote = quote;
    }
}
```

1. Creates an entry in the `ServiceHolder` array for the service. `ServiceHolder` is an inner class used to keep track of the properties of a service, including its name, the name of its class, its start type (automatic, manual, or disabled), and a reference to the running service object itself.

2. Uses `Class.forName()` to load the service's class and calls `newInstance()` to create an instance of it.

3. If the service is designated as "automatic," its `start()` method is called.

The reverse process happens in the servlet's `destroy()` method. It goes through the array of `ServiceHolder` objects and calls the `stop()` method of any active services. The `doGet()` method performs two tasks:

Figure 14-30

The Properties File
Used to Configure
Services

```
# =================================================
# This is the properties file for the
# ServiceManager servlet.
# =================================================
#
# Services
#
# This is a comma-delimited list of keys that point to
# services in this properties file.
#
# Example:
#
# services=Hello,Speller,QOTD
#
services=Hello,Qotd
#
# For each service, there must be three entries:
#
# name:   the display name of the service
# class:  name of the Java class implementing the service
# start:  'automatic','manual','disabled'
#
# Example:
#
# myService.name=My Service
# myService.class=ijs.app.services.MyService
# myService.start=automatic
#

# Hello service
Hello.name=Hello Service
Hello.class=ijs.app.services.HelloService
Hello.start=manual

# Quote of the day service
Qotd.name=Qotd Service
Qotd.class=ijs.app.services.QotdService
Qotd.start=automatic
```

1. Reports the status of all configured services in an HTML table, showing the service name, its current status (started or not), and its configured startup mode (see Figure 14-32). The format of this display is similar to the Windows NT services control panel applet.

2. Handles requests to start and stop services. The table contains the appropriate start or stop hyperlink, depending on whether the service is currently running. These hyperlinks contain a `serviceNumber` parameter and an `action` code so that the `ServiceManager` servlet knows what action to perform on which service.

▬▬ ▬▬ ▬▬ ▬▬
Figure 14-31

The Service-
Manager Servlet

```java
package ijs.app.services;

import java.io.*;
import java.net.*;
import java.util.*;

import javax.servlet.*;
import javax.servlet.http.*;

/**
 * This class is a platform-independent means of
 * launching and controlling background server processes,
 * similar to Windows NT services or Unix daemon processes.
 * The class should be run as an automatically
 * loaded servlet.
 * <P>
 * The list of services to be run is loaded from
 * a properties file, whose name is specified as
 * an initialization parameter.
 * <P>
 * Each service to be run must implement the
 * ijs.app.services.Service interface, which
 * requires it to support three methods:
 * <UL>
 * <LI><CODE>start()</CODE>
 * <LI><CODE>stop()</CODE>
 * <LI><CODE>isRunning()</CODE>
 * </UL>
 * <P>
 */
public class ServiceManagerServlet extends HttpServlet
{
   /**
    * A local class that holds information about a service.
    */
   class ServiceHolder
   {
      String  name;
      String  className;
      String  startType;
      Service service;
   }

   /**
    * An array of holder objects, one for each loaded service.
    * The array is initialized in the init() method.
    */
   private ServiceHolder[] services =
      new ServiceHolder[0];

   /**
    * Performs servlet initialization
    * @exception ServletException if a servlet exception occurs
    */
   public void init(ServletConfig config)
      throws ServletException
      {
```

Figure 14-31
(Continued)

```
super.init(config);

// Read the list of services.  Each service must
// have the following fields:
//
// (name=)   Display name
// (class=)  Service class name
// (start=)  'automatic','manual','disabled'

try {
    String fileName = getInitParameter
        ("servicesFileName");
    log("servicesFileName=[" + fileName + "]");
    if (fileName == null)
        throw new RuntimeException
        ("No servicesFileName init parameter found");

    Properties prop = new Properties();

    log("Opening " + fileName);
    InputStream in = new FileInputStream(fileName);
    log(fileName + " opened");

    prop.load(in);
    log("Properties loaded");
    in.close();

    // Get the services key.  This is a comma-delimited
    // list of services to be loaded

    String serviceKeyString =
        prop.getProperty("services");
    log("services=[" + serviceKeyString + "]");

    if (serviceKeyString == null)
        throw new RuntimeException
        ("services key not found");

    // Create a vector of services

    Vector sv = new Vector();
    StringTokenizer st =
        new StringTokenizer(serviceKeyString, ",");

    while (st.hasMoreTokens()) {
        String keyPrefix = st.nextToken();
        log("loading " + keyPrefix);

        String key;

        // Get the service name, class,
        // and start parameters

        key = keyPrefix + ".name";
        String name = prop.getProperty(key);
        log(key + "=[" + name + "]");
        if (name == null)
```

```
                          throw new RuntimeException
                             (key + " key not found");

             key = keyPrefix + ".class";
             String className = prop.getProperty(key);
             log(key + "=[" + className + "]");
             if (className == null)
                throw new RuntimeException
                   (key + " key not found");

             key = keyPrefix + ".start";
             String startType = prop.getProperty(key);
             log(key + "=[" + startType + "]");
             if (startType == null)
                throw new RuntimeException
                   (key + " key not found");

             // Check the startup mode

             boolean autoStart = false;
             if (startType.equalsIgnoreCase("automatic")) {
                autoStart = true;
             }
             else
             if (startType.equalsIgnoreCase("manual")) {
             }
             else
             if (startType.equalsIgnoreCase("disabled")) {
                // Ignore this service
                continue;
             }
             else
                throw new RuntimeException
                   (startType + " is invalid for " + key);

             // Instantiate the service class

             log("Loading " + className + " class");
             Class cls = Class.forName(className);
             log(className + " class loaded");

             log("Instantiating " + className);
             Object obj = cls.newInstance();
             log(className + " instantiated");

             Service service = (Service) obj;

             // Start it if requested

             if (autoStart) {
                log("Starting " + name);
                service.start();
                log(name + " started");
             }

             // Save it in the vector of services
```

Figure 14-31
(Continued)

```java
            ServiceHolder holder = new ServiceHolder();
            holder.name      = name;
            holder.className = className;
            holder.startType = startType;
            holder.service   = service;

            sv.addElement(holder);
        }

        // Make an array out of the vector

        log(sv.size() + " services loaded");
        services = new ServiceHolder[sv.size()];
        sv.copyInto(services);
    }
    catch (Exception e) {
        throw new UnavailableException(this, e.getMessage());
    }
}

/**
 * Shuts down remaining services
 */
public void destroy()
{
    for (int i = 0; i < services.length; i++) {
        ServiceHolder holder = services[i];
        if (holder.service.isRunning()) {
            try {
                log("Shutting down " + holder.name);
                holder.service.stop();
                log(holder.name + " stopped");
            }
            catch (IOException e) {
                log("Could not stop "
                    + holder.name
                    + ": "
                    + e.getMessage());
            }
        }
    }
    super.destroy();
}

/**
 * Handles a GET request
 * @param request the servlet request object
 * @param response the servlet response object
 * @exception ServletException if a servlet exception occurs
 * @exception IOException if an I/O exception occurs
 */
public void doGet(
        HttpServletRequest request,
        HttpServletResponse response)
    throws ServletException, IOException
{

    response.setContentType("text/html");
```

Figure 14-31
(Continued)

```java
PrintWriter out = response.getWriter();

// Start or stop a service if requested

String msg = null;
String sn = request.getParameter("service");
String action = request.getParameter("action");
if ((sn != null) && (action != null)) {
   try {
      msg = performAction(action, sn);
   }
   catch (Exception e) {
      msg = e.getMessage();
   }
}

// Show the status message and the list of
// loaded services

StringBuffer sb = new StringBuffer();

sb.append("<HTML>");

sb.append("<HEAD>");
sb.append("<TITLE>Service Manager</TITLE>");
sb.append("</HEAD>");

sb.append("<BODY>");
sb.append("<H3>Service Manager</H3>");
if (msg == null)
   msg = services.length + " services loaded";
sb.append("<PRE>" + msg + "</PRE>");

sb.append
("<TABLE BORDER=1 CELLPADDING=2 CELLSPACING=0>");

sb.append("<TR>");
sb.append("<TH WIDTH=200>Service Name</TH>");
sb.append("<TH WIDTH=80>Status</TH>");
sb.append("<TH WIDTH=100>Startup</TH>");
sb.append("<TH>Start</TH>");
sb.append("<TH>Stop</TH>");
sb.append("</TR>");

for (int i = 0; i < services.length; i++) {

   ServiceHolder holder = services[i];

   sb.append("<TR>");
   sb.append("<TD>");
   sb.append(holder.name);
   sb.append("</TD>");
   sb.append("<TD>");
   sb.append(holder.service.isRunning()
             ? "started"
             : " ");
   sb.append("</TD>");
```

```
        sb.append("<TD>");
        sb.append(holder.startType);
        sb.append("</TD>");
        sb.append("<TD>");
        if (!holder.service.isRunning()) {
            sb.append("<A HREF=\"");
            sb.append(request.getRequestURI());
            sb.append("?service=");
            sb.append(i);
            sb.append("&action=start");
            sb.append("\">");
            sb.append("start");
            sb.append("</A>");
        }
        else {
            sb.append(" ");
        }
        sb.append("</TD>");
        sb.append("<TD>");
        if (holder.service.isRunning()) {
            sb.append("<A HREF=\"");
            sb.append(request.getRequestURI());
            sb.append("?service=");
            sb.append(i);
            sb.append("&action=stop");
            sb.append("\">");
            sb.append("stop");
            sb.append("</A>");
        }
        else {
            sb.append(" ");
        }
        sb.append("</TD>");
        sb.append("</TR>");
    }

    sb.append("</TABLE>");
    sb.append("</BODY>");
    sb.append("</HTML>");

    out.println(sb.toString());
}

/**
 * Starts or stops a service, returning a status message
 */
protected String performAction(
        String action,
        String serviceNumberString)
    throws Exception
{
    // Get the index of the service within the
    // services array

    int serviceNumber = Integer.parseInt
        (serviceNumberString);
```

Figure 14-31
(Continued)

```
if ((serviceNumber < 0) ||
    (serviceNumber >= services.length))
    throw new IllegalArgumentException
    ("service number ["
        + serviceNumber
        + "] is not between 0 and "
        + (services.length - 1));

// Perform the action

ServiceHolder holder = services[serviceNumber];

// Start

if (action.equals("start")) {

    if (holder.service.isRunning())
        throw new RuntimeException
        (holder.name + " is already running");

    try {
        holder.service.start();
        return holder.name + " started";
    }
    catch (IOException e) {
        return "Could not start " + holder.name
            + ": " + e.getMessage();
    }
}

// Stop

if (action.equals("stop")) {

    if (!holder.service.isRunning())
        throw new RuntimeException
        (holder.name + " is not running");

    try {
        holder.service.stop();
        return holder.name + " stopped";
    }
    catch (IOException e) {
        return "Could not stop " + holder.name
            + ": " + e.getMessage();
    }
}

    throw new IllegalArgumentException
    ("Unknown action [" + action + "]");

}

/**
 * Handles a POST request
 * @param request the servlet request object
 * @param response the servlet response object
```

Figure 14-31
(Continued)

```
 * @exception ServletException if a servlet exception occurs
 * @exception IOException if an I/O exception occurs
 */
public void doPost(
      HttpServletRequest request,
      HttpServletResponse response)
    throws ServletException, IOException
  {
    doGet(request, response);
  }
}
```

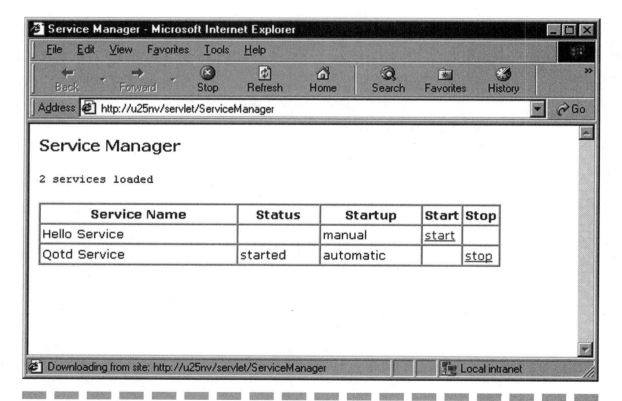

Figure 14-32 ServiceManager Status Panel

The final installation step is to register the ServiceManager as an autostart servlet. Table 14-1 shows the means used by several popular servlet engines.

TABLE 14- 1

	JRun 2.3.3
Properties file	`servlet.`**`<alias>`**`.preload=true` **property in** `jsm-default/ services/`**`<service name>`**`/properties/servlets.proper- ties`
	JRun 3.0*
Properties file	`<load-on-startup>`*n*`</load-on-startup>` **element in the** `<servlet>` **entry for the servlet in the Web application's** WEB- INF/web.xml **file.**
	ServletExec 2.2
Properties file	**Specify the servlet alias in the** `servlets.startup` **property in** `ServletExec/ServletExec Data/`**`<server name>`**`/servlets. properties` **or, using the** `admin` **servlet, specify a nonzero entry in the servlet's** `Init Load Order` **parameter.**
	ApacheJServ 1.0
Properties file	**Add the servlet alias to the** `servlets.startup` **property in** `ApacheJServ/conf/zone.properties`.

*JRun 3.0 was in beta at the time this was written. Some configuration details may be different in the production release.

14.8   The Four Fours

Strategic technology issues and business cases notwithstanding, you also can use servlets to help your kids with their homework. An old but still popular mathematics puzzle involves combining exactly four fours using only elementary arithmetic operations to make an expression that equals 1, 2, and so on, as high as possible. For example,

```
1= 4 + ((4/4) - 4)
2= (4*4) / (4+4)
3= ((4*4) - 4) / 4
...
```

For any given target value, there may multiple solutions or no solutions at all, depending on which arithmetic operations are allowed.

In this section we will develop an interactive Web-based calculator that will find all possible symbolic expressions that make a given set of numbers equal a specified target number. We will not restrict ourselves to four fours; the user will be able to choose any set of integers and any target number.

Describing the Symbolic Operations

First, we need to describe the arithmetic operations we can perform. It would be nice to be able to add and remove operations to make the problem more interesting, so we shall represent operations as objects implementing a common interface (called `Operation`). The interface is shown in Figure 14-33.

Classes that implement `Operation` must provide three methods:

- `int evaluate(Number a, Number b)`. Given two `java.lang.Number` objects, this method will perform its operation and return the result as an integer. We use the `java.lang.Number` class for the input parameters because it is the superclass of `java.lang.Integer` and another class we are about to develop. This will allow us to perform the operation on any type of numeric operands.

- `boolean isDefined(Number a, Number b)`. Operations may not be defined for all pairs of operands. For example, division is undefined for $b = 0$. This method returns true or false, depending on whether there is a defined value for the operation when performed on numbers a and b (in that order).

- `boolean isCommutative()`. A *commutative* operation is one which has the same value when performed on (a, b) as it does on (b, a) for all

Figure 14-33

The Base Interface for Symbolic Arithmetic Operations

```
package ijs.app.four4s;

/**
 * The methods that an operation must implement
 */
public interface Operation
{
    /**
     * Returns the integer value of performing
     * the function on the two specified numbers
     */
    int evaluate(Number a, Number b);

    /**
     * Returns true if the operation is defined
     * for the specified number pair.
     */
    boolean isDefined(Number a, Number b);

    /**
     * Returns true if the operation is commutative
     */
    boolean isCommutative();
}
```

possible choices of a and b. Addition is commutative, for example, whereas subtraction is not. This method will allow us to cut down the number of possibilities we have to evaluate later on.

Figures 14-34, 14-35, 14-36, and 14-37 show the addition, subtraction, multiplication, and division classes that implement Operation. In addition to the Operation interface methods, each class overrides the toString() method to display its mathematical symbol.

What we are looking for in this problem is symbolic expressions, not just numbers. Figure 14-38 shows a class named Term that keeps track of an operation and two operands, able to report its value either as an integer or in human-readable symbolic form. Term is a subclass of java.lang.Number, so instances of it can be passed to an operation's evaluate() and isDefined() methods. This also will allow us to create nested Term objects made up of other terms, resulting in expressions of any complexity we care to build, still retaining the ability to get both their numeric value and their symbolic form.

Figure 14-34

The Addition Operation Class

```
package ijs.app.four4s;

import java.io.*;

/**
 * The addition operation
 */
public class Addition implements Operation, Serializable
{
    public int evaluate(Number a, Number b)
    {
        return a.intValue() + b.intValue();
    }

    public final boolean isDefined(Number a, Number b)
    {
        return true;
    }

    public final boolean isCommutative()
    {
        return true;
    }

    public String toString()
    {
        return "+";
    }
}
```

Figure 14-35
The
Subtraction
Operation Class

```java
package ijs.app.four4s;

import java.io.*;

/**
 * The subtraction operation
 */
public class Subtraction implements Operation, Serializable
{
    public int evaluate(Number a, Number b)
    {
        return a.intValue() - b.intValue();
    }

    public final boolean isDefined(Number a, Number b)
    {
        return true;
    }

    public final boolean isCommutative()
    {
        return false;
    }

    public String toString()
    {
        return "-";
    }
}
```

The Solution Algorithm

To solve the problem, we will use the brute-force method of enumerating all possible permutations of the numbers and operations, selecting only those that have the desired value. The algorithm we will use to enumerate the permutations is this:

```
Let S be the set of numbers
Let F be the set of allowed operations
If there is only one element in S, return its symbolic value
Otherwise,
For each pair (a, b) in S:
    For each operation (op) in F:
        If op is defined on (a, b):
            Let c = op(a, b)
            Let S' be the set composed of c and the subset of S
            resulting from the removal of a and b
            Call this algorithm recursively on S'
            If op is not commutative:
                If op is defined on (b, a):
                    Let c = op(b, a)
                    Let S' = {c + (S - a - b)}
                    Call this algorithm recursively on S'
```

Figure 14-36

The
Multiplication
Operation Class

```
package ijs.app.four4s;

import java.io.*;

/**
 * The multiplication operation
 */
public class Multiplication implements Operation, Serializable
{
    public int evaluate(Number a, Number b)
    {
        return a.intValue() * b.intValue();
    }

    public final boolean isDefined(Number a, Number b)
    {
        return true;
    }

    public final boolean isCommutative()
    {
        return true;
    }

    public String toString()
    {
        return "*";
    }
}
```

Figure 14-39 lists a class that implements this algorithm, storing its results in a solutions hashtable keyed by the integer value of the expression. Each entry in the hashtable is itself a hashtable of the string values of all expressions that have the same numeric value.

All that remains is the JSP page that drives the solver class, as shown in Figure 14-40. It creates an instance of the ijs.app. four4s.Problem class as a JavaBean and prompts for a set of numbers and a target number. It sets these properties of the bean and then invokes its getSolutions() method for the target number. The results are displayed in symbolic form, as shown in Figure 14-41.

Figure 14-37

The Division
Operation Class

```java
package ijs.app.four4s;

import java.io.*;

/**
 * The integer division operation
 */
public class Division implements Operation, Serializable
{
    public int evaluate(Number a, Number b)
    {
        return a.intValue() / b.intValue();
    }

    public final boolean isDefined(Number a, Number b)
    {
        int bv = b.intValue();
        return (bv != 0) && ((a.intValue() % bv) == 0);
    }

    public final boolean isCommutative()
    {
        return false;
    }

    public String toString()
    {
        return "/";
    }
}
```

Figure 14-38
A Class That
Groups an
Operation and
Two Numbers in
Symbolic Form

```java
package ijs.app.four4s;

import java.io.*;

/**
 * A <CODE>Term</CODE> is a pair of numbers
 * and an operation.  It has both a numeric
 * value and a symbolic representation.
 */
public class Term extends java.lang.Number
    implements Serializable
{
    private Operation op;
    private Number a;
    private Number b;
    private int value;

    public Term(Operation op, Number a, Number b)
    {
        this.op = op;
        this.a = a;
        this.b = b;
        value = op.evaluate(a, b);
    }

    public String toString()
    {
        return "("
            + a.toString()
            + " "
            + op.toString()
            + " "
            + b.toString()
            + ")";
    }

    public long longValue()
    {
        return (long) value;
    }

    public int intValue()
    {
        return value;
    }

    public double doubleValue()
    {
        return (double) value;
    }

    public float floatValue()
    {
        return (float) value;
    }
}
```

▰▰ ▰▰ ▰▰ ▰▰

Figure 14-39

A Class Containing
an Algorithm to
Solve the
Generalized Four
Fours Problem

```java
package ijs.app.four4s;

import java.io.*;
import java.util.*;

/**
 * A puzzle consisting of a set of numbers and operations.
 * A solution to the puzzle consists of arranging all the
 * numbers using any of the specified operations to arrive
 * at an expression equal to a given number.  For example,
 * if the numbers are 2, 3, 5, and 11, and the target
 * number is 10, one solution is
 * <PRE>
 * 11 - (5 / (2 + 3))
 * </PRE>
 * In general, there may be many solutions for any given
 * target number, or no solution.
 * <P>
 * The problem is often called the Four 4's, with the set
 * of numbers being {4, 4, 4, 4} and the objective being
 * to find solutions for each number 1, 2, ..., as far
 * as possible.
 */
public class Problem implements Serializable
{
    // =============================================
    //     Constants and global variables
    // =============================================

    public static final Operation[] op = {
        new Addition(),
        new Subtraction(),
        new Multiplication(),
        new Division(),
    };

    // =============================================
    //     Instance variables
    // =============================================

    /**
     * The original set of numbers in the problem
     */
    private Number[] numbers;

    /**
     * A table of solutions to the problem.
     * Each entry in this table is itself a Hashtable
     * of individual terms all having the same
     * integer value.
     */
    private Hashtable solutions;

    // =============================================
    //     Constructors
    // =============================================
```

Figure 14-39
(Continued)

```
/**
 * Creates a new empty problem.
 */
public Problem()
{
    this(new Integer[0]);
}

/**
 * Creates a new problem from an array
 * of generic Number objects.
 */
public Problem(Number[] inputs)
{
    setNumbers(inputs);
}

// ===========================================
//     Instance methods
// ===========================================

/**
 * Sets the list of numbers this problem will evaluate
 */
public void setNumbers(Number[] inputs)
{
    int n = inputs.length;

    numbers = new Number[n];
    for (int i = 0; i < n; i++)
        numbers[i] = inputs[i];
    solutions = new Hashtable();

    enumerate(numbers, solutions);
}

/**
 * Returns the list of all possible values
 */
public int[] getPossibleValues()
{
    int n = solutions.size();
    int[] list = new int[n];
    Enumeration ekeys = solutions.keys();
    for (int i = 0; i < n; i++) {
        Integer key = (Integer) ekeys.nextElement();
        list[i] = key.intValue();
    }

    // Sort the list in numeric order

    for (int i = 0; i < n-1; i++) {
        for (int j = i+1; j < n; j++) {
            if (list[i] > list[j]) {
                int temp = list[i];
                list[i] = list[j];
                list[j] = temp;
```

Figure 14-39
(Continued)

```
            }
        }
    }

    return list;
}

/**
 * Returns all known solutions for the
 * given integer value.
 */
public String[] getSolutions(int target)
{
    Integer key = new Integer(target);
    Hashtable entry = (Hashtable) solutions.get(key);
    if (entry == null)
        return null;

    int n = entry.size();
    String[] list = new String[n];
    Enumeration ekeys = entry.keys();
    for (int i = 0; i < n; i++)
        list[i] = (String) ekeys.nextElement();

    return list;
}

// ===========================================
//     Class methods
// ===========================================

/**
 * Make all possible combinations of the
 * specified numbers and operations.
 */
protected static void enumerate
    (Number[] numbers, Hashtable solutions)
{
    final int n = numbers.length;

    // If there is only one number in the set,
    // there is no need to enumerate further.

    if (n == 1) {

        // File this number (which is actually
        // an expression consisting of all the
        // numbers in the original set) in the
        // solution hashtable according to its
        // integer value.

        Number number = numbers[0];

        // In the interests of time, consider only
        // nonnegative solutions

        int value = number.intValue();
```

Figure 14-39
(Continued)

```
if (value >= 0) {

    // Use the number's integer value as the key
    // into the solution table

    Integer key = new Integer(value);
    Hashtable entry = (Hashtable) solutions.get(key);

    // If this is the first solution found for
    // this value, the solutions table entry will
    // not exist.  Create a new one in that case.

    if (entry == null) {
        entry = new Hashtable();
        solutions.put(key, entry);
    }

    // Add this solution to the solution table
    // entry for this value

    String s = number.toString();
    entry.put(s, s);
}
}

// If there is more than one number in the set,
// find all solutions using a recursive algorithm:
//
// For each pair (p, q) of numbers in the set:
//
//     For each operation f:
//
//         Create the subset consisting of
//         the set with p and q removed but
//         with f(p,q) added.
//
//         Evaluate this subset for all solutions.
//
//         If the operation is not commutative,
//         do the same thing with f(q, p).
//
//     end for
//
// end for

else {

    // Choose each pair (p,q) in the set

    for (int i = 0; i < n-1; i++) {
        final Number p = numbers[i];
        for (int j = i+1; j < n; j++) {
            final Number q = numbers[j];

            // Evaluate p and q with each
            // available operation
```

```
            for (int k = 0; k < op.length; k++) {
                Operation operation = op[k];
                if (operation.isDefined(p, q)) {
                    Number pq = new Term(operation, p, q);
                    Number[] subset = null;
                    subset = removeFromSet(numbers, p);
                    subset = removeFromSet(subset, q);
                    subset = addToSet(subset, pq);
                    enumerate(subset, solutions);
                }
                if (!operation.isCommutative()) {
                    if (operation.isDefined(q, p)) {
                        Number qp = new Term(operation, q, p);
                        Number[] subset = null;
                        subset = removeFromSet(numbers, q);
                        subset = removeFromSet(subset, p);
                        subset = addToSet(subset, qp);
                        enumerate(subset, solutions);
                    }
                }
            }
        }
    }
  }
}

/**
 * Returns a new array of Number objects
 * with the first occurrence of the specified
 * Number removed.
 */
public static Number[] removeFromSet
    (Number[] set, Number number)
{
    // Find first occurrence of number

    for (int i = 0; i < set.length; i++) {
        if (set[i].equals(number)) {
            Number[] subset = new Number[set.length-1];
            System.arraycopy(set, 0, subset, 0, i);
            System.arraycopy(set, i+1, subset, i,
                (set.length - (i+1)));
            return subset;
        }
    }

    // The number was not in the set

    return set;
}

/**
 * Returns a new array of Number objects
 * with the specified Number added.
 */
public static Number[] addToSet
    (Number[] set, Number number)
{
    Number[] superset = new Number[set.length+1];
    System.arraycopy(set, 0, superset, 0, set.length);
    superset[set.length] = number;
    return superset;
}
```

```jsp
<%@ page errorPage="ErrorPage.jsp"
        import="java.io.*,java.util.*,ijs.app.four4s.*"
        %>
<%--
    Create a bean to keep track of the numbers and
    solutions.
--%>

<jsp:useBean id="problem" class="ijs.app.four4s.Problem"/>

<HTML>
<HEAD>
<TITLE>Four 4's Problem</TITLE>
</HEAD>
<BODY>
<H3>Four 4's Problem</H3>
<%
    String submitted = request.getParameter("submitted");
    String list = request.getParameter("list");
    String target = request.getParameter("target");
%>
<FORM>

<%--
    Use a hidden field to indicate whether the
    form has been submitted or is just now
    being generated.
--%>

<INPUT NAME="submitted" TYPE="HIDDEN" VALUE="1">

<%-- Prompt for the set of numbers --%>

Number set:
<INPUT NAME="list" TYPE="TEXT" SIZE="16"
<%= list == null ? "" : ("VALUE=\"" + list + "\"") %>
>

<%-- Prompt for the target number --%>

Target number:
<INPUT NAME="target" TYPE="TEXT" SIZE="8"
<%= target == null ? "" : ("VALUE=\"" + target + "\"") %>
>

<%-- The submit button --%>

<INPUT TYPE="SUBMIT" VALUE="Go">
<P>
</FORM>
<%
    // If numbers were specified, start the problem

    if (submitted == null) {
%>
    Enter a list of integers in the <B>number set</B>
    field above<BR>
```

Figure 14-40
(Continued)

```
                    and a number to be found as an expression of
                    them<BR>
                    in the <B>target</B> field.
<%
    }
    else {

        // Extract the list of numbers

        StringTokenizer st = new StringTokenizer(list, " ,");
        int n = st.countTokens();
        if (n == 0)
            throw new RuntimeException
            ("No numbers specified");

        Number[] numbers = new Number[n];
        for (int i = 0; i < n; i++) {
            String token = st.nextToken();
            try {
                numbers[i] = new Integer(token);
            }
            catch (NumberFormatException e) {
                throw new RuntimeException
                (token + " is not an integer");
            }
        }

        // Send the list of numbers to the problem

        problem.setNumbers(numbers);

        // Extract the solutions

        int value = Integer.parseInt(target);
        String[] solutions = problem.getSolutions(value);
        if (solutions == null)
            throw new RuntimeException
            ("No solutions found for " + target);
%>

<H4><%= solutions.length %> solutions found
    for target=<%= target %></H4>

<%     for (int i = 0; i < solutions.length; i++) { %>

<%= value %> = <%= solutions[i] %><BR>

<%     } %>
<% } %>
</BODY>
</HTML>
```

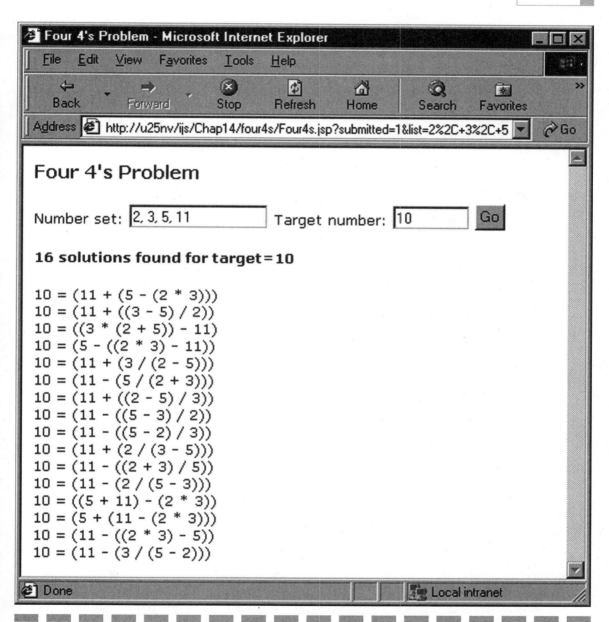

Figure 14-41 Using the Four Fours JSP Page to Solve {2, 3, 5, 11} for 10

APPENDIX A

SERVLET API REFERENCE

This appendix describes each class in the three servlet packages:

```
javax.servlet
javax.servlet.http
javax.servlet.jsp
```

For each class, the following sections are included:

- Class name
- Context (full name, type, superclass, interfaces implemented)
- Class description
- Summary of constructors, fields, and methods
- Details of each constructor or method, including its signature and a description of its operation.

The classes are presented in alphabetical order, as are the methods in each class.

Cookie

Context

Full name:	`javax.servlet.http.Cookie`
Type:	**Class**
Extends:	`java.lang.Object`
Implements:	`java.lang.Cloneable`

Description

A cookie is a small collection of key/value pairs that a servlet sends to a requester. The requester (usually a Web browser) is asked to store the information locally and return it the next time it makes a request the same URL.

Servlet engines can use cookies to store session information that is unique to a particular client. This use is transparent to the servlet author. You also can explicitly send and receive cookies with the `HttpServletResponse.addCookie()` and `HttpServletRequest.getCookies()` methods, respectively.

Be aware that users can refuse to accept cookies, so your application should handle this case.

Summary

```
// Constructors
public Cookie(String name, String value);
// Methods
public Object clone();
public String getComment();
public String getDomain();
public int getMaxAge();
public String getName();
public String getPath();
public boolean getSecure();
public String getValue();
public int getVersion();
public void setComment(String purpose);
public void setDomain(String pattern);
public void setMaxAge(int expiry);
public void setPath(String uri);
public void setSecure(boolean flag);
public void setValue(String newValue);
public void setVersion(int v);
```

Constructors

Cookie

Signature:
```
public Cookie(String name, String value);
```
Description:
Creates a new cookie with the specified name and value.

Methods

clone

Signature:
```
public Object clone();
```

Description:

Returns a copy of the cookie.

getComment

Signature:

```
public String getComment();
```

Description:

Returns the cookie's comment field or `null` if no comment was set.

getDomain

Signature:

```
public String getDomain();
```

Description:

Returns the cookie's domain, if one was specified; otherwise returns `null`.

getMaxAge

Signature:

```
public int getMaxAge();
```

Description:

Returns the maximum number of seconds that the cookie should be stored before it is deleted. Note that this is relative to the time that `setMaxAge()` was called, not the current time.

getName

Signature:

```
public String getName();
```

Description:

Returns the cookie name. Note that there is no `setName` method; you must set the cookie's name in the constructor.

getPath

Signature:

```
public String getPath();
```

Description:

Returns the path under which the cookie is visible. A request for any URL in that path or any of its subdirectories will cause the cookie to be returned. See RFC 2109 for more information about cookie paths.

getSecure

Signature:
```
public boolean getSecure();
```
Description:

Returns true if the user agent (browser) will return cookies using a secure protocol.

getValue

Signature:
```
public String getValue();
```
Description:

Returns the cookie's value.

getVersion

Signature:
```
public int getVersion();
```
Description:

Returns the cookie protocol version:

0—Original Netscape specification

1—RFC 2109 specification

setComment

Signature:
```
public void setComment(String purpose);
```
Description:

Sets the cookie's comment field to the specified string.

setDomain

Signature:
```
public void setDomain(String pattern);
```
Description:

Sets the cookie's domain. A domain can be used to restrict the cookie's visibility to a subset of servers in a particular addressing scheme. The domain name is converted to lowercase before it is stored. If no domain is specified, the cookie is returned only to the server that sent it. See RFC 2109 for details.

setMaxAge

Signature:
```
public void setMaxAge(int expiry);
```

Description:

Specifies the length of time in seconds that the cookie should persist. A positive or zero value requests the browser to delete the cookie after the specified interval. A negative value requests the browser to keep the cookie active only for the duration of the current browser instance.

setPath

Signature:

```
public void setPath(String uri);
```

Description:

Specifies a path in which the cookie should be visible. If a path of /servlet/abc is specified, for instance, then the cookie will be returned along with any requests for a URL containing that path, e.g., /servlet/abc/def. If no path is specified, / is assumed. The path must include the servlet that sets the cookie. See RFC 2109 for more details about cookie paths.

setSecure

Signature:

```
public void setSecure(boolean flag);
```

Description:

Tells the user agent (browser) whether to return the cookie using a secure protocol or not.

setValue

Signature:

```
public void setValue(String newValue);
```

Description:

Sets the cookie's value to the specified string.

setVersion

Signature:

```
public void setVersion(int v);
```

Description:

Sets the cookie protocol version:
0—Original Netscape specification
1—RFC 2109 specification

GenericServlet

Context

Full name:	`javax.servlet.GenericServlet`
Type:	**Abstract class**
Extends:	`java.lang.Object`
Implements:	`javax.servlet.Servlet`
	`javax.servlet.ServletConfig`
	`java.io.Serializable`

Description

A base class for servlets that do not use HTTP protocol-specific features. `GenericServlet` implements the basic elements of all servlets:

- Initialization
- Request handling
- Destruction

The only method that must be overridden is `service`, which actually handles requests.

`HttpServlet`, the base class for HTTP servlets, is more commonly used than `GenericServlet`.

Summary

```
// Constructors

public GenericServlet();

// Methods

public void destroy();
public String getInitParameter(String name);
public Enumeration getInitParameterNames();
public ServletConfig getServletConfig();
public ServletContext getServletContext();
public String getServletInfo();
public void init()
    throws ServletException;
public void init(ServletConfig config)
```

```
   throws ServletException;
public void log(String msg);
public void log(String message, Throwable t);
public abstract void service(ServletRequest req, ServletResponse res)
   throws ServletException, IOException;
```

Constructors

GenericServlet

Signature:
```
public GenericServlet();
```
Description:

An empty constructor that performs no work. Any servlet initialization should be done in the `init` method.

Methods

destroy

Signature:
```
public void destroy();
```
Description:

Called by the servlet engine when the servlet is unloaded. Servlet authors can override this method to release any allocated resources. In `GenericServlet`, this method simply logs the fact that it was executed.

getInitParameter

Signature:
```
public String getInitParameter(String name);
```
Description:

Given an initialization parameter name, returns the value of the parameter. If no such parameter exists, returns `null`.

getInitParameterNames

Signature:
```
public Enumeration getInitParameterNames();
```
Description:

Returns an `Enumeration` of the names of all the initialization parameter that exist for this servlet.

getServletConfig

Signature:

```
public ServletConfig getServletConfig();
```

Description:

Returns the `ServletConfig` object associated with this servlet.

getServletContext

Signature:

```
public ServletContext getServletContext();
```

Description:

Returns the `ServletContext` object associated with this servlet.

getServletInfo

Signature:

```
public String getServletInfo();
```

Description:

Returns a `String` containing identifying information about this servlet to the servlet engine. Returns an empty string if you do not override this method.

init

Signature:

```
public void init()
throws ServletException;
```

Description:

A version of `init` that does not explictly store the `ServletConfig` object. This method is called by `init(config)` in `GenericServlet`.

init

Signature:

```
public void init(ServletConfig config)
throws ServletException;
```

Description:

Initializes the servlet. This method is called by the servlet engine when the servlet is first loaded. No requests will be serviced until this method completes. If you detect an error during initialization, you should throw an `UnavailableException` so that the servlet engine will not try to handle requests with this servlet.

If you override this method, you must take care to call `super.init(config)` so that the `ServletConfig` is stored in the servlet instance.

log

Signature:
```
public void log(String msg);
```
Description:
Writes a log message consisting of the servlet's class name and the specified message.

log

Signature:
```
public void log(String message, Throwable t);
```
Description:
Writes a log message that includes the specified exception or error and a stack trace.

service

Signature:
```
    public abstract void service(ServletRequest req,
ServletResponse res)
        throws ServletException, IOException;
```
Description:
Handles a request. All the information about the request is encapsulated in a `ServletRequest` object and the response in a `ServletResponse`. This is the only method that subclasses of `GenericServlet` are required to override.

HttpJspPage

Context

Full name: `javax.servlet.jsp.HttpJspPage`
Type: Interface
Superinterface: `javax.servlet.jsp.JspPage`

Description

A subinterface of JspPage that is implemented by HTTP-specific classes generated by a JSP engine. The JSP engine will automatically create a _jspService() method that contains all the scriptlet code defined in the page. The JSP author should not override this method.

Summary

```
// Methods

public void _jspService(HttpServletRequest request,
HttpServletResponse response)
    throws ServletException, IOException;
```

Methods

_jspService

Signature:
```
    public void _jspService(
      HttpServletRequest request,
      HttpServletResponse response)
        throws ServletException, IOException;
```
Description:
    The body of the JSP page as generated by the JSP engine.

HttpServlet

Context

Full name:	javax.servlet.http.HttpServlet
Type:	**Abstract class**
Extends:	javax.servlet.GenericServlet
Implements:	java.io.Serializable

Description

An abstract base class for servlets that operate in an HTTP environment. HttpServlet is a thin extension of GenericServlet that provides specific methods for HTTP GET, POST, PUT, DELETE, HEAD, OPTIONS, and TRACE requests. The service() method determines the HTTP request type and invokes the appropriate method.

A typical HttpServlet subclass will override doGet(), doPost(), or both but not service().

Summary

```
// Constructors

public HttpServlet();

// Methods

protected void doDelete(HttpServletRequest req, HttpServletResponse
resp)
    throws ServletException, IOException;
protected void doGet(HttpServletRequest req, HttpServletResponse resp)
    throws ServletException, IOException;
protected void doOptions(HttpServletRequest req, HttpServletResponse
resp)
    throws ServletException, IOException;
protected void doPost(HttpServletRequest req, HttpServletResponse
resp)
    throws ServletException, IOException;
protected void doPut(HttpServletRequest req, HttpServletResponse resp)
    throws ServletException, IOException;
protected void doTrace(HttpServletRequest req, HttpServletResponse
resp)
    throws ServletException, IOException;
protected long getLastModified(HttpServletRequest req);
protected void service(HttpServletRequest req, HttpServletResponse
resp)
    throws ServletException, IOException;
public void service(ServletRequest req, ServletResponse res)
    throws ServletException, IOException;
```

Constructors

HttpServlet

Signature:
```
    public HttpServlet();
```

Description:

Default (empty) constructor. Performs no work. All servlet initialization should be performed in the init() method inherited from GenericServlet.

Methods

doDelete

Signature:

```
    protected void doDelete(HttpServletRequest req,
HttpServletResponse resp)
        throws ServletException, IOException;
```

Description:

Handles an HTTP DELETE request. As with doPut(), this type of request is generally not initiated directly by a Web browser.

doGet

Signature:

```
    protected void doGet(HttpServletRequest req,
HttpServletResponse resp)
        throws ServletException, IOException;
```

Description:

Handles an HTTP GET request. By default, does nothing except return an error indicating that the servlet does not handle the GET method.

Servlet authors that override doGet() typically will perform the following steps:

1. Read and handle HttpServletRequest parameters
2. Get an output stream by calling either getWriter() or getOutputStream() in the HttpServletResponse object.
3. Set the Content-Type header in the response object.
4. Write the output HTML page.

doOptions

Signature:

```
    protected void doOptions(
```

```
   HttpServletRequest req,
   HttpServletResponse resp)
      throws ServletException, IOException;
```
Description:

Handles an HTTP OPTIONS request and returns a list of methods that the HTTP server supports. This method is generally not overridden.

doPost

Signature:
```
protected void doPost(
   HttpServletRequest req,
   HttpServletResponse resp)
      throws ServletException, IOException;
```
Description:

Handles an HTTP POST request. By default, does nothing except return an error indicating that the servlet does not handle the POST method.

Servlet authors that override doPost() typically will perform the following steps:

1. Read and handle HttpServletRequest parameters.
2. Get an output stream by calling either getWriter() or getOutputStream() in the HttpServletResponse object.
3. Set the Content-Type header in the response object.
4. Write the output HTML page.

doPut

Signature:
```
protected void doPut(
   HttpServletRequest req,
   HttpServletResponse resp)
      throws ServletException, IOException;
```
Description:

Handles an HTTP PUT request. The name of the resource to be written can be found by calling the request object's getRequestURI() method, and the resource data itself can be read from the request object's input stream. HTML forms do not support the PUT method; this type of request generally is not initiated directly by a Web browser.

doTrace

Signature:

```
protected void doTrace(
  HttpServletRequest req,
  HttpServletResponse resp)
    throws ServletException, IOException;
```

Description:

Handles an HTTP TRACE request and echoes back the request headers. This method is generally not overridden.

getLastModified

Signature:

```
    protected long getLastModified(HttpServletRequest
req);
```

Description:

Returns the time (in milliseconds since January 1, 1970) that the request object was last modified or -1 if the time is not known. The default implementation always returns -1.

service

Signature:

```
protected void service(
  HttpServletRequest req,
  HttpServletResponse resp)
    throws ServletException, IOException;
```

Description:

The main entry point for HTTP requests. This method determines the request method (GET, POST, etc.) and dispatches the request to the appropriate handler method (doGet(), doPost(), etc.) In the case of the GET method, it tries to determine if the resource has been modified since it was last requested. If not, it returns just an HTTP NOT_MODI-FIED status line. This method generally is not overridden.

service

Signature:

```
public void service(
  ServletRequest req,
  ServletResponse res)
    throws ServletException, IOException;
```

Description:
A convenience method that converts a protocol-neutral request to an HTTP request, if possible, and then invokes the HTTP-specific `service()` method.

HttpServletRequest

Context

Full name:	`javax.servlet.http.HttpServletRequest`
Type:	Interface
Superinterface:	`javax.servlet.ServletRequest`

Description

Encapsulates all information about an HTTP request: its parameters, attributes, headers, and input data.

Summary

```
// Methods

public String getAuthType();
public Cookie getCookies();
public long getDateHeader(String name);
public String getHeader(String name);
public Enumeration getHeaderNames();
public int getIntHeader(String name);
public String getMethod();
public String getPathInfo();
public String getPathTranslated();
public String getQueryString();
public String getRemoteUser();
public String getRequestedSessionId();
public String getRequestURI();
public String getServletPath();
public HttpSession getSession();
public HttpSession getSession(boolean create);
public boolean isRequestedSessionIdFromCookie();
public boolean isRequestedSessionIdFromUrl();
public boolean isRequestedSessionIdFromURL();
public boolean isRequestedSessionIdValid();
```

Methods

getAuthType

Signature:
```
public String getAuthType();
```
Description:

If the server uses an authentication scheme like BASIC or SSL, returns the name of this scheme; otherwise returns null.

getCookies

Signature:
```
public Cookie getCookies();
```
Description:

Returns an array of all the Cookie objects that were sent with this request. Returns null if no cookies were sent.

getDateHeader

Signature:
```
public long getDateHeader(String name);
```
Description:

Given a request header name, converts the corresponding header value into a Date object, which is returned as a long value (the number of milliseconds since January 1, 1970). If the specified request header does not exist, returns -1.

getHeader

Signature:
```
public String getHeader(String name);
```
Description:

Returns the string value of the specified request header or null if the named header is not found in the request.

getHeaderNames

Signature:
```
public Enumeration getHeaderNames();
```
Description:

Returns an Enumeration of all the header names found in this request. If there are no headers, returns either null or an empty Enumeration, depending on the servlet engine.

getIntHeader

Signature:

```
public int getIntHeader(String name);
```

Description:

Given a request header name, converts the corresponding header value into an integer and returns the integer value. If the specified request header does not exist, returns −1.

getMethod

Signature:

```
public String getMethod();
```

Description:

Returns the HTTP method contained in the first line of the request, i.e., GET or POST.

getPathInfo

Signature:

```
public String getPathInfo();
```

Description:

Returns the substring of the request URL that follows the servlet name or null if there is no additional path information. Same as the CGI variable PATH_INFO.

getPathTranslated

Signature:

```
public String getPathTranslated();
```

Description:

Returns the substring of the request URL that follows the servlet name converted to a real filesystem path or null if there is no additional path information. Same as the CGI variable PATH_TRANSLATED.

getQueryString

Signature:

```
public String getQueryString();
```

Description:

Returns the substring of the request URL that follows the "?" or null if there is no query string. Usually found only in GET requests. Same as the CGI variable QUERY_STRING.

getRemoteUser

Signature:

```
public String getRemoteUser();
```
Description:

Returns the user name if HTTP authentication is active and the user had logged in. Returns `null` otherwise. Same as the CGI variable REMOTE_USER.

getRequestedSessionId

Signature:

```
public String getRequestedSessionId();
```
Description:

Returns the value of the session ID returned by the client. Usually the same as the current session but may refer to an old expired session. Returns `null` if the request does not specify a session ID.

getRequestURI

Signature:

```
public String getRequestURI();
```
Description:

Returns the substring of the request URL starting with the protocol name (e.g., `http://`) if present, and extending to but not including the query string (which starts with "?").

getServletPath

Signature:

```
public String getServletPath();
```
Description:

Returns the substring of the request URL that refers to the servlet, excluding any additional path information or query string. Same as the CGI variable SCRIPT_NAME.

getSession

Signature:

```
public HttpSession getSession();
```
Description:

A convenience method that returns the value of `HttpSession.getSession(true)`.

getSession

Signature:

```
public HttpSession getSession(boolean create);
```

Description:

Returns the current HttpSession object or creates a new one (if the create parameter is true). The returned value depends on whether the session already exists and whether the create parameter is true or false:

Session Exists	create	Returned
False	false	null
False	true	New session
True	false	Existing session
True	true	Existing session

isRequestedSessionIdFromCookie

Signature:

```
public boolean isRequestedSessionIdFromCookie();
```

Description:

Returns true if the request session ID was received from a Cookie as opposed to being sent as part of the request URL.

isRequestedSessionIdFromUrl (deprecated)

Signature:

```
public boolean isRequestedSessionIdFromUrl();
```

Description:

An old alias for isRequestedSessionIdFromURL().

isRequestedSessionIdFromURL

Signature:

```
public boolean isRequestedSessionIdFromURL();
```

Description:

Returns true if the request session ID was received as part of the request URL as opposed to being sent from a Cookie.

isRequestedSessionIdValid

Signature:

```
public boolean isRequestedSessionIdValid();
```

Description:

Returns `true` if the request specifies the ID of a valid, active session.

HttpServletResponse

Context

Full name: `javax.servlet.http.HttpServletResponse`

Type: Interface

Superinterface: `javax.servlet.ServletResponse`

Description

Encapsulates all information about the response generated for an HTTP request, including response headers, the status code, and the output stream.

Summary

```
// Fields
public static final int SC_ACCEPTED;
public static final int SC_BAD_GATEWAY;
public static final int SC_BAD_REQUEST;
public static final int SC_CONFLICT;
public static final int SC_CONTINUE;
public static final int SC_CREATED;
public static final int SC_FORBIDDEN;
public static final int SC_GATEWAY_TIMEOUT;
public static final int SC_GONE;
public static final int SC_HTTP_VERSION_NOT_SUPPORTED;
public static final int SC_INTERNAL_SERVER_ERROR;
public static final int SC_LENGTH_REQUIRED;
public static final int SC_METHOD_NOT_ALLOWED;
public static final int SC_MOVED_PERMANENTLY;
public static final int SC_MOVED_TEMPORARILY;
public static final int SC_MULTIPLE_CHOICES;
public static final int SC_NO_CONTENT;
public static final int SC_NON_AUTHORITATIVE_INFORMATION;
```

```
public static final int SC_NOT_ACCEPTABLE;
public static final int SC_NOT_FOUND;
public static final int SC_NOT_IMPLEMENTED;
public static final int SC_NOT_MODIFIED;
public static final int SC_OK;
public static final int SC_PARTIAL_CONTENT;
public static final int SC_PAYMENT_REQUIRED;
public static final int SC_PRECONDITION_FAILED;
public static final int SC_PROXY_AUTHENTICATION_REQUIRED;
public static final int SC_REQUEST_ENTITY_TOO_LARGE;
public static final int SC_REQUEST_TIMEOUT;
public static final int SC_REQUEST_URI_TOO_LONG;
public static final int SC_RESET_CONTENT;
public static final int SC_SEE_OTHER;
public static final int SC_SERVICE_UNAVAILABLE;
public static final int SC_SWITCHING_PROTOCOLS;
public static final int SC_UNAUTHORIZED;
public static final int SC_UNSUPPORTED_MEDIA_TYPE;
public static final int SC_USE_PROXY;

   // Methods

public void addCookie(Cookie cookie);
public boolean containsHeader(String name);
public String encodeRedirectUrl(String url);
public String encodeRedirectURL(String url);
public String encodeUrl(String url);
public String encodeURL(String url);
public void sendError(int sc)
   throws IOException;
public void sendError(int sc, String msg)
   throws IOException;
public void sendRedirect(String location)
   throws IOException;
public void setDateHeader(String name, long date);
public void setHeader(String name, String value);
public void setIntHeader(String name, int value);
public void setStatus(int sc);
public void setStatus(int sc, String sm);
```

Methods

addCookie

Signature:
```
    public void addCookie(Cookie cookie);
```
Description:
Writes a `Set-Cookie` header for the specified `Cookie`.

containsHeader

Signature:
```
    public boolean containsHeader(String name);
```

Description:

Returns `true` if the response already contains a header with the specified name.

encodeRedirectUrl (deprecated)

Signature:

```
public String encodeRedirectUrl(String url);
```

Description:

An old alias for `encodeRedirectURL()`.

encodeRedirectURL

Signature:

```
public String encodeRedirectURL(String url);
```

Description:

Supports session tracking by optionally appending the encoded session ID as a parameter in a URL intended to be used with `sendRedirect()`. This is not necessary if the client supports cookies. The servlet engine makes this determination; it is always safe to filter URLs to be written through this method.

encodeUrl (deprecated)

Signature:

```
public String encodeUrl(String url);
```

Description:

An old alias for `encodeURL()`

encodeURL

Signature:

```
public String encodeURL(String url);
```

Description:

Supports session tracking by appending the encoded session ID as a parameter in the specified URL if necessary. This is not necessary if the client supports cookies. The servlet engine makes this determination; it is always safe to filter URLs to be written through this method.

sendError

Signature:

```
public void sendError(int sc)
  throws IOException;
```

Description:

Sets the HTTP status code to the specified value. The response object is committed after this method is called; any further writing to it has no effect.

sendError

Signature:
```
public void sendError(int sc, String msg)
  throws IOException;
```
Description:

Sets the HTTP status code to the specified value and sets the status message. The response object is committed after this method is called; any further writing to it has no effect.

sendRedirect

Signature:
```
public void sendRedirect(String location)
  throws IOException;
```
Description:

Sets the HTTP status code to 302 (moved temporarily) and writes a `Location` header with the specified value. The user agent (Web browser) usually will interpret this response and request the new URL automatically.

setDateHeader

Signature:
```
public void setDateHeader(String name, long date);
```
Description:

Writes a response header with the specified name and a correctly formatted date value.

setHeader

Signature:
```
public void setHeader(String name, String value);
```
Description:

Writes a response header with the specified name and value.

setIntHeader

Signature:
```
public void setIntHeader(String name, int value);
```

Description:

Writes a response header with the specified name and a string-formatted integer value.

setStatus

Signature:
```
public void setStatus(int sc);
```
Description:

Sets the HTTP status code for this response.

setStatus (deprecated)

Signature:
```
public void setStatus(int sc, String sm);
```
Description:

No longer valid. Use `sendError(int sc, String msg)` instead.

HttpSession

Context

Full name: `javax.servlet.http.HttpSession`

Type: Interface

Superinterface: None

Description

An `HttpSession` is a repository of named references to objects belonging to a user's browser session. This repository remains active in the server between user requests. A session has a unique session ID assigned by the server that the client keeps track of and passes back with each subsequent request.

A session is created by calling the `HttpServletRequest.getSession(true)` or `HttpServletRequest.getSession()` method. The session ID is then passed to the client either by a cookie or as a parameter in a generated URL. The session is considered "new" until the client joins it, that is, until the client passes back the session ID in a subsequent request. The `isNew()` method can be used to determine this.

Objects are stored in the session using the `putValue()` method and can be retrieved with the `getValue()` methods. If an object in a session implements the `HttpSessionBindingListener` interface, it will be notified whenever it is bound to or unbound from a session.

Summary

```
// Methods

public long getCreationTime();
public String getId();
public long getLastAccessedTime();
public int getMaxInactiveInterval();
public HttpSessionContext getSessionContext();
public Object getValue(String name);
public String getValueNames();
public void invalidate();
public boolean isNew();
public void putValue(String name, Object value);
public void removeValue(String name);
public void setMaxInactiveInterval(int interval);
```

Methods

getCreationTime

Signature:
```
public long getCreationTime();
```
Description:
Returns the time the session was created in milliseconds from January 1, 1970.

getId

Signature:
```
public String getId();
```
Description:
Returns the session ID.

getLastAccessedTime

Signature:
```
public long getLastAccessedTime();
```

Description:

Returns the time the session was last accessed in milliseconds from January 1, 1970.

getMaxInactiveInterval

Signature:

```
public int getMaxInactiveInterval();
```

Description:

Returns the maximum number of seconds this session can remain active between requests. If the time interval is exceeded, the servlet engine is permitted to terminate it.

NOTE: *Some servlet engines erroneously treat this value as milliseconds or minutes. You should verify this method's operation if you depend on it being correct.*

getSessionContext (deprecated)

Signature:

```
public HttpSessionContext getSessionContext();
```

Description:

Formerly returned a reference to the HttpSessionContext.

getValue

Signature:

```
public Object getValue(String name);
```

Description:

Returns the object with the specified name if it exists in the session or null if it does not.

getValueNames

Signature:

```
public String getValueNames();
```

Description:

Returns an array of the names of all objects in this session or an empty array if there are none.

invalidate

Signature:

```
public void invalidate();
```

Description:

Closes the session, calling `valueUnbound()` for any `HttpSessionBindingListener` objects bound to the session.

isNew

Signature:

    public boolean isNew();

Description:

Returns `true` if a session has been created but the client has not yet issued a request with that session ID.

putValue

Signature:

    public void putValue(String name, Object value);

Description:

Stores a reference to an object in the session under the specified name. If the object implements the `HttpSessionBindingListener` interface, the servlet engine calls its `valueBound()` method.

removeValue

Signature:

    public void removeValue(String name);

Description:

Removes a reference to an object in the session with the specified name. If the object implements the `HttpSessionBindingListener` interface, the servlet engine calls its `valueUnbound()` method. Ignored if the specified value does not exist in the session.

setMaxInactiveInterval

Signature:

    public void setMaxInactiveInterval(int interval);

Description:

Specifies the maximum number of seconds this session can remain active between requests. If the time interval is exceeded, the servlet engine is permitted to terminate it.

NOTE: *Some servlet engines erroneously treat this value as milliseconds or minutes. You should verify this method's operation if you depend on it being correct.*

HttpSessionBindingEvent

Context

Full name:
`javax.servlet.http.HttpSessionBindingEvent`

Type: **Class**

Extends: `java.util.EventObject`

Implements: **Nothing**

Description

An event object that is passed as a parameter to the `valueBound()` and `valueUnbound()` methods of an `HttpSessionBindingListener`. Using methods in the event object, the `HttpSessionBindingListener` can get the name by which it was bound and a reference to the `HttpSession` itself.

Summary

```
// Constructors

public HttpSessionBindingEvent(HttpSession session, String name);

// Methods

public String getName();
public HttpSession getSession();
```

Constructors

HttpSessionBindingEvent

Signature:
```
    public HttpSessionBindingEvent(
       HttpSession session, String name);
```
Description:
    Creates a new `HttpSessionBindingEvent` object for the specified session using the specified name.

Methods

getName

Signature:
```
    public String getName();
```
Description:
Returns the name by which the object is known to the session.

getSession

Signature:
```
    public HttpSession getSession();
```
Description:
Returns the session to which the object is bound.

HttpSessionBindingListener

Context

Full name:	`javax.servlet.http.HttpSessionBinding-Listener`
Type:	Interface
Superinterface:	`java.util.EventListener`

Description

If an object implements this interface, it is notified when it is bound to or unbound from an `HttpSession`. The object must provide `valueBound()` and `valueUnbound()` methods, each of which has an `HttpSessionBindingEvent` parameter that allows the object to determine its name and the session to which it belongs.

Summary

```
// Methods

public void valueBound(HttpSessionBindingEvent event);
public void valueUnbound(HttpSessionBindingEvent event);
```

Methods

valueBound

Signature:

```
public void valueBound(HttpSessionBindingEvent
event);
```

Description:

   Called when this object is bound to an HttpSession.

valueUnbound

Signature:

```
public void valueUnbound(HttpSessionBindingEvent
event);
```

Description:

   Called when this object is unbound from an HttpSession.

HttpSessionContext

Context

Full name:	javax.servlet.http.HttpSessionContext
Type:	Interface
Superinterface:	None

Description

Formerly a means of getting the set of active HttpSession objects maintained by the servlet engine. *Deprecated as of Servlet API 2.1 for security reasons.*

Summary

```
// Methods

public Enumeration getIds();
public HttpSession getSession(String sessionId);
```

Methods

getIds (deprecated)

Signature:

```
public Enumeration getIds();
```

Description:

Formerly returned an Enumeration of the active HttpSession objects in the servlet engine.

getSession (deprecated)

Signature:

```
public HttpSession getSession(String sessionId);
```

Description:

Formerly returned the HttpSession having the specified ID.

HttpUtils

Context

Full name:	javax.servlet.http.HttpUtils
Type:	Class
Extends:	java.lang.Object
Implements:	Nothing

Description

A utility class providing methods useful in HTTP servlets.

Summary

```
// Constructors

public HttpUtils();

// Methods
```

```
public static StringBuffer getRequestURL(HttpServletRequest req);
public static Hashtable parsePostData(int len, ServletInputStream in);
public static Hashtable parseQueryString(String s);
```

Constructors

HttpUtils

Signature:

```
public HttpUtils();
```

Description:

Default (empty) constructor. Performs no work.

Methods

getRequestURL

Signature:

```
public static StringBuffer getRequestURL(
    HttpServletRequest req);
```

Description:

Returns the entire URL used for the specified request. Includes the protocol, server name, port number (if other than the default), and file name. Does not include the query string.

parsePostData

Signature:

```
public static Hashtable parsePostData(
    int len, ServletInputStream in);
```

Description:

Reads the servlet request input stream for the specified length and parses it into key/value pairs by calling parseQueryString().

parseQueryString

Signature:

```
public static Hashtable parseQueryString(String s);
```

Description:

Given a query string containing URL-encoded parameters and values, returns a Hashtable containing the parsed names and values. In the hashtable, the parameter name is the key, and the corresponding value is an array of strings. If the parameter occurs only once, the array length is one; otherwise, there are multiple entries in the array. See `java.net.URLEncoder` for specifics of how the decoding is done.

JspEngineInfo

Context

Full name:	`javax.servlet.jsp.JspEngineInfo`
Type:	**Abstract class**
Extends:	`java.lang.Object`
Implements:	Nothing

Description

A class that provides information about the JSP engine. An instance of this class is returned by the `JspFactory.getEngineInfo()` method.

NOTE: *This class is designed primarily for use by JSP engine developers.*

Summary

```
// Constructors

public JspEngineInfo();

// Methods

public abstract String getImplementationVersion();
```

Constructors

JspEngineInfo

Signature:
```
    public JspEngineInfo();
```
Description:
    JspEngineInfo **object.**

Methods

`getImplementationVersion`

Signature:
```
public abstract String getImplementationVersion();
```
Description:
Returns the JSP engine's implementation version number.

JspFactory

Context

Full name:	`javax.servlet.jsp.JspFactory`
Type:	Abstract class
Extends:	`java.lang.Object`
Implements:	Nothing

Description

A class that provides factory methods for creating the objects necessary to support the JSP environment. Includes a static method for assigning the default `JspFactory`.

NOTE: *This class is designed primarily for use by JSP engine developers.*

Summary

```
// Constructors

public JspFactory();

// Methods

public static synchronized JspFactory getDefaultFactory();
public abstract JspEngineInfo getEngineInfo();
```

```
public abstract PageContext getPageContext(
     Servlet servlet,
     ServletRequest request,
     ServletResponse response,
     String errorPageURL,
     boolean needsSession,
     int buffer,
     boolean autoflush);
public abstract void releasePageContext(PageContext pc);
public static synchronized void setDefaultFactory(JspFactory deflt);
```

Constructors

JspFactory

Signature:
```
public JspFactory();
```
Description:

Creates a new JspFactory object.

Methods

getDefaultFactory

Signature:
```
public static synchronized JspFactory
getDefaultFactory();
```
Description:

Returns the currently registered JspFactory object.

getEngineInfo

Signature:
```
public abstract JspEngineInfo getEngineInfo();
```
Description:

Returns the JspEngineInfo object for this JSP implementation.

getPageContext

Signature:
```
public abstract PageContext getPageContext(
   Servlet servlet,
   ServletRequest request,
   ServletResponse response,
   String errorPageURL,
```

```
        boolean needsSession,
        int buffer, boolean autoflush);
```
Description:

Returns the `PageContext` object. Calling this method causes the `PageContext.initialize()` method to be invoked and causes the following attributes to be set:

- The requesting servlet
- The `ServletConfig` for the requesting servlet
- The `ServletRequest` object
- The `ServletResponse` object
- The URL of the JSP's error page, if one was specified
- Whether the JSP needs an HTTP session
- The buffer size
- Whether the buffer should be autoflushed on overflow

These resources are released when the `releasePageContext()` method is called.

NOTE: *A call to this method is automatically generated by the JSP engine and should not be coded by the JSP author.*

releasePageContext

Signature:

```
        public abstract void releasePageContext(PageContext
pc);
```
Description:

Releases the `PageContext`, including any resources obtained when `getPageContext()` was invoked.

NOTE: *A call to this method is automatically generated by the JSP engine and should not be coded by the JSP author.*

setDefaultFactory

Signature:

```
        public static synchronized void setDefault-
Factory(JspFactory deflt);
```
Description:

Sets the default `JspFactory` object. Should only be called by the JSP engine itself.

JspPage

Context

Full name: `javax.servlet.jsp.JspPage`

Type: Interface

Superinterface: `javax.servlet.Servlet`

Description

A subinterface of `Servlet` that is implemented by classes generated by a JSP engine. The `jspInit()` and `jspDestroy()` methods can be overrided by the JSP author to perform what the `Servlet` `init()` and `destroy()` methods do.

Summary

```
// Methods

public void jspDestroy();
public void jspInit();
```

Methods

jspDestroy

Signature:
```
    public void jspDestroy();
```
Description:
    A method invoked when the generated JSP servlet is destroyed. This method should be overridden instead of `destroy()`.

jspInit

Signature:
```
    public void jspInit();
```
Description:
    A method invoked when the generated JSP servlet is initialized. This method should be overridden instead of `init()`.

JspWriter

Context

Full name: `javax.servlet.jsp.JspWriter`

Type: **Abstract class**

Extends: `java.io.Writer`

Implements: Nothing

Description

A subclass of `java.io.Writer` that is used to write JSP output. Its role is primarily the same as `java.io.PrintWriter`. This class is instantiated by the generated `_jspService()` by calling the underlying servlet's `getWriter()` method, which makes it illegal later to call `getOutputStream()`.

The "out" implicit variable is an instance of this class.

Summary

```
// Fields

protected boolean autoFlush;
protected int bufferSize;
public static final int DEFAULT_BUFFER;
public static final int NO_BUFFER;

// Constructors

protected JspWriter(int bufferSize, boolean autoFlush);

// Methods

public abstract void clear()
   throws IOException;
public abstract void clearBuffer()
   throws IOException;
public abstract void close()
   throws IOException;
public abstract void flush()
   throws IOException;
```

```
public int getBufferSize();
public abstract int getRemaining();
public boolean isAutoFlush();
public abstract void newLine()
    throws IOException;
public abstract void print(boolean b)
    throws IOException;
public abstract void print(char c)
    throws IOException;
public abstract void print(char s)
    throws IOException;
public abstract void print(double d)
    throws IOException;
public abstract void print(float f)
    throws IOException;
public abstract void print(int i)
    throws IOException;
public abstract void print(long l)
    throws IOException;
public abstract void print(Object obj)
    throws IOException;
public abstract void print(String s)
    throws IOException;
public abstract void println()
    throws IOException;
public abstract void println(boolean x)
    throws IOException;
public abstract void println(char x)
    throws IOException;
public abstract void println(char x)
    throws IOException;
public abstract void println(double x)
    throws IOException;
public abstract void println(float x)
    throws IOException;
public abstract void println(int x)
    throws IOException;
public abstract void println(long x)
    throws IOException;
public abstract void println(Object x)
    throws IOException;
public abstract void println(String x)
    throws IOException;
```

Constructors

JspWriter

Signature:

```
protected JspWriter(int bufferSize, boolean
autoFlush);
```

Description:

Creates a new JspWriter object of the specified size and autoflush attribute.

Methods

clear

Signature:
```
public abstract void clear()
    throws IOException;
```
Description:

Clears the page buffer. Throws an `IOException` if the buffer has already been cleared (i.e., if a full buffer of data has already been written to the output stream).

clearBuffer

Signature:
```
public abstract void clearBuffer()
    throws IOException;
```
Description:

Clears the page buffer. Does not throw an `IOException`.

close

Signature:
```
public abstract void close()
    throws IOException;
```
Description:

Flushes and closes the stream.

flush

Signature:
```
public abstract void flush()
    throws IOException;
```
Description:

Flushes the output stream.

getBufferSize

Signature:
```
public int getBufferSize();
```
Description:

Returns the buffer size in bytes.

getRemaining

Signature:
```
public abstract int getRemaining();
```
Description:
Returns the number of bytes available in the buffer.

isAutoFlush

Signature:
```
public boolean isAutoFlush();
```
Description:
Returns an indication of whether the JSP autoFlush flag is set.

newLine

Signature:
```
public abstract void newLine()
    throws IOException;
```
Description:
Writes the system line.separator string.

print

Signature:
```
public abstract void print(boolean b)
    throws IOException;
```
Description:
Writes a Boolean value (true or false).

print

Signature:
```
public abstract void print(char c)
    throws IOException;
```
Description:
Writes a single character.

print

Signature:
```
public abstract void print(char s)
    throws IOException;
```

Description:
Writes an array of characters.

print

Signature:
```
public abstract void print(double d)
    throws IOException;
```
Description:
Writes the string equivalent of a double-precision floating-point number.

print

Signature:
```
public abstract void print(float f)
    throws IOException;
```
Description:
Writes the string equivalent of a floating-point number.

print

Signature:
```
public abstract void print(int i)
    throws IOException;
```
Description:
Writes the string equivalent of an integer.

print

Signature:
```
public abstract void print(long l)
    throws IOException;
```
Description:
Writes the string equivalent of a long integer.

print

Signature:
```
public abstract void print(Object obj)
    throws IOException;
```
Description:
Writes the output of an object's toString() method.

print

Signature:
```
    public abstract void print(String s)
      throws IOException;
```
Description:
Writes a string.

println

Signature:
```
    public abstract void println()
      throws IOException;
```
Description:
Writes the line separator, terminating the current line.

println

Signature:
```
    public abstract void println(boolean x)
      throws IOException;
```
Description:
Writes a Boolean value (true or false) and terminates the current line.

println

Signature:
```
    public abstract void println(char x)
      throws IOException;
```
Description:
Writes a single character and terminates the current line.

println

Signature:
```
    public abstract void println(char x)
      throws IOException;
```
Description:
Writes an array of characters and terminates the current line.

println

Signature:
```
    public abstract void println(double x)
      throws IOException;
```

Description:

Writes the string equivalent of a double-precision floating-point number and terminates the current line.

println

Signature:
```
    public abstract void println(float x)
       throws IOException;
```
Description:

Writes the string equivalent of a floating-point number and terminates the current line.

println

Signature:
```
    public abstract void println(int x)
       throws IOException;
```
Description:

Writes the string equivalent of an integer and terminates the current line.

println

Signature:
```
    public abstract void println(long x)
       throws IOException;
```
Description:

Writes the string equivalent of a long integer and terminates the current line.

println

Signature:
```
    public abstract void println(Object x)
       throws IOException;
```
Description:

Writes the output of an object's toString() method and terminates the current line.

println

Signature:
```
    public abstract void println(String x)
       throws IOException;
```

Description:
> Writes a string and terminates the current line.

PageContext

Context

Full name:	`javax.servlet.jsp.PageContext`
Type:	Abstract class
Extends:	`java.lang.Object`
Implements:	Nothing

Description

`PageContext` is a wrapper object that encapsulates all the details of a single invocation of a JSP to handle a request. It contains methods to initialize and release the session, writer, request, and response objects. It also provides methods to set and retrieve attributes in the various namespaces accessible to the JSP.

A `PageContext` object is created and initialized by the `JSPFactory` when its `getPageContext()` method is called and released when its `releasePageContext()` is called. These two method calls are automatically performed by code generated by the JSP engine.

Summary

```
// Fields

public static final String APPLICATION;
public static final int APPLICATION_SCOPE;
public static final String CONFIG;
public static final String EXCEPTION;
public static final String OUT;
public static final String PAGE;
public static final int PAGE_SCOPE;
public static final String PAGECONTEXT;
public static final String REQUEST;
public static final int REQUEST_SCOPE;
public static final String RESPONSE;
```

```
public static final String SESSION;
public static final int SESSION_SCOPE;

// Constructors

public PageContext();

// Methods

public abstract Object findAttribute(String name);
public abstract void forward(String relativeUrlPath)
    throws ServletException, IOException;
public abstract Object getAttribute(String name);
public abstract Object getAttribute(String name, int scope);
public abstract Enumeration getAttributeNamesInScope(int scope);
public abstract int getAttributesScope(String name);
public abstract Exception getException();
public abstract JspWriter getOut();
public abstract Object getPage();
public abstract ServletRequest getRequest();
public abstract ServletResponse getResponse();
public abstract ServletConfig getServletConfig();
public abstract ServletContext getServletContext();
public abstract HttpSession getSession();
public abstract void handlePageException(Exception e)
    throws ServletException, IOException;
public abstract void include(String relativeUrlPath)
    throws ServletException, IOException;
public abstract void initialize(
    Servlet servlet,
    ServletRequest request,
    ServletResponse response,
    String errorPageURL,
    boolean needsSession,
    int bufferSize,
    boolean autoFlush)
    throws IOException, IllegalStateException,
IllegalArgumentException;
public abstract void release();
public abstract void removeAttribute(String name);
public abstract void removeAttribute(String name, int scope);
public abstract void setAttribute(String name, Object attribute);
public abstract void setAttribute(String name, Object o, int scope);
```

Constructors

PageContext

Signature:
```
public PageContext();
```
Description:
    The default (empty) constructor.

Methods

findAttribute

Signature:

```
public abstract Object findAttribute(String name);
```

Description:

Searches the page, request, session, and application scopes (in that order) for the specified attribute, returning the value of the first match. If the attribute does not exist in any scope, returns null.

forward

Signature:

```
public abstract void forward(String relativeUrlPath)
    throws ServletException, IOException;
```

Description:

Calls the forward() method associated with a Request-Dispatcher for this servlet. See javax.servlet. Request-Dispatcher for details.

getAttribute

Signature:

```
public abstract Object getAttribute(String name);
```

Description:

Returns the specified attribute in page scope or null if the attribute does not exist.

getAttribute

Signature:

```
public abstract Object getAttribute(String name, int
    scope);
```

Description:

Returns the specified attribute in the indicated scope or null if the attribute does not exist. Scope choices are indicated with the following constants:

```
PageContext.PAGE_SCOPE
PageContext.REQUEST_SCOPE
PageContext.SESSION_SCOPE
PageContext.APPLICATION_SCOPE
```

getAttributeNamesInScope

Signature:

```
public abstract Enumeration getAttributeNamesInScope(
    int scope);
```

Description:

Returns an Enumeration of attribute names in the specified scope. See getAttribute(String name, int scope) for a list of scope values.

getAttributesScope

Signature:

```
public abstract int getAttributesScope(String name);
```

Description:

Returns the scope of the first attribute of the specified name. See getAttribute(String name, int scope) for a list of scope values.

getException

Signature:

```
public abstract Exception getException();
```

Description:

Return the Exception object passed to an ErrorPage.

getOut

Signature:

```
public abstract JspWriter getOut();
```

Description:

Returns the JspWriter for this response.

getPage

Signature:

```
public abstract Object getPage();
```

Description:

Returns the servlet associated with this PageContext.

getRequest

Signature:

```
public abstract ServletRequest getRequest();
```

Description:

Returns the ServletRequest associated with this PageContext.

getResponse

Signature:

```
public abstract ServletResponse getResponse();
```

Description:

Returns the ServletResponse associated with this PageContext.

getServletConfig

Signature:

```
public abstract ServletConfig getServletConfig();
```

Description:

Returns the ServletConfig associated with this PageContext.

getServletContext

Signature:

```
public abstract ServletContext getServletContext();
```

Description:

Returns the ServletContext associated with this PageContext.

getSession

Signature:

```
public abstract HttpSession getSession();
```

Description:

Returns the HttpSession for this request (or null).

handlePageException

Signature:

```
public abstract void handlePageException(Exception)
   throws ServletException, IOException;
```

Description:

Used to process an unhandled exceptions thrown by the current page. Calls the ErrorPage if one is active.

include

Signature:

```
public abstract void include(String relativeUrlPath)
   throws ServletException, IOException;
```

Description:

Calls the include() method associated with a RequestDispatcher for this servlet. See javax.servlet.RequestDispatcher for details.

initialize

Signature:
```
public abstract void initialize(
Servlet servlet,
ServletRequest request,
ServletResponse response,
String errorPageURL,
boolean needsSession,
int bufferSize,
boolean autoFlush)
throws IOException, IllegalStateException,
IllegalArgumentException;
```
Description:

Stores the `servlet`, `request`, `response`, `errorPageURL`, `needsSession`, `bufferSize`, and `autoFlush` attributes and makes the appropriate implicit variables available to the JSP. This method is called by the `getPageContext()` method and should not be called directly by the JSP author.

release

Signature:
```
public abstract void release();
```
Description:

Performs the opposite of `initialize`, releasing the `PageContext` and the resources it acquired. This method is called by the `releasePageContext()` method and should not be called directly by the JSP author.

removeAttribute

Signature:
```
public abstract void removeAttribute(String name);
```
Description:

Searches the page, request, session, and application scopes (in that order) for the specified attribute, removing the first matching attribute.

removeAttribute

Signature:
```
public abstract void removeAttribute(String name, int
scope);
```

Description:

Removes the attribute associated with the specified name and scope. Scope choices are indicated with the following constants:

```
PageContext.PAGE_SCOPE
PageContext.REQUEST_SCOPE
PageContext.SESSION_SCOPE
PageContext.APPLICATION_SCOPE
```

setAttribute

Signature:

```
public abstract void setAttribute(String name, Object
attribute);
```

Description:

Sets the specified attribute with page scope. `setAttribute` `(String name, Object o, int scope)` can be used to set attributes in other scopes.

setAttribute

Signature:

```
public abstract void setAttribute(String name, Object
o, int scope);
```

Description:

Sets the specified attribute in the specified scope. Scope choices are indicated with the following constants:

```
PageContext.PAGE_SCOPE
PageContext.REQUEST_SCOPE
PageContext.SESSION_SCOPE
PageContext.APPLICATION_SCOPE
```

RequestDispatcher

Context

Full name:	`javax.servlet.RequestDispatcher`
Type:	Interface
Superinterface:	None

Description

An interface implemented by an object that can forward requests to another resource (such as a servlet or JSP). The servlet engine creates `RequestDispatcher` objects in response to the `ServletContext getRequestDispatcher(String url)` method.

Summary

```
// Methods

public void forward(ServletRequest request, ServletResponse response)
    throws ServletException, IOException;
public void include(ServletRequest request, ServletResponse response)
    throws ServletException, IOException;
```

Methods

forward

Signature:
```
public void forward(
   ServletRequest request,
   ServletResponse response)
   throws ServletException, IOException;
```
Description:

Forwards the `ServletRequest` and `ServletResponse` objects to another resource for processing. The request is considered closed after the `forward()` method is called, and further actions in the original servlet have no effect.

include

Signature:
```
public void include(
   ServletRequest request,
   ServletResponse response)
   throws ServletException, IOException;
```
Description:

Invokes the request on another resource and merges its output with this servlet's output. This enables a servlet to call another (to generate standard headings or footers, for example).

Servlet

Context

Full name:	`javax.servlet.Servlet`
Type:	Interface
Superinterface:	None

Description

This interface defines the basic set of methods that all servlets implement. Most servlets implement this interface indirectly by subclassing either `HttpServlet` or `GenericServlet`.

Summary

```
// Methods

public void destroy();
public ServletConfig getServletConfig();
public String getServletInfo();
public void init(ServletConfig config)
   throws ServletException;
public void service(ServletRequest req, ServletResponse res)
   throws ServletException, IOException;
```

Methods

destroy

Signature:
```
    public void destroy();
```
Description:

Called by the servlet engine when it is about to unload a servlet. This gives the servlet the opportunity to release any resources it owns.

NOTE: *Calling this method does not actually unload the servlet. You can call this method yourself, but it has no effect on the life cycle of the servlet.*

getServletConfig

Signature:

```
public ServletConfig getServletConfig();
```

Description:

Returns the `ServletConfig` object associated with this servlet. The `ServletConfig` provides access to the `ServletContext` and the initialization parameters.

getServletInfo

Signature:

```
public String getServletInfo();
```

Description:

Returns a string containing identifying information about the servlet. Intended to provide descriptive information to a servlet engine administration program. The contents of the string are up to the servlet author but should not contain any HTML markup tags.

init

Signature:

```
public void init(ServletConfig config)
    throws ServletException;
```

Description:

This method is called by the servlet engine when the servlet is first loaded. It must complete successfully before the servlet engine will pass the servlet any requests.

service

Signature:

```
public void service(ServletRequest req, Servlet-
Response req)
    throws ServletException, IOException;
```

Description:

Called by the servlet engine to handle a servlet request.

ServletConfig

Context

Full name: `javax.servlet.ServletConfig`

Type: Interface

Superinterface: None

Description

An interface providing methods to access a servlet's `ServletContext` object and any initialization parameters that it has.

Summary

```
// Methods

public String getInitParameter(String name);
public Enumeration getInitParameterNames();
public ServletContext getServletContext();
```

Methods

getInitParameter

Signature:

```
public String getInitParameter(String name);
```

Description:

Returns the initialization parameter having the given name. The means of specifying initialization parameters is vendor-specific. The value returned is a single `java.util.String`.

getInitParameterNames

Signature:

```
public Enumeration getInitParameterNames();
```

Description:

Returns an `Enumeration` of the names of the initialization parameters. The enumeration will be empty if there are no parameters.

getServletContext

Signature:

```
public ServletContext getServletContext();
```

Description:
Returns a reference to the `ServletContext`.

ServletContext

Context

Full name:	`javax.servlet.ServletContext`
Type:	Interface
Superinterface:	None

Description

`ServletContext` defines the interface between a servlet and the servlet engine in which it runs.

Summary

```
// Methods

public Object getAttribute(String name);
public Enumeration getAttributeNames();
public ServletContext getContext(String uripath);
public int getMajorVersion();
public String getMimeType(String file);
public int getMinorVersion();
public String getRealPath(String path);
public RequestDispatcher getRequestDispatcher(String urlpath);
public URL getResource(String path)
    throws MalformedURLException;
public InputStream getResourceAsStream(String path);
public String getServerInfo();
public Servlet getServlet(String name)
    throws ServletException;
public Enumeration getServletNames();
public Enumeration getServlets();
public void log(Exception exception, String msg);
public void log(String msg);
public void log(String message, Throwable throwable);
public void removeAttribute(String name);
public void setAttribute(String name, Object object);
```

Methods

getAttribute

Signature:

```
public Object getAttribute(String name);
```

Description:

Given an attribute name, returns the object in the servlet context that corresponds to it. Returns `null` if no such attribute exists.

getAttributeNames

Signature:

```
public Enumeration getAttributeNames();
```

Description:

Returns an `Enumeration` of the names of all attributes in the servlet context.

getContext

Signature:

```
public ServletContext getContext(String urlpath);
```

Description:

Given a URL on the server, returns a `ServletContext` object for it. If the URL does not exist or does not represent a servlet, returns `null`.

getMajorVersion

Signature:

```
public int getMajorVersion();
```

Description:

Return the major servlet API number.

getMimeType

Signature:

```
public String getMimeType(String file);
```

Description:

Given a file name, returns the file's MIME type.

getMinorVersion

Signature:

```
public int getMinorVersion();
```

Description:

Returns the minor servlet API number.

getRealPath

Signature:

```
public String getRealPath(String path);
```

Description:

Given a server-relative path name, returns the absolute path that corresponds to it.

getRequestDispatcher

Signature:

```
public RequestDispatcher getRequestDispatcher(String
    urlpath);
```

Description:

Given a URL, returns a RequestDispatcher for it.

getResource

Signature:

```
public URL getResource(String path)
   throws MalformedURLException;
```

Description:

Given a path, returns the corresponding resource from the servlet's Web application. Returns null if no resource is mapped to the specified path.

getResourceAsStream

Signature:

```
public InputStream getResourceAsStream(String path);
```

Description:

Given a path, returns an input stream for the corresponding resource from the servlet's Web application. Returns null if no resource is mapped to the specified path.

getServerInfo

Signature:

```
public String getServerInfo();
```

Description:

Returns the server name and version.

getServlet (deprecated)

Signature:
```
public Servlet getServlet(String name)
   throws ServletException;
```
Description:

Formerly used to get a reference to a servlet given its name. This method is deprecated and should no longer be used. Sun indicates that it will be permanently removed in some future version of the API.

getServletNames (deprecated)

Signature:
```
public Enumeration getServletNames();
```
Description:

Formerly used to get an enumeration of the names of all the servlets in the servlet context. This method is deprecated and should no longer be used. Sun indicates that it will be permanently removed in some future version of the API.

getServlets (deprecated)

Signature:
```
public Enumeration getServlets();
```
Description:

Formerly used to get an enumeration of all servlets in the servlet context. This method is deprecated and should no longer be used. Sun indicates that it will be permanently removed in some future version of the API.

log (deprecated)

Signature:
```
public void log(Exception exception, String msg);
```
Description:

Formerly used to write a stack trace and the given message in the servlet engine's log file.

log

Signature:
```
public void log(String msg);
```
Description:

Writes the given message in the servlet engine's log file.

log

Signature:

```
public void log(String message, Throwable throwable);
```

Description:

Writes a stack trace and the given message in the servlet engine's log file.

removeAttribute

Signature:

```
public void removeAttribute(String name);
```

Description:

Removes the attribute in the servlet context with the specified name, if it exists.

setAttribute

Signature:

```
public void setAttribute(String name, Object object);
```

Description:

Stores a reference to the specified object in the servlet context under the given name.

ServletException

Context

Full name:	javax.servlet.ServletException
Type:	Class
Extends:	java.lang.Exception
Implements:	Nothing

Description

The base class for servlet exceptions.

Summary

```
// Constructors

public ServletException();
public ServletException(String message);
public ServletException(String message, Throwable rootCause);
public ServletException(Throwable rootCause);

// Methods

public Throwable getRootCause();
```

Constructors

ServletException

Signature:
```
    public ServletException();
```
Description:

Default (empty) constructor, which simply calls the superclass constructor.

ServletException

Signature:
```
    public ServletException(String message);
```
Description:

Creates a new ServletException with the specified message text.

ServletException

Signature:
```
    public ServletException(String message, Throwable
    rootCause);
```
Description:

Creates a new ServletException with the specified message text and a reference to another exception that caused this one.

ServletException

Signature:
```
    public ServletException(Throwable rootCause);
```

Description:
    Creates a new `ServletException` with default message text and a reference to another exception that caused this one.

Methods

getRootCause

Signature:
    `public Throwable getRootCause();`
Description:
    For a `ServletException` caused by another exception or error, this method will return that other exception or error.

ServletInputStream

Context

Full name: `javax.servlet.ServletInputStream`
Type: Abstract class
Extends: `java.io.InputStream`
Implements: Nothing

Description

A subclass of `java.io.InputStream` that provides a means of reading both binary data and text lines from an HTTP request. A servlet gets access to this stream by calling the `getInputStream()` method in the servlet request object.

Summary

```
// Constructors

protected ServletInputStream();
```

```
// Methods

public int readLine(byte b, int off, int len)
    throws IOException;
```

Constructors

ServletInputStream

Signature:
```
protected ServletInputStream();
```
Description:

Default constructor. Performs no work.

Methods

readLine

Signature:
```
public int readLine(byte b, int off, int len)
    throws IOException;
```
Description:

Reads bytes from the input stream and copies them into the specified byte array starting at the specified offset. Stops reading when either the specified length is exceeded or a newline character is found (which is also copied into the byte array). Returns the number of bytes read or -1 at end of file.

ServletOutputStream

Context

Full name:	`javax.servlet.ServletOutputStream`
Type:	Abstract class
Extends:	`java.io.OutputStream`
Implements:	Nothing

Description

A subclass of `java.io.OutputStream` that can be used for writing binary data back to the client. A servlet gets access to this stream by calling the `getOutputStream()` method in the servlet response object.

NOTE: `getOutputStream()` *cannot be called if you have already called* `getWriter()` *for the same request.*

Summary

```
// Constructors

protected ServletOutputStream();
// Methods

public void print(boolean b)
    throws IOException;
public void print(char c)
    throws IOException;
public void print(double d)
    throws IOException;
public void print(float f)
    throws IOException;
public void print(int i)
    throws IOException;
public void print(long l)
    throws IOException;
public void print(String s)
    throws IOException;
public void println()
    throws IOException;
public void println(boolean b)
    throws IOException;
public void println(char c)
    throws IOException;
public void println(double d)
    throws IOException;
public void println(float f)
    throws IOException;
public void println(int i)
    throws IOException;
public void println(long l)
    throws IOException;
public void println(String s)
    throws IOException;
```

Constructors

ServletOutputStream

Signature:
```
protected ServletOutputStream();
```
Description:
Default constructor. Performs no work.

Methods

print

Signature:
```
public void print(boolean b)
    throws IOException;
```
Description:
Prints a Boolean value (as either `true` or `false`) with no CRLF at the end.

print

Signature:
```
public void print(char c)
    throws IOException;
```
Description:
Prints a single character with no CRLF at the end.

print

Signature:
```
public void print(double d)
    throws IOException;
```
Description:
Prints the string value of a double-precision floating-point number with no CRLF at the end.

print

Signature:
```
public void print(float f)
    throws IOException;
```

Description:

Prints the string value of a single-precision floating-point number with no CRLF at the end.

print

Signature:
```
public void print(int i)
    throws IOException;
```
Description:

Prints the string value of an integer with no CRLF at the end.

print

Signature:
```
public void print(long l)
    throws IOException;
```
Description:

Prints the string value of a long integer with no CRLF at the end.

print

Signature:
```
public void print(String s)
    throws IOException;
```
Description:

Prints a string with no CRLF at the end.

println

Signature:
```
public void println()
    throws IOException;
```
Description:

Prints a CRLF (carriage return–line feed).

println

Signature:
```
public void println(boolean b)
    throws IOException;
```
Description:

Prints a Boolean value (as either true or false) followed by CRLF at the end.

println

Signature:
```
public void println(char c)
  throws IOException;
```
Description:

Prints a single character followed by CRLF at the end.

println

Signature:
```
public void println(double d)
  throws IOException;
```
Description:

Prints the string value of a double-precision floating-point number followed by CRLF at the end.

println

Signature:
```
public void println(float f)
  throws IOException;
```
Description:

Prints the string value of a single-precision floating-point number followed by CRLF at the end.

println

Signature:
```
public void println(int i)
  throws IOException;
```
Description:

Prints the string value of an integer followed by CRLF at the end.

println

Signature:
```
public void println(long l)
  throws IOException;
```
Description:

Prints the string value of a long integer followed by CRLF at the end.

println

Signature:
```
public void println(String s)
    throws IOException;
```
Description:
Prints a string followed by a CRLF at the end.

ServletRequest

Context

Full name: `javax.servlet.ServletRequest`

Type: Interface

Superinterface: None

Description

Encapsulates all information about a servlet request, including its parameter names and values, attributes, and input stream. `HttpServletRequest` extends this interface for HTTP-specific features.

Summary

```
// Methods

public Object getAttribute(String name);
public Enumeration getAttributeNames();
public String getCharacterEncoding();
public int getContentLength();
public String getContentType();
public ServletInputStream getInputStream()
    throws IOException;
public String getParameter(String name);
public Enumeration getParameterNames();
public String getParameterValues(String name);
public String getProtocol();
public BufferedReader getReader()
    throws IOException;
public String getRealPath(String path);
public String getRemoteAddr();
public String getRemoteHost();
public String getScheme();
public String getServerName();
```

```
public int getServerPort();
public void setAttribute(String key, Object o);
```

Methods

getAttribute

Signature:
```
public Object getAttribute(String name);
```
Description:

Returns the value of the specified attribute or null if it does not exist. Servlet attributes are typically created by the servlet engine and are vendor-specific.

getAttributeNames

Signature:
```
public Enumeration getAttributeNames();
```
Description:

Returns an Enumeration of the names of all attributes in this request. The enumeration will be empty if the request has no attributes.

getCharacterEncoding

Signature:
```
public String getCharacterEncoding();
```
Description:

Returns the name of the character encoding style or null if none is used.

getContentLength

Signature:
```
public int getContentLength();
```
Description:

Returns the length of the request data or −1 if not known. Same as the CGI variable CONTENT_LENGTH.

getContentType

Signature:
```
public String getContentType();
```
Description:

Returns the content type or null if not known. Same as the CGI variable CONTENT_TYPE.

getInputStream

Signature:
```
public ServletInputStream getInputStream()
  throws IOException;
```
Description:

Returns the servlet input stream.

getParameter

Signature:
```
public String getParameter(String name);
```
Description:

Returns the value of the named request parameter or `null` if the parameter does not exist.

getParameterNames

Signature:
```
public Enumeration getParameterNames();
```
Description:

Returns an `Enumeration` of the names of all parameters in this request.

getParameterValues

Signature:
```
public String getParameterValues(String name);
```
Description:

Returns an array of the values of the specified request parameter. Ordinary single-valued parameters will have an array of length 1. Parameters having more than one value (such as checkboxes or selection lists) can return a multiple-entry array.

getProtocol

Signature:
```
public String getProtocol();
```
Description:

Returns the protocol name, including the major and minor version numbers. Examples are `HTTP/1.0` or `HTTP/1.1`. Same as the CGI variable `SERVER_PROTOCOL`.

getReader

Signature:
```
public BufferedReader getReader()
  throws IOException;
```
Description:

Returns the servlet input stream as filtered through a `java.io.InputStreamReader()` object.

getRealPath (deprecated)

Signature:
```
public String getRealPath(String path);
```
Description:

Formerly returned the specified path as an absolute path in the Web server file system. Use `ServletContext.getRealPath()` instead.

getRemoteAddr

Signature:
```
public String getRemoteAddr();
```
Description:

Returns the IP address of the client sending the request. Same as the CGI variable REMOTE_ADDR.

getRemoteHost

Signature:
```
public String getRemoteHost();
```
Description:

Returns the host name of the client sending the request. Same as the CGI variable REMOTE_HOST.

getScheme

Signature:
```
public String getScheme();
```
Description:

Returns the name of the scheme (e.g., http, https, or ftp) used by this request.

getServerName

Signature:
```
public String getServerName();
```

Description:

   Returns the name of the server receiving the request. Returns the host name of the server that received the request. Same as the CGI variable SERVER_NAME.

getServerPort

Signature:

   public int getServerPort();

Description:

   Returns the port number of the server receiving the request (e.g., 80 for typical HTTP servers). Same as the CGI variable SERVER_PORT.

setAttribute

Signature:

   public void setAttribute(String key, Object o);

Description:

   Stores an attribute in this request. The attribute can be retrieved with getAttribute(). Throws an IllegalStateException if the attribute already exists in the request.

ServletResponse

Context

Full name: javax.servlet.ServletResponse

Type: Interface

Superinterface: None

Description

Encapsulates all information about the response generated for a request, including response headers, the status code, and the output stream. HttpServletResponse extends this interface for HTTP-specific features.

Summary

```
// Methods

public String getCharacterEncoding();
public ServletOutputStream getOutputStream()
   throws IOException;
public PrintWriter getWriter()
   throws IOException;
public void setContentLength(int len);
public void setContentType(String type);
```

Methods

getCharacterEncoding

Signature:
```
public String getCharacterEncoding();
```
Description:
Returns the name of the character set encoding for this response.

getOutputStream

Signature:
```
public ServletOutputStream getOutputStream()
   throws IOException;
```
Description:
Returns the ServletOutputStream for this response. Cannot be called if getWriter() has already been called for this response.

getWriter

Signature:
```
public PrintWriter getWriter()
   throws IOException;
```
Description:
Returns a PrintWriter for this response. Cannot be called if getOutputStream() has already been called for this response.

setContentLength

Signature:
```
public void setContentLength(int len);
```

Description:

Indicates to the client the length of the content written to the response.

setContentType

Signature:
```
public void setContentType(String type);
```
Description:

Sets the content type.

SingleThreadModel

Context

Full name:	`javax.servlet.SingleThreadModel`
Type:	Interface
Superinterface:	None

Description

An interface that can be implemented by a servlet to indicate to the servlet engine that multiple threads cannot be used to access the `service()` method concurrently. This ensures that servlets will handle only one request at a time. There are no methods in this interface; it is simply a marker to indicate that it wants this behavior.

NOTE: *Although this makes a single instance of the servlet thread-safe within its own* service() *method, it does not prevent multiple instances from accessing external resources at the same time.*

Methods

None.

UnavailableException

Context

Full name:	`javax.servlet.UnavailableException`
Type:	Class
Extends:	`javax.servlet.ServletException`
Implements:	Nothing

Description

A subclass of `ServletException` thrown by a servlet when it can no longer handle requests, either temporarily or permanently.

Summary

```
// Constructors

public UnavailableException(int seconds, Servlet servlet, String msg);
public UnavailableException(Servlet servlet, String msg);

// Methods

public Servlet getServlet();
public int getUnavailableSeconds();
public boolean isPermanent();
```

Constructors

UnavailableException

Signature:
```
public UnavailableException(int seconds, Servlet
servlet, String msg);
```
Description:
   Creates a new `UnavailableException` for the specified servlet with the specified error message indicating that the servlet is temporarily unavailable. Accepts an integer indicating the number of seconds the servlet is expected to be unavailable. If the number is zero or negative, no estimate is available.

UnavailableException

Signature:

```
public UnavailableException(Servlet servlet, String
msg);
```

Description:

Creates a new UnavailableException for the specified servlet with the specified error message indicating that the servlet is permanently unavailable.

Methods

getServlet

Signature:

```
public Servlet getServlet();
```

Description:

Returns a reference to the disabled servlet.

getUnavailableSeconds

Signature:

```
public int getUnavailableSeconds();
```

Description:

Returns the estimated number of seconds the servlet is expected to be unavailable. If the time is negative or zero, no estimate is available. Note that the time is relative to when the exception was created, not the current time.

isPermanent

Signature:

```
public boolean isPermanent();
```

Description:

Returns a flag indicating whether the servlet is permanently unavailable or not.

APPENDIX B

HTTP HEADER QUICK REFERENCE

This appendix describes the headers defined in the HTTP specification. Headers are ordinary key/value pairs that describe the client or server, the resources to be transmitted, and the characteristics of the connection. An HTTP message can contain four different types of headers:

- *General headers.* These can be used either in a request or a response and relate to the transaction as a whole rather than to specific resources. Examples of general headers include Cache-Control, Connection, Date, Pragma, Transfer-Encoding, Upgrade, and Via.
- *Request headers.* These allow a client to pass information about itself and the form of response it is expecting. Examples include Accept, Authorization, If-Modified-Since, and User-Agent.
- *Response headers.* These are used by a server to pass information about itself and the response. Examples include Location, Server, and WWW-Authenticate.
- *Entity headers.* These define information about the resource being transferred. Can be used either in a request or a response. Examples include Content-Length and Content-Type.

Headers are all written in the same format: the header name (which is case-insensitive), a colon, one or more spaces, the header value, and a CRLF (carriage return–line feed).

Servlets have complete access to both request and response headers. Incoming headers can be read using the getHeader(String name) method of the HttpServletRequest object. There are also special-purpose methods getIntHeader(String name) and getDateHeader(String name) that will parse and convert headers in numeric or date format. The list of headers in a request can be retrieved with the getHeaderNames() method. Likewise, outgoing (response) headers can be written with the HttpServletResponse object's setHeader(String name, String value), setIntHeader(String name, int value), and setDateHeader(String name, Date value) methods. Outside of servlets, Java classes in general have access to HTTP headers through analogous methods in the java.net.URLConnection object.

For a more detailed discussion of HTTP, refer to the full specification, RFC 2068. This can be found on the Web at *http://www.freesoft.org/ CIE/RFC/2068/index.htm*.

Header Name	Description
Accept	Specifies media types that the client is able to handle, in order of preference. Multiple types may be specified in a comma-separated list. Wildcards are acceptable. Example: `Accept: image/jpeg, image/pjpeg, image/png, */*`
Accept-Charset	Specifies character sets that the client is able to handle, in order of preference. Multiple types may be specified in a comma-separated list. Wildcards are acceptable. Example: `Accept-Charset: iso-8859-1,*,utf-8`
Accept-Encoding	Specifies the encoding mechanisms that the client understands. Example: `Accept-Encoding: gzip,compress`
Accept-Language	Specifies the list of natural languages that the client prefers. Example: `Accept-Language: en,de`

Accept-Ranges	A response header that allow the server to indicate that it will accept requests for parts of a resource at a given offset and length. The value of the header is the unit of measure in which range requests are understood. Example:
	
	`Accept-Ranges: bytes`
	
	`Accept-Ranges: none`

Age	Allows the server to specify the length of time in seconds that has elapsed since the response was generated on the server. This header is primarily used with cached responses. Example: `Age: 30`
Allow	A response header that specifies a list of HTTP methods supported by the resource in the request URI. Example: `Allow: GET, HEAD, PUT`
Authorization	A request header used to specify the credentials (the realm and encoded user ID and password) necessary to access a resource. Example: `Authorization: Basic YXV0aG9yOnBhaww=`
Cache-Control	A general header used to specify caching directives. Example: `Cache-Control: max-age=30`

Header Name	Description

Connection	A general header used to indicate whether or not to keep the socket connection open. Examples:
	
	`Connection: close`
	
	`Connection: keep-alive`

Content-Base	An entity header that specifies the base URI for resolving relative URLs within the entity. If the `Content-Base` header is not specified, then relative URLs are resolved using either the `Content-Location` URI (if it is present and absolute) or using the request URI. Example: `Content-Base: http://www.ipfoods.com`
Content-Encoding	A modifier to the media type that indicates how an entity has been encoded (zipped, compressed, etc.). Example: `Content-Encoding: gzip`
Content-Language	Used to specify the natural language of the data in the input stream. Example: `Content-Language: en`
Content-Length	Specifies the length in bytes of the data contained in the request or response. Example: `Content-Length: 382`
Content-Location	Specifies the location (URI) of the resource contained in the request or response. If this is an absolute URL, it also functions as the base from which relative URLs in the entity are resolved. Example: `Content-Location: http://www.ipfoods.com/newsletter`
Content-MD5	An MD5 digest of the entity body, used as a checksum. The sender and receiver both compute the MD5 digest. The receiver compares its computed value against the value transmitted in this header. Example: `Content-MD5: <base64 of 128 bit MD5 digest>` MD5 is described in RFC 1321.
Content-Range	Sent with a partial entity body; indicates the low and high byte offset of the section to be inserted. Also indicates the total length of the entity body. Example: `Content-Range: 1001-2000/5000`
Content-Type	Indicates the MIME type of an entity body sent or received. Example: `Content-Type: text/html`

Header Name	Description
Date	The date at which the HTTP message was sent. Example: `Date: Mon, 06 Mar 2000 18:42:51 GMT`
ETag	An entity header that assigns a unique identifier to the resource being sent. For resources that can be requested using more than one URL, the `ETag` can be used to determine whether the same resource is actually sent. Example: `ETag: "208f-419e-30f8dc99"`
Expires	Specifies a date after which the entity should be considered stale. Example: `Expires: Mon, 05 Dec 2008 12:00:00 GMT`
From	A request header giving the email address of the human user who controls the user agent. Example: `From: webmaster@ipfoods.com`
Host	The host name (and, optionally, port number) of the resource being requested. This field is mandatory for requests made using HTTP/1.1. Example: `Host: www.ipfoods.com`
If-Modified-Since	If included with a GET request, makes the request conditional on the last modification date of the resource. If this header is present and the resource has not been modified since the specified date, a 304 (not modified) response should be returned. Example: `If-Modified-Since: Wed, 01 Mar 2000 12:00:00 GMT`
If-Match	If included in a request, specifies one or more entity tags (see `ETag`). The resource is only sent if its `ETag` matches one in the list. Example: `If-Match: "208f-419e-30f8dc99"`
If-None-Match	If included in a request, specifies one or more entity tags (see `ETag`). The operation is only performed if the resource's `ETag` matches none of the entries in the list. Example: `If-None-Match: "208f-419e-30f8dc99"`

If-Range	Specifies an entity tag (see `ETag`) for a resource that the client already has a copy of. Must be used together with a `Range` header. If the entity has not been modified since the last time it was retrieved by the client, the server will send only the range specified; otherwise, it will send the entire resource. Example:
	
	`Range: bytes=0-499`
	
	`If-Range: "208f-419e-30f8dc99"`

Header Name	Description
If-Unmodified-Since	Similar to but opposite in sense from If-Modified-Since. The requested entity is only returned if it has not been modified since the specified date. Example: If-Unmodified-Since: Wed, 01 Mar 2000 12:00:00 GMT
Last-Modified	Specifies the date and time the requested resource was last modified. Example: Last-Modified: Wed, 08 Mar 2000 12:00:00 GMT
Location	Used to redirect the requester to another location for a resource that has moved. Used in conjunction with a 302 (moved temporarily) or 301 (moved permanently) status code. Example: Location: http://www2.ipfoods.com/index.jsp
Max-Forwards	A request header used with the TRACE method to specify the maximum number of proxies or gateways through which the request can be routed. Proxies or gateways should decrement the number before passing on the request. Example: Max-Forwards: 3
Pragma	A general header that sends implementation-specific information. Example: Pragma: no-cache
Proxy-Authenticate	Similar to WWW-Authenticate, but designed to request authentication only from the next server in the request chain (a proxy). Example: Proxy-Authenticate: Basic realm=Admin
Proxy-Authorization	Similar to Authorization, but not intended to pass any further than a proxy server in the immediate server chain. Example: Proxy-Authorization: Basic YXV0aG9yOnBBoaWw=
Public	Lists the set of methods supported by the server. Example: Public: OPTIONS, MGET, MHEAD, GET, HEAD
Range	Specifies a unit of measure and a range of offsets from which a partial resource is requested. Example: Range: bytes=206-5513
Referer	A (misspelled) request header field that indicates the original resource from which a request was made. For HTML forms, this is the address of the Web page containing the form. Example: Referer: http://www.ipfoods.com/product/search.html

Header Name	Description

Retry-After	A response header field sent by a server in conjuction with a 503 (service unavailable) status to indicate how long to wait before requesting the resource again. The time can either be a date or a number of seconds. Examples:
	
	`Retry-After: 180`
	
	`Retry-After: Thu, 09 Mar 2000 16:45:15 GMT`

Server	A response header that indicates the identity and version number of the Web server software. Example: `Server: Apache/1.3.9 (Win32)`
Transfer-Encoding	A general header that indicates the type of transformation that has been performed on the message body that should be reversed by the receiver. Example: `Transfer-Encoding: chunked`
Upgrade	Allows a server to specify a new protocol or protocol version. Used in conjunction with the 101 (switching protocols) response code. Example: `Upgrade: HTTP/2.0`

User-Agent	Specifies the type of software used to make the request (typically, a Web browser). Examples:
	
	`User-Agent: Mozilla/4.0 (compatible; MSIE 5.0; Windows NT; DigExt)`
	
	`User-Agent: Mozilla/4.7 [en] (WinNT; I)`

Vary	A response header field used to signal that the response entity was selected from the available representations of the response using server-driven negotiation. Example: `Vary: *`
Via	A general header containing a list of all intermediate hosts and protocols used to satisfy the request. Example: `Via: 1.0 fred.com, 1.1 wilma.com`
Warning	A response header used to supply additional information about the status of a response. Example: `Warning: 99 www.ipfoods.com Asparagus is getting stale`
WWW-Authenticate	A response header challenging the user agent to supply a user ID and password. Used in conjunction with the 401 (not authorized) status code. Expects an `Authorization` header in reply. Example: `WWW-Authenticate: Basic realm=ipfm_mgmt`

APPENDIX C

SERVLET ENGINES

In order to host servlets from your Web server, you need a servlet engine. A servlet engine is a Web server add-on component that intercepts and handles servlet requests. There are a number of products that do this, most of which are available free or as free evaluation versions over the Internet. This appendix describes the three that were used in this book. A more complete list can be found at *http://java.sun.com/products/servlet/industry.html.*

JSWDK

Sun Microsystems provides a freely downloadable basic servlet engine in its JavaServer Web Development Kit (JSWDK 1.0). It includes a simple Web server for stand-alone operations. JSWDK is a development system and not suitable for production use. It can be downloaded from *http://java.sun.com/products/jsp/download.html.*

JRun

JRun is a widely used commercial servlet engine produced by Allaire Corporation. It handles the Java Servlet API 2.1 and JavaServer Pages 1.0. The most recent production version is JRun 2.3.3. There are three versions available for download:

- *JRun.* Freely downloadable development version, limited to five concurrent connections.
- *JRun Pro.* Supports unlimited concurrent connections, multiple JVMs, and remote administration.
- *JRun Pro Unlimited.* All the features of JRun Pro, plus unlimited concurrent JVMs.

Version 3.0 of JRun is in the works, promising streamlined administration, improved performance, and full support for the Servlet API 2.2,

JSP 1.1, and Web applications. Allaire's JRun products can be downloaded from *http://www.allaire.com/Products/JRun.*

ServletExec

New Atlanta Communications, Ltd., offers ServletExec, which operates in the Servlet API 2.1 and JSP 1.0 environment, and ServletExec Debugger. ServletExec supports the following Web servers:

- Microsoft IIS and PWS on Windows 95/98/NT
- Netscape FastTrack and Enterprise Server on Windows NT, Solaris, and other Unix variants
- Apache on Windows NT, Solaris, Linux, and other Unix variants

Mac OS Web servers such as WebSTAR and AppleShare IP

ServletExec products can be downloaded from the New Atlanta Web site at *http://www.newatlanta.com/downloads.html.*

Apache JServ

Apache JServ is a noncommercial, freely downloadable servlet engine from the Apache Software Foundation. A copy of JServ is included on the CD-ROM accompanying this book. JServ features Servlet API 2.0 compliance and uses simple text-based configuration files. At present, it works only with the Apache Web server. There are external add-on modules that enable JServ to support

- Server-side includes (using Apache JSSI)
- A Web publishing framework (with Cocoon)
- JSP (with the GNUJSP servlet)

More information about JServ can be found at the Apache Web site at *http://java.apache.org/jserv/index.html.*

Tomcat

The JSWDK and Apache JServ products are being merged into a single, open-source project jointly developed by Sun Microsystems and the

Apache Software Foundation. The project, code-named *Tomcat*, will become the official reference implementation of Java Servlets and JavaServer Pages. Beta versions of Tomcat are available at *http://jakarta.apache.org*.

INDEX

ommerce solutions in
Inc. Formerly a con-
ked for seven years at
s experience as a pro-
A native of Corvallis,

Phil can be reached at author@philhanna.com.